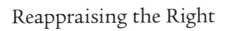

Reappraising the Right

Reappraising the Right

The Past and Future of American Conservatism

George H. Nash

ISI BOOKS

Wilmington, Delaware

Nash, George H., 1945–
    Reappraising the right : the past & future of American conservatism / George H. Nash.
        p. cm.
    Includes bibliographical references and index.
    ISBN 978-1-935191-65-0 (cloth : alk. paper)

        1. Conservatism—United States. 2. United States—Politics and government. 3. United States—Intellectual life. I. Title.

JC573.2.U6N37 2009
320.520973—dc22   2009017090

Published in the United States by:

ISI Books
Intercollegiate Studies Institute
Wilmington, Delaware 19807-1938
www.isibooks.org

                    Manufactured in the United States of America

To

Annette Y. Kirk

and

Charles W. Dunn

Contents

vii

Contents

Introduction

Conservatism at the Crossroads

In the American election year of 2008, as Barack Obama glided unexpectedly toward the White House, a new political narrative took hold among
the chattering classes: the conservative era, the Age of Reagan, was said to
be ending. According to liberal writers like George Packer and E. J. Dionne,
the once mighty conservative intellectual and political movement that had
dominated the nation's debates since the late 1970s had fallen into moribun-
dity and disarray.[1]

A few conservative pundits seemed half-inclined to agree. Yuval Levin,
a frequent contributor to National Review Online, sensed "intellectual
fatigue" among his ideological allies and added, "The conservative idea fac-
tory is not producing as it did."[2] Another rising conservative commentator,
Jonah Goldberg, commenced a column in *USA Today* in mid-2008 by quoting the writer-humorist Philander Johnson: "Cheer up, for the worst is yet to
come." Although Goldberg went on to insist that the conservative movement
had "a lot of life left in it," his bon mot captured the mood of trepidation
gripping many around him as the election approached.[3]

Some—especially in the subset of right-wing thinkers known as paleoconservatives—were more acerbic. At a paleocon website in August 2008,
Austin Bramwell posted a piece provocatively entitled "Is the Conservative
Movement Worth Conserving?"[4] Elsewhere, Patrick Buchanan—the preeminent paleoconservative spokesman in the country—expressed his dismay
at the conservative establishment by paraphrasing an aphorism attributed to
Eric Hoffer: "Every great cause begins as a movement, becomes a business,
and eventually degenerates into a racket."[5]

Such sentiments did not dissipate with the defeat of the Republican Party—that imperfect vehicle of modern conservatism—at the polls later in the year. Some weeks before the election, Sam Tanenhaus, the editor of the *New York Times Book Review*, asserted in print that the conservative movement in America had entered "its last and genuinely decadent phase."[6] Some weeks *after* the election, his prognosis became grimmer still. Writing in the *New Republic*, he offered an "intellectual autopsy" of the movement under the title "Conservatism Is Dead."[7]

Once again voices on the Right could be found who at least partly agreed with him. Within days of the election, Jeffrey Hart—a longtime senior editor of *National Review* who left the magazine in 2008 and endorsed Obama— declared at a liberal website: "Movement conservatism, RIP."[8] A few months later, at the national meeting of the conservative Philadelphia Society, the political scientist Claes Ryn—a distinguished traditionalist conservative—bluntly suggested that "the so-called conservative movement" needed "[C]hapter 11 reorganization."[9]

Most activists and intellectuals on the Right, however, seemed less convinced of their movement's supposed bankruptcy than of its need for a speedy escape from the political wilderness into which it had been cast. But how, on what terms, and under whose banner? Just a week after the traumatic election, Rod Dreher, the leading journalistic advocate for the persuasion known as "crunchy conservatism," predicted that "the scattered and demoralized armies of the right" would soon engage in a ferocious "civil war."[10] The very next day, the neoconservative columnist David Brooks asserted in the *New York Times* that "the battle lines" had "already been drawn in the fight over the future of conservatism." In one "camp," he contended, stood those he dubbed the "Traditionalists," including the radio talk show hosts Rush Limbaugh and Sean Hannity and an "alliance of Old Guard institutions" such as Americans for Tax Reform and the Family Research Institute. These, said Brooks, were committed to returning to the "core ideas" of the Republican Party, like cutting taxes and reducing the size of government. In the other "camp," he wrote, were "Reformers" like himself, *National Review*'s Ramesh Ponnuru, and the *Wall Street Journal*'s Peggy Noonan, committed not to "slashing government" but to "modernizing" Republican "priorities" for "new conditions."[11]

In the aftermath of the Democrats' decisive victory, signs multiplied that Dreher and Brooks were correct. At times in the long winter of 2009 it seemed that a class war of sorts had broken out on the Right as "elitists" confronted "populists" over such issues as the place of religious conservatives in the coalition. At the vortex of much of this disputation was the radio superstar Limbaugh, who—with twenty million or more listeners per week—commanded a larger audience than any other conservative in the land. Early in 2009, upon saying of President-elect Obama, "I hope he fails," Limbaugh triggered a national media firestorm that Democratic Party strategists and the Obama administration gleefully tried to exploit.[12]

But not all of Limbaugh's detractors were on the Left. In *The American Conservative* magazine, John Derbyshire accused the practitioners of "lowbrow talk radio" of "catering to reflex rather than thought" and of inhibiting a potentially "much more worthwhile project: the fostering of a middlebrow conservatism."[13] Writing in *Newsweek*, the neoconservative author David Frum claimed that Limbaugh was "kryptonite, weakening the GOP nationally"—especially with independents and women.[14] Limbaugh and his defenders duly returned verbal fire, and few denied that, however polarizing, he was "a huge benefit to the Right."[15] By the time the tempest subsided, his national radio audience had nearly doubled in size.[16]

Beneath all this intramural squabbling lay philosophical and strategic fault lines of sobering importance. How should American conservatives regain their footing in the new political terrain? Should they go "back to basics" and proclaim their principles with renewed fervor, after the frustrations and muddled compromises of the past eight years? Or should they calm down and concentrate on devising fresh public policy initiatives designed to attract a putatively centrist and pragmatic electorate? Should they militantly reaffirm their antistatist convictions or reluctantly concede that, like it or not, "big government" was here to stay? How much—if at all—should the conservative message be revised and its tone modulated? In what way, if any, should the movement itself be reconfigured?

These questions recalled a dilemma that Whittaker Chambers had described to William F. Buckley Jr. in another time of conservative anguish, more than fifty years earlier. "Those who remain in the world," Chambers observed, "if they will not surrender on its terms, must maneuver within its terms. That is what conservatives must decide: how much to give in order to survive at all; how much to give in order not to give up the basic principles." All this, he predicted, would lead to "a dance along a precipice."[17]

In 2009 a new era of conservative maneuvering began. At the dawning of the Age of Obama, many conservatives feared that Chambers's precipice had drawn closer than ever. Yet as unfriendly as the world may have looked to them, in truth it was a far less lonely place for conservatives than it had been in 1953 when a young don from Michigan named Russell Kirk brought forth a book he originally intended to call *The Conservatives' Rout.*[*] In the early 1950s, only three small conservative publishing houses existed in the United States. By 2009 the outlets for conservative expression were exponentially more numerous, and conservative books like Mark Levin's *Liberty and Tyranny* were often bestsellers. In 1953 *National Review*—the flagship journal for conservatives—did not yet exist. In the spring of 2009 the magazine's circulation surged to more than 200,000. The Internet, meanwhile, pulsated with right-wing websites and blogs. If nothing else, a market for conservative discourse had developed and appeared to be self-sustaining—a point for conservatives to remember amidst the encircling gloom.

Even the internal arguments on the Right were in their way a sign of vitality, and as 2009 wore on, the gallows humor of 2008 gave way to a more proactive mood. The "tea party" demonstrations were a notable case in point. Hyped though the phenomenon may have become in sympathetic media, the fact remained that on April 15, 2009, hundreds of thousands of ordinary Americans citizens came together, voluntarily, at sites all over the nation, *on a work day*, to protest the perceived leftward lurch of the new administration in Washington. In the annals of American conservatism such a swift and far-flung mobilization was without precedent.

Perhaps the most hopeful portent for conservatives, paradoxically, was the audacity and perhaps hubris of their ideological foes. As the Obama administration and its congressional supporters galloped to the left (or so conservatives judged), the threat of a crippling "civil war" on the Right seemed to diminish. Embattled conservatives could not afford such an indulgence. More quickly than many observers expected, President Obama's initiatives galvanized his intellectual and political opponents. During the campaign of 2008, Governor Sarah Palin's nomination for vice president—and the tumultuous reaction to it—had reinvigorated millions of despondent grassroots conservatives. The reality of liberalism *in power*, in 2009, bestirred them even more. It began to appear not only that they must resist but that they had a fighting chance to recover lost ground.

Nevertheless, there was no concealing the depth of the challenges that the American Right now faced. The multiplicity of "camps" and factions under its umbrella—neocons, paleocons, crunchy cons, libertarians, and more—attested to the fissiparous tendencies among them: not a *fatal* flaw

---

[*] The title, of course, became *The Conservative Mind.*

(conservatives had survived and transcended these tensions for decades), but a complicating fact of life just the same. The very success of conservatives at building institutions since the 1970s had bred another peril that columnist Ross Douthat called "cocooning"[18]: conservative voices there were aplenty as Obama took office, but were they reaching *and persuading* anyone outside their own precincts?

Long-term trends also seemed problematic. Make a list, as Ronald Brownstein and David Wasserman have done, of all the counties in the United States with at least twenty thousand people. Then look at the one hundred "best educated" of these counties: those having the highest percentage of college graduates, defined as people over the age of twenty-five with a bachelor's degree or higher. Most of these counties—America's so-called Diploma Belt—used to be Republican. By the early twenty-first century this was no longer the case. In 1988 the Democratic presidential candidate carried only thirty-six of these one hundred counties. In 2008 the Democratic candidate won seventy-eight of them.[19]

Another datum sent a similar warning signal to conservatives. According to exit polling statistics cited by political analyst Michael Barone, Americans aged thirty and over divided their votes almost evenly in the 2008 presidential election—50 percent for Barack Obama, 49 percent for his opponent, John McCain. But among voters twenty-nine and under, Obama won by a margin of 66 percent to 32 percent. It was the widest "generation gap" in the history of American exit polling[20]—and probably in the history of the United States.

There was no certainty, of course, that these and other demographic trends would continue. Wars, recessions, scandals, and other unforeseeable events could alter the political landscape at any time. But if the disappointments of the Bush presidency and the 2008 election taught conservatives anything, it was that they could no longer take their political prosperity for granted. If they wished to know what tomorrow, and the day after, might bring, they would need to heed the somewhat unconservative advice of the computer scientist Alan Kay: "The best way to predict the future is to invent it."

But again: how, on what terms, and under whose banner? "When you come to a fork in the road," said Yogi Berra, "take it." By 2009 American conservatives sensed that they, too, had come to a fork in the road—or at least to a painful bump. As they pondered uneasily which turn (if any) to take, the need for reflection and reappraisal grew apparent. From Vermont to Virginia to Michigan—and innumerable other locations as well—conservatives ·

young and old were forming study clubs and discussion groups and revisiting the intellectual and spiritual sources of their movement. At places like the Alexander Hamilton Institute in upstate New York and the Colloquium on the American Founding at Amherst College, bands of conservative professors, college students, and alumni were analyzing current discontents and seeking renewal in the light of the foundational principles of Western civilization. Peering forward, as it were, through a glass darkly, many conservatives felt impelled also to look back, the better to find a compass for the journey ahead.

Which brings us to the book in your hands. For more than three decades I have been a historian of American conservatism, particularly of its intellectual manifestations. During that time the conservative movement, once inchoate and marginalized, has grown in intellectual sophistication and political heft to become a competitive presence in our public life.

Yet as I travel and lecture around the country to college students and other audiences, I am struck by how little of this history people actually know, including many who self-identify with the conservative community. In our age of "saturation media" (as George Will calls it)—focused on the sound bites and squalls of the eternal Present—it is hard, even for professed *conservatives*, to take stock and stay connected to their heritage, even when a deeper acquaintance with it might yield a bracing perspective on present predicaments.

In *Reappraising the Right* I attempt to supply such perspective. In 1976 I made my first major foray into this territory in my book *The Conservative Intellectual Movement in America Since 1945*. Since then I have returned to this subject often, from many angles, exploring topics not covered (or covered only briefly) in the original book. As the conservative intellectual community has matured and diversified, the range of my inquiries has necessarily expanded. The book before you is one product of these labors.

I have grouped its contents into five distinct clusters. The chapters in Part I examine some of the traditions, institutions, books, and personalities that laid the foundations for the modern American Right. I consider, for example, the immense importance of "think tanks" in erecting the infrastructure that has undergirded conservative public policy formulation for a generation. I take the measure of some of the books and essays that decisively shaped conservative consciousness during the Age of Reagan. Above all, I reassess the careers and significance of such founding fathers of the modern Right as Russell Kirk, Friedrich Hayek, and Richard Weaver—as well as others, less remembered, who deserve recognition.

Some of these figures, as you will see, were unabashed contrarians, even toward one another—a useful reminder that conservatism is not the same as conformity. Indeed, paraphrasing Emerson, one might say that whoso would be a conservative must be a *non*conformist (dissenting at times from others who adopt the same label). In any case, I hope that these chapters convey to readers a sense of the fortitude, independence of spirit, and earnestness of those who came to exemplify the conservative mind after World War II—individuals whose words and thoughts (and in some cases, personal sacrifices) created the patrimony upon which succeeding generations have drawn.

Anyone with a smidgen of knowledge of conservatism is aware of William F. Buckley Jr. (1925–2008). In Part II, I focus on this extraordinary man and his legacy, notably the magazine, *National Review*, that he founded and sustained for more than half a century. In these days when anyone can consult a variety of conservative periodicals by simply going online or visiting the nearest bookstore, it is easy to forget that life, for conservatives, was not always so easy. The remarkable rise of *National Review* testifies to a truth we too often lose sight of: that it is people (not "forces") who make history, and that (in Calvin Coolidge's words) "[n]othing in the world can take the place of persistence." Another lesson, perhaps, for contemporary conservatives to ponder.

In Part III, I investigate a relatively neglected subject: the impact of Jewish activists on the evolution of the American Right. For many readers the chapters in this section will come as a surprise. After all, are not most Jewish voters in the United States politically liberal? While that is true, it does not capture the entire story. Even before *Commentary*, under the editorship of Norman Podhoretz, joined the ranks of American conservatism (a story told in chapter 24), the Jewish contribution to conservative causes was notable, as my chapter on the Jewish "forgotten godfathers" at *National Review* discloses. The essays in Part III underscore one of the themes of the volume before you: American conservatism is a wide river with many tributaries.

Part IV of *Reappraising the Right* may startle some readers even more. Why, in a book on the history and future of conservatism, should there be a series of chapters devoted to Herbert Hoover? Was he not an unabashed Progressive, even a proto–New Dealer? Did he not, as president, cause—or at least exacerbate—the Great Depression?

I have no doubt that many readers will turn to Part IV with this set of preconceptions in their heads. In recent years Herbert Hoover has been no hero to the American Right. Indeed, it would be hard to find a commendatory reference to him in any conservative or libertarian publication since the 1980s. For reasons that I elucidate in chapters 25 and 28, he has become—almost uniquely among our modern presidents—a "political orphan," unwelcome in liberal and conservative pantheons alike. Particularly during the "Great Recession" of 2008–9, the Internet reverberated with denouncements of his record by bloggers Left and Right, eager to draw ideological lessons from his perceived mishandling of the Great Depression.

Unfortunately, much of this partisan hunt for a "usable past" obscured not only Hoover's larger record in and out of office but also the intricate history of American conservatism. Few of the indictments of his anti-Depression policies stopped to scrutinize the political and ideological context in which he struggled. Few remarked upon the extent to which, during the campaign of 1932 and the rest of his life, he battled *against* Franklin Roosevelt and the New Deal. Few noticed that in his books *American Individualism* (1922) and *The Challenge to Liberty* (1934) Hoover articulated a vision of American exceptionalism and a critique of statism that conservatives (and others) might study with profit. Few recorded that during his long and extraordinarily productive ex-presidency he was a stalwart patron of right-wing causes and publications like *Human Events*, a supporter of William F. Buckley Jr. and Senator Robert Taft, and a revered grandfather figure for most conservatives in his latter days. Few realized that he came to regard his creation of the Hoover Institution on War, Revolution and Peace at Stanford University as his greatest benefaction to the American people. Toward the end of his life and long afterward, his pioneering archive and think tank became an intellectual redoubt for American conservatives.

All this, and more, has been lost from view in the maelstrom of current contentions. There is much about Hoover's record and political philosophy that might intrigue and even instruct today's conservatives if they can get past what they *think* they know about him and become more adequately acquainted with his career. To quizzical readers of Part IV I say, then: read on.

Finally, in Part V, I turn more directly to the question of the hour: the future of the conservative movement. Historians are not necessarily good prognosticators, but by deliberately taking a longer view we can try to liberate our readers from the provincialism of the present. With Franklin Roosevelt again being acclaimed on the Left as the salvific modern president, how should conservatives come to terms with his New Deal? How will Ronald Reagan—the perceived antithesis of Roosevelt—be remembered by history?

What is Reagan's lasting legacy for his fellow conservatives? And what are the prospects for the intellectual and political force that he so much personified? These are some of the questions I address in my final chapters.

For readers impatient for a sneak preview, let me say here simply that, come what may in the long run, it appears to this historian that in the short run, at least, conservatives will participate importantly in our national conversation. Conservatism in America is not dead.

One more introductory observation: *Reappraising the Right* is not a manifesto. It is not a how-to manual for winning the next election. It is a work of scholarship and reflection intended for readers of all persuasions seeking a better understanding of American conservatism and therefore a better understanding of our times.

In the current political climate, perplexed conservatives especially may decide to turn its pages, and I hope they do—in search not of instant formulas for success but of something deeper and more sustaining: enhanced perspective on who they are, where they came from, and what they believe. Gaining that, they may more wisely face the future—and perhaps even invent it.

"The only thing new in the world," said Harry Truman, "is the history you don't know." In the pages that follow, I hope readers discover much that is both new and worth knowing.

Part I

Conservatism Reappraised:
Traditions, Institutions, Books, People

1

Pilgrims' Progress:
America's Tradition of Conservative Reform

"Is the American Experience Conservative?" That was the title of a lecture that I delivered at the Heritage Foundation in Washington, D.C., on September 29, 1987, just after the bicentennial celebration of the Constitution. I adapted the lecture for publication, under the above title, in the Fall 1991 issue of Policy Review, *from which the text below is taken. Portions of the lecture and subsequent article appeared previously in* Imprimis.

As the opening paragraphs of this lecture/article make clear, certain concerns about the health of the conservative movement were on my mind two decades ago. They are on my mind still, in 2009, as I put this essay before you.

As the unifying and invigorating struggles of the 1980s recede from consciousness, disturbing signs of sectarianism have begun to afflict the conservative movement. One thinks of the increasingly feisty "exchanges of views" among certain neo- and paleoconservatives. One thinks of the well-publicized differences among leading conservative commentators over the Gulf War and the objectives of American foreign policy. Even as the overall infrastructure grows, generating a neverending flow of conferences and policy studies, one wonders at times whether we are witnessing a laudable division of labor in the mold of Adam Smith or a subtle process of parallel fragmentation. Each ideological tendency in the movement now has its own network of scholars, foundations, think tanks, and periodicals. But few conservative institutions, it seems, embrace and attempt to unite these sometimes fractious components of the Grand Alliance. No wonder that more than one observer has openly suggested that conservatism's moment of glory has passed.

During the first decades after World War II, the emerging intellectuals of the American Right were repeatedly obliged to establish their historical legitimacy—to demonstrate that the American heritage they presumed to defend was authentically conservative. During the 1970s and 1980s, this preoccupation with the past gradually subsided. As conservatives came to influence public discourse, they found it less and less necessary to validate their claim to be indigenous. Whatever their roots or lineage, they were, undeniably, achieving results in the intellectual and political marketplace. Their very success was proof enough that they "belonged."

Now, however, the wheel of good fortune seems to be stalling, as the battles over judges Robert Bork and Clarence Thomas make clear. For what the judges' opponents are really asserting is that Bork, Thomas, and by implication the entire conservative intellectual movement are marginal, eccentric, and dangerous—not part of the mainstream at all. To the opponents of these nominations, the American political tradition evidently consists of only two legitimate forces: "progressive" liberalism, entrenched in the courts and elsewhere since 1933, and the "pragmatic," accommodating Center, willing to ratify liberalism's victories with the doctrine of stare decisis. Aware that he who controls the past controls the future, the cultural commissars of "political correctness" now seem intent on constructing an image of the past that equates conservatism, and American civilization itself, with racism and oppression. If they succeed, tomorrow will be theirs.

For all these reasons, it seems appropriate to reexamine the American experience and contemporary conservatism's relationship to it. More particularly, I wish to identify some of the core values of our past—values that American conservatism ought to stand for. Perhaps by stepping back from the current tumult and reflecting anew upon what America has meant, today's conservatives can regain both perspective and purpose.

FIRST NEW NATION

From the days of the Puritans to the age of Ronald Reagan, a sense of uniqueness and of destiny has infused the American character. On board the ship *Arbella* as it sailed for New England in 1630, John Winthrop admonished his Puritan brethren: "[W]e must consider that we shall be as a city upon a hill, the eyes of all people are upon us." A century and a half later, Hector St. John de Crèvecoeur, a Frenchman who had settled in New York, pronounced in a classic little book a famous question: "What then is the American, this new man?" And he prophesied: "Here individuals of all nations are melted into a new race of men, whose labors and posterity will one day cause great changes in the world."

On the back of our one-dollar bill is a replica of the Great Seal of the United States. One side of the seal features a majestic bald eagle holding arrows and an olive branch in its talons. The reverse side of the seal, however, is less familiar—and, I think, more revealing. It shows a pyramid—an unfinished pyramid—with the date 1776 engraved in Roman numerals on its base. Below the pyramid is a motto: *Novus Ordo Seclorum*—"A New Order of the Ages."

Adopted by the Continental Congress in 1782, the Great Seal of the United States symbolized America's self-image as it embarked upon nationhood. America, the seal suggested, was not simply another nation-state; it represented something novel in history. Moreover, it portended the future—"a new order of the ages," a break with the past. The Old World, with its kings, oligarchies, and regimes of oppression, was to be left behind forever. Now, in a vast and nearly empty land, there would be constructed a republic "conceived in liberty," as Lincoln later put, and dedicated to a proposition, a creed, a set of truths held to be self-evident. America was to be a polity created by conscious design, an unprecedented experiment in self-government on a continental scale.

From its inception in 1776, the American republic has been identified with the hopes and future of mankind. The United States, to borrow a phrase from Seymour Martin Lipset, was "the first new nation," and Americans and Europeans alike have probed the implications of this event. Said Alexis de Tocqueville in *Democracy in America* in the 1830s: "I confess that in America I saw more than America; I sought there the image of democracy itself. . . ." For Tocqueville, as for so many observers, America exemplified the contours of the future.

In other ways than the political, America has long been perceived as an untraditional society. To millions upon millions of immigrants through decade after decade of our history, America has been a land of opportunity, a refuge from the constricted, decadent, stratified, class-bound, traditional societies of Europe. Is it surprising that during our Civil War the British aristocracy was sympathetic to the "feudal" South, while the British working class favored the more "modern" North? America has beckoned precisely because it appeared to be different from the Old World.

STUPENDOUS SOCIAL ENERGY

What has America promised? It has promised freedom: free land, upward mobility, equality of opportunity, a chance to start over. It has been a land of stupendous social energy, a land wherein has flourished, as in no other society before or since, the social type known as the self-made man. Benjamin Franklin is said to have remarked that America is a country where we ask of a person not "Who is he?" but "What can he do?" In our commitment to a society based on individual merit and equality of opportunity, we Americans have adopted two of the core values of modernity.

Still another way in which America has exhibited its modernity is in its dedication as a society to progress—or, to use a better word, to "improvement." Implanted deep in the American psyche is a conviction that social conditions around us do not have to be that way—that if evils exist we can eradicate them, that if, for example, corrupt politicians hold office we can throw the rascals out, that we are the masters of our fate and the captains of our souls. Passivity and fatalism are not a part of our national character. If we encounter obstacles that seem insuperable, our creed tells us that we can move on. This is one reason, I suspect, why California, and more recently Alaska, have held so much allure for the American imagination: They are states where, all else failing, we can go and start over. We are a restless people; half of us change residences every five years. Has there ever been a society as mobile, as kinetic, as our own?

IMPULSE FOR IMPROVEMENT

This relentless American impulse for improvement—of society and of oneself—has taken the most various forms. Think of the extraordinary edifice of higher education that Americans in two centuries have established: from small liberal arts colleges to behemoth universities. Think of the assumptions about human nature behind this commitment, and think also about its expansiveness: Americans increasingly seek education not just for a privileged elite but for ever broader segments of the population. A far higher percentage of Americans attends college than in any other country in the world. And consider this: has there ever been a society as incessantly productive of reform movements as our own? I refer not only to such preeminent crusades as those for emancipation of the slaves, universal suffrage, and regulation of the trusts, but also of such causes as temperance, prison reform, aid to the Indians, the creation of orphanages, abolition of child labor, even the health food movement. "What is man born for but to be a Reformer . . . ?"

wrote that enormously popular American philosopher, Ralph Waldo Emerson. We are, I repeat, a restless people, and many of us believe that even our inner selves can be re-formed. It is a remarkable, and remarkably modern, notion.

Let me offer another example. As a nation Americans have long been enamored of entrepreneurship, invention, and technology. From Eli Whitney to Thomas Edison, from Henry Ford to Charles Lindbergh, from the Wright brothers to the astronauts, from the automobile to the home computer and VCR: no other society has honored science—above all, applied science—as lavishly as has ours. I do not know how many inventions have been patented in the United States in the past hundred years, but I would not be surprised if the total exceeded that of all other industrial nations combined.

THE AMERICAN DREAM

This interest in technology, in gadgetry, and in shaping and reshaping our environment reflects another aspect of the American temperament. We Americans like to think of ourselves as an optimistic, problem-solving people. During the election campaign of 1980, Ronald Reagan repeatedly denounced the drab, defeatist notion that America's challenges were insuperable, that our expectations must be lowered forever, that the "era of limits" had arrived. It was a theme that was persuasive to millions. In his inaugural address, Reagan declared:

> The crisis we are facing today [requires] our willingness to believe in ourselves and to believe in our capacity to perform great deeds; to believe that together with God's help we can and will resolve the problems which now confront us.
>
> And after all, why shouldn't we believe that? We are Americans.

Surely it is significant that in our discourse we speak of something called the American Dream. No one ever talks about the British Dream, the Russian Dream, or the Japanese Dream. But the American Dream—that is something else. Instinctively, we comprehend what it means: It means opportunity—opportunity to achieve, to ascend the ladder, to transcend our origins, however humble. We sense that this is distinctively an American dream, that it is inextricably interwoven with our self-definition as a people. We sense further that ours is a land where dreams, often enough, find fulfillment, and that our society is unusual because of it.

TOM PAINE AND HERBERT HOOVER

This belief in American uniqueness and destiny, then—of America as a trail-blazing society—has been deeply embedded in our historical consciousness. It is not the sole property of the Left. Consider this quotation:

> It was not because it was proposed to establish a nation but because it was proposed to establish a nation *on new principles*, that July 4, 1776, has come to be regarded as one of the greatest days in history. [emphasis added]

Who said this? Tom Paine? William O. Douglas? No; it was Calvin Coolidge in 1926. Now consider these words:

> By a classless America our forefathers meant far more than a sociological expression. There were to be no stratifications in life that handicapped the rise of any boy from the bottom to the top. The human particles should move freely in the social solution. . . . This idea of a fluid class-less society was unique in the world. It was the point at which our social structure departed from all others.

Who wrote this paean to a classless America? Hubert Humphrey? Eugene Debs? Jane Fonda? No; it was Herbert Hoover in 1940.

Or consider these lines from the poem "America For Me," written by Henry van Dyke many years ago and recited, significantly enough, at the Republican national convention in 1980:

> 'Tis fine to see the Old World, and travel up and down
> Among the famous palaces and cities of renown,
> To admire the crumbly castles and the statues of the kings,
> But now I think I've had enough of antiquated things.
>
> So it's home again, and home again, America for me!
> My heart is turning home again, and there I long to be,
> In the land of *youth* and *freedom* beyond the ocean bars,
> Where the air is full of sunlight and the flag is full of stars.

* * * * * * * * *

6

I know that Europe's wonderful, yet something seems to lack;
The *Past* is too much with her, the people looking back.
But the glory of the Present *is to make the Future free,*—
We love our land for what she is and *what she is to be.*

Oh, it's home again, and home again, America for me!
[emphasis added]

America is different: It represents youth, freedom, energy, a better future. This is a vision that has been central to our national identity.

EUROPE: THE BURDEN OF HISTORY

Several years ago, I participated in a conference of German and American conservatives held in Bad Godeberg, West Germany. The subject was the "Reagan Revolution" and its implications for the Atlantic alliance. I was fascinated, during those four days, by the differences in outlook and temperament between the America delegation and its European hosts. The Americans tended to be ebullient and practical, filled with specific suggestions for getting things done. Do we want to advance the cause of conservatism? Then, the Americans would say, let us organize: set up conferences, establish think tanks, found journals and newspapers, work from the grass roots. The Germans, in contrast, seemed much less "activist," more constrained by a sense of limitation, and elitist rather than populist in their approach to institutions and mechanisms of social change.

Above all, I was struck by the differences in attitudes toward history among the conferees. For most Americans at the meeting, history seemed to begin with the Carter administration, and when answering questions, Americans focused quickly on the present. When the Germans answered questions, their remarks might begin with learned references to the revolution of 1848 and work down gradually (sometimes very gradually) toward the present. For the Americans, the past was prologue; for the Germans, it was a weight. As one German intellectual said to me during the conference, "Our [German] history is a burden and a curse." I returned home with a deeper appreciation of the distinctiveness of the American experience.

Perhaps by now you discern the point I am making. If, as the social scientists tell us, the process of modernization entails social mobility, economic freedom, and the breakdown of class barriers; if it means equality of opportunity, increased popular participation in politics, and equal justice

7

under the law; if it means a social order that is not static and hierarchical but dynamic and future-oriented; if it means technological innovation and a spirit of improvement, then America for two hundred years—at least in its own self-understanding—has been a modernizing, not a traditional, society.

ELOQUENT DISSENTERS

There have been dissenters from these trends, to be sure, and sometimes the dissenters have been eloquent. In his bicentennial history of Illinois, Professor Richard Jensen has even reinterpreted American history as in substantial measure a conflict between "modernizers" and "traditionalists." Mark Twain, for instance, scorned the American penchant for uplift. "To do good is noble," Twain observed. "To instruct others in doing good is just as noble and much easier." Among twentieth-century American critics of the modernizing ethos, one thinks above all of Albert Jay Nock, H. L. Mencken, and the Southern Agrarians who published *I'll Take My Stand* in 1930: "superfluous men," Robert Crunden has called them, brilliant men, but men whose dissent only underscored the prevailing orthodoxy of their time. Most Americans—at least most Americans who got things done in this society—saw themselves as creators of a modern, progressive civilization. The quintessential American, a British visitor shrewdly remarked in 1898, is "a highly electric Anglo-Saxon." Until well into the twentieth century, America was predominantly, in more than one sense of the term, a Yankee nation.

Now I am generalizing broadly, of course. And you will note that I am dealing with perceptions and ideals. But the "most potent force in society," Herbert Hoover once reminded us, "is its ideals." From the late eighteenth century to the early twentieth, the dominant American ideal has been (to use a current term) "democratic capitalism." And in the long perspective of Western history, democratic capitalism has been a virtual synonym for modernization.

We must now examine an unsettling paradox. Today over much of the earth, the ideals of the American experiment—political equality and participation, entrepreneurial freedom and economic growth, social fluidity and equality of opportunity—enjoy immense prestige, as the suicide of communism accelerates. And yet these same ideals are also mocked and despised, and nowhere with more intensity than in certain enclaves in America itself.

DEFECTION OF THE INTELLECTUALS

The profound defection of many of the West's most distinguished intellectuals from the American ethos of democratic capitalism is one of the most stunning and disturbing features of our time. It is a phenomenon that has many roots—far more than I can analyze here. But clearly it is linked to the rise, within the last century or so, of a new conception of modernity. Unlike the modernizing principles to which I have referred earlier, this "new modernity" (as I shall call it) has not been primarily political or economic in its orientation. It has been, at bottom, literary, aesthetic, and in a way, spiritual. The pioneers of this consciousness are familiar enough to all: names like Nietzsche, Kierkegaard, and Sartre; Ibsen, Gide, and Baudelaire; Pound, Picasso, and the early Albert Camus. Again, I must generalize and simplify, but few will deny that at the heart of this new modernity was a sense of relativism, negation, and despair. Where the "old modernity" asserted that certain truths were self-evident, the new modernity denied that universal truths exist. Where the old modernity was bourgeois, the new modernity was bohemian, contemptuous of bourgeois culture. Where the old modernity tended to be optimistic (after all, would not tomorrow be better than today?), the new modernity was not. Where the old modernity tended to be rationalistic, the new modernity explored the irrational and the absurd. Where the old modernity offered liberation from external constraints—from the barriers of class, race, national origin, and arbitrary government—the new modernity preached liberation from inner constraints—from traditional morality, from artistic convention, from rationality itself. Where the old modernity concentrated on getting ahead in the world and was relatively indifferent to questions of ultimate meaning, the new modernity was haunted by the conviction that life has no ultimate meaning, that God (as Nietzsche put it) is dead.

There is little doubt that this "new modernity" or modernism, as some have labeled it, has penetrated very deeply into our civilization. How is it that this counterculture has become so pervasive? Writing in *National Review* in 1970, Jeffrey Hart offered one answer:

> During the past [generation] there has occurred a sort of cultural explosion: paperbacks, Eliot reading his poems to 50,000 students in a Midwestern football stadium, LP records, . . . Mailer and Genet and de Sade appearing in mass circulation journals, the op-art and pop-art and porno phenomena.

All of these things, along with affluence, the GI Bill and the assumption, implicit in democratic theory and increasingly the premise of government action, that absolutely everyone must go to college, have now given rise to a vast student proletariat. Twenty-five years ago, about 10 percent of the college-age population attended college; today the percentage approaches 50 and it will continue to climb. Much of this proletariat absorbs the attitudes of the adversary culture. . . .

CLASH OF MODERNITIES

Looking back at my own education, I can attest to the acuity of Professor Hart's remark. Attending college in the 1960s, I was exposed to books like Paul Goodman's *Growing Up Absurd* and Norman O. Brown's *Life Against Death*, to plays like *Waiting for Godot* and the *Marat/Sade*. Teaching at Harvard in the early 1970s, I had a student tell me one day that all values are without rational foundation, that one can only choose arbitrarily among them. This was pure existentialism, of course, but where had he acquired such ideas?

And as the "new modernity" has percolated down through our culture, the values of the "old modernity" have come increasingly to seem old-fashioned. Listen to the voices that dominate our public discourse. Listen carefully the next time someone uses the term "Protestant ethic" or "middle-class values" or "equality of opportunity" and see whether you do not detect a note of irony or condescension. Surely it is significant that the political embodiment of these values in America at present is the Republican Party, the conservative party. It is in the Republican Party and among people called conservatives and neoconservatives that one still hears the rhetoric of upward mobility and achievement, of liberty and free-market capitalism as the hope of all nations. The ideals of modernity—of the old modernity, that is—have become the property of the conservatives.

Now does this clash of "modernities" really matter? Does it matter that the ideology of modernism has become a virtual orthodoxy among the secular intelligentsia? Does it matter that, as Midge Decter once observed, there is spreading through our society a conviction that "nothing is worth dying for"? Yes, it does matter, for two reasons. First, few men and women can live in a spiritual vacuum for long. If their society seems meaningless, they will in rage and frustration find or create meaning somewhere, even in violence, decadence, and revolution. Second, no society can survive without some sense of its own goodness. If many Americans no longer believe in our system, there are others in the world who believe in theirs—and are willing to enforce their beliefs at gunpoint.

Now is there a historical relationship between the "two modernities"? I have presented them as antagonists, but could there be some dialectical process by which the one inexorably gave birth to the other? Is there, in other words, an inevitable declension from democratic capitalism to socialist nihilism? There is a verse by Goldsmith that my New England ancestors used to recite:

Ill fares the land
To hastening ills a prey
Where wealth accumulates
And men decay.

More recently, Joseph Schumpeter, Daniel Bell, and others have suggested that capitalism creates the intellectual class that will ultimately destroy it—indeed, that capitalism generates its own fatal "cultural contradictions": that capitalism, with its ceaseless incitements to instant gratification of every taste, no matter how debased, eventually destroys the cultural matrix of decency, sobriety, and self-restraint upon which it—and republican self-government—depend.

Is this thesis true? Is the "new modernity" the necessary offspring of the old? In short, is the American way of life inherently and irremediably flawed?

Religious Roots

I do not believe that it is. But if I am correct, it is because of a fundamental constitutive element of the American ethos that I have not yet mentioned. Consider again the Great Seal of the United States. It contains, as I have said, the motto *Novus Ordo Seclorum* and the image of an unfinished pyramid. But hovering above the pyramid is a symbolic unblinking eye: the eye of God. And placed above that is another Latin motto, *Annuit Coeptis*, meaning "He has favored [our] undertaking." Americans, I said earlier, are a restless people, but as Tocqueville long ago recognized, we have not been restless in everything, particularly in the realm of our formative philosophic and moral beliefs. And a powerful reason for this remarkable constancy amidst so much flux is that America, since the beginning, has evolved within a context of Christian religious belief.

I am not saying that the Founding Fathers sought to establish a Christian commonwealth or that America's public institutions have been explicitly religious in character. I am saying that the impulses described earlier in this essay—the impulses that I have called the "old modernity"—have operated, at least until recently, within a predominantly and persistently religious culture. If the "new modernity" has not yet triumphed among us, it is because American culture has been molded and guided by the non-modern and profoundly civilizing force of our Judeo-Christian religious heritage. In short, if the American polity and economy are in some sense modern, American culture—at the level of ultimate beliefs about God and man—has been and perhaps remains primarily conservative.

The United States, then, is a modern nation. But it is not only a modern nation, and in this fact may lie the fate of the American experiment. Liberty, said Alexis de Tocqueville, "cannot be established without morality, nor morality without faith." If America is to survive, its indisputably modern elements must be conjoined with what Russell Kirk has called the "permanent things," spiritual things and the institutions that sustain them. Without this fusion, the American experiment may fail—not because it is a regime of liberty but because liberty alone cannot instruct us how to live. It is what we *do* with our liberty that will determine our country's future, and for that guidance we must turn outside the marketplace and the polling booth. If the old modernity is not to succumb to the relativism and anti-religious nihilism of the new, it will have to draw on transcendent, premodern sources—on religious faith—to infuse our lives with meaning. Edmund Burke said it well in his *Letter to a Member of the National Assembly* (1791):

> Society cannot exist unless a controlling power upon will and appetite be placed somewhere, and the less of it there is within, the more there must be without. It is ordained in the eternal constitution of things, that men of intemperate minds cannot be free. Their passions forge their fetters.

It is the duty of conservatives—even while accepting and celebrating the ideals of the "old modernity"—to forge the internal checks and balances that will channel those ideals toward the "permanent things" and thus give spiritual substance to the "opportunity society."

12

BLESSINGS OF LIBERTY

It is not, perhaps, commonplace for you to hear a conservative scholar celebrate the ideals of the "old modernity" and invoke it as a paradigm of value against its detractors. Still, if any of you are tempted to say that democratic capitalism is not worth purifying and preserving, or to conclude that the American experiment is too "modern" for your taste, I would ask you to indulge in a little act of imagination. Imagine that when you leave this room you will be arrested and perhaps tortured for unlawful assembly; in large portions of the world at this very moment, this would be your fate. Imagine that you could not obtain employment because of a government whim; it happened to Lech Walesa. Imagine that if you could not find a job, you would be expelled from the city where you are now living; only yesterday this was the case in the Soviet Union. Imagine that if you were a school teacher and identified yourself as a Christian, you were then assigned to a dead-end job far from home. It is happening in China today.

The American heritage of which we are the heirs has bequeathed us the "blessings of liberty." Freedom—to worship, to travel, to select and change careers. Freedom—to write, to publish, to attend meetings. Let us not lightly disparage these blessings. Even as new hope germinates in the liberated nations of East Central Europe and the crumbling internal empire of the Soviet Union, let us remember: free societies are a rarity in human history, and as the Kurds and Kuwaitis can tell you, they have their merits still.

American conservatives, then, unless they wish to live lives of reclusive despondency, must defend and civilize, not repudiate, the free society they have inherited. It will not, I believe, be easy; at times it will entail, in Whittaker Chambers' unforgettable metaphor, "a dance along a precipice." But in a culture of spreading nihilism and incivility, American conservatives must cherish their roots and perceive their true enemies with clarity. Against the disparagements and competing mythologies of the Left, they must affirm the vitality and validity of the American Dream.

2

Engines of "Idea Power":
The Rise of Conservative Think Tanks

This essay is drawn from a speech delivered on September 26, 1991, at the President's Club dinner of the Indiana Policy Review Foundation in Indianapolis. The speech was subsequently published and distributed by the foundation.

Some years ago the journal *Science* published a fictitious interview with the director of a mythical think tank known as the Breakthrough Institute. The director, whose name was given as "Dr. Grant Swinger," was said to be chairman of the board of the Center for the Absorption of Federal Funds. The *Science* reporter asked "Dr. Swinger" to give some examples of his institute's accomplishments. "Well," he said, his staff had "resolved the conflict between teaching and research." "How?" the reporter asked. "By doing neither," the director replied.

The term "think tank" is a comparatively new one in our language. Although coined in the 1940s, it only acquired its current meaning in the 1960s, when it was used to describe such military-oriented research organizations as the Rand Corporation. Since then the term has been applied to a widening array of entities engaged in the study of governmental policy, both foreign and domestic. We have come a long way since think tanks could be thought of simply as contractors who absorb federal funds.

As the scope of the term has expanded, so has the phenomenon it labels. If by the expression "think tank" one means any organization conducting research relating to public policy, then there are now at least 1,200 think tanks in the United States.

Increasingly, it seems to me, our political discourse is being shaped by the "war of ideas" in which these institutions engage. One cannot listen very long to National Public Radio, for example, without hearing about studies by such organizations as the Urban Institute or the Center for Defense Information. Similarly, one cannot scan the conservative media without quickly encountering references to the Manhattan Institute, the Ethics and Public Policy Center, the Political Economy Research Center, and innumerable others. Indeed, as a historian of conservatism in America I am repeatedly impressed by the degree to which the contemporary conservative movement has become less theoretical and introspective in recent years and ever more interested in concrete issues of legislation. If there has been a characteristic mode of conservative expression in the past decade, it has not been the rarefied tome of political philosophy, economic theory, or cultural criticism. It has been, above all, the policy study.

What is occurring in Washington, D.C., is now happening at the grass roots as well. Just seven years ago not a single conservative think tank existed at the state or municipal level in the United States. Now there are at least thirty-six. Clearly this is no passing fad. Instead, we are witnessing a massive elaboration of an impulse, an exuberant exfoliation on what was once a slender tree.

As a student of conservatism I have been asked to reflect upon the increasingly visible role of think tanks in the conservative community. In order to do so, I propose that we step back from our present preoccupations and consider this phenomenon in historical perspective. What does the efflorescence of think tanks across the nation tell us about our conduct of public life? What does it disclose about where we have come as a polity and where we are going?

Although ideologically motivated centers of research and advocacy are now a familiar part of the conservative landscape, it may surprise you to learn that the existence of such organizations—whether on the Right *or* the Left—is a comparatively recent development in American history. It was only seventy-five years ago, in 1916, that the first organization in this country to focus exclusively on national public policy issues was founded. This was the Institute for Government Research; eleven years later it merged with two other groups to become the Brookings Institution. On the conservative side of the street, the Hoover Institution on War, Revolution and Peace—created in 1919 as an archive of documentation on World War I and its consequences—did not enter the domestic policy field until the 1960s. The American Enterprise Institute, although founded in 1943, did not become a dynamic "player" in Washington, D.C., until twenty years later. The Hudson Institute, now located in Indianapolis, was only established in 1961; the Center for Strategic and International Studies a year later. The Heritage Foundation did not come into existence until 1973 and did not become preeminent until just a decade ago. With few exceptions the creation of conservative think tanks is less than a generation old. The state-level manifestations of this trend, of course, are scarcely out of their swaddling clothes.

Such facts naturally raise a question: why this spectacular recent upsurge? The first, and most obvious, reason is that there is a perceived need for such institutions, a need for the kind of "product" that they produce. As conservatism since the 1970s has moved from theory to practice, from the Ivory Tower (if you will) to the marble corridors of political power, the demand for practical application of conservative principles has intensified. And that is what think tanks are: formulators and marketers of applied conservatism. At the state and local level, this demand has been fueled by the conviction that too many conservatives ignored their roots during the Reagan era when all the action appeared to occur inside the Beltway.

But *why* this seemingly insatiable need for think tanks and the specialized work that they do? Why the need, and why now? A deeper explanation begins to emerge when we consider the definition of a think tank offered by a leading student of the subject. The primary function of a think tank, he argues, is "to act as a bridge between knowledge and power." This definition points us toward a second reason for the emergence of the think tank as a distinctive social institution in our time: the continuing growth of government and the deepening politicization of our society. As government at all levels expands its regulatory grasp, the terrain for policy studies, and hence for think tanks, grows apace. Surely there would be less occasion for bridge-building between the spheres of knowledge and power if the jurisdiction of power were circumscribed and reduced.

Yet why, one might ask, does the exercise of power require specialized knowledge at all? Here we come to a third reason for the growth of think tanks of all persuasions: the reigning assumption, now deeply embedded in our culture, that the purpose of government is to promote social change and that governing and policymaking are identical. If government is to improve the human condition, does it not need expertise for guidance? And who will supply it if not trained scientists—social scientists, economic scientists, physical scientists, and other practitioners of what has been called "idea power"? Increasingly, it seems, no governmental body, even at the local level, can make a significant decision in this country without first acquiring heaps of detailed knowledge in the form of studies, reports, impact statements, and elaborate assemblages of data.

This symbiosis of politics and putative expertise brings me to another reason for the current proliferation of think tanks: the increasing "intellectualization" of our politics. Again, the trend is relatively recent in its impact upon the American Right. About forty years ago, Senator Robert Taft—the "Mr. Conservative" of his day—was asked whether he had read Russell Kirk's new book *The Conservative Mind*, one of the formative works of the postwar conservative renaissance. "No," the senator replied, and added with a chuckle, "You remind me of [James] Thurber's *Let Your Mind Alone*." Taft remarked that he was a politician, not a philosopher. Today, just a generation later, the wall between politicians and "philosophers" has virtually disappeared. This is a remarkable change. Surely it says much about our current conduct of politics that most members of Vice President Quayle's senior staff hold doctorates.

We have come far indeed from the time of H. L. Mencken, who said that in politics you have to rise above principle. Today the mark of a presidential candidate is a commitment to high principle (at least before the election) reinforced by reams of position papers drawn up by task forces of experts residing in think tanks.

Feeding this "intellectualization" of our politics is an extraordinary demographic datum: In the United States of America, for the first time in the history of the planet, a majority of men and women are seeking some form of postsecondary education. As tens of millions of people have become exposed in the past thirty years to academic disciplines and modes of discourse, there has been created an enormous consumer market for ideas, or at least words. The swelling of the ranks of the educated and (in some cases) the indoctrinated has had tremendous implications for the style of our politics. For example, have you ever wondered about the profusion of political slogans on T-shirts, buttons, and automobile bumper stickers—another peculiar phenomenon of our time? Surveys have shown that the more education a person attains, the more likely he or she is to view politics in ideological terms. All of this creates new opportunities for those who disseminate political ideas.

For think tanks there is an additional implication of this trend: as more people become better educated, the pool of idea producers also expands. There are now more than 100,000 Ph.D.s in the United States, an increase of more than 50 percent since the late 1960s. A cynic might remark that this growing mass production of intellectuals is proof of Say's Law: that the supply of expertise creates its own demand. More intellectuals, more think tanks!

Another underlying factor promoting the creation of think tanks is technological. With the advent of desktop publishing and fax machines, it has become easier for organizations to disseminate their products (such as issue papers and newsletters) to their target audiences.

Still another reason for the multiplication of think tanks, at least of conservative ones, is the growing uncongeniality of academia for conservative scholars. The increasing aggregation of conservative policy centers has provided havens for more than a few refugees from the inhospitable world of "political correctness." Without perhaps being fully conscious of what they have being doing, conservatives have begun to create an alternative network in which intellectuals on the Right can conduct their work without harassment. If the winds of academe continue to blow at gale force from the left, this will only provide further incentive for some conservative think tanks to evolve into outposts of advanced research in the social sciences—a substitute, in short, for decadent universities.

Other factors also help to account for the profusion of think tanks: the decentralized structure of American politics, to take an obvious example. But by now I have said enough to indicate that the rise of this form of political/intellectual organization is indicative of powerful historical tendencies that have acquired additional velocity in recent years. Increasingly these currents are affecting Middle America, thus opening a new frontier for this expression of intellectual energy.

I wish now to turn to the future. As conservatives continue to develop institutions, particularly in the states, in service to our cause, it appears to me that several challenges loom. The first is a direct consequence of success. When I began research on American conservatism back in the 1970s, my principal sources included perhaps half a dozen journals. Since then, the publication of conservative books, articles, columns, and policy studies has become an avalanche. As I survey this veritable torrent of print, a haunting, practical question relentlessly intrudes: who can possibly *read* all this material? Who indeed reads more than a smattering of it? For all the brave talk of targeting elite opinion-molders, what evidence do we have that the people who ought to read this output really do so systematically? I myself am not a professional marketer of ideas. But I am a consumer of ideas, and I have the uncomfortable feeling that most conservative literature, alas, is unread—or read only by the already converted. As conservative think tanks generate ever more journals, monographs, pamphlets, conference papers, and op-ed pieces—which I applaud—it seems imperative that we devise ways of measuring the effectiveness of this gargantuan effort.

The second challenge is more subtle, and it, too, is a product of prosperity. In the past decade or so, each constituent element in the conservative coalition—libertarian, traditionalist, anti-Communist, neoconservative and New Right—has occupied and assiduously cultivated its own niche, complete with supporting scholars and publications. Such a division of labor can be—and I think generally has been—beneficial. But as time goes by it also carries a risk: the risk of attenuation of the willingness to cooperate. The contemporary conservative intellectual movement is in a way like a hand, comprising five separate but associated digits. If any one of these is severed and removed, or tries to function to the exclusion of the others, the hand as a whole loses effectiveness. As the number of conservative think tanks increases, and as the process of differentiation stretches into the states and cities, conservatives must avoid the sectarian temptation and remember that the Grand Alliance is greater than its parts.

The final problem confronting conservative think tanks is in my view the profoundest of all. The world of public policy is precisely that: a *public* world revolving around legislation and administration. As our society politicizes, we must of necessity operate on that turf. But as conservatives, especially, should understand, not every issue in life is neatly reducible to a policy to be resolved through expertise and political action. As Russell Kirk, among others, has taught us, the proper ordering of the state is ultimately dependent upon the kind of order that prevails in the private sphere.

And here I wonder whether conservative research and advocacy groups are doing nearly enough. Consider the campaign, enthusiastically endorsed and spearheaded by conservatives including the Indiana Policy Review Foundation, for greater parental choice in education—that is, choice of the schools which their children will attend. I do not oppose this movement, but a nagging question recurs: who among us is articulating the values on which parents will exercise their choice?

Suppose conservatives win this policy battle; what then? By what criteria will parents expend their educational vouchers? Does it matter? Will conservative leaders simply say, "The parents know best," and move on to other issues? Or will we strive to educate the parents—a task that will take us beyond the purely public sphere?

Again I ask: who among the conservatives is attempting to mold and purify—and not simply criticize—the social mores which ultimately determine the limits of political possibility? Are we conservatives paying enough attention to value-formation in the larger society as opposed to value-application in the legislatures and courts? A society may be outwardly free and prosperous yet rotting intellectually and spiritually at the core.

It is therefore essential that conservatives not aim all their ammunition at legislators, bureaucrats, and editorial writers, important though these people obviously are. Here, it seems to me, lies an opportunity for the burgeoning family of state-level think tanks. Such organizations, by their very location, are closer than most of their elders to the world of everyday people leading everyday lives. By carefully establishing networks of influence at the relatively nonintellectual grass roots—via such mediating institutions as civic and service clubs—conservative intellectual activists in the states may be able to develop new mechanisms for what one conservative theorist has called "the reclamation of cultural power." This is no minor matter, for tomorrow's public policy debates may be lost unless today's cultural battles are won.

The emergence of state-level think tanks, then, is a welcome development on the American Right. It has great potential. Nearly two hundred years ago Edmund Burke declared, "The only thing necessary for the triumph of evil is for good men to do nothing." In Indiana and elsewhere, good men and women have taken his words to heart—with results that give me confidence that conservatism in America has a future as well as a past.

Modern Tomes:
Conservative Writings That Changed Our Minds between the 1970s and the 1990s

This appraisal of contemporary conservative writings appeared in the July–August 1997 issue of Policy Review *under the title "Modern Tomes."*

A number of years ago, the writers Malcolm Cowley and Bernard Smith invited a group of American intellectuals to identify the nonfiction books of recent decades that had most impressed them and had to some extent influenced their thinking. The result was an intriguing volume entitled *Books That Changed Our Minds*. In it, eleven contributors analyzed such classics as *The Education of Henry Adams* and Oswald Spengler's *Decline of the West*.

The Cowley–Smith anthology came to mind recently when the editors of *Policy Review* asked me to compile a list of the most important and influential works advancing conservative ideas in the past twenty years. At first the task seemed simple, as obvious candidates sprang quickly to consciousness. Then it became more daunting, as the sheer scope of conservative literature since 1977 came into view. How to extract from this vast and specialized cornucopia a mere ten or fifteen titles? Moreover, many conservative books of the last two decades have been intellectually important and richly deserving of recognition but not, alas, as influential as they ought to be. Many other conservative writings in this period have been primarily of intramural significance—applauded inside the movement but unfortunately little noticed outside it.

How, then, should we navigate the rapids? It is here that the Cowley–Smith volume of years ago suggests a decisive criterion: Which writings of a conservative character in the past twenty years can be said to have changed minds? Which have discernibly altered America's public conversation and (in some cases) its public policy?

What follows, then, is neither an exhaustive canon of recent conservative "great books" nor a mechanical compendium of bestsellers. It is, rather, a chronological list of twelve books, two articles, and two speeches that, at least as much as many others, have given the intellectual climate of our time a conservative cast.

"A WORLD SPLIT APART"
Commencement address, Harvard University (June 8, 1978)
Aleksandr Solzhenitsyn

Exiled from the Soviet Union in 1974, the acclaimed author and dissident came to the West a hero of the resistance to Communist tyranny. The message he brought with him, however, was profoundly discomfiting to liberal and "pragmatic" Americans in the post-Vietnam era of détente. In an astonishing commencement address at Harvard, Solzhenitsyn decried the moral cowardice, flaccidity, materialistic self-indulgence, and misuses of freedom in the West and accused its ruling elites of a loss of "civic courage" in the face of Communist evil.

How had this predicament come to pass? For Solzhenitsyn, it was nothing less than a civilizational catastrophe literally centuries in the making. At Harvard—the academic capital of secular, liberal modernity—he unabashedly traced the West's "present debility" to a defective worldview "born in the Renaissance" and unleashed politically by the Enlightenment: "the calamity of an autonomous, irreligious humanistic consciousness." Liberating "imperfect man" from "the moral heritage of Christian centuries," and proclaiming man's autonomy "from any higher force above him," "rationalistic humanism" had eventually produced, in the twentieth century, a world scarred by materialistic decadence, "moral poverty," and spiritual deprivation. "Humanism that has lost its Christian heritage," he added, could not prevail against materialistic communism.

In his searing indictment of atheistic humanism, and in his call for fundamental spiritual renewal transcending the "ossified formulas of the Enlightenment," Solzhenitsyn expressed with remarkable force themes espoused by American conservatives from Whittaker Chambers to the Religious Right of today.

THE WAY THE WORLD WORKS (1978)
Jude Wanniski

Hailed by Irving Kristol as the "best economic primer since Adam Smith," this book introduced the world to the intellectual counterrevolution of the 1970s known as supply-side economics. Together with Arthur Laffer, Jack Kemp, Robert Bartley, and others, Wanniski articulated a growing assault on a vulnerable Keynesian orthodoxy and—in the process—converted much of the GOP to a new orthodoxy of its own, centered on economic growth and cuts in tax rates. Two decades later, tax cuts remain at the core of conservative Republicanism.

BREAKING RANKS (1979)
Norman Podhoretz

If much of modern conservatism is a revolt against the 1930s and the New Deal, much of contemporary neoconservatism is a revolt against the 1960s. No one has explored the interior history of this decade more trenchantly than Norman Podhoretz in *Breaking Ranks*. The editor of *Commentary* from 1960 to 1995, Podhoretz believes that "clarity is courage," and in this memoir he tells the story of his journey from liberalism to radicalism to neoconservatism with a clarity that brought him contumely from former allies. By publicly defecting from the Left and critiquing it so effectively, Podhoretz undermined two widespread assumptions in left-of-center circles: the belief that history, in the long run, always favors "progressive" causes, and the belief that only liberalism and radicalism are respectable points of view. By destroying the automatic equation of liberalism with intelligence and of "progressivism" with progress, Podhoretz and his fellow neoconservatives made it impossible for the Left to condescend any longer to the Right. The terrain of public debate in America was transformed.

"DICTATORSHIPS AND DOUBLE STANDARDS"
Commentary (November 1979)
Jeane Kirkpatrick

When this seminal essay appeared, American foreign policy was floundering. Pro-American but authoritarian regimes in Nicaragua and Iran had just given way to anti-American and even more authoritarian ones—and all with the befuddled collaboration of the U.S. government. Fettered by an idealistic concern for human rights, the administration of Jimmy Carter seemed increasingly unable to differentiate friend from foe.

At this critical juncture in the Cold War, Kirkpatrick, a Georgetown professor and a registered Democrat, propounded two arguments that conservatives eagerly seized upon. Traditional, authoritarian autocracies, she asserted, are less repressive, less disruptive of the lives of the people, and less systemically evil than revolutionary regimes of the Left with their utopian and totalitarian ideologies. And traditional, authoritarian regimes are more "susceptible of liberalization" and eventual democratization than leftist ones led by Marxist revolutionaries.

Kirkpatrick's article led to her becoming the U.S. ambassador to the United Nations in the Reagan administration. (Ronald Reagan himself read and admired this essay.) Just as important, it provided American policymakers a powerful conceptual framework for making necessary distinctions between greater and lesser evils in their prosecution of the Cold War. This article helped to relieve what was threatening to become a paralyzing tension between realism and idealism in American foreign policy.

FREE TO CHOOSE (1980)
Milton and Rose Friedman

In early 1980, as the nation's economy groaned under the burden of soaring inflation and unemployment, Nobel laureate Milton Friedman—America's most famous free-market economist—hosted a ten-part series on public television entitled *Free to Choose*. In the spring, he and his wife published a companion volume by the same name; it became the bestselling nonfiction book of the entire year. In it they explained with unrivaled lucidity their classical liberal philosophy of freedom and applied it to a host of policy issues. At the end of *Free to Choose*, the authors ventured to declare that Americans were "waking up." "We are recognizing the dangers of an overgoverned society, coming to understand . . . that reliance on the freedom of people to control their own lives in accordance with their own values is the surest way to achieve the full potential of a great society." A few months later, Ronald Reagan was elected president. In *Free to Choose*, the Friedmans helped to catalyze the intellectual ferment that produced the "Reagan Revolution."

WEALTH AND POVERTY (1981)
George Gilder

If Jude Wanniski was the most ardent propagandist for supply-side economics, writer George Gilder has been called its theologian. Appearing at the dawn of the Reagan era, *Wealth and Poverty* audaciously propelled the case for capitalism upward, out of the mundane sphere of taxation and public policy and onto the higher plane of morality and metaphysics. Where even some defenders of the free market had heretofore been willing to give but two cheers for capitalism, Gilder unashamedly gave three. His book was an ode to entrepreneurship as marvelously creative, basically altruistic, and veritably moral. "A successful economy depends on the proliferation of the rich," he asserted. Successful entrepreneurs were "the heroes of economic life."

Scorning the gloom-and-doom ideologies of the stagnant 1970s, he proclaimed: "Our greatest and only resource is the miracle of human creativity in a relation of openness to the divine." Here was a book worthy of Reagan's buoyant vision of America. By fearlessly extolling the moral promise of entrepreneurial capitalism, and by mounting a lively assault on the modern welfare state, Gilder not only authored an unusual and refreshing apologia for freedom and creativity. He also strengthened growing populistic sentiment on the Right against managerial elitists who presume to guide entire economies.

THE SPIRIT OF DEMOCRATIC CAPITALISM (1982)
Michael Novak

By the early 1980s, it was increasingly plain that socialism in practice had failed and that capitalism had proven far more beneficial to the human race. And yet, despite its undeniable triumphs, wrote Michael Novak, not one theologian—Christian or Jewish—had ever evaluated the "theological significance" of this extraordinarily successful form of political economy.

In *The Spirit of Democratic Capitalism*, Novak—a Roman Catholic social theorist and historian—elucidated the spiritual and moral foundations of "democratic capitalism" as an interlocking unity embracing a market economy, a democratic polity, and a moral-cultural matrix animated by "ideals of liberty and justice for all." By examining democratic capitalism at the level of ideals and values, and by declaring its superiority to socialism at this level, Novak contributed powerfully to the intellectual rehabilitation of this system of social organization, particularly among Christian thinkers. His book became an antidote to that strange but fashionable brew of Christianity and Marxism in the 1970s and 1980s known as "liberation theology."

Reflections of a Neoconservative (1983)
Irving Kristol

In his introduction to this collection of essays, the longtime editor of the *Public Interest* observed that neoconservatism "aims to infuse American bourgeois orthodoxy with a new self-conscious intellectual vigor, while dispelling the feverish mélange of gnostic humors that, for more than a century now, has suffused our political beliefs and has tended to convert them into political religions." In the past twenty years, no conservative or neoconservative has done more to carry out this mission. Much of Irving Kristol's work has occurred quietly, in his encouragement of the scholarship and institution-building that have powered the conservative cause. But much of his contribution has taken the form of incisive and influential essays published in the *Wall Street Journal* and various magazines. *Reflections* is an excellent collection of these pieces, mostly written in the late 1970s and early 1980s. This anthology should be supplemented by Kristol's *Neoconservatism: The Autobiography of an Idea* (1995).

Address to the National Association of Evangelicals
(March 8, 1983)
Ronald Reagan

This was the unforgettable speech in which the president of the United States forthrightly labeled the Soviet Union an "evil empire." "The real crisis we face today is a spiritual one," Reagan went on; "at root, it is a test of moral will and faith." In prose that proved to be prophetic, he added: "I believe that communism is another sad, bizarre chapter in human history whose last pages even now are being written."

For American conservatives and for friends of freedom everywhere, Reagan's address was a bracing affirmation of truth, an ideological shot heard round the world. It is not too much to suggest that the conservative president's unapologetic verbal offensive against communism—of which this speech was a classic expression—was one of the catalytic agents that set the Soviet Union on the path to extinction.

Modern Times (1983, rev. 1991)
Paul Johnson

No conservative's bookshelf should be without this provocative reinterpretation of twentieth-century history emphasizing the staggering evil wrought by "the rise of moral relativism, the decline of moral responsibility, the repudiation of Judeo-Christian values," intellectual hubris, and the unconstrained, ideologically driven State. To those who believed that "an enlarged state could increase the sum total of human happiness," the British ex-socialist Johnson taught otherwise. In the twentieth century, he said, the State "had proved itself an insatiable spender, an unrivaled waster," and "the greatest killer of all time." For conservatives of every persuasion—libertarian, traditionalist, anti-Communist, neoconservative, and Religious Right—Johnson's volume provided an invaluable history lesson and counterweight to the deadly progressivist utopianism of our times.

The Naked Public Square (1984)
Richard John Neuhaus

In the decade or so before this book appeared, a startling political awakening of Protestant evangelicals and other religious conservatives occurred, to the consternation of many liberal Americans. Were not the Moral Majority and its allies, they thought, threats to democracy and tolerance? Although often sharply critical of the religious New Right, Richard John Neuhaus—himself a Christian cleric—was even more disturbed by a regnant ideology of militant secularism that was driving religion and religiously derived values from the nation's public life. If our "public square" remains thus denuded, he warned, democracy itself would be at risk. For the "naked public square" would not stay empty; the vacuum would be filled by false gods and tyrants much more intolerant (and intolerable) than traditional religion. A "public ethic" necessary for the survival of American democracy, Neuhaus contended, "cannot be reestablished unless it is informed by religiously grounded values." The "religious base of the democratic experiment" must be rearticulated.

The Naked Public Square remains a *locus classicus* for the argument that people of faith have a right and obligation to participate in public affairs—not only for their own sakes but for the health of our common polity. This book endures as a formidable obstacle to secularist triumphalism.

Losing Ground (1984)
Charles Murray

It was not enough for conservatives in the 1980s to preach the virtues of democratic capitalism and supply-side economics. They needed a credible empirical critique of the liberal politics of compassion. In 1984, Charles Murray delivered it. Deploying an array of statistical indices of social well-being, Murray documented an astounding pattern: From 1950 to the mid-1960s, the condition of America's poor (including blacks) gradually improved, only to deteriorate—often severely—after 1965. Indeed, the "number of people living in poverty," Murray reported, "stopped declining just as the public-assistance program budgets and the rate of increase in those budgets were highest."

Whence this staggering and unexpected reversal of the trendlines? Why did so many of America's poor become worse off in the 1970s than they had been in the early 1960s? Murray's answer was equally stunning: The War on Poverty—the crown jewel of Lyndon Johnson's Great Society—wrought devastating havoc on the poor. The War on Poverty—compassionate liberalism in action—"changed the rules of their world," encouraged behavior that was "destructive in the long term," and subsidized its own "irretrievable mistakes." "We tried to remove the barriers to escape from poverty," said Murray, "and inadvertently built a trap."

Murray's book was immediately and sometimes harshly criticized from the Left. But as a sophisticated social scientist who had done his homework, he could not be ignored. *Losing Ground* still stands as one of the most powerful indictments of liberal social policy ever written by a scholar on the Right.

"DAN QUAYLE WAS RIGHT"
The Atlantic (April 1993)
Barbara Dafoe Whitehead

By the 1990s, alarming patterns of social deviancy and regression had begun to appear far beyond the poor and underclass. The structure of the family itself seemed to be disintegrating, and politicians were taking note. In a 1992 speech, Vice President Dan Quayle called for a renewed "public commitment" to "our Judeo-Christian values," including marriage, and added:

> It doesn't help matters when prime time TV has Murphy Brown—a character who supposedly epitomizes today's intelligent, highly paid, professional woman—mocking the importance of fathers, by bearing a child alone, and calling it just another "lifestyle choice."

For his pains Quayle was scathingly berated, and the cause of "family values" was mocked. The actress who played Murphy Brown received an honorary degree at an Ivy League university. How surprising, then, that less than a year later an *Atlantic* article suggested boldly that Quayle was right.

Barbara Dafoe Whitehead—not known as a conservative—assembled a panoply of data demonstrating what to conservatives seemed obvious: The widespread dissolution of intact, two-parent families had been harmful for millions of children. Once more the liberationist ethos of the 1960s stood indicted by its undeniable consequences. The "vast natural experiment in family life" in the past twenty-five years, said Whitehead, had yielded "the first generation in the nation's history to do worse psychologically, socially, and economically than its parents."

Whitehead's article—appearing as it did in a liberal magazine—undoubtedly did much to legitimate conservative perspectives on a central issue in the "culture wars." "Family values" now became everyone's concern. Of course, many on the Left seemed to prefer to talk about children and their "villages" (rather than parents) as the key elements in the social equation. Whitehead, however, stressed the importance of families, a more conservative formulation. Like many other articles by conservatively oriented analysts in the 1990s, her essay exemplified the growing validation by social-science research of traditional moral teachings: what Rudyard Kipling called "the gods of the copybook headings."

THE BOOK OF VIRTUES (1993)
William Bennett

If the social agenda of religious conservatives could be summed up in a phrase, it might be (to borrow from Gertrude Himmelfarb) "the re-moralization of society." But in the face of profound social disorientation, vulgar relativism and hedonism, and a "naked"—even hostile—public square, how does one do this? In 1993, William Bennett resorted to an unconventional stratagem: He compiled a massive anthology of moral tales and poetry designed to teach children such virtues as self-discipline, responsibility, courage, perseverance, and honesty. By drawing primarily upon the classic wisdom of Western civilization, by writing openly of the need for "moral literacy," and by unflinchingly labeling his collection a book of virtues, Bennett set himself against the postmodernist and decadent sensibilities so prevalent in elite and popular culture. His anthology became a bestseller.

Bennett's venture is a useful reminder that conservative concerns encompass more than economics, political theory, and public policy. The preservation of a humane and civil society requires the constant replenishment of the moral and spiritual sources of our conduct. In this respect, conservatism is a private as well as a public philosophy.

THE VISION OF THE ANOINTED (1995)
Thomas Sowell

In the past two decades, the conservative social scientist Thomas Sowell has produced a barrage of important books on race and ethnicity, political philosophy, and other subjects. Of these, the most wide-ranging, yet laser-like in its intensity, is *The Vision of the Anointed: Self-Congratulation as a Basis of Public Policy*. In this withering polemic, Sowell lays bare the underlying assumptions and baneful consequences of "the prevailing vision of our time," a vision "dangerously close to sealing itself off from any discordant feedback from reality." It is the predominant vision of the American intelligentsia and its followers: a "self-anointed elite" that sees itself as morally and intellectually superior to the rest of us. Sowell deftly contrasts this elite's worldview—liberalism—with the "tragic vision" of conservatives. The "anointed," for example, quite literally consider reality to be "socially constructed" and therefore capable of being "deconstructed" and reconstructed at will. For them the world is "a very tidy place" where "human nature is readily changeable" and social problems can be "solved."

But Sowell does not stop here. Invoking a wealth of social-science data and other documentation, he concludes that in area after area of American life, the liberal vision of the anointed has brought about "social degeneration" and immense devastation since the 1960s. Ours has been an era, he says, of "self-inflicted wounds" inflicted by "supposedly 'thinking people'" who fancied themselves "wiser and nobler than the common herd." "Seldom," he finds, "have so few cost so much to so many." For a concise, morally impassioned, and relentless arraignment of contemporary liberalism in theory and practice, look no further than this book.

NOT WITHOUT HONOR: THE HISTORY OF AMERICAN ANTICOMMUNISM (1996)
Richard Gid Powers

When Richard Powers began work on this book, he tells us, he believed that "anticommunism displayed America at its worst." Instead, "I came to see in anticommunism America at its best." From a liberal academic in the 1990s, these are unexpected words, and *Not Without Honor* is an unexpected book: a comprehensive, scholarly history of American anticommunism in which the contribution of many conservatives—including William F. Buckley Jr. and Ronald Reagan—receives respectful, even sympathetic, treatment.

Powers, to be sure, is severely critical of some manifestations of the anti-Communist impulse. To the irritation of some on the Right, he differentiates sharply between those he deems "responsible anticommunists" (including Buckley, Norman Podhoretz, and the anti-Communist Left) and those he disapprovingly labels "countersubversives": above all, Senator Joseph McCarthy and his fellow conspiracy-hunters. In his desire to rescue anticommunism from McCarthyism, Powers does not, perhaps, take full measure of what James Burnham called "the web of subversion" that existed in America in the early years of the Cold War. Still, in a climate of academic opinion long dominated by anti-anti-Communist biases, *Not Without Honor* presents American resistance to communism as an essentially honorable and even noble cause. For conservatives—and for a balanced historical memory—this is a long step forward.

Taken all together, these works remind us of how far conservatism has traveled since William F. Buckley Jr., in *Up From Liberalism*, mourned "the failure of the conservative demonstration." Since then, and with increasing power and frequency, conservatives have made their "demonstration" in the demanding arena of public debate. Of course, there is always more to do as the challenges multiply and as our age (in Whittaker Chambers's words) "finds its own language for an eternal meaning."

4

The Quiet, Libertarian Odyssey of John Chamberlain

This review of John Chamberlain's autobiography, A Life with the Printed Word, *was published in the March 1983 issue of the* American Spectator.

One day in late 1955, an unassuming, middle-aged man appeared at the office of the fledgling *National Review*, found an unoccupied chair, and sat down. After peering at a typewriter for a few moments, he proceeded to punch the keys. Forty-five minutes later, he departed. After this ritual had repeated itself once a week for several months, a young *National Review* staffer grew indignant. On all his visits, she protested, the typewriter repairman had never examined her machine.

This "typewriter repairman," it turned out, was *National Review*'s lead book reviewer, John Chamberlain. Coming to the office for his weekly assignment, he would quietly compose his review at the typewriter with seemingly effortless grace. Then, his work completed, he would silently slip out of the office—careful not to disturb his colleagues laboring at their own projects.

These qualities of calmness, solicitude, and self-effacement are abundantly reflected in John Chamberlain's newly published autobiography. For more than half a century now, Chamberlain has been leading, as he puts it, "a life with the printed word." And what an abundant life it has been! In 1926, fresh out of Yale, he became a cub reporter for the *New York Times*; within three years he was assistant editor of the *Times*'s Sunday book review. In 1933, at the astonishingly young age of thirty, he rose to the eminence of daily book reviewer for the *Times*. For the next four years, he turned out five book reviews a week (plus sundry other essays) and solidified his reputation (in one authority's words) as the "finest critic of his generation." In the late thirties and forties, he occupied positions of influence at *Fortune*, *Life*, and *Time* under Henry Luce, with a professorship at Columbia's School of Journalism on the side. In the fifties, he was a founding editor of the *Freeman*, an editorial writer for the *Wall Street Journal*, and a valued contributor to *National Review*. In the sixties, he became one of the most respected of conservative columnists.

Along the way, he raised three children and wrote several books (including two libertarian classics, *The Enterprising Americans* and *The Roots of Capitalism*). Today, in his eightieth year, John Chamberlain continues indefatigably to expound the philosophy of "voluntarism" and free-market capitalism with the same robust reasonableness that has won him journalistic admirers for five decades.

Such a life is ample subject indeed for an autobiography, and one can only be pleased that Chamberlain has written his. But the importance of *A Life with the Printed Word* transcends the particularities of a richly successful career. For like so many other American conservative luminaries since 1945, Chamberlain in his youth was a man of the radical Left. How was it that this supporter of Norman Thomas in 1932 became a Reaganite a generation later? How did a quasi-socialist of the thirties come to write the foreword to Hayek's *Road to Serfdom* in 1944? What, in short, prevented Chamberlain from becoming (in his words) "just another New York liberal" in middle age? The story of his intellectual journey from Left to Right is the principal subject of this absorbing memoir.

One source of Chamberlain's evolution lay in his temperament. A New England Yankee who came of age in the 1920s, he shared his generation's artistic and civil libertarianism and its apolitical distrust of crusading fanaticism. He never lost these early attitudes. Even in the politics-drenched thirties, Chamberlain retained some of his youthful skepticism of concentrated power. Indifferent to the early New Deal, he was drawn instead to the Brandeisian trust-busting philosophy of his friend Leon Henderson and to nonconformists of the Left like John Dos Passos (whose own intellectual odyssey rather strikingly resembles Chamberlain's).

The sheer act of reading, one suspects, also helped to rescue Chamberlain from stultifying leftist conformity. Reviewing a book a day for the *Times*, he discovered authors like Albert Jay Nock, the grandfather of libertarianism, and Max Eastman, who had been to Moscow and seen not the future but the truth. Later on he encountered Rose Wilder Lane and Isabel Paterson, whose *God of the Machine* "hit me like a ton of bricks" in 1943. Chamberlain must surely be one of the best-read journalists of all time; the very act of confronting an endless variety of books for review shielded him from the certitudes of the cultural commissars. Chamberlain the literary critic, one senses, could never surrender his independence to anyone's party line.

Still another factor nudging him from the Left was his experience with the Communists and their sympathizers. The most harrowing episode occurred when Walter Duranty, the *Times*'s famed Moscow correspondent, "almost casually" remarked to Chamberlain one day that three million Russians had died in a deliberate, artificial famine. (It was Stalin's method of liquidating the kulaks.) Chamberlain was aghast. How could Duranty be so callous about this gigantic horror? And why had he never even reported this story in his dispatches? Soon afterward, Chamberlain himself mentioned the murderous famine in one of his book reviews. Immediately the Communist journal *New Masses* demanded proof: Chamberlain replied by citing Duranty as his source.

Now the fat was really in the fire. In danger of losing his visa from the Soviet government, Duranty denied that he had ever said anything. The Communists, meanwhile, denounced Chamberlain with fury. Suddenly Chamberlain's reputation for veracity—and his job at the *Times*—were in peril. Fortunately, a fellow *Times* journalist, Simeon Strunsky, came forward in Chamberlain's defense: Duranty had also told Strunsky about the famine. Without this in-house corroboration, Chamberlain would likely have been fired by the *Times* and his journalistic career perhaps destroyed.

Although Chamberlain remained a man of the Left for most of the thirties, he was never a Communist. Instead, he became known in Party circles as a "dissident radical," suspect and unreliable because of his friendship with ex-Communist intellectuals.

And so an independent man of the Left he might have remained, had it not been for one event that decisively set him on the road to the Right. In 1936, through his friend Archibald MacLeish, Chamberlain joined the staff of *Fortune*. For the next decade, as a senior journalist for the Luce publications, Chamberlain had an extraordinary opportunity to study and write about the workings of American business.

It was a revelation. Freed from the environs of Greenwich Village, he began to explore a world that his literary and leftist friends never saw: the functioning world of capitalism, of free-market creativity. Traveling around the country on assignments for *Fortune*, he encountered entrepreneurs who were every bit as capable and interesting as the literati he had left behind. Increasingly, Chamberlain's anticapitalist preconceptions dissolved. Business leaders, he discovered, were not necessarily Babbitts after all. The American economy was not "mature" and permanently stagnant. The market system *worked*. The more he examined the dynamic intricacies of the private sector, the stronger grew his commitment to voluntarism. His antipolitical impulses likewise deepened. Washington "does not originate much," he writes in these memoirs; "a country can only be happy and prosperous by keeping its politicians on a taut leash."

Eventually Chamberlain came to believe that the truly significant economic story of the thirties was not that of New Deal intervention in the economy (which failed in any case to end the Depression). It was the pioneering efforts of risk-taking entrepreneurs and technological innovators. It was they, not the politicians and regulators, who "saved the day for us in war and established the basis for the huge postwar expansion." And, Chamberlain adds, "If I hadn't broken out of the tight little world of literary New York and gone to work for Harry Luce, I would never have seen what still eludes our Arthur Schlesingers and the others who write what passes for our 'history.'"

The opportunity to observe American business, then, liberated Chamberlain from the Left. Reading, writing, observing, he had *studied* his way out of collectivism. From the mid-1940s on, he has been a stalwart defender of entrepreneurial capitalism and an effective spokesman for the conservative movement.

All this and more Chamberlain recounts in these never-strident memoirs—a veritable travelogue through the ideological battlegrounds of half a century. It is a book filled with acute observations of people—of Henry Luce and Charles Lindbergh, Whittaker Chambers and Willi Schlamm, of journalists of the Center, Left, and Right. At times one wishes that this compact autobiography were twice as long, that Chamberlain had favored us with even more impressions of his stellar array of acquaintances, and with more about himself. In fifty-seven years of journalism, he has known so many of the great. After completing this volume one yearns for him to tell us more.

But such expansiveness, one suspects, would be out of character for this soft-spoken New Englander. "Of all the autobiographies of ideological explorations," writes William F. Buckley Jr. in his introduction, "John Chamberlain's is surely the most soft-throated in the literature." It is a book, too, that is singularly free from rancor. Indeed, despite a career of journalistic advocacy, and an unfashionably journey from Left to Right, Chamberlain seems never to have made an enemy or lost a friend.

To those who have made his acquaintance, this remark will cause no surprise. Back in the sixties, a Harvard professor mordantly observed that academe is a place where men of principle outnumber men of honor. John Chamberlain is a man of principle; to those who know him personally, he is a man of rare decency as well. In this age of self-advertisement, it is a pleasure to read a book by a distinguished journalist so unassuming that he could be mistaken for a typewriter repairman. *A Life with the Printed Word* is more than an illuminating trek through our times. It is the memoir of a gentleman.

5

Whittaker Chambers:
The Ambivalent Icon

This review of Whittaker Chambers: A Biography, *by Sam Tanenhaus, appeared in the May 1997 issue of the* American Spectator *under the title "The Ambivalent Icon."*

Next year will mark the fiftieth anniversary of the most sensational espionage case in American history. In August 1948 Whittaker Chambers, a senior editor at *Time*, testified before the House Un-American Activities Committee that he had been an underground Communist in the 1930s and had known as Communists a number of U.S. government employees in Washington. Among these was an up-and-coming State Department officer named Alger Hiss. Chambers told the committee that in 1938 he had broken from the murderous Soviet apparatus he served and had tried unsuccessfully to persuade his friend Hiss to do the same.

In the ensuing decade Chambers had carved out a brilliant career as a protégé of Henry Luce. Hiss, meanwhile, had become a high-ranking State Department official and a trusted member of the American delegation to the Yalta conference in 1945. Suave, elegant in appearance, and well-connected, he seemed to epitomize New Deal liberalism, committed to progressive social change and a peaceful world.

In the summer of 1948, as the Cold War turned more rancorous, Whittaker Chambers's testimony stunned the nation. When Hiss, who was by then president of the prestigious Carnegie Endowment for International Peace, aggressively denied under oath Chambers's charges and sued him for slander, Chambers astounded the nation further by producing a cache of secret government documents given to him by Hiss ten years before. Some were notes in Hiss's own handwriting. Others were copies of highly confidential State Department materials—typed, it was later established, on Hiss's own home typewriter. Instead of turning these items over to his Russian spymaster in 1938, Chambers had held onto them as protection against reprisal by Stalin's hit men. Now, ten years later, he and Hiss stood exposed before their country not just as once-concealed Communists but as spies.

Chambers's electrifying disclosure carried even greater implications. If his testimony was correct—and the purloined documents offered powerful corroboration—Soviet Russia had organized a massive espionage ring in the 1930s which had penetrated the upper echelons of the Roosevelt administration. Even worse: Chambers had warned the U.S. government about the spy ring in 1939, and the government had seemingly done nothing about it. (When an intermediary went to Roosevelt with Chambers's information, FDR brusquely rebuffed him. The story, he angrily declared, "isn't true.") For Republican politicians like Representative Richard Nixon (who helped to break open the case), the Chambers testimony took on new significance. Not just communism, but the policy of liberal American officialdom *toward* communism, was now at issue. Suddenly (as the saying went) a generation was on trial: the generation of the New Deal and the "Red Decade."

Chambers admitted and repented his terrible past. By 1948 he had striven for nearly a decade—through crusading journalism at *Time*—to awaken America to the menace of Soviet communism. Alger Hiss, however, made no such confession or atonement. Insisting that he was neither a Communist nor a spy, the former diplomat asserted his innocence with growing implausibility.

Initially, at least, the luminaries of American liberalism (including Eleanor Roosevelt) believed him. In August 1948 President Truman himself denounced the congressional inquiry as a "red herring" created by reactionary Republicans. Distinguished Americans such as Felix Frankfurter and Adlai Stevenson agreed to serve as character witnesses for Hiss. But in 1950, after two traumatic trials, Hiss was convicted of perjury (and, implicitly, espionage) and sentenced to five years in prison. For the rest of his life he and his supporters claimed he had been framed.

For most Americans at the time, the verdict was persuasive. Astonishing as it initially seemed to some, it was Chambers—the self-confessed Communist, pudgy and unprepossessing—who had told the truth. It was

Hiss, the "liberal"—well-dressed, well-spoken, a graduate of Harvard Law School—who had lied. The popular understanding of the case was immeasurably strengthened in 1952 by the publication of Chambers's *Witness*, a work properly acclaimed as one of the classic American autobiographies. It was further reinforced in 1978 by Allen Weinstein's volume *Perjury*, which concluded, after exhaustive study, that Hiss was guilty as charged.

Still, old myths die hard, and in some circles on the left a cult of agnosticism lingers on. Questioned recently on *Meet the Press*, Anthony Lake—President Clinton's erstwhile nominee to direct the CIA, no less—opined that the evidence of Hiss's guilt was not "conclusive." And when Hiss himself died last November at ninety-two, both ABC and NBC television news implied that he had been an innocent victim of anti-Communist hysteria. The passions of fifty years ago are not dead yet.

Along now comes Sam Tanenhaus with the first full-length biography of the enigmatic man at the center of this drama. For those who have read *Witness* or *Perjury*, much of *Whittaker Chambers* will be familiar. But Tanenhaus, a tenacious researcher, has adduced much new and important detail, including evidence from long-closed archives in Budapest and Moscow. The result is a skillfully crafted narrative that further substantiates Chambers's testimony and removes all reasonable doubt of Hiss's guilt.

Tanenhaus's book is much more, however, than an updated account of a famous controversy. It is the gripping story of a tormented man who embraced a false god, committed crimes in its name, repudiated it in fear and loathing, and then bravely bore witness against it at great personal and professional cost.

Born in 1901, Chambers seemed fated for an unconventional life. His father was a commercial artist and bisexual who deserted his family for two years to lead an alternative lifestyle, and who held himself aloof from his wife and sons when he returned. His mother, a child of economically fallen gentry, struggled desperately to keep up appearances and raise her boys to be somebody. The family's home was spiritually barren. Religious influences were nil, except for a German-language tutor who tried to convert Whittaker to Christian Science. During much of his youth Chambers was a self-conscious outsider, immersed in a private world of literature, including *Les Misérables*, his favorite novel.

In 1920 Chambers entered Columbia University, where he impressed students and professor alike with his literary talent. But something was profoundly amiss. How does a college freshman whose hero in 1920 was

Calvin Coolidge become a Communist five years later? In a lucid account of Chambers's college experience, Tanenhaus depicts his subject as a tortured religious seeker, groping anxiously for meaning and purpose in a world he perceived as sick and dying. Tanenhaus emphasizes the horrifying disintegration of Chambers's home life in these years: an ordeal culminating in his younger brother's suicide in 1926. To Chambers, who had begun to devour leftist and Communist literature, his middle-class family's travails were emblematic of the malaise of a decadent civilization. The self-assured, totalitarian zealotry of the Communists offered an alternative.

Tanenhaus does not emphasize—although Chambers himself later did—the role of the university's liberalism in subverting the certitudes of callow conservatives like himself. "By the end of my sophomore year at Columbia," Chambers later wrote, "I had ceased to be a conservative. I was nothing." God was merely a "convention." Truth was "wholly relative." His mind was a "vacuum" whose "law" was skepticism. The professorial skeptics at Columbia, he said, had "absolutely nothing" to put in the place of the "traditional beliefs" that they had destroyed in him. For a young man of Chambers's temperament and inner turmoil, genteel negations could not satisfy. He thought Leninist communism could.

So Chambers at age twenty-four became a Communist and remained one for twelve more years. A gifted writer and translator, he eventually became editor of the Communist-dominated monthly, *New Masses*. By 1932 he was (in one writer's words) "the hottest literary Bolshevik" in New York. His short story "Can You Make Out Their Voices?" won him international acclaim on the Left.

Then, at the height of his literary fame, Chambers was abruptly ordered underground into the clandestine world of Soviet-orchestrated espionage. Dispatched to Washington in 1934, he soon met Alger Hiss, among others. The apparatus he encountered was no penny-ante affair. He later calculated that he knew of seventy-five different underground Communists in the nation's capital. Many were in key agencies and had good career prospects; some held Ivy League degrees. From Hiss and others, Chambers regularly collected sensitive government documents, copies of which he delivered to Soviet intelligence officers in New York. Even today the full historical significance of this operation cannot be fathomed. Some of the State Department documents that Hiss provided, for example, could have helped the Russians to break American diplomatic codes. Perhaps someday we will learn about all this in Moscow. But for now the files of Russian military intelligence, for which Chambers worked, remain inaccessible.

For several years Chambers served, in Tanenhaus's words, as the "linch-pin of an efficient espionage apparatus." But as the Stalinist purges of the late 1930s gained momentum, he grew appalled—and increasingly frightened. One by one, Communists of his acquaintance were summoned to Moscow and their doom. Ominously, his own Soviet handler ordered him to visit the Soviet Union—a command he managed to evade. Repelled by the mon-strous evil in which he was enmeshed, Chambers finally bolted in 1938—convinced, he told his wife, that he was leaving the winning for the losing side. He turned to Christianity and dedicated himself to combating commu-nism through his journalism. At *Time* he relentlessly fought in-house leftists and naifs who thought that Joseph Stalin's intentions were benign. Cham-bers made enemies by his anti-Soviet editing and his unabashed rewriting of his foreign correspondents' reports. But as Tanenhaus notes, his grasp of the direction of current history was far more accurate and even prophetic than that of his ideological foes.

Then, in 1948, came the subpoena which shattered Chambers's life yet again and thrust him reluctantly onto the national stage. While the Hiss legal team vainly strained to demolish his credibility, pro-Hiss partisans subjected him to a malicious whispering campaign that Arthur Schlesinger Jr. called "one of the most repellent of modern history." Pilloried on the witness stand as a moral leper and a liar, the beleaguered ex-Communist came to feel that he was a witness in another sense: a martyr for a faith that might yet redeem the West at its moment of supreme crisis. Thus in his monumental mem-oir of 1952, he tried to point America—though he doubted he would suc-ceed—back to the spiritual moorings that alone could save it in its struggle against atheistic communism. In this respect he anticipated Solzhenitsyn (with whom he is briefly compared by Tanenhaus).

Chambers died in 1961. In his final decade he became an icon and ambivalent godfather of postwar conservatism. Here Tanenhaus carefully documents Chambers's deep misgivings about Joseph McCarthy, his uneasy relationship with *National Review*, his denunciation of Ayn Rand, and his various deviations from 1950s-style conservatism. Although Tanenhaus is correct about these particulars, he perhaps makes too much of them. For all Chambers's reservations about *National Review* and McCarthy, he still called himself "a man of the Right." But where William F. Buckley Jr. and his allies wished to "stand athwart history yelling Stop," Chambers the inveter-ate pessimist judged the conservative cause to be nearly hopeless, doomed to maneuver precariously within the terms set by the socialist tide of modern history. Hence his dissent from doctrinaire conservative sectarianism and his support for that Republican tactician par excellence, Richard Nixon.

Not everyone will be comfortable with the portrait that emerges from this impressive biography. Tanenhaus discloses some of the less-than-saintly aspects of Chambers's life: his bohemian lifestyle in the 1920s; his "Party marriage" and other affairs; his early homoerotic poetry and long struggle with homosexuality. Some readers may be put off—as many acquaintances were in Chambers's lifetime—by his self-created aura of inscrutability and what a colleague at *Time* called his "suppressed air of melodrama," as well as his attempt in *Witness* and other writings to find transcendent meaning in his ordeal. For some, his effort had the grandeur of a religious pilgrimage. For others, his words seemed portentous.

Even now, nearly forty years after death, this man engenders controversy. Why? Why (in Tanenhaus's words) the "passionate belief of so many" that Alger Hiss "must be innocent no matter what the evidence?" Quoting the critic Leslie Fiedler, Tanenhaus supplies an answer: Chambers effectively challenged the liberal "dogma" that in every political controversy "the liberal *per se* is the hero." By successfully impugning Hiss, he destroyed the Left's illusion—still strong in 1948—that "mere liberal principle" was "in itself a guarantee against evil."

Chambers, too, believed that he was confronting liberalism head-on—and not just its superiority complex. "The simple fact," he subsequently wrote, "is that when I took up my little sling and aimed at communism, I also hit something else. What I hit was the forces of the great socialist revolution, which, in the name of liberalism . . . has been inching its ice cap over the nation for two decades." To Chambers, twentieth-century liberals and Communists were *both* revolutionaries who shared an underlying vision: the replacement of "the power of business" by "the power of politics." These were fighting words in 1948—and long afterward.

Characteristically, however, Chambers the man of faith did not stop there. For him the ultimate meaning of the turbulent Hiss case—and of his own sad, self-convicting witness—was religious. For the crisis of the twentieth century, he held, was at bottom a crisis of faith. Communism, he explained in *Witness*, was fundamentally a religion—man's "great alternative faith"—whose seductive promise was: "Ye shall be as gods." Its vision was "the vision of man without God," of "man's mind displacing God as the creative intelligence of the world." To Chambers, militant communism—the faith of Alger Hiss—posed an inescapable choice: "God or Man, Soul or

Mind, Freedom or Communism." In this irrepressible conflict, Chambers believed, secular liberalism was on the wrong side.

And that, one suspects, is the final reason his voice still speaks to us: his stark, uncompromising indictment of modern liberalism. To moderate liberals his utterances have seemed to be fanatical nonsense. Tanenhaus (evidently a moderate liberal himself) asserts reproachfully the "awful fact" that Chambers's "worldview . . . helped bring McCarthyism into existence." Add to the mix his penchant for punditry, and the temptation arises to conclude that here was a man who read Spengler and Dostoevsky a little too often.

But before we glibly dismiss his ruminations, consider this: the growing divergence in late twentieth-century America between our secularized liberal elites and the so-called Religious Right. Looking back on the late 1940s, do we not see the same cleavage that Chambers called the "jagged fissure" at the heart of the Hiss case: the chasm between "the enlightened and the powerful" (who were frequently pro-Hiss) and "the plain men and women of the nation" (who believed Chambers)? God or Man, Soul or Mind: Chambers's formulation may seem facile. But as the "culture wars" of the nineties intensify, substantial numbers of Americans believe that at the root of our troubles is indeed a conflict of visions.

Because his own life was riven by this conflict, and because he so movingly strove to fathom its meaning, Chambers intrigues and jars us even now. "The witness is gone," Arthur Koestler wrote at Chambers's death. "[T]he testimony will stand." But not just his testimony in a legal sense. The political and spiritual fault lines that he identified continue to shake, revealing issues of fundamental import that vex us still. Even in death, the witness of Whittaker Chambers is not yet history.

6

Searching for Conservatism's Essence:
The Investigations of John P. East

John P. East was a noted conservative political scientist who served as a United States senator from North Carolina between 1981 and 1986. This essay was my Introduction to his book The American Conservative Movement: The Philosophical Founders *(Regnery Books, 1986).*

If there is a single philosophical premise that distinguishes recent American conservatism, it is the conviction that "ideas have consequences." We live in a decade in which, for the first time in generations, the ideas of self-identified conservatives seem ascendant—an era in which the arguments of "academic scribblers" of the Right are being translated, however imperfectly, into public policy.

Such a moment, like all transitional moments, is marked by both exhilaration and anxiety: exhilaration at the attainment of influence so long yearned for; anxiety lest the very possession of influence breed complacency and corruption of the intellect. How does one navigate from the realm of scholarship and "high thinking" to the world of political maneuver and compromise? How does one, in Whittaker Chambers's phrase, successfully "dance along a precipice" between principle and pragmatism, contemplation and activism, unyielding philosophic truth and flexible managerial expediency?

At such times of uncertainty, when the way forward seems so obscure, it is always useful to rediscover the intellectual perspective that impelled us to action in the first place. In the book before us, Senator John East has done just that. He has written a series of essays not on "issues of the eighties," prospects for the next election, or some other ephemeral topic, but on a subject he clearly deems more fundamental: the formative political theory of the "Founding Fathers" of modern American conservatism.

It is a book, first of all, about scholars: in particular, seven learned and dedicated men who laid the theoretical foundations for today's American Right.* These were not the only architects of the conservative renascence, to be sure—a fact Mr. East would no doubt be the first to acknowledge. Other uncommon men and women—professors, journalists, politicians, builders of the infrastructure of conservative institutions—have played indispensable roles as well. But it is the seven individuals he has selected, Mr. East contends, who did the most to infuse American conservatism with intellectual substance and coherence—who made it, in short, a formidable movement of ideas.

At one level this book may be read as a straightforward exposition of the thought of conservatism's "philosophical founders." As such it has real value—and not just for those who may be curious to learn more about the intellectual origins of the Reagan Revolution. In these busy days few of us have the time or inclination to immerse ourselves systematically in the writings of those whose hard-won insights we perhaps too casually adopt as our own. Senator East's lucid essays are therefore especially welcome. By concisely reintroducing us to our heritage, he offers a timely refresher course on the philosophy that undergirds our strivings.

Mr. East's book, however, has more than a narrowly pedagogical purpose. What emerges from his meticulous *explications de texte* is a subtle but persistent emphasis on the underlying theoretical unity of modern conservatism. He observes that despite all the manifest variations in content and in style, the conservatism of these "Founding Fathers" does in fact have discernible "common denominators." This "philosophical core" is the Great Tradition of classical and Judeo-Christian thought, against which are arrayed the fanatic legions of heretical, secular modernity. Conservatism for Senator East is ultimately and essentially spiritual in character. The personal virtues it celebrates—such as piety, humility, and self-sacrifice—require an "openness to transcendence" and acceptance of the God-given nature of things. It is part of Mr. East's intention, one suspects, to recall American conservatives to their inescapably religious roots. Quietly he reminds us that conservatism properly understood is not only a philosophy of government but of self-government, that conservatism at its best is a meditation not simply on what to think but on how to live.

Mr. East does not conceal the unresolved tensions in contemporary conservative thought—particularly the problematic place of the libertarian perspec-

---

* The seven scholars were: Russell Kirk, Richard M. Weaver, Frank S. Meyer, Willmoore Kendall, Leo Strauss, Eric Voegelin, and Ludwig von Mises.

tive in the larger conservative firmament. Consider this sentence that he quotes from Ludwig von Mises: "The keystone of Western civilization is the sphere of spontaneous action it secures to the individual." For conservatives of all persuasions this is a brilliant perception; freedom for the individual is indeed at the center of Western experience. No one contemplating the totalitarianism of a Soviet Union or a Vietnam, the fates of a Solzhenitsyn or a Sakharov, the forced collectivization of an Ethiopia or Cambodia today, or Maoist China yesterday, will disdain the ineffable preciousness of individual liberty.

Yet as we simultaneously contemplate the accelerating nihilistic decadence around us—a phenomenon of which Mr. East takes frequent note—questions relentlessly intrude. Is all "spontaneous action" necessarily good? Are all individual choices equally valid and equally to be left alone? What is the proper response of conservatives (and of a conservative government) to those who "choose" drugs, pornography, and other forms of self-degrading behavior? What, in brief, should we *do* with our freedom? How *ought* we to live? As most of Senator East's conservative theorists teach us, the conservative mission is not coterminous with removing obstacles to individual initiative in the marketplace.

Another theme emerges from these essays. All of the scholars Mr. East examines were men of integrity who throughout their long careers stood resolutely against the times. Despite their often lonely status, and the costs—both pecuniary and professional—that it imposed, they did not become misanthropic pessimists. Instead they remained men of courage and even (Mr. East shows) men of hope. Hope and affirmation, the belief that virtuous men and women can make a difference, that error and evil can yet be held at bay: This, not despairing passivity, marked the seven whose intellectual labors are here analyzed. It is an example, Mr. East obviously believes, that can inspire and hearten us now.

It is said that the owl of Minerva takes its flight at twilight, that we can fully comprehend our heritage only when it is receding into the irrecoverable past. Thanks to books like Senator East's, the twilight need not become darkness. He has given us a study of the "first principles" of American conservatism as propounded by some of its most distinguished theorists. He has not only thereby rendered homage to famous men. He has illuminated (in Robert Frost's words) "the truths we keep coming back and back to."

7

Friedrich Hayek and the
American Conservative Movement

This lecture was given at a national student conference hosted by the
Intercollegiate Studies Institute in Indianapolis in April 2004.

In the opening chapter of his magisterial book *The Conservative Mind*, Russell Kirk asserted: "Men of ideas, rather than party leaders, determine the ultimate course of things." Our conference today attests to the truth of Kirk's remark.

I wonder how many of you are struck, as I am, by the unusual nature of this gathering. We have come together today from all over the United States to examine the legacy of a book: a book published sixty years ago last month in Great Britain. It is a work not of fiction, poetry, drama, personal philosophy, or religion—fields that address the universals of the human condition—but, in its author's own words, a "political book," intended to be a tract for the times. The times in which this book appeared have long since vanished, yet the book remains and holds its power to persuade.

In fact, this little book—Friedrich Hayek's *Road to Serfdom*—is now almost universally hailed as a classic, a volume that transcends the vicissitudes of time. A few years ago, at the turn of the millennium, it was widely rated by scholars as among the one hundred most significant books of the twentieth century. Some commentators placed it in the top ten. It has been called the "single most influential political book published in Britain" in the twentieth century. It has been translated into several dozen languages, including, most recently, Hebrew. During the Cold War it circulated among the anti-Communist underground in eastern Europe and the Soviet Union.

Since his death in 1992, at the age of nearly ninety-three, Friedrich Hayek has been acclaimed as the ablest philosopher of liberty in the twentieth century. Some have compared him to Adam Smith. Writing in the *New Yorker* four years ago, one analyst went so far as to state that "on the biggest issue of all, the vitality of capitalism, he was vindicated to such an extent that it is hardly an exaggeration to refer to the twentieth century as the Hayek century."

But if *The Road to Serfdom* has achieved iconic status, it is useful to ask: how did this happen? That, in part, is my assignment here. My focus will be less on the substance of the book than on its reception—and especially its impact upon the conservative intellectual community that began to coalesce after its publication. The history of this book, as well as its argument, is illuminating.

In the spring of 1944 a book called *The Road to Serfdom* appeared in Britain and soon caused a great storm. It was not written by a native Englishman but by an Austrian émigré named Friedrich Hayek, then teaching at the London School of Economics. As World War II enveloped Europe, he grew increasingly alarmed about the tendency toward governmental planning of the economy and the consequences of this trend for individual liberty. Writing to the American pundit Walter Lippmann in 1937, Hayek lamented: "I wish I could make my 'progressive' friends . . . understand that democracy is possible only under capitalism and that collectivist experiments lead inevitably to fascism of one sort or another." He decided to write a learned polemic, which he dedicated "to the Socialists of all parties."

The thesis of Hayek's work was simple: "Planning leads to dictatorship"; "the direction of economic activity" inevitably necessitates the "suppression of freedom." By "planning" Hayek did not mean any kind of preparation by individuals or governments for the future; he meant only "central direction of all economic activity according to a single plan." Such comprehensive controls, he argued, would necessarily be arbitrary, capricious, and ultimately destructive of liberty.

Economic control is not merely control of a sector of human life which can be separated from the rest; it is the control of the means for all our ends. And whoever has sole control of the means must also determine which ends are to be served, which values are to be rated higher and which lower—in short, what men should believe and strive for.

Collectivism, in short—all collectivism—was inherently totalitarian; "democratic socialism" was illusory and "unachievable." Pointing to Nazi Germany as the incarnation of his fears, Hayek argued that "the rise of fascism and nazism was not a reaction against the socialist trends of the preceding period but a necessary outcome of those tendencies." In other words, fascism was not the ugly face of capitalism but a species of collectivism. His book, in short, was no academic matter. The path to socialism which Britain was taking was the very path Germany had already chosen: the road to serfdom.

Against this specter Hayek opposed "the abandoned road" of individualism and classical liberalism. The "fundamental principle" of this creed was "that in the ordering of our affairs we should make as much use as possible of the spontaneous forces of society, and resort as little as possible to coercion." This did not mean, Hayek insisted, that government should be inactive; he strenuously denied that his brand of liberalism was identical with laissez faire. Instead, he proposed the concept of the Rule of Law: "[G]overnment in all its actions is [to be] bound by rules fixed and announced beforehand." There was, he contended, a world of difference between his version of the liberal state and the centralized, capricious, privilege-granting, collectivist state.

The response to Hayek's work in Great Britain was immediate. The first printing sold out in about a month. Intended "as a warning to the socialist intelligentsia of England," *The Road to Serfdom* incited many readers to vigorous reply. The eminent economist Lord Keynes, who had been Hayek's great rival in the 1930s, told Hayek privately that it was a "grand" book which said "so well what needs so much to be said." So important a challenge did it offer to the proponents of state planning and classical socialism that a prominent Labour Party M.P. wrote and published a book-length rebuttal.

The British reception of Hayek's book was mild and restrained, however, compared to its fate in the United States following publication on September 18, 1944. Hayek had given "little thought" (he later wrote) to the book's "possible appeal" to American readers. In fact, three American publishing houses—at least one of them apparently motivated by political opposition to Hayek—rejected it. When the University of Chicago Press finally published the volume, it printed only 2,000 copies. As Hayek later recalled, his book was "not intended for popular consumption."

Hayek's expectation was wrong. Instantly his book was recognized not just as a scholarly polemic, but as a work of extraordinary timeliness. Within a week of publication the publisher ordered a second printing of 5,000 copies. Only nine days after publication the publisher requested a third printing of 5,000 more. The next day it doubled that to 10,000. Within a few days of publication the publisher received requests to translate *The Road to Serfdom* into German, Dutch, and Spanish. By the spring of 1945 the book had gone into a seventh printing. And all this was occurring while World War II was still being fought. "Seldom," wrote one observer, "have an economist and a nonfiction book reached such popularity in so short a time."

Many book reviewers contributed to the growing controversy and book sales with excited and sometimes extravagant remarks. In the *New York Times Book Review*, the veteran journalist Henry Hazlitt proclaimed *The Road to Serfdom* "one of the most important books of our generation," comparable in "power and rigor of reasoning" to John Stuart Mill's *On Liberty*. Another reviewer predicted that Hayek's work might become a "milestone in a critical age," like Thomas Paine's *The Rights of Man*. Meanwhile, the hostile *New Republic* editorialized that Hayek's work was having little scholarly impact and was simply being used by reactionary business interests. Stuart Chase, a noted liberal journalist and advocate of national economic planning, asserted that Hayek's volume was fulfilling a "deep spiritual need in American men of affairs" for "the fundamentalist doctrine that those of us beyond fifty were brought up on." Writing early in 1946, Professor Charles Merriam, a wartime vice-chairman of the National Resources Planning Board, vehemently dismissed Hayek's book as "one of the strange survivals of obscurantism in modern times." Even in academic circles the debate became tempestuous, so much so that the editor of the *American Economic Review* took the unusual step of publishing two reviews of the book. Needless to say, they disagreed.

No one was more startled—and admittedly embarrassed—by the American uproar than the scholarly Professor Hayek himself. As he later observed, the emotions the book engendered amazed him. He had written his book (as he later put it) for a "small circle of people"—mainly "British progressives"—who were "actively struggling with the difficult questions which arise in the field where economics and politics meet." He hoped to persuade a few of these leaders of opinion that "they were on an extremely dangerous path." Why, then, should such a work aimed at experts and written by an Austrian émigré living in London stir the passions of Americans? Perhaps it was true, as the *New Republic* charged, that chambers of commerce and businesses were boosting demand for the book by bulk orders, thereby concealing its actual public appeal. But why should they have bothered? And if, as one critic alleged, Hayek had merely presented "an old nostrum attractively packaged," why should many liberals (new style) have become so angry and even dismayed?

First, we need to note several accidental or fortuitous factors that helped to transform the publication of Hayek's book into a media phenomenon. On the Sunday following its publication the book received a glowing, front-page review in the *New York Times Book Review*. Even more than today, the *New York Times* in the 1940s was an arbiter of intellectual fashion. By giving the lead review space to *The Road to Serfdom*, the *Times* signaled that here was a book of importance. This judgment ensured that Hayek's book would be stocked in bookstores and reviewed elsewhere.

Even more remarkably, the man the *Times* selected to do the review was no leftwing enemy of Hayek's position but instead the pro-free-market journalist Henry Hazlitt. Some of you may recognize him as the author of a pro-capitalist book, *Economics in One Lesson*, which went on to sell over half a million copies. Hayek's book could not have received a friendlier send-off in the media capital of the United States.

A second unexpected development was the decision of the *Reader's Digest* to condense the book for its subscribers. The *Digest* published the condensation—done by a former Marxist, Max Eastman—in its April 1945 issue and arranged for the Book-of-the-Month Club to distribute copies of the condensed version. Eventually more than 600,000 reprints of this condensation were disseminated. Today, when the *Reader's Digest* is often associated with doctor's offices and the magazine racks of supermarkets, it is hard to remember that in 1945 it was a cultural transmission belt of considerable importance. Every month it sold millions of copies. Moreover, its owner, DeWitt Wallace, was a conservative, and the magazine had a conservative tilt. The *Digest*'s condensation of *The Road to Serfdom* put the book into the mental universe of Middle America.

As it happened, the April 1945 issue of *the Reader's Digest* appeared just as Hayek visited the United States on a prearranged lecture tour of a few universities. Upon arriving in New York, the professor was told by his American sponsor that (thanks to the *Digest*) he had become famous and that the original plan had been called off. He was now to go on a lecture tour of the whole country. The visiting scholar was astonished.

"I can't do that," he said, "I have never done any public lecturing."
"Well, that's all arranged, you must try and do it."

"When do we begin?"

"Oh, you are late already. . . . You start tomorrow morning at Town Hall in New York."

Hayek did not know what Town Hall was. He thought it must be a woman's club. The next morning on his way downtown, he asked his chairman: "Well, what sort of audience do you expect?"

"The hall holds three thousand, but there's overflow."

"My God. I have never done such a thing. What am I supposed to lecture on?"

"Oh, we have called the tune, 'Law and International Affairs.'"

"My God, I have never thought about it. I can't do this."

"Everything is announced, they are waiting for you."

"So" [Hayek later recalled], "I was ushered into this enormous hall with all kinds of apparatus which are strange to me. At that time they had dictating machines, microphones, all completely new to me. My last recollection is, I asked the chairman, 'Three-quarters of an hour?'"

"'Oh no, it must be exactly one hour, you are on the radio.'"

"So I got up on a subject on which I had no idea, and I still know that I began with the sentence, 'Ladies and gentlemen, I suppose you will all agree when I say'—I didn't know yet what I was going to say."

Fortunately, Hayek—who had never before given a popular lecture—managed to entrance the crowd. The lecture—and the tour that followed—proved to be a triumph. More importantly for the long run, he established many contacts that would prove useful in the intellectual counterrevolution that he had launched with his book.

By now the Austrian-born professor was something of a celebrity in the Anglo-Saxon world. Upon his return to Great Britain in the spring of 1945, he suddenly found himself an issue in the British general election campaign. On the evening of June 4, Prime Minister Winston Churchill delivered the Conservative Party's political broadcast on national radio. Churchill had evidently been reading *The Road to Serfdom* before his speech, which contained a fiery brew of Hayekian substance and Churchillian rhetoric:

No Socialist Government conducting the entire life and industry of the country could afford to allow free, sharp, or violently-worded expressions of public discontent. They would have to fall back on some form of Gestapo, no doubt very humanely directed in the first instance. And this would nip opinion in the bud; it would stop criticism as it reared its head, and it would gather all the power to the supreme party and the party leaders, rising like stately pinnacles above their vast bureaucracies of Civil Servants, no longer servants and no longer civil. And where would the ordinary simple folk—the common people, as they like to call them in America—where would they be, once this mighty organism had got them in its grip?

Socialism, Churchill thundered, "is inseparably interwoven with totalitarianism and the abject worship of the State."

Churchill's "Gestapo speech" (as it came to be called) was widely criticized as excessive, and it may have cost his party the election. The next evening the Labour Party leader, Clement Attlee, scorned Churchill's attack as merely a "second hand version of the academic views of an Austrian, Prof. Friedrich August von Hayek, who is very popular just now with and supplies ideas to the Conservative party." There was perhaps a bit of innuendo here. Hayek did not use his middle name (August), but the Socialists did when they referred to him, possibly underscoring the fact that he was foreign-born. Furthermore, although Hayek was by now a naturalized British subject, Attlee called him an Austrian—an oblique reminder, perhaps, of another Austrian against whom Britain had just fought a war: Adolf Hitler.

For his part, Professor Hayek immediately informed the press that he was "a teacher of economics, not a politician," and had "no connection whatever with the Conservative Party." But the incident probably only increased his notoriety among British and American intellectuals.

But adventitious factors alone—the *New York Times Book Review*, the *Reader's Digest* condensation, the successful American lecture tour, and the "Gestapo speech"—cannot account for the response to *The Road to Serfdom* in the mid-1940s. After all, why would 3,000 people turn out to hear an economist at a Town Hall forum in 1945? Clearly, something deeper was going on.

One such factor was identified by Hayek himself several years later. In contrast with Great Britain, he said, where the issue of freedom versus planning had become a familiar one by 1945, the United States remained at the stage of enthusiasm. For many American intellectuals the ideal of a "new kind of rationally constructed society" still seemed novel, vibrant, and "largely unsoiled by practical experience." To criticize such heady beliefs was to attack something nearly sacred.

Some years later William F. Buckley Jr. made a similar point when he described *The Road to Serfdom* as "a squirt of ice water . . . in an age swooning with passion for a centralized direction of social happiness and economic plenitude."

This leads to another reason for the American Left's reaction to Hayek's book. It had not, after all, been such a long time since modern liberalism (statism to its detractors) had attained power in America. It had not been so terribly long—twelve years, in fact, in 1945—since professors, lawyers, and many others had turned to Washington, D.C., and to President Roosevelt for a New Deal. For many of these people, one suspects, the pleasures and gains of those days were not quite consolidated in 1945. Theirs was still an uncertain triumph, not yet ratified by time and consensus. Consequently, when a bold challenge like Hayek's appeared, it could not be airily dismissed. It was a threat, and it had to be vigorously repulsed.

Such responses were not long in coming. In the *American Political Science Review* Professor Charles Merriam, a leading apostle of planning who had angrily debated Hayek on the radio, denounced *The Road to Serfdom* as a "confused," "cynical," and "over-rated work of little permanent value." In a book provocatively entitled *The Road to Reaction*, Herman Finer criticized Hayek so harshly and sweepingly that Hayek himself described that book as "a specimen of abuse and invective which is probably unique in contemporary academic discussion." In the *New Republic*, Alvin H. Hansen, the leading American acolyte of Keynesian economics, published a four-page critique which concluded: "Hayek's book will not be long lived. There is no substance in it to make it live." He conceded only that it would "momentarily" arouse discussion and prompt some useful "self-examination." That was the most he would allow Hayek: the role of a gadfly.

Meanwhile the *New Republic*, in its editorial columns, asserted that the heavy sales of *The Road to Serfdom* were coming from orders placed by "business interests" who were using Hayek's "doctrine" to defend practices that the professor himself disapproved of. Hayek's worldly success, it sniffed, "amounts to little more than an indignity."

Yet if, at war's end, many self-designated progressives, for all their power and prominence, may still have felt insecure, the American Right did not know it. There a far different sentiment prevailed. Outnumbered and beleaguered, it could only rejoice when a compelling restatement of its case appeared. And that was precisely part of Hayek's significance: He enabled those who felt routed to draw the lines and confidently take sides once more. At last they had a champion who made the enemy squirm. It is a measure of their rout and of the paucity of libertarian thought in America in this period that they were obliged to rely on an Austrian professor for leadership.

And here we must emphasize a crucial point. In 1945 no coordinated classical liberal or conservative intellectual community existed in the United States. To be sure, there were eloquent dissenters here and there, including Hayek's mentor and fellow expatriate Ludwig von Mises, who published two trenchant books of his own in 1944. Still, in 1945 classical liberal thinking was its nadir of influence among American intellectuals. After all, had not the recent Great Depression definitively discredited capitalism and the individualist ethos which had sustained it? When Hayek and others like him came along in the mid-1940s to suggest otherwise, they gave the American Right something it desperately needed: an infusion of academic prestige.

There was another reason why *The Road to Serfdom* appealed to the American Right at this juncture. Hayek believed fervently in the power of ideas. His book was a study of the development of pernicious ideas. Implicit in his whole approach was the conviction that good ideas can defeat bad ones. For many of his readers, this was a message of hope. Institutionalized error could be rectified.

With the publication of *The Road to Serfdom*, Hayek had thrown his pebble into the pond and had created a bigger splash than he had ever expected. Let us now consider some of the ripple effects.

For Hayek personally the immediate effects were bittersweet. His book had made him famous, but fame was a double-edged sword. Hayek, in fact, paid dearly for his deviation from statist orthodoxy. For the next thirty years he was marginalized in his profession, and he knew it. To most of his peers he had become that dreaded beast, an "ideologue." No longer interested in purely technical economics, he increasingly turned toward issues of political and social philosophy—and away from the mathematical modeling that intrigued so many of his younger colleagues. He had also committed, in the eyes of many of his peers, the cardinal academic sin of writing a popular book. For a time Hayek seemed to share some of these very sentiments. He wrote later on that he "long resented being more widely known by what I regarded as a pamphlet for the time than by my strictly scientific work."

But there were compensations. *The Road to Serfdom* established Hayek as the world leader of the intellectual opposition to socialism and set him on a path that took him in 1949 to the University of Chicago, where he joined the prestigious Committee on Social Thought. There, for a decade, he worked on his magnificent volume *The Constitution of Liberty* (published in 1960), a tome that he hoped would be the equivalent of *The Wealth of Nations* for the twentieth century. While at the University of Chicago, he became a founding patron of the *New Individualist Review* and lectured under the auspices of the Intercollegiate Society of Individualists, now known as the Intercollegiate Studies Institute, or ISI. But even in the United States he did not find his path completely easy. It was a sign of the uncongenial intellectual climate in which he struggled that he was obliged to rely upon an American foundation to pay his salary at the University of Chicago.

Another ripple effect of *The Road to Serfdom* became discernible in 1947 when Hayek founded the Mont Pelerin Society, an international network of classical liberal, or free-market, thinkers that still exists today. Building on the contacts he had made while publicizing *The Road to Serfdom*, Hayek brought together nearly forty prominent scholars—seventeen of them from the United States—for the founding meeting near Mont Pelerin in Switzerland. The personal impact was powerful, as one of its participants, Milton Friedman, recognized. "The importance of that meeting," he said, "was that it showed us that we were not alone." The Mont Pelerin Society soon became a kind of international "who's who" of classical liberal scholars—a venue for exchanging ideas and (as we might say) for networking. Slowly a community was being created: a community of intellectuals dedicated, in Hayek's words, to "the rehabilitation of the idea of personal freedom especially in the economic realm."

The expanding influence of *The Road to Serfdom* can be measured in other ways, in the individuals whose minds and lives it changed. In Britain, an avid early reader was a university student named Margaret Roberts, whom we know today as Margaret Thatcher. Another British subject who discovered the book was a man named Antony Fisher, who became so enthralled by it that he contacted Hayek and asked him what he (Fisher) might do to reverse the socialistic tide. Hayek advised him to establish a research organization that could reach the intellectuals and disseminate classical liberal ideas. In 1957 Fisher did precisely that. The Institute of Economic Affairs (or IEA), based in London, became a clearinghouse for Hayekian thought and the intellectual backbone of Thatcherite conservatism. The indefatigable Fisher went on to organize free-market think tanks in Canada and the United States, including the Manhattan Institute in New York. In 1981 he founded the Atlas Economic Research Foundation, a facilitator of free-market think tanks all over the world. Think of it: for Fisher this all started with his reading the *Reader's Digest* version of *The Road to Serfdom*.

In the United States, one can find similar instances of lives redirected and transformed by this book. Frank Meyer, a Communist apparatchik in the late 1930s and early 1940s, later wrote that at a "crucial moment" in his life Hayek's book "played a decisive part" in liberating him from Marxism. Meyer went on to become the book review editor of *National Review* and one of the outstanding conservative intellectual figures of the 1950s and 1960s. Another reader of Hayek, it appears, was Ronald Reagan. A decade ago some would have scoffed at this suggestion. But we now know that Reagan was a closet intellectual, and the skeptics scoff no more. We must also not overlook the effective role of intellectual conveyor belts like the Intercollegiate Studies Institute, which distributed copies of *The Road to Serfdom* (and many other books) to college students after ISI's founding more than half a century ago.

By the early 1950s the free-market revival which Hayek launched had come a long way from the storm cellar days of the decade before. The march of "hot socialism" had been checked. In 1954 Professor H. Stuart Hughes of Harvard put it this way:

> The publication ten years ago of F. A. Hayek's *The Road to Serfdom* was a major event in the intellectual history of the United States. . . . [I]t marked the beginning of that slow reorientation of sentiment—both in academic circles and among the general public—toward a more positive evaluation of the capitalist system which has marked the past decade.

"That slow reorientation of sentiment." Libertarianism and capitalism had become intellectually defensible again.

At this point an important contextual observation is in order. The conservative movement in America after World War II was a confluence of many intellectual currents, of which Hayekian liberalism was but one. In addition to the classical liberals, there were religious and cultural traditionalists, ex-Communist Cold Warriors, and, more recently, the Religious Right and the neoconservatives. Hayek, although of course an anti-Communist, was identified with only one branch of this emerging coalition.

Moreover, Hayek did not want to surrender the word liberal as the best description of his viewpoint. In a striking passage in the 1956 paperback edition of *The Road to Serfdom*, he argued that "true liberalism" was not identical with conservatism and that it was dangerous to confuse them. A few years later, he published an essay bluntly entitled "Why I Am Not a Conservative," an essay apparently aimed at the revival of conservative thought associated with Russell Kirk's book *The Conservative Mind*.

Although Hayek in that essay seemed to have classical European conservatism in mind, his critique contributed to his problematic standing on the American Right. To some traditionalist conservatives he was a secular rationalist with a utopian streak and an overly sanguine view of unguided human nature. To Russell Kirk, for instance, an economic order cannot "long endure apart from a moral order," a truth that he felt Hayek had insufficiently learned. For Kirk the world "never is governed by little tracts and pamphlets." He may have put *The Road to Serfdom* in that category.

Fundamentally Hayek wanted human societies to develop spontaneously in freedom—the best way to cope with the unknown. For theistic conservatives, however, man's root problem is not ignorance (a failing of the mind), but sin (a failing of the heart).

For his part, Hayek styled himself an "Old Whig." An agnostic, he called the philosophical skeptic David Hume his "great idol." Yet he also, in an interview in the 1980s, identified himself as a "Burkean Whig." He was a classical liberal, it seems, with conservative inclinations.

For most Americans who took the label "conservative," this was enough for them to include him in their pantheon.

It is probable that *The Road to Serfdom* and its author would have receded eventually into obscurity had not the unexpected occurred: in 1974, to his astonishment, Hayek received the Nobel Prize in economics. The award conferred prestige that the academy had long denied him. It gave the elderly professor a new lease on life, it gave American conservatives a sense of buoyancy and of having "arrived," and it renewed public interest in the little book that had made him famous. Hayek lived until 1992, long enough to see the Thatcherite revolution in Britain, the Reagan Revolution in America, and the collapse of the Soviet Union and its evil empire. By the time of his death, approximately 250,000 copies of *The Road to Serfdom* had been sold. I do not know how many copies have been distributed since his death, but today a veritable Hayek "industry" has sprung up, as his works are collected, biographies are written, and scholarship about him flourishes. *The Road to Serfdom*, I suspect, has a long shelf life ahead.

More than forty years ago, Richard Weaver—another of modern conservatism's founding fathers—ruminated aloud about the most important thing that conservative intellectuals could do. His answer? They could write what he called "unshakable books." My lecture today has focused on one such endeavor. Many of you in this audience are contemplating academic careers. As you do so, I offer you this final thought. I ask you to reflect upon the extraordinary history of *The Road to Serfdom*. Very few of us will ever achieve the stature of its author. But those of us who choose the academic life can strive, as Hayek did, to write unshakable books. This, perhaps, is the final lesson of *The Road to Serfdom* for American conservatives: be like Hayek. Aim high. Persevere. You just might change the course of history.

8

The Place of Willmoore Kendall
in American Conservatism

This essay was presented as a conference paper at the University of Dallas in 1997 and published in John A. Murley and John E. Alvis, eds., Willmoore Kendall: Maverick of American Conservatism *(Lexington Books, 2002).*

In a conversation with a friend in the 1940s, Willmoore Kendall remarked that he had a "messianic urge."[1] It was neither the first nor the last time that this brilliant political scientist and preacher's son revealed an inordinate passion for greatness. In the early 1930s, when a young Kendall contemplated a career in journalism, the journalistic philosopher-king of the day, Walter Lippmann, was for a time his role model.[2] A few years later, as a man of the far Left, he announced that his "purpose in life" was "to become a great Socialist publicist" and tried vehemently but vainly to convert his Methodist father to communism.[3] By the mid-1940s, having written a path-breaking doctoral dissertation on John Locke, Kendall apparently entertained the hope of becoming an American Locke, or perhaps the Thorstein Veblen of the political science profession.[4]

It is not uncommon for young men of great gifts to dream dreams. But Kendall's desire for a kind of secular immortality did not disappear with advancing years. During his middle age, by which time he had become a man of the Right, he indicated to a friend that he wanted to be, for the contemporary era, an American equivalent of Edmund Burke. And in 1963, as this native of rural Oklahoma prepared to accept what would be his final academic appointment—at the University of Dallas—he wrote: "At Dallas, I can be Moses back from the forty years of his preparation, among *his* people."[5]

Lippmann, Locke, Veblen, Burke, Moses: clearly, Willmoore Kendall was a man of high ambition—an ambition (in Jeffrey Hart's words) "conceived in national and even world-historic terms."[6] If at first glance this trait may seem disconcerting, it will appear less so when one recalls that Kendall was a child prodigy who learned to read at the age of two, entered the eighth grade at the age of eight, graduated from high school at thirteen, and entered Northwestern University that same year as the youngest college student in the United States. Surrounded by high expectations and public adulation from an early age, Kendall was a man of formidable ability, and he knew it. To a considerable degree, one can interpret his early career as a search for a calling worthy of this self-knowledge—and his later career as a quest to give intellectual leadership to those he perceived to be leaderless.

It is Kendall the would-be "American Burke" whom I propose to examine in this chapter. More specifically, it is Kendall's place in the American conservative movement that I shall consider. Or, more properly, reconsider, for it was over twenty years ago that I first wrote about him in a journal article, and then in a book about conservative intellectuals.[7] Having offered a detailed appraisal of him there, I do not wish merely to repeat it here. But some subjects do bear reinvestigation. In the case of Kendall, the passage of more than thirty years since his death affords an appropriate opportunity for another look at a person who surely deserves it.

When Kendall died in 1967 at age fifty-eight, his close friend and fellow political scientist Charles S. Hyneman asserted that "few of his generation in American political science can match his claim for attention over the decades immediately ahead."[8] Just three years later, Jeffrey Hart, a conservative professor and senior editor of *National Review*, echoed him. "Willmoore Kendall," Hart declared, "remains, beyond any possibility of challenge, the most important political theorist to have emerged in the twenty-odd years since the end of World War II."[9] Nevertheless, in the three decades since his passing, Kendall has not received the kind of scholarly attention commensurate with these judgments. To be sure, he has not been entirely ignored. In 1970, his book *The Basic Symbols of the American Political Tradition* (coauthored with George W. Carey) was published.[10] In 1971 came a hefty collection of his essays, entitled *Willmoore Kendall Contra Mundum*.[11] In the mid-1970s, there appeared a lengthy article about him in *Modern Age*,[12] as well as an analysis of his thought by John P. East in the *Political Science Reviewer*.[13]

In the 1980s, he was the subject of appreciative essays by the conservative scholars Gregory Wolfe and Samuel Francis.[14] From time to time, one will find mention of Kendall in places like the polemics of Harry Jaffa and the writings of Kendall's friend Garry Wills.[15] And, if secular immortality can be conferred by novelists, Kendall has the distinction of earning a claim to it by being the inspiration for a short story by Saul Bellow.[16]

No, Willmoore Kendall has not been forgotten. But in comparison with the other founding fathers of modern American conservatism, he has not been abundantly remembered—certainly not as much as the tributes to him at his death might lead us to expect. In the last twenty years, for instance, William F. Buckley Jr., Richard Weaver, James Burnham, and Whittaker Chambers have been the subjects of biographies or monographs; similar studies of Frank Meyer and Ludwig von Mises are underway. Both Russell Kirk and Irving Kristol have been honored by Festchriften, while Friedrich Hayek and Milton Friedman, as far back as the 1970s, received the Nobel Prize in economics. There is today a Russell Kirk Center for Cultural Renewal, a Ludwig von Mises Institute, and a Wilhelm Röepke Institute. There is a Leo Strauss "industry" and an Eric Voegelin "industry," but nothing similar for Willmoore Kendall.

Why not? Three factors go far toward providing an explanation. First, unlike most of the other founders of the conservative intellectual movement after 1945, Kendall died a comparatively young man, before his projected oeuvre could be said to be complete. Second, he was a scholar who for the most part wrote essays and reviews rather than books.[17] Although his output as an essayist was respectable in quantity and often stunning in quality, I suspect that there is a tendency, among intellectuals, to study and memorialize those who leave their thoughts behind in the form of finished books rather than scattered articles (however luminous).

Here one must note two data of importance for understanding Kendall's scholarly productivity. First, he was an inveterate writer of letters. Indeed, he must have been one of the most prolific correspondents of the twentieth century, and he rarely confined his missives to a single page. I do not know how many letters—often startlingly long and argumentative—that he produced during his career; they must have numbered in the thousands. I myself have read hundreds of them (including one handwritten twenty-nine-page-long tour de force!), not counting hundreds more that he exchanged with his father from boyhood until his father's death in 1942.[18] For a historian, Kendall's prodigious letter-writing is a godsend. But in the end, one cannot help noting pensively how much of his time and energy went into this fugitive form of self-expression, time and energy that might have gone into formal publications. In fact, one could cull from his surviving correspondence a tantalizing list of books and articles that he intended to write but never completed: works with titles such as *Jean-Jacques Rousseau and the Doctrine of Majority Rule*, *Confessions of an American Imperialist Reactionary*, and *Doctrine and Strategy for Contemporary American Conservatism*.

A second crucial datum is this: to his enduring credit, Willmoore Kendall never stopped thinking, and, in middle age, his intellectual journey took him into new territory, represented by his conversion to Roman Catholicism and his discovery of the scholarly "revolution" wrought by Leo Strauss and Eric Voegelin. How many middle-aged academics—or academics of any age—have the ability and courage to reexamine their premises fundamentally and thereupon reorient their careers? Kendall did. He once remarked that he was, so far as he knew, the only political theorist of his generation who had "absorbed" the Straussian and Voegelinian "revolutions."[19]

But there was a price for this reorientation: For a time it slowed him down. Hence, for a combination of reasons—both intellectual and personal—there hung about Kendall from his Yale days (1947–61) onward, an aura of aspirations unfulfilled: a barrier toward rendering him his due.

In a memorial tribute to Kendall in 1968, Charles Hyneman observed that his friend's "contributions to professional literature" were "less than they could have been, less than they would have been if he had not had such a raging compulsion to expose error and force recognition of sound principles here and now." Hyneman's words point us toward the third and most important reason for Kendall's still somewhat shadowy place in the conservative pantheon: his own "volatile" personality and intellect.[20] Extraordinarily bright, he was also extraordinarily argumentative—"a walking sign of contradiction" (said a friend) "who lost no time, on a first meeting, contradicting you."[21] Kendall's "raging compulsion to expose error" evidently took root very early, during his stormy relationship with his blind and brilliant father. In 1935, when Willmoore was only twenty-six, his father remarked that his boy seemed "ridden, as a consequence of his inheritance, by a demon of evangelistic fervor."[22] Whatever the psychosocial sources of this behavior, Kendall, in his adulthood, never abandoned what a one-time colleague at *National Review* called "his most characteristic role—the cross-examiner, the inspired heckler, the nemesis of evasion and cloudy-mindedness, the hound of heresies."[23] Unfortunately for his own career—and, no doubt, for his long-term reputation—not everyone took as much pleasure from this probing as he did. As Professor Hyneman once remarked, Kendall "thought it his proper business to expose the fraudulent and set the well-meaning right." It was a "service," Hyneman delicately added, "that was not always asked for and perhaps usually not appreciated."[24]

Kendall's brash combativeness and love of debate were not his only note-worthy characteristics.[25] A superlative teacher and generous dissertation advisor, he inspired and profoundly altered the lives of a number of students. He could also be, by all accounts, a very demanding person.[26] A professor at the University of Dallas was struck by Kendall's ability to produce "absolute hatred" and "absolute devotion" in the same student.[27] At *National Review*, where he was a senior editor for eight years, it was said that he was never on speaking terms with more than one associate at once. According to William F. Buckley Jr., to whom he was a mentor at Yale and an intimate friend until the 1960s, Kendall's calendar of personal relationships was "inscrutable, the only givens being that he must not be on speaking terms with more than three people at any one time."[28]

In short, well before his death Willmoore Kendall had achieved the status of a legend, and long after his death, too. In a sense, he was a victim of his own genius and eccentricities. So colorful was he, and so fascinating, that there has been a tendency to remember him more as "the most unforgettable character I've met" than as a deep and daring conservative thinker.

It was not simply Kendall's personality that inhibited an appreciation of his achievement as a conservative. His own piercing intellect had the same effect. As Leo Paul S. de Alvarez has noted, Kendall's brand of conservatism was "unique." "It was typical of the man" (de Alvarez has written) "that he struck out alone to form his own vision of America, a vision that no one else who called himself a conservative seemed to share."[29] While original-ity and nonconformity can, by their very conspicuousness, attract disciples, too much intellectual distance—especially from the audience one hopes to instruct—can, in the short run at least, be self-defeating. To some degree, that happened to Kendall. Within the conservative movement, as well as the political science profession, he remained to the end the Great Dissenter.

What were the terms of his dissent? During the last dozen years of his life, Kendall became engrossed in an overarching project: an attempt to delineate the essence of American conservatism. Time and again, in articles and speeches, he asked: What *was* conservatism, anyway? What were the "basic issues" (or the "ultimate issue") that divided American conservatives from their liberal foes?[30] He even began two books on the subject (both, alas, never finished): *Sages of Conservatives* (a series of essays about fellow conservative theorists) and the previously mentioned *Doctrine and Strategy for Contemporary American Conservatism*.

One reason Kendall embarked upon this enterprise was his deepening conviction that the intellectual leadership of contemporary conservatism was, in his words, "a poor lot," full of "false teachers."[31] In 1964 he declared publicly that the conservative movement—"assuming that is that we are a movement"—was "rent not only by divided counsels, but also by sharply conflicting views of political reality and, above all, of the American political system itself, and the proper role of Conservatives with respect to its proper functioning, its good health, and its preservation." Repeatedly, he charged, the conservatives had been "intellectually unprepared" for onslaughts from the Left. Indeed, he felt tempted to say, the movement seemed "to be in the *business* of being unprepared intellectually for the next thrust of the Liberal Revolution; the Conservatives never do their homework until after they have flunked the exam."[32]

One way to illuminate Kendall's estrangement from his presumed intellectual allies is to identify the strands of conservative thought that he rejected. If the conservative intellectual movement from 1945 to 1967 was a coalition of three broad groupings—libertarian, traditionalist, and anti-Communist[33]—it is instantly apparent that Kendall did not belong to the first category. He was not—nor had he ever been—a libertarian. In part, perhaps, because he had immersed himself in John Maynard Keynes's writings while a Rhodes Scholar at Oxford in the 1930s, he never embraced free-market economics as the crux of his belief system. As a professor at Yale in the late 1940s, he twitted a procapitalist student named William F. Buckley Jr. "You" (Kendall would tell Buckley in class) "don't know a damn thing about economics."[34] Kendall even questioned the almost sacrosanct conservative belief (championed by Milton Friedman and others) that political freedom and economic freedom were inseparable.[35] To be sure, Kendall was no socialist. But like the ex-Trotskyist James Burnham, whose journey from Left to Right in some ways resembled his own, he never worshiped at the altar of laissez faire.

Nor did he accept the "history lesson" and political theory commonly espoused by libertarian conservatives of his day, a viewpoint encapsulated in a militant defense of individual rights and freedoms against the state. For this version of the conservative creed (which we might call Goldwaterism), Kendall exhibited little patience. Not only was he both publicly and privately critical of Goldwater (whom he considered "very bad news for the cause");[36] the whole notion that America's political tradition was one of "individual rights," he asserted, was a "Liberal lie."[37] *His* conservatism, Kendall announced in 1963, had "sworn no vow of absolute fidelity either to free enterprise à la von Mises, or to a certain list of 'rights' à la John Chamberlain, or to a certain holy trinity of government functions à la . . . Frank Meyer, or to revolving-door mistrust of political authority as such à la Frank Chodorov."[38] Contrary to those conservatives who exalted individual liberty as the highest political good and denounced Big Government—even government per se—as evil and dangerous, Kendall asserted boldly that neither government nor even energetic government was inherently evil at all. *The Federalist* (a book he revered as his political bible) should (he believed) have taught conservatives otherwise.[39]

Nor did Kendall fit in comfortably with much of the traditionalist wing of the emerging conservative revival, particularly with those who extolled Edmund Burke as conservatism's supreme mentor for today. While Kendall found Burke conceptually useful,[40] he also believed that much of Burke's thought was irrelevant to America's heritage. And that, for Kendall, was crucial. If American conservatism was going to make any difference, he argued, it must be grounded in *American* experience and expressed in *American* vocabulary. It must, in other words, be accessible to the political marketplace where, in his view, the battles between Right and Left were being fought.

What, after all, were conservatives (said Kendall) but "those who are defending an established order against those who seek to undermine or transform it"? That being the case,

> I make no sense . . . of calling "Conservative" the man who takes a dim view of his country's established institutions, feels something less than at home with its way of life as it actually lives it, finds it difficult to identify himself with the political and moral principles on which it has acted through its history, dislikes or views with contempt the generality of the kind of people his society produces, and—above all perhaps—dissociates himself from its Founders, or at least holds them at arms' length. Such a man may be the better or nobler or wiser for all this dim-viewing and the yearning-away from; he may be right as rain. But I fail to see where you can get by calling him a Conservative (or where he gets by calling himself one).[41]

Kendall, then, repudiated the "Burke 'cultists'"[42]—and one self-styled Burkean above all: Russell Kirk. By the early 1960s, Kendall was convinced that Kirk—author of *The Conservative Mind* and a leading eminence on the intellectual Right—must be shunted aside as an influence on the conservative movement.[43] Privately Kendall called his own *The Conservative Affirmation* (1963) a "declaration of war" against Kirk.[44] In the unpublished *Sages of Conservatism* and an essay on Richard Weaver, Kendall made his "war" overt.[45]

To Kendall, Kirk's inadequacies were manifold: He wrote "with an eye too much to Burke and not enough to the Framers" of the Constitution. He had insufficient grasp of *American* conservatism and the *American* tradition, particularly as explained by *The Federalist*. He was "too far above the fray" and too lacking in clarity about the actual issues in the ongoing conservative-liberal "war" to serve as a good guide to the conservative "resistance." His definition of conservatism was muddled, and on some issues he was really a liberal. Kendall also objected to Kirk's "defeatism"—his sense that contemporary conservatism was fighting a noble but losing battle. In truth, Kendall countered, the conservative cause (properly understood) had not been routed at all. Privately, Kendall contrasted Kirk's "literary" conservatism with his own "marketplace conservatism, not very elegant."[46]

Clearly, a conservative intellectual who, in 1964, found both Russell Kirk and Barry Goldwater to be flawed teachers was a man who marched to a different drummer. With respect to the third stream of conservative consciousness after 1945, however—unyielding, Cold War anticommunism—Kendall the staunch anti-Communist fit right in. Like many of the Right's other founding fathers, he had once been a man of the far Left, and like nearly all conservative intellectuals, he considered prosecution of the Cold War to be a moral and strategic imperative. But even here, Kendall set himself apart. Not content with advocating containment of, or even rollback of, world communism, in the early years of the Cold War he openly advocated that the United States initiate a first strike against the Soviet Union: that is, wage a "preventive war."[47] His position scandalized the liberal community at Yale. At home, he approved in principle the deportation of American Communist leaders to Russia and urged the extirpation of Communist influence in American life—not on the liberal premise that domestic Communists were a "clear and present danger" to our national security (he did not think they were) but for the good and sufficient reason that the American people, as a "closed" society, had the right to banish a subversive movement that was totally antithetical to their way of life.

Unlike many other conservatives, who eventually acquired doubts about Joseph McCarthy and McCarthyism, Kendall was an unabashed and thoroughgoing "McCarthyite"—and remained one long after the senator from Wisconsin and his cause had been defeated.[48] In that role—a tenured professor for McCarthy—he was a very rare bird. McCarthyism, he declared, in a speech that he probably delivered in the early 1960s, was one of the two roots of "the contemporary American Conservative movement." "Conservatives," he added, "now know, from McCarthy's example, who are the right people to carry battles to."[49] Kendall's "egghead McCarthyism" (as he himself called it) did not appear to isolate him from fellow conservatives.[50] But his persistent and flamboyant articulation of it illustrated his tendency to test the limits of all orthodoxies—even his own. In that respect it subtly accentuated his apartness from the conservative mainstream.

Not that Kendall left such a perception open to any doubt. As his examination of conservatism's fundamental tenets proceeded in the 1960s, the "hound of heresies" cheerfully publicized his differences with his confreres. The preface to *The Conservative Affirmation* crackled with subtle and not-so-subtle jibes at their positions. To further enliven matters, Kendall invented epithets for his fellow conservatives, epithets that he planned to use in his projected *Sages of Conservatism*. He dubbed Russell Kirk "the Benevolent Sage of Mecosta." Frank Meyer was "the False Sage of Woodstock." James Burnham—a leading conservative strategist of the Cold War—was "the Muscleminded Sage of Kent." William F. Buckley Jr. was "the Young Sage of Stamford." Kendall even had epithets for himself; one was "the Worried Sage of Northford."[51]

In all of this one can detect, perhaps, an element of rivalry. It must have vexed Kendall that other conservative "sages"—including his onetime protégé Buckley—were gaining prominence as spokesmen for the cause, while he, the best-trained conservative political theorist in the country, was suffering discrimination bordering on ostracism in his profession. Be that as it may, Kendall's often devastating wit (which even today sparkles on the printed page) may well have driven further a wedge between himself and his associates on the Right. Certainly it could not have comforted his compatriots around *National Review* to know that he was preparing to cross-examine them in print: with the goal, no less, of lessening their influence over the conservative movement.

So much for the varieties of conservatism that Kendall was against. Let us turn now to what he stood for. While it is obviously impossible to explicate his teachings thoroughly in a few paragraphs,[52] we can quickly get to the core. Kendall's "essence" may, in fact, be stated quite succinctly. To a degree unique among conservatives of his era, be believed in the fundamental virtue, and capacity for self-government, of the American people. And he conceived his mission to be the intelligent defense of the institutions and constitutional morality through which, since 1787, the American people had manifested their impulse toward self-government. Unlike those conservatives who thought of themselves as a forlorn, antimajoritarian remnant in danger of being consigned to the ash heap of history, Kendall fearlessly and confidently insisted that conservatives had not been routed, and need not be routed, if only they could acquire the right mentors.

Why was Willmoore Kendall so different from other conservatives in this respect? Why, even in the face of the demise of McCarthy and the debacle of the Goldwater campaign, did he continue to exude what William F. Buckley Jr. called his "baffling optimism"?[53] Two closely related factors account for this remarkable divergence from the prevailing conservative persuasion. First, Kendall seems to have felt an almost mystical identification with "the people"—*his* people: the inarticulate men and women between the Appalachians and the Rockies.[54] On its face it seems odd. He did not, after all, spend much time among them after leaving home as a young man. A cosmopolitan college professor, fluent in three languages, he was at least as much at home in Oxford, Paris, and Madrid as (let us say) in Tulsa. But there it is. When he came to Dallas in 1963, he felt that he was coming home. In some of his commentary upon the failings of the conservative movement, one even senses a note of pity, on Kendall's part, for the suffering people at the grassroots—deeply moral and betrayed by their supposed "betters," who were assailing the people's cherished way of life. Kendall has been called a "prophet of the heartland."[55] To put it another way, he was one of the first conservative intellectuals to articulate conservatism in "populist" terms as the voice of the "silent majority."

Second, Kendall's commitment to popular self-government was linked to a powerful disposition that underlay his career: his lifelong distrust of elites. Like so many other traits, his anti-establishmentarianism probably had its origins in his relationship with his father (the first establishment of his life). He did not, however, outgrow it. As a radical majority-rule democrat in the 1930s, he detested undemocratic governing minorities, whether "economic royalists" at home or Stalinists in Republican Spain. In 1940–41, he fought against an establishment, led by Franklin Roosevelt, which, as he saw it, was maneuvering America into a foreign war. At Yale University in the late 1940s and 1950s, he took on the emerging liberal establishment, a new class which he perceived to be profoundly at odds with his country's traditional institutions and values. But he did not stop here, and the following is key to understanding his place in American conservatism. *When the Right itself began to develop an establishment,* Kendall rebelled. Iconoclast to the end, he put more faith in the wisdom of the people (whom he perhaps idealized) than in the intellectual icons and princes with whom he associated. For Kendall, in every phase of his life, the primary threat to the good society came not from below but from above.

What, finally, may be said about Kendall's contribution to post-1945 conservatism in the perspective of the past thirty-five years? (I refer not to Kendall the political theorist or intellectual historian but to Kendall the conservative seer and strategist.) Obviously, much has occurred in America since his death—much that, presumably, would appall him: the various multiplying "rights" revolutions (such as the "right" to abortion); the rise of a media elite and an "imperial judiciary"; the growing plebiscitary elements in the political process; and the intensifying "civil war potential" in American society (something he feared), exemplified by our "culture wars" and the growing ideology of a totally "open" society.

Despite these changes, Kendall, if he were here, might point to three accomplishments for which conservatives should remember him. First, he helped to *Americanize* contemporary conservatism by pointing conservatives back to their own past—above all, to the founding documents and arrangements of their polity. He did so, moreover, in a manner and idiom that remain fresh and arresting a generation later. Second, he helped to *politicize* the conservative movement: that is, he taught it to "keep its eye" on Congress and on the health of the American system. (There was more at stake, in other words, than day-to-day public policy questions and economics.) Third, he bequeathed to conservatives a conception of politics as a battleground between a "liberal revolution" and a conservative "resistance." It was a struggle requiring "doctrine" and "strategy." Kendall's military metaphors may seem unsettling, but for him the issues to be decided were profound: the open society (we might say "diversity") versus orthodoxy; philosophical relativism (and all its consequences) versus the truth embodied in the Western tradition; and government by deliberate sense of the people's representatives, acting under God, versus government by plebiscitary passions or manipulative minorities.

Kendall tried to discern the big picture; he tried to educate conservatives to do so, too. He also bequeathed to conservatives a set of questions—perhaps the ultimate questions for evaluating his project. Is his vision of the American conservative cause still valid? Are the "virtuous people" still virtuous? Do they (or do enough of them) still truly carry the Great Tradition "in their hips"? Is Kendall's "baffling optimism" still justified?

Perhaps we, the living, are too close to the sound and fury of today's debates to know for certain. But on one point we all can agree. When one thinks of the gravity of these questions, and of the rousing analytical rigor with which he would address them, one wishes that Willmoore Kendall were here to give his answer.

9

The Life and Legacy of Russell Kirk

I delivered this lecture at the Heritage Foundation in Washington, D.C., on June 22, 2007. My remarks were then published by the foundation as No. 1035 in its Heritage Lectures series. I reproduce the text here with a few minor revisions.

In the book of *Ecclesiasticus* it is written: "Let us now praise famous men, and our fathers that begat us." We gather today to honor the memory of a famous man, a man who earned his fame by writing about those who, in an intellectual and spiritual sense, were our fathers. In the great chain of being that we call Western civilization, Russell Kirk was a sturdy link.

Some years ago, a young libertarian wrote a book entitled *It Usually Begins with Ayn Rand*. I do not know how many young conservatives in 2007 would say that their intellectual awakening began with the books and essays of Russell Kirk. But certainly many among us can testify to his influence and especially to the impact of his masterful book *The Conservative Mind*.

As most everyone knows, *The Conservative Mind* was Russell Kirk's magnum opus. More than fifty years after its publication, it remains in print in several languages. For most scholars, the publication of a book of this distinction would be the culmination of a career. For Kirk, who was only thirty-four at the time, it was just an opening salvo. In the years to come, he founded two influential journals (*Modern Age* and the *University Bookman*); published a regular column for more than two decades in *National Review*; wrote a major biography of T. S. Eliot and a classic history entitled *The Roots of American Order*; did more than anyone living to revive Edmund Burke as a fountainhead of conservative thought; completed a superb memoir called *The Sword of Imagination*; and churned out a prodigious torrent of other writings.

How prodigious? According to Charles Brown, who has just completed a comprehensive bibliography of Kirk's works, Dr. Kirk wrote 26 nonfiction books, 9 volumes of novels and collected short stories, 255 book reviews, 68 introductions and forewords to other peoples' books, 814 essays and short pieces published in periodicals, and nearly 3,000 newspaper columns. Among all the founding fathers of modern American conservatism, only William F. Buckley Jr. rivaled him in productivity.

Surely, a man of such phenomenal intellectual output and versatility deserves to be honored, and so Kirk has been and continues to be. At the Heritage Foundation, for example, you will find a portrait of him on the wall. If you exercise your imagination a little, you may hear echoes of his voice in the Heritage auditorium, where he delivered more than fifty lectures in a little over a decade.

Sometimes it is hinted that Kirk is slowly becoming a forgotten figure. The evidence suggests otherwise. Many of his books remain in print, and others are in the pipeline for republication. Today we celebrate the most recent addition to his bibliography: a collection of his most outstanding essays, impressively edited by Professor George Panichas.[1] The title of this volume, *The Essential Russell Kirk*, is doubly meaningful. It suggests, first, that the essays therein contain the essence of Kirk's teaching, and secondly, that Kirk himself is essential—essential to American conservatism. I hope you will read this splendid volume and agree.

No, Kirk has not been forgotten, nor is he likely to be anytime soon. And yet there is a sense, at least in some corners of the American Right, that in 2007, thirteen years after his passing, Kirk has come to be a figure more admired than studied. Some observers have suggested that much of the praise heaped upon Kirk since his death has been "empty homage" by people who covet his prestige but care little for his teaching. Others lament that American higher education—the recurrent target of Kirk's fusillades—seems more degraded than ever, at least by the standards Kirk struggled to uphold.

Is Kirk's conservatism, then, a "live option" for Americans in 2007? To put it another way: Is Russell Kirk still essential? Before we can ponder these questions, we need a clearer sense of just what kind of conservatism he espoused and of where he fits in the jigsaw puzzle of modern American conservatism.

BOOKISH AND PRECOCIOUS

To understand his message, we need to know the messenger. Who was Russell Kirk? He was born in 1918 in the village of Plymouth, Michigan, a few miles outside Detroit. His father was a railroad engineer who dropped out of school before the sixth grade. In Plymouth, and in the hamlet of Mecosta in the "stump country" of central Michigan, Kirk lived and grew to young adulthood. A romantic traditionalist by instinct, as it were, he came early to share his father's prejudices against the "assembly-line civilization" already penetrating Michigan under the aegis of Henry Ford.

Kirk was a shy boy, bookish and precocious. By the impressionable age of eight he was devouring the novels of the man he later called his "literary mentor," Sir Walter Scott. The imprint on the boy's imagination was indelible. By the time he was ten (he tells us), he had read all of the works of Victor Hugo, Charles Dickens, and Mark Twain. By the time he was a teenager, Kirk's cast of mind was fixed. Growing up almost as an only child (his one sibling, a sister, was seven years younger), he lived in a world of old houses, old villages, old books, and elderly relatives, many of whom believed in spirits and ghosts.

After graduating from high school in 1936, Kirk entered Michigan State College (now Michigan State University), whose spirit of "conformity," utilitarianism, and "dim animosity toward liberal education" grated against his sensibility. Possessing little money (the Great Depression was still on), he lived frugally, subsisting much of the time on a diet of peanut butter and crackers, and graduated as a history major in 1940.

For the next year, Kirk was a graduate student in history at Duke University, where he wrote a master's thesis later published as *Randolph of Roanoke*. In it he clearly sympathized with the antebellum Virginian's aristocratic, states' rights agrarianism. During this year, the young scholar from Michigan began to get acquainted with the conservative South. He read approvingly the Southern Agrarian manifesto, *I'll Take My Stand*. For the rest of his life, he considered himself a "Northern Agrarian."

In the summer of 1941, Kirk found himself working at Henry Ford's Greenfield Village. Even before his experiences at the Ford company, Kirk had developed a distaste for big business, big labor, and big government. His year or so at Ford did nothing to change his attitude. Indeed, his dislike of bureaucracy and what he called federal "parasites" was, if anything, increasing. He denounced the military draft as "slavery." He published his first scholarly article, in which he advocated a return to "Jeffersonian principles." All in all, his was the Midwestern libertarian conservatism of Senator Robert Taft.

Kirk's drifting ended abruptly in August 1942, when he was drafted into the army. For nearly four years he lived in the desolate wastes of Utah (and, later, at a camp in Florida) as a sergeant in the Chemical Warfare Service. In one respect, Kirk's wartime experience proved to be invaluable: As a clerk with largely routine duties, he found a large amount of time to read. And read he did—Albert Jay Nock's *Memoirs*, Chesterton's *Orthodoxy*, Irving Babbitt's *Democracy and Leadership*, the political thought of Walter Bagehot, and countless classics of English and ancient literature.

After his discharge from the army in 1946, Kirk was appointed an assistant professor of history at his alma mater, Michigan State. On the side, he founded and operated a used bookstore. But the young scholar with antiquarian interests was not long for the world of East Lansing. In 1948, Kirk—who was partly Scottish by ancestry—undertook doctoral studies at the University of St. Andrews in Scotland. In 1952, he earned the university's doctor of letters degree—the only American ever to do so.

YEARS AT ST. ANDREWS

The years 1948 to 1952 were more than just a time of intensive study, however. In many ways they set the mold for the rest of Kirk's career. Already deeply attached to rural and ancestral ways, and already an Anglophile in his literary tastes, Kirk fell deeply in love with his ancestral homeland. There, he became a connoisseur of ancient castles, old country houses, and the lore of old St. Andrews. There, and in rural England, which he avidly explored on foot, he found "the metaphysical principle of continuity given visible reality." There, Russell Kirk found a way to live. Some years later, he himself became a country squire, as we shall see, recreating at the old family house in Mecosta something of the lifestyle he had cherished in Scotland. Not without reason did he come to refer to himself as "the last bonnet laird of the stump country."

The St. Andrews experience affected Kirk in another way: It powerfully reinforced his staunchly classical philosophy of education. Reflecting some years later upon his St. Andrews days, when he had lived in a garret and skimped on the consumption of food, he wrote:

It is good for a student to be poor. Getting and spending, the typical American college student lays waste his powers. Work and contemplation don't mix, and university days ought to be days of contemplation.

For the rest of his life, Kirk held unswervingly to his approach to higher education, embodied in St. Andrews, and excoriated the decadence symbolized for him by Michigan State.

In still another way, St. Andrews left an indelible imprint upon this highly imaginative young man. Even before he arrived in Scotland, Kirk knew—as he later wrote—that "[m]ine was not an Enlightened mind." It was (he said), "a Gothic mind, medieval in its temper and structure."

> I did not love cold harmony and perfect regularity of organization; what I sought was variety, mystery, tradition, the venerable, the awful. I despised sophisters and calculators; I was groping for faith, honor, and prescriptive loyalties. I would have given any number of neo-classical pediments for one poor battered gargoyle.

In misty, medieval St. Andrews and the Scottish countryside, Kirk found enough to nourish his imagination for the remainder of his life. His later gothic novel, *Old House of Fear*, was set in Scotland. It sold more copies than all his other books put together.

Finally, it was at the University of St. Andrews that Kirk discovered—or more precisely, discovered more deeply—the great intellectual hero of his life: Edmund Burke. To Kirk's Midwestern, grassroots, American conservatism, and to his "aristocratic" literary humanism, was now added another layer of thought: Burkean traditionalism, which Kirk acclaimed as "the true school of conservative principle." Burke's writings formed the basis for his doctoral dissertation, which was published in 1953 as *The Conservative Mind*.

GIVING CONSERVATIVES AN IDENTITY

Of the detailed substance of Kirk's book, I will say little, since most of you, I presume, have already read it. But its significance for American conservatism deserves further comment. What Kirk did was to demonstrate that intelligent conservatism was not a mere smokescreen for selfishness. It was an attitude toward life with substance and moral force of its own. A century earlier, John Stuart Mill had dismissed conservatives as "the stupid party." In 1950, an eminent American literary critic had dared to assert that liberalism was "the sole intellectual tradition in the United States." After the appearance of *The Conservative Mind*, the American intellectual landscape assumed a different shape. Kirk's tour de force breached the wall of liberal condescension. He made it respectable for sophisticated people to identify themselves as men and women of the Right.

Above all, *The Conservative Mind* stimulated the development of a self-consciously conservative intellectual movement in America in the early years of the Cold War. In the words of the book's publisher, Henry Regnery, Kirk gave an "amorphous, scattered" opposition to liberalism an "identity."

All this was a remarkable accomplishment for a single volume by a little-known author in 1953. The magnitude of Kirk's achievement becomes even more impressive when we observe that *The Conservative Mind* was not, in the conventional sense, a political book. In its 450 pages he laid out no elaborate agenda for legislation. Instead, he tirelessly reminded his readers that political problems were fundamentally "religious and moral problems" and that social regeneration was a goal which required action at levels beyond the political and economic. This is one reason why *The Conservative Mind* has outlived the special circumstances of its birth: It focuses our attention on ends and not just on means.

Kirk did this, moreover, by fearlessly grounding his conservatism in religion, particularly Christianity. In an age of predominantly secular public discourse, he unabashedly spoke of the soul and of his conviction that God rules society. In an age of the growing hegemony of the social sciences, he defiantly quoted poetry and wrote ghostly fiction with a moral twist. Indeed, I can think of no conservative in the past half century who resorted as frequently as did Kirk to works of literature to buttress his social and political commentary. You will find abundant evidence of this in Professor Panichas's volume.

The author of *The Conservative Mind* was not indifferent to the worldly concerns of politics and economics. A little later in his career, for example, he helped to launch the Goldwater-for-President movement. But fundamentally, Kirk realized that political activism was not his calling. He was, rather, a moralist and man of letters whose vocation, as he saw it, was to remind us of the truths embodied in the permanent things.

THE BOHEMIAN TORY

It was to these truths that Kirk returned, in more ways than one, in 1953. In that year—the very year he became an academic celebrity—Kirk courageously resigned his teaching position at Michigan State—appalled, he wrote, by the administration's deliberate dumbing-down of educational standards. (The president of the university at the time had only one earned degree: a bachelor of science degree in poultry husbandry. Kirk disparaged him as a "chickenologist.") Preferring "unsalaried independence" (as he put it) to the corrupting mediocrity of academe, he took up the uncertain life of a professional writer and lecturer. Declining a host of academic job offers, he instead went back to remote Mecosta, Michigan (pop. 200), and to the old family house on Piety Hill, to live with his widowed grandmother and two maiden great aunts.

In his history of *National Review* published last year, Professor Jeffrey Hart, who knew Kirk, described him as a "self-invented work of art, prodigiously learned." By the mid-1950s his distinctive persona seemed complete. Not yet married, the peripatetic bachelor proudly called himself a "Bohemian Tory." He defined a bohemian as "a wandering and often impecunious man of letters or arts, indifferent to the demands of bourgeois fad and foible." He hated television, which he called "Demon TV." He refused to drive an automobile, which he labeled a "mechanical Jacobin."

It is entirely possible that Kirk would have remained a brilliant, if somewhat reclusive, social critic, writing for literary journals and Sunday supplements, had not William F. Buckley Jr. come calling in Mecosta in 1955. Buckley was about to launch a conservative magazine called *National Review*, and he wanted Kirk to write a regular column for it. To Buckley's delight, Kirk immediately agreed to do so. But to Buckley's dismay, his host refused to be identified on the magazine's masthead as one of its editors. And therein hangs a tale which illuminates much about modern American conservatism and Kirk's place in it.

RIVALS FOR INTELLECTUAL LEADERSHIP

For in 1955, Kirk's Burkeanism was not the only school of right-wing thought vying for prominence. Another intellectual tendency, known in those days as "classical liberalism" or "individualism" but generally known to us today as libertarianism, was also stirring in the United States. Among its adherents, broadly speaking, were such free-market economists as Friedrich Hayek, Ludwig von Mises, and Milton Friedman, and the novelist Ayn Rand.

To Russell Kirk, "true conservatism"—Burke's conservatism—was utterly antithetical to unrestrained capitalism and the egoistic ideology of individualism. "Individualism is social atomism," he exclaimed; "conservatism is community of spirit." Spiritually, he said, individualism was a "hideous solitude." On one occasion Kirk even criticized "individualism" as anti-Christian. No one, he asserted, could logically be a Christian and an individualist at the same time.

Such sentiments, which Kirk expressed with gusto in *The Conservative Mind* and elsewhere, did not exactly endear him to libertarians. Nor did his frequent fulminations against classical liberalism and the gospel of Progress. In 1955, the editor of the libertarian *Freeman* magazine, a man named Frank Chodorov, commissioned a critical article on Kirk and his so-called new conservatism. The author of the article was an argumentative libertarian (and former Communist) named Frank Meyer. The trouble with Kirk and his allies, said Meyer, was a lack of grounding in "clear and distinct principle." For all the froth and evocative tone of their writings, they failed utterly to provide a crisp analytic framework for opposing the real enemy—collectivism—that was threatening to engulf us all. Kirk had no standards, said Meyer, no principle for distinguishing between what was good and bad in the status quo. Meyer was additionally angered by Kirk's sweeping condemnation of "individualism." The fiery ex-radical, who believed that "*all* value resides in the individual," felt that Kirk did not comprehend the principles and institutions of a free society. To underscore the point, Meyer's attack on Kirk was given the title "Collectivism Rebaptized."

For Kirk, such an assault was disagreeable, if not surprising, considering its source. Far more disturbing to him was what transpired next. As it happened, Kirk in 1955 was in the process of founding his own journal—*Modern Age*—when Meyer's blast appeared. Someone—Kirk believed it was either Meyer or Chodorov—sent a copy of Meyer's critical article to every member of Kirk's board of advisors. To Kirk this was a blatant attempt to undercut him with his sponsors and perhaps kill *Modern Age* in its womb. So when Kirk learned that Buckley intended to publish Meyer and Chodorov in *National Review*, the Bohemian Tory declined to be listed on the masthead as an editor. He was not about to accept any appearance of responsibility for publishing the likes of Chodorov and Meyer, whom he labeled "the Supreme Soviet of Libertarianism." And when Kirk discovered that Chodorov and Meyer had been placed on the new magazine's masthead, he ordered Buckley to remove his own name from that page, where he had been briefly listed as an associate and contributor. Kirk vowed that though he might write for the same magazine as Meyer and Chodorov, he would not be "cheek by jowl with them in the masthead."

Buckley, who was trying to forge conservatism's diverse elements into a coalition, was perturbed. He insisted that Meyer was not out to "get" Kirk and undermine his influence—although Kirk had what he considered evidence to the contrary. But Kirk did not relent. For the next twenty-five years, he wrote steadily for *National Review*—in fact, wrote more for it, I believe, than any other person except possibly Buckley himself. But he did not add his name to its masthead. He remained *in National Review* but not quite of it.

It is not possible to give you here a full account of the subsequent feud (as some have called it) between Kirk and Frank Meyer. So far as I know, they never met nor fully reconciled, though they did correspond and did, I think, develop a measure of respect for each other. Interestingly, each became a convert to Roman Catholicism—Kirk in 1964 and Meyer on his deathbed in 1972. Perhaps, in the end, they were not so far apart as it seemed.

Nevertheless, for a long time they personified the two polarities in post-war conservative thought: Meyer the arch-libertarian, for whom freedom to choose was the highest political good, and Kirk the arch-traditionalist, who sought to instruct his readers on the proper choices. The important point is that the difference between them was more than personal. Other conservative intellectuals in the 1950s and beyond were also disturbed by Kirk's seemingly nostalgic and indiscriminate yearning for a premodern world. Kirk's repeated invocation of "the wisdom of our ancestors" was no doubt useful, the conservative scholar Richard Weaver remarked on one occasion, but the question was: Which ancestors? "After all," said Weaver, "Adam is our ancestor. . . . If we have an ancestral legacy of wisdom, we have also an ancestral legacy of folly. . . ."

Nor was Meyer the only rival with whom Kirk had to contend for intellectual leadership of the emerging conservative movement. Another was the political scientist Willmoore Kendall, who had been one of Buckley's mentors at Yale. Never a man to shy from a rough-and-tumble argument, Kendall openly repudiated what he called the "Burke 'cultists'"—above all, Russell Kirk. Privately, Kendall called his own book *The Conservative Affirmation* (1963) a "declaration of war" against Kirk.

So much for Kirk's critics on the Right. Suffice it to say here that from the mid-1950s forward Kirk responded vigorously to the challenges hurled against his formulation of the conservative creed. Toward doctrinaire libertarianism (especially as expounded by someone like Ayn Rand), he remained utterly uncompromising. It was, he declared in the 1980s, "as alien to real American conservatism as is communism." It was "an ideology of universal selfishness," and he added: "We flawed human creatures are sufficiently selfish already, without being exhorted to pursue selfishness on principle." To those who asserted that his Burkean conservatism was insufficiently principled and mired in historical contingency, he reinterpreted Edmund Burke as a thinker in the "natural law" tradition—a tradition transcending national borders and mutable social conditions. To those who thought that Kirk slighted the role of reason in his defense of what he called the Permanent Things, he increasingly grounded his insights on what he termed the moral imagination. To those who disparaged his conservatism as an alien hothouse plant, he reaffirmed Burke's intellectual influence on American statesmen and emphasized the premodern roots of American order. Repeatedly, for example, he highlighted the most conservative features of the American War for Independence and its culminating achievement, the Constitution.

It is sometimes said that as men become old, they revert to the political mindset of their youth. In the final decade of his life, Kirk, it seems to me, returned more overtly—at least in his politics—to the noninterventionist, Taftite, bedrock conservatism of his boyhood. He did so, in part, under the stress of the growing quarrel between the so-called neoconservatives and their traditionalist right-wing critics, the most militant of whom took the label of paleoconservatives. In this imbroglio, which still continues today, a number of Kirk's friends, such as M. E. Bradford, were firmly in the paleo-conservative camp, and toward it Kirk tended to gravitate. In 1988, in a controversial address at the Heritage Foundation, he mixed considerable praise for the neoconservatives with mordant criticism. The next year he permitted his name to go on the masthead of the paleoconservative monthly *Chronicles*, where it remained for approximately three years until he took it off. In 1991 he condemned the first Gulf War as an arrogant and imprudent "war for an oil-can." The next year he served as chairman of Patrick Buchanan's presidential campaign in Michigan.

In general, though, Kirk tried to stay aloof from the factional infighting that was once again afflicting the Right. Early in his career, he had described himself as one who played "a lone hand," and to a considerable extent he succeeded. It is one reason why, at his death in 1994, he was so widely respected by his fellow conservatives.

THE BENEVOLENT SAGE OF MECOSTA

There was another reason for this respect, which I must touch upon before closing. In 1964, at the age of almost forty-six, Russell Kirk married. In the next eleven years he became the father of four daughters. With his new station in life came new duties; as he remarked in his memoirs, "married men require money." The years ahead brought little diminution in the pace of his intellectual activity, nor could there be, with a growing family to support. In a 12-month period between mid-1967 and mid-1968, for example, he delivered about 150 lectures around the country.

Although married life imposed new obligations on Kirk, it also created new opportunities to increase his influence on American conservatism. With his wife, Annette, as his helpmeet, the Bohemian Tory evolved into a Tory squire and paterfamilias: the laird of Piety Hill. Willmoore Kendall privately called him "the Benevolent Sage of Mecosta"—a designation I think Kirk would have enjoyed.

And like all sages, he attracted inquiring students to his door. With the assistance of the Intercollegiate Studies Institute, he held periodic conferences—called Piety Hill seminars—at his home in Mecosta: scores of them over a period of twenty years. According to Annette, a total of two thousand students and professors participated in these events. For some it was a life-changing experience. With the help of the Wilbur Foundation, the impecunious refugee from what he called Behemoth University created his own informal campus in Mecosta—an endeavor that persists today in the Russell Kirk Center for Cultural Renewal. If he had not married, probably none of this would have happened, and his impact on American conservatism would have been less.

What, finally, may we say about Kirk's place in the galaxy of American conservatism? First, a word about his message. More than any other conservative writer of his era, he elevated the tone and substance of conservative discourse. As Gregory Wolfe has put it, he was a "bridge-builder" to "the classics of our culture." Whatever we may think about his interpretation of Burke, or of the American Revolution, or of any other past or present controversy, Kirk's legacy as a moralist endures. He elevated our discourse—and our vision.

Secondly, a word about the messenger. Kirk's antimodern persona did not win universal approbation on the American Right. It attracted some and repelled others. And it raised a perennial challenge for those who would propagate his teachings: Namely, how adversarial toward modernity can one become without losing one's ability to influence one's fellow men and women? We might call this the dilemma of traditionalist conservatism in untraditional times.

Here Kirk himself gave us a clue on how to resolve it. In the words of an old Christian hymn, "This Is My Father's World." Russell Kirk knew this, and because of that, he never withdrew bitterly into a "hideous solitude." He never gave up on communicating with the world around him. "This Is My

Father's World," and as Kirk liked to say, cheerfulness keeps breaking in. He did not let his critique of modernity lead him into the Slough of Despond.

Of Kirk's career, it can well be said that he took the road less traveled by. No doubt he paid a price for his independence—in diminished income, in caricature at times, and in lost prestige among the American professoriate. And yet his labors bore fruit, as the scintillating volume *The Essential Russell Kirk* attests.

In a way, Kirk's life illustrates the truth of a remark attributed to the historian Peter Viereck: "If you stand still long enough, sooner or later you're avant-garde." Russell Kirk did not stand still all his life, but on the issues that truly mattered he stood his ground. And because he did, we, his grateful heirs, can carry on.

10

The Memoirs of Forrest McDonald, Conservative Historian

This is a review of Forrest McDonald, Recovering the Past: A Historian's Memoir *(2004). The review appeared in the Spring 2005 issue of* Modern Age *under the title "A Conservative Historian's Memoir."*

As a talented college athlete in the 1940s, Forrest McDonald hoped to become a major league baseball player. He might well have succeeded, had he been able to hit a curve ball. Fortunately for students and scholars of American history, he soon discovered where his greater aptitude lay.

This is among the revelations that enliven Professor McDonald's new memoir, *Recovering the Past*. For nearly half a century now, McDonald, a historian, has been publishing scintillating studies of the political, economic, and intellectual origins of the American republic, along with substantial works on American economic history. Such titles as *E Pluribus Unum, Novus Ordo Seclorum* and *Alexander Hamilton: A Biography* have earned honored places on fellow scholars' shelves. His 1987 Jefferson Lecture at the National Endowment for the Humanities (reprinted in this memoir) is a luminous introduction to the intellectual world of the Founding Fathers. If, as Richard Weaver once said, conservative intellectuals need to produce "unshakable books," McDonald, an unabashed conservative, has more than fulfilled his quota.

On the dust jacket of his latest volume, McDonald's publisher acclaims him as "a legend in his own time." He has earned this reputation not only for his scholarship and productivity (more than fifteen books to date), but also for the way in which he has scaled the academic heights. In a profession long dominated by liberals and leftists, he has fearlessly challenged the regnant orthodoxy and lived to tell the tale.

Recovering the Past: A Historian's Memoir is that tale. It is the story of a young Texas Ph.D., brimming with "boundless self-confidence and inexhaustible energy," whose first major book, *We the People* (1958), dealt a devastating blow to Charles A. Beard's "economic interpretation" of the Constitution. It is the story of "a barefoot boy in the Ivy League" (as he styles himself) who was unafraid to speak his mind, come what may. It is the intellectual adventure story of a prolific historian whose curiosity seemed never to dissipate. Each book he completed was followed by another.

Along the way, the young iconoclast made enemies. In Wisconsin, where he worked during much of the 1950s, his first book, a history of the state's public utility industry, "elicited howls of rage" from the local Progressive newspaper and dark mutterings that he was a "tool of the power trust." The resulting "political fracas" nearly cost him his job and his career. At Brown University, where he taught during much of the 1960s, his outspoken criticism of the university's racial policies earned him a unanimous rebuke by the faculty and a warning by the university's president that McDonald "would never receive another salary increase at Brown." At Wayne State University, where he taught next, he was eventually honored as the institution's "most distinguished faculty member," but quit after the faculty voted to unionize. Finally, he found his way to the University of Alabama, where he taught—it seems contentedly—until his retirement.

All these tempests—and more—McDonald recounts with zest in this candid and highly readable memoir. He is particularly deft at depicting the nasty academic politics that he encountered, as well as the historiographical milieu in which he worked. Deeply devoted to standards of excellence in his calling, he does not hesitate to identify historians he considers incompetents and knaves. A master practitioner of the historian's craft, he disdains the pedants and ideologues who, to his dismay, have come to dominate his profession. In the preface to *Recovering the Past*, he announces that he has written his book not for his colleagues in the professoriat but for "that elusive critter called the general reader, or, more precisely, for the vast number of people who genuinely love history for its own sake which, as will become evident, I regard as eliminating a sizable majority of professional historians."

Nor does McDonald conceal his own political sympathies. He declares bluntly in his memoir that "for all its faults, this country has more to be proud of and less to be ashamed of than any other nation on the face of the earth." "I did not set out to prove that proposition," he adds; "my instincts and my research led me to it, and I have little patience for those who say otherwise." Lest there be any doubt about the matter, this cheerful contrarian has blithely illustrated his memoir with photographs of himself meeting Ronald Reagan, Richard Nixon, and George W. Bush. It takes a healthy supply of insouciance (and humor) to do that.

How, one wonders, was McDonald able to survive and prosper in his chosen profession? For one thing, not even his fiercest enemies could deny his intellectual attainments. He was bright and formidably learned, and they knew it. For another, he made his early reputation in the golden age of the late 1950s, when sound scholarship could still prevail over ideological purity in the distribution of academic honors and rewards. By the time the polarizing upheavals of the sixties occurred, he was safely tenured.

Geography, too, helped to immunize him against leftist academic fashion. At the University of Texas in the late 1940s, he admits, he received a somewhat provincial education, which left him "blissfully ignorant of the subjectivist-relativist-presentist philosophy" so pervasive in history departments elsewhere. He thereby escaped indoctrination by osmosis at a critical period in his intellectual development.

Above all, McDonald survived and thrived because he was not by temperament a party-line ideologue and was unfazed by the imprecations of those who were. Unlike too many of his fellow historians who let their present-day policy agendas control their interpretation of the past, McDonald refused to distort his subjects in this way. He has studied history, he explains, "because it gives me pleasure, and I do not care whether my writing has implications for current policy." This willingness to study the past for its own sake—coupled with a deeply ingrained independence of mind and spirit—enabled McDonald to chart his own path, free from the conformist passions of his peers.

And what a fruitful pathway it has been. As much as any American historian since 1950, McDonald liberated his profession from its thralldom to the notion that the Constitution of 1787 was the product of the selfish machinations of wealthy interest groups. More broadly, in a series of powerful books McDonald demonstrated both the intellectual complexity and grandeur of the American Founding. In the process he helped to expose what he calls the "fundamental flaw" in the scholarship of the so-called New Historians led by Charles A. Beard: "their utterly unsophisticated conception of economic activity as the exploitation by the wealthy of the poor, laborers, farmers, and small businessmen." In his influential biographies of Alexander Hamilton and Samuel Insull, among other writings, McDonald helped to combat the condescending hostility toward capitalism that long afflicted the writing of American history.

McDonald was less successful at slaying the simplistic worldview that underlay the "progressive" historians' approach: their belief that history at bottom is a struggle between "good people" and "bad people," between victims and victimizers, and that the duty of the historian is to side with the aspirations of the "good." It is a mental habit that remains all too seductive today. But thanks in part to the scholarly labors of McDonald, at least one stultifying manifestation of it—crude economic determinism—is no longer in vogue among historians. The historiography of the American experience is much the richer for its demise. For this, conservatives especially, as defenders of the American regime of ordered liberty, have reason to be grateful to Professor McDonald.

This does not mean that McDonald's own brand of conservatism is neatly predictable. Although a Texan by birth and a farmer by avocation (he once bought a tractor with his lecture earnings), he is clearly no Southern Agrarian. Among the Founding Fathers his hero appears to be Hamilton, whose zealous commitment to creating a dynamic, money-based, private enterprise economy—McDonald tells us—helped to energize and revolutionize American society. Indeed, this reviewer once heard McDonald remark that the United States would have become a bunch of banana republics had it not been for Hamilton's vision and genius. Conversely, McDonald is no venerator of the Jeffersonians, whom he describes in his memoir as privileged reactionaries, "swimming against the tide of history" and "determined to resist the emergence of the modern world." Nor does he march to the dissident beat of antistatist libertarianism, as his magisterial book *The American Presidency: An Intellectual History* (1994) attests. There he concludes that the institution of the presidency "has been responsible for less harm and more good, in the nation and the world, than perhaps any other secular institution in history." In *Recovering the Past* he reveals that he agrees with Alexander Hamilton that the Bill of Rights was "unnecessary and pernicious." These are not the convictions of a simon-pure libertarian.

McDonald, one suspects, enjoys being a provocateur. Like many intellectuals on the Right after the Second World War, he has cherished his independence and has refused to become an organization man, particularly when the "organization" (in his case, the history profession) was full of liberals and leftists.

One puzzle, though, he does not quite resolve in his memoir: How did he become, to use his own word, an "archconservative"? By his own admission he was not always one. In 1948, he tells us, he voted for Harry Truman for president; in 1952, for Adlai Stevenson. By 1964, however, he was a public supporter of Barry Goldwater. Why this transition? He does not explicitly say.

To be sure, an alert reader of *Recovering the Past* can make some educated guesses. In "progressive" Madison, Wisconsin, in the 1950s, the young Texan ran afoul of an "extremely left wing" subculture which distrusted Southerners in general and McDonald, a friend of the "power trust," in particular. It did not help that McDonald was believed to be writing a critical book about Charles A. Beard, a patron saint of Progressive intellectuals. A frank desire to show up the "Wisconsin crowd" helped motivate McDonald to write *We the People*, as he acknowledges in a marvelous anecdote in his memoir. Exposure to Wisconsin-style leftism undoubtedly drove him to the Right.

Still, one wishes that McDonald had expatiated on his evolution as a conservative—an unusual trajectory, to say the least, for an upwardly mobile scholar of his generation. This leads us to the one limitation (a self-imposed limitation, we suspect) of this otherwise excellent memoir: It is focused almost exclusively on McDonald's career as a professional historian. About his youth, personal life, and extracurricular interests we learn comparatively little.

By and large, this is probably as it should be. It is, after all, as a professional historian that he has made his mark. At times, however, one finds oneself yearning for glimpses of the scholar at ease, beyond the confines of his purely professional pursuits. McDonald, for instance, has long been associated with the conservative intellectual community, yet his book contains almost no references to conservative leaders or causes. Such conservative luminaries as Russell Kirk and M. E. Bradford—whom McDonald knew—go unmentioned. Similarly, he informs us that he found Richard Nixon (whom he met for dinner in 1992) to be "awesomely learned about history; it was rather like spending an evening with, say, John Adams." From a historian of McDonald's stature this is a remarkable tribute; it leaves this reader hungry for substantiating detail. Perhaps, in some future book or essay, McDonald will favor us with such broader reminiscences.

For now, we can savor this latest addition to his oeuvre. "Men hit only what they aim at," said Thoreau. Throughout his career Forrest McDonald has aimed well and consistently hit his target. In *Recovering the Past* we learn with pleasure how he did it.

11

E. Victor Milione
(1924–2008)

These remarks were delivered at a memorial service in Arlington, Virginia, on April 11, 2008, and are published here in slightly modified form.

Members of the Milione family, ladies and gentlemen:
This afternoon we celebrate the life and accomplishment of one of the pioneers of American conservatism. During his more than fifty years as a conservative activist, E. Victor Milione seldom stood in the spotlight. Perhaps for this reason, his leadership was often easy to overlook. But there was one realm in which his achievement could be discerned and measured. Quietly, doggedly, unobtrusively, for most of his adult life Milione devoted himself to building the influential institution known to us today as the Intercollegiate Studies Institute.

To appreciate Milione's imprint upon ISI, and—through it—the larger world of American conservatism, we must turn for a moment to another man, the institute's founder: Frank Chodorov. Chodorov was an uncompromising libertarian. A temperamental aginner and near-anarchist, he once remarked: "As for me, I will punch anyone who calls me a conservative in the nose. I am a radical."

In 1950 Chodorov published an article in *Human Events* urging the creation of a national network of Individualist Clubs to combat the ascendancy of socialistic thinking among the nation's college students. In a separate article he proposed what he called a "fifty-year project" to implement such an intellectual counterrevolution on the campus.

Chodorov did not expect anything concrete to emerge from his published musings. Imagine his astonishment, then, when he received an unsolicited check in the mail for $1,000 from none other than J. Howard Pew. Thoroughly taken aback, and having no definitive plan for using the check, Chodorov told Frank Hanighen of *Human Events* that he thought he would simply return it. Hanighen's advice was sage and swift: "Never send money back."

Not long afterward, Chodorov established the Intercollegiate Society of Individualists. At first, ISI was little more than a vehicle for distributing libertarian literature to a scattered student remnant. Then, about a year after its founding, a friend of ISI in the Midwest raised the princely sum of $6,000 for its activities. As Chodorov later told the story:

> That made me rich. So, I hired Vic Milione to run the outfit and to visit schools in the East. . . . I told him, "Vic, I have this money and as long as it lasts, you will get $75 a week and expense money. You'll have to take your chances on the future."

Milione, then about thirty years old, had been working for an organization called Americans for the Competitive Enterprise System. It tells us much about him that he decided to take the chance.

So in 1953 Milione entered the service of ISI. His roles were many: part fundraiser, part office manager, part traveling salesman for a cause. He was a bit like a trade union organizer, except that the "union locals" he organized consisted of college students, entirely self-selected and governed by the ethos of voluntarism.

It was well for ISI that Milione joined its management. Chodorov, the president and visionary individualist, had some quirky business habits. When checks arrived in the mail he would deposit them, but he did not keep copies of his letters acknowledging the gifts. As ISI's current president Kenneth Cribb, will tell you, that was no way to build a donor base.

This, then, was Vic Milione's first notable contribution to ISI: he brought order into its struggling operations. For a time, after the $6,000 bonanza ran out, he even worked without salary and expense money until he could secure additional funds. If ISI was Chodorov's baby, it was Milione, as much as anyone, who raised the child to maturity.

But Milione was more than simply ISI's chief operating officer. Eventually he became its president himself, with a vision and missionary impulse of his own. Here we come to the second crucial contribution that he made to ISI. Frank Chodorov was not a conventionally religious man. For many years, he was a vehement atheist. Toward the end of his life, as he sought a firm metaphysical foundation for his philosophy of individual rights, he reluctantly accepted what he called the "God-idea." But at most, his was a vaguely deistic religion without a deity.

Milione, on the other hand, was a Roman Catholic, convinced (as he once put it) that the "basic premises of conservatism" include the conviction that "this is a God-centered universe" and that "man is a part of that creation." To Milione the fundamental purpose of ISI was to preserve Western civilization, a civilization that was religious at its core.

Over the years Milione broadened ISI's mission to encompass more than a Chodorovian crusade against collectivism. Without Milione at its helm, ISI might easily have evolved in an exclusively libertarian direction. Instead, he made it a home for the traditionalist wing of conservatism as well. In so doing, he averted the seductive shoals of sectarianism and helped to enlarge the conservative mainstream.

In the process, he exerted an influence far beyond the campuses where ISI pursued its mission. The ecumenical Philadelphia Society, for example, was at its inception something of an ISI alumni society. Fittingly, Milione belonged to the society for nearby forty years and was elected to the well-deserved rank of distinguished member.

As we sum up and honor his accomplishments, two final comments come to mind. First, I am struck anew by how humble ISI's origins were in the 1950s and by how resolutely Milione persevered in those formative years, when funding was scarce and worldly wisdom might easily have prompted him to move elsewhere.

But "perseverance" does not quite say it all. Few people, I think, will persevere for long in adversity unless some transcendent purpose impels them. So it was with Milione's mentor Frank Chodorov. At the end of his seminal proposal for a "fifty-year project" to reclaim the American mind, Chodorov asked: "Is the effort worth while? To which one offers as answer another question: What in life is more worth while than the pursuit of an ideal?"

Well, we know how Vic Milione answered that question. For his idealism, his fortitude, and his priceless institutional legacy, we salute him.

12

Ernest van den Haag
(1914–2002)

This tribute appeared in the Spring 2003 issue of the University Bookman.

With the death of Ernest van den Haag on March 21, 2002, the conservative movement lost one of its most redoubtable intellectual warriors in the decades after World War II. And the *University Bookman* lost one of its longtime friends and supporters.

Like so many of conservatism's postwar "founding fathers," van den Haag was a former radical and refugee from totalitarian Europe. Born in Holland and raised in Italy, he was a twenty-three-year-old Communist and law student at the University of Florence when Mussolini's Fascist government imprisoned him in 1937. He spent most of the next two years in solitary confinement. Upon his release, he made his way to France, where he briefly studied psychiatry at the Sorbonne, only to be arrested by the French as an "enemy alien" in the early months of World War II. In 1940, as the French regime collapsed before the Nazi onslaught, van den Haag escaped from his French concentration camp and crossed into Spain—literally dodging bullets along the way. From there he traveled to Portugal and thence, by ship, to the United States. It was an adventure reminiscent of the movie *Casablanca.*

When van den Haag reached America, his speaking knowledge of English was nonexistent. His first jobs were as a busboy and vegetable seller in New York City. Somehow he gained admission to the graduate school of the University of Iowa, from which he earned a master's degree in economics in

1942. Returning to New York, he met Sidney Hook, whom he credited with converting him from communism. "I was a youthful fool," van den Haag remarked years later about his student days in Europe. After encountering Hook (who seems to have become something of a mentor), the immigrant from Italy abandoned Marxist radicalism forever.

After serving in the U.S. Office of War Information during World War II, van den Haag settled down to an academic career in New York City, including teaching positions at New York University, the New School for Social Research, and Fordham University. Although he earned his doctorate in economics at NYU, the fields of sociology, psychology, and social philosophy interested him more. During the 1950s and 1960s he was a rara avis in academia: a credentialed social scientist and unabashed conservative. Even more improbably, after being psychoanalyzed he became a psychoanalyst himself—a profession that he practiced on the side for nearly three decades.

In 1957, while having lunch with Sidney Hook, van den Haag chanced to meet William F. Buckley Jr., who sent him a copy of *National Review*. Before long, the learned professor was contributing articles to Buckley's magazine, an association that endured for the next forty-five years. As his reputation grew among conservatives, so did his ties to the conservative insurgency. In 1960, he contributed to the inaugural issue of the *University Bookman* and remained associated with its work for many years. He was also an active trustee of the *University Bookman*'s sponsor, the *Educational Reviewer*. He belonged to the Philadelphia Society and served as its president in 1978–79. In the 1980s, he was affiliated with the Heritage Foundation. At Fordham University, he was the John M. Olin Professor of Jurisprudence and Public Policy for six years.

As a disciplined academic, van den Haag authored several provocative books, including such gems as *The Jewish Mystique* (1969), *Political Violence and Civil Disobedience* (1972), and *Punishing Criminals: Concerning a Very Old and Painful Question* (1975).

The latter volume established him instantly as a leading authority on American criminology. In the next two decades, he acquired a reputation as one of the most formidable scholarly advocates of the death penalty for the crime of murder.

The émigré social scientist also published more than two hundred articles. The short essay, in fact, was the perfect vehicle for his potent mix of fearless iconoclasm, relentless logic, and erudition. And fearless he was, challenging liberal and leftist sacred cows down the line: from the United Nations to the minimum wage, from sex education to pornography, from feminism to foreign policy, from *Brown v. Board of Education* to the handling of urban riots. At times, his defiance of conventional thinking bordered on the outrageous, at least to liberal sensibilities. Asked, in 1972, why he preferred Richard Nixon to George McGovern for the presidency, he replied briskly, "I would rather be governed by a knave than by a fool."

As on the printed page, so on the public platform, van den Haag combined analytic trenchancy with a seemingly inexhaustible reservoir of pertinent expertise. The one-time law student loved disputation. He was willing, he said, to debate anybody about anything. In the 1980s he often did so under the auspices of the Heritage Foundation. Time and again, his opponents were both appalled and confounded by what one of them called his "irreverent unorthodoxy." Like the roadrunner in the cartoon, he always seemed to be a step ahead of his adversaries. By the time they had grasped the subtleties of his argument, he had sped on to another point.

William F. Buckley Jr. once described van den Haag as a "tuning fork of reason in the cacophonous world of social science." But not everyone on the Right liked the sound that his "tuning fork" made. In 1960 he startled readers of *National Review* with a defense of Keynesian economics. In 1979, again in *National Review*, he published a scathing critique of libertarianism. Idiosyncratic on the issue of abortion, he asserted that a human embryo was only potentially human during its first three months of existence. Hence he would allow abortions until a recognizably human fetus was formed. On these and other issues he was unafraid to be a deviationist.

Most troublingly for many conservatives, van den Haag throughout his career seemed impervious to the truth claims of religion. In 1950, he asserted publicly that religion could not be "logically justified," although he granted that religion was a "useful" and "necessary" "opiate," essential for the stability of a free society. This was a strictly pragmatic argument that he apparently never disavowed. He also strenuously rejected the idea of natural law. Nature does not tell us how to live, he countered; it merely gives us choices. "I do not know where nature got the authority to tell me what to do," he declared. Asked a few years ago why he felt that murder was bad, he replied simply, "I feel it." His intuition told him so. He added that he had not found a better answer.

Not surprisingly, in his later years, van den Haag—ever the contrarian—asserted (contra Christianity) that people own their lives and are therefore free to end their lives if they so choose. Although by no means a libertarian, he nevertheless contended in the late 1990s that people should have the "right to die" without governmental interference.

In essence, van den Haag's was a deeply skeptical and secular brand of conservatism, grounded not in religious faith but upon a recognition of the limits of reason in the pursuit of social betterment. Perhaps, having nearly lost his life as a young man in thrall to an orthodoxy, he could never again commit himself to another one.

Or did he? Toward the end, his intimate friend William F. Buckley Jr. discerned signs that the irreverently unorthodox émigré was mellowing on the subject of religion. In a letter to Buckley in the mid-1990s, van den Haag announced that he was a "convert" to Roman Catholicism "in substance but not in form." "I stayed away for a long time from the Church," he added, "except in the most formal sense and I am only now making my way back." How he reconciled this turn with his public positions on natural law and suicide, he evidently did not say. But in 2002, just a few weeks before his death, he requested a Catholic funeral, which in due course he received. In the end, this urbane and worldly scholar apparently saw—and at last transcended—the limits of his own agnosticism.

With his heavy European accent, trademark cigars, and aura of the bon vivant, van den Haag was an unforgettable figure on the conservative scene. But those who knew his writings will remember him most for his withering dissection of the pretentious political orthodoxies of our age. At a time when conservatism was out of fashion among the intelligentsia, he gave conservatives a bracing example of mental rigor, forensic tenacity, and the courage of unconventional conviction.

13

The Influence of Richard Weaver's
Ideas Have Consequences on American Conservatism

This essay was first presented as a conference paper at a symposium on Richard Weaver held at Belmont Abbey College. It was then published in Ted J. Smith III, ed., Steps Toward Restoration: The Consequences of Richard Weaver's Ideas *(ISI Books, 1998).*

On April 3, 1963, Richard M. Weaver was found dead in his small apartment in Chicago, precisely one month after his fifty-third birthday. The conservative intellectual community in America was stunned. Already an esteemed member of this community, Professor Weaver was immediately eulogized as a scholar and moralist of unusual power—indeed, as "one of the ablest cultural critics of our times."[1]

In the three-and-one-half decades since Weaver's death, his reputation among conservatives has remained high. In 1984, when his first published book—*Ideas Have Consequences*—appeared in a new paperback edition, the distinguished sociologist Robert Nisbet pronounced it "one of the few authentic classics in the American political tradition."[2] Four years later, the preeminent conservative publisher Henry Regnery cited *Ideas Have Consequences* as one of just three books "which provided the intellectual basis for the modern conservative movement."[3] (The other two were Friedrich Hayek's *Road to Serfdom* and Russell Kirk's *The Conservative Mind*.) In 1996, when the first biography of Weaver was published, the one-time Marxist historian Eugene Genovese asserted in the *New Republic* (no less) that Weaver "deserves to rank among the most significant intellectuals of America in this century."[4]

The continuing acclaim for Weaver on the American Right has been matched by devoted efforts to honor his memory. In 1964 the Intercollegiate Society of Individualists (now known as the Intercollegiate Studies Institute) established a Richard M. Weaver Fellowship program for graduate students.[5] Thirty-five years later its beneficiaries include many of the best conservative scholars in American academia. In 1983 the Rockford Institute in Illinois created an annual Richard M. Weaver Award for Scholarly Letters; since then, some of the finest historians and social critics in the United States have received it.[6]

Meanwhile Weaver's writings—the basis for his reputation—have continued to be disseminated. During his lifetime Weaver published only three books, but between 1964 and 1970 four more came out posthumously, in part because of the exertion of his intellectual heirs.[7] Nor has interest in his work waned over the years. In 1987 the Liberty Press brought out a collection of Weaver's essays on Southern history and literature.[8] That same year President Edwin J. Feulner Jr. of the Heritage Foundation—himself a former Weaver Fellow—selected Weaver's brilliant essay "Up From Liberalism" for national distribution.[9] In 1995 the Intercollegiate Studies Institute produced a paperback edition of his *Visions of Order*.[10] Thus it has come about that more of Weaver's oeuvre has appeared in book form after his death than before it. And all this time, *Ideas Have Consequences* has remained almost continuously in print: a remarkable datum in itself. How many other books published in 1948, one wonders, managed to stay in print a mere five years, let alone fifty?

As conservative testimonials to Weaver's importance have multiplied, academia has begun to take notice. Since the late 1980s, Weaver has been the subject of no fewer than three doctoral dissertations, five master's theses, two biographies (with a third on the way), one monograph, an anthology of appreciative essays, and a steadily increasing number of scholarly articles.[11] In fact, there now exists more serious scholarship about Richard Weaver than about any other founding father of modern American conservatism, except for Eric Voegelin and Leo Strauss. To put it another way: in the past decade a Weaver "industry" has sprung up—not, to be sure, as large as the Strauss and Voegelin "industries," but one whose potential for growth seems assured.

At first glance the burgeoning interest in Weaver may seem puzzling. A reserved and unassuming bachelor, he was neither a campus celebrity nor a charismatic public speaker. A professor in the undergraduate college of the

University of Chicago, he left behind no corps of talented graduate students to build on his intellectual edifice. In the variegated world of the intellectual Right, one frequntly hears of Straussians and Voegelinians, Austrian School economists and Chicago School economists, Burkeans and even Objectivists, but no Weaverites. Indeed, shortly after Weaver died, a friend remarked that "he was much admired, but seldom imitated."[12] Yet for all these apparent limitations, this "shy little bulldog of a man"[13] soon attained nearly iconic status in the pantheon of American conservatism.

Three factors help us to understand why. First, in the estimation of those who came to know him, Richard Weaver was a "remarkable" man.[14] "Still water runs deep," says the proverb, and many who befriended him sensed that here was no ordinary college professor but a figure of truly "great depths."[15] Time and again, in the appraisals of Weaver that his friends and colleagues composed over the years, one finds moving references not just to his mind but to his character: to his "dogged integrity," "rugged honesty," courage, "quiet heroism," and modesty.[16] For those who knew him personally, Weaver was a figure of genuinely moral stature.[17]

It was not just that he was an exceptionally disciplined scholar who worked literally seven days a week, or that his lifestyle seemed so austere and monastic that a friend compared him to a "little gnome."[18] No, there was something else that his friends discerned in him and found deeply affecting: a sense of vocation to which, with "almost consuming passion," he devoted himself.[19] Weaver's life was "a crusade to reestablish belief in the reality of transcendentals," a friend wrote in 1970.[20] Another friend said that Weaver kept his mind "fixed on the far goal of a grand reordering of a splintered society."[21] Weaver himself once remarked that he had been powerfully influenced by his mentor John Crowe Ransom's concept of the "unorthodox defense of orthodoxy."[22] But however one defines his calling, there is little doubt that, to a degree unusual among academics of his time, Weaver saw himself not just as a seeker of knowledge but as a soldier in a great spiritual and intellectual battle.[23] No wonder his fellow conservatives admired him. He "never gave an inch on the fundamentals,"[24] one of them asserted. This, too, was part of the reason he fascinated—and continues to fascinate—the Right.

Weaver's mode of living seemed to enhance his quiet mystique. Living alone in a rented hotel room during most of his years in Chicago, he appeared to make few concessions to the modern world. Although he owned an automobile for most of his adult life, he found driving in Chicago to be nerve-wracking and soon gave up the effort. Nearly every summer, in fact, during his University of Chicago years, he escaped the uncongenial Windy City for his beloved ancestral home town of Weaverville, North Carolina, where (it is said) he cultivated a little plot of land with a horse-drawn plow, never a tractor. He insisted on traveling from Chicago to Weaverville by train. Only rarely in his life did he consent to fly a plane. "You have to draw the line somewhere," he said.[25]

Secondly, since 1963, this native Tarheel has increasingly been recognized as belonging to a vibrant, twentieth-century tradition of Southern conservatism, extending from the authors of *I'll Take My Stand* in 1930 to M. E. Bradford and Marion Montgomery in the 1990s. One scholar has concluded that Weaver was "the most influential southern conservative since the Agrarians."[26] Another has labeled him "the Saint Paul of the Vanderbilt Agrarians. He was born too late to be one of the twelve, but with the possible exception of Donald Davidson, he became the movement's most vigorous and eloquent defender."[27] No longer perceived (as he sometimes was in his lifetime) as a kind of solitary genius, Weaver can now be seen in context. In the community of scholarship there is now a thriving Southern Agrarian "industry" (if that is not an oxymoron), and Richard Weaver has become part of it. It is the second reason he has not been forgotten.

But neither Weaver's personal qualities nor his prominence in the great Southern Agrarian chain of being, would alone sustain his reputation among American conservatives were it not for a third fact—his books—and for one book above all. In a separate article, Ted J. Smith III has explained how *Ideas Have Consequences* came to be written. In this essay we shall examine how *Ideas Have Consequences* came to be read—read and assimilated—by the conservative intellectual movement since World War II. There is universal agreement among conservatives that this slender volume had "profound" and "seminal" importance.[28] According to Robert Nisbet, it "launched the renascence of philosophical conservatism in this country."[29] How, then, did its influence manifest itself? In what ways did this book change minds?

When *Ideas Have Consequences* appeared in 1948, its publisher (the University of Chicago Press) anticipated that the book would cause a sensation. Investing heavily in advertising, the press ordered an initial printing of 7,500 copies.[30] The publisher's judgment was quickly vindicated: Within two years *Ideas Have Consequences* received more than one hundred reviews, to the amazement of its author.[31] Weaver had been warned that his opus would provoke wrathful rejoinders, and so, in some quarters, it did.[32] Readers—

both pro and con—seemed to respond to it vehemently, he told his ideological soulmate Donald Davidson.[33]

But if the author of *Ideas Have Consequences* soon found himself under furious assault from the Left, he must have been heartened by the plaudits he received from a number of scholars who were to become luminaries of the postwar intellectual Right. In the *Kenyon Review*, Eliseo Vivas—later to be a friend of Weaver—acclaimed him as "an inspired moralist."[34] In the *Journal of Politics*, Willmoore Kendall, a conservative political scientist and teacher of William F. Buckley Jr., unabashedly nominated Weaver for "the captaincy of the anti-Liberal team."[35] Still another conservative who discovered *Ideas Have Consequences* in its first month of existence was a young historian and bookstore proprietor in East Lansing, Michigan, named Russell Kirk. Quickly recognizing the importance of Weaver's volume, Kirk displayed it prominently in his bookshop and invited its author to address a literary society in East Lansing. Thus began a close and lifelong friendship.[36] Kirk was impressed by the "uncompromising intrepidity" of *Ideas Have Consequences* and publicly saluted its author as "one of the most courageous men in America."[37] He also extolled Weaver's "iron logicality," and bestowed upon him the epithet "the Calvin of criticism."[38] For Kirk and Kendall—and no doubt for others on the Right—one source of the book's appeal was its outspoken repudiation of what Kirk called "ritualistic liberalism."[39] As Kendall put it in his review, Weaver's "real enemy" was "the more or less typical American liberal."[40]

In the cases of Kirk, Vivas, and Kendall, it is safe to say that Weaver to them was a kindred spirit rather than a mentor. But in at least one crucial instance, the influence of *Ideas Have Consequences* went much deeper. Among its early readers was a former Communist Party functionary named Frank S. Meyer. Already disillusioned with communism, Meyer in 1948 was not yet a man of the Right. By his own account, *Ideas Have Consequences* exerted a huge influence on his "personal development towards conservatism." Even more importantly, Weaver's book, in Meyer's words, "adumbrated . . . the informing principle" of postwar American conservatism: "the unity of tradition and liberty." It was *Ideas Have Consequences*, Meyer later declared, which provided "much of the inspiration" for his own salient contribution to conservative thought: the position known as "fusionism." In 1970 a grateful Meyer called the publication of *Ideas Have Consequences* "the *fons et origo* of the contemporary American conservative movement."[41]

If *Ideas Have Consequences* had decisively affected the life of only one man, Frank S. Meyer—the key conservative theorist of the early 1960s—it would have to be accorded a significant footnote in our intellectual history. But of course the impact of Weaver's first published book was more far-reaching than that. "It will shock," Paul Tillich predicted, and shock it did.[42]

For Weaver's book was nothing less than a sustained philippic against the smugness and shibboleths of the twentieth century. "This is another book about the dissolution of the West," he announced in his very first sentence.[43] By the end of the first page he had labeled modern man a "moral idiot," seemingly incapable of distinguishing "between better and worse."[44] By page three he had propounded a sweeping thesis: that the disintegration of Western civilization was directly traceable to an "evil decision" six hundred years earlier. Enticed by the "fateful doctrine of nominalism" espoused by William of Occam, Western civilization had abandoned its belief in transcendental values or "universals" and thus the position that "there is a source of truth higher than, and independent of, man." "The defeat of logical realism by nominalism in the great medieval debate," Weaver asserted, was "the crucial event in the history of Western culture."[45]

For the next 184 pages Weaver unsparingly delineated what he held to be the "consequences" of this intellectual revolution. With ruthless candor he flayed the idols of the age: the Whig theory of history; the doctrine of progress; "the fallacy of scientism"; the hubris of technology; "the fetish of material prosperity"; "the worship of comfort"; industrialism; materialism; pragmatism; empiricism; liberalism; democracy; relativism; "the insolence of material success"; the "disorganizing heresy" of equality; "the foolish and destructive notion of the 'equality' of the sexes"; and more. At times his audacity was breathtaking. "Has the art of writing proved an unmixed blessing?" he asked.[46] After a coruscating indictment of the modern mass media (the "Great Stereopticon"), he asserted: "How . . . can one hesitate to conclude that we would live in greater peace and enjoy sounder moral health if the institution of the newspaper were abolished entirely?"[47] In other startling passages he condemned jazz music ("the clearest of all signs of our age's deep-seated predilection for barbarism") and dismissed impressionist art as an expression of nominalism and "egotism" in painting.[48] But Weaver was not engaged in cheap, attention-seeking pyrotechnics. The decadence, moral chaos, and rampant immersion in sensation that had engulfed the West were not happenstance, he insisted. They were products of a centuries-long intellectual retreat from first principles, from true knowledge (the knowledge of universals), and from the integrative "metaphysical dream" of the Middle Ages.

It is sometimes assumed that *Ideas Have Consequences* appeared in 1948 like a bolt from the blue, disturbing the complacency of mid–twentieth-century America. This was not really true. In the aftermath of World War II, the market for Weaver's cultural critique was in fact considerable. Just the year before, Arnold Toynbee had published a one-volume condensation of his six-volume *A Study of History*, a monumental inquiry into the rise and fall of civilizations. Toynbee's book was one of the spectacular publishing events of 1947. It even received a *Time* magazine cover story written by Whittaker Chambers, soon to be another of postwar conservatism's founding fathers.[49] In 1948, Professor Toynbee followed up with a book entitled *Civilization on Trial*; it, too, was heavily reviewed.[50] Few conservatives became as despairing as Chambers, who told William E Buckley Jr. in 1954 that it was "idle to talk about preventing the wreck of Western civilization. It is already a wreck from within."[51] But the fear that the West *might* be dying was widespread. As the threat of another world war invaded public consciousness, the question "Whither Western civilization?" was very much in the air. *Ideas Have Consequences* both benefited from and gave voice to this mood of cultural angst.

Nor is it correct to say that *Ideas Have Consequences* was an exceptionally original book, although its thesis—that Western civilization's troubles began with the nominalist controversy of the fourteenth century—appears to have been uniquely Weaver's. To the contrary: *Ideas Have Consequences* was in many ways a derivative book, and in identifying what it derived from, one can begin to understand its appeal to American conservatives.

Where, in 1948, was Richard Weaver "coming from"? Some hostile readers of *Ideas Have Consequences* quickly associated him with a "chain of reaction" allegedly headquartered at the University of Chicago, where Robert Hutchins and the philosopher Mortimer J. Adler—"the Divine Doctors of the Great Books Movement"—had been propagating a neomedievalist gospel for years.[52] The semanticist S. I. Hayakawa labeled this movement "Neo-Scholasticism." Hutchins and Adler, he said, were its "neon lights"; Richard Weaver, Russell Kirk, and Eric Voegelin were among its "dim bulbs."[53] While Weaver, an ardent Platonist, shared much of the pedagogical and metaphysical worldview promulgated by Hutchins and his allies, the young English professor drew most of his inspiration from other sources. His references in his book to "sentimental humanitarianism" reflected his exposure to Irving Babbitt and the New Humanists, about whom Weaver had written his master's thesis in 1934.[54] His concept of "the spoiled-child psychology" (the subject of his fourth chapter) he took from the Spanish philosopher José Ortega y Gasset, whom he quoted twice in his book.[55] Indeed, *Ideas Have Consequences* forcefully reminded more than one reader of Ortega's 1930 classic, *The Revolt of the Masses*.[56] Above all, Weaver's worldview in 1948 derived, as we now know, from the Southern Agrarians, whose earnest disciple, by the mid-1940s, he had become.[57] In his mordant criticisms of industrialism and technology, in his negative appraisal of urban man and urban living, and in his plea for a society based on "distinction and hierarchy," he resembled no one so much as the authors of the Agrarian manifesto, *I'll Take My Stand*.[58] It was no coincidence. Not surprisingly, some of these very Agrarians had been his teachers in graduate school.[59]

Far, then, from being sui generis, *Ideas Have Consequences* was a luminous example of a diverse and well-established literary tradition of "cultural pessimism," whose past exponents had included Oswald Spengler. As usual, Weaver himself minced no words about it. "Cultural decline is a historical fact," he declared emphatically in his book; " . . . to establish the fact of decadence is the most pressing duty of our time. . . ."[60] In deliberately hard-hitting and unequivocal prose,[61] he uttered concerns that "cultural pessimists" and "declinists" had been expressing for years. In Weaver, the ideology of cultural pessimism gained an eager recruit, at a time when the ideology of progressivism was tottering.[62]

This leads us to the first great contribution that *Ideas Have Consequences* made to the conservative cause after 1945. By linking the rise of modernity to cultural disintegration, it put modernity itself on trial. By standing outside modernity and depicting it as a problem, Weaver dramatically extended the mental horizon of the postwar Right. The crisis of the West, as he diagnosed it, was not simply one of foreign policy (the battle against communism) or economics (the fight against the New Deal). No, said Weaver, Western man faced a *civilizational* catastrophe, born of "unintelligent choice" and philosophic error deep in our past.[63] It was to be a central tenet of "traditionalist" conservatism for years to come.

This idea of Weaver's soon had consequences of its own. Among those whom *Ideas Have Consequences* persuaded that the West's crisis was "total" was a young conservative activist named E. Victor Milione. In 1953 Milione became associated with the Intercollegiate Society of Individualists; eventually, he became ISI's president, serving in that capacity for more than twenty years. Armed with Weaver's insight, Milione contended that ISI must not focus narrowly on politics or economics. It must instead address "the 'total crisis,' the crisis of culture." Reflecting in part Milione's Weaverian vision, ISI initiated—and sustains to this day—a broadly interdisciplinary approach to its mission.[64] In a conservative intellectual community often preoccupied by short-term contests over public policy, ISI maintains the long view—thanks in considerable measure to Richard M. Weaver.

Coupled with Weaver's critique of modernity in *Ideas Have Consequences* was a second theme that wielded enormous influence over the postwar conservative mind: his unalloyed moral and metaphysical absolutism. Not surprisingly, relativistic liberals castigated him for it, finding in his "metaphysical certitudes" the intellectual scaffolding for authoritarianism.[65] But Weaver was not to be deflected. Truth, universals, and transcendentals were real, he insisted. Forty years before the vogue of nihilistic postmodernism, he discerned and indicted the growing "inroads" of relativism, "with its disbelief in truth."[66] With remarkable prescience he warned:

> The denial of universals carries with it the denial of everything transcending experience. The denial of everything transcending experience means inevitably . . . the denial of truth. With the denial of objective truth there is no escape from the relativism of "man the measure of all things."[67]

By insisting upon the existence and knowability of objective truth, and by looking (as he put it) "toward an ontological realm which is timeless,"[68] Weaver exerted an upward pull on American conservatives. Not for him (or them) a form of conservatism mired in expediency and mindless pragmatism. Following Weaver (and a little later, Russell Kirk), conservatives asserted instead their fealty to an "objective moral order" and the "permanent things." Thus in 1960, when the Young Americans for Freedom was born, its founding manifesto affirmed belief in "certain eternal truths" and "transcendent values."[69] The unapologetic philosophical absolutism of the crusading conservatives of the early 1960s owed much to the worldview and rhetorical tone of *Ideas Have Consequences*.

A third way in which *Ideas Have Consequences* made its imprint on conservatives was its encouragement of what might be called a Roman Catholic interpretation of modern history. At a time when most Americans probably interpreted the story of Western civilization as an ascent from the benighted Middle Ages, Weaver turned the entire chronicle upside down. It was the Middle Ages, he argued, which had evinced "a comparatively clear perception of reality"—in fact, "a greater awareness of realities than our leaders exhibit today."[70] It was "the unfixing of relationships in the fourteenth century," he said, which had set the West on its course of "social disintegration."[71] Although *Ideas Have Consequences* deliberately avoided religious exhortation, its biases were noticeable. "The metaphysical right of religion went out at the time of the Reformation," he asserted.[72] "For four centuries every man has been not only his own priest but his own professor of ethics, and the consequence is an anarchy which threatens even that minimum consensus of value necessary to the political state."[73]

So palpable was Weaver's yearning for the lost metaphysical unity of the Middle Ages that one Protestant reviewer of *Ideas Have Consequences* denounced its author as "a propagandist for a return to the medieval papacy."[74] To another reviewer (a Roman Catholic), Weaver appeared to be advocating "the catholicity of Catholicism," only to stop "just short of saying it"—"dead in his tracks"—"as if he had suddenly seen something."[75] Other reviewers noted with amusement that Weaver's "pure Platonism" put him to the right of Thomas Aquinas.[76]

Weaver, of course, was not a Roman Catholic but an inactive Protestant, who in later years occasionally attended Episcopal church services in Chicago.[77] While his worldview was basically Christian,[78] he was not a man to verbalize his religious faith, and its precise doctrinal content remains uncertain.[79] (One point that does seem clear is that he felt little affinity for the fundamentalist Protestantism of the Bible Belt.)[80] But whatever Weaver's innermost religious convictions, the implicitly Catholic neomedievalism of *Ideas Have Consequences* made its mark on American conservative intellectuals, not a few of whom eventually converted to the Roman Catholic faith.[81] Like John Hallowell's *Main Currents in Modern Political Thought* (1950) and Eric Voegelin's *The New Science of Politics* (1952), *Ideas Have Consequences* popularized a historical paradigm for conservatives in which the founding events of modernity—including the Reformation—came to be seen as critical episodes in the decline of the West. Thus did Richard Weaver, a Protestant from North Carolina, contribute to the noticeably Roman Catholic and Anglo-Catholic coloration of traditionalist American conservatism in the first two decades after World War II.

A fourth influence of Weaver's book on the postwar Right was subtler, but equally profound. It lay in his firm conviction that ideas—above all, "our most basic ideas of human destiny"—were the decisive determinants of the course of civilizations.[82] Weaver was not the only conservative theorist to assert this after 1945, but he was one of the first and most compelling. In the wake of *Ideas Have Consequences*, a new genre of conservative criticism proliferated: distinctively intellectual histories and genealogies of declension, all seeking to answer the question: "When did Western civilization take its wrong turning?" Although their answers differed in details, one theme was invariant. Not machines, not the "class struggle," not impersonal social "forces," but ideas: these were the engines of history.[83]

In a way this was, for conservatives, a source of hope. For if (as Weaver argued) a "falsified picture of the world"[84] had produced pernicious consequences for Western civilization, then perhaps a correct picture of the world would yield better consequences. If the world today is as it is because of the sheer, unfathomable weight of impersonal forces, then resistance to its pressures may well be futile. But if our world is the product of ideas in our heads, maybe we can reform our world by changing our ideas.

Such was the hopeful prospect which Weaver held out in *Ideas Have Consequences*. The intellectual history he taught, and which countless conservatives absorbed, was antimaterialist, antideterminist, antifatalist.[85] In a remarkable sentence that he wrote elsewhere shortly before he began *Ideas Have Consequences*, he asserted: "We can will our world."[86] For conservatives seeking the origin of present travails in intellectual error, it was a bracing message. *We can will our world.* Error can be refuted. Ideas have consequences.

But if this is so, it follows that the creators and purveyors of ideas—notably teachers, writers, rhetoricians, and college professors—have a supreme role to play in the redemption of our culture. It was a lesson Weaver explicitly taught in the penultimate chapter of his book, wherein he recommended the study of poetry, rhetoric, dialectic, and foreign languages as ways of restoring "the metaphysical community of language" and even "our lost unity of mind."[87]

And that leads to the fifth way in which *Ideas Have Consequences* molded postwar conservatism in its early years: It encouraged cultural traditionalists to think of themselves as a civilized aristocracy in revolt against the masses and their idols. It should not escape notice that *Ideas Have Consequences* was written by an English professor at a time when more than a few custodians of the humanities in America were appalled by the growing evisceration of the traditional liberal-arts curriculum. For conservatives and other votaries of humane learning, Weaver's outspoken attacks in his book on the cult of "progress," on the "fallacies" of scientism and technology, and on the "specialist" as "a man possessed of an evil spirit,"[88] had strong appeal. Here was a man unafraid to rebuke the ignoramuses (both lettered and unlettered) who were systematically subverting the life of the mind in America. When Weaver contrasted Europe in the Middle Ages (where "the possessor of highest learning was the philosophic doctor")[89] with the contemporary United States (where scientists, technicians, and specialists "at the borderline of psychosis"[90] held sway), the "philosophic doctors" of 1948 approved. His fighting words helped to instill in them a renewed sense of the worth of their cause.

In one area, though, Weaver's assault on the enemies of civilization did not appear to resonate, at least not at first: his scathing denunciations of the bourgeoisie and its value system. *Ideas Have Consequences* contained more than a dozen references to the bourgeoisie or middle class; not a single one of these allusions was favorable. The middle class, he asserted, was "besotted."

> Loving comfort, risking little, terrified by the thought of change, its aim is to establish a materialistic civilization which will banish threats to its complacency. It has conventions, not ideals; it is washed rather than clean. The plight of Europe today is the direct result of the bourgeois ascendancy and its corrupted worldview.[91]

To Weaver the "bourgeois mentality" was "psychopathic in its alienation from reality."[92] The world that "the bourgeoisie finds congenial" was "inane." He accused the middle class of spreading the "infection" of "egotism" and self-seeking, leading to "a fragmentation of society which cannot stop short of complete chaos."[93] He asserted that the bourgeoisie "first betrayed society through capitalism and finance."[94] He scorned as "Philistine" the notion that happiness in life consisted of "a job, domesticity, interest in some harmless diversion such as baseball and fishing, and a strong antipathy toward abstract ideas."[95] He attacked "the worship of comfort" as a "form of debauchery" and contrasted it with his own philosophy that "life means discipline and sacrifice."[96]

Such vehemence invites the suspicion that some bitter personal experience may have underlain Weaver's aspersions on the bourgeoisie, and that, indeed, appears to have been the case.[97] But whatever the origin of Weaver's fiercely anti–middle class sentiments, they did not catch on with most of his confreres on the Right. Nor did his similar strictures on "finance capitalism," industrialism, and commercialism. There were fundamentally two reasons for this. First, the developing conservative movement after World War II had a second component very different from the religious/literary traditionalism exemplified by Weaver. This was the classical liberal or libertarian wing of the Right, and for it individual freedom—including economic freedom—was the summum bonum. As these two disparate streams of resistance to modern liberalism came together in the 1950s, this very fact limited the audience on the Right for all-out critiques of middle America and the economics of private enterprise.

Secondly, in *Ideas Have Consequences* and elsewhere, Weaver himself muted the antibourgeois thrust of his analysis, notably by his eloquent defense of individual, small-scale property ownership as "the last metaphysical right." To be sure, Weaver made it plain that he was defending property ownership for metaphysical reasons, not materialistic ones, and that his advocacy of "the distributive ownership of small properties" had nothing whatsoever to do with the "abstract" property arrangements wrought by "finance capitalism." "Big business and the rationalization of industry," he asserted, "abet the evils we seek to overcome."[98] Yet what was his scheme of independently owned homes, farms, and local businesses if not a version of a middle-class ideal? Although he did not label it as such, Weaver had endorsed the via media of Southern Agrarianism. If no partisan of what he called "monopoly capitalism," neither did he welcome what he disapprovingly labeled "pagan statism."[99] He wanted private property to be a "sanctuary" against the omnipotent State.[100] This fact probably helped to assuage the discomfort some of his conservative readers might otherwise have felt.

As it happened, Weaver's apologia for individually owned private property as "the last metaphysical right" turned out to be one of the most influential legacies of *Ideas Have Consequences.* Not only did it open a bridge to the free-market conservatives; more importantly, it enabled conservatives to vindicate private property rights in language that did not look like a rationalization of materialistic acquisitiveness. Unintentionally or not, Weaver helped to elevate the conservative "case" on this issue to a higher plane. It was an important service.

As for Weaver's castigation of the bourgeoisie, his intention in *Ideas Have Consequences* may not have been as anticapitalist as it might have appeared. When he had used the word "bourgeois" (he explained as the book started to circulate), he had been thinking of the kind of Americans whose highest aspiration was ownership of a Buick. Philistines, in short—people with shriveled souls.[101] These were the kind of bourgeois he had evidently met during his unhappy years of teaching at Texas A & M University, just prior to his conversion to Southern Agrarianism: the sort of people Sinclair

Lewis had satirized in *Babbitt*, and whom H. L. Mencken had derided as the "booboisie." In part, then, the publication of *Ideas Have Consequences* was another skirmish in a long-running culture war between "alienated" literary intellectuals and a middle America they perceived as crass and materialistic. Weaver's passionately antibourgeois rhetoric was probably perceived by his fellow conservatives through that lens, and they would have been right. In 1948 Weaver was closer to Mencken than to Marx.

There is another sense in which it could be said that *Ideas Have Consequences* influenced American conservatism after 1945. If Weaver created the book, the book created him as a conspicuous public intellectual of the Right. In the late 1940s and 1950s Weaver became a friend of many leading figures in the conservative renascence. One of these, Henry Regnery, published Professor Weaver's second book, *The Ethics of Rhetoric*, in 1953.[102] In 1955 Weaver became a contributor to *National Review* at its founding and remained so listed on its masthead until his death.[103] Eleven years earlier, in a letter to Cleanth Brooks, Weaver had declared modern liberalism to be exhausted and had yearned for a journalistic alternative to the cheap and dishonest liberalism being expounded (he said) in leading periodicals.[104] In William F. Buckley Jr.'s *National Review* he got his wish. During the next eight years he contributed thirty-six articles and reviews to its pages.[105] *National Review*, he told Buckley, was indispensable.[106]

Another conservative quarterly publication with which Weaver became affiliated was the academic quarterly *Modern Age*, launched by Russell Kirk in 1957. Weaver contributed the lead article to the inaugural issue, and several additional pieces in the next few years.[107] As an associate editor of *Modern Age* from late 1959 to 1963, he worked hard to assure its success.[108] He also had charge of its book review section.[109]

Still another conservative organization that Weaver embraced was the Intercollegiate Society of Individualists, now the Intercollegiate Studies Institute, founded in 1953. In the late 1950s he joined the society's board of directors.[110] In the next several years he lectured under the organization's auspices to campus audiences and prepared three essays which it circulated as pamphlets.[111] Weaver was openly proud of his association with ISI, and pleased that its influence was expanding.[112] He esteemed the institute highly, he wrote to a friend in early 1963.[113] Barely two weeks later, and just four days before his death, he told an acquaintance that the work ISI was doing was admirable.[114]

The link with the Intercollegiate Society of Individualists, one suspects, was good for Weaver. It gave him an appreciative audience of conservative youth and drew him away, on occasion, from the almost monastic discipline of his daily life. It was also good for *Ideas Have Consequences.* In 1959, the year that Weaver's book first appeared in a paperback edition, E. Victor Milione distributed approximately six hundred copies through ISI.[115] In the next four decades, ISI disseminated literally thousands of additional copies to college students and graduate students throughout the United States.[116] Thanks to the paperback revolution, and more especially to Milione and his associates, *Ideas Have Consequences* experienced a kind of second birth.

Meanwhile, as Weaver grew closer to the growing conservative youth movement, there were signs that he was beginning to modify some of the antimodernism of *Ideas Have Consequences.* Not in a wholesale manner: as late as 1959, in the Foreword to the paperback reprint of his book, Weaver wrote that he "saw no reason, after the lapse of more than a decade, to retreat from the general position of social criticism" he had offered.[117] Still, on at least a few telltale issues, he appeared to be changing his mind. In early 1961, for instance, the board of directors of the Intercollegiate Society of Individualists had under consideration a proposal by William F. Buckley Jr. to change the organization's name, on the grounds that "conservative" was now the movement's label and that the strange-sounding word "individualist" was an obstacle to the society's success.[118] Despite Professor Weaver's denunciation of the term "individualism" in *Ideas Have Consequences,*[119] he opposed Buckley's recommendation. The name Intercollegiate Society of Individualists had always seemed appropriate to him, he protested.[120] Nor was this a momentary lapse on Weaver's part. That same year he became one of three original editorial advisors of the *New Individualist Review,* a journal founded by graduate students of Friedrich Hayek at the University of Chicago. The new publication had decidedly libertarian leanings, and, fittingly enough, its two other faculty sponsors were professors Hayek and Milton Friedman. If Weaver felt any intellectual embarrassment about serving on the same masthead with two of the staunchest defenders of free-market capitalism in the Western world, the record does not show it. He remained an advisor to the *New Individualist Review* until his death.[121]

By far the strongest evidence of a developing reorientation in Weaver's conservatism appeared in an address delivered in April 1959 at the University of Wisconsin and delivered again at an ISI-sponsored gathering in Chicago in September 1962. On the latter occasion his lecture was entitled "How to Argue the Conservative Cause."[122] Although it is possible to find continuities between the contents of this speech and *Ideas Have Consequences,* two themes were startlingly novel. First, Weaver asserted that, in the great contemporary debate over communism and collectivism, the vast majority of the American people were soundly committed to the conservative cause: the cause of freedom. It was the intellectuals and educated people, he said, who had absorbed liberal and collectivist ideas, while it was people farther down the social scale who had remained mostly untainted. From an intellectual nonconformist who less than a dozen years before had excoriated bourgeois complacency and "the spoiled-child psychology of the urban masses," it was a remarkable reversal. The ordinary citizen, Weaver now told his listeners, was a sensible fellow. The one-time antagonist of philistinism now found virtue in middle America. Weaver was in a new frame of mind that April day, a frame of mind that anticipated the coming era in which conservatives would shuck off their minority-mindedness and proclaim themselves the vanguard of the silent majority.

Even more surprising was the second new theme in Weaver's 1959/1962 speech: his rousing defense of the American economic system. An economy rooted in freedom, incentives, and initiative, he proclaimed, had rewarded Americans with the best standard of living in world. Capitalism—yes, capitalism—had produced an incomparable cornucopia of plenty. Weaver exhorted listeners not to feel guilty or defensive about the material achievements of their capitalist system. A society founded upon freedom of enterprise, he averred, was a natural product of unchanging human nature. Such a society, he predicted, would survive.

It is impossible to know where Weaver might have taken these arguments in the years ahead. Less than seven months after he gave this lecture for the second time, he died. Moreover, around the time he was publicly praising capitalism for its bounteousness, he was also continuing to write sympathetically about Southern Agrarianism and contemplating a return to the South to teach. To the end of his days he remained a critic of industrialism and technological "progress."[123] Nevertheless, by the last years of his life Weaver had significantly softened the militantly antimaterialistic, antibourgeois, anticapitalist biases of *Ideas Have Consequences*. Perhaps at the height of the Cold War against an atheistic and collectivist enemy, the United States of America looked better to him than it had in the late 1940s. In his 1959/1962 speech on the "conservative cause," he appeared to think so. To Weaver on these occasions, the United States of America was a success to be celebrated against its leftist critics.

All this is, perhaps, a useful reminder that important thinkers do not stop thinking and that authors sometimes outlive their earliest books. But books—

and particularly, great books—can outlive their authors, and such was the fate of Weaver's *Ideas Have Consequences*. When Weaver died in 1963, his writings did not die with him. "Strong books, like high deeds, confer immortality," Russell Kirk wrote at the time, and his words proved prophetic.[124] In the first three decades (and more) after Weaver's death, *Ideas Have Consequences* continued to be read, admired, and cited on the American Right.[125] The very phrase "Ideas have consequences" became a cliché, as conservatives (reflecting Weaverian thinking) engaged in what they called "the battle of ideas."

Yet even as conservatives everywhere acclaimed Weaver, a subtle change in their perception of him now occurred: a tendency to see in him a mirror for their own preoccupations. This in itself was a tribute to his importance: His intellectual legacy was deemed valuable enough to be argued over and claimed. But it meant that from now on, to some degree, the author of *Ideas Have Consequences* would be a contested figure on the Right.

One of the first to appropriate Weaver after his passing was Frank S. Meyer, the chief ideologist of the fractious conservative movement in the 1960s. In 1964 Meyer—hard at work on articulating the philosophical synthesis called fusionism—dedicated a book on the subject to the memory of Weaver, whom he labeled the "pioneer and protagonist of the American conservative consensus."[126] In 1970 (as noted earlier), Meyer contended that *Ideas Have Consequences* was the veritable fountainhead of his fusionist philosophy. Meanwhile, in 1965, Willmoore Kendall—conservatism's great contrarian—used a review of Weaver's posthumous volume *Visions of Order* to berate the "high priests" of the conservative establishment from which Kendall was increasingly estranged. Weaver's conservatism was "unique," said Kendall; only Weaver, among his fellow conservatives, stood on the "right" side on certain pivotal issues.[127] When one of Kendall's bêtes noires, Russell Kirk, eulogized Weaver in the Foreword to *Visions of Order*, Kendall accused Kirk of trying to make Weaver into his "alter-ego."[128]

As various conservatives sought (as it were) to "capture" Weaver for their agendas, an event occurred which drastically altered their perception of him: the publication, in 1968, of a slightly expanded version of his 1943 doctoral dissertation, under the title *The Southern Tradition at Bay*. During his lifetime Weaver had often published articles on Southern subjects, including sharp criticisms of racial integration and the emerging civil rights movement.[129] But none of the three books he published in his lifetime had been overtly Southern in content. Moreover, he had taught nearly twenty years at the University of Chicago, no Southern citadel. It was only five years after his death that the profoundly formative, Southern Agrarian dimension of his thought became fully apparent. From this point forward, the prevailing interpretation of Weaver was unequivocal: He was "the most prominent disciple of the Vanderbilt Agrarians"[130]—indeed, their "best expositor"[131]—and even "the most unreconstructed of them all."[132]

The growing recognition of the Agrarian roots of Weaver's conservatism soon had reverberations on the Right. Traditionalist Southern conservatives speedily hailed him, both as a prophet of the evils of modernity and as a dogged defender of the antimodern South. In the 1970s a group of his admirers attempted to establish a Richard M. Weaver College in South Carolina.[133] In the 1980s and early 1990s the *Southern Partisan* printed two largely unknown addresses by him at family reunions many years before, as well as a lengthy cover story lauding his achievement.[134] Whenever the Agrarians and their disciples were discussed, Weaver's name was likely to be mentioned with respect.[135]

Not surprisingly, the increasing emphasis on Weaver's Southernness evoked a fresh interpretation of *Ideas Have Consequences*. With *The Southern Tradition at Bay* belatedly in print, it now seemed to some conservatives that *Ideas Have Consequences* should be read as a companion volume to it, an indictment not just of modernity-in-general but of Northern modernity in particular. But if Weaver was now to be understood not as a conservative-in-general but as a quintessentially *Southern* conservative, a new possibility opened up: *Ideas Have Consequences* could become a weapon against Yankees—including Yankee conservatives—with whom latter-day Southern Agrarians and their allies had their differences.

And this is precisely what happened in the 1980s, as a vocal movement of (often Southern) "paleoconservatives" (as they came to be called) dissented from the prevailing conservatism of Ronald Reagan's America. Writing in the thirtieth-anniversary issue of *National Review* in 1985, the emerging paleoconservative writer Chilton Williamson Jr. asserted bluntly that Richard Weaver would not have been "comfortable" with the "new breed" of "boisterous," optimistic conservatives, "entirely devoid of the tragic sense," who had come to prominence in the Reagan era. No, said Williamson, Weaver had seen "more deeply" than "the GOP boosters of the Eighties" the "socially and morally destructive aspects of that form of industrial capitalism we call the West."[136]

The deployment of Weaver's writings as artillery in sectarian strife intensified in the late eighties and nineties during the bitter ideological war between paleoconservatives and neoconservatives, a controversy in which one of Weaver's staunchest admirers, M. E. Bradford, was a protagonist.[137] As the neoconservative ideology of "democratic capitalism" gained popularity, becoming the semi-official creed of the Reaganites, embattled paleoconservatives turned to what they called the Old Right for countervailing intellectual ammunition. And no one on the Old Right seemed more useful than Weaver. If Irving Kristol was the "godfather" of neoconservatism, Richard Weaver seemed to acquire a comparable stature among paleoconservative champions of the "Old Republic."[138]

From a paleoconservative perspective, the enlistment of Weaver in their army made sense. What could be more glaring than the gulf between the stern antimodernism of *Ideas Have Consequences* and the cheerful American exceptionalism of Ronald Reagan? What could be more antithetical to Reagan's "supply-side economics" than what Eugene Genovese claimed was the "deep anticapitalism" of Weaver's conservatism?[139] Indeed, had not this gulf existed since the infancy of the postwar conservative revival? In the 1950s, in the very years that Weaver was questioning such "god terms" as "progress" and "science,"[140] Reagan had been a spokesman for General Electric, whose corporate motto was: "Progress is our most important product." No wonder, then, that in 1996 a Southern devotee of Weaver argued in *National Review* that Weaver's conservatism had "nothing in common" with the defense of capitalism.[141]

In appropriating Weaver for their purposes in this way, the paleoconservatives were relying almost exclusively on the early Weaver—the scourge of "progress" and "bourgeois capitalism" in *Ideas Have Consequences*—not on the Cold War conservative who had heaped praise on American capitalism in 1959 and 1962. It was Weaver the cultural declinist whom they quoted, not the conservative activist who openly identified his cause with middle America in the late 1950s and early 1960s. Of course, few conservatives of any stripe appeared to realize that by 1959 Weaver had begun to attenuate, in some respects, the cultural pessimism he had adopted so fervently in the 1940s when he had felt "condemned" to live in "darkest Chicago."[142] But perhaps it would not have mattered if they had. For *Ideas Have Consequences* was a powerful book, and by 1963 it had taken on a life of its own.

And then, in the 1990s, just as Southern traditionalists and others were reaffirming Weaver's status as an "intellectual saint,"[143] a surprising twist in the Weaver saga occurred. For the first time, Weaver himself came under significant fire from the Right.[144] In 1992, in a book portentously entitled

The Conservative Crack-Up, R. Emmett Tyrrell Jr. accused Weaver of encouraging "a sense of political futility" among conservatives after World War II. If Weaver was right that the "dissolution of the West" had begun with the acceptance of nominalism in the fourteenth century, then—Tyrrell asked with exasperation—"what the hell could be done about it?" Tyrrell conceded that Weaver's "dismal scholarship had its virtues": It directed readers to "important things, the nature of man, the quality of men's souls." Unfortunately, said Tyrrell, Weaver's writings were "more likely to move his readers to political despair than to enthusiastic, back-slapping political action."[145]

Tyrrell's frustration was echoed a year later by Samuel Francis, a Southern paleoconservative disciple of James Burnham. In an essay pungently entitled "Ideas and No Consequences," he asserted that modern American conservatism was a failure. One large reason, he declared, was that the movement's intellectuals, including Weaver, had been guilty of an "abstract and abstruse intellectualism" which had helped to doom their cause to "irrelevance." Men like Weaver, Eric Voegelin, and Leo Strauss, said Francis, had practiced a "formalistic and normative approach" to political theory, an approach "reluctant to admit that some things, even ideas, fail." The Old Right, charged Francis, had been "too uxoriously wedded to Weaver's principle that 'Ideas Have Consequences.'" It had too often responded to "the civilizational crisis it perceived" by indulging in "a pretentious medievalism," attraction to "archaic social and political forms such as the antebellum South," and other brands of "romanticism" and "archaism." "Ideas do have consequences," Francis acknowledged, "but some ideas have more consequences than others," in part because "some ideas serve human interests and emotions . . . while other ideas do not." The Old Right "intelligentsia" had fallen short, said Francis, because American culture contained "no significant set of interests to which its ideas could attach themselves." Lacking a social base from which to resist the "managerial revolution," the "hyperintellectualism of the Old Right" had collapsed in futility.[146]

As if these blows to Weaver's iconic status were not enough, in 1996 Jeffrey Hart delivered another. Hart's target was not *Ideas Have Consequences* but the Southern Agrarian vision that undergirded it. To Hart, this was precisely Weaver's weakness: His "Southernness" had rested upon just that—a vision, a dream, "an abstraction from historical reality." Rejecting the argument that "capitalism" and "tradition" were irreconcilable, Hart retorted that the conservative, antebellum South so cherished by Weaver had itself been "capitalist" at its core. The very "essence" of the early nineteenth-century

Southern economy had been "trade and money." Clearly Hart had little patience with Weaver's oft-quoted contention that the Old South had been a feudal society, *"the last non-materialist civilization in the Western World."*[147] To Hart, Weaver's "polarizations" between the South and North, between "traditional community and capitalism," were "abstractions masquerading as actual entities." Although Hart did not criticize *Ideas Have Consequences* overtly, he suggested that its author, leading a life of "isolation," "seemed to forget what lived, non-abstract social existence is like." For Hart, Weaver was "an uncertain guide to a fully imagined American conservatism."[148]

The unexpected emergence of a critique of Weaver's thought from within the Right raised many questions. Fifty years after the publication of *Ideas Have Consequences*, was its reign as a conservative classic finally ending? Had Weaver (at least the early Weaver) been too abstract and formalistic, too imbued with Platonism, too convinced of the primacy of ideas? Had his interpretation of the decline of the West stretched conservatives' mental horizon too far, to the point of neomedieval archaism and irrelevance? During most of his career Weaver had been a determined standard-bearer for two powerful intellectual traditions: cultural pessimism about modernity and (the other side of the coin) the philosophy of Southern Agrarianism. Had he perhaps been too devoted a paladin? In his quest for a true and coherent "metaphysical dream," did his own "dream" become a confining ideology?

As conservatives celebrated *Ideas Have Consequences'* fiftieth anniversary, few could deny that much of Weaver's worldview seemed more remote than ever from the "lived, non-abstract social existence" of late twentieth-century America: his admiration for "the chivalry and spirituality of the Middle Ages,"[149] for instance; his unqualified assaults upon science and technology; his celebration of a regime of "distinction and hierarchy"; his blasts at the middle class. As Americans, including conservative Americans, logged on to the Internet, invested in the stock market, and anticipated the third millennium, few gave any sign of repudiating the institutions of modernity. If an antimodernist revolution of this magnitude had been Weaver's objective, his cause seemed truly lost.

And yet, as Russell Kirk remarked in the mid-1950s, Weaver's writings, "once read, ferment in the mind."[150] As the Cold War abroad yielded in the 1990s to "culture wars" at home, the perception of cultural disintegration and decline, to which Weaver in 1948 gave classic expression, appeared to be making a comeback on the Right. If true, the life of *Ideas Have Consequences* was not yet over. In 1996 Robert Bork produced a telling volume in this vein under the title *Slouching Towards Gomorrah*; it was a national bestseller.[151] In the late 1990s the American conservative community seemed divided between "optimists," who believed the future of Western civilization to be promising, and "pessimists," who judged the West's moral foundations to be collapsing with frightening speed. For conservatives of the latter persuasion, *Ideas Have Consequences* had lost neither its persuasiveness nor its punch.

What a remarkable book *Ideas Have Consequences* had turned out to be. In the 1940s an unknown English instructor at the University of Chicago had set out to be a diagnostician of the decadence of the West. If, fifty years later, certain elements of his book appeared antiquated, its power to provoke seemed undiminished. Too much of its account of the consequences of moral and epistemological relativism had proven to be almost eerily prescient. In *Ideas Have Consequences* Weaver warned: "We approach a condition in which we shall be amoral without the capacity to perceive it and degraded without means to measure our descent."[152] In the America of the late 1990s, many conservatives felt that Weaver's prophecy had come true.

As *Ideas Have Consequences* started its second half century in print, there was every reason to believe that it would be read for a long while yet.

14

Francis Graham Wilson:
A Conservative Scholar's Wisdom

This is a review of Francis Graham Wilson's book The Case for Conservatism, *republished in 1991 with a new Introduction by Russell Kirk. My review appeared in the* University Bookman *that same year.*

Forty years have passed since Francis Wilson first published the three lectures contained in this elegant reprint edition, and it is important to remember the context in which they first appeared. Conservatism in 1951 was not yet a respectable political designation, especially in the precincts of academe where Wilson, a political scientist, toiled. Indeed, the regnant opinion among American intellectuals of the time was that only liberalism could engage serious minds and that conservatism was merely an expression of prejudice, resentment, or avarice.

That the "conservative spirit in politics" is both intellectually defensible and politically imperative was the thesis which Professor Wilson took upon himself to prove in these lectures, first delivered at the University of Washington. Despite the daunting magnitude of his task, Wilson could take some comfort from the changing circumstances of his listeners. Sobered by liberalism's failures and fragmentation at home, and disturbed by the relentless aggression of communism abroad, many American academics in the early 1950s were willing, if only fleetingly, to concede that perhaps a "conservative moment" had arrived. For a largely liberal audience, then—skeptical but not implacably hostile—Wilson initially formulated his case. In the process he helped to catalyze the emergence of an articulate, intellectual Right in the Cold War era.

According to Wilson, conservatism is "primarily a spirit animating political behavior," a "way of life," and "a manner of judging life." It is not, however, lacking in "primary values" or certain permanent characteristics, of which he identified five. First, conservatism attempts to discern a "pattern in history" that will yield "clues" as to what is feasible or infeasible in the "management of politics." Second, unlike those on the Left who consider man to be perfectible if only his institutions can be reformed or destroyed, conservatives hold that man by his very nature is a mixture of good and evil, of rationality and irrationality. He is "a child of God," who is sinful yet also "capable of living up to the standards of reason, provided he is taught to do so, and provided, in Christian thought, that he is aided by grace." Man, in other words, can improve, but the process is slow; utopia is a costly illusion. Third, conservatives believe in a fixed "moral order in the universe," a "criterion of life" applicable to all people regardless of their social class. Fourth, conservatives insist that the power of government must be limited and that the "preservation of liberty" depends in part upon "the moderation of the impact of government on the individual." Finally, conservatives defend the institution of private property, which they regard as crucial for the survival and "moral function" of the family.

Having defined his terms, so to speak, Wilson was anxious to demonstrate that the conservative approach to politics was critically relevant to contemporary problems. In this respect *The Case for Conservatism*, examined a generation later, displays some of the marks of a *livre de circonstance*. Time and again, for instance, Wilson alluded to the struggle in the late 1940s and early 1950s to arrest the march of militant communism in western Europe. The "idea of an inevitable class struggle," he remarked at one point, "is the most terrible illusion of our time." The "primary characteristic of political conservatism" at present, he asserted, was "its defense of traditional democracy" on an "international scale." While discussing the American Revolution, he declared that "there is no mystery in the conservative as a revolutionary, for it has often been so. It is so today among those who would preserve the continuity of Western society against the encroachment of Slavic ideology." Much of Wilson's expressed concern in these lectures for constitutional government, free elections, and "social reconstruction" arose from his recognition that the fate of Europe and of the civilization of the West were imperiled as never before by totalitarianism.

Wilson also undertook to identify the conservative contribution to America's own political development and thereby to refute the glib contention that only liberalism had rooted itself on these shores. Conservatism "has served its function in America and it has made our history," he argued. Not surprisingly, he extolled *The Federalist* (which he ranked with the works of Edmund Burke in creating "the modem conservative spirit in politics"), and he called attention to the contribution of Paul Elmer More (the "greatest of our intellectual conservatives"). He noted approvingly that "the principles of economic progress," as expounded by certain American economists, comprised "one of the lasting elements in American conservative theory." He shrewdly observed that an essential component of "the defense of the American system has been the promise of opportunity to the willing hand, and the assurance that ordinary men can and do share in our wealth more than in other lands."

Wilson, of course, realized that principled conservatives can never hold out the prospect (as irresponsible radicals can) of the complete eradication of pain and tragedy from the human condition. Still, he sensed the importance of providing every member of a society with "the hope that progress can be made," and he recognized that America historically had offered such hope. Without succumbing to utopian temptations and fantasies, he knew that conservatism as a public philosophy must be committed to the possibility of social betterment.

In the course of his lectures, Wilson made a number of quietly provocative observations that foreshadowed later cleavages in the conservative movement. He disparaged laissez faire economics as a doctrine just as "millenarian" as Marxism and stressed that postwar conservatism, while necessarily antisocialist, must accept changes in "economic arrangements." He taught that conservatism "learns to forget the lost cause and the irrelevant tension." In the face of Communist tyranny, he unabashedly exhorted conservatives to defend "the democratic tradition" and pointedly dismissed the aristocratic and monarchic conservatism of prewar Europe as an ineffectual anachronism. At the conclusion of his second lecture, he said bluntly:

> Whatever else it may be, conservatism, as a spirit in politics, is an eternal demand for political moderation, and for an evolving continuity, in which reform may be attained without the psychiatric fury of nationalism or the intransigent hatred of revolutionary Marxism.

Such "middle way" sentiments, of a kind espoused by many postwar Christian Democrats in western Europe, could not have pleased those on either side of the Atlantic who were seeking a more fervent and formulaic basis for political battle.

Indeed, reading this volume more than a generation after its appearance, one is struck by how undoctrinaire and unprogrammatic it is. Wilson's case for conservatism was not a plea for a specific set of public policies. In fact, he argued, conservatism is decidedly not a "fixed program" at all, and much conservative literature (including that of the early nineteenth century, when modern conservatism was born) is now obsolete. One is struck, too, by the unpolemical character of the author's prose. In part, no doubt, this quality reflects his temperament and training. Wilson was a political theorist, not a policy analyst or media commentator. While a scholar of sturdy conviction, he was evidently disinclined to indulge in rancorous debate. Moreover, as an avowed conservative in a profession dominated by antithetical currents of thought, he perhaps deliberately eschewed confrontation for conversation, the better to make himself heard.

In any case, forty years later what most impresses this reviewer is not the overall content of these lectures (some of which is now dated) but the epigrammatic insights one encounters along the way. For example, these observations by Wilson:

> . . . the conservative defense of the moral order, the moral order that has emerged from Jewish, Roman, and Christian tradition, is the only answer we have today to the corrosive doctrine of the class struggle. . . . Ideas and a common spirit can unite a people, but material interests most surely divide. And if we are spiritual eunuchs it is easy for us to kill each other in a struggle for unlimited power and for the wealth that the common efforts of all may have produced in any society.
>
> The conservative criticism of our age is that some liberals have turned . . . from humanity, from the expansion of freedom for the individual, to a culture bolshevism that can only be expressed in moral trickery and tyranny.
>
> If we seek for the ultimate conflict between the conservative and the revolutionary spirit in politics, we shall find it in our conceptions of human nature.

Political tracts rarely transcend their origins, and political books that are both temperate in tone and unprogrammatic in prescription are not apt to become bestsellers. *The Case for Conservatism* was not a bestseller in

1951, and it was soon overshadowed by other contributions to the scholarly canon of the Right. Nevertheless, it is good to have this volume back in print. Francis Wilson was one of the founding fathers of the post-1945 conservative renascence. In these pioneering lectures he distilled much wisdom and helped to give an intellectual movement its identity.

15

Hillsdale College:
A Model for Conservatives

For more than a generation Hillsdale College in Michigan has held a place of prominence in the conservative firmament. This brief essay suggests some reasons why. Originally published as the Foreword to Arlan K. Gilbert, The Permanent Things: Hillsdale College, 1900–1994 *(Hillsdale College Press, 1998), it is reprinted here in slightly modified form.*

In the vast archipelago of institutions of higher learning scattered throughout the United States, Hillsdale College is a very small island. As of 1997, more than twelve million Americans were enrolled as either full- or part-time undergraduate students in the nation's colleges and universities. Of this multitude, just under twelve hundred—or fewer than one in ten thousand—had come to Hillsdale.

Yet raw numbers are rarely a true measure of historical significance. Individuals, not faceless aggregations, make history. The Declaration of Independence was signed by just fifty-five men. The Constitution was formally adopted by thirty-nine. When the Pilgrims on the *Mayflower* landed at Plymouth, they numbered barely one hundred souls. In the Middle East, two thousand years ago, Jesus of Nazareth had but twelve disciples.

So, too, with colleges and universities: There the power of ideas—and of a few courageous people articulating these ideas—can count for far more than massive enrollments, amplitude of endowment, or magnificence of the physical plant. So, today, it is with Hillsdale College. Situated far from the great concentrations of political, financial, and cultural power in our society, it has nevertheless attained a standing nearly unique in American higher education, and one greatly disproportionate to its size and resources.

How has this come to pass? Almost a decade ago, Arlan K. Gilbert began to answer this question by researching the remarkable history of the institution where he himself has taught for nearly four decades. In *Historic Hillsdale College*, he traced the Hillsdale saga from its origins in the 1840s to the dawn of the twentieth century. In *The Permanent Things*, he advances his narrative from 1900 to the present, thereby completing a sesquicentennial history project that has surely been a labor of love.

Every good college deserves a devoted chronicler, and in Professor Gilbert Hillsdale College has a worthy one. For his efforts the entire Hillsdale community, past and present, as well as friends and visitors like myself, can be grateful. But not every college has a distinctive story to be told, and here Professor Gilbert has a great advantage. *The Permanent Things* is more than a proud recital of one college's struggles and glories; of its dedicated professors and administrators; of the rhythms and lore of its campus life; of lustrous triumphs on diamond, field, and track. All that is here, of course, and properly so, but there is more.

For in this volume, like its predecessor, Professor Gilbert reminds us that Hillsdale College has been an institution with a mission: a liberal arts college tenaciously committed to traditional learning, Judeo-Christian values, and independence from external control. "History is philosophy learned from examples," an ancient Greek scholar asserted. In the volume at hand Professor Gilbert illuminates not only the details of Hillsdale's history but the controlling philosophy that has increasingly set it apart.

Two themes dominate his narrative. The first, quite simply, is *survival.*

In the mid-nineteenth century, Hillsdale and many other small Midwestern colleges had been "founded" (in one writer's words) "amid hard conditions with poverty as their endowment, self-sacrifice as their spirit, Christian living as their goal, [and] American freedom as their medium."[1] It was an ennobling experience, but not without recurrent suffering and strain. For much of the twentieth century, Gilbert records, Hillsdale teetered on the verge of financial collapse. Time and again, only the most sacrificial exertions and the intervention of a few benefactors saved the school from imminent ruin. On occasion the college had to borrow money just to meet its monthly payroll. During the Great Depression the faculty came to resemble impecunious missionaries, with the lowest salaries of any college professors in Michigan. As late as the 1950s the possibility of closure hung over Hillsdale.

Only in the past quarter century has Hillsdale achieved security. The key, Professor Gilbert documents, has been Hillsdale's extraordinary success in building a national constituency beyond its relatively slender pool of alumni and its limited geographical base. Through such vehicles of outreach as *Imprimis*, the Center for Constructive Alternatives, and the Shavano Institute for National Leadership, the college has acquired a following—both intellectual and financial—which has permitted it, in a single generation, to transform itself from a fragile and essentially regional institution into one of national prominence.

Hillsdale could not have accomplished this, however, if it had not stood for something—if, indeed, its message and mission had not resonated with hundreds of thousands of Americans who had never seen its campus. This leads us to the second overarching theme of Professor Gilbert's story: *resistance*.

Resistance—repeatedly—to the snares of governmental regulation and the corrupting lure of governmental aid. Resistance to the ethos of utilitarianism regnant in state-subsidized universities and community colleges. Resistance, in the name of Christian convictions and traditional learning, to the secularist, permissive, and even nihilistic impulses that have vitiated so much of academe in recent decades. It is this quality of persistent opposition to the drift of things that has won Hillsdale a legion of admirers.

Yet if Hillsdale for more than a century has exemplified a creed of rugged individualism (in the best sense), one must still ask: Why? Why here and not elsewhere? Why has *this* college, almost alone, managed to defy the seemingly inexorable law of entropy, under which institutions over time abandon the faith and intent of their founders? No doubt the college's frontier origins, and its initial links with the Freewill Baptists, had something to do with the principled independence which it has assiduously cultivated. "Just as the twig is bent, the tree's inclined." Yet frontiers do not last forever, and the college's links to the separatistically inclined Baptists have long since vanished. So the question recurs: how has Hillsdale, in this century, maintained *its* traditions when so many institutions of similar background have forsaken theirs?

It is a question I invite readers to ponder as they read Professor Gilbert's book. Therein they will find many clues. Let me mention two.

First, this little Michigan college appears to have been blessed over the years by an unusual number of "inner-directed" administrators, professors, and—not to be overlooked—trustees who genuinely believed in their mission, even when adversity threatened to overwhelm them. For them, Christian faith, a liberal arts education, and independent living were causes to be cherished, not mantras to be intoned on ceremonial or fundraising occasions. One of the hardest things to keep alive in this world is a tradition. One way or another, Hillsdale's guardians did it. Professor Gilbert's book helps us to understand how.

Second, the very fact that Hillsdale's financial footing was so precarious for so long seems to have reinforced the college's commitment to its core beliefs. Hillsdale has never been so prosperous that it could take its existence for granted. Because it has always had to earn its future, it has repeatedly had to convince others that it deserves a future. Hence it could not grow rusty in explaining its reason for being.

Nor, one trusts, will it be tempted to grow rusty now, as recognition and reward crown its sturdy defense of the "permanent things." For even as Hillsdale prospers, the disorientation of American academic life accelerates. There is countervailing work to be done—the work that Hillsdale College was founded to do. In *The Permanent Things*, Professor Gilbert has given us the story of his college to this point. If Hillsdale remains true to its mission—as I expect it will—we may be confident that someday his books will be part of a multivolume series.

16

The New Counterculture:
Rod Dreher and the Crunchy Cons

This review of Rod Dreher's book Crunchy Cons *appeared in the* Wall Street Journal *on February 21, 2006, under the title "The New Counterculture."*

Rod Dreher, a columnist and editor at the *Dallas Morning News*, is a self-confessed member of the vast right-wing conspiracy. As a lapsed Protestant who converted to Roman Catholicism several years ago, he is an unabashed religious and social conservative. He has little use for the morally relativist and libertine tendencies of modern liberalism. Too often, he says, "the Democrats act like the Party of Lust."

But Mr. Dreher is also a passionate environmentalist, a devotee of organic farming, and a proponent of the New Urbanism, an antisprawl movement aimed at making residential neighborhoods more like pre-suburban small towns. He dislikes industrial agriculture, shopping malls, television, McMansions, and mass consumerism. Efficiency—the guiding principle of free markets—is an "idol," he says, that must be "smashed." Too often, he claims, Republicans act like "the Party of Greed."

Four years ago, Mr. Dreher coined the term "crunchy conservatism" (as in crunchy granola) to describe hybrids like himself: political right-wingers with countercultural sensibilities. Now, in a book based largely on interviews and his own experience, he explores the type in depth. But *Crunchy Cons* is not a pallid work of sociology. It is a rousing altar call to spiritual secession from an America that Mr. Dreher sees as awash in materialism, consumerism, and "lifestyle-libertarian" thinking.

In Mr. Dreher's view, consumer-crazed capitalism makes a fetish of individual choice, and, if left unchecked, "tends to pull families and communities apart." Thus consumerism and conservatism are, for him, incompatible, a fact that mainstream conservatives, he says, simply do not grasp. He warns that capitalism must be reined in by "the moral and spiritual energies of the people." It is not politics and economics that will save us, he declares. It is adherence to the "eternal moral norms" known as the "Permanent Things."

And the most permanent thing of all is God. At the heart of Mr. Dreher's family-centered crunchy conservatism is an unwavering commitment to religious faith. And not just any religious faith, but rigorous, old-fashioned orthodoxy. Only a firm grounding in religious commitment, he believes, can sustain crunchy conservatives in their struggle against the radical individualism and materialism he decries. Nearly all the crunchy cons he interviews are devoutly Christian or orthodox Jewish believers who are deliberately ordering their lives toward the ultimate end of "serving God, not the self"—often at considerable financial sacrifice.

Mr. Dreher sees *Crunchy Cons*, in part, as "a handbook of the resistance." He advocates homeschooling. He applauds community-supported agriculture, small businesses, simple living, historic preservation, and much else that promotes a "sacramental" (non-utilitarian) sense of life. You cannot be truly conservative today, he avers, without being countercultural.

These themes, of course, are not new, as Mr. Dreher acknowledges. He cites E. F. Schumacher's decentralist 1973 classic *Small Is Beautiful*. He approvingly mentions Richard Weaver (1910–63), the author of *Ideas Have Consequences*, and Wendell Berry, a contemporary agrarian poet and essayist. Above all, he extols Russell Kirk, the author of *The Conservative Mind* and a tireless defender of the "Permanent Things." Mr. Dreher, in short, identifies himself with the venerable traditionalist school of conservatism that reaches back to Kirk, the Southern Agrarians, and beyond: a communitarian conservatism profoundly disturbed not only by secular liberalism but also by the relentless dynamism of modern commercial life.

And therein lies the significance of *Crunchy Cons*. It is a reminder of the enduring tension on the right between those for whom the highest social good is freedom—the emancipation of the self from statist restraint and oppressive custom—and those for whom the highest social good is virtue: the formation of character, the cultivation of the soul.

Fortunately, Mr. Dreher is not a dour sermonizer. He is a lively writer with a talent for quotable prose ("the point of life is not to become a more satisfied shopper"), and his sense of humor and self-deprecation help to temper his stem-winding style. He also recognizes that not everyone can afford to withdraw from the mainstream or follow the nearly monastic path that he keeps pointing to. Still, he hopes that his fellow crunchy cons and Birkenstocked Burkeans will have the courage, born of religious conviction, to resist the tides of modernity as much as they are able.

Because Mr. Dreher offers no detailed blueprint for cultural renewal, some may dismiss his book as just another lifestyle manifesto. This would be a mistake. Like it or not, Mr. Dreher raises concerns that will not go away. America today is more broadly free and prosperous than any society in human history. We are gloriously "free to choose." But choose what?

Part II

William F. Buckley Jr. and the
Advent of *National Review*

17

God and Man at Yale Revisited

I presented this paper at a conference on "Faith, Freedom, and Higher Education" held at Grove City College in April 2009. The conference was organized and hosted by the college's Center for Vision and Values.

In early 2008, William F. Buckley Jr.—the "patron saint" of American conservatives[1]—died at the age of eighty-two at his home in Connecticut. Best known as the founder and longtime editor of *National Review*, and as the host for more than thirty years of the television show *Firing Line*, he had led one of the most productive lives in the history of American journalism. During his nearly sixty years in the public eye, he published more than 50 books (both fiction and nonfiction); dozens of book reviews; more than 800 editorials, articles, and remarks in *National Review*; several hundred articles in periodicals other than *National Review*; and approximately 5,600 syndicated newspaper columns. He gave hundreds of public lectures around the world (often at the rate of seventy or more a year), conducted 1,429 separate *Firing Line* programs, and may well have composed more letters than any American who has ever lived.

Conservatives like to say that "ideas have consequences." Certainly the aphorism is applicable to the sizzling writings of William F. Buckley Jr. Of all his books, undoubtedly the most consequential was his very first, *God and Man at Yale*. Written when he was barely twenty-five years old, it has stayed in print almost continuously for nearly six decades. For the student of faith, freedom, and higher education in America, the story of *God and Man at Yale* remains a tale worth knowing.

William F. Buckley Jr. was born in 1925 into a large and rambunctious Roman Catholic family presided over by his wealthy, ultraconservative father, an oilman from Texas. From an early date it was evident that he was going to make his mark upon the world. Upon entering Yale University in 1946 (after military service in the Second World War), he quickly became a Big Man on Campus, a formidable member of the debating team, a ubiquitous conservative polemicist, and in his senior year, a member of the prestigious Skull and Bones society. From early 1949 to early 1950 he served as the chairman (editor-in-chief) of the undergraduate *Yale Daily News*, from which perch he fired conservative editorial fusillades at liberal targets, much to the discomfiture of the faculty and administration.

By his senior year, Buckley—although personally popular—was increasingly distressed by the pedagogical drift of things at Yale. Brought up to be a devout Christian and staunch "individualist" (in today's parlance: a free-market conservative or libertarian), he was appalled by the rampant secularism, atheism, and socialistic sentiments that he discerned inside and outside the classroom—and by official Yale's seeming indifference to these threats. He therefore responded eagerly when Yale's administration invited him to become the undergraduate speaker at the university's annual Alumni Day ceremonies on February 22, 1950.

Buckley prepared a speech depicting Yale as a university that had lost its moorings and "mission." So long as Yale persisted in its "fanatical allegiance to *laissez-faire* education," he wrote, "she will lead her students nowhere." It was time, he argued, for Yale's trustees to define their institution's purpose and to take measures to "imbue her students with that same purpose."[2]

When President Seymour of Yale and his advisers saw an advance copy of Buckley's text, they were aghast. In the president's words, it was nothing less than "an attack upon the Yale faculty" and totally inappropriate for the occasion. The administration promptly requested Buckley to revise his draft. Buckley reluctantly agreed to tone it down a little but refused to alter its substance. Instead, he offered to withdraw from the program completely if his text were still deemed unacceptable. To his astonishment, just one day before the event, President Seymour accepted his offer. The alumni audience, he told Buckley, would have been "upset" by his proposed speech.[3]

In Buckley's later word, Yale's suppression of his Alumni Day address was the "catalyst" for what happened next.[4] Shortly after his graduation in 1950, he embarked upon a systematic, book-length case study of the educational environment at Yale as it had impinged upon his faith and political philosophy. The informal motto of the university was "For God, for Country, and for Yale." With the daring and aplomb that had helped to make him an undergraduate luminary, he entitled his book *God and Man at Yale: The Superstitions of "Academic Freedom."*

In his Foreword, Buckley came swiftly to the point. "I myself believe," he wrote, "that the duel between Christianity and atheism is the most important in the world. I further believe that the struggle between individualism and collectivism is the same struggle reproduced on another level. I believe that if and when the menace of communism is gone, other vital battles, at present subordinated, will emerge to the foreground. And the winner must have help from the classroom."[5]

Alas, he reported, neither orthodox Christianity nor traditional American beliefs in free enterprise and limited government were receiving much help from the classrooms of his alma mater. He had entered Yale looking to it "for allies against secularism and collectivism."[6] Instead, despite its façade of "detached impartiality," the "net impact" of Yale's educational offerings was distinctly *anti*-Christian and scornful of the free-market philosophy pioneered by Adam Smith. Acting under the "protective label" of "academic freedom," Yale had become an example of "one of the most extraordinary incongruities of our time: the institution that derives its moral and financial support from Christian individualists and then addresses itself to the task of persuading the sons of these supporters to be atheistic socialists."[7]

In two bluntly worded chapters, Buckley attempted to substantiate his claims. He asserted that Yale's department of religion was neither "a source of pervasive Christian influence" nor, indeed, of *any* influence upon most undergraduates. He charged that some of Yale's most popular professors (whom he named) were publicly hostile to Christianity, even in the classroom. One noted professor of religion had even called himself "80 percent atheist and 20 percent agnostic."[8] In many of the social science departments, Buckley continued, secularist biases were pervasive. In fact, he asserted, not a single department at Yale was "uncontaminated with the absolute that there are no absolutes, no intrinsic rights, no ultimate truths."[9] Although a Christian presence could be found in Yale's extracurricular activities, much of it was of a nondoctrinal, do-good variety—no substitute for "classroom exposition and guidance."[10] Christian *students* there certainly were at Yale, wrote Buckley, but they received little sustenance from either the faculty or the administration.

In the realm of economics, Buckley reported, the intellectual climate was more disturbing still. Citing chapter and verse from the pro-Keynesian textbooks and teachings of Yale's department of economics, he portrayed a department committed to a "revolution": "one that advocates a slow but relentless transfer of power from the individual to the state." [11] Not only was Yale's economics curriculum riddled with Keynesian biases and critiques of traditional capitalism; the favored textbooks completely ignored critiques of the liberal Keynes by distinguished free-market scholars like Friedrich Hayek, author of *The Road to Serfdom*. To Buckley, it was proof that Yale—its pious protestations of neutrality notwithstanding—was deliberately and dangerously tilting to the Left. The "net influence of Yale economics" was "thoroughly collectivistic," he charged. "Individualism is dying at Yale, and without a fight." [12]

Buckley did not stop with documenting "Yale's intellectual drive toward agnosticism and collectivism."[13] In an audacious display of counterrevolutionary fervor, he called upon the university's alumni—if they agreed with him—to "interfere" and set Yale's "educational policy" aright.[14] Invoking a consumer sovereignty model for university governance, he argued that the university's alumni—its "consumers"—were the ultimate "governing body" and "ultimate overseers" of Yale's product.[15] He reminded his readers that Yale was a *private* educational institution and that its graduates had both a right and a duty to insist that their alma mater instill the "value orthodoxy" that they themselves believed in.[16]

To achieve this objective, Buckley knew that he must pierce the carapace of Yale's protective ideology: what he provocatively called the "superstitions" of "academic freedom." It was "the shibboleths of 'academic freedom,'" he thundered, which had thwarted efforts to "Christianize Yale" for many years.[17] It was the "hoax" of "academic freedom" which had provided a convenient smokescreen for incoherent "*laissez-faire* education." At one point, he asserted that Yale already possessed a "value orthodoxy"; *he* proposed only to "narrow" it. In place of the secularist and collectivist tendencies currently ascendant at Yale, he would implant an orthodoxy grounded in the truths of Christianity and individualism. And he would enforce it: If a socialist were found to be teaching at Yale he would be barred from doing so because he was "inculcating values that the governing board at Yale consider to be against the public welfare."[18] If the "overseers" of a university "have embraced democracy, individualism, and religion," he said, then "the attitudes of the faculty ought to conform to the university's."[19]

The fearless controversialist conceded that some professors would be discharged (and some "ought to be discharged") if he succeeded. But "no one not apathetic to the value issues of the day," he countered, could "in good conscience contribute to the ascendancy of ideas he considers destructive of the best in civilization." "If the majority of Yale graduates believe in spiritual values and in individualism" (as Buckley assumed), "they cannot contribute to Yale so long as she continues in whole or in part to foster contrary values." As for the dogma of "academic freedom": "[I]n the last analysis," it "must mean the freedom of men and women to supervise the educational activities and aims of the schools they oversee and support."[20]

To the young alumnus, these concerns were not trivial. The "educational institutions" of the West are "the nerve center of civilization," he contended. All too often, the "guardians of this sustaining core of civilization" had "abdicated their responsibility to mankind."[21]

God and Man at Yale was published on October 15, 1951, by the Henry Regnery Company, a small, conservative publishing house in Chicago. Within a week the first printing of 5,000 had sold out.[22] In its first six months, the volume sailed through four more printings and sold 25,000 copies—an extraordinary feat for a little-known author writing about a seemingly obscure topic.[23] The volume's sales were fueled by lively publicity in the press. *Time, Life,* and *Newsweek* ran articles about it.[24] The *Saturday Review*—a highly influential, literary weekly—gave the book *two* reviews (one pro, one con).[25] In all, something like one hundred periodicals weighed in with articles and commentaries. Clearly Buckley had touched a sensitive nerve.

Several adventitious factors contributed to the book's astonishing sales. With the assistance of his father, Buckley poured $16,000 (a substantial figure) into publicity; the fund enabled Regnery to advertise the book aggressively and to mail a circular to 40,000 Yale alumni.[26] John Chamberlain's laudatory introduction to the book also gave it a boost; Chamberlain (Yale class of 1925) was a respected journalist and former daily book reviewer of the *New York Times*. Partly it was a matter of felicitous timing: *God and Man at Yale* was launched just four days before Yale celebrated its 250th anniversary, a milestone much noted in the press. The timing was no coincidence: Buckley and his father successfully pressured Henry Regnery to speed the book into print in time to benefit from Yale's publicity.[27]

Interest in Buckley's broadside was also stimulated by its sheer novelty and effrontery. Here was a dashing young alumnus of Old Eli—and a member of Skull and Bones, no less!—publicly skewering his alma mater for straying from true religion and sound economics. No one had ever seen anything quite like it. *Life* magazine compared the book to the "brat who comes to the party and tells the guests that their birthday boy is secretly a dope addict."[28] *Time* dubbed Buckley a "rebel in reverse": "a fire-eating youthful conservative."[29]

There was more to the story, however, than that. In his Foreword Buckley prophesied that his volume would evoke "bitter opposition."[30] Barely a month after publication, he confessed that he had been "naïve beyond recognition." The opposition had been more vituperative than he had ever dreamed. "I should have known better, of course, for I had seen the Apparatus go to work on other dissenters from the Liberal orthodoxy, and I respected the Apparatus and stood in awe of it...."[31]

Instead of loftily ignoring Buckley's polemic, official Yale reacted to it (in one journalist's words) "with all the grace and agility of an elephant cornered by a mouse."[32] Even before the book was published, President Griswold of Yale (who had not yet read it) privately condemned it and attempted to induce Buckley to withdraw it.[33] Three months before the publication date, Yale's trustees secretly created a committee of alumni to investigate "the intellectual and spiritual welfare" of the university—an obvious preemptive act of damage control. The existence of the committee was disclosed four days before Buckley's book appeared. Early in 1952, without once mentioning Buckley by name, the committee announced triumphantly that all was well at Yale: Its investigation had found not a single faculty member who was "trying to undermine or destroy our society" or to "indoctrinate" students with "subversive theories." Nor was Yale encouraging irreligion or atheism; religious life at the university was said to be "deeper and richer than it has been in many years." For good measure, the committee ringingly extolled the principles of academic freedom and affirmed that a university's "business" was "to educate, not to indoctrinate its students."[34]

McGeorge Bundy (Yale class of 1940 and now a Harvard professor) was not so inclined to beat around the bush. In a blistering review essay in the November 1951 *Atlantic Monthly*, Bundy excoriated *God and Man at Yale* as "dishonest in its use of facts, false in its theory, and a discredit to its author." He labeled Buckley "a twisted and ignorant young man whose personal views of economics would have seemed reactionary to Mark Hanna."[35] Bundy subsequently denied that Yale's administration had designated him to "deliver the counterattack" or that he had been "approached" by Yale's administration "in any way whatever." He did not reveal that after accepting the assignment from the *Atlantic Monthly's* editor (a Yale man), he himself had approached Yale and had spent a day with President Griswold discussing the forthcoming review point by point.[36] Delighted by Bundy's scathing assault (which he confessed to a "kind of savage pleasure" in composing), Yale's administration promptly ordered 2,000 reprints, which it handed out to inquiring alumni.[37]

Bundy's "intemperate performance" (as Buckley soon labeled it)[38] was but one cloudburst in a torrent of vituperation that rained down upon the young Yale graduate in the months ahead. Even today, nearly six decades later, one is startled by the vehemence of many of the rejoinders to Buckley's criticisms. In the *Yale Daily News*, professor of religion Theodore M. Greene—one of Buckley's targets—called the book "pure fascism": "he would transform Yale into the most dogmatic, hidebound institute for orthodox propaganda."[39] In the *Saturday Review,* Chad Walsh asserted that what Buckley "really proposes is that the alumni of Yale should turn themselves into a politburo, and control the campus exactly as the Kremlin controls the intellectual life of Russia."[40] A reviewer in the *New Republic* accused Buckley of advocating "precisely" the "methods" used in Fascist Italy, Nazi Germany, and Communist Russia.[41] A reviewer in the *Journal of Bible and Religion* worried that Buckley's book might become "the campaign pamphlet of a totalitarian movement to assume control of all American higher education."[42] Irate reviewers compared him to Torquemada, Savanarola, and Joseph Goebbels (Adolf Hitler's minister of propaganda).

At Yale itself, a professor of economics assailed the book as "authoritarian" in its educational theory and as "scurrilous and boorish in its reference to individuals."[43] In *The Progressive*, Yale professor of law Fred Rodell, a militant liberal, called it (among other things) "dishonest," "balderdash," and a "barbarian bleat" by "one bigoted boy" against his alma mater.[44] In the scholarly *Yale Law Journal*, Vern Countryman—another very liberal Yale law professor—began his review this way: "Once upon a time there was a little boy named William Buckley. Although he was a little boy, he was much too big for his britches." In the ensuing twelve-page review essay, Countryman never again referred to Buckley by his surname. Instead, the professor condescendingly called him "Willie" and "little Willie."[45]

It was Frank Ashburn, however—respected headmaster of the Brooks School and a trustee of Yale University—who hurled the most sensational accusation. *God and Man at Yale*, he wrote in the *Saturday Review,* "stands as one of the most forthright, implacable, typical, and unscrupulously sincere examples of a return to authoritarianism that has appeared. . . . This book is one which has the glow of a fiery cross on a hillside at night. There will undoubtedly be robed figures who gather to it, but the robes will not be academic. They will cover the face."[46]

Why was the liberal reaction to *God and Man and Yale* so extravagantly antagonistic? Why the heated, even hysterical allusions to Nazis, the Spanish Inquisition, and the Ku Klux Klan? Why, in particular, in Buckley's later words, the "remarkably virulent" response by Yale itself?[47]

In the case of Yale's administration, the immediate motivation was financial. Shortly before *God and Man at Yale* was published, one of the university's trustees told John Chamberlain that the book would cost the institution a million dollars.[48] It was not an irrational apprehension. Buckley's treatise contained an explicit summons to Yale's alumni to rise up and assert control of their alma mater—and a stern warning that they should not "support" it if it encouraged values they deemed "inimical to the public welfare."[49] If Buckley's factual case against Yale's gained credence, the university might suffer a crippling decline in alumni giving.[50]

If Yale's administration feared a financial backlash, Yale's liberal professors (and, by extension, liberal and leftist professors elsewhere) feared something else: a loss of academic power—and conceivably employment— if Buckley's challenge to "academic freedom" and his theory of consumer (alumni) sovereignty took root. Again, this was not an entirely implausible specter. In 1951 and 1952 the Cold War against Communist Russia and China was raging. At home growing numbers of Americans, championed by Senator Joseph McCarthy (among others), feared that Communists and their fellow travelers had penetrated the U.S. government and other institutions, including the universities. At the University of California, professors had been required by authorities to sign "loyalty oaths" (swearing that they were not Communists) as a condition of holding their jobs. (One of the California dissenters who refused to sign—and was then fired—soon received an honorary degree from Yale.)[51] In this highly charged context, Buckley's stentorian call for new "value orthodoxy" at his alma mater—and for the dismissal of professors who deviated too far from it—seemed genuinely alarming. More irritating still to many liberal professors, "this little Neanderthaler" (as Countryman called him)[52] was mocking *their* "religion," *their* orthodoxy—the sacred creed of academic freedom—in the name of— of all people—the alumni. The alumni! It was a horrifying thought. Liberal academia was filled with *refugees* from the philistine world that alumni supposedly inhabited. If Buckley was disgusted by the perceived intolerance and hypocrisy of liberal Yale, many a liberal professor in 1952 was equally vexed by the perceived anti-intellectualism of "McCarthyite" America.

Even some Yale alumni shared this negative perception of their own fellow graduates. Not long after *God and Man at Yale* appeared, Buckley chanced to meet the Reverend Henry Sloan Coffin, chairman of Yale's alumni committee that had been set up to evaluate Yale's health (and refute Buckley's book). Said Coffin gruffly to his youthful nemesis: "Why do you want to turn over Yale education to a bunch of boobs?"[53]

The rancor of the controversy intensified further when some of Buckley's fiercest critics took aim at what they considered the key to the entire controversy: his Roman Catholicism.[54] To McGeorge Bundy, writing in the *Atlantic Monthly*, it seemed "very strange," even impudent, for an "ardent" Catholic like Buckley to "offer a *prescription*, pretending to speak for Yale's true religious tradition" (which was Protestant). It was "stranger still," Bundy added darkly, for Buckley to offer "no word or hint" in his book of his "special allegiance."[55] In a similar vein, Fred Rodell accused Buckley of dishonestly concealing his "very relevant church affiliation."[56] To Bundy there were "pronounced and well recognized differences between Protestant and Catholic views on education in America"—differences that disqualified Buckley from trying to reform historically Protestant Yale.[57]

Bundy's "religious" criticism of *God and Man at Yale* found echoes among Yale's defenders. According to Henry Sloan Coffin (a former president of Union Theological Seminary), Buckley's book was plainly "distorted by his Roman Catholic point of view." Yale—said Coffin—was a "Puritan and Protestant institution by its heritage." Buckley "should have attended Fordham or some similar [i.e., Catholic] institution."[58] Behind the scenes, Yale's president and his allies disparaged the book as the work of a Catholic zealot far outside Yale's Protestant mainstream.[59] In the words of one of President Griswold's closest associates: Buckley's proposed reforms would turn Yale into "a small town parochial academy."[60]

What was going on here? Why these angry allusions to Buckley's religious faith? In 1951, Yale had come far from its eighteenth-century origins as a college for Congregational ministers, but it remained generically Protestant in its ambience. To the mainline Protestant custodians of Yale's image and self-understanding, Buckley's untimely manifesto was a retrograde, Catholic attack on their cherished Protestant values: Protestants, they believed, stood for individual freedom of conscience (and its supposed derivative, academic freedom); Catholics stood for "indoctrination" and "a religion of external authority."[61] From this perspective, Buckley's appeal for a new "value orthodoxy" looked like nothing less than a disguised attempt to impose a "Catholic" model of education upon "Protestant" Yale.

It is difficult to know how deeply Yale's advocates believed this. Invoking anti-Catholic biases was an easy way to marginalize their accuser among most Yale alumni. But the early 1950s were not the post-Vatican II, ecumenical era with which we today are familiar. The late 1940s and early 1950s, in fact, were a time of considerable tension between Roman Catholics and other religious groups in the United States. These were the years when Francis Cardinal Spellman and Eleanor Roosevelt argued vehemently in public about government aid to parochial schools and when President James B. Conant of Harvard urged the abolition of all private schools in the country. This was the era when the philosopher Sidney Hook asserted that "there is no academic freedom in Catholic colleges."[62] Perhaps most revealing of the intellectual climate of this period was the publication in 1949 of Paul Blanshard's muckraking *American Freedom and Catholic Power*, which depicted the Roman Catholic Church hierarchy as an authoritarian threat to American liberty and democracy.[63] (Coincidentally, Blanshard's brother, who was not an orthodox Christian, taught philosophy at Yale; Buckley labeled him "an earnest and expansive atheist.")[64] Blanshard's bestselling broadside was hugely popular in liberal academic circles.[65]

It was into this stormy religious environment that Buckley strode in October 1951 with his stunning appeal for a creedal university.

Rather ironically, under the circumstances, Buckley soon found himself under attack from prominent Roman Catholics as well—not for his strictures on secularism in education but for the other foundation of his critique of Yale: his procapitalist, economic "individualism." Both *Commonweal* and *The Pilot* charged him with advocating socioeconomic "heresy." Catholic commentators claimed that his laissez faire economic philosophy flagrantly contravened the social teachings of the Church, as encapsulated in recent papal encyclicals.[66]

To Buckley, it must have seemed at times that most of the intelligentsia was against him. Pilloried by Bundy and others as a "violent," "unbalanced," and "twisted" ignoramus, and chastised by liberal Catholics as a heretic in his economics, the young author discovered that even some of his allies on the Right were less than enamored of his views. While *God and Man at Yale's* factual findings evoked many plaudits in conservative circles,[67] conservative academics were cool about his proposed cure. Friedrich Hayek, from whom Buckley badly wanted a blurb for the book, declined to give him one; the great economist objected strenuously to Buckley's chapter on academic freedom.[68] Russell Kirk, another rising conservative luminary, was also unpersuaded. In his book *Academic Freedom* (1955), he condemned Buckley's "individualism" as anti-Christian, and asserted that Buckley's "program of indoctrination" would be "ruinous to his aims": "the preservation of American religious faith, constitutional government, and free economic institutions." Attempting to steer clear both of "indoctrinators" and "doctrinaire liberals," Kirk asserted that Buckley's remedy would be "worse than the disease."[69] Other conservatives expressed similar qualms.[70]

Both then and later, Buckley fought back hard against his critics. To those who furiously accused him of advocating "fascism," he rejoined that "irresponsible, irreproachable education by an academic elite" was itself a kind of fascism.[71] What, he wondered, was "fascistic" about "a summons to free citizens freely associated, exercising no judicial or legislative power, to communicate their ideals at a private college through the appropriate selection of texts and teachers"? What was authoritarian about the ideals he professed and "sought to serve": "the ideals of a minimalist state, and deference to a transcendent order"?[72] He continued to hold that "academic freedom" was the doctrine "that most successfully impedes the growth of Christianity in precisely the culture where it could most efficaciously take root and spread, the student mind."[73]

As for supposedly slyly and dishonestly concealing his Catholicism, he insisted that the matter was irrelevant. In his book he had evaluated Yale's religious condition using a carefully nondenominational understanding of Christianity. Moreover, he had submitted a draft of his chapter on religion in advance to an interfaith group of religious counselors at Yale, every one of whom had agreed that there was nothing peculiarly Catholic about his treatment of the subject.[74] As for the "fashionable Catholic journals" which had condemned him as a "heretic," the antistatist libertarian was unrepentant. Too many "Christian modernists," he later observed, believed that "the road to Christianity on earth lies through the federal government."[75]

Nor did Buckley back down after the bitter brouhaha subsided. When he published a twenty-fifth anniversary edition of *God and Man at Yale* in the mid-1970s, he prepared a comprehensive new introduction in which he again lambasted Yale's loss of "mission" and rebutted the arguments and slurs of his enemies. "I cannot come to terms," he confessed, "with a university that accepts the philosophical proposition that it is there for the purpose of presenting 'all sides' of 'any issue' as impartially and as reasonably as possible."[76] Again and again in his later years, he insisted that the "teaching part of a college" should be "animated by certain values," and that the alumni "should have the final voice on the values that a college seeks to promote and cherish." It was "nihilistic," he averred, "to assume that all values are exactly equal, which is what the concept of academic freedom tells you. . . ." If any university that he had attended had on its faculty "more than a fair share of professors who taught error," he remarked in 1978, he would withhold his financial contributions and "even campaign aggressively against it."[77]

In 1952, after more than six months of acerbic commotion, the tempest over *God and Man at Yale* tapered off. But the fault lines persisted, with long-term consequences. For Yale itself, the immediate consequences were surprisingly few. Contrary to its panicky fears (and Buckley's hopes), there was no insurrection by the Yale alumni to reform their alma mater along Buckleyite lines. "Yale's challenge," Buckley wrote sardonically, "has always been to flatter its alumni while making certain they should continue impotent," and so far as he was concerned, it succeeded.[78] What another conservative rebel, M. Stanton Evans (Yale class of 1955), called "the monumental lethargy of the alumni" seemed undisturbed.[79] In the fiscal year in which Buckley's book appeared, alumni contributions to Yale actually increased.[80]

The failure of Yale's alumni to mobilize and "proceed to govern the university"[81] exposed a serious chink in Buckley's armor. What if the alumni were not reliable reformers? What if they bought into the ideology of academic freedom and the anything-can-be-taught practices of "*laissez-faire* education"? Even worse, what if, over time, a majority of graduates of Yale and other elite universities turned out to be secular, collectivistic liberals?

In his book and elsewhere, Buckley conceded that if secular collectivism was what Yale's alumni truly wanted, that was "their privilege." In that case, he said, he would have "nothing more to say."[82] But in 1951, at least, he considered Yale's existing educational "emphases" to be "directly opposed to those of her alumni."[83] As the Cold War era of the 1950s gave way to the tumultuous sixties, he had reason to reconsider. In 1968, he ran as an insurgent conservative for a seat on the Yale Corporation (board of trustees). The contest aroused tremendous excitement. Yale alumni voted in record numbers. Buckley lost decisively—to a liberal.[84]

So in 1951–52 Yale repulsed the perceived Torquemada at its gates. Outwardly, at least, little changed in New Haven. For Buckley, however, the consequences of the battle were both immediate and enormous. With an inadvertent assist from Yale's wrathful "apparatus," a star was born: Within weeks he was a national celebrity. Much more importantly, a *conservative* star was born: The controversy catapulted the debonair debater to the forefront of the emerging conservative intellectual and journalistic community in the United States. Without the *succès de scandale* of *God and Man at Yale*, Buckley might never have successfully founded the conservative *National Review* in 1955. It quickly became the preeminent conservative publication in the United States. Without Buckley, the movement might have floundered indefinitely in its search for sophisticated leadership.

In 1982 John Chamberlain, who had lent his considerable prestige to Buckley's maiden effort, observed that Buckley, "more than any single figure, has made conservatism a respectable force in American life."[85] Ideas have consequences, and so do books. *God and Man at Yale* set Buckley on the road to becoming arguably the most important public intellectual in American life in the past half century.

For Buckley, then, despite the immediate pain, the outcome was exceedingly positive. Not so, at first, for the two men who had helped to launch his intrepid volume. After John Chamberlain contributed his supportive introduction, he never again received an invitation to write for the prestigious *Yale Review*, to which he had contributed for many years. The mild mannered man of letters was "nearly ostracized" by the Yale academic community.[86] Henry Regnery also felt the sting of those who (in Buckley's words) "preached the virtues of an open mind."[87] Angered by Regnery's dissemination of *God and Man at Yale*, the Great Books Foundation at the University of Chicago canceled his lucrative contract to publish its Great Books series.[88] Chamberlain was unfazed and later wrote regularly for Buckley's magazine. Regnery, too, recovered and became for a generation the leading publisher of conservative books in the United States.

God and Man at Yale had even broader consequences for American conservatism. Although not the first twentieth-century book to voice conservative criticisms of liberalism in higher education,[89] it was the first to become a *cause célèbre* and bestseller. Six decades later *God and Man at Yale* remains the *locus classicus* for what is now a burgeoning genre of conservative social criticism: the exposure of liberal bias and hypocrisy in American higher education. Soon Buckley's volume had successors and imitators in books and articles with titles like *Collectivism on the Campus* and "God and

Woman at Vassar."[90] In more recent years, books like *Poisoned Ivy* (a book about Dartmouth College), *Tenured Radicals*, and *Illiberal Education* have owed something of their inspiration to Buckley's pioneering exposé.[91]

God and Man at Yale and the ensuing brouhaha had another, more subtle influence on conservative intellectuals: It introduced a permanently populist dimension into their critique of academe. Although conservatives have long decried the decadence and degradation of standards in higher education, it was Buckley who first argued that the problem inhered in a power structure controlled by a self-serving elite. In 1951 he referred to it as the "Apparatus." The epithet of choice, for conservatives, soon became the "liberal establishment": preaching freedom but practicing a monopoly; preaching tolerance but all too often willing to demonize conservative dissenters as bigoted and "fascist." Although Buckley himself was a highly intelligent individual, the *God and Man at Yale* experience gave him a lifelong distrust of liberal intellectual arrogance: "these haughty totalitarians who refuse to permit the American people to supervise their own destiny."[92] It was Buckley who in 1963 mordantly remarked: "I am obliged to confess that I should sooner live in a society governed by the first two thousand names in the Boston telephone directory than in a society governed by the two thousand faculty members of Harvard University."[93]

Buckley's proposed solution to liberal academic malfeasance, however, never caught on. With the partial exception, in recent years, of Dartmouth College (where conservative alumni have elected several of their number to the college's governing board), there have been few, if any, successful efforts by conservative college graduates to exercise effective supervision over their alma maters. In the years since 1951, conservatives and libertarians have developed other strategies to counter the perceived liberal stranglehold on higher education. They have tried going around entrenched faculties and biased courses by circulating conservative literature through organizations like the Intercollegiate Studies Institute and the Collegiate Network of alternative student newspapers. Here and there they have created beachheads in the form of academic centers at certain universities; the James Madison Program in American Ideals and Institutions at Princeton is a notable example. They have built an impressive array of think tanks in Washington, D.C., and elsewhere, where conservatively inclined scholars can pursue advanced studies—and influence public policy—outside the inhospitable confines of academic institutions. They have helped to build the National Association of Scholars into a powerful voice for "reasoned scholarship" and standards of excellence in colleges and universities. They have established the Foundation for Individuals Rights in Education (FIRE), which has come to the legal defense of college students oppressed by the ravages of political correctness. And they have cultivated such faith-friendly outposts as Grove City College—an institution William F. Buckley Jr. admired.[94]

Nearly sixty years after its publication, *God and Man at Yale*'s historical significance is clear. For Yale, the book offered an unwelcome snapshot of an institution in slow recessional from the Christian matrix formed by earlier generations. The ensuing altercation was a noisy episode in the creeping secularization and de-Protestantization of America's elite universities, a process definitively traced by George Marsden in *The Soul of The American University*.[95] For Buckley and his fellow conservatives, it was a critical moment in forging an intellectual resistance to these and other trends sanctioned by the statist and secularizing ideology called modern liberalism.

Nearly sixty years later, *God and Man at Yale* has gone through three distinct editions and continues to sell: quite an achievement for a *livre de circonstance* in 1951. But then, as events proved, it was not a *livre de circonstance* at all. Today the book lives on because its courageous author, in his admittedly "callow" way,[96] raised enduring questions concerning faith, freedom, and education that continue to roil American public life. When all is said and done, what is the purpose of a college or university? Who should define and oversee the fulfillment of its goals? Its faculty? Its students? Its administrators? The parents and alumni who foot most of the bills? The federal government, which now, nearly everywhere, intrudes?

And what are the solemn responsibilities of a university—to its scholars, to its matriculants, to its heritage, and to the surrounding civil society that permits it to be free?

Perhaps the final lesson of *God and Man at Yale* is this. Just as it has been said that war is too important to leave to the generals, so is education too serious a pursuit to entrust to any single, unaccountable authority.

18

William F. Buckley Jr. the Writer

This is my introduction to William F. Meehan III, ed., William F. Buckley Jr.: A Bibliography *(ISI Books, 2002).*

Every year in the United States more than 60,000 books are published in the English language, along with millions of articles in literally thousands of periodicals. How does one "access" (in the current jargon) this relentless torrent of new knowledge? The Internet helps, but it hardly suffices. For most students and scholars, it is still necessary to turn to those unpretentious instruments of research known as bibliographies.

We live in a Golden Age of Bibliography, as a quick trip to an academic library will demonstrate. Go to the reference room, and there you will find an ever-increasing array of bibliographic finding aids on nearly every subject imaginable. Only rarely, though, will these volumes be devoted to the works of a single human being. And for good reason: very few people write enough—and enough that is worthwhile—to warrant the labor of a formal compilation.

In the bibliography at hand we have a luminous exception to this rule. For more than fifty years now, William F. Buckley Jr. has been a buoyant presence in American public life. Editor, debater, columnist, lecturer, television host, he has been a peerless and indefatigable champion of the conservative cause. His persona, vocabulary, and voice must be among the most recognizable in the entire Western world.

Throughout these decades Buckley has been a prolific practitioner of the written as well as the spoken word. Just how prolific, William Meehan's bibliography makes astonishingly clear. Consider a few statistics gleaned from the pages that follow. Between 1951 and the end of the year 2000, William F. Buckley Jr. wrote and published: 34 nonfiction books; 15 books of fiction; 81 book reviews; 56 introductions, prefaces, and forewords to other people's books; 222 obituary essays; more than 800 editorials, articles, and remarks in *National Review*; more than 350 articles in periodicals other than *National Review*; and more than 5,000 syndicated newspaper columns, at the rate of two or three per week.

Nor is this all that he has committed to paper. For years he received hundreds of letters a week and answered them. By now he may well have composed more correspondence than any American who has ever lived. At Yale University, where his papers are deposited, his *unpublished* files (mostly incoming and outgoing correspondence) comprise nearly a thousand hefty boxes.

The magnitude of Buckley's writing achievement becomes even more astounding when we remember its context. In the past five decades Buckley has scarcely been a cloistered wordsmith. His daily writing has occurred in the midst of myriad grueling responsibilities, including: editing a national opinion magazine; hosting the longest-running show in the history of public television (1,429 separate programs in 33 years); and lecturing on the public platform from coast to coast (at the rate of 70 or more lectures a year for years). Not to mention such "minor" diversions along the way as running for mayor of New York City; serving on the U.S. delegation to the United Nations; attending to family and business interests; playing a musical instrument at a near-professional level of competence; and sailing across the Atlantic and Pacific oceans on his yachts.

How has he done it? Obviously Buckley is a rapid and ready writer, a fact to which I myself can attest. In the mid-1970s I had an appointment to see him at *National Review's* headquarters in New York. As it happened, Bill was running a bit late that day. When the appointed hour arrived, he leaned out of his office and said: "I have a column to write. See you in twenty minutes."

At that point Buckley was still using a typewriter for his compositions. But within a decade or so he had become an aficionado of computers, as I again can attest. About a dozen years ago, during a telephone conversation, he suddenly asked me whether I was using a personal computer for my

149

own writing. No, I admitted. He was amazed. "George!" he exclaimed. "The computer is the greatest invention since—the pencil!"

But innate verbal virtuosity and the wonders of word processing cannot begin to explain Buckley's prodigious literary output. He was, after all, churning out a stream of polished prose long before word processors were invented. Closer to the crux of the matter, I think, is something else: Despite the frenetic condition of "overdrive" that has characterized his lifestyle since youth, Buckley is a writer of extraordinary discipline. As Dr. Meehan observes in his preface, in thirty-nine years of writing a twice- and thrice-weekly newspaper column (that's thirty-nine *years*), Buckley has missed his filing deadline exactly four times. In each instance it was because of illness. It is a feat fit for inclusion in the *Guinness Book of World Records*. One wonders whether he somewhere discovered and took to heart the aphorism of the Victorian novelist Anthony Trollope: "There is no greater human bliss than twelve hours of work, and only six hours in which to do it."

Yet even self-discipline cannot entirely account for Buckley's productivity as a writer—certainly not if the word "discipline" evokes an image of doggedness and strain. Buckley's workload may be heavy and importunate, but his resultant prose is neither labored nor dull. His is not the compulsive writing of a workaholic. Indeed, one does not sense while reading it that its author is at work at all.

And here, I think, we reach the essence of the issue. Vice President Richard Cheney recently remarked that you do not experience stress in what you love to do. Perhaps this is Buckley's secret also. If—as someone has said—Toryism is enjoyment, then Bill Buckley is the quintessential Tory.

But of course it is not just Buckley's productivity that we celebrate in this comprehensive bibliography. It is the substance and distinctive style of his written work. And this leads us to the fundamental premise of the volume that Dr. Meehan has assembled: namely, that the contents therein deserve to be consulted—not just now, not just for a season, but on into the indefinite future. A bibliography, by its very nature, affirms that its contents are *not* ephemeral, that they are and will be worth reading for a long time to come.

For three reasons Buckley's oeuvre merits such an affirmation. First, his career has almost precisely coincided with two of the most fateful dramas in the history of Western civilization: the struggle against totalitarian communism abroad and the concurrent struggle to bolster the foundations of liberty at home. For half a century, these have been the overarching issues of our public discourse and the defining themes of Buckley's own writings. It has been an ideological age in which words and ideas have supremely mattered. To these great debates Buckley has memorably contributed. He has done so, moreover, not as an aloof and solitary observer but as a paladin of organized conservatism: as a preeminent voice, that is, for millions of Americans. When the history of the second half of the twentieth century is written, wise scholars will study his writings as an invaluable guide to the intellectual life of our times.

Secondly, Buckley's commentaries will survive because they encompass much more than the epiphenomena of politics. In his fifty-plus years in the public arena, the most diverse subjects have engaged his curiosity: religion, music, literature, art, philosophy, pedagogy, language, sailing—in a word, the vast cultural matrix out of which our political life evolves. Like his friend and near contemporary Tom Wolfe, Buckley is a penetrating critic of our peculiar manners and morals. Long after the political minutiae of yesteryear fade from memory, we will, I predict, continue to be fascinated by Buckley's observations on the way we lived then.

Above all, Buckley's works are destined to endure because their enduring subject is people and because their author is a person of singular joie de vivre. If Buckley, like a latter-day Walter Lippmann, had spent the past fifty years declaiming loftily about Issues of the Day, his prose would eventually be forgotten, save by a historian or two. But Buckley has not primarily been a policy analyst or abstract theorist. He has been, rather, a cheerful controversialist and, in the process, a collector of an incredible gallery of friends. Even his political antagonists are his friends.

Eventually historians of our era will want to understand not only the weighty issues we debated but the character and personality of the debaters. To Buckley they will turn happily for insight. For not only has he known and befriended most of the principals; he has studied and written about them, with a keenness and vivifying wit that will long be savored.

Nowhere is his gift for personal portraiture better displayed than in the 222 obituary essays that Dr. Meehan has catalogued—appraisals composed under acute time pressure and often amidst feelings of personal loss. A very interesting book could be compiled from these columns. I hope that Bill finds the time someday to do so.

For now, however, we shall be content with the several thousand literary works that he *has* created—and with the knowledge that he continues to produce and plan still more. Because of William Meehan's efforts, high school students, college students, graduate students, teachers, professors, and others now have an excellent entree into the life and times of a remarkable American.

To Dr. Meehan, then, we give our thanks for a meticulous and timely piece of scholarship. And to William F. Buckley Jr., still active in his mid-seventies, we offer our gratitude and the whispered words: "Write on!"

19

Creation Story:
Building the House of Conservatism

This is a review of Niels Bjerre-Poulsen's Right Face: Organizing the American Conservative Movement 1945–65, *published in 2002. My appraisal appeared in the May 5, 2003, issue of* National Review.

In the ever-quickening tumult of current political debate, it is easy to forget that American conservatism has become middle-aged. Fifty years ago this spring, Russell Kirk published *The Conservative Mind*. Forty-three years ago next September, Young Americans for Freedom was born. Later this year the Intercollegiate Studies Institute will celebrate its fiftieth anniversary. In two years *National Review* will do the same.

What happens when a political movement reaches maturity? For those within its ranks, the impulse grows to proclaim success and salute its intrepid founders. For those outside its ranks, passion yields to curiosity: How, they wonder, did such a phenomenon come into prominence and power? In short, present-mindedness gives way slowly to self-consciousness and to the historian's quest for deeper understanding.

So it is with contemporary American conservatism. Long neglected by most serious scholars, conservatism in the last half decade has suddenly become a historiographical frontier.

Among the new generation of historians who have discovered conservatism from the outside is Niels Bjerre-Poulsen, an associate professor of American studies at Copenhagen Business School. Like most of his confreres, Bjerre-Poulsen is less interested in conservatism's intellectual history than in its "political mobilization." Conservative ideology, that is, is less fascinating to him than the vehicles by which this ideology was carried into the political arena. In *Right Face*, he tells the story of how, in the first two decades after World War II, a "would-be political elite" of conservatives set out to "institutionalize their political ideas" and create a powerful "network" of influences and advocacy.

And what a story it is. In the late 1940s and 1950s, the American Right was a hodgepodge of uncoordinated intellectual and political figures—religious traditionalists and doctrinaire classical liberals, business tycoons and zealous ex-Communists, leftover isolationists and crusading Cold Warriors, near-anarchists and converts to Catholicism, learned college professors and rambunctious McCarthyites—united principally in their opposition to communism and to Franklin Roosevelt's New Deal. How to forge out of such discordant elements an effective resistance to their "collectivist" enemies?

As Bjerre-Poulsen explains, the process unfolded on essentially two fronts. In the 1950s, conservative leaders concentrated on developing an infrastructure of journals and related transmission belts for conservative discourse. Here *National Review*, founded in 1955, was preeminent. In its first decade or so of existence, NR—under William F. Buckley Jr., James Burnham, Frank Meyer, and William Rusher—functioned as the general staff of the conservative movement, as its clearinghouse of news and ideas, and increasingly as its gatekeeper and arbiter of respectability. Without the intellectual coherence and camaraderie supplied by its leading journal, the conservative movement would not have become what it aspired to be: a political force determined to put its ideas into action.

Intellectual consolidation was Phase One. Phase Two commenced a few years later. In 1960 Buckley and his allies founded Young Americans for Freedom, an invaluable source of talent for future battles and future conservative leadership. In 1962 came the creation of the New York Conservative Party in the very belly of the liberal beast. Above all (and this forms the bulk of Bjerre-Poulsen's story), between 1960 and 1964 enthusiastic and disciplined conservative activists successfully captured the biggest political vehicle of all—the Republican Party—in their drive to nominate Barry Goldwater for the presidency.

Bjerre-Poulsen clearly has a multifaceted tale to tell. One theme that vividly emerges from it is the many pitfalls that conservatives had to overcome in their struggle to build a viable counterestablishment. Some conflicts were philosophical: the enduring tension between libertarians and traditionalists. Some were geopolitical and strategic: the residual isolationism of the

Old Right versus the Cold War interventionism of the New. Some were temperamental and tactical: between elitists who saw themselves as an antipolitical Remnant and populists who wanted to rouse the "silent majority."

Time and again these difference of perspective clashed: in polemics at and around *National Review*; in power struggles at *Human Events* and *The Freeman*; in the pitched battle at the Republican national convention of 1952; and in the ambivalent response of conservative intellectuals to Senator Joseph McCarthy. The early attempts to create a conservative community were fraught with strife. Nevertheless, what Bjerre-Poulsen narrates is mainly a success story. As he makes clear in a brief epilogue on conservatism from 1965 to the present, the Goldwater campaign was not the beginning of the end; it was, for embattled conservatives, the end of the beginning.

All this and more Bjerre-Poulsen covers with clarity and insight. He is particularly effective in linking the internal history of *Human Events* and *The Freeman* to the larger ideological rifts within the Right in the first postwar decade. He notes astutely how McCarthyism ushered in a more majoritarian consciousness among conservatives and how McCarthyite anticommunism served as a bridge between former isolationists and emerging Cold Warriors. He recounts how Buckley and *National Review* dealt with the dilemma posed by the rise of the John Birch Society. He discloses the catalytic, behind-the-scenes achievements of conservatism's PR guru, Marvin Liebman. He deftly illuminates the surprising friction that arose between Barry Goldwater and his conservative kingmakers in 1963–64.

Indeed, after reading this book some may wonder whether conservatives were prudent to put so many eggs in the reluctant Goldwater's basket in the years before his presidential run. Their campaign to secure Goldwater's nomination was brilliant, but (as Bjerre-Poulsen shows) the campaign's chosen vessel proved to be flawed. The conservatives constructed their "network," and it survived the debacle of Goldwater's defeat. Still, as conservatives ruefully learned, infrastructure alone is not enough unless it produces sound leaders.

But if Bjerre-Poulsen's book is by and large a story of success, its tone is by no means triumphant. In his epilogue he insists that in the years since 1980 (and 1994) no conservative "revolution" has "swept the country." Conservatism, he acknowledges, has become "institutionalized and professionalized." It has held onto its power base in the Republican Party. Its organizational work has been "a major success." But it has not, he says, replaced "the New Deal order," nor has it yet devised a "coherent political program" capable of winning "sustained" victories at the polls.

Bjerre-Poulsen is also highly skeptical of the "fusionist" brand of conservatism (long associated with *National Review*) that endeavored to reconcile libertarian and traditionalist visions of the good society. A true fusion of these perspectives, he claims, never happened in the 1950s and 1960s: The conservative coalition "remained a shotgun marriage" held together "almost entirely" by antipathy to "New Deal liberalism."

Many conservatives will strongly contest this categorical dismissal—at the level of everyday experience, if not of abstract theory. Talk to an average conservative today and you will likely find a harmonious mix of libertarian and traditionalist sentiments. Fusionism remains the de facto conservative consensus. But Bjerre-Poulsen is probably correct to note that, since the 1970s, organized libertarianism and organized traditionalism have increasingly gone their separate ways. What this portends for conservatism's future as a coalition is problematic.

Bjerre-Poulsen's judgment on these points raises the issue of his own angle of vision toward his subject. As with so many historians who are now writing about conservatism, this Danish scholar's political sympathies appear to lie on the left. Occasionally these biases surface. Thus he refers to the Communist subversion controversy of the late 1940s and early 1950s as the "second Red Scare": a tendentious term employed by some historians to connect the episode with the discredited Red Scare of 1919–20. (The very word "scare," of course, carries the pejorative message that anti-Communist concerns at the time were groundless.) Similarly, he repeatedly labels McCarthyism a "witch-hunt," again suggesting by his terminology that the furor over communism in America in the early Cold War lacked any valid foundation. Bjerre-Poulsen does not argue this point; he simply seems to assume that it is self-evident.

He is more overtly critical of conservatives when he analyzes their response to the civil rights movement in the late 1950s and 1960s. At one point he describes conservatives' constitutional objections as "in most instances . . . sheer hypocrisy."

Fortunately—whether one agrees with him or not—these lapses into judgmentalism are infrequent and generally unobtrusive. Nor does his opining emanate altogether from one direction. He is pointedly unimpressed by the efforts of certain left-of-center social scientists in the 1950s to depict the resurgent Right as a form of social pathology. While Bjerre-Poulsen is unafraid to evaluate his subject, he does not (for the most part) argue with it—a welcome sign of intellectual maturity. Like most of the younger historians (including liberal ones) who are now tilling the field of conservative history, Bjerre-Poulsen has sufficient detachment to treat his topic respectfully. This is a mighty step forward.

In essence, *Right Face* is a concise, analytical survey of a twenty-year struggle by conservative activists to establish a sustainable beachhead in American public life. As a survey, the book cannot cover individual episodes in substantial detail. For a fuller rendering of the 1964 Goldwater campaign, readers will want to consult Rick Perlstein's *Before the Storm*; for the story of YAF, Gregory L. Schneider's *Cadres for Conservatism*; for the New York Conservative Party, George J. Marlin's *Fighting the Good Fight*; for broader accounts of conservatism's political trajectory, Lee Edwards's *The Conservative Revolution* and Jonathan M. Schoenwald's *A Time for Choosing*.

But what *Right Face* necessarily lacks in narrative depth, it more than compensates for in breadth and incisiveness. Bjerre-Poulsen's compact but comprehensive volume is a worthwhile addition to the historiography of American conservatism. And he underscores a valuable point. Conservatives like to say that ideas have consequences, and it is true. Every institution chronicled in this book was the embodiment of ideas that eventually blossomed into organized political activity. Ideas are crucial in motivating people; "consequences," after all, do not just happen by chance. From 1945 to 1964 and beyond, the power of intellectual conviction propelled countless conservatives into self-sacrificing action year in and year out, in fair weather and foul. As the conservative movement of 2003 enters a comfortable middle age, this is a history lesson worth remembering.

20

Jeffrey Hart's History of *National Review*

My appraisal of Professor Hart's book appeared in the January 30, 2006, issue of National Review *under the title "Re: Us."*

Fifty years ago last autumn, William F. Buckley Jr. launched a "journal of opinion" for "radical conservatives." *National Review*, he announced in its opening issue, stood "athwart history, yelling Stop." Fifty years later, his daring venture had not only defied the tides of history but had altered their course.

How did this happen? Like many another little magazine, it could easily have foundered on the shoals of ideological disaster. It could have become a voice of carping irrelevance, the plaything of an isolated sect. Instead, it grew to refine and then to redefine the mainstream of American public life. In *The Making of the American Conservative Mind*, Jeffrey Hart aims to tell us why.

In many ways Hart is ideally equipped for this task. A reader of *National Review* since its inception, and one of its senior editors since 1969, he has both observed and participated in its development. Along the way he has come to know nearly all the intellectuals who put their imprint on its pages. His appraisals, in this book, of such men as Russell Kirk, Frank Meyer, Willmoore Kendall, and James Burnham are astute and illuminating. For these alone his book should not be missed.

The Making of the American Conservative Mind is not a formal, scholarly history. Part chronicle, part memoir, it might best be described as a rich, discursive meditation on *National Review*'s encounter with the world. How Buckley's magazine dealt with the John Birch Society, Barry Goldwater, Richard Nixon, Ronald Reagan, and much more: All are part of Hart's kaleidoscopic narrative.

His book is, however, a meditation with a theme. For Hart, *National Review*'s half-century of public engagement conveys a lesson. There is, he avers, a moral to the story. As Hart sees it, the history of *National Review* is a "Quest Narrative: the quest for a politically viable and thoughtful American conservatism." In pursuit of this objective, he says, the magazine has repeatedly oscillated between an "ideal right-wing Paradigm and realistic Possibility." Time and again it has been forced to choose between ideological purity and what Buckley called "the politics of reality." This enduring tension between Idea (or desire) and Actuality was related, in Hart's telling, to another question: Just what kind of journal of opinion did *National Review* aspire to be—the voice of a backwater "bayou" or a guide for the national "mainstream"? Did the journal wish to convert the liberal establishment it steadily assailed or to destroy it and replace it with something else? Did it hope to speak to an educated elite or to the "silent majority"?

In shaping the magazine's outlook and message, no one (save Buckley) was more crucial, according to Hart, than James Burnham. Readers of *National Review* know Burnham as the magazine's foreign-policy guru and author of a regular column on "The Third World War" (i.e., the Cold War). But as Hart demonstrates, the former Trotskyist's influence at the magazine was even greater than those roles might suggest. Tirelessly he pushed it, both in style and substance, toward the "mainstream," and away from what he deemed to be dogmatic posturing. Quietly and persistently, he lobbied for what Hart calls "prudential," "flexible," and "strategic" conservatism, in opposition to the stubborn, sectarian "utopianism" of some of his colleagues. At a time when many at NR were ardent Goldwaterites, Burnham pined for Nelson Rockefeller for president. The feisty journal never went that far, but Burnham succeeded (says Hart) in convincing Buckley that *National Review*, to be influential, must always maneuver within sight of the political center.

Burnham is clearly Hart's hero, a man he hails as "indispensable" to *National Review*'s success. Not surprisingly, Hart examines the magazine's encounter with "actuality" through Burnhamite lenses. He argues, for instance, that *National Review* was quite wrong about its early bête noire, Dwight D. Eisenhower, whom the magazine refused to endorse for reelection in 1956. Relying upon recent revisionist historical scholarship, Hart lauds Eisenhower as a model of "prudential conservatism"—and as one of the three most successful presidents of the twentieth century. Similarly, he interprets *National Review*'s obstreperous defense of Joseph McCarthy as an early episode in the magazine's "recurrent struggles between wish and reality."

More controversially, Hart bluntly accuses the contemporary right-to-life movement—an integral part of conservative reality since the 1970s—of "utopian," even "Jacobinical" tendencies. Invoking the sainted name of Edmund Burke, he asserts that a complete ban on abortion in America will never happen. The *Roe v. Wade* decision, he says, and the "women's revolution" that preceded it reflect "a relentlessly changing social actuality" that simply cannot be revoked by legal fiat. The women of America, he opines, "will not surrender control of their reproductive capacity."

Curiously, Hart, a Roman Catholic convert, never really addresses the morality of abortion. Instead, he offers William James's "philosophy of experience" as a "sounder guide to morality" than natural-law thinking and appears to counsel accommodation to putatively irreversible social trends.

Summing up his excursion through *National Review*'s history, Hart asserts that the magazine taught America conservatives "how to think"—that is, how to argue their case in the arena and avoid the pitfalls of doctrinaire "utopianism." On the whole he is proud of the magazine's extraordinary achievements. It courageously resisted the "hard utopianism" of the Communists and the "soft utopianism" of the liberals. It defended the validity of the nation-state and the need for national defense. It championed free-market economics and successfully subverted socialist orthodoxy.

But Hart is critical, too, and worried. Over the years, in his opinion, *National Review* has neglected aesthetic issues and conservation of the natural environment. Above all, he is dismayed by what he regards as a rising tide of *unconservative* ideology and sentiment on the American right—a tide embodied, for him, in the "hard Wilsonian" foreign policy of George W. Bush and the idealistic fervor of his Evangelical allies.

This leads us to the moral of Hart's story, which erupts with muffled fury toward the end of his book. "Ideology," he warns, "is always wrong because it edits reality and paralyzes thought." Wilsonianism, he adds—whether "hard" or "soft"—is a "snare and a delusion" in foreign policy and "far from conservative" in spirit. And Protestant Evangelicalism—a crucial element in today's conservative coalition—he deems inherently "antitraditional" and not reliably conservative at all. About the faith-driven "actuality" of contemporary conservatism, Hart, the disciple of Burnham, is an unhappy man.

In part his discomfiture illustrates how profoundly the landscape of American conservatism has changed since 1955. In *National Review*'s first twenty-five years, conservatives were a defiant minority comprising three elements: libertarians, traditionalists, and Cold Warriors. Since 1980 two more have come aboard: the neoconservatives and the interfaith Religious Right. During *National Review*'s second quarter-century, intellectual conservatism has become more majoritarian and less "aristocratic" in its self-understanding, and more hopeful, even ambitious, in its bearing. Meanwhile conservative institutions, activists, and culture warriors have proliferated from the Beltway to the blogosphere. Although *National Review* remains highly influential in this new environment (and increasingly so through National Review Online), its original role as the movement's tutor and counselor—its Burnhamite role—is no longer uncontested. And Burnham-style "strategic" conservatism—so dominant during the magazine's "outsider years"—has given way to a politics of greater expectations.

What, then, should we make of Hart's interpretation of NR's first half-century? Certainly the tug-of-war between ideals and "actuality" has been *one* theme in *National Review*'s history, and one worth pondering during our current discontents. As a corrective to ideological hubris, Hart's morality tale is instructive. But prudential conservatism teaches more than one lesson. "The politics of reality," unchecked, can be a snare. Realism itself can become a confining ideology. Adjustment to "actuality" carries its own peril in a too-easy assumption that the future must always resemble the present.

Hart extols Ronald Reagan as a prudent conservative, and Reagan certainly was not reckless. But he was also an optimistic, proactive, and quintessentially *idealistic* conservative, determined to alter the reality of the Cold War. And he did.

American conservatism at its Reaganite best is a combination of impulses—of realism and idealism, of prudence and hope, of worldly sobriety and faith-based aspiration. If *National Review* can keep this reality in focus, it will have much to teach us during its next fifty years.

But first, let us pause and enjoy Hart's spirited stroll down memory lane.

21

Family Album:
National Review at Work and Play

My review of Linda Bridges' and John R. Coyne's book Strictly Right: William F. Buckley Jr. and the American Conservative Movement *appeared in the May 28, 2007, issue of* National Review. *It appears here with a few minor revisions.*

In recent years books about *National Review* have become a cottage industry. In 2004 came William F. Buckley Jr.'s literary autobiography, *Miles Gone By*. In 2005, his sister Priscilla's *Living It Up at* National Review. In 2006, Jeffrey Hart's volume *The Making of the American Conservative Mind*. This wave is no effusion of nostalgia. *National Review* is now regarded as the most influential political magazine of the past half century. And who knows its history better than those who made it?

In *Strictly Right* Linda Bridges and John R. Coyne Jr. have added a lively contribution to this genre. They are well placed and qualified for the task. Bridges has worked at *National Review* since college, and is now an editor at large. Coyne is a former associate editor, feature writer, and Washington correspondent for the magazine. Both are *National Review* insiders, with an insider's feel for the dynamics of the enterprise.

Strictly Right is partly an informal history *of National Review*, partly a biographical portrait of its founding editor, and partly a chronicle of modern American conservatism. But whereas Bill and Priscilla Buckley have written sparkling memoirs, and Jeffrey Hart a provocative intellectual history, Coyne and Bridges have successfully done something else. They have compiled, as it were, a behind the-scenes family album, filled with glimpses of the NR family at work and play.

From its inception *National Review* has always had some of the earmarks of a family business. William F. Buckley Jr., the founder and editor, owned the entire voting stock. Early on he hired his sister Priscilla, an accomplished journalist, to provide ballast. Eventually she became managing editor, a post she held for more than a quarter of a century. Other Buckley siblings— notably Aloise Buckley Heath—made their appearance in the magazine's pages. And Bill's race for the New York City mayoralty in 1965 paved the way for his campaign manager—his brother Jim—to enter politics himself and become in 1970, "the sainted junior senator from New York."

Successful families require hands-on fathers, and *National Review* in its youth was no exception. Not quite thirty years old when the magazine's first issue appeared, Bill Buckley seemed miscast for his role. The brash and dashing polemicist from Yale did not exactly resemble Robert Young in *Father Knows Best*. But precisely because he was younger than most of his colleagues (and controlled the voting stock), Buckley was able to keep NR's house from collapsing. As Bridges and Coyne explain, *National Review* had more than its share of contentious personalities: men like Frank Meyer, Willmoore Kendall, Brent Bozell, and William Schlamm, among others. Buckley the sharp-tongued debater discovered that he needed—and possessed—the "fatherly" diplomatic skills to keep his sometimes cantankerous colleagues from upending their common endeavor.

Successful families also need steadying rituals. Bridges and Coyne astutely describe the lubricating rituals and customs that made *National Review* function with increasing harmony: the fortnightly editorial conferences, the dinners at Paone's, the annual *Messiah* party before Christmas, even the occasional practical jokes. Whether from instinct or from what Edmund Burke would have called the unbought grace of life, Buckley saw to it that working at *National Review* was never simply a job. He made it fun. For his devoted staff it became a way of life.

It was a way of life routinely leavened by laughter—another secret of familial survival. Be prepared to chuckle and guffaw when you read the book. *Strictly Right* abounds with examples of the humor that served as a bonding agent between the magazine's helmsman and his crew. Like the time someone asked Buckley why Senator Robert Kennedy refused to appear on Buckley's television talk show, *Firing Line*. "Why," Buckley replied, "does the baloney reject the grinder?" Or the time Henry Gibson asked Buckley on *Laugh-In* why he was always seated when he appeared on television. Couldn't he think on his feet? Buckley retorted: "It's very hard to stand up carrying the weight of what I know."

Sometimes the magazine's playful insouciance led its editors to push the envelope, to the discomfiture of those who thought NR insufficiently serious for its own good. Bridges and Coyne recount how, in 1971, after the leak of the top-secret Pentagon Papers to the *New York Times* during the Vietnam War, the senior editors of *National Review* prepared a sensational issue containing their own purported cache of leaked government documents. It was a hoax, skillfully concocted by the senior editors themselves. Buckley and his cohorts wanted to demonstrate that the liberal, antiwar media could be taken in by forged documents so long as their contents were "inherently plausible." The NR editors succeeded: The media, temporarily duped, were outraged by the prank.

But not just the media. NR's own publisher, who was not let in on the joke beforehand, was furious. This reviewer knows a conservative who spent hours studying NR's elaborate forgeries—only to learn that he had been wasting his time. I do not think he ever read *National Review* again.

Such high-spiritedness undoubtedly buoyed the NR family in its formative years. But humor alone was not sufficient. Back in the 1950s, it became fashionable to say that "the family that prays together, stays together." In a way, this was true of the folks at *National Review*. At no time, of course, did the magazine's editors promulgate a confessional statement or adhere to a single religious faith. Individuals of many religious traditions (and no tradition) contributed to its pages and still do. Nevertheless, it is noteworthy how many of *National Review's* founding generation were either ardent Roman Catholics (like the Buckleys) or friendly fellow travelers of the Catholic Church. A remarkable number of the magazine's principal contributors—including Willmoore Kendall, Jeffrey Hart, Russell Kirk, Brent Bozell, and Frank Meyer—became Catholic converts. At least two others—Ernest van den Haag and James Burnham—were lapsed Catholics who returned to the fold shortly before their deaths.

Although NR was never, in any formal sense, a "Catholic magazine" (as left-wing critics sometimes alleged), Catholic Christianity shaped the worldview of many, maybe most, of its inner circle. A Christian sensibility formed the subtext—and context—for much of NR's brand of conservatism. It was another tie that bound the NR "tribe" together.

Strictly Right is not an exhaustive history of its subject. Organized as an episodic narrative, it largely eschews interpretation for a diet rich in anecdotes. But patterns, willy-nilly, emerge. Bridges and Coyne provide fresh insight, for example, into the enduring tug-of-war in the magazine between what Jeffrey Hart calls "prudential conservatism" (exemplified by James Burnham) and more aggressively ideological formulations (championed by Frank Meyer and William A. Rusher, among others).

The authors also bring into focus the magazine's own evolution. For the first ten years or so of its existence, *National Review* was more than an upstart journal of opinion; it could plausibly claim to be American conservatism's Central Command. It had the field of conservative advocacy journalism largely to itself, and its political allies were largely out of power. During this phase of the magazine's history, issues of doctrine and intellectual self-definition were at the apex of its agenda.

By 1980, *National Review*'s status had begun to change. Many of its early intellectual giants no longer wrote for its pages. Richard Weaver, Willmoore Kendall, and Frank Chodorov had died in the 1960s; Frank Meyer in 1972. In 1978 James Burnham suffered a debilitating stroke. In 1980 Russell Kirk ceased writing his regular column after twenty-five years of unflagging service.

Coincidentally, the advent of the Nixon administration—and, far more significantly, the Reagan administration—shifted the center of gravity in American conservatism decisively toward Washington, the world of politics and the think tanks—and away from the intelligentsia and its flagship journal.

The magazine remained influential, of course—in some ways, even more so. Its editor in chief was increasingly honored as (in Hart's words) "the most influential journalist since Walter Lippmann." But 1980 undeniably marked a turning point. American conservatism—and *National Review* itself—had reached adulthood. The movement's Silver Age, the Age of Reagan, superseded the fabled Golden Age of NR's youth.

Bridges and Coyne's family album invites such ruminations. It also turns its strobe lights on relatively unfamiliar sides of Buckley's life, including his relationship with his talented son (and fellow author), Christopher, and with Bill's witty, Canadian-born wife, Pat. Even close friends of Buckley will discover things about him that they did not know when they peruse this delectable book.

In Bridges and Coyne's affectionate portrait of their chief, two traits stand out. The first is how restless and adventurous he has been. Whether driving to work in Manhattan on a Honda motor scooter (as he did for several years), or sailing the Atlantic and Pacific oceans in little yachts, or driving down a winding mountain road in the Azores at sixty miles per hour, the founder of *National Review* has never been a stereotypical stodgy Tory.

The other trait that *Strictly Right* illuminates is Buckley's astonishing drive and productivity. In nearly sixty years (and counting) in the public eye, he has published fifty-four books, hundreds of magazine articles, and several thousand newspaper columns. He has hosted one of the longest-running public-affairs shows in the history of television; delivered uncounted hundreds of public lectures; run for mayor of New York City; played a musical instrument at a near-professional level of competence; touched foot on all seven continents; and quite possibly written more letters than any other American who has ever lived.

All this raises an obvious question: How could one man accomplish so much and still find time to edit *National Review*? Was Buckley—as some have hinted—an absentee landlord?

Bridges and Coyne vigorously dispute this suggestion. They note that between 1955 and 1990 (when Buckley retired from the helm), he personally edited the editorial section of the magazine about three-quarters of the time, hired and dismissed columnists, commissioned articles, and "made the final decision" on virtually all signed contributions to his journal. Whether in the office or out of it, "his was the controlling intelligence."

But the authors acknowledge that it was a loyal team led by Priscilla that handled most of the daily editorial responsibilities. And therein lay the final key to the survival of the *National Review* family: Over time it became an extended family, an institution, a fortress against human foibles and mortality. But institutions, we know, are not impersonal beings. They are animated by the character of their founders. At the end of *Strictly Right* Bridges and Coyne perceptively remark that among Buckley's multifaceted achievements one more deserves recognition: He was a gifted "institution builder" who created a great journalistic enterprise and held it together.

Just so. No one else could have done it. At *National Review* it took a Bill Buckley to raise a family.

Part III

Conservatism and the American Jewish Community

22

Jews for Joe McCarthy:
The Rise and Fall of the American
Jewish League Against Communism

I presented this paper at a conference on "McCarthyism in America" held at the National Archives in Washington, D.C., on February 9, 2000—the fiftieth anniversary of the speech in Wheeling, West Virginia, that catapulted Senator Joseph McCarthy to national political prominence. My essay is published here for the first time.

I

In the early autumn of 1947 Benjamin Schultz was a little-known rabbi in Yonkers, New York. He was also a man with a mission.

Born in 1906, Schultz was a graduate of the University of Rochester and of the Jewish Institute of Religion founded by Rabbi Stephen S. Wise. Since 1935 Schultz had been spiritual leader at Temple Emanu-El in Yonkers. Since 1944 he had also been a journalist, with at first one column and then two in the weekly *National Jewish Post*.[1] An ardent anti-Communist, Schultz increasingly used his columns and other writings to highlight the Soviet Union's persecution of the Jews and the Communist Party's penetration of American Jewish life. He did not hesitate to criticize prominent American Jewish leaders and agencies—including the eminent Stephen S. Wise, who had ordained him—for failing, in Schultz's judgment, to notice and combat the growing Red menace.[2]

As the Cold War between the Soviet Union and the West intensified at home and abroad in 1947, Schultz's crusade acquired a new dimension. With the assistance of the reporter Frederick E. Woltman of the *New York World-Telegram*, who had recently won the Pulitzer Prize for exposing Communist infiltration of labor and political groups, Schultz prepared a similar exposé of the Communists' "penetration of religion" in the United States.[3] The Yonkers rabbi prepared his case carefully; each article was filled with names, dates, and quotations. Before the articles were published, an official of the Anti-Defamation League of B'nai B'rith reviewed them and made various changes.[4] The *World-Telegram* also took steps to maximize the articles' impact by sending a promotional letter in advance to the New York clergy.[5]

On October 14, 15, and 16, 1947, Schultz's series appeared in the *World-Telegram* under the headline "Commies Invade the Churches."[6] Protestants, Jews, and Catholics each received a column. Citing by name various left-wing clerics who had collaborated with Communist-controlled organizations, the rabbi declared: "Communists have a foothold in our churches. Many key Protestant and Jewish leaders are their dupes or willing pawns. Catholic-born labor leaders and glamorized celebrities use their 'faith' to lure Catholics into helping communism."[7] The Communists were "working hard on Jew, Protestant, and Catholic," said Schultz, in order to "soften America for Soviet aggression." It was "time to drive them from the church. And from the temple, too."[8]

The Yonkers rabbi's articles evoked a considerable stir. In New York City the militantly anti-Communist *Jewish Daily Forward* applauded the series and said that it had brought "honor and prestige" to Schultz's temple.[9] The national commander of the American Legion was so impressed that he distributed copies to every legion chaplain in the United States.[10] But Schultz's essays would probably have been forgotten had it not been for his critique therein of one man: his one-time teacher and patron, Stephen S. Wise.

In 1947 Wise, at age seventy-three, was a towering figure in American Jewry. President of the American Jewish Congress, prominent Zionist, and a celebrated clergyman, he was also an outspoken liberal who unabashedly endorsed candidates for public office and warmly espoused liberal causes. Wise was never a man to shrink from public controversy. As the Cold War worsened in the late 1940s, he grew increasingly fearful that it would turn hot.[11] He did not hesitate to condemn Winston Churchill's "Iron Curtain" speech of 1946 as "one of the most mischievous and hurtful utterances ever made by a person of authority and responsibility."[12] Committed to the goal of world peace, the renowned rabbi apparently joined a number of "peace committees" that turned out to be Communist fronts.[13]

And this, to Rabbi Schultz, was wrong. Back in the summer, in an article published by the *New Leader*, Schultz had expressed the hope that Wise would "disown these people soon" and "desist from giving comfort to elements that are the opposite of what he stands for."[14] Now, in the *World-Telegram*, Schultz repeated his public criticism. He asserted that the Jewish People's Fraternal Order—"a fraternal and propaganda arm of the Communist Party"—was seeking to "utilize leading Jews and does snare some for the party."

> Thus, Rabbi Stephen S. Wise, one of the leading rabbis in America and a non-Communist, lent his prestige to a rally of this Communist front on Jan. 23, 1946. Moreover, he declared that: "Not a select few founded the Soviet government. The people did." Two months later the rabbi in a sermon called for giving Russia the atomic bomb know-how. He defended Soviet expansion and blamed it on our "withholding the atomic bomb secret."

Schultz emphasized that "less than one per cent" of America's 5,000,000 Jews were "Communistic." But others, he added, were "liberals who've been sold on Stalin's 'liberalism.'"

> Dr. Wise, for instance, sincerely believes that liberals and Communists can work together against Fascism, as certain Protestant bishops and ministers also believe. Thus believing, they lend their name to sinister groups.[15]

As it happened, this was not the first time that Wise had been criticized by anti-Communist Jews for his attitude toward the Soviet Union and its American supporters. Some months earlier, the *Jewish Daily Forward* had attacked Wise as "Chief Rabbi of our Communists," a charge duly reported by Schultz in the *National Jewish Post*.[16] Nor was it the first time that Schultz himself had chided Wise in print, to Wise's "disgust."[17] But it was one thing for the Yonkers rabbi to reprove his mentor in comparatively obscure publications like the *New Leader* and *National Jewish Post*. It was quite another to do so in a major New York newspaper. Perhaps for this reason, when Wise learned of Schultz's statements about him in the *World-Telegram*, the distinguished rabbi exploded in wrath:

> I brand him [Schultz] as a professional and probably profiteering Communist baiter, as unworthy to be even a member, not to say a Rabbi, of a Jewish congregation. His column on Rabbis and the Communist line is not only mendacious but utterly and inexcusably vicious.[18]

171

Ignoring the advice of a friend that Schultz respond to Wise (if he must) in a respectful manner, the Yonkers clergyman instead struck back hard.[19] Nowhere in Wise's reply (noted Schultz) did he "deny the facts cited in the three articles" or "make the slightest attempt to deny the very brief and mild reference I made to him." Wise, he said, was dodging the issue. Adding fuel to the flames, he asserted bluntly that Wise had "consistently" given encouragement to the Communist movement in the United States by joining and speaking before Communist fronts.[20]

If Wise was angered by Schultz's published critique, the New York Board of Rabbis was infuriated. To Schultz's colleagues in the rabbinate, the venting of charges against Wise in the press—and by a graduate of his own seminary, whom he had ordained—was an act of staggering impropriety, akin to announcing in the press that one's own father was a drunkard.[21] Swiftly, a special committee of the board asked Schultz to appear before it. Instead, he requested an adjournment because he was "tied up" in Yonkers "protecting myself" against an effort to "oust" him from his temple.[22] But the rabbinical board was in no mood to wait. On October 22—only six days after the final installment of the *World-Telegram* series—an angry board met to consider what to do.

At first the body was ready to expel Schultz outright. But one rabbi present warned that it could not do this without first holding a public hearing, at which Schultz might very well accuse more rabbis of Communist sympathies.[23] Unwilling, apparently, to contemplate such a spectacle, the board settled for a unanimous resolution of condemnation. Schultz, it charged, had cited various clergy and organizations in his articles as "either Communists, Communist dupes, or Communist sympathizers." In so doing, he had employed "the 'smear technique' of the scandalmonger, a technique entirely inappropriate for a rabbi." Furthermore, he had "endeavored to bring into question the loyalty and Americanism of religious teachers whose record for sincerity and patriotism is unimpeachable." The board therefore asked Schultz to apologize publicly "to those whom he has wronged," and to atone for his "obvious infraction" of the commandment, "Thou shalt not bear false witness against thy neighbor." If he did not, it declared that it might have to act to "protect the integrity of the rabbinate."[24]

Instead of repenting, Rabbi Schultz counterattacked. Nowhere, he told the press, did the board's resolution deny any of the specific allegations he had made. It was un-American, he charged, to condemn his articles "without investigation and without a hearing." The board's resolution, he asserted, was "an example of viciousness and unfairness."[25]

Certainly Schultz had some reason to feel aggrieved. The rabbis had censured him for bearing false witness against his neighbor, but where had his witness been demonstrated to be false? He stood accused of engaging in a "smear technique," but what precisely constituted the smear? Nowhere, for instance, had he called Rabbi Wise a Communist, or pro-Communist, or even (explicitly) a Communist dupe. Instead, citing Wise's own words and deeds, he had labeled the noted rabbi a sincere "non-Communist," whose behavior toward the Communists (in Schultz's view) was terribly misguided.

In the weeks following the appearance of his *World-Telegram* series, apparently not a single person challenged Schultz's factual claims.[26] But in the hurricane of antagonism that now enveloped him, the veracity of his articles seemed almost irrelevant. Coming from some other (and nonclerical) source, the substance of Schultz's polemic might have been accepted as fair comment. But to his clerical critics the substance evidently did not matter. To them he was a man who had publicly besmirched the reputation of his own teacher and had attacked other religious leaders as well.[27] For years to come he would be a virtual outcast among his fellow rabbis.[28]

Benjamin Schultz's troubles had just begun. For several years, the board of trustees of his congregation had been dissatisfied with his extracurricular activities and (in their view) his neglect of his pastoral duties.[29] The appearance of the *World-Telegram* series was evidently the last straw. On October 20, the board asked Schultz to resign. When he refused, the board proceeded with plans for a congregational meeting on October 26 to ponder his fate.[30]

In a statement to the press the board's chairman denied that Schultz's anti-Communist activities had anything to do with its displeasure.[31] Schultz disagreed. The board's request for his resignation, he asserted, had come because of his articles in the *World-Telegram*.[32] With the board now recommending his dismissal to the congregation, the embattled rabbi made it plain that he would not go quietly.[33] In a telegraphic fusillade to the *National Jewish Post* he thundered:

> It is apparent that the disciples of Rabbi Wise and those innocents who have been whiplashed into this frenzy against me by a small but vociferous pro-Communist clique are better organized than the large majority of Jewry, who have a warm devotion to American principles and to freedom of thought and expression for religious leaders and others.[34]

But Schultz was not wholly without resources. His articles in the *World-Telegram* had come to the attention of George Sokolsky, the vehemently anti-Communist (and Jewish) columnist for the Hearst press. Traveling up to Yonkers from New York City, Sokolsky urged Rabbi Schultz's board of trustees to reconsider its decision.[35] More ominously, he warned that if Schultz were fired Sokolsky would publicly berate the congregation for punishing Schultz because of his anticommunism.[36] In the wake of Sokolsky's intervention, the board abruptly cancelled its congregational meeting.[37] Schultz had been saved.

Or had he? Less than two weeks later, on November 4, the feisty rabbi unexpectedly resigned from his Yonkers pastorate. He did so (he informed the press) "because of continued pressure following my board of trustees' previous failure to oust me for my anti-Communist articles." Schultz disclosed that the trustees were now boycotting his religious services in a body and were threatening to do so "all this year." Only three weeks after his sensational series in the *World-Telegram*, the rabbi who had wanted to drive Communists from the temple had been driven instead from his own.[38]

Despite Schultz's allusion to the pressure against him, his departure from Temple Emanu-El was not entirely coerced. At least one close rabbinical friend maintained that if Schultz had truly wanted to, he could have mobilized his local supporters and survived. Instead, the friend contended, Schultz had *chosen* to leave because he had a new career, as an anti-Communist, in mind.[39] Schultz himself seemed to acknowledge as much in 1949 when he told a congressional committee that he had resigned "because this evil of communism was so great and international in its scope that I desired to wage the fight against it in a larger field."[40]

Whether Schultz, in the last analysis, gave up his pastorate unwillingly, or whether he left because he craved a "larger field" for his activism, the immediate result was the same. The author of "Commies Invade the Churches" was now unemployed.

As it happened, he would not be out of work very long.

II

Benjamin Schultz was by no means the only Jewish anti-Communist who was disturbed by the Communist presence in American Jewish life in the late 1940s. The veteran writer and editor Eugene Lyons was another. A former Communist sympathizer who had been disillusioned while a newspaper correspondent in Moscow between 1928 and 1934, Lyons had gone on to write *The Red Decade: The Stalinist Penetration of America* (1941) and innumerable attacks on communism and its apologists. In 1946–47 he and a number of other Jewish anti-Communists helped to launch *Plain Talk*, a monthly magazine devoted to exposing Soviet machinations abroad, Communist subversion at home, and the moral and intellectual failings of Popular Front liberalism. Isaac Don Levine became the journal's editor, Lyons eventually one of its contributing editors, Ralph de Toledano for a time its managing editor, and Alfred Kohlberg (reputed head of the "China Lobby") its publisher and principal bankroller.[41]

Although Jewish writers were prominent in the *Plain Talk* circle, the magazine was not a Jewish periodical, and Lyons, for one, considered that more must be done to combat Communist influence among his people. From his perspective there was much work to do. While very few American Jews were Communists, in the mid-1940s a disproportionate number of American Communists were of Jewish origin.[42] Certain labor unions with heavy Jewish membership were Communist-controlled. The 50,000-member Jewish Peoples Fraternal Order—cited by the attorney general in 1947 as a Communist front—was "an organizational and financial bulwark of the Communist Party" and of its chief newspapers, the *Daily Worker* and Yiddish language *Freiheit*.[43] Meanwhile, in the aftermath of the recent world war against Hitler, the Communist Party was assiduously portraying itself (and the Soviet Union) as friendly to Jewish interests, including the establishment of a State of Israel in the Middle East.[44]

To Lyons the time had come to marshal opposition to the Communists' dangerous cultivation of the Jews. For years he had been advocating the creation of a grassroots, Jewish organization for this purpose. In late 1946 and 1947 he and several friends met in his home from time to time to discuss the idea. At last, in November 1947—the very month of Rabbi Schultz's departure from his synagogue—Lyons, Levine, Kohlberg, Sokolsky, and several others decided to found the American Jewish League Against Communism.[45]

Incorporated in February 1948, the league publicly announced its formation in mid-March.[46] "We Americans of Jewish faith and tradition have banded together to oppose the menace of communism," its platform proclaimed. "Throughout history, the Jews have been the victims of tyranny, even as they are now the first target of totalitarian dictatorship." Communism, "like Fascism and Nazism," was "the enemy of Judaism, a religion stressing liberty and the sanctity of the individual." Both "as Americans and as Jews," the league pledged to battle "Communist aggression," which was "forcing a new slavery upon large sections of the free world."

The league had no intention of keeping a low profile. In its manifesto it vowed to "expose and resist with all the lawful resources at our command every Communist effort to bore from within Jewish, as well as all religious, life." It vowed to "educate the Jewish public on the extent and danger of Communist infiltration in Jewish organizations and institutions" and to "turn the spotlight of pitiless publicity" on efforts by "Communist agitators" to "exploit Jewish grievances for sinister and disloyal ends." It pledged to "unfold the horrible and long-suppressed truths" about Soviet persecution of Jewish culture and religion in Russia, as well as the fate of thousands of Zionists and Jewish religious leaders in Soviet prisons and "slave labor camps." It promised to publicize the "economic destitution" that Communist dictatorships had wrought upon Jewish populations. And it proposed to serve as a "clearing-house in the fight for freedom and against Communism."[47]

The league's founding chairman (and largest financial supporter) was the wealthy businessman Alfred Kohlberg, soon to be a leading participant in the debate over "who lost China."[48] Its initial national advisory council comprised fifty-one people, including Levine, Lyons, Sokolsky, and Lawrence Fertig, a columnist for the *New York World-Telegram.* Another prominent council member was Benjamin Gitlow, former general secretary of the Communist Party of the United States. Although the hard-line anti-Communists around *Plain Talk* were the catalysts of the new venture, the organizers clearly hoped to forge a broad coalition. Thus the first national advisory council included a Democratic member of Congress from New York City (Abraham J. Multer), an official in the New York State Liberal Party, the managing editor of the *Menorah Journal*, two Orthodox rabbis in the Bronx, and two officials in the anti-Communist International Ladies Garment Workers Union.[49] The union itself was a source of some of the league's early funding.[50]

The AJLAC's architects now confronted the challenge of converting their rhetoric into a program. Here they faced the multiple possibilities implicit in their charter. Of the league platform's seven stated "principles," the first three concentrated on exposing Communist infiltration and agitation at home. The next three focused on persecution of the Jews abroad. The seventh "aim and purpose" (to "act as a clearing-house") suggested an ambition to place the league at the vortex of all anti-Communist activism in the United States. Would the infant league try to pursue these goals with equal vigor? Or would it veer in one direction more than another?

Among the league's founders there seems to have been some difference of opinion, although it is unclear how much they realized it at the time. Levine envisaged an educational organization that would teach Jews "the facts about Communism" and operate "within the synagogues, among Jews."[51] Kohlberg seems to have conceived the league as a more militant entity that would "fight Communist infiltration into Jewry."[52] The two visions were not necessarily incompatible, but they might yield very different approaches.

Clearly much would depend on the executive director who would implement the league's program and serve as its face to the world. On March 14, 1948, the league disclosed its choice: Rabbi Benjamin Schultz.[53]

Since the appearance of Schultz's *World-Telegram* series the previous October, Lyons and his cohorts had become acquainted with the rabbi, who attended at least two meetings of the league's organizing committee as a guest in late 1947 and early 1948. A month or so before the league was publicly launched, Isaac Don Levine asked Schultz whether he might like to work for it. Schultz was eagerly receptive. So, too, it seems, after interviewing him, were most of the committee members, including Kohlberg, who promptly agreed to pay the league's bills (including Schultz's salary) for the opening months of its existence.[54]

And so, on March 14, it was Rabbi Schultz who informed the press of the new anti-Communist enterprise headquartered in Manhattan. The "Communist minions of Stalin are infiltrating all walks of life, in all religions without exception," he declared. The aim of the American Jewish League Against Communism was "to ferret out all Communist activity in Jewish life, wherever it may be."[55] Caught up, perhaps, in the thrill of the moment, he exclaimed: "My pulpit is 220 West 42d Street in New York and my congregation is America."[56]

The league and its energetic executive director hit the ground running. In its early months of operation the AJLAC repeatedly denounced attempts by Communists and their front organizations to manipulate pro-Zionist sentiment among American Jews.[57] At a time when the Soviet Union and its American sympathizers were trumpeting their support for the new nation of Israel, the AJLAC warned Jews not to be deceived. "Communists are no friends of Zion," it said.[58] They were simply using "Jewish troubles" as "bait and propaganda."[59]

On May 15, 1948, in the first hours of Israel's existence, the American Committee of Jewish Writers, Artists, and Scientists held a massive "Salute to the Jewish State" rally in New York City at which President Truman was booed, the Soviet Union was applauded wildly, and Andrei Gromyko of the Soviet Union was acclaimed as "a stable fighter for freedom."[60] The AJLAC labeled the event a "Communist-staged rally" and its sponsoring committee a "pro-Communist front" that had been set up to "take the heat off the Communists" after the Soviet Union's "brutal execution" of two leading Polish-Jewish labor leaders.[61] A few months later the league accused the Communist Party of deliberately inciting "racial tension" and of inflaming grievances among American minority groups—a charge that led to Schultz's testifying before a congressional committee about Communist activity among Jews.[62]

Speaking before one such committee in 1949, Schultz declared: "I resent the fact that the Communist Party has a Jewish section. It was largely because they raised the Jewish issue that my organization was founded."[63]

In its first year, the league made a particular effort to publicize the travail of Jews behind the Iron Curtain and to unmask "the anti-Semitic myth that Jews somehow benefit from Communist regimes."[64] Undoubtedly its most impressive achievement in this area was its commissioning of *Soviet Russia and the Jews* (1949), a fifty-one-page, scholarly pamphlet by an exiled Russian-Jewish scholar, Gregor Aronson. The pamphlet was one of the first publications—the league later said it was *the* first—to document the Soviet Union's growing campaign of anti-Semitism, anti-Zionism, and systematic suppression of traditional Jewish culture.[65] For Aronson's sponsors it was powerful proof that the Soviet Union had not been "good for the Jews."[66]

The league had more on its agenda, however, than refuting Communist propaganda and issuing "pitiless publicity" about front groups. In a pamphlet about itself in early 1949 it asserted: *"Like every other American racial and social group,* the Jewish community has been deeply infiltrated by the Communists. The first and most vital job of our league is to expose and combat that infiltration."[67] In 1948 and 1949, the league and its executive director increasingly turned their verbal artillery in this direction.

On May 31, 1948, Schultz, testifying before the Senate Judiciary Committee as a private individual, endorsed the Mundt-Nixon bill, which would require Communist and Communist front organizations to register with the federal government. "There is not a particle of truth," he said, to the Communist "propaganda" claim that the bill was a threat to Jews. "It is an anti-Communist bill. The vast majority of Jews are against communism, and the bill has nothing to do with them." The "attempt to smear the bill as anti-Jewish," he opined, was "nefarious."[68]

A year later Schultz testified even more forcefully in behalf of similar proposed legislation called the Mundt-Ferguson bills. America, he said, was menaced by a "new style war against it—the internal war of infiltration—that is, of Communist aggression against our democratic institutions. This internal war is waged by persons of Communist sympathies who are trained to seem to be what they are not."

> The Mundt-Ferguson bills are designed to smoke these people out, and to smoke out the organizations—innocent-appearing—through which they work. . . .
>
> The plain truth is that the Mundt-Ferguson bills are a great tribute to democracy. . . . There is no "enforced silencing" in this bill. There are no restrictions on speech. There is only an insistence that the public has the right labels.
>
> These bills are repressive if the pure-food laws are repressive. Pure-food laws protect the public by preventing fraudulent labels. These bills are the pure-food laws of the American intellect. They insist on truthful labels for groups and persons.[69]

Back in New York, Schultz and his league focused increasingly on the "internal war of infiltration." Their principal targets were the Jewish Peoples Fraternal Order and its parent organization, the "notoriously pro-Communist" International Workers Order, which the attorney general had determined in 1947 to be a Communist front.[70] Early in 1949 the league asked the New York City Board of Education to prevent the IWO from using public school buildings for children's classes after normal school hours.[71] The IWO (or, more precisely, the JPFO) had been conducting such classes in seven public schools as part of its network of fifty-three such schools devoted to what one historian has called "education and ideological socialization of the young."[72] The JPFO's schools purported to offer "Jewish education." The American Jewish League Against Communism retorted that it was not Jewish in a religious sense at all. These schools taught "the Communist religion"—"the religion of atheism"—the AJLAC charged. They were "'fronts' for Communists and for the training of potential Communist leaders." The IWO, it alleged, wanted to use public school facilities "to attach an air of respectability to things they teach.[73] After a contentious public hearing in which Rabbi Schultz was a participant, the Board of Education voted unanimously to bar the IWO from use of New York City's schools.[74]

Fresh from this victory the AJLAC sought other ways to marginalize Communist influences in the state of New York. It endorsed the state's Feinberg Law, which forbade the employment of Communist Party members in the public schools.[75] In 1949, the league demanded an investigation of the chief of the New York Public Library's Jewish division because he was a sponsor of the School of Jewish Studies, cited by the Department of Justice as a subversive organization. In this instance the league was rebuffed.[76] But it could take considerable satisfaction from one thing: It was being heard.

By the end of the league's first year of operation, its organizers had considerable reason to be cheered. According to Schultz, it had "several thousands" of members in twenty-two states.[77] Its booklet on *Soviet Russia and the Jews* had won plaudits in the press.[78] Most gratifying of all, perhaps, was the league's growing prestige in veterans' and anti-Communist circles. At its first anniversary luncheon on May 2, 1949, its speakers included Brigadier-General Julius Klein (past national commander of the Jewish War Veterans) and a California Congressman named Richard M. Nixon.[79]

Rabbi Schultz, in fact, seemed especially popular among veterans, who evidently perceived him as something of a martyr to the cause of anticommunism.[80] Time and again he addressed veterans' gatherings around the country.[81] In April 1948, the Catholic War Veterans of New York State presented him one of its annual Americanism awards for having "traced the godless ideology of communism into the sacred precincts of the house of God and baring the penetration to public view."[82] It was the first of many such honors that he received from such organizations in the next few years.[83] In January 1950 came still greater recognition when the American Legion invited the American Jewish League Against Communism and several dozen other organizations representing fifty million Americans to form a grand alliance called the All-American Conference to Combat Communism. At the conference's founding meeting Rabbi Schultz was appointed to the permanent executive council.[84]

During his first year as executive director, Schultz also attempted to cement ties with other religious groups, particularly Roman Catholics. He advocated creation of an interfaith commission to combat Communist infiltration of churches and synagogues—and of Protestant and Catholic leagues against communism that would parallel his own.[85] He lauded Francis Cardinal Spellman of New York City for protesting the Communists' arrest of Cardinal Mindszenty in Hungary.[86] And when Schultz's antagonist, Rabbi Stephen S. Wise, asserted publicly that "the largest of Christian churches [the Roman Catholic Church] is unequivocally for war," the American Jewish League Against Communism apologized to the chancellor of the Catholic University of America. Wise's views, said the AJLAC, were not those of the American Jewish community.[87]

There was one group, however, where the league and its executive director were *not* winning favor: the leadership of American Jewry. From the beginning, such "mainstream" Jewish agencies as the American Jewish Committee and Anti-Defamation League of B'nai B'rith harbored deep reservations about the American Jewish League Against Communism. Just one month after the league was founded, and in response to numerous inquiries, the Civil Rights Division of the ADL prepared and circulated to the ADL's regional offices a memorandum on the embryonic league. Although the ADL's document took no explicit stand on the AJLAC, it dwelt at length on Rabbi Schultz's recent quarrel with his rabbinical critics.[88] Clearly some parts of the Jewish "establishment" considered the rabbi from Yonkers to be a loose cannon.

The Jewish defense agencies' staffs and leaders had more than merely personal qualms about Schultz. To many of them, the very idea of a *Jewish* league against communism was troubling and offensive. The Catholics and Protestants had no such counterparts, they noted. Why should Jews as Jews be singled out? To them the league, in its clamorous crusade to dissociate Jews from communism, was actually reinforcing the anti-Semitic myth that Jews were Communists. The more the league declaimed against Communist infiltration of Jewish communal life, the more it fed the false perception that Jews above all others were of suspect loyalty.[89]

The Jewish establishment also resented the league's claim that it was "the only group dealing specifically and courageously with the problem of Communist intrusion in the Jewish community in America."[90] While the league acknowledged that other Jewish organizations were also fighting the Communist menace, they were not (it said) doing so "exclusively." Only it was "exclusively" committed to this single mission.[91] To Jewish critics of the league, this carried the imputation that they were not doing enough. Nor did they care for the brash newcomer's announcement that it intended to coordinate the anti-Communist "efforts of important Jewish leaders in the old Jewish organizations."[92]

Even more worrisome to Jewish officialdom was the league's growing indulgence in what its critics called "vigilantism," to the detriment (they believed) of civil liberties. To the heavily liberal leadership of the principal Jewish defense and communal agencies, for example, the Mundt-Nixon and Mundt-Ferguson bills, as well as the Feinberg law in New York, were dangerous threats to free speech and American democracy. In 1948 and 1949 many of them went on public record in opposition to these countersubversive measures.[93] They were not amused when Rabbi Schultz took the opposite side.[94]

To some of them, it seemed that Schultz was indiscriminately calling Jewish individuals and organizations "red" when they were actually "pink."[95]

Nor were Jewish public relations professionals pleased when the Joint Committee Against Communism in New York was founded in early 1950 in the AJLAC's own offices, with Schultz as its coordinator. The Joint Committee described itself as "an interfaith patriotic coalition." Its membership seemed largely to consist of local veterans who, like Schultz, wished to root out the remaining Communists in their midst.[96] To one prominent staff member of the American Jewish Committee, the new Joint Committee was merely a front for Schultz's ever-expanding witch hunt.[97]

For its part, the AJLAC insisted that it was not providing fodder for the anti-Semites. To the contrary, it argued that the very existence of a Jewish league against communism proved the "base untruth" of the anti-Semitic bromide that all Jews were Communists.[98] Time after time, the league emphasized publicly that the great majority of Jews were not Communists and that Judaism and communism were completely antithetical.[99] To those who charged that anticommunism was at times a convenient mask for anti-Semites the league replied that the notion of a link between anti-Semitism and anticommunism was a Communist-sponsored canard.[100] But on the increasingly vexatious issue of civil liberties—and of how far the crackdown on domestic Communists and their allies should go—there was little that the league could say to mollify its liberal Jewish critics. The gap between them—already substantial in 1949—was to grow wider.

In January 1950, S. Andhil Fineberg of the American Jewish Committee informed his colleagues that the AJLAC was doing more harm than good and that the American Jewish Committee should now take steps to weaken it. He suggested that pro-league Jewish war veterans be told that the league's approach to Communist-fighting was wrong. He urged that an unimpeachable anti-Communist be commissioned to write an article for the Jewish press explaining that a special league of Jews against Communism (when no other ethnic or religious groups had analogous societies) was both unnecessary and harmful.[101]

Fineberg's stance was particularly significant because he himself was a staunch anti-Communist who headed the American Jewish Committee's staff committee on communism for several years in the 1950s. Within the AJC, he was on the relatively conservative side of its spectrum.[102] He was also a rabbi and an old friend of Benjamin Schultz, whom he had helped to save from expulsion from the rabbinate.[103] If even Fineberg thought that Schultz and the AJLAC should now be thwarted, it was a sign of how tenuous the league's footing in the Jewish community really was.

Despite Fineberg's recommendation, the AJC took no immediate action, perhaps because it feared that Schultz might attack it as a Communist dupe.[104] But it did advise the Jewish War Veterans against a league offer to merge its veterans division into the JWV, in return for the JWV's adopting the league's program of exposing Communist infiltration among veterans groups.[105] And in midsummer, an AJC official initiated a quiet investigation of the league. He discovered that it apparently had only three to four hundred dues-paying members and a paltry annual budget of about $30,000.[106]

By September 1950, relations between the American Jewish Committee and the American Jewish League Against Communism—as evidenced by their correspondence—had become increasingly tense and disputatious.[107] By now, too, the AJC was telling inquirers that the league had no standing in the Jewish community, that it was unaffiliated with any Jewish organizations, and that most of its board of advisers were nonentities.[108] But the AJC had not yet publicly criticized Schultz and his colleagues.

Then, in August 1950, a dramatic incident occurred which brought the conflict between the league and its Jewish adversaries into the open. On August 27 the National Broadcasting Company cancelled the fall premiere of the *Henry Aldrich Family* television show after it received numerous protests against the assignment of the actress Jean Muir to a leading role. Among the reported protestors were the American Legion, the Catholic War Veterans, and the American Jewish League Against Communism.[109] The complainants acted because Muir's name was included in a recently published book called *Red Channels*, which itemized the past left-wing associations of numerous Hollywood personalities.[110] Muir immediately denied that she had ever been a Communist or pro-Communist, but the next day, the show's sponsor announced that she had been dropped from the cast entirely because she was a "controversial personality" whose appearance might harm the sale of the sponsor's products.[111]

Despite Muir's indignant denials, the veteran anti-Communist polemicist (and AJLAC director) Eugene Lyons was not convinced. Muir, he wrote later, had a long and well-documented record of involvement with pro-Communist, "Stalinoid outfits," and had been known in Hollywood as "a bitter and fervid adversary" of those who were fighting Communist party-line "influences in the actors' guilds."[112] Be that as it may, the case of Jean Muir instantly became a cause célèbre among many American liberals (including some leaders of the American Jewish Committee), to whom the fired actress was a victim of reckless vigilantes.[113] Among these—or so it seemed in some liberals' eyes—was Benjamin Schultz, who had demanded Muir's dismissal on August 26 on behalf of his Joint Committee Against Communism in New York. A few days later, he announced to the press that the Joint Committee had created a radio committee "to 'police' the radio and television networks, producers and entertainers trying to 'sell' Communist ideas." The firing of Muir, he said portentously, was "only the beginning."[114]

The American Civil Liberties Union now sprang into the fray with an investigation, which led to a 1952 book on blacklisting in which Schultz was cast in a decidedly unfavorable light.[115] But Schultz did not have to wait until 1952 to be rebuked by liberal organizations for his role in the Muir affair. To the leadership of the American Jewish Congress, American Jewish Committee, and Anti-Defamation League of B'nai B'rith, the wayward rabbi and his league had now gone too far. On December 26, 1950, in a joint statement on communism and civil liberties, the three Jewish organizations roundly condemned the "irresponsible vigilantism" manifested in recent "slanderous attacks" on "personalities in the political and entertainment world" by self-appointed "defenders of America against Communism." It deplored "the activity of any organization employing the name 'Jewish' in its title, which resorts to smear tactics and character assassination. We especially deplore such activity on the part of a rabbi."

No "racial or religious group," the statement continued, "can serve its own interests and that of the public by maintaining special anti-Communist agencies." The three Jewish defense agencies deemed it "regrettable that any group of Jews should set themselves apart from the well-established bodies of organized Jewry and give the impression that its members have a special interest in combating communism."[116]

There could be no mistaking the target of these words. But perhaps out of fear of an unseemly public quarrel or a lawsuit, the joint declaration did not mention Schultz or the league by name, nor was the statement released to the general or Anglo-Jewish press. It was printed only in the official publications of the three signatories.[117]

Meanwhile, a few weeks earlier, the American Legion-sponsored All-American Conference to Combat Communism (AACC) had held a convention in Buffalo. There Edwin J. Lukas, director of the American Jewish Committee's Civil Rights Division, had succeeded in blocking Schultz's renomination to the Conference's executive council. Joseph Woolfson of the

AJC had replaced him. The removal of Schultz had not been easy to effect because of his popularity with many of the delegates. But for Lukas and his AJC colleagues it was a welcome development. A man whom they regarded as an irresponsible fanatic would no longer be the Jewish representative on the conference's governing board.[118]

The American Jewish League Against Communism's leadership was furious at Schultz's ouster—and apoplectic when they learned the reason why. Someone, it seems, had informed the AJC that Schultz was advocating an American Legion boycott of the coming American tour of the Israeli Philharmonic Orchestra because he deemed its co-conductor, Leonard Bernstein, to be pro-Communist. Convinced (he later said) that the informant was reliable, Lukas had passed on the damaging tip to a member of the AACC's nominating committee who had thereupon insisted that Schultz not be reappointed to the executive board.

Schultz vehemently denied the allegation, accused Lukas of peddling injurious falsehoods, demanded that Lukas issue a public retraction, and hinted broadly that he would otherwise file a libel suit. The legion official to whom Schultz had allegedly spoken also denied the story. Lukas, however, stood his ground, contending that his source of information was reliable. But when Alfred Kohlberg, the league's chairman, requested a copy of an AJC investigator's report on the incident, Lukas replied that the AJC's Investigative Division would not release the document "for security reasons." An infuriated Kohlberg promptly accused Lukas himself of inventing the story. To this depth had relations between the AJC and the AJLAC now sunk.[119]

Schultz's removal from the All-American Conference's governing board was soon overshadowed by an even more acrimonious verbal brawl. Late in 1950 Congress enacted, over President Truman's veto, a sweeping antisubversive law known as the Internal Security Act (or McCarran Act, after its principal sponsor). Leading Jewish organizations vigorously opposed the legislation as "a violation of traditional American guarantees of individual freedom" and appealed to Truman to veto it.[120] The American Jewish League Against Communism, predictably, felt otherwise.

Then, in January 1951, President Truman, by executive order, created a nonpartisan Commission on Internal Security and Individual Rights, headed by Admiral Chester W. Nimitz. The nine-member panel of distinguished citizens, the president said, would investigate how "a free people can protect their society from subversive attack without at the same time destroying their own liberties."[121] To Senator Pat McCarran and a chorus of hard-line anti-Communists, Truman's initiative looked suspiciously like an attempt to undercut the investigative prerogatives of Congress and the newly enacted Internal Security Act. Eventually, the powerful senator used a legal technicality to prevent the Nimitz Commission from ever carrying out its assignment.[122]

Among those who quickly attacked the president's decision was the increasingly peripatetic Benjamin Schultz. Speaking before the Women's Patriotic Conference on National Defense in Washington, D.C., on January 27, Schultz charged that "respected military and naval names" were now being "deliberately used to cover up the pro-Red guilt" of the Truman administration's past. Specifically, Nimitz himself was being used to "whitewash an evil pro-Communist situation" and "hamper a real security check" by Senator McCarran. But the rabbi did not stop there. While allowing that Nimitz ("a naval hero") was "sincere and loyal," Schultz declared that the admiral's "*record* on tolerance of pro-Communists" was "bad." As proof Schultz cited Nimitz's recent vote, as a regent of the University of California, to retain forty professors who had refused to sign a loyalty oath for state employees. Schultz conceded that the members of the presidential commission were all "fine people," but none, he said, was an expert on "the international communistic conspiracy."

Warming to his theme, Schultz asserted that General George Marshall ("a really fine person" and "a great Army man") was another "'fall guy' in this military name plot." A few years before, while Marshall was chief of staff, army orientation courses had "largely followed the Communist Party line," especially about the Chinese Communists, although Marshall had not realized it. What Schultz appeared to be saying was that Marshall's prestige had been exploited by unnamed individuals to conceal Communist subversion in the U.S. military.[123]

Schultz's remarks about Nimitz and Marshall received little notice in the nation's press. But they elicited both outrage and consternation among the leaders of organized American Jewry. Only three days after Schultz's speech, the National Community Relations Advisory Council (NCRAC)—comprising the American Jewish Committee, American Jewish Congress, Anti-Defamation League of B'nai B'rith, Jewish Labor Committee, Jewish War Veterans of the USA, and Union of American Hebrew Congregations—issued a blistering denunciation of Schultz for his "infamous" attack on "the patriotism and moral character of two great Americans": Marshall and Nimitz. "Such irresponsible attacks impair the fight against Communism," the NCRAC leaders asserted. "Rabbi Schultz in no way represents any section of the American Jewish community and the major Jewish organizations repudiate and condemn his repeated resort to vilification and slander of reputable Americans on the pretext of combatting Communism."[124] The next day, the New York Board of Rabbis added its own words of reproach, blasting Schultz and the league for "irresponsible character assassination" and "indiscriminate and unpatriotic denunciation of our revered military heroes" (Nimitz and Marshall).[125]

To Schultz, the extraordinary public rebuke from the Jewish establishment must have seemed uncomfortably reminiscent of the Rabbi Wise incident in 1947. Could not his critics read what he had said? He had not challenged the loyalty and patriotism of Admiral Nimitz; he had questioned his judgment and the use to which his well-earned prestige was being put. Schultz was far from alone in believing that the Nimitz Commission was intended to be a weapon in Truman's battles with congressional anti-Communists. Nor was he alone in noticing that Nimitz, as a university regent, had revealed himself to be on the "liberal" side of the Communist/civil liberties issue, and that none of the commission members was an expert in communism.[126] But Schultz weakened his case by his swipe at General Marshall (who was not on the Nimitz Commission) and by emotive verbal flourishes about "fall guys," "plots," and "pro-Red guilt." In the superheated atmosphere of early 1951, one suspects that Schultz's critics were listening less to his substantive charges than to the impassioned rhetoric in which he clothed them.

In any case, the NCRAC's unprecedented outburst now precipitated a fiery row with Kohlberg that erupted at repeated intervals for the next two years. By early February 1951, the American Jewish Committee had received information that Kohlberg and Schultz were supposedly launching an all-out campaign to harass Jewish organizations. Later that month, Kohlberg issued a lengthy reply to the NCRAC in the form of a printed letter to the members of the American Jewish League Against Communism. Kohlberg claimed that the NCRAC agencies had misrepresented Schultz's remarks about Nimitz and Marshall. More dramatically, he now openly accused the Jewish agencies of carrying on a three-year, undercover campaign of "abuse" and "vilification" of the league—"mostly by word of mouth"—with the intent "to destroy the League and its active officials." Why? Kohlberg offered two reasons: 1) the "entrenched" Jewish bureaucracies did not "like competition"; and 2) the "large staffs" of these organizations contained "a certain number of Communist Party members" and "a vast majority of either strong or mild sympathizers with Communism." The "Directorates" of the Jewish organizations were being manipulated by their "pinko staffs."[127]

It is unnecessary to discuss in detail all the epistolary firecrackers that Kohlberg's letter ignited. For a time the threat of libel suits hung in the air.[128] By now, of course, the chasm between the AJLAC and its critics was unbridgeable. What the Jewish agencies perceived as reckless vigilantism, the league saw as "aggressive anti-Communism." What Jewish leaders considered the principled defense of civil liberties Kohlberg scorned as "confusion and ignorance" abetted by "pinko staffs."[129] Finally, in 1952, through the good offices of George Sokolsky, representatives of the ADL and the AJLAC met informally and decided, in effect, to call a truce. While each party continued to believe in the correctness of its own technique of fighting communism, they agreed that it could serve "no useful purpose" to lambaste each other in public.[130]

An armistice between the league and the American Jewish Committee proved more difficult to arrange. In the spring of 1953 certain members of the league obtained a copy of an AJC memorandum earlier that year in which the league was severely—some thought savagely—criticized. Once again tempers flared, accusations flew, and Kohlberg threatened to initiate a lawsuit.[131] One AJC official believed that Kohlberg was using the threat to intimidate the AJC into silence.[132] In the end, Kohlberg and the chairman of the AJC's executive committee held a kind of summit conference, at which the AJC representative promised to instruct his staff to make no personal attacks on individual members of the league. But to Kohlberg's disappointment the American Jewish Committee leader refused to commit his agency to a policy of public and private silence about the league.[133] And there, apparently, the dispute was left to lie.

The harsh, protracted wrangling with the Jewish establishment—and the incidents which provoked it—proved costly to the league. In September 1950, in the wake of the Jean Muir incident, Isaac Don Levine resigned—disturbed, he said, by the league's "public relations policies" and its failure to consult him about some of its actions.[134] A few months later Brigadier General Julius Klein (who had become a director) also quit, upset by what he considered to be Schultz's "smearing" of General Marshall and Admiral Nimitz.[135] In the spring of 1951 Representative Abraham Multer resigned.[136] One by one, it seemed, those who had been on the center-left side of the league's original coalition were abandoning ship.[137]

That spring S. Andhil Fineberg of the American Jewish Committee assured a Jewish newspaper that the league was declining in strength and would continue to do so. It was being stifled by a dearth of publicity and by other Jewish organizations' adoption of "intelligent anti-Communist programs" far larger than anything the league could do. Fineberg professed to be amused at opponents of anti-Communist hysteria "becoming hysterical over something as insignificant as the League."[138]

Not that Schultz and his colleagues had given up trying. In 1951 and 1952 the league's executive director became increasingly interested in Communist influences in the New York state school system. He demanded that a state commission examine school textbooks, and his Joint Committee Against Communism cited eighteen faculty members at Brooklyn College who had been (in the committee's words) "seriously involved with organizations or activities cited as subversive."[139] He took part in the uproar over allegedly Communist teachers at Sarah Lawrence College and reportedly asked the Senate Judiciary Committee to open an investigation of the nation's colleges and universities.[140]

At times Schultz himself was the victim of misrepresentation. Late in 1951, for instance, the *New York Times* erroneously reported that Schultz had accused Brigadier General Julius Klein, Admiral Nimitz, and General Marshall of "pro-communism."[141] Schultz protested to the *Times* that he had said no such thing in his speech in Washington the previous January. The *Times* publicly acknowledged that the stenographic transcript of Schultz's remarks proved that he was right.[142]

To the rabbi and his allies, a liberal "smear brigade" (as Schultz called it) was attempting to destroy him.[143] Privately, Eugene Lyons conceded that Schultz was not an able politician and that he had a lot to learn about winning friends and influencing other people.[144] But to Lyons, this did not excuse what he publicly termed "a vile whispering campaign" against Schultz at the time of the Wise affair and a "vicious attack" on Schultz by the Anti-Defamation League in 1948.[145] To Lyons and others like him, the beleaguered rabbi was (in the words of a New York veterans group) a man who had "contributed tremendously to the national welfare by his brilliant exposé" of the Communist threat "at the risk of sacrificing his reputation through slanderous accusations."[146]

There now occurred a perceptible shift in the league's operations. Rebuffed by, and without influence among, organized Jewry, in 1952, 1953, and 1954 the AJLAC crafted a new niche for itself: cheerleader for the anti-Communist crusade led by Senator Joseph McCarthy.

In part this development probably reflected the wishes of Chairman

Kohlberg, who met McCarthy in early 1950 and quickly became a close friend and adviser.[147] Before long, Kohlberg's detractors gave him the epithet "the Jewish Joe McCarthy."[148] In part also the league's growing identification with McCarthy reflected its own evolution into a countersubversive organization. Like the Wisconsin senator, the league had been pouring most of its energies into identifying Communists, fellow travelers, and dupes on the American home front.

In any case, between 1952 and 1954, one of the most conspicuous boosters of McCarthy and his "ism" in New York state and beyond was Rabbi Schultz. In December 1952, to the horror of many Jews who considered McCarthy a dangerous demagogue and protofascist, Schultz's Joint Committee Against Communism in New York organized a lunch in the senator's honor in New York City. The rabbi presented McCarthy an award for his "historic and sacrificial battle against subversion in high places" and labeled McCarthyism "a term of honor."[149] In 1952 the AJLAC itself awarded a plaque to Roy Cohn, a noted young anti-Communist attorney who was soon to become Senator McCarthy's chief counsel.[150] In 1953 it presented a citation to G. David Schine, a consultant to the senator's investigations subcommittee. On this occasion Schultz declared that "those who are for McCarthy are complete Americans" because they recognized the danger of communism and wished to combat it.[151] In 1953 the league also presented an award to Chairman Harold H. Velde of the House Committee on Un-American Activities at a luncheon in New York City attended by virtually the entire committee.[152] And when, in midyear, Schultz himself received the annual Americanism award of the Westchester County, New York, American Legion, congratulatory letters and telegrams poured in from Vice President Richard Nixon, J. Edgar Hoover, Bernard Baruch, Joseph McCarthy, and other anti-Communist luminaries.[153] Never had the league's prestige among fellow Cold Warriors been so high.

More and more now, the league seemed to be hitching its wagon to McCarthy's shooting star. In mid-1954, when Roy Cohn resigned under fire as counsel to McCarthy's subcommittee, the indefatigable Schultz—by now an experienced hand at these matters—organized and presided over a banquet in Cohn's honor at the Hotel Astor. More than 2,000 people, including McCarthy himself, applauded the zealous lawyer whom Schultz called "the symbol of the people's revolt against politicians soft on treason, professors soft in the head and writers talking softly about Hiss and Oppenheimer, but loudly against McCarthy and Cohn."[154] Skillfully combining (in one observer's words) "the airs of clergyman and toastmaster," the rabbi exclaimed:

"America is for Cohn; the people are for Cohn; he stands for McCarthyism. God bless it."[155]

But McCarthy, like Cohn before him, was now heading for a fall. Late in the autumn of 1954, as the Wisconsin senator faced impending censure by his colleagues, his fervent rabbinical booster attempted to rescue him. To the dismay of Jewish liberals and some veterans, Schultz announced plans for a pro-McCarthy "march on Washington" on Veterans Day.[156] In response to objections against a political demonstration on a sacred holiday, and to the ugly connotations of the word "march," Schultz converted the event into a "solemn convocation" at Constitution Hall.[157] On the evening of November 11, more than three thousand McCarthy partisans, led by Schultz himself—including 873 on a special train from New York City—jammed into the hall for a rally. Like the conductor of an orchestra, the rabbinical master of ceremonies led them in singing a song: "Nobody's for McCarthy (But the People)." Late in the evening McCarthy himself unexpectedly entered the hall; the crowd went wild. Schultz gave McCarthy a plaque; McCarthy gave Schultz a hug. The rabbi's embrace of McCarthy and his cause was now literal.[158]

Although the American Jewish League Against Communism did not technically sponsor the Washington, D.C. rally (the Joint Committee Against Communism did),[159] both the league and its executive director paid a penalty for such acts of political theater. In response to numerous inquiries from Jewish communities, the National Community Relations Advisory Council circulated to its constituent organizations copies of the Jewish agencies' condemnations of Schultz in 1950 and 1951. In a cover memorandum, the NCRAC's executive director contended that Schultz's behavior had repeatedly offended and embarrassed most American Jews. The NCRAC organizations, he added, considered Schultz's actions to be helpful, rather than hurtful, to the Communists.[160]

In early December 1954 came another blow. With the quiet assistance of at least one staff member of the American Jewish Committee, the *New York Post* published a massive, five-part investigative series called "The Strange Case of Rabbi Schultz," whom it derisively dubbed "a rabbinical Revere seeking to alert the Jewish community to the joys of mccarthyism [sic]."[161] In the eyes of his enemies, he was no longer just an ogre but an object of ridicule.

While Schultz had been out mounting the rhetorical parapets for Cohn and McCarthy, the league itself had been languishing. In mid-1954 George Sokolsky confessed to a friend that it was completely broke, unable to raise sufficient funds in the Jewish community.[162] Alfred Kohlberg complained that while small contributions to the league were increasing, gifts from large contributors were becoming very difficult to sustain. He suspected that major donors were being advised or pressured to stop giving.[163] Schultz, too, claimed that "organizational pressures" against the AJLAC were intensifying and that dozens of "ugly instances" of "suppression and censorship" of the league occurred in 1954.[164]

Whatever the truth of these allegations, by late 1954 the American Jewish League Against Communism was only a shadow of its purported former self. In 1951 Schultz had told an Ohio newspaper reporter that the league had 30,000 members.[165] Three-and-a-half years later, Eugene Lyons was asked whether the "concept" or "operation" of the league had changed since 1948. "Only in dimension," he replied. "Instead of hundreds of thousands, we have hundreds."[166]

On December 2, 1954, the United States Senate voted 67–22 to condemn Joseph McCarthy for abusive misconduct toward two senate committees during his tempestuous five-year career as a Communist-hunter. Could the Jewish league that had become a virtual fan club survive his political demise?

III

Early in 1955, Alfred Kohlberg, recovering from a heart attack, retired as the AJLAC's president and took the title of honorary president. George Sokolsky became the league's new president and Roy Cohn the chairman of the executive committee.[167]

At first little seemed to change. Perhaps to compensate for the beating Rabbi Schultz had recently taken from the *New York Post* and others, the league organized yet another testimonial dinner—this time for the rabbi himself—on April 20, 1955. Before an assemblage of seven hundred people in a New York City hotel, Schultz heard himself extolled by Senator McCarthy as a "gallant warrior" and "indispensable" figure in "the anti-Communist fight" of the past ten years. Schultz's "most distinguished service," McCarthy continued, had been his work as "founder" and "guiding star" of the American Jewish League Against Communism. The league and its executive director's "most valuable contribution" was that "they dramatically symbolize the eternal hostility" between Judaism and communism. Along with Kohlberg, Lyons, Gitlow, and other Jewish anti-Communists, Schultz—declared McCarthy—had exposed "the malicious myth that persons of the Jewish faith and Communists have something in common."[168]

Eleven days after this testimonial banquet, Schultz addressed a large

Loyalty Day rally in White Plains, New York.[169] On June 2 he was given the honor of offering the opening prayer at a session of the United States Senate; it was, said a friendly journalist, "the proudest moment of his life."[170]

While Schultz was again doing what came naturally—anti-Communist preaching—Sokolsky was struggling to give the rickety league a fresh start. He obtained significant help from several Jewish businessmen, notably Victor Emanuel, chairman of the AVCO Corporation, and Lewis Rosenstiel, the founder of Schenley Industries.[171] Emanuel even joined the board of directors.[172] Bernard Baruch was another quietly generous contributor, as he evidently had been for a number of years.[173]

Sokolsky also attempted to beef up the organization's program. Thanks to donations from Emanuel and another Jewish benefactor, the league distributed free copies of Don Whitehead's *The FBI Story* to every conservative and reform rabbi in the United States.[174] The league also began to take note of and condemn "false anti-Communists": known anti-Semites who were exploiting the anti-Communist cause for their hateful purposes.[175] Sokolsky was determined, he said, to attract a better class of membership and enhance the league's stature as a Jewish organization among Jews.[176]

Still, it was tough going, as he admitted to Kohlberg in 1956. His disappointments, he said, had been unbelievable. Individuals had promised to join and had then backed off. The league had been fought as if it were an enemy of the United States.[177]

Indeed, for all of Sokolsky's exertions, the league's visible program in the late 1950s consisted of little more than periodic luncheons in New York City at which it presented awards to anti-Communist dignitaries like David Lawrence and Senator William Knowland.[178] Such well-attended events were good for a modicum of press coverage but little more. The league was beginning to look less like a think tank than a private club.

In early 1958 Kohlberg resigned from the AJLAC's honorary presidency and directorate.[179] Although he pledged $5,000 to its coffers for the year ahead, he seems to have concluded that its continued existence was pointless.[180] By now observers at its testimonial lunches were noticing that few of the attendees at these functions were Jewish. One guest jokingly suggested that the league consider changing its name to the American Jewish-Irish Anti-Communist Committee.[181]

At the beginning of 1960 President Sokolsky suspended the league's operations because (he later said) of insufficient funds.[182] A few months later Alfred Kohlberg—long the league's single largest financial supporter—died in New

York City.[183] Even before these developments, another problem had begun to beset the organization: growing friction between its executive director and its president.[184] Anxious to enhance the league's acceptability among its putative constituents, Sokolsky was dismayed by what he perceived as Schultz's inability or unwillingness to go out and proselytize among his fellow Jews.[185] Schultz's side of the story is less clear, but he appears to have come to dislike both Sokolsky and Roy Cohn.[186] Perhaps he missed the old days when, presumably with Kohlberg's approval, he had traveled extensively as a lecturer on communism to veterans and patriotic societies. In any case, by 1960, and evidently well before, Schultz had begun to regret his financial dependence upon the league and to yearn for a return to the rabbinate.[187] Sometime in 1960, he resigned, or was dropped, as the league's executive director.[188]

Schultz was now disillusioned with his former employers, his disenchantment exacerbated by the league's failure (for a time at least) to pay him his back salary.[189] With the assistance of a couple of rabbinical friends, including S. Andhil Fineberg of the American Jewish Committee, he obtained a position as rabbi of a congregation in Brunswick, Georgia, in 1960.[190] In 1962 he became rabbi of a congregation in Clarksdale, Mississippi.[191]

Schultz's fervently anti-Communist convictions and penchant for speechifying now came back to haunt him and again threaten his career. The rabbi arrived in Mississippi only a few weeks before the compulsory racial integration of the University of Mississippi and resultant rioting that led to the U.S. Army's patrolling the formerly all-white campus. That October, in the midst of the Cuban missile crisis, Schultz addressed a local women's club in Clarksdale. "What America needs is more Mississippi, not less," he declared. He urged President Kennedy to withdraw federal troops from Ole Miss "because our enemy is not here. Our enemy is communism."

If Mississippi had its way, Castro would not be in Cuba now. Washington would not have installed him there.

If Mississippi had prevailed, the Berlin Wall would have been torn down as soon as it went up. But then, the Russians would not have been there in the first place.

If Mississippi had prevailed, pro-Communists would be off American college faculties. Corruption of our youth would stop.

If Mississippi with its States' Rights philosophy had its way, big government, provocative dictatorship and eventual national bankruptcy would be thrown out the window.

If Mississippi had its way, "red-baiter" would be a term of honor and "flag-waver" would not be a dirty word. Traditional patriotism would again sweep the land to strengthen our people inwardly, and insure victory in the international crisis. As it is, America is losing. It is losing mostly because of decay among its own intellectuals.

Schultz called upon "the dedicated clergy of our state and the South generally to demand that our Northern preachers fight the Cold War for America, even if it means less time for them to attack the South."[192]

Schultz's widely reported speech—and a similar, though less passionate, talk to a Rotary club a few months later[193]—shocked his Mississippi colleagues in the reform rabbinate, some of whom vowed never to set foot in Clarksdale as long as he was there.[194] They not only strongly disapproved of what he said but of when and how he said it, and of the fact that he—a rabbi and a newcomer—had injected himself so melodramatically into politics.[195] They also were incensed that his speeches had given comfort to Mississippi's arch-segregationist, white citizen's council movement, which published excerpts of his Clarksdale address in its monthly journal.[196]

Then and later Schultz insisted, in all apparent sincerity, that his Clarksdale speech had not been a defense of racial segregation. He had, in fact, never mentioned segregation at all. What he had intended to do, he said, was to give a boost to Mississippians' morale during a time of crisis in which the state (in his opinion) was being unfairly besmirched. By "more Mississippi, not less" he had meant (he said) the state's anticommunism, not its racial institutions.[197] While conceding several years later that he was philosophically opposed to federal usurpation of governmental power, he asserted that he was not anti-black. In fact, he pointed out, the blacks of his community had asked him to deliver the eulogy for Martin Luther King Jr. at a huge memorial service after the civil rights leader was assassinated in 1968.[198]

Not for the first time, the controversial rabbi apparently had been a victim of misunderstanding induced in part by his oratorical flamboyance and political tone-deafness. Arriving in the Magnolia State in 1962, he perceived the world around him in terms of his Cold War ideology—not, as his rabbinical colleagues did, in terms of the growing domestic upheaval over civil rights. And so, for years to come, the rabbi from Clarksdale had to endure the suspicion that he was a defender of the racial status quo and white supremacy.

In late 1962 and early 1963, with the assistance of his old friend S. Andhil Fineberg, and under great pressure from reform rabbis in the region, Schultz tempered his rhetoric and patched up relations with his colleagues.[199] The "rabbinical Revere" never abandoned his anti-Communist views, which he expounded from time to time in the years ahead. Always a popular speaker before civic groups, he eventually became a district governor of Rotary International. Evidently well-liked by his congregation in Clarksdale, he died there in 1978. After all the strife of yesteryear, his career appeared to have a happy ending.[200]

Meanwhile, back in New York, George Sokolsky had been struggling to revive the American Jewish League Against Communism. In 1960 he hired an up-and-coming conservative public relations consultant named Marvin Liebman to reorganize and reactivate the moribund organization.[201] In May 1961 Sokolsky announced in a membership solicitation mailed to Jewish leaders that the AJLAC was being revived. The reason for its renewed activity, he said, was that "the situation of the Jew in the Soviet world is so unspeakably horrible that some organization must exist in the United States that is devoted to this noble cause of combatting communism from a Jewish standpoint."[202]

Once again the leadership of American Jewry disagreed. Although the American Jewish Committee made no public pronouncement against the league, it distributed to its area directors and others a memorandum containing information (supplied by Fineberg) about the league. It suggested that the AJLAC was both unnecessary and (by its very existence) implicitly derogative of the anti-Communist work of other Jewish organizations. It pointed out that, during the league's life, no other Jewish agency had ever collaborated with it.[203] The advisory was undoubtedly intended to dissuade any who inquired from joining Sokolsky's organization. In Boston, where a number of people had received his appeal for new membership, the Jewish Community Council declared it to be "gratuitous and unnecessary for any Jewish group to assume the specialized role indicated by" the AJLAC.[204] There was little sign that the league would be able to breach these barriers.

Nevertheless, Sokolsky and his band soldiered on. As of early 1962 the reorganized board of directors included a number of old names—Sokolsky as chairman, Cohn as president, and Lyons and Morrie Ryskind among the vice presidents—as well as some new ones. Marvin Liebman was now its executive secretary; Bernard Baruch continued to be a generous donor.[205]

Early that year—as the John Birch Society and other groups on the far Right rose into prominence—the American Jewish League Against Communism returned to the limelight with a well-advertised testimonial dinner for Chairman Sokolsky. The featured speaker, Senator Thomas Dodd of Connecticut, spoke on "The Mortal Struggle"; the league distributed 25,000 copies of his address.[206] A couple of weeks later the renascent league made another splash with a public endorsement of the House Committee on Un-American Activities, for whose abolition a number of American liberals—including some rabbis—had recently called. The league took this step, it said, both because it supported the committee and because it wished to underscore its conviction that the vast majority of American Jews supported the anti-Communist work of government agencies.[207] Out in California, the Los Angeles chapter of the league feted the chairman of the House committee at the chapter's fourteenth anniversary dinner, which was publicized in a full-page advertisement in a Jewish newspaper. The advertisement included a commendatory message from J. Edgar Hoover.[208] For a time it appeared that the league was back in business to stay, a beneficiary of the new surge of right-wing populism in the early 1960s.

Unfortunately for Sokolsky and his associates, one manifestation of this sentiment was to provoke a disastrous crisis. Among the increasingly popular evangelists of the anti-Communist gospel in 1962 was the Christian Anti-Communist Crusade and its charismatic director, Fred C. Schwarz. An Australian doctor and a born-again Christian whose Jewish father had converted to Christianity, Schwarz was viewed with suspicion by some American Jews, who found the very name of his organization to be troubling. Skeptical officers of the ADL, in particular, scrutinized his activities and literature for signs of anti-Semitism and denounced him as a right-wing extremist. Schwarz protested his innocence. Many indignant conservatives, including Eugene Lyons and Marvin Liebman, believed that Schwarz and his program were entirely free of anti-Semitism and had been unjustly maligned.[209]

George Sokolsky was decidedly not among Schwarz's defenders, inside and outside the AJLAC. For reasons that are not entirely clear, Sokolsky conceived an antipathy to Schwarz so intense that it became a source of public comment and a bone of furious contention with his league associates.[210] Sokolsky was irate when Rabbi Max Merritt of the AJLAC's Los Angeles chapter accepted a major financial contribution to the chapter from a non-Jewish backer of Schwarz. The league, Sokolsky declared, did not take money from non-Jews.[211] The league's chairman also apparently took umbrage when Merritt offered a prayer at one of Schwarz's Anti-Communism Schools.[212] By the time the dust settled, Merritt had been expelled from the League's executive committee and ordered not to use the league's name.[213] The Los Angeles chapter of the organization was now extinct; Merritt and Ryskind thereupon established a new entity: the Jewish Council Against Communism.[214]

Convinced that Dr. Schwarz was not an anti-Semite, Marvin Liebman telephoned the Anti-Defamation League on May 2, in a vain attempt to arrange a conference between its staff and the Australian physician.[215] Sokolsky was livid and promptly upbraided Liebman in scathing terms.[216] That same day Liebman submitted his resignation as the AJLAC's executive secretary and announced that he would help Schwarz to organize his forthcoming "Greater New York School of Anti-Communism."[217] Two days later, in a stinging letter, Sokolsky accused Liebman of (among other things) selling himself to Schwarz for the money.[218]

It is not known how Sokolsky reacted when another AJLAC stalwart, Eugene Lyons, addressed the Christian Anti-Communist Crusade's rally in Madison Square Garden in late June.[219] But such squabbling did not matter much longer. On December 12, 1962, Sokolsky died in New York City at the age of sixty-nine.[220]

Roy Cohn—once Joseph McCarthy's right-hand man and still his defender— now assumed full command of what was left of the league. At a lunch attended by more than three hundred people in New York City on May 23, 1963, he presented its first George E. Sokolsky Award to Francis Cardinal Spellman.[221] A few days later, a local liberal columnist poked fun at the affair and labeled the league one of "the late Joe McCarthy's surviving front organizations."[222]

And with that the fifteen-year-old American Jewish League Against Communism lapsed into obscurity. Never again did the *New York Times* report on its testimonial lunches and dinners. Although the organization was still around as late as 1978 (with Cohn as its president), its existence, to all appearances, had become purely nominal.[223] When Cohn died in 1986, in all likelihood the vestigial league died with him.[224]

IV

At the end of the day, what had the league accomplished?

Perhaps its proudest boast was that it was "the first American organization to expose and document the Communist anti-Jewish policies" of Soviet Russia and its satellites in the late 1940s.[225] Its 1949 study *Soviet Russia and the Jews*, by Gregor Aronson, was apparently "the first English-language booklet" to be published on this subject.[226] In the late 1940s and early 1950s, the American Jewish Committee and other Jewish organizations commissioned numerous books, articles, and other studies detailing what one AJC executive termed "the desperate realities of Jewish life behind the Iron Curtain."[227] But in this area, at least, the American Jewish League Against Communism seemed to be ahead of the curve.

The league could also claim some credit—though this was not among its original purposes—for counteracting anti-Semitism among non-Jews, particularly on the pro-McCarthy far Right. In 1950, for instance, the U.S. Army and Navy discovered that many recruits to the armed forces believed that the Communist conspiracy was led by Jews. To refute this false conception, the navy invited Rabbi Schultz to address its sailors, including a gathering of ten thousand recruits at a camp in the South.[228] As a tireless and effective lecturer to Legionnaires and other groups identified in Jewish minds with the reactionary Right, Schultz ventured into precincts where few other Jews cared to go. There, his message—that most Jews were anti-Communists, that no true Jew could be a Communist, that atheistic communism and Judaism were eternal foes—probably helped to undermine anti-Semitic stereotypes, as some of his Jewish critics conceded.[229] Of course, to them Schultz's very singularity severely limited his usefulness: If one lone rabbi was a McCarthyite, what message did that send McCarthyites about the rest of the Jews? By relentlessly drawing attention to Communists still active in the Jewish community, Schultz—in the opinion of his liberal Jewish opponents—conveyed a distorted impression of the scope of the problem.[230]

Certainly in its early years the AJLAC contributed its share to the "pitiless publicity" that helped to delegitimate the Communist and fellow-traveling subculture in American life during the post–World War II decade. Though handicapped by a chronic lack of resources (from 1948 to 1960, Rabbi Schultz was its sole professional employee), the league exhibited a considerable capacity for generating sound and fury. To be sure, many of its targets—such as the Jewish Peoples Fraternal Order—were already increasingly unpopular in the Jewish community. It was the American Jewish Committee, not the league, which spearheaded the campaign that expelled the JPFO from Jewish communal organizations in the early years of the Cold War.[231] There is scant evidence that the AJLAC made much difference in this battle.[232] Still, its bark, if not its bite, gave it some prominence—and for a time, substantial prestige on the Right.

But on balance, the league's successes, in its own terms, were small ones, and judged by its initial hopes it was a failure. It never overcame the opposition of the Jewish establishment and never successfully mobilized a base among Jewish voters. It never became the coordinator of all Jewish anti-Communist activity. As time went on, and as the league's countersubversive mission overwhelmed its educational one, its constituency changed. Instead of serving as an anti-Communist emissary to his fellow Jews, Schultz became (in the *New York Post*'s words) "a Jewish missionary to the militant right."[233] Such a role had its attractions and advantages, but pro-McCarthy theatrics were not what the league had been established to perform. George Sokolsky, in the late 1950s, realized this and tried to restore the league to its Jewish foundations. It was too late.

Why had it failed? In 1960 Sokolsky attributed its difficulties to personalities. Kohlberg, for example, had few contacts with the Jewish community before he helped to establish the league. Sokolsky himself, though the son of a rabbi and an observant Jew, had married outside his faith, and his son had converted to Roman Catholicism. Rabbi Schultz, Sokolsky went on, had borne his own liabilities stemming from his altercation with his rabbinical associates in 1947. And Roy Cohn had reminded everyone of Joseph McCarthy.[234]

Sokolsky's analysis was astute, so far as it went. Throughout its existence, the league was saddled by its fateful decision to hire Schultz as its first executive director. It was also undoubtedly handicapped by the fact that several of its key officers—though accomplished in their own professions—were unaffiliated with the organized Jewish community.[235] And that was crucial. Although the league's initial board of directors reflected a number of potential blocs of support (such as the garment workers union), Schultz and Kohlberg evidently made little effort after that to establish close ties with Jewish institutions other than the Jewish War Veterans. Not that such an initiative would have yielded much; from the outset the league encountered skepticism, which soon turned into hostility, from the Jewish defense agencies. Still, the league's combative tactics and mutterings about "pinko staffs" did not help. By the time it sought a nonaggression pact with the ADL and AJC in 1952 and 1953, there was no reservoir of goodwill upon which to draw.

But the league's encumbrances transcended personalities, tactics, and the isolation—both imposed and self-imposed—from which it suffered. Fifty years later, one is struck by how hard it was for the league and its non-Communist critics to communicate with one another during the McCarthy era. How different their mindsets and points of reference turned out to be. Looking right, the Jewish defense agencies—strongly liberal and civil-libertarian in their political ideology—perceived appalling crudeness, fanaticism, and the threat of resurgent anti-Semitism. To them the American Jewish League Against Communism was a coterie of fanatic reactionaries whose ideology was both repellent and potentially dangerous. The enemy abroad was the Communists, but at home the present danger was on the Right.

Looking left, Kohlberg and the AJLAC perceived (in addition to Communists and their sympathizers) foolish liberals whose understanding of the Communist menace was flawed—liberals who at times seemed more concerned for the civil liberties of traitors than for uprooting the web of subversion on American soil. At the peak of the McCarthy era, each side saw the other as hysterical—and at times got nearly hysterical saying so.

Beneath this intellectual chasm lay the bedrock question of just what anticommunism really meant. In 1951, S. Andhil Fineberg remarked that there was a difference between fighting communism and fighting Communists.[236] The Jewish defense agencies tended to want to combat communism, leaving exposure of individual Communists to the government, and abhorred anything that smacked of private "vigilante" action.[237] (Here, no doubt, the historical analogy of Nazi Germany weighed on their minds.) Kohlberg and his allies, by contrast, wanted to expose Commun*ists*—people—and drive them out of the public square. To them the Communist Party and its apologists were not a normal political movement deserving of constitutional protection but a fifth column—a conspiracy—directed and sustained by an expansionist foreign power. It followed, in their minds, that carriers of this armed doctrine should be deprived of any ability to affect public policy during a time of war—the "war of infiltration" that had already begun. If one side in the anti-Communist debate tended to focus on the fallacies and evil consequences of the doctrine, the other side—in addition to that—focused on its carriers.

And so the blood on both sides rose to a boil. Fifty years later it still simmers as historians try to understand the conflict of visions that occurred in that unhappy time.

23

Forgotten Godfathers:
Premature Jewish Conservatives and
the Rise of *National Review*

Originally a paper presented at a conference on Jewish conservatism, this essay was published in the combined June/September 1999 issue of American Jewish History.

I

For historians of the ideologically riven twentieth century, the migration of writers and artists from Left to Right is a familiar phenomenon. But sometimes those who make it are not familiar, and sometimes their ultimate destination is a surprise.

The subject of this essay is seven American Jews who made this intellectual journey: seven men who, by the mid-1950s, found themselves "prematurely" on the political Right at a time when most intellectuals—including Jewish intellectuals—stood somewhere to the left of center. Unlike the pilgrimage of the often Jewish neoconservatives who came to prominence in the Reagan era, the trek that these seven took did not begin with the traumas of the 1960s. Instead, it took place an entire generation before the epithet "neoconservative" was coined.

Our subject is seven Jews, but in a way our story begins with a gentile. In November 1955 an adventurous young conservative named William F. Buckley Jr. founded a magazine that was destined to alter the ideological climate of late twentieth-century America. Much has been written about Buckley's *National Review*.[1] But one fact has not been given as much attention as it deserves: of the thirty-one names that appeared on the original masthead of *National Review,* no fewer than five were Jewish.[2]

In some respects the association of these men with the fledging venture was not surprising. Each (as we shall see) had a good reason for being there. Nor was their appearance on the masthead an act of tokenism. Each was a personal friend of Buckley's, and each contributed substantially to the insurgent journal in the years ahead.

But from another perspective the conspicuous Jewish presence at *National Review* at its inception presents a puzzle, for in 1955 much of the American Right was not exactly attractive to American Jews. Many conservative activists of the early 1950s—including Buckley himself and Senator Robert Taft—had been isolationists before Pearl Harbor, not a position shared by many Jews. Moreover, after World War II, Taft—the Mr. Conservative of his day—had angered Jews and others by his publicly expressed constitutional objections to the Nuremberg war crimes trials.[3] Another conservative hero, Senator Joseph McCarthy, seemed to many Jews a dangerous demagogue reminiscent of Adolf Hitler. Behind all this discomfiture lay the unpleasant fact that parts of the American Right were not free from anti-Semitism—a taint, as it happened, that Buckley was determined to efface.

Not surprisingly, then, few Jewish intellectuals embraced Buckley's embryonic magazine. In 1956, barely six months after *National Review* started publishing, the American Jewish Committee's monthly journal, *Commentary,* published a ferocious assault on it by Dwight Macdonald. His article was entitled "Scrambled Eggheads on the Right," a caption supplied by a young assistant editor named Norman Podhoretz.[4] In its first decade of existence *National Review* and its editor in chief clashed heatedly with the Anti-Defamation League of B'nai B'rith, particularly over what Buckley regarded as the ADL's own defamation of Dr. Frederick Schwarz and his Christian Anti-Communism Crusade.[5] For their part, Arnold Forster and Benjamin R. Epstein of the ADL, in their 1964 book *Danger on the Right,* labeled Buckley "one of the leading fellow travelers of the American Radical Right."[6] Not surprisingly again—given all this commotion and the negative stereotype of conservatism that Buckley had to overcome—*National Review's* influence on the American Jewish community was initially slight. In 1960 Buckley revealed to a friend that less than one percent of his magazine's readers were Jewish.[7]

Nevertheless, the fact remains that a striking number of *National Review's* original luminaries were Jews. Indeed, without them the magazine might never have gotten off the ground, for if Buckley was the founding father of the journal, its unlikely godfather was an Austrian Jewish emigré journalist named William S. Schlamm. It was Schlamm (1904–78), a former advisor to Henry Luce, who "conceived the idea" of *National Review,* persuaded Buckley to make it a reality, and then worked assiduously with him to launch the enterprise.[8] It was Schlamm who suggested that the youthful Buckley become editor in chief and owner of the magazine's entire voting stock, sage advice that helped *National Review* avoid the shoals of factionalism.[9] It was Morrie Ryskind (1895–1985), a prize-winning playwright and Hollywood screenwriter, who organized a series of crucial fundraising receptions for the projected magazine at his home in Beverly Hills.[10] As a result, Buckley achieved more financial success with Ryskind's California friends than with anyone else except his own father.[11] When *National Review* made its debut, Schlamm became one of its principal editors and Ryskind one of its "associates and contributors" as well as a founding member of its board of directors.[12]

Three more Jewish writers were present, as associates and contributors, at *National Review*'s creation. Eugene Lyons (1898–1985), a senior editor of *Reader's Digest,* was virtually the incarnation of the "premature anti-Communist." An ardent Bolshevik sympathizer in the 1920s, he had lost his illusions while a correspondent in Moscow between 1928 and 1934. His resultant *Assignment in Utopia* (1937) became one of the most powerful anti-Communist classics of the twentieth century.[13] Frank S. Meyer (1909–72), a former high-ranking functionary in the British and American Communist parties between 1931 and 1945, was by 1955 a fervent libertarian in quest of the philosophical foundation for a valid American conservatism. Frank Chodorov (1887–1966), a friend of Buckley's since the 1940s, was an even purer libertarian for whom the coercive State was the veritable "enemy of society." In 1952, in the most consequential act of his career, Chodorov had founded the Intercollegiate Society of Individualists (ISI) as the first step in a fifty-year campaign, as he put it, to reverse "the socialization of the American character."[14] The society's first president was William F. Buckley Jr.[15]

If Buckley and Schlamm had had their way *National Review* would have lured still another Jewish conservative into its founding ranks, Ralph de Toledano, as managing editor. Toledano (1916–2007), an established editor at *Newsweek,* declined the invitation.[16] Nevertheless, within a few months he began writing articles for the new magazine, thereby inaugurating an association that has lasted more than forty years. In 1960 his name, too, joined *National Review*'s masthead.[17]

Shortly after Buckley's journal appeared, a congratulatory letter arrived from a young Jewish public relations executive in New York named Marvin Liebman.[18] Before long Liebman himself was writing occasionally for the magazine. Far more importantly, in the coming decade and beyond, he emerged as the outstanding fundraiser, organizer, and coordinator of "agitation-propaganda" for a vast apparatus of conservative causes associated with *National Review*. In the process, Liebman later reminisced, Buckley became his best friend and "unquestionably the most important figure in my life."[19]

The willingness of these seven Jewish intellectuals to affiliate with *National Review* in its infancy raises an intriguing question. How are we to explain their public endorsement of Buckley's journal? Clearly, on a personal level, the young editor showed himself ready to hire talent without regard for religious creed or ethnic origin. Moreover, in the years ahead he firmly dissociated his magazine (and the cause it represented) from anti-Semitic bigotry.[20] Of particular concern to him, in the late 1950s, were growing manifestations of anti-Semitism at the right-wing monthly *American Mercury*. Buckley was appalled and inclined (he told Morrie Ryskind) to "blast" the *Mercury* publicly.[21] Finally, on April 1, 1959, citing "pathologically irresponsible editorial material" in that magazine's current issue, Buckley issued a memorandum to writers for *National Review*. Henceforth, he announced, *National Review* would not include on its masthead names which also appeared on the masthead of the *American Mercury*.[22] The "insidious anti-Semitism that lurks in the corners of the *Mercury*," Buckley told a correspondent some months later, "has caused considerable damage." *National Review*, he declared, was attempting to protect both itself and its readers from "the stain of association with positions that gravely damage the cause of true conservatism."[23]

On another front, the Roman Catholic Buckley was perturbed by the fairly common impression, in these early years, that *National Review* was essentially a Catholic magazine.[24] In part, it appears, to counteract this perception, Buckley deliberately looked for a non-Catholic in 1961 to serve as *National Review*'s first religion columnist.[25] His choice was the distinguished Jewish theologian and sociologist Will Herberg. Significantly, Herberg was delighted to accept.[26] In the next decade he contributed numerous articles and the weight of his prestige to the magazine.

All this, presumably, pleased the seven Jewish writer-activists who so publicly cast their lot with *National Review* in the mid-1950s.[27] It also helps to explain Buckley's intense irritation with his liberal critics at the Anti-Defamation League. In a feisty exchange with the ADL's national chairman,

Dore Schary, in 1967, Buckley declared, "I have been credited with doing more than any single man in the history of the modern conservative movement to expunge anti-Semitism, to the extent that it lurked in the conservative movement. Over a period of fifteen years I have been relentlessly hostile to anyone who has approached me at *National Review* attempting to traffic in racial prejudice."[28]

Yet Buckley's vigilant opposition to anti-Semitism, his rejection of right-wing extremism, and his relentless efforts to elevate conservatism's standing among intellectuals cannot alone explain the Jewish dimension of his magazine at its birth. However welcoming and ecumenical, even he could not have drawn Schlamm, Ryskind, and the rest into his magazine's orbit unless they themselves had been prepared to enter it. The question therefore recurs: How did these seven individuals develop their affinity for *National Review*-style conservatism? How did they arrive at Buckley's journalistic hostelry when most other Jews could scarcely countenance such a trip? Who *were* these seven Jewish nonconformists, and what does their nonconformity reveal about their experience as Jews in America?

II

In many ways these men were typically Jewish. With the possible exception of Frank Meyer, all were first- or second-generation Americans. Three (Lyons, Schlamm, and Toledano) were born abroad. Three others (Chodorov, Liebman, and Ryskind) were born in New York of immigrant parents from eastern Europe. Except for Schlamm, who was born in the Austro-Hungarian empire and educated in Vienna, the rest spent most or all of their boyhood in the vicinity of New York City.[29] Whether it was the Lower East Side, the Lower West Side, Brooklyn, or nearby Newark, New Jersey, the sidewalks of New York were for most of them a formative cultural milieu.

Their family circumstances varied. Schlamm's father was a merchant in Galicia, Meyer's father a successful New York lawyer, Toledano's father a Paris-educated newspaper correspondent. Toledano, the only Sephardic Jew in this group, came from a long line of rabbis and other Jewish leaders, including some who had attained great eminence in medieval Catholic Spain. The rest had humble origins and—in the case of Chodorov, Lyons, and Ryskind—direct exposure to the hard world of the New York slums.[30]

Despite these obstacles, the seven soon displayed another characteristic of Jewish immigrants and immigrants' sons: upward mobility. In an era when only a small fraction of American high school graduates went on to college, every one of the seven received at least some higher education.[31] Highly articulate, they published, in the course of their careers, more than fifty books. Five of the seven wrote autobiographies.[32]

These premature Jewish conservatives had something else in common: Each, in his youth, had been a student radical. Frank Chodorov, the oldest, was the most idiosyncratic. A temperamental "aginner" and self-styled "individualist," Chodorov as a boy instinctively disliked the Socialist "pundits" who pontificated in the "coffee saloons" on Grand Street.[33] Socialists, he came to believe, had "an intuitive urgency for power, power over other people."[34] As a college student at Columbia (in the class of 1907) he "fought it out with the socialists," arguing that "man's management of man is presumptuous and fraught with danger."[35] Instead, Chodorov became enamored of anarchism until he discovered that the anarchists "took a dim view" of private property, "without which, it seemed to me even then, individualism was meaningless."[36]

But it was not radical politics which gripped Chodorov's soul in his college years. Stung by repeated anti-Semitic insults during his freshman year, when he had the temerity as a Jew to play on the football team, he began to search for the cause of this "horrible thing." In short order he found his answer: Religion was "at the bottom of social discords." Religion was "the cause of all strife."[37] Flush with this "discovery," Chodorov became a militant atheist and embarked, in his own words, on an "anti-God crusade." For the next dozen years or so, he remained "loyal" to his cause.[38]

Morrie Ryskind, the next oldest, took a more conventional route to the Left. As a member of the class of 1917 at the Columbia School of Journalism, he was admired for his humorous writings in student publications. But when war clouds descended over the United States in 1916–17, Ryskind's activism turned serious. Fervently opposed to American entry into World War I, he joined the Intercollegiate Society of Socialists, distributed antiwar pamphlets on street corners, and wrote editorials against American intervention. Then, when the United States declared war in April 1917, Columbia's president, Nicholas Murray Butler—previously an advocate of neutrality—instantly and vociferously became prowar. Disgusted by what he saw as Butler's "tone of righteousness" and "abdication of principles," Ryskind promptly satirized "Czar Nicholas of Columbia" in the campus humor magazine. The students laughed—but not Butler. When Ryskind refused to apologize or resign as editor of the magazine, he was expelled from Columbia University, just six weeks before he would have graduated.[39]

A few years later, after stints in journalism and public relations, Ryskind launched a sparkling career as a scriptwriter for Broadway musicals and Hollywood films, including several of the Marx Brothers' greatest comedies. (Groucho Marx was even the best man at Ryskind's wedding.) Still something of an antiwar liberal and supporter of leftish causes in the 1920s, Ryskind combined political conviction and devastating satire in *Strike Up the Band* (1930) and *Of Thee I Sing* (1931), for which, in 1932, he shared the Pulitzer Prize.[40] In 1932, he voted for Norman Thomas for president.[41] As late as 1936, he counted himself a member of the Old Guard faction of the Socialist Party.[42]

The other Jewish conservatives-to-be went further. In 1919, at the age of fifteen, "Willi" Schlamm—still in Vienna—joined the Communist youth movement. By the age of twenty-one, he was editor-in-chief of the Austrian Communist Party's periodical, *Die Rote Fahne [Red Flag]*.[43] Across the Atlantic, Eugene Lyons's initiation into radical activity had been even swifter. Arriving in New York City from Russia as a boy of nine, he had been bitterly disillusioned by the poverty and class conflict into which he had been thrust. "I thought myself a 'socialist' almost as soon as I thought at all," he later wrote.[44] He dreamed of becoming a writer for "my side of the class war."[45] As a college freshman in 1917, Lyons rejoiced at news of the Russian Revolution. The Bolshevik coup later that year seemed an equally glorious event.[46] During the 1920s, as a journalist and committed leftist, Lyons threw himself into the defense of Sacco and Vanzetti and worked in the New York office of the Soviet news agency Tass for four years. "Unhesitatingly I cast my lot with the communists," he said.[47] In 1927 he was chosen to be the United Press's correspondent in Moscow. Although never a formal member of the Communist Party, he was an enthusiast nonetheless, determined to use his new journalistic post "in the further service of that cause."[48]

While Lyons was settling down in Moscow, Frank Meyer was on a similar journey. Between 1929 and 1932, Meyer was an undergraduate at Oxford University. In late 1931, dissatisfied by the Labour Party's "reformism," he joined the Communist Party of Great Britain. Within a few months he was the national secretary of the party's student bureau and overseer of several hundred disciplined party members in British universities.[49]

A few years later—in late 1937 or early 1938—a fourteen-year-old Marvin Liebman joined the Young Communist League in New York City and happily plunged into the thriving party subculture in that city.[50] Across town Ralph de Toledano—seven years older than Liebman—was studying at

Columbia in its class of 1938 and feeling the "pull" of the Communist tide.[51] For a number of reasons Toledano felt ambivalent about Columbia's student Communists and did not join the Young Communist League (though asked to do so).[52] But he lived, as he later recorded, on the Communist Party's "cozy periphery" and "quarreled with the Communists only over tactics, strategy and degree."[53]

Yet if the seven subjects of this essay started out on the Left, they did not remain there indefinitely. Chodorov, again, took the most unusual path. Along about 1915 he read—and then repeatedly reread—Henry George's *Progress and Poverty*. Each time he did so, he later recalled, "I felt myself slipping into a cause."[54] For the rest of his life, Chodorov was a disciple of Henry George and an uncompromising libertarian antistatist.[55] From 1937 to 1942 he was the director of the Henry George School of Social Science in New York, which he built into a flourishing institution.[56] Proclaiming himself a "radical" in the cause of individual liberty and "historic liberalism," he took up journalism in the 1940s and wrote books with titles like *One Is a Crowd* and *The Income Tax: Root of All Evil*.[57] In the first decade after World War II, his unadulterated libertarianism influenced many younger conservatives, including William F. Buckley Jr.[58]

For our other Jewish radicals it was nothing so esoteric as Henry George that catalyzed their turn to the Right. In one way or another, it was the encounter with communism. Expelled from the Communist ranks for deviationism in 1929, Willi Schlamm became a prominent anti-Nazi and anti-Stalinist newspaper editor in central Europe during the 1930s. In 1938 he fled to the United States, where he soon found work as a columnist at the anti-Stalinist *New Leader*. In 1941 he joined the editorial staff of *Fortune*. By the end of World War II, he had risen in the ranks to become a foreign policy advisor and senior assistant to Henry Luce, editor-in-chief of *Time*, *Life*, and *Fortune*. Gradually the "non-Marxian socialist" found himself drifting toward the Right.[59]

Two other true believers could tell similar stories. Having seen at first hand the face of totalitarianism and Red terror in Russia between 1928 and 1934, Eugene Lyons was not about to remain mute. His *Assignment in Utopia* was only the opening salvo in a lifelong campaign to awaken Americans to the evil and danger of communism. For Frank Meyer the process of disillusionment took longer. In 1934 the young Communist firebrand returned to the United States, where he rose in the ranks of the American Communist Party as a dedicated member of its Stalinist cadre. During service in the army in World War II, Meyer's ideological armor began to crack. He was outside the Communist cocoon now, and he had time to think. In 1944 Friedrich Hayek's antisocialist polemic, *The Road to Serfdom*, shook Meyer further. By now he was on the Browderite right wing of the American Communist movement. In 1945 Earl Browder himself—the head of the party— was suddenly purged. Meyer, who bitterly fought this Stalin-imposed switch in the party line, left soon after. No longer in thrall to a god that had failed, he retreated to a reclusive sanctuary in Woodstock, New York, to put his life back together and decide what he really believed.[60]

What Schlamm, Lyons, and Meyer experienced inside the Communist domain, Ryskind and Toledano encountered on the fringe. During the mid-1930s Ryskind still considered himself a man of the left of center. He voted for Franklin Roosevelt's reelection in 1936 and wrote occasionally for *The Nation*.[61] But the gifted comic writer, who by now had moved to Hollywood, soon ran into a rapidly growing Communist presence in the film industry, including the Screen Writers Guild, in which he was active. As an Old Guard Socialist in 1936, Ryskind had opposed the Socialist Party's decision to form a united front with the Communists; he had no faith in the Communists' commitment to civil liberties.[62] Eugene Lyons's *Assignment in Utopia* reinforced his anti-Communist convictions.[63] When Ryskind—never timid about expressing himself—began criticizing Roosevelt's court-packing scheme and the Moscow purge trials, he was accused of being a Trotskyite and of selling out to Wall Street and the Hollywood movie moguls. Liberal acquaintances stopped asking him to their homes. He had mocked the illiberal pieties of Popular Front liberalism.[64]

For Ralph de Toledano it was a similar story. The Moscow show trials, Lyons's *Assignment in Utopia*, and the bloody Stalinist subversion of the Spanish Republic in the Spanish civil war helped to lift the "red haze" in which he had been living.[65] Above all, the monstrous Hitler-Stalin pact of 1939 dispelled Toledano's lingering hesitations and made him a convinced anti-Communist.[66] As he emerged from "the valley of the Red Shadow"[67] he, too, endured the ire of once-close friends who now called him a "fascist."[68]

In 1940 Toledano joined the editorial staff of the anti-Stalinist *New Leader*, where Willi Schlamm had also taken refuge.[69] Bit by bit the young Columbia graduate's political education continued. Early in 1943 Toledano's friend, the emigré Italian anarchist Carlo Tresca, was mysteriously murdered in New York City—a victim, Toledano had reason to believe, of a Communist assassin under orders from the Kremlin. For the young editor at the *New Leader*,

Tresca's killing "was a landmark on the road to anti-Communism. . . . My war against communism suddenly acquired a very personal dimension."[70]

In their deepening revulsion against communism, the seven Jewish intellectuals did not content themselves with becoming mere ex-radicals. To their new political orientation they brought the same fervor that had characterized their youth. At the Luce publishing empire during the 1940s the voluble Schlamm was an energetic member of the anti-Communist faction and an ally of a soon-to-be-famous ex-Communist (and *Time* editor) named Whittaker Chambers.[71] Between 1939 and 1944, Eugene Lyons edited the *American Mercury* and used its pages repeatedly to warn Americans not to trust our wartime ally, Soviet Russia.[72] In 1947, as the Cold War intensified, he became a contributing editor of the newly founded anti-Communist monthly *Plain Talk,* edited by another Jewish ex-radical, Isaac Don Levine.[73] (Ralph de Toledano was the magazine's first managing editor.)[74] In the years to come, Lyons and others churned out anti-Communist literature in profusion, including Toledano's and Victor Lasky's runaway bestseller, *Seeds of Treason* (an account of the Hiss-Chambers espionage case), and Frank Meyer's *The Moulding of Communists.*[75]

Meanwhile, on the West Coast, Morrie Ryskind became increasingly embroiled in the civil war between Communists and anti-Communists that tore Hollywood apart in the 1940s.[76] In 1947, he testified as a "friendly witness" at the House Un-American Activities Committee's hearings on Communist infiltration of the motion picture industry.[77] He paid a severe price for his cooperation. When publicity-conscious industry representatives hinted ahead of time that he should soft-pedal his testimony, he refused— and was promptly blacklisted. Up to then he had been earning as much as $75,000 per script as one of the ten highest paid writers in Hollywood. After he testified, he never received another cent. The more celebrated "unfriendly witnesses" known as the Hollywood Ten were not the only film industry professionals to be deemed "unemployable."[78]

Marvin Liebman, the youngest of the lot, took longer to reach the Right. An ex-Communist in 1945 at the age of twenty-two (he quit the party when his hero Earl Browder was expelled),[79] he nevertheless remained on the Left several more years. But the party's clichés were losing their luster, and doubts about the party line were intruding. Then, in 1951, Liebman met Elinor Lipper, a German Jew who had spent eleven years in an infamous Soviet slave labor camp in Siberia. In two horrific hours she told him her story and destroyed his remaining "emotional ties" with the Soviet Union. For Liebman, it was a "catharsis," a "turning point in my life."[80] Soon the public relations executive was raising funds for refugees from Communist countries and for a widening array of anti-Communist causes.[81]

Yet anticommunism alone cannot explain the full journey upon which these Jewish activists now embarked. There were, after all, many Jewish anti-Communists at the time who remained on the Left—in the trade-union movement, for example. Some other factor must have been operative here; what was it? In a word, it was a concurrent disenchantment with liberalism.

For Morrie Ryskind—already uneasy about Rooseveltian hubris and the drift of the New Deal's domestic agenda—the final blow was Roosevelt's decision to seek a third presidential term in 1940. Ryskind was appalled by this "horrendous insult to our political heritage." Registering for the first time ever as a Republican, he donated $10,000 to Wendell Willkie's presidential campaign and even wrote the Republican candidate's campaign song ("We Want Willkie").[82]

Ryskind's reaction to the imperial Roosevelt presidency was no passing spasm. In 1948 and 1952 he ardently supported Robert Taft's presidential candidacy.[83] Along the way he became active in the Beverly Hills Republican Club where, in 1951, he met an impressive young guest lecturer: William F. Buckley Jr.[84]

For most of the others, it was not liberalism's domestic policies that first propelled them to the Right. It was liberalism's response to the menacing evil of communism. In 1941 Eugene Lyons—premature as usual—published *The Red Decade: The Stalinist Penetration of America*. It was a scathing exposé of Communist influence on American life in the late 1930s—and of the fatuities (and worse) of Popular Front liberalism.[85] During World War II, Lyons continued to fret about Communist penetration of the American labor movement and other institutions.[86] Cheerfully accepting the label "Red-baiter,"[87] he denied in the late 1940s and early 1950s that the United States was succumbing to anti-Communist hysteria.[88] "The danger today," he wrote in 1953, "is not hysteria but complacency."[89]

Lyons's revulsion against Popular Front liberalism and its anti–anti-Communist prejudices found an echo in Ralph de Toledano. In the immediate aftermath of World War II, Toledano was still on the anti-Stalinist Left. He belonged to the Liberal Party and briefly joined Americans of Democratic Action.[90] But in 1948, while covering the sensational Hiss-Chambers case for *Newsweek*, Toledano became sickened by many liberals' response to the controversy.[91] He also became acquainted with Whittaker Chambers.

"From the start," the *Newsweek* journalist later wrote, "I knew that I had come upon the most significant friendship of my life."[92] Its impact was profound. With Chambers as the "catalyst," Toledano made his "break with the liberals in 1948" and initiated a long, soul-wrenching reexamination of his fundamental beliefs.[93] Like Chambers, Toledano came to see the twentieth-century crisis of the West as a fundamentally religious conflict between theistic and atheistic views of man—a war in which secular liberalism was on the wrong side.[94]

And so, in the late 1940s and 1950s, the conviction grew among the nascent Jewish conservatives that not just communism but liberalism itself was terribly flawed. There were many indicia of their deepening disillusionment. In 1948, for instance, at a time when the late Franklin Roosevelt was a hero to most American Jews, Eugene Lyons boldly published a laudatory biography of Roosevelt's rival, Herbert Hoover.[95] Lyons, in fact, became a friend of Hoover's and repeatedly extolled him as a great man.[96] Ralph de Toledano also became a friend and admirer of "the Chief" (as Hoover was known to his intimates).[97]

Nowhere, though, was the Jewish conservatives' growing estrangement from liberalism more evident than in their behavior during the McCarthy era of 1950–54. Privately some of them were well aware of Senator Joseph McCarthy's deficiencies.[98] But in public word and deed nearly all of them became, if not defenders of McCarthy personally, then critics of his critics as well as strong believers in the basic legitimacy of the ongoing congressional investigations of Communist activity in the United States.[99] Eventually two of them (Ryskind and Schlamm) became affiliated for a time with the John Birch Society.[100]

For most of the premature Jewish conservatives, the McCarthy controversy was a bridge to William F. Buckley Jr. In 1954 Schlamm wrote a stirring prologue to Buckley's and L. Brent Bozell's *McCarthy and His Enemies*. Not only that, Schlamm helped to edit their manuscript—a collaboration that paved the way for his fateful suggestion that Buckley launch *National Review*.[101] When *McCarthy and His Enemies* was ready for publication, Toledano supplied an enthusiastic endorsement.[102] Meyer also admired the book, while Ryskind was so delighted that he undertook a personal campaign to boost its sales in California.[103]

Eventually the storms of the McCarthy era subsided. But the furies they unleashed helped to drive many emerging conservatives—including some of our Jewish conservatives—into a hardening repudiation of liberalism and all its works. Toledano, for one, came to believe—like his hero/mentor, Whittaker Chambers—that communism was the "military phase" of "a great revolution which was destroying a civilization built on religious and moral imperatives."[104] It was a revolution, moreover, in which secular, relativistic liberals were "tortured allies" of the atheistic Communists.[105] Searching for a conservative alternative, Toledano concluded that anticommunism alone was not enough. Anticommunism was "not conservative unless it aimed at more than the military manifestation of the Communist threat."[106] In rejecting communism one must also reject liberalism, which shared its underlying "theorems" and worldview.[107]

Frank Meyer, the aspiring conservative theoretician, was the most tireless exponent of this perception of the organic, philosophical unity of the Left. The "Bolshevik revolution" and the "Roosevelt revolution" had "parallel" aims, he contended. Each sought to bring into power "an elite dedicated to the principled suppression of the freedom of men as innate centers of will."[108] "The primacy of society and the state over the individual," he said, was "the essence of collectivism."[109] Both liberalism and communism shared this bedrock assumption. Time and again, in the years ahead, Meyer would maintain that liberalism and communism were "forms of the same revolutionary movement."[110]

Not for Meyer and the others, then, Arthur Schlesinger Jr.'s famous dictum that the welfare state was the best defense against communism. *Their* enemy was what Toledano called the "Coercive State"—in *all* its manifestations.[111] The championing of individual liberty against the State was a clarion theme in nearly all the Jewish conservatives' later writings.[112] Meyer, characteristically, composed the most elaborate formulation in a book of political theory entitled *In Defense of Freedom* (1962). "My intention in writing this book," he proclaimed, "is to vindicate the freedom of the person as the central and primary end of political society."[113] Society and the state are "made for individual men, not men for them."[114]

Having seen Leviathan up close—either as Communists, near-Communists, or anti-Communists—these Jewish ex-radicals seemed to cherish their freedom all the more.

III

By 1955, then, our seven subjects were firmly ensconced on the American Right—"out of step" (in Chodorov's words) with the dominant intellectual climate of their day.[115] They were also Jews, surely aware that few of their brethren shared their political affiliations. There is little sign that this fact caused them anguish.[116] Indeed, their nonconformity, in many cases, extended to things Jewish.

With the possible exception of Schlamm and Lyons, who seem not to have written about the subject, all of our group were brought up as Jews and exposed to various degrees of Jewish tradition and religious observance.[117] As upwardly mobile Jewish immigrants and immigrants' children, most (and probably all) of them experienced the sting of anti-Semitism. Morrie Ryskind never forgot an anti-Semitic incident he endured at the Algonquin Round Table in the 1920s.[118] Nor did Marvin Liebman ever forget the terrible anti-Semitic taunts he received while in the U.S. Army in World War II.[119] Ralph de Toledano felt the pain of "social" anti-Semitism at *Newsweek* in the 1950s.[120] Anti-Semitism at Princeton may have caused Frank Meyer to drop out in the late 1920s and attend Oxford instead.[121] And, as mentioned earlier, anti-Semitic insults at Columbia transformed Frank Chodorov into a crusading atheist.

Years later, as conservatives, some of these Jews noticed anti-Semitism on the Right and protested against it. When the anti-Semitic blight appeared at the *American Mercury* in 1955, Toledano declared that he would "have no part of a publication which even flirts with the anti-Semites."[122] Ryskind, too, was upset by anti-Semitism at the *American Mercury* and urged *National Review* to denounce it.[123] As a consummate organizer of conservative and anti-Communist causes, Liebman also was acutely aware of (and sometimes the target of) anti-Semitism in the fever swamps of the far Right.[124]

At times, some of these conservatives evinced their Jewish consciousness in other ways. On a number of occasions, Lyons wrote articles about the plight of Jews under communism and attacked the canard that communism was a Jewish product.[125] He also endeavored strenuously to awaken the Jewish community to the Communist danger by helping to organize, in 1948, the American Jewish League Against Communism.[126] Ryskind became an active member of this organization.[127] Some years later, after it had become moribund, Liebman was invited to make an effort to revive it.[128]

Yet what stands out most about the seven, as a group, was that they were not—at least publicly—very demonstrative about their religious and ethnic identity. The first chapter of *Assignment in Utopia*—in which Lyons discusses his youth on the Lower East Side of New York—contains no explicit acknowledgment that he is Jewish. Similarly, in Toledano's memoir, *Lament for a Generation*—which chronicled both his political and religious evolution—there was only a single reference to his Jewish ancestry.[129] According to a close friend, Frank Meyer in his later years took a "carefully distant view . . . of his own Jewishness."[130] For Chodorov, *his* Jewishness was a fact (and a subject of lifelong curiosity) but not something otherwise to be made much of. Writing in 1948, he declared bluntly, "I am a Jew. Not that anyone cares, least of all myself."[131]

There is, perhaps, a ready explanation for this phenomenon. As first- and second-generation immigrants, these Jews no doubt felt an urge to assimilate. Moreover, striving to make it in a society where anti-Semitism was still strong, they may have sensed that it would do them little good to advertise their marginality. The middle decades of the twentieth century, in any case, were not a time when upwardly mobile professionals emphasized their ethnicity.

But even allowing for these considerations of time and place, what remains noticeable about these Jewish conservatives is how individualistic they were—and how willing to deviate from the Jewish mainstream. Chodorov was an antiwar isolationist in 1939–41 and lost his job at the Henry George School because of it.[132] In 1948 Ryskind supported Robert Taft's presidential quest despite initial displeasure at Taft's criticism of the Nuremberg war crimes trials.[133] During the Cold War, Lyons wrote fairly frequently for Catholic publications, where his anti-Communist expertise and commentary were welcome.[134] Toledano, too, wrote at times for Catholic periodicals; his 1947 pamphlet *How Communism Demoralizes Youth* (which he prepared for the Catholic Information Society) cost him a position as a youth leader in the Ethical Culture movement.[135]

Indeed, several of the Jewish conservatives showed their willingness to criticize severely the Jewish establishment of their day. In 1951 Lyons publicly accused the Anti-Defamation League of a "vicious attack" on the executive director of the American Jewish League Against Communism.[136] In 1962 he publicly battled the ADL over Dr. Frederick Schwarz's Christian Anti-Communism Crusade and addressed a rally organized by Schwarz in Madison Square Garden.[137] In 1964 Willi Schlamm accused "New York Jews" of "casting suspicion on every man of the American Right for rabid anti-Semitism"—a "neurotic readiness" that was both dangerous and unfounded.[138] A year later Toledano, in his syndicated column, berated the Anti-Defamation League for being more interested in denouncing the "radical right" than in combating growing anti-Semitism among American blacks.[139]

This readiness to swim against the current was especially evident in the group's response to the great issue for American Jews of the 1940s and 1950s: Zionism and the creation of the State of Israel. Chodorov, the arch-individualist, was outspokenly anti-Zionist and bitterly resented the arguments of militant Zionists. "There is a strident group in this country," he wrote in 1952, "who insist that American citizenship does not absolve the Jew from loyalty to Israel, that he is in fact vested with dual citizenship, the stronger of which, judging from their demands for financial help, is in the newly acquired half. That is silly . . . if loyalty to Israel is the identification of a Jew, then I declare unequivocally that I am not one."[140] Fiercely rejecting "the yoke of dualism," he twice reviewed favorably books by Rabbi Elmer Berger, a leading American anti-Zionist.[141] Zionism was not Judaism, Chodorov asserted, but rather "the mania of a nationalist-minded group."[142]

Chodorov was not alone in his anti-Zionist orientation. Ryskind became a friend of Rabbi Berger and repeatedly urged Buckley, in the late 1950s, to meet him.[143] According to Buckley, Schlamm was "utterly uninterested" in Israel when they worked together in the mid-1950s.[144] Meyer also was initially skeptical about the wisdom of the creation of Israel (because of the displacement of Arabs in the region). On one occasion, his son recalled, Meyer asked, "Couldn't they have put Israel somewhere else?"[145] But by 1967, and probably before, Meyer had changed his mind and become an ardent supporter of Israel as an outpost of Western civilization in the Cold War.[146] Anticommunism, and perhaps Jewish pride, altered his perspective.[147]

Yet on this issue the seven Jewish conservatives were not united. The two youngest (and perhaps that fact is significant) had a very different attitude toward the Zionist cause. Not long after quitting the Communist Party in 1945, Liebman joined the American League for a Free Palestine, the American arm of the Palestinian Jewish underground army known as the Irgun. In late 1946 he sailed from New York as purser of a Jewish refugee ship, the *Ben Hecht,* only to be captured by the British navy and sent to a detention camp in Cyprus. Upon his release he returned to the United States, where he became a fundraiser for Israeli causes.[148]

All this happened while Liebman was still on the Left. During the 1950s and 1960s, his fundraising career took a conservative turn, and his Zionist activism apparently subsided (at least from public view). But Liebman seems never to have abandoned his pro-Israel sentiments.[149] As with Meyer, anticommunism buttressed Liebman's identification with Israel.

Of the seven Jews in our survey only Toledano seems to have been publicly supportive of Israel in the 1950s.[150] And an Israeli sympathizer he remained. In 1969, evidently for the first time, he journeyed to Israel as a guest of its government. The trip, he told a rabbinic friend, was one of the most moving travel experiences of his life.[151] In 1970—despite all his criticisms, years before, of the Truman administration's handling of the Communist issue— he contemplated writing a biography of President Truman, for whom he now had great respect. One reason, he said, was Truman's crucial role in the creation of Israel.[152]

But if Toledano, in this instance, was unrepresentative of our group, in another and critical respect he fit right in. With the exception of Ryskind— who apparently never lost his ancestral faith—every one of these Jewish conservatives grew up either outside of, or in open rebellion against, Judaism.[153] In 1898, at the impressionable age of eleven, Frank Chodorov attended a Yom Kippur service in a local synagogue. There he spied a man he knew—a man with a thoroughly "bad reputation"—earnestly, very earnestly, saying his prayers. The boy began to wonder: "Could one day of hard prayer in a synagogue wash out the sins of a whole year? Is God bought off so cheaply?" When his mother could give him no convincing answer, young Chodorov rebelled. It was "my last trip to the synagogue," he later wrote.[154] So far as is known, in the remaining sixty-eight years of his life he never went to a synagogue again.

Nor, in this area, was Chodorov out of step. Frank Meyer's religious background was Reform Judaism, not Orthodox, but he, too, was an intellectual rebel as a teenager and rejected his religious heritage quite early.[155] Toledano was a Sephardic Jew, proud of his distinguished lineage, and his home environment was not untouched by religious influences.[156] But by the age of twelve, he had concluded that he did not believe in God. His father, an agnostic, sent him to an Ethical Culture school, where he encountered the "sterile rationalism" of people who believed that "to be categorical about truth was a form of fanaticism." At Columbia, he shared in the prevailing "invincible and optimistic materialism" of the campus. Inducted into the U.S. Army in 1943, he refused to allow it to affix the letter C (for Catholic), P (for Protestant) or H (for Hebrew) to his dogtags. He continued to resist "the pressures of religious affiliation." After the war he became editor of the Ethical Culture Society's monthly, *The Standard,* where in 1946 he penned and published a secular humanist credo.[157]

Lyons, too, had become a rationalist and religious skeptic while young and apparently never wavered from his nonfaith.[158] He sent his daughter to the same Ethical Culture preparatory school that Toledano had attended.[159] About Schlamm's religious upbringing little is known, but as a Communist at the age of fifteen he presumably—and probably zestfully—imbibed the doctrinal atheism of his Marxist comrades. As for Liebman, his boyhood had been rich with temple attendance, celebration of religious holidays, and exposure to "Jewish traditions."[160] But as a teenage Communist he, too, presumably put religion behind.

In later years every one of these Jews (except Lyons and Ryskind) experienced a "return to religion," a spiritual awakening that paralleled their political-intellectual migration. But curiously, and perhaps significantly, in no instance did their theological journeys take them unreservedly back to the Judaism of their forebears.

Once more, Chodorov's path was all his own. Prodded in part by Henry George's *Progress and Poverty,* he struggled to discover a metaphysical underpinning for his philosophy of individual rights. Where could one find an inviolable *basis* for such rights, he asked himself, if not in "an order of things outside man and his works"? Slowly and reluctantly the zealous atheist felt compelled to accept what he called the "God-idea"—faith that in nature one could discern "immutable law." It was not organized religion that he embraced, only "religion itself, which is merely faith in the possibility of an explanatory pattern of constancies." His was an abstract, vaguely deistic religion without a deity.[161] Beyond that he would go no further.[162]

Frank Chodorov, it seems safe to say, was sui generis. Far more typical, in his religious yearnings, was Ralph de Toledano. A few years after World War II, the young Jewish rationalist underwent a religious conversion—an ineffable experience of God's grace that he recounted evocatively in his *Lament for a Generation.*[163] A growing friendship with the ex-Communist and Quaker mystic Whittaker Chambers—with whom he felt a deep spiritual affinity—played a substantial part in Toledano's spiritual rebirth. "Somehow, through you," he told Chambers in 1951, "I returned to my faith in God."[164]

But what institutional form, if any, would Toledano's renewed faith now take? An accomplished poet and music critic as well as a journalist, he seemed thoroughly at home with Christian sacred music and writings.[165] As a Spanish-speaking Sephardic Jew who loved Spanish literature, he seemed equally moved by Sephardic rituals and by the Roman Catholic mass.[166] Growing up Sephardic in New York City, he felt a closer "kinship" with the Spanish-Catholic poet and philosopher Miguel de Unamuno than with the Yiddish-speaking Ashkenazic Jewish intellectuals he met on Second Avenue. In fact, he came to feel that "if Jews were somehow alien in America, Sephardic Jews were alien twice over; once in America and once among the Ashkenazim."[167]

Like Whittaker Chambers, Toledano evidently considered converting to Roman Catholicism in the 1950s. On one occasion, he sent a copy of one of his books to a famous Catholic bishop. It bore the inscription: "From a Catholic fellow traveler."[168] But Toledano "could never forget" the wrong that the Catholic Church, through the Spanish Inquisition, had perpetrated on his kin nearly five centuries before: In 1492 his distinguished ancestor Daniel de Toledo and his relatives, along with all other Jews living in Spain who refused to convert to Christianity, were expelled from that country. For Toledano this late-medieval act of "ethnic cleansing" proved an insuperable hurdle.[169] His own subsequent theological ruminations were, by his own acknowledgment, unorthodox—neither conventionally Judaic nor conventionally Christian.[170]

If Toledano at least glanced toward Rome, Willi Schlamm went virtually all the way. In the mid-1950s he told William F. Buckley Jr. that he considered himself a "Christian fellow traveler" and that the main reason he did not convert was pride.[171] In 1960 he remarked to a German journalist, "Spiritually, without question, I tend toward Christianity."[172]

Then, in 1964, this emigré "coffeehouse Viennese Jewish intellectual" (as Buckley called him)[173] produced an entire book on the subject of Jewish identity: *Wer ist Jude?* [*Who Is a Jew?*].[174] In it Schlamm asserts that the creation of the State of Israel now permits the solution of the dilemma of Jewish existence in the Diaspora. Thanks to Israel, Jews of the Diaspora need no longer feel an obligation to remain Jewish. A radical voluntarist (as one reviewer described him), he argues that Jewish identity is now a matter of choice.[175]

According to Schlamm, there are only two valid choices for a Jew wishing to remain a Jew. One could become a "national" Jew and emigrate to Israel, or one could become a religious Jew but otherwise assimilate into one's host country. A Jew is anyone who wants to be a Jew. He calls for Judaism to become a religion open to all—indeed, for both Jews and Christians to proselytize. He discusses Simone Weil and Henri Bergson, Jews who had become Christian but had not wanted to be baptized because they did not want to be disloyal to their own people. But now, thanks to the establishment of Israel, Jewish survival is assured—and individual Jews of the Diaspora are free to choose their own religion without feelings of guilt or embarrassment.

Ironically, in the end Schlamm never quite chose any of his alternatives. He did not move to Israel, he did not return to Judaism, and he did not formally convert to Christianity. But according to a close friend, he did become a "Christian by conviction" who (though never baptized) received, when he died, a Catholic burial service officiated by a Carmelite priest.[176]

If Schlamm—in the words of this same friend—"died at the very gates of the Church," the two remaining Jews in our group entered inside.[177] In the late 1970s, Marvin Liebman—by then in his fifties—became spiritually restless and began to seek a religious home. In 1980 he was baptized into the Roman Catholic Church; William F. Buckley Jr. and Buckley's sister were his godparents.[178]

It was Frank Meyer whose journey from Jerusalem to Moscow to Rome was the most tortuous one (and possibly the most revealing). Not too long after his teenaged rebellion against Judaism, Meyer found himself at Oxford where, in 1931, he faced a choice: He could become a Communist or he could become a Catholic. Why? Because these were the two great bodies of thought that gave answers and guidance about what to do in the crisis that the world was in. Christianity, he had concluded, was the only serious alternative to communism.[179] For a time he was tempted by the arguments of two brilliant Catholic intellectual priests, Martin D'Arcy and Ronald Knox, who were then affiliated with Oxford University.[180] But in late 1931, communism won the battle for his mind.

When Meyer broke with the Communist Party in 1945 and undertook, over the next several years, to reconstruct his worldview, he conspicuously did not return to the lost Judaism of his boyhood.[181] In fact, for the rest of his life he had very little contact with the American Jewish community.[182] Apparently Judaism's emphasis on community repelled him.[183] Having just escaped the fearful regimentation of the Communist Party, he was not about to submit to any authority—even a spiritual one—that might circumscribe what a friend called his "endangered individuality."[184]

Instead, in the late 1940s and 1950s he began to consider himself a Christian, although one who abstained from any denominational affiliation.[185] More particularly, despite a confessedly powerful attraction to the Roman Catholic Church, he held back for years from entering its portals. For one thing, he told Buckley in 1954, "I'm a Jew, and it's always harder, especially if there's persecution going on.[186] Like Toledano, he could not forget past injustices. For another thing, he found the Church and some of its doctrines "collectivist."[187] He disagreed with its position on abortion.[188] He speculated once that he might become an Episcopalian because that church permitted more doctrinal diversity, but the liberal political bent of the Episcopal Church ultimately scared him away.[189]

Finally, in 1972, as he lay dying of cancer, the time for decision arrived. Virtually to the end he raised objections.[190] But on April 1, 1972, Meyer ceased to argue and was baptized a Catholic. That very same day he died.[191]

Of the seven Jewish conservatives who became associated with *National Review,* then, two became Catholics outright, one became Catholic in his beliefs, and one (for a time at least) was a "fellow traveler." It is a singular datum. Was it a coincidence, or was there some larger significance to it?

In matters so personal it is probably best not to speculate too much. But a few conjectures do seem worth offering. First, as the premature Jewish conservatives made their peregrination to the Right, the Jewish religious and political establishment of the day could not have seemed appealing to them. To the extent that Jewish religious and communal institutions were publicly identified with liberal causes (and with social justice defined in liberal terms), they could not have seemed a plausible haven for exradicals who had rejected *all* left-of-center ideologies as variants of the same false god. Prizing their hard-won individuality, and placing a very high value on liberty, some of these nonconformists seemed noticeably averse to the communal emphases of Jewish thought and practice. Believing (as Schlamm argued in *Wer ist Jude?*) that the Christian faith directed its adherents away from the collective and toward the "individual person," they evidently found it congenial to gravitate in the same direction themselves.[192]

But why, then, did they turn to Rome? It is noteworthy that (except for Meyer, who considered the middle way of Anglicanism) none of these Jewish conservatives seems to have seriously contemplated becoming a Protestant.[193] Perhaps the mainline Protestant denominations of the era appeared too liberal or too bland. Certainly Protestant fundamentalism would have seemed exotic, if indeed these Jews were even aware of it. There is no evidence that they were.

What remained was the Roman Catholic Church, rigorously anti-Communist (surely an attractive attribute) and projecting an image of continuity in a world of flux. And although William F. Buckley Jr. did not have much of a personal role in their religious reorientation,[194] the milieu of *National Review*-style conservatism which these Jews entered was one in which Roman Catholic and Anglo-Catholic influences were prominent.[195] Perhaps this distinctive cultural environment subtly influenced the theological as well as the political outcome of these Jews' journeys from Left to Right.

In any case, the fact is worth pondering that—unlike many Jewish conservatives of the 1990s, who are rediscovering Judaism (including Orthodoxy)—nearly all of the Jews of the *National Review* circle felt unable or unwilling, in their generation, to make the same choice.[196]

IV

And so, by the late 1950s, seven gifted Jewish intellectuals had made their way to *National Review*. In 1957, after a falling out with Buckley, Schlamm returned to Europe, where, for the next two decades, he had a turbulent career as a lecturer, newspaper columnist, editor, and author of bestselling books. An exuberant advocate of hardline policies towards the Soviet Union, he was hated by the German Left, which called him a warmonger, demagogue, and fascist.[197] But Schlamm's break with Buckley was not ideological, and in the 1960s he contributed a number of articles to *National Review*.

Morrie Ryskind and Eugene Lyons also wrote for *National Review,* as did Toledano, who became the magazine's music critic as well as its pseudonymous Washington correspondent for a time. After Frank Chodorov's stroke in 1961, his professional activity ceased, but by then his beloved Intercollegiate Society of Individualists was an established entity with thousands of members. Renamed the Intercollegiate Studies Institute in 1966, it is today one of the most important stars in the conservative intellectual galaxy.

Frank Meyer, too, found his niche at *National Review*. Cheerfully argumentative, relentless in his pursuit of truth, he was known as the magazine's "house metaphysician" and chief ideologist.[198] His regular column was aptly entitled "Principles and Heresies." In the 1960s he became the principal architect of "fusionism," an influential attempt to reconcile conservatism's divergent theoretical tendencies. Marvin Liebman, meanwhile, became, in Buckley's words, "a one-man public-relations industry" for conservative and anti-Communist causes and the "principal administrative organ" for Young Americans for Freedom and other key conservative organizations.[199] His skills earned him comparison with Willi Munzenberg, the legendary Communist organizer of Popular Front activism during the 1930s.[200]

Each of these Jewish contrarians, then, in his own way, left his mark upon American conservatism. Without them the movement would have been much poorer. Clearly, among Jews, they represented a minority. In part because of their premature political affiliation with the American Right, in part because of their own distance from the American Jewish community, they constituted a kind of lost generation and are today, for the most part, little remembered outside conservative circles.

Still, the very existence of these "forgotten godfathers" of American conservatism—and of others beyond the scope of this essay—should make historians pause.[201] At the very least their remarkable careers suggest that in servatism—and of others beyond the scope of this essay—should make historians pause.[201] At the very least their remarkable careers suggest that in the 1940s and 1950s the American Jewish community was more politically diverse than is usually thought.

24

Joining the Ranks:
Commentary and American Conservatism

First given at a conference on the history of Commentary *in 2003, this essay was published in Murray Friedman, ed.,* Commentary *in American Life (Temple University Press, 2005).*

I

Probably no American journal of opinion has been more praised and pilloried in the last thirty years than *Commentary* has, under the editorship of Norman Podhoretz and Neal Kozodoy, and no political tendency or ideology has been more analyzed and remarked on than the phenomenon called neoconservatism, with which *Commentary* has been identified since the early 1970s. On the subject of neoconservatism, at least four full-length books have been written, along with several dissertations, numerous anthologies and memoirs, and uncounted newspaper and magazine articles—not to mention a stream of "background" works, as it were, about the "New York Intellectuals."[1]

Confronting this unending avalanche of scholarship, apologia, and polemic, one is reminded of an anecdote told about Albert Einstein. Called on to speak at an after-dinner ceremony, he arose and declared simply, "There is nothing new to say."

Yet, on reflection, at least one part of the story merits further investigation. Most of the now-extensive literature on neoconservatism has tended to concentrate on its early years, when Norman Podhoretz and his allies staged an intellectual insurrection against the American Left. Relatively less attention has been paid to the rest of the story: the years in which the deradical-ized journal joined forces with the American Right. It is *Commentary*'s pro-cess not of "breaking ranks," but of joining ranks—the ranks of American conservatism—that will be the focus of the pages that follow.

II

In its nearly sixty years of existence, *Commentary* has gone through three distinct ideological phases. The first (1945–59), under its founding editor Elliot Cohen, may be labeled "Cold War liberalism." The second (1960–late 1960s), under his successor Norman Podhoretz, might be called left/liberal-ism or "New Leftism." The third, which Podhoretz initiated in 1970, was a repudiation of the second phase and a comprehensive assault on the Left in all its guises. To this third period (still ongoing), critics and scholars have affixed the label "neoconservatism."

We need not tarry long over the origins of this third chapter in *Commentary*'s political evolution. In three powerful memoirs and other writings, Podhoretz has explained in detail the reasons for his break with his erst-while comrades. To say that in 1970 *Commentary*'s editor launched a com-prehensive critique of "the Sixties" might be acceptable shorthand. To be somewhat more specific, Podhoretz and likeminded friends were appalled by the furious anti-Americanism, neo-isolationism, and anti-anticommunism permeating the New Left in the later years of the Vietnam War and by the concurrent "cultural revolution of the 60's."[2] They were equally alarmed by what they saw as the craven capitulation of the liberal elite to the swelling left-wing tide and by the emergence of a corrosively antibourgeois "adver-sary culture" sustained by this very elite.

Many elements fueled the nascent neoconservatives' apprehensions: destructive student radicalism on the campuses, the traumatic 1967 New York City teachers' strike (which pitted blacks against Jews), the eruption of anti-Semitism in parts of the black community as black protest swept beyond the traditional civil rights agenda to demands for "black power" and even revolution, the rising cry for racial quotas in colleges and universities, and the shocking appearance of anti-Semitism and hostility to Israel on the American Left in the aftermath of the 1967 Six-Day War. For all these reasons and more, Podhoretz concluded that the time had come for *Commentary*, and for Jews in general, to defend "the liberal democratic order in America" against the ideas of those, "especially on the radical Left," who were working to destroy it.[3]

Commentary's public volte-face began with the magazine's June 1970 issue.[4] For the next several years, every issue bristled with articles challenging the icons and shibboleths of the Left. That this was no passing intellectual squabble was apparent by 1972, when the magazine's editor and his new allies vehemently opposed the leftist presidential candidacy of George McGovern. In a portent of things to come, that year Podhoretz voted to reelect President Richard Nixon. It was the first time he—and many other disaffected liberals—had ever cast a ballot for a Republican.[5]

The spectacle of ex-radicals and chastened liberals loudly rebelling against the transmogrification of American liberalism—a revolt against the Left from within—quickly aroused the interest of the nation's media.[6] Among those who were particularly intrigued were the editors of America's principal conservative magazine, *National Review,* headquartered (like *Commentary*) in New York City. In March 1971 *National Review* took approving note of *Commentary*'s right turn in an editorial invitingly entitled "Come On In, the Water's Fine."[7] A year later, one of *National Review*'s senior editors, James Burnham—an ex-Marxist himself, and thus in some ways a "premature neoconservative"—analyzed the intellectual journey that the *Commentary* circle was taking. To Burnham, the new ideological grouping had two characteristics: "a break with liberal doctrine" coupled with a retention of "the emotional gestalt of liberalism." In his judgment, it was an "uneasy dualism" indicative of a "transitional state" that was "bound to develop further into a more integral outlook."[8]

Meanwhile, *National Review*'s editor in chief, William F. Buckley Jr., had been getting acquainted with Norman Podhoretz. In 1972 the two began to correspond.[9] In one letter, Buckley acclaimed the "superb job" that Podhoretz was doing at *Commentary*.[10] Early in 1973, Podhoretz invited Buckley—evidently for the first time—to contribute to a *Commentary* symposium.[11] It was a subtle sign of the changing ideological landscape.

Such gestures were all the more significant in the light of *Commentary*'s past unfriendliness to *National Review*. Back in 1956, scarcely six months after Buckley's magazine was founded, *Commentary* had published a scathing attack on it, written by Dwight Macdonald. His article was called "Scrambled Eggheads on the Right," a title supplied by a young assistant editor named Norman Podhoretz.[12] In 1965 *Commentary* had struck again, this time with an article by Richard H. Rovere entitled "The Conservative Mindlessness." According to Rovere, the "rightist intellectuals" clustered around Buckley had produced "almost nothing but insults to the intelligence."[13]

Whatever their past ideological differences, by 1972 Podhoretz and Buckley had discovered common ground—so greatly had the political terrain shifted since the early 1960s. In part, perhaps, their developing friendship illustrated the old adage that the enemy of my enemy is my friend. More profoundly, it reflected the growing congruence between the Cold War liberalism that Podhoretz was now trying to revive and the Cold War conservatism championed by *National Review*. When it came to resisting Soviet imperialism abroad and détentist illusions (or worse) at home, the readers of *Commentary* could increasingly appreciate *National Review* (and vice versa).

For Podhoretz, another factor permitted these first modest steps toward dialogue, and eventual alliance, with the respectable Right. In the wake of the harrowing Arab-Israeli war of 1967, the editor of *Commentary* had vowed with renewed determination to defend the state of Israel "relentlessly" against its enemies and to "stand up for Jewish interests in America" whenever they were threatened.[14] Where, he asked publicly in 1971, were these threats to be found? In "the ideological precincts of the Radical Left," he answered, where hostility to Israel had merged with a "larger hostility among intellectuals to America, to middle-class values, to industrialism, to technology, and even to democracy." The "most active enemies of the Jews," he insisted, were now on the far Left, not on the "ideological Right."[15] It was an assertion profoundly counter to Jewish historical experience abroad—and profoundly consequential for the unfolding direction of *Commentary*.

If the conservative editors of *National Review* were encouraged by *Commentary*'s tilt toward "right-wing liberalism,"[16] the Jewish magazine's erstwhile friends on the Left were infuriated. To them Podhoretz and company had become "apostates and lunatics"[17]—in a word, traitors. Socialists like Irving Howe and Michael Harrington were particularly incensed—and perhaps particularly worried by the new movement's potential. In 1974 Howe and Lewis A. Coser edited an entire volume of essays critical of the pernicious phenomenon. They entitled their book *The New Conservatives*.[18] To compound the insult (in their circle the word "conservative" was no honorific), Harrington and others disseminated a taunting epithet that caught the fancy of the media. Podhoretz and his ilk, they charged, had become "neoconservatives."[19]

Not surprisingly, the *Commentary* circle did not take kindly to this tendentious label. In an elementary sense, of course, by veering away from the radical Left, Podhoretz and company had necessarily moved toward the Right. But not, they vigorously argued, *into* the Right. Time and again, Podhoretz and other *Commentary* stalwarts insisted that they were really (once again) true liberals, striving to rescue an honorable political tradition from those who were trying (as Podhoretz's wife, Midge Decter, said) to "abscond with its good name."[20] They were liberals—unabashed, anti-Communist, Cold War liberals—endeavoring to revive the Vital Center after its collapse during the intellectuals' civil war over Vietnam. In substantial measure, Podhoretz was attempting to revert to *Commentary*'s first phase, its pre-1960 phase: the days when it had affirmed "hard" anticommunism, moderate reformism, and the essential goodness of American civilization.

Here we come to a crucial point about the opening stage (roughly 1970–79) in *Commentary*'s turn to the Right: it was a turn only, not a conversion. Podhoretz himself (and various contributors to *Commentary*) might reach out cautiously to Buckley's *National Review,* and even occasionally socialize with conservative intellectuals, but they did not embrace *National Review*-style conservatism, or its political vehicle, the Republican Party.

Why not? For one thing, as self-defined liberals and Democrats, they were not yet ready to give up on their party of heritage. In December 1972, just after the McGovern election debacle, Podhoretz and many other intellectuals associated with *Commentary* organized the Coalition for a Democratic Majority to recapture the Democratic Party from the McGovernites.[21] In 1975 and 1976, many of these same right-wing liberals rallied to the presidential candidacy of Senator Henry Jackson (D-WA). These efforts ultimately failed, of course, but it took several years for neoconservative activists to recognize they could not go home again.

Another impediment to realignment lay in the neoconservatives' perception of the landscape beyond the precincts of liberalism. It was one thing to consort with a dashing conservative like Buckley, a verbalist and controversialist like themselves. It was quite another thing to contemplate joining the Republican Party of Richard Nixon. To the gathering clan of neoconservatives—heavily Northeastern, disproportionately Jewish, and at home in the intellectual hothouse of New York—the Republican Party represented the alien and boring world of business, country clubs, and small-town America. As for Nixon himself, although many neoconservatives had preferred him to McGovern (faute de mieux), the Republican president's Cold War policy of détente seemed a feeble foundation for the revival of American power and self-confidence that they craved.[22]

Still another brake on *Commentary*'s rightward drift arose in the mid-1970s in the person of Daniel Patrick Moynihan. In 1975 the revisionist liberal professor and former government official published in *Commentary* a passionate summons to the United States to stand up and defend its liberal democratic principles at the United Nations against the anti-American, anti-democratic, and illiberal attacks cascading from its ideological foes in the Third World.[23] Within weeks, Moynihan found himself appointed American ambassador to the United Nations, where for the next eight months he waged a spirited counterattack and reaffirmation of American values. So popular did he become that in 1976, in part at Podhoretz's urging, Moynihan sought the Democratic senatorial nomination in New York.[24] After first defeating two leftists in the party's primary, Moynihan ousted the conservative Republican incumbent—William F. Buckley Jr.'s brother—in the fall election. For Podhoretz, writing as a "centrist liberal" three years later, Moynihan's victory represented a triumph of a man of "the old liberal tradition" over "the kind of conservative who might more properly have been called a radical of the Right."[25]

For the next three years, Senator Moynihan was *Commentary*'s hero and the bearer of its political aspirations.[26] As long as Moynihan was a potential contender for the presidency, the right-wing liberals now known as neoconservatives could dream of redeeming the Democratic Party and resuscitating the Cold War liberalism for which they stood. As long as such a project seemed viable, their trek to the Right would be hesitant and incomplete.

Beneath these political circumstances and calculations, however, deeper inhibitions were at work. Although increasingly aware of the failure of Great Society liberalism (a lesson taught by that other neoconservative journal par excellence, *The Public Interest*),[27] the *Commentary* circle during the 1970s continued to believe in the welfare state—in contrast, they believed, to the conservatives at *National Review*, who appeared unreconciled even then to the New Deal.[28] Moreover, many of *Commentary*'s writers had grown up poor during the Great Depression and did not share what they perceived as conservative antipathy to the labor movement.[29] To *Commentary*-style neoconservatives in the making, the leadership of America's labor unions was resolutely anti-Communist, which was more than they could say about some business leaders.[30] (Here again, neoconservatives seemed to conflate conservative intellectuals with Republicans.)

Militant, evangelistic anticommunism, of course, was to be the great bonding agent between Buckleyite conservatism and the new variant stirring around *Commentary*. Here too, however, there was a difference—at least in some neoconservative minds—that may have imparted some sense of distance from the Right. In the 1950s, Norman Podhoretz has written, he vigorously disputed the "antisecularist" contention (held by conservatives like Buckley and Whittaker Chambers) that the salient difference between the Communist and Western worlds was that "they were godless and we were not":

> I did not, that is, accept the idea that the cold war was a war between atheism and religious faith. What in my view separated us from them was that we were free and they were not, that our political system was democratic and that theirs was totalitarian.[31]

It is difficult to know how much such a difference of perspective was still operative twenty years later, but it does bring back to mind James Burnham's observation in 1972 that the neoconservatives had broken with liberalism's "doctrine" but not with its "gestalt." And two powerful elements in the liberal gestalt of the 1970s (and later) were a suspicion of religiously based discourse and a conviction that conservative intellectuals were at best eccentrics, not to be taken seriously by open (i.e., liberal) minds.

Beyond the "policy gap" between *Commentary* and mainstream conservatism, then, there lay a "culture gap" that had not yet been bridged. Although little has been written about this subject, one has a sense that, to much of the *Commentary* circle of the mid- and late 1970s, the existing conservative intellectual community was an unimpressive lot.[32] In this largely unspoken attitude, *Commentary* may have been influenced by the much-quoted words of its literary patron saint (and Podhoretz's mentor), Lionel Trilling. Back in 1950 (in *The Liberal Imagination*), Trilling had famously declared that "no conservative or reactionary ideas" were in "general circulation" in the United States and that liberalism was the country's "sole intellectual tradition."[33] Trilling was wrong, as Podhoretz later acknowledged,[34] but the eminent literary critic's pronouncement long reverberated through the corridors of academia, reinforcing a subtle superiority complex that distorted liberal judgment of conservatism until quite recently.

Yet if—for all these reasons—*Commentary* had not yet come all the way into the water, *National Review*-style conservatives could applaud its progress, and did.[35] As former Leftists, Podhoretz and his colleagues had an advantage: They knew their enemy intimately and knew how to breach its armor.[36] Even more important, as writers and academics who had made their reputation while on the Left, the neoconservatives could not be contemptuously ignored. In the hierarchy of the American intelligentsia, their credentials and status were unassailable. This meant that—to the consternation of their enemies—they could reach an audience largely impervious to the arguments of marginalized conservatives.

As the 1970s unfolded, then, the self-styled "centrists" around *Commentary* did not "convert"—not yet.[37] But the political tide was now running against them. Increasingly appalled by Soviet expansionism abroad and by the fecklessness and flaccidity of the American response, the born-again Cold Warriors at *Commentary* became ever more estranged from the administration of President Jimmy Carter. One historian of neoconservatism has labeled the years 1976–80 the time of "Searching for Truman."[38] One might just as aptly label it "Waiting for Moynihan." But in 1979, Senator Moynihan—a politician now—signaled that he had no intention of challenging Carter's renomination, thereby depriving Podhoretz and others of their would-be paladin.[39] The vaunted middle ground of Cold War liberalism had become a will-o'-the-wisp.

Thus, in 1980, Norman Podhoretz and a host of right-wing liberals of the *Commentary*/Henry Jackson/Daniel Moynihan stripe rallied to the candidacy of the man whose celebration of American virtues and whose anti-Communist fervor most closely resembled their own: Ronald Reagan. Initially, in a private meeting in 1979, Podhoretz had not been impressed by Reagan's intellect.[40] Nevertheless, after nearly a decade of contention with former soulmates on the left-of-center, the editor of *Commentary* had learned a lesson: "that one ought to join the side one was now on instead of engaging in a futile attempt to change the side one used to be on."[41] In 1980, Podhoretz voted unhesitatingly for Reagan for president and even published a pro-Reagan foreign policy manifesto entitled *The Present Danger.*[42] When Reagan won the election in a landslide, a jubilant Podhoretz declared in *Commentary* that the Republican Party had a "truly historic opportunity" to "reverse the decline of American power."[43]

It was a new era, and not just for Republicans. During the 1970s, *Commentary* had mounted a relentless critique of the American Left from the right (but not from within the Right), thereby helping to create an intellectual climate receptive to Reaganism. In the political crucible of 1980, the magazine's liberal inhibitions disappeared. In 1980 *Commentary* and its editor crossed the Rubicon.

III

With the inauguration of President Reagan in 1981, a new chapter in *Commentary*'s turn to the right commenced—a chapter that, in its essential features, continues to unfold. The minutiae of the story line need not detain us. What is more interesting—and revealing—is the evolving interplay between the now unabashedly neoconservative magazine and the larger political and intellectual constellation that it joined.

In the early 1980s, for the first time since the mid-1960s, *Commentary* had a sympathetic audience in Washington. Not only were its monthly issues avidly read inside the Beltway, but many of its former contributors and allies (including Podhoretz's son-in-law) attained positions of influence in the Reagan administration, particularly in the foreign policy and military establishments.[44] The prime example of this nexus was Jeane Kirkpatrick, whose 1979 article in *Commentary* on "Dictatorships and Double Standards" had profoundly impressed Ronald Reagan and had led to his selection of her to be his administration's ambassador to the United Nations.[45] If, as some like to say, the function of intellectuals is to "speak truth to power," *Commentary* in the early 1980s was superbly situated for the task.

Politically, then, the Reagan years were *Commentary*'s moment in the sun. However, with newfound influence came a subtle change of circumstances. Although *Commentary* was never a house organ of the Reagan administration or the Republican Party, the neoconservatives for whom it spoke were not free-floating intellectuals, either. They were now part of a wider conservative coalition embracing five distinctive elements: libertarians—defenders of free-market economics and personal liberty against socialism and the metastasizing, regulatory, welfare state; traditionalists—defenders of traditional social mores and morals (the "permanent things") against the corrosive acids of modernity, especially secular liberalism; Cold Warriors—specialists in the military and geopolitical struggle against communism and the Soviet "evil empire"; the Religious Right—evangelical Protestants, Roman Catholics, and Orthodox Jews engaged in grassroots resistance to a deepening cultural revolution waged by a secular, liberal elite against Judeo-Christian morality and institutions; and the neoconservatives themselves. Although the neoconservatives shared, to varying degrees, the concerns of the other constituents of the conservative grand alliance, the fact that they now belonged to an alliance was to pose eventual problems for *Commentary*.

As the neoconservatives quickly settled into the Reaganite landscape, signs of their adaptation to the new zeitgeist multiplied. Gone now was any lingering public resistance to the label that had been pinned on them.[46] More interesting still, gone now—or at least going—was the abstract and reflexive commitment to the welfare state that had kept many fledgling neoconservatives from accepting *National Review*-style economics.[47]

Why? In part, no doubt, like much of America, the *Commentary* circle had been "mugged by reality"—the reality of stagflation during the presidency of Jimmy Carter. In part, too, the writers for *Commentary* were influenced by the trenchant critique of Great Society liberalism emanating from *The Public Interest,* edited by neoconservatism's "godfather," Irving Kristol. Nor was the *Commentary* circle unaware of the spectacular appearance in the late 1970s of a new body of thought called supply-side economics, of which Kristol was the leading impresario.[48] More than ever, conventional welfare-state liberalism seemed problematic.

Not surprisingly, then, in the 1980s *Commentary* became an ardent exponent of capitalism.[49] Fittingly enough, it was Podhoretz's wife, Midge Decter, who edited one of the classic pro-capitalist tracts of the decade, George Gilder's *Wealth and Poverty.*[50] *Commentary* also publicized the pathbreaking work of the neoconservative scholar Michael Novak, whose *The Spirit of Democratic Capitalism* (1983) became the locus classicus of a new moral and theological case for the American economic system.[51] By extolling capitalism not just pragmatically but philosophically ("democratic capitalism"), *Commentary* contributed substantially to the intellectual counterrevolution against the Left. In so doing, the magazine altered not only the national climate of opinion but also its own mooring on the ideological spectrum.

In the realm of foreign policy, *Commentary*'s trajectory during the 1980s was somewhat different. Already militantly anti-Communist and supportive of aggressive resistance to the Soviet empire, the magazine changed little in this area after the 1980 election: Its hard-line Cold War posture was already congruent with Ronald Reagan's. Ideological compatibility was one thing, however; programmatic implementation another. Here, to its surprise and distress, the magazine found itself frequently to the right of the Reagan administration. At times Podhoretz and other *Commentary* writers sternly criticized the Reagan team for failing to prosecute the Cold War energetically enough and for succumbing to détentist illusions about the Soviet Union.[52] On one occasion, the criticism elicited a telephone call to Podhoretz from Reagan himself.[53]

Yet if the *Commentary* neoconservatives were now fulfilling James Burnham's prophecy that they would develop "a more integral outlook," a troubling question was beginning to take form by the mid-1980s—not on the Left, from which *Commentary* had long since broken ranks, but on the intellectual Right: Was the neoconservatives' worldview truly conservative? Aside from being zealous anticommunists, did they belong on the Right at all?

To an increasingly angry group of traditionalists, who took the label "paleoconservatives," the answer was emphatically no. The "neocons" (they argued) were "impostors" and "interlopers," who despite their recent rightward journey remained essentially secular, Wilsonian, and welfare-statist in their philosophy.[54] In other words, not conservative at all. Where, for example, traditional conservatives had opposed communism in the name of Western civilization, the neoconservatives of the 1980s did so (said their right-wing critics) in the name of a grandiose, neo-Wilsonian ideology of "global democratic capitalism." As if (said disgusted "paleos") "capitalism" and "global democracy" were the essence of the conservative cause.

The conflict between the two factions first surfaced in 1981, when President Reagan selected the Brooklyn-born neoconservative William Bennett (over the Texas traditionalist Professor M. E. Bradford) to chair the National Endowment for the Humanities after a lobbying battle that left many wounds. Bradford, a prolific scholar and disciple of the anticapitalist Southern Agrarian writers of the 1930s, was a popular figure in the conservative intellectual community, but on three counts he was politically vulnerable: he had opposed the 1964 Civil Rights Act, he had supported George Wallace for president in 1968 and 1972, and in his scholarly writings he had excoriated Abraham Lincoln. Seizing on this record, his neoconservative antagonists derailed his nomination, to the undying outrage of some of his supporters.[55]

Partly, perhaps, out of deference to the ecumenical tone of the Reagan administration, the clash between the neocons and their rivals stayed mostly out of view for several years, but the feud publicly erupted again in 1986, when Bradford and his allies subjected the neoconservatives to a scathing critique at the annual meeting of the conservative Philadelphia Society and in the *Intercollegiate Review*.[56] The fat was now in the fire. In 1989 and 1990, the lingering animosities flared into a firestorm that threatened to sunder the conservative alliance.

The outbreak of the "conservative wars" (as the *New Republic* labeled them) unleashed a torrent of analysis, mostly by aggrieved paleoconservatives and liberal journalists eager to document the "conservative crackup."[57] At one level, the problem was cast in personal and political terms: Some paleoconservatives accused the neocons of capturing the leading conservative grant-making foundations and deliberately defunding more genuinely conservative challenges to the status quo.[58] According to the preeminent traditionalist author Russell Kirk, the neoconservatives had "behaved as if they were the cadre of political machines . . . eager for place and preferment and power, skillful at intrigue."[59] Another traditionalist scholar, Stephen Tonsor, was more blunt:

> It has always struck me as odd, even perverse, that former Marxists have been permitted, yes invited, to play such a leading role in the conservative movement in the twentieth century. It is splendid when the town whore gets religion and joins the church. Now and then she makes a good choir director, but when she begins to tell the minister what he ought to say in his Sunday sermons, matters have been carried too far.[60]

Most observers agreed that the differences between the neoconservatives and other conservatives went deeper than the rough-and-tumble of coalition politics. Some stressed sociological factors: The neoconservatives at *Commentary* and elsewhere tended to be city folk, often New Yorkers, Jewish, and formerly Marxist, in contrast to the paleoconservatives, who were based in the South and Midwest.[61] Moreover, most neoconservative scholars (it was claimed) seemed to be social scientists, susceptible to meliorist temptations; traditionalist conservatives, in contrast, tended to find their home in the humanities.[62] A recurrent refrain on the paleo Right was that the neoconservatives had simply not escaped the prison of their philosophical premises: In their worldview they were liberals and modernists still. Far from supporting "diversity in the world," said Russell Kirk, the neoconservatives "aspire to bring about a world of uniformity and dull standardization, Americanized, industrialized, democratized, logicalized, boring."[63] It was noteworthy that what to neoconservatives were good words ("Americanize" and "democratize") were to Kirk and his followers the distasteful vocabulary of liberalism.[64]

There, as much as anywhere, lay the rub. To Stephen Tonsor, the neoconservatives were still trapped in "the halfway house" of secularized modernity. True conservatism, he averred, had its roots in Roman and Anglo-Catholicism; its culture was not alienated modernity but "Christian humanism." The neoconservative phenomenon was "a transmogrification of 'the New York intellectuals' . . . who, in turn, reflected the instantiation of modernity among secularized Jewish intellectuals." He boldly called on the neoconservatives (so many of whom were Jewish) to renounce their "cultural modernism" and return (if they "wish us to take their conservatism seriously") to "the religious roots, beliefs, and values of our common heritage."[65]

Initially the neoconservatives said little in print about these fusillades. One exception was a 1988 article in *Commentary* which argued that, when all was said and done, neoconservatism was closer to the American mainstream than was its rival. The "fundamental difference" between the two bodies of thought, the *Commentary* writer asserted, was that neoconservatives belonged to "the tradition of liberal democratic modernity," whereas the paleoconservatives were "heirs to the Christian and aristocratic Middle Ages." The neoconservatives espoused the principles of "individual liberty, self-government, and equality of opportunity"; their antagonists affirmed religious (especially Christian) belief, prescription, and hierarchy. From this perspective, the writer argued, it was neoconservatism, not paleoconservatism, that was "both genuinely American and genuinely conservative."[66] Once more *Commentary* was positioning itself in the center, between the far Right and far Left.

If the sectarian strife had proceeded at this level of abstraction, it might eventually have subsided into a sullen truce. But amid the sound and fury of paleoconservative indignation, worried neoconservatives thought they discerned something more: the resentful rumblings of neoisolationist nativism and, in a few cases, anti-Semitism.

For Norman Podhoretz in particular, who had long felt a special responsibility to defend "Jewish interests," the apparent recrudescence of long-suppressed anti-Semitism on the Left and the Right was profoundly disturbing. Never one to shy from journalistic contention, between 1986 and the early 1990s he publicly accused several paleoconservatives of anti-Semitic utterances.[67] The editor of *Commentary* was most perturbed by the pugnacious, paleoconservative journalist Patrick Buchanan, whose public remarks on Israel and related subjects Podhoretz judged to be indisputably anti-Semitic.[68]

Podhoretz's dismay intensified when Buchanan turned politician in 1991 and vowed to "take back" the conservative movement from the neocon cabal.[69] Fiercely and defiantly "nationalist" (rather than "internationalist"), skeptical of "global democracy" and entanglements overseas (including the Middle East), and fearful of the effect of Third World immigration on America's Europe-oriented culture, Buchananite paleoconservatism increasingly resembled nothing so much as the American Right before the onset of the Cold War. When Buchanan himself campaigned for the presidency in 1992 under the pre–World War II "isolationist" banner of "America First," his symbolism seemed deliberate and complete. To Jewish neoconservatives who vividly recalled Charles Lindbergh's aspersions about "the Jews" at an America First antiwar rally in 1941, Buchanan's revival of pre-1945, "Old Right" conservatism was not pleasant to contemplate.

The political aspirations of Patrick Buchanan triggered another round of conservative discord, in which Podhoretz and *Commentary* conspicuously participated.[70] Podhoretz, to put it mildly, was not amused when *National Review,* for "tactical" reasons, briefly supported Buchanan's presidential campaign against President George Bush in 1992.[71] So heated did the atmosphere become on the Right, especially over the sensitive issue of anti-Semitism, that William F. Buckley Jr.—the paterfamilias of the conservative intellectual movement—was moved to publish an entire book on the subject in 1991.[72] To the immense pleasure and relief of Podhoretz, Buckley came down largely on the side of the neoconservatives.[73]

Beyond the passions and particularities of the moment, what was going on? In retrospect, it is clear that from the mid-1980s to the mid-1990s, American conservative intellectuals became embroiled in a great transitional struggle for self-definition. When President Reagan retired in 1989, they lost the unifying hero who had embodied each component of the five-part conservative coalition. When the Cold War ended soon after, they lost much of the ideological cement and imperative to cooperate that had held them together and suppressed deviationist tendencies. In 1990 William F. Buckley Jr. retired as editor of *National Review*—another sign that the American Right was entering a new phase. With the leadership of the conservative movement seemingly up for grabs, and with a strange, new, post–Cold War world now looming, the possibility seemed real that the conservative community might revert to its pre–Cold War, pre-Buckleyite roots.

For the embattled editor of *Commentary* and his fellow neoconservatives, the stakes in this transition were especially high. For nearly a decade, Podhoretz had made his political home on the Right. For nearly two decades he had contended that there was far more anti-Semitism on the American Left than on the Right. To his Jewish readers and others, Podhoretz had cited William F. Buckley Jr.'s long and honorable record of keeping *National Review* free of any anti-Semitic taint.[74] In effect, Podhoretz had been asserting that it was now safe for a Jew to be a conservative. What if he were wrong?

When the polemical dust finally settled in the mid-1990s, it became clear that Podhoretz's apprehensions had not materialized. The political and intellectual landscape on the Right was far more congenial to the neoconservatives than to their paleoconservative adversaries. Although Buchanan and his brethren continued to compete in the public square (in 2002 he launched a new magazine),[75] both politically and intellectually the "Old Right" remained on the margin of the conservative movement. The conservative establishment had not been overthrown.

Why not? Why—to put the question differently—did mainstream conservatism seem increasingly indistinguishable from its neoconservative variant? To some paleoconservatives, the answer was unflattering: conservative media and institutions had been systematically co-opted and corrupted, by money from neoconservative-dominated foundations, by misplaced friendship, and by the fear of being labeled anti-Semitic.[76] Whatever the truth of such allegations in individual cases, deeper intellectual currents were at work. Back in 1972, long before *Commentary* joined the conservative ranks, the "premature neoconservative" James Burnham declared in *National Review* that much conservative "doctrine" had become "more and more obviously obsolescent."[77] So, for better or worse, it turned out to be. In the late 1970s and 1980s, conservative intellectuals increasingly accepted—in practice if not quite in principle—the continued existence of the welfare state.[78] What was Ronald Reagan's "safety net" but an acknowledgment by conservatives that some form of governmental aid to the needy would always be with us? What, indeed, was supply-side economics (in part a neoconservative invention) but an effort not to dismantle the State (an impossibility), but to shrink its importance by enlarging the private sector through economic growth?

On another front—race relations—the conservative movement also shifted toward the center, making peace with the civil rights legislation of the 1960s (and the memory of Martin Luther King Jr.) but drawing the line against quotas and reverse discrimination. Here, as in economic policy, the older conservative community's dominant perspective increasingly converged with that of the neoconservatives.[79]

The *Commentary*-style neoconservatives were changing, too, however, although more, perhaps, in their gestalt than in their doctrine. In their enthusiastic embrace of "democratic capitalism" during the 1980s and their growing recognition of the "social pathologies" of the welfare state, Podhoretz and his associates had come a long way from the liberal and radical biases of their youth.[80] And when the Cold War preoccupations of the 1970s and 1980s yielded to the "culture wars" of the 1990s, Podhoretz increasingly explored the moral and religious dimensions of contemporary issues—and in terms that nearly every conservative could applaud.[81] Here again, perceived barriers between "secular" neoconservatives and "religious" traditional conservatives were fading away.

In no respect was this rapprochement more remarkable than in the willingness of *Commentary* in the 1990s to defend another crucial part of the conservative coalition: the Religious Right. Although the faith-based conservatives included Orthodox Jews and rabbis, the bulk of the movement consisted of Roman Catholics and evangelical Protestants, led first by Jerry Falwell's Moral Majority organization and then by Pat Robertson's Christian Coalition.

It is no exaggeration to say that the political awakening of theologically conservative Christians in the 1980s stirred enormous anxiety among American Jews. Conditioned by centuries of European experience to fear the political Right and the populist manifestations of Christian militancy, apprehensive Jews now perceived both elements to be arising simultaneously in America. As the energized Christians pushed their agenda (notably about abortion) into the public arena, Jews who had been taught to equate the "Jewish interest" with liberalism and secularism were greatly vexed. How could such a phenomenon possibly be good for the Jews? And why, some of them must have asked themselves, was *Commentary*—a Jewish magazine—cohabiting a political dwelling with people like *that?*

Yet (and the evidence was undeniable) Pat Robertson and other Christian conservative leaders were vocally and strenuously supportive of Israel—as much as, if not more than, any other non-Jewish segment of the American population. Should Jews reject such potentially useful allies in the defense of the Jewish state?

For the *Commentary* circle of Jewish neoconservatives, the issue became acute in mid-1994, when the Anti-Defamation League (ADL) of B'nai B'rith published a 193-page report condemning the Religious Right for an "assault on tolerance and pluralism in America."[82] According to the ADL's national director, the Religious Right indulged in "a rhetoric of fear, suspicion and even hatred that stains the democratic process."[83] Such an attack was not in itself surprising: The ADL had long been critical of spokesmen for American conservatism.[84] What was newsworthy was the response to the ADL by Jewish neoconservatives. In short order, Podhoretz's wife collected the signatures of seventy-five Jewish leaders, including many contributors to

Commentary, on a full-page advertisement in the *New York Times* under the headline "Should Jews Fear the 'Christian Right'?" The Jewish signatories accused the ADL of perpetrating an act of "defamation" and "bigotry" against conservative Christians. They asked, how was "the political activity of Christian conservatives" tantamount to "an assault on pluralism"? "The separation of church and state is not the same thing as the elimination of religious values and concepts from political discourse." More pointedly still, the Jewish neoconservatives remarked, "Judaism is not, as the ADL seems to suggest, coextensive with liberalism." "Above all," they concluded, on the issue of "the survival of Israel," Jews "have no more stalwart friends than evangelical Christians."[85]

Clearly the neoconservative defense of the Christian Right contained an element of pragmatic calculation: Pat Robertson and his followers were friends of Israel, and hence good for the Jews. Norman Podhoretz himself, in a 1995 article in *Commentary,* made this very point in the course of absolving Robertson of the charge (by leftist critics) of anti-Semitism.[86] But Podhoretz was willing to go even farther: "Who's afraid of the religious Right? Not I," he announced in *National Review* in 2000. Not only was he not afraid of the Religious Right, he actually believed that it possessed "certain positive virtues." It had reminded America of her "religious foundations"—the "capital" on which her "democratic system still draws"—and it had "acted as an often lonely source of resistance to the complete triumph of relativism in our culture and libertinism in our behavior."[87]

Here, in plain view, was yet another bridge that now linked *Commentary*-style neoconservatives to their compatriots on the Right. Neoconservative hostility to the antinomian countercultural upheaval of the 1960s blended nicely with conservative revulsion against the "liberationist" trends of the 1990s. How far Podhoretz and his allies around *Commentary* had traveled from the "halfway house" of modernity—and from the predominantly secular and liberal Jewish community. Liberal Jews might still worry about the threat of a "Christian America." Neoconservative Jews were more alarmed about living in an *anti*-Christian America—a harsh, atheistic, morally disorienting world that was a menace to everyone, including Jews.[88]

Yet if *Commentary*-style neoconservatives increasingly shared the Religious Right's moral concerns, this did not mean that they had succumbed to cultural despair. This became apparent in late 1996 and 1997, when a new storm blew in from a totally unexpected direction: the religious magazine *First Things,* edited by Podhoretz's neoconservative friend Richard John

Neuhaus. In a symposium entitled "The End of Democracy? The Judicial Usurpation of Politics," Neuhaus and his colleagues charged that the American judiciary had become so brazenly imperialistic and so utterly divorced from Biblical morality in its rulings that it constituted a threat to the very foundations of the American political order. Millions of Americans, Neuhaus asserted, were becoming profoundly alienated from their government. Citing Nazi Germany as an analogy, he wondered aloud whether the time might be near when "conscientious citizens" could "no longer give moral assent to the existing regime." The symposium also seemed to hint that active resistance to unjust laws—including civil disobedience and "morally justified revolution"—might someday be necessary.[89]

The *First Things* symposium was deliberately provocative, and no one was more provoked than Norman Podhoretz and some of his fellow neoconservatives. Although Podhoretz had long been critical of the imperial judiciary, he was outraged at what he deemed an irresponsible, seditious, anti-American outburst that was uncomfortably reminiscent of the radical Left's attack on the American "regime" in the 1960s. "I did not become a conservative in order to be a radical," he told Neuhaus, "let alone to support the preaching of revolution against this country."[90] To Podhoretz and such allies as the historian Gertrude Himmelfarb, the symposium's questioning of the legitimacy of the American regime was beyond the pale of responsible conservative discourse.[91] Two neoconservative scholars severed their association with *First Things* in protest.[92]

In the next several months, the conservative intellectual community, including the *Commentary* circle, plunged into a new and highly publicized civil war—or so it seemed for a time.[93] So incendiary was the subject matter, and so distinguished were the polemicists, that the media strained to put labels on the feuding factions. It was said to be a war between "neocons" and "theocons," Straussian political philosophers and Catholic Thomists, even Jews and Christians.[94] One commentator, an Orthodox rabbi, denied that the split was between Jews and Christians at all. It represented, rather, a division

between the orthodox believers of either faith on one hand, and bourgeois conservatives on the other. Most of the neocons are defending bourgeois stability and respectability; Father Neuhaus, on the other hand, realizes that much of the American right is not clear about the basic civilizational crisis. That's because he is an orthodox Catholic, while most of the neocons are *not* orthodox Jews.[95]

The rabbi may have had a point about Podhoretz and some of the neo-conservatives associated with *Commentary*. Perturbed though Podhoretz was by the ravages wrought by the 1960s counterculture and its heirs, he did not believe that the "traditionalists" were losing the culture war. It seemed instead than an "armistice" was in the making.[96] Rejecting what he called "the anti-Americanism of the Right," he emphatically did not see his native land as mired in irredeemable decay.[97] To the contrary, it was in a mood of profound gratitude that he published in 2000 a memoir revealingly entitled *My Love Affair with America*.[98]

Although Podhoretz initially feared that the *First Things* symposium had created the "most consequential" fissure of all on the contemporary Right,[99] the explosive controversy soon subsided, as both sides pulled back from the rhetorical brink.[100] Despite all the verbal pyrotechnics and journalistic drumrolling, the intellectual Right did not inwardly secede from the American regime in 1997. For Podhoretz, this turn of events came as a great relief. In 1995, he had retired as *Commentary*'s editor; as he later remarked, he was now "too old to seek for yet another political home."[101]

IV

In March 1996, a few months after his retirement, Podhoretz published in *Commentary* a lengthy "eulogy" for neoconservatism. The movement, he announced, was "dead," a victim "not of failure but of success."[102]

The retired editor enumerated some of the ways that the neoconservative movement had altered the "character" and "ethos" of American conservatism as well as the larger course of American history. "More passionately and more effectively than any other group," he asserted, the neoconservatives had exposed the "lies" of 1960s radicalism. "[M]ore passionately and more effectively than any other group," the neoconservatives had undertaken the task "of rebuilding intellectual and moral confidence in the values and institutions on which American society rests"—values that he unashamedly lauded as those of "the bourgeois democratic order."[103]

"The bourgeois democratic order": In this one phrase Podhoretz spoke volumes about the kind of conservatism that he and *Commentary* had come to espouse. In 1945, *Commentary* had been born into a marginal, impoverished, immigrant-based subculture and an intellectual milieu that touted "alienation" and "critical nonconformity" as the true marks of the intellectual vis-à-vis his own culture. Two generations later, *Commentary* stood in the mainstream of American culture, and even of American conservatism, as a celebrant of the fundamental goodness of the American regime, and Norman Podhoretz, an immigrant milkman's son, was its advocate. It was a stunning achievement.

In his list of neoconservative successes, however, there was one that Podhoretz omitted, though in the long run it may prove to be the most important of all. It concerns *Commentary*'s effect on the Jewish community. In his recent autobiography, *A Jew in America*, Rabbi Arthur Hertzberg (who officiated at Norman Podhoretz's wedding to Midge Decter) recounts how he did not join his neoconservative friends in their turn to the Right after the trauma of the Six-Day War. Hertzberg shared the incipient neoconservatives' outrage at "the betrayal of Israel" by many liberals "in its moment of need," but

> I could not agree with them that political and social liberalism was to be abandoned. I did not see the conservatives in America flocking to the banner of racial equality or abjuring their own long-standing habits of excluding Jews wherever and whenever they could. . . . I refused to believe that Jews could find dependable allies in that part of American society that had almost always excluded them and held them in social contempt.[104]

Hertzberg was referring, of course, to American conservatism as he perceived it in the 1960s. But his refusal to believe that Jews could find "dependable allies" on the Right bespoke an adamantine resistance to conservatism that has by no means disappeared among American Jews—an ideological headwind against which *Commentary* has had to contend since 1970.

Commentary under Podhoretz did not, of course, convert the majority of American Jews to its brand of conservatism, but it did accomplish something almost as momentous: It made conservatism a respected and unignorable presence in the Jewish community. Like William Lloyd Garrison's *Liberator*, it was heard.

At least as important, *Commentary* opened a door to a new generation of conservative Jewish writers, not just by publishing some of their work in its pages but by the compelling example of its own history. For if *Commentary*-style neoconservatism lost its distinctiveness in the 1990s, the decade also witnessed another phenomenon: the emergence of a host of postneoconservative Jewish journalists and scholars into the front ranks of American conservatism.[105] A few of them—like John Podhoretz and William Kristol—

were literally the offspring of neoconservative parents, but all of them, in a sense, were *Commentary*'s children—not because they were true neoconservatives (leftists who turned Right) but precisely because they did not need to be: *Commentary* had helped to clear the ground before them. Thanks to the labors of Podhoretz and his generation, it was now respectable—and, indeed, hardly worthy of comment—to be both a Jew and a conservative.

With that achievement, Podhoretz had earned the right to retire. Neoconservatism may be dead, but its legacy thrives. Thanks in no small measure to *Commentary*, it may be said of today's mainstream Right: "We are all neoconservatives now."

Part IV

Herbert Hoover:
A Neglected Conservative Sage?

25

Herbert Hoover: Political Orphan

This appraisal originated as a "Tower Talk" at the Hoover Institution on War, Revolution and Peace in 1988. The Hoover Institution Press subsequently printed it, in slightly modified form, as a pamphlet, Herbert Hoover: Political Orphan (1989). *It is reproduced here with a bit of updating and a few other minor revisions.*

Many of you are no doubt familiar with a statement attributed to Abraham Lincoln: "You can fool some of the people all of the time, and all of the people some of the time, but you can't fool all of the people all of the time." Some of you may also be familiar with a version of this remark attributed to H. L. Mencken. According to him: "You can fool some of the people all of the time and all of the people some of the time—and that's enough!" And some of you may have heard of another mordant observation that has been ascribed to Mencken: "In politics a man must learn to rise above principle."

In 2009 it is easy to be cynical about politics. But no cloud of expediency surrounds the man whose career I shall examine in this essay. In the three-quarters of a century since he left the presidency, few observers have accused Herbert Hoover of "fooling the people" or "rising above principle."

Yet around Hoover, more than 40 years after his death and 135 after his birth, clouds of a different sort remain to be dispelled—an intellectual fog that even now impairs our clear perception. Where in the spectrum of American statesmanship does he belong? A hero of libertarians like Rose Wilder Lane and John Chamberlain in the 1950s, he is today routinely castigated by libertarians as the true father of the New Deal interventionist state. A vehement anti-Communist, a friend of Joseph McCarthy and Richard Nixon, Hoover was nonetheless hailed in the 1970s by some New Left historians as a profound critic of global, interventionist anticommunism. A proud sponsor of *Human Events*, *The Freeman*, and other conservative causes after World War II, an ally of William F. Buckley Jr. in the founding of the *National Review* in 1955, Hoover in more recent years has been stigmatized in conservative media as a cheerless apostle of balanced budgets and high taxes. Acclaimed in his day as "the greatest Republican of his generation," he was likened in the 1980s—even on the Right—to Jimmy Carter.

Surely it is noteworthy that one of Ronald Reagan's first acts as president was to hang a portrait of Calvin Coolidge in a prominent place in the White House and that he was known to quote Franklin Roosevelt (but not Hoover) in his speeches. It is noteworthy, too, that in the 1990s a leading conservative politician of the time, Jack Kemp, contrasted Reaganomics with what he called "Hooverism." Today, during the "great recession" of 2009, the airwaves and the blogosphere reverberate with aspersions cast upon Hoover from the Right.

If contemporary conservatives no longer claim Hoover as one of their own, contemporary liberals have scarcely rushed to embrace him. To be sure, it is now possible to find among liberal historians and commentators expressions of respect for Hoover and of sympathy for his struggle as president—sentiments liberals of the New Deal era would never have uttered. In fact, in the 1990s Hoover probably received more sympathetic coverage in left-of-center journals and newspapers than in right-of-center ones. In Congress, his most persistent defender during the past generation was the liberal Republican senator from Oregon, Mark Hatfield. Nevertheless, in 1996, when Arthur Schlesinger Jr. asked a very liberal group of historians to rank the American presidents, their composite judgment was that Hoover was an outright failure. When *Time* in 1998 asked nine historians—again nearly all of them liberal—to judge the seventeen presidents of the twentieth century, Herbert Hoover finished dead last.

Even nonliberal scholars seem half-inclined to agree. In 1998 the Intercollegiate Studies Institute asked thirty-eight conservative historians and political scientists to evaluate America's chief executives. In this survey, Hoover barely made it to the "below average" category, just ahead of the presidential failures.

So it is that we confront a curious datum: Early in the twenty-first century, eight decades after he entered the White House, Herbert Hoover remains to a considerable degree a political orphan, unwelcome in liberal and conservative pantheons alike.

Underlying this bipartisan aversion has been a continuing ambiguity in Hoover historiography. Somehow, despite all the research and analysis, he remains an elusive figure. Was he, historians have wondered, an ossified nineteenth-century liberal or a sophisticated, twentieth-century "corporate liberal"? A spokesman for big business or a proto-New Dealer? A quintessential product of rural and small-town America or a modern managerial elitist? A failed adherent of "rugged individualism" or a rejected prophet whose message is valid still?

Many factors account for the historical haze that continues to envelop this man. First, there is the sheer breadth and duration of his career. Born in 1874 in a little Iowa farming community, Hoover was orphaned before he was ten. By the time he was twenty-one, he had worked his way through Stanford University and had entered his chosen profession of mining engineering. At the age of twenty-four, he was superintendent of a gold mine in the desolate outback of Western Australia. By the age of twenty-seven, he had managed a gigantic coal-mining enterprise with 9,000 employees in northern China and had survived a harrowing brush with death in the Boxer Rebellion. By 1914, at the age of forty, Hoover was an extraordinarily successful mining engineer who had traveled around the world five times and had business interests on every continent except Antarctica.

With the outbreak of World War I, Hoover rose to international prominence as founder and director of the Commission for Relief in Belgium, a humanitarian relief agency that ultimately brought food to more than nine million French and Belgian civilians a day—an unprecedented undertaking in world history. After serving as head of President Woodrow Wilson's wartime Food Administration, he returned to Europe after the armistice for ten months as director-general of the American Relief Administration, organizing the supply of food for starving millions, facilitating the emergence of stable economies, and helping thereby to check the advance of Bolshevik revolution in central Europe. Thanks in considerable measure to the relief efforts of Hoover and his staff, perhaps one-third of the population of Europe was saved from privation and death.

In the 1920s, when he served as secretary of commerce under presidents Warren Harding and Calvin Coolidge, it was said that Hoover was undersecretary of every other department as well. Indeed, one distinguished historian has jocularly remarked, "While Hoover had only one term in the presidency he had almost as many years in the White House as Franklin Roosevelt." Certainly it seems correct to say that Hoover was the most influential man in American public life between 1921 and 1933. The first man to have his image transmitted over television (in 1927), the first president to have a telephone permanently on his desk, Hoover after his four years in the White House lived longer as a former president (thirty-one-and-a-half years) than any other former chief executive in our history.

These were strenuous years, too; even in his mid-eighties he worked eight to twelve hours a day. Between the ages of eighty-five and ninety, he published seven books. From Wilson to Eisenhower, he served five presidents of the United States. He wrote incessantly. A bibliography of his published writings and addresses contains over 1,200 entries.

When Herbert Hoover died in 1964, he had lived ninety extraordinarily productive years, including a full fifty in public service. It was a record that in sheer scope and duration may be without parallel in American history.

If the formidable magnitude and variety of Hoover's accomplishments have tended to retard a complete assessment of his place in history, a second factor also has contributed, and that is the personality and character of the man himself. From the time he entered public life in World War I, there was always something enigmatic about him. Blunt, laconic, protective of his personal privacy, with an aura about him of impersonal efficiency, Hoover was not an easy man to understand. Many contemporaries were puzzled by him. *Who's Hoover?* was the title of a book written about him in 1928. "Is Hoover Human?" asked a noted magazine article that same year. But if Hoover seemed almost machinelike to some, very few doubted his ability. Said a well-known Quaker to a friend about to visit Secretary of Commerce Hoover: "Don't let him get thy goat. He'll sit there and hear thee talk, and so far as thee can tell thee might just as well be talking to a stump or a stone, but he'll not miss a thing." He was right.

Hoover's reticence and taciturnity, his tendency as an administrator to rely on intermediaries to achieve his objectives while he quietly master-minded their efforts from behind the scenes: these and other traits have made it difficult to discern his true, often catalytic role in crucial episodes throughout his career. So, too, with his benefactions: From the time he was a college graduate he systematically concealed his charitable acts toward others, preferring to give anonymously through surrogates. In the mid-1930s,

Hoover's brother estimated that Hoover had given away more than one-half of his profits for benevolent purposes. Characteristically, however, he did it without fanfare, with the result that even today the enormous extent of his benefactions is not fully known.

Given this panoply of character traits (some of them no doubt arising from his early orphanhood), it is not surprising that for many people Hoover has long remained what a famous journalist called him in 1928: "an enigma easily misunderstood."

A third, more concrete factor has also contributed to the lingering perplexity about Hoover. It was only in 1966 that the bulk of his papers, comprising literally millions of documents, became available to scholars for the first time at the Herbert Hoover Presidential Library in Iowa. With this stroke, all previous Hoover historiography was rendered, if not obsolete, at least subject to new and skeptical scrutiny. Only then could the "real" Herbert Hoover, so to speak, emerge from obscurity. Moreover, since the mid-1960s, new, Hoover-related collections have become available at the Hoover Institution on War, Revolution and Peace, and old collections have been admirably processed by professional archivists, thereby facilitating research and permitting the task of historical revisionism to accelerate.

All of this helps to explain the continuing lack of consensus about our thirty-first president. To these factors we must add one more. Hoover left office in 1933 during the greatest national trauma since the Civil War. For a generation after he left the White House, he was the focus of highly personalized historiography in which he was portrayed as either the hero, or more frequently as the villain, of a great moral drama culminating in the New Deal.

Although the former president had his defenders among popular historians and journalists, far more influential among professional historians were highly critical accounts of his presidency in such books as Arthur Schlesinger Jr.'s *The Crisis of the Old Order* (1957). In the early, heroic phase of New Deal historiography, the tendency to moralize about Hoover was strong, and the moralizing was mostly to his detriment. It has taken a long time for this impulse to subside, and, indeed, it has not vanished even yet.

Nevertheless, with the passage of time, the receding of partisan emotion, and the opening of the Hoover papers, we have entered a new era in Hoover scholarship. For the first time, it is becoming possible to take proper measure of this unusual man.

In the autumn of 1928, as Hoover was seeking the presidency, a certain mediocrity was running for city council in Augusta, Georgia. The candidate apparently knew his limitations, for he announced in his campaign advertisements, "I know I'm not much, but why vote for less?" With Herbert Hoover we do not, so to speak, have to "vote for less." For unlike most men in politics then or since, Hoover *had* a social vision, a coherent sense of what he was doing in public life—and why.

How, then, shall we understand this political orphan? I suggest we begin by asking how he understood himself. A son of Quaker parents living in Iowa a decade after the Civil War, Hoover grew up in a Republican village where the only Democrat, as he remembered it, was the town drunk. Identifying himself in 1910 with the Progressive wing of the Republican Party, he contributed financially in 1912 to Theodore Roosevelt's Bull Moose campaign. Early in 1920, in response to pleas that he run either as a Democratic or Republican candidate for president, Hoover first labeled himself an "independent progressive," alienated from Republican reactionaries and Democratic radicals alike. A few weeks later he declared a Republican affiliation and allowed his name to be placed on the ballot in California. After losing that state's primary to Senator Hiram Johnson, Hoover declared:

> I do not believe that this country is either reactionary or radical. I believe that the country at heart is progressively liberal. . . . I believe that the better way to secure needed reforms in political, social and economic conditions is through the progressive element in the Republican Party.

This, then, was Hoover's self-image in 1920, near the beginning of his active career in American politics. It was also how others perceived him. Early that year the *New Republic*, Justice Louis Brandeis, Walter Lippmann, and numerous other members of the "progressive" wing of American politics supported him for the presidency. It is very possible that he could have obtained the Democratic nomination. Franklin Roosevelt supported him. In a letter that historians like to quote, Roosevelt declared: "[Hoover] is certainly a wonder, and I wish we could make him President of the United States. There could not be a better one." Early in 1921, when Hoover was selected for President-elect Harding's cabinet, it was only after Harding quelled the opposition of the old guard of the Republican Party.

Herbert Hoover was a man of action, a man for whom the highest purpose of life was practical achievement. But he also was capable of philosophical reflection. Late in 1922, in a book entitled *American Individualism*, he expounded his understanding of the American sociopolitical system.

According to Hoover, the revolutionary upheavals of World War I and its aftermath had produced a world in ferment. In this cauldron, collectivist ideologies alien to America were competing for the minds of men and women. To Hoover, who had just seen in postwar Europe the vicious results of blending "bestial instincts" (as he called them) with idealistic, humanitarian jargon, the need for a definition of the American system was urgent. He called this alternative "American Individualism."

By this term he did not mean unfettered, old-fashioned laissez faire. Hoover was anxious that individual initiative always be stimulated and rewarded; initiative, in fact, was one of the character traits he most admired. Progress, he declared, "is almost solely dependent" on the few "creative minds" who "create or who carry discoveries to widespread application." These minds, he said, must be free to "rise from the mass." But "the values of individualism," he argued, must be "tempered"—tempered by "that firm and fixed ideal of American individualism—*an equality of opportunity.*" Equality of opportunity, "the demand for a fair chance as the basis of American life"—this, in Hoover's words, was "our most precious social ideal."

Hoover did not believe that equality of opportunity was automatically self-sustaining in a modern, technological economy. As a Progressive, he believed that some governmental regulation and legislation (such as antitrust laws and inheritance taxes on large fortunes) were necessary to prevent economic coagulation, *inequality* of opportunity, and the throttling of individual initiative. Like many other Progressives, Hoover abhorred the notion of a rigid, class-conscious society. To him it was imperative that "*we keep the social solution free from frozen strata of classes.*" As he put it some years later, the uniqueness of American society lay in its ideal of a "fluid classless society." It was, he said, "the point at which our social structure departed from all others."

Hoover was not (to use today's terminology) a libertarian. Nor was he a "rugged individualist" in the Social Darwinist sense. He did not believe that an advanced economy could function without regulation. In fact, he often explicitly rejected the philosophy of laissez faire, which he defined as "every man for himself and the devil take the hindmost." It was, he stated, an outmoded social doctrine which America had abandoned "when we adopted the ideal of equality of opportunity—the fair chance of Abraham Lincoln."

In the context of 1921–33, Hoover was undoubtedly a governmental "activist." As secretary of commerce he took the initiative in national waterway development, radio regulation, aviation regulation, stabilization of the coal and railroad industries, abolition of the twelve-hour day in the steel industry, and elimination of industrial waste. He was one of the foremost exponents of governmental public-works expenditures as a form of countercyclical economic policy. Nominated in 1928 over the opposition of the Republican Party's old guard and some elements of big business, Hoover conceived his term of office as a reform presidency and set to work with characteristic drive. When the Great Depression came, the federal government under President Hoover responded with unprecedented intervention in a peacetime economy. This, he said later (and approvingly) "is hardly laissez-faire."

But if Hoover was not a free-market purist, neither was he a proto-New Dealer. It is absolutely crucial, if we are to understand him, that we comprehend the nature, guiding purpose, and boundaries of his activism. Time and again he insisted that the form and extent of governmental involvement in the economy must be carefully defined, and above all, kept consistent with the broad American traditions of voluntary cooperation, local self-government, and individual initiative. The purpose of Hoover's limited governmental regulation was to strengthen and preserve American Individualism, not to subvert or supplant it.

How was this to be done? As Hoover perceived it, the fundamental role of the federal government was to stimulate the private sector to *organize and govern itself.* "I believe cooperation among free men can solve many problems more effectively than government," he declared in 1937. During the 1920s and early 1930s, Hoover in office willingly used government as a device to facilitate this cooperation—through publicity, collection and dissemination of statistical data, and the convening of conferences of private-sector representatives. Between 1921 and 1924 alone, to take but one example, Hoover's Commerce Department sponsored over nine hundred such conferences on the single subject of efficiency and standardization.

Certainly there was much of the modernizer, the technocrat, and the efficiency engineer in Hoover. Indeed, in some quarters during the 1920s he came to be regarded as an aggrandizing bureaucrat. Franklin Roosevelt, for instance, told a friend in 1928 that Hoover "has always shown a most disquieting desire to investigate everything and to appoint commissions and send out statistical inquiries on every conceivable subject under Heaven. He has also shown in his own Department a most alarming desire to issue regulations and to tell businessmen generally how to conduct their affairs."

Hoover, then, was no enemy of innovation. He believed in the conscious, rational use of modern social science for the amelioration of social ills. Gather the facts, publicize them, and devise solutions that avoid the myopic partisanship of electoral politics (for which he had profound distaste): Here, too, he showed the influence of pre-1914 Progressivism.

Yet we must not lose sight of the fact that for all of Hoover's reforming and modernizing impulses, he also had a conserving purpose: the preservation, in an urban, industrial society, of the American tradition of equal opportunity. Whenever possible, Hoover searched for noncoercive, decentralized, cooperative arrangements to solve such problems as unemployment. In the 1920s, for instance, long before Social Security, he tried to encourage insurance companies to establish a private system of old-age pensions. He organized and skillfully led such private institutions as the American Child Health Association and the Better Homes in America movement, the latter devoted to the profoundly conservative goal of wide diffusion of home ownership. He mobilized the resources of great private foundations in the cause of scientific and social research, such as studies of the business cycle. While an activist (for his time) in the use of governmental power, he employed it repeatedly to facilitate the growth of *non*governmental, mediating institutions.

Hoover's idiosyncratic blend of progressivism and antistatism pleased neither the Left nor the Right. Difficult to pigeonhole, he had little support among the class of professional politicians, with whom, as an outsider in office, he had to deal. Not surprisingly, during his presidency his relations with Congress were abysmal. He labeled one senator "the only verified case of a negative IQ." When in 1930 one of Hoover's granddaughters was born, his first response was, "I'm glad she doesn't have to be confirmed by the Senate." In a whimsical mood one day, he remarked, "There ought to be a law allowing the President to hang two men a year, and without being required to give any reason."

With the advent of the Democrats to power in 1933, Hoover, for the first time in his public life, found himself "in opposition." In the years ahead, he endeavored to define his social philosophy in the face of the challenge posed by the New Deal. "The impending battle in this country," he told an associate shortly after Roosevelt's first hundred days, would be between "a properly regulated individualism" and "sheer socialism." "That," he said, was "likely to be the great political battle for some years to come." As the months passed, Hoover increasingly identified his own philosophy as that of "historical liberalism" and excoriated the collectivist, regimenting "false liberalism" of the New Deal. "The New Deal," he said, "having corrupted the label of liberalism for collectivism, coercion, [and] concentration of political power, it seems 'Historic Liberalism' must be conservatism in contrast." And so, in the last third of his life, Hoover, the former Bull Mooser, the self-styled Progressive Republican of the 1920s, became a counterrevolutionary: a defender of what he called "true liberalism."

It was once remarked of Hoover that he was "too progressive for the conservatives and too conservative for the radicals." Such, I suspect, will be the response of some who appraise him today. Clearly there are elements of his thought that do not appeal to contemporary American conservatives: his energetic expansion of the federal government's role in economic life in the 1920s and 1930s, for instance; his unequivocal repudiation of laissez faire; his faith in social science research as a basis for the rational reordering of our institutions. Some conservatives may be troubled by a feeling that Hoover conceived society as something to be deliberately, continuously, and endlessly reformed.

Yet if parts of Hoover's philosophy have an unconservative sound, it is also abundantly evident that he was not a modern liberal. First, as a tireless exponent of voluntarism, he emphatically repudiated the statist philosophies of communism, socialism, fascism, and the New Deal. Unlike some of his contemporaries, Hoover never abandoned his aversion to the overweening regulatory state. He recognized in burgeoning bureaucracy a pernicious enemy of the creative impulses upon which freedom and prosperity depend. "True liberalism," he declared, "is found not in striving to spread bureaucracy but in striving to set bounds to it."

Secondly, unlike many latter-day liberals, Hoover did not believe that government exists for the primary purpose of redistributing wealth. To be sure, he believed, as he stated in 1936, that "economic fair play" required that "the economically more successful must through taxes or otherwise help bear the burdens" of "victims of misfortune and of the ebb and flow of economic life" by "providing for old age, unemployment, better homes, and health." Hoover accepted, if you will, as Ronald Reagan later did, the concept of a "safety net" provided by government and paid for by taxation. Also, as mentioned earlier, he favored stiff inheritance taxes on large fortunes. Yet he did so not out of a socialistic yen to "soak the rich" or penalize success but because the notion of a wealthy, insulated, privileged class perpetuating its economic power for generations was anathema to his philosophy of American Individualism. Everyone should be free, he believed, to rise in the world, as he had done, without artificial encumbrance. Equality of opportunity, not equality of result, was his governing principle. "The human particles," he said, "should move freely in the social solution."

Another set of concerns that tended to separate Hoover from the liberalism of his day was his abiding interest in fostering productivity and economic growth. For all his efforts in the 1920s to rationalize and stabilize the economic order, Hoover never lost his vision of America as a perpetual frontier. How he inveighed at the "economy of scarcity" that he believed the New Deal was imposing on our nation. "The notion that we get richer and more prosperous by producing less," he said in 1936, "is about as progressive as a slow-motion film run backwards." How he criticized the view, popular in the 1930s and again in the 1970s, that the era of American abundance was over and that the frontiers of opportunity were closing:

> When we concede that progress is ended we concede that hope and new opportunity have departed. That is the concept of a static nation. It is necessarily the philosophy of decadence. No society can become static, it must go forward or back. . . . No society will function without confidence in its future opportunities.

Fundamentally, he was interested in multiplying wealth, not dividing it. And unlike many of his foes on the Left, he knew that the creation of wealth does not occur by accident.

Finally, more than any other man who has held the presidency, Hoover was profoundly acquainted with the social systems of the Old World. He had seen, as he later put it, "the squalor of Asia, the frozen class barriers of Europe." He had seen the haughty oligarchies of the Right, the bloody tyrannies of the Left, and the hatreds, injustices, and miseries they engendered. He had seen the terrible consequences of imperialism, war, and revolution as few Americans ever had. And he had seen America in contrast.

This perception of contrast between the Old World and New was the experiential core of Hoover's social philosophy, and it had a profoundly conservative effect on him. It gave him a lifelong understanding of America as a uniquely free, humane, classless society that had come closer to implementing its ideals than any other nation on earth. Hoover judged the imperfections of the American system not as a person of the Left might—by theoretical standards never before realized and perhaps impossible to attain. He judged it as a conservative would—in the historical and comparative perspective of other societies, other experiments, and other ideologies that had failed.

Some years ago, a member of the British Parliament addressed his constituency during an election campaign. Concluding his remarks, the orator proclaimed, "These are our principles. If you do not like them, we have others." Unlike this amiable cynic, Herbert Hoover was a man of principles—principles that found their touchstone in the concept of "equality of opportunity." Orphan, engineer, humanitarian, statesman, he was the veritable embodiment in his lifetime of a formative ideal in our history: the ideal of upward mobility. Since the time of Abraham Lincoln, the American people by and large have stood for this principle and for the only kind of society in which such a principle makes sense: a free, dynamic, capitalist society, a society of promise and hope, in which men's and women's fulfillment in life is determined not by group identity or arbitrary governmental decree but by their own inner resources—by merit. For as long as Americans cherish this ideal and strive to create a society based upon it, they will find appeal in the philosophy and vision of Herbert Hoover.

26

The "Great Enigma" and the "Great Engineer": The Political Relationship of Calvin Coolidge and Herbert Hoover

This essay was first presented at a symposium at the Library of Congress in 1995. It is reprinted here from the subsequent volume of conference papers: John Earl Haynes, ed., Calvin Coolidge and the Coolidge Era *(Library of Congress, 1998).*

In the spring of 1923, Calvin Coolidge had been vice president of the United States for a little more than two years, but his hold on office was anything but sure. In the highest echelons of the Republican Party, speculation was rising that the enigmatic and laconic New Englander would not be renominated. Senators in his own party were said to be searching for someone else. Indeed, at the beginning of April a large contingent of Republican Progressives from the West—about forty members of Congress in all—publicly made it known that they wanted Assistant Secretary of the Navy Theodore Roosevelt Jr. to replace Coolidge as the Republicans' vice presidential nominee in 1924.[1]

Coolidge's growing vulnerability was not surprising. Since taking his oath of office in 1921, he had made little impression on official Washington. To be sure, he had dutifully attended Cabinet meetings, presided over the Senate, and otherwise comported himself with propriety. But his impact upon public policy had been slight.

Then, just four months later, before the "Dump Coolidge" sentiment could crystalize, Warren Harding unexpectedly died, catapulting "Silent Cal" into the White House. Acutely aware that he was an accidental presi-

261

dent, Coolidge felt morally bound to carry on Harding's policies until the next election. This in turn meant that the new president would keep his predecessor's Cabinet intact.

Among the Cabinet secretaries whom Coolidge thus retained was a man just two years younger than he, a man who was already making a powerful impression on the Republican administration: Secretary of Commerce Herbert Hoover. Since entering the Cabinet in 1921 over the bitter objections of the Republican old guard, Hoover had rapidly established himself as one of the ablest and most influential of Harding's advisers. Within months, Hoover had transformed his hitherto quiescent Cabinet agency into a bureaucratic dynamo. A tireless exponent of efficiency, he had launched a national campaign to eliminate waste in industry, an effort that included literally hundreds of Commerce Department–sponsored conferences on product standardization and related subjects. With Harding's approval, he had taken the initiative in the development of regulatory frameworks for the pioneering industries of civil aviation and radio. In the field of labor relations, he had played a key role in the settlement of the traumatic national coal and railroad strikes of 1922 and in the elimination of the twelve-hour day in the steel industry in 1923. Waterway development, farm relief, and foreign trade: into these fields, and more, Hoover had energetically ventured, usually with the admiring support of the president. Hoover is "the smartest 'gink' I know," Harding had remarked one time to a friend. In the president's Cabinet only Secretary of State Charles Evans Hughes had wielded comparable influence. Not surprisingly, on Harding's final western trip in 1923, Herbert Hoover had gone with him and had helped to ghostwrite some of the president's last official utterances.[2]

If the serious, hard-driving Hoover and the genial, flaccid Harding had been an unlikely political twosome, the pairing of Hoover and Calvin Coolidge was to be, if anything, stranger still. In 1895 each man had graduated from college: Coolidge from Amherst on the east coast, Hoover from Stanford University in California. From that point on, their careers could hardly have been more divergent. Hoover had become a globe-trotting mining engineer and financier who later calculated that he had spent a total of two years of his life on ships at sea. Coolidge had become a lawyer and politician in a small city only ten miles from his alma mater. By 1914 Hoover had traveled around the world several times, including such exotic locales as the Australian outback, the jungles of Burma, and China during the Boxer Rebellion. Coolidge, by contrast, had traveled outside the United States only once—to Montreal, Canada, for his honeymoon—and had otherwise journeyed rarely, if ever, more than a hundred miles from his adopted hometown of Northampton, Massachusetts. In World War I and its aftermath, Hoover had become an associate of Woodrow Wilson, a participant in the Versailles peace conference, and a humanitarian responsible for saving millions of Europeans from hunger and death. Coolidge, in the same period, had ascended the "escalator" of elective office in Massachusetts.

Each man was a hereditary Republican. In 1920 each had been a dark horse candidate—and thus a rival of the other—for the Republican presidential nomination that ultimately went to Harding. But here, too, their differences overshadowed their commonality. In 1912 Hoover had supported Theodore Roosevelt's Bull Moose campaign for the presidency. In 1918, as a leading member of President Wilson's wartime administration, he had publicly endorsed Wilson's call for the return of a Democratic Congress in the off-year election. In 1920 he had first declared himself an "independent progressive" before affirming a Republican affiliation. During this same period, Coolidge had been a paragon of party regularity and, by 1920, a symbol of safety and conservatism.[3]

These distinctions in background and career experience were reinforced by profound differences in the two men's temperaments. Hoover was a veritable workaholic, filling his calendar with appointments from morning till night and using lunches and dinner parties for intense discussions of public business. It was not uncommon for him to converse with thirty different visitors in a single afternoon. Coolidge, who in his boyhood had seemed destined to die young of tuberculosis, had a much less robust constitution and was obliged to conserve his energy constantly. Thus, as president, Coolidge received no visitors in the afternoon (except upon request) and required as much as ten hours of sleep per day. Concern for his fragile health was one of the motifs of Coolidge's presidency.[4]

In part, no doubt, because of these basic physiological dissimilarities, the two men's approaches to governance differed markedly. Coolidge's speeches were often patriotic homilies, long on idealism and devoid of controversy. Secretary of Commerce Hoover's speeches tended to be policy statements, replete with data and proposals for action. Coolidge was legendarily cautious and vigilant. "I have never been hurt by what I have not said," he once declared.[5] Secretary Hoover, though he could be equally cautious, nevertheless generated an unending blizzard of speeches, congressional testimony, and press releases, all carefully compiled by his office staff into reference volumes that they called the "Bible." Coolidge was a competent and well-informed chief executive who generally preferred, when a problem arose, to delegate it to the appropriate governmental agency. Hoover, as secretary of commerce (and later as president) would delegate, too—and then immerse himself in the troublesome matter anyway. Coolidge's "ideal day," H. L. Mencken once remarked, "is one on which nothing whatever happens." Hoover's ideal day— nay, his typical day—was marked by incessant activity at a pace few men could equal.[6]

The two men also responded very differently to criticism. When Coolidge entered public life, he decided (he once told a visitor) that he would not let abuse annoy him any more than he could help.[7] Hoover was just the opposite. Widely known for possessing one of the thinnest political skins in Washington, he sedulously kept track of all press criticism of himself and sought (usually through surrogates) to rebut what he labeled "smears" and "mud." On one occasion early in Coolidge's presidency, Hoover angrily complained to the president about editorial criticism of the secretary of commerce in *Wallaces' Farmer*. "Do you mean to say," Coolidge replied, "that a man who has been in public life as long as you have bothers about attacks in the newspapers?" "Don't you?" Hoover retorted, citing a savage critique of Coolidge in a recent issue of the *American Mercury*. "You mean that one in the magazine with the green cover?" Coolidge answered; "I started to read it, but it was against me, so I didn't finish it."[8] Imbued with an "emotional need to take things easy,"[9] Coolidge, wherever possible, tried to avert stress and risk. Hoover, in his own words, had a "naturally combative disposition"[10] and an eagerness to take command.

Even the two men's political philosophies seemed to reflect their unlike temperaments. To Coolidge, the purpose of government was not to do good but "to prevent harm." When governments attempted to "do good," he told a friend, "they generally got themselves and other people into trouble."[11] "A great many times if you let a situation alone it takes care of itself," the president told a news conference in 1924.[12]

Hoover, by contrast, was an avid "policy wonk" with a passion to implement his ideas. "I know how to make money and that no longer interests me," he remarked one time to a friend. "I don't fully know how Government may best serve human beings. That does interest me."[13] If Coolidge (in Hoover's slightly disdainful words) was "a real conservative, probably the equal of Benjamin Harrison,"[14] Hoover was a trained engineer. And engineers are taught to alter their environment, not leave it alone.

Between the instinctively noninterventionist Yankee president and his instinctively interventionist secretary of commerce, then, there lay a considerable experiential, psychological, and even philosophical gulf. "If you see ten troubles coming down the road," Coolidge told Hoover, "you can be sure that nine will run into the ditch before they reach you and you have to battle with only one of them." "The trouble with this philosophy," Hoover later wrote, "was that when the tenth trouble reached him he was wholly unprepared, and it had by that time acquired such momentum that it spelled disaster."[15]

With all of these disparities in outlook, some measure of friction between the two men was well-nigh inevitable. When Hoover entered the Harding Cabinet, some had predicted that the aggressive secretary of commerce would soon be out of office. Hoover had indeed clashed with a number of his fellow Cabinet officers, some of whom regarded him as a bureaucratic meddler.[16] One Treasury Department official labeled him "Secretary of Commerce and Under-Secretary of all other departments."[17] Still, he had managed to get along with his tolerant boss in the White House, and that had sufficed. But now Hoover's benevolent patron was gone, and a new chief executive was in charge. Would the ubiquitous secretary of commerce have the same success with Coolidge as he had enjoyed with Warren G. Harding?

For the next five-and-a-half years, the "Great Enigma" in the White House and the "Great Engineer" at the Commerce Department dominated the American political landscape.[18] Although some of the vagaries of their interaction are no doubt lost to history, the record is sufficient to disclose the basic pattern. Behind the façade of official etiquette and party regularity, one finds an evolving and increasingly tense relationship. By exploring its contours and intricacies, we may illuminate some of the political dynamics of a far from placid decade.

Hoover's early contacts with Coolidge showed every sign of cordiality and cooperation. Barely two months after President Coolidge took office, his secretary, C. Bascom Slemp, wrote to Hoover: "I can not tell you how many things I feel we are dependent on you about." When Coolidge unveiled his legislative program in his first State of the Union address on December 6, 1923, many of his recommendations reflected Hoover's interests. Even more significantly, when Coolidge submitted his first budget to Congress a few days later, Hoover's Department of Commerce was one of only two Cabinet agencies to escape the president's budget-cutting axe.[19]

In the months ahead, other manifestations of presidential support for Hoover occurred. One of Hoover's most ambitious goals as secretary of commerce was the development of America's inland waterways: a project that he believed would yield enormous economic benefits. Already, in 1921, President Harding had appointed him chairman of a commission to negotiate an interstate compact for taming the Colorado River. Another component of Hoover's vision was construction of a seaway that would link the Great Lakes with the Atlantic Ocean. On March 14, 1924, President Coolidge appointed him chairman of the St. Lawrence Commission of the United States, with authority to negotiate with its Canadian counterpart. One more arrow had been added to Hoover's expanding quiver of governmental responsibilities.[20]

Still another area where Hoover and Coolidge found common ground was agricultural policy, the most contentious (and, for the Republican Party, the most divisive) issue of the 1920s. In the aftermath of World War I, the nation's corn and wheat belt had plunged from prosperity into recession, exacerbated by surplus production. As the crisis lengthened, farmers and their congressional allies clamored for federal assistance. Much of their agitation crystalized into support for a massive interventionist proposal known as the McNary-Haugen bill, under which a U.S. government export corporation would buy surplus crops at a remunerative domestic price and sell them abroad at whatever price the foreign market offered. Hoover vehemently opposed the price-fixing McNary-Haugen plan, which he considered thoroughly unsound. Instead, he argued for credit reform and a nationwide system of voluntary marketing cooperatives by the farmers themselves, with the assistance of a federal marketing board. Hoover clearly was no disciple of laissez faire, but he vigorously objected to overt governmental price-fixing and direct governmental operation of business. "No one can sit in the middle of the Federal Government and watch the operation of bureaucracy, even in its best sense," he said in 1927, "and have any confidence whatever as to its ability to buy, sell, and distribute commodities and services."[21]

By the spring of 1924, an early version of the McNary-Haugen bill was before Congress, and Coolidge's Cabinet was split. Secretary of Agriculture Henry C. Wallace openly favored the legislation; Hoover emphatically did not. On this and other issues (including bitter jurisdictional disputes between the two agencies), the two men's differences had degenerated into bureaucratic warfare. Coolidge did not intervene in their feuding. With an eye, probably, on the coming presidential election and the farm vote, the president refrained from definitive comment on the McNary-Haugen bill. But from the legislation that he *did* support in 1924—including encouragement of marketing cooperatives—there is little doubt that his position on farm relief was much closer to Hoover's than to the McNary-Haugenites'. Although the McNary-Haugen bill was defeated in Congress in June 1924 (thanks in part to Hoover's influence with Congress), it would come up again and again in the next four years. In the initial battle to defeat it, a bond had been forged between Hoover and Coolidge. It was to be the most important and consequential bond of their relationship.[22]

In the early months of Coolidge's presidency, Hoover had another opportunity to cement his ties to his new chief. In November 1923, California's prickly Progressive Republican senator, Hiram Johnson, announced that he would seek the Republican presidential nomination in 1924. Since Coolidge also was presumed to be a candidate (a surmise that he soon confirmed), an intraparty brawl seemed in the offing. Johnson was already an archenemy of his fellow Californian Hoover, who had challenged him in California's presidential primary in 1920 and whose supporters had been trying ever since to remove Johnson as an obstacle to Hoover's presidential ambitions. With Hoover's assistance, his California faction swung into action in behalf of Coolidge's candidacy. Hoover himself publicly endorsed the president shortly before the California primary. When the votes were counted in California, Coolidge had administered a humiliating defeat to Johnson, thereby clearing the last hurdle to an easy nomination. More gratifying, perhaps, to Hoover, his well-organized supporters had secured his ascendancy over Johnson in the California Republican Party: a decisive step in Hoover's own quest for the White House.[23]

As it happened, Hoover nearly found himself on the ticket as Coolidge's running mate in 1924. As the Republican national convention convened in Cleveland that June, the only uncertainty was the party's choice for vice president. Hoover's name was prominently mentioned as a possibility. But Coolidge was reportedly averse to Hoover's leaving the Cabinet, and at any rate, wanted Senator William Borah of Idaho to balance the ticket. In the wee hours of the morning of June 12, Coolidge's campaign manager, William M. Butler, notified party leaders that this was Coolidge's wish and that the hitherto resistant Borah would accept.[24]

Now followed nearly twenty-four hours of confusion that may have changed the course of American history. Awakened at his home in the middle of the night, Borah announced emphatically that he would not accept a vice-presidential nomination. With the Idaho maverick out of the picture, Butler floated the name of another progressive, Judge William Kenyon of Iowa. Unable to stomach a man they deemed too radical and irregular, party hierarchs demanded that President Coolidge personally request Kenyon's selection. Contacted at the White House by telephone, Coolidge (who had previously adopted a "hands off" attitude toward the matter) declined to comply. The lid was now very much off the kettle.

The first ballot for vice president ended inconclusively. Then, on the second ballot, the delegates stampeded to former Governor Frank Lowden of Illinois, only to have him telegraph the convention a few hours later that *he* would not accept the nomination. Desperate to contain the deepening disarray, Butler now ordered that Hoover be chosen as Coolidge's running mate. It was too late. Throughout the convention many party leaders had resented the tactless ways of Butler, and now they took their revenge. On the third ballot they nominated Charles G. Dawes, who received 682½ votes to 234½ for Hoover. The bulk of Hoover's support came from California, Massachusetts (controlled by Butler), and southern delegations controlled by the Coolidge administration. On the final ballot, Hoover had been the candidate of the Coolidge forces, and he had lost.[25]

There is no evidence that Butler had designated Hoover on any direct instructions from the White House. But it is unlikely that Butler would have tried if he had thought that President Coolidge would disapprove. For his part, Hoover pronounced himself "more than happy" at Dawes's selection and privately asserted that his own "greatest opportunity for public service lay elsewhere."[26] It is, in fact, hard to envision such a hyperactive man spending the next four years presiding over the U.S. Senate.

In the ensuing presidential contest, Hoover actively campaigned for the Coolidge-Dawes team. In late October, the secretary of commerce even ghostwrote a presidential telegram (which Coolidge then issued under his own name) endorsing federal development of the Colorado River, including "a great dam at Boulder Canyon or some suitable locality."[27] And when Coolidge was elected in a landslide, Hoover was quick to telegraph his congratulations. Coolidge replied that he was "deeply grateful to you for all that you have done in behalf of the cause for which we both stand." This exchange was more than a formality. A few days after the election, Coolidge asked Hoover to remain in the Cabinet. The secretary of commerce eagerly accepted.[28]

Two months later, however, a curious new development occurred. Just before the November election, Hoover's antagonist, Secretary of Agriculture Henry C. Wallace, had died in office. Seizing the opportunity to install a more compatible man in his place, Hoover immediately recommended that the president appoint William Jardine of Kansas, an economist "opposed to all paternalistic legislation" (meaning McNary-Haugenism).[29] Instead, Coolidge appointed another individual who would serve ad interim for a few months.

Then, on January 15, 1925, Coolidge informed the press that he was considering transferring Hoover himself to the Department of Agriculture. Using his official disguise of "White House Spokesman," Coolidge announced that the Secretaryship of Agriculture was a very important post at the present time and that he (Coolidge) was seeking a man of large business experience who could fill it and institute a plan of cooperative marketing (Hoover's favorite solution to the farm crisis). Coolidge's public courtship of Hoover was surprising behavior for a man who was generally secretive about his appointments. Even more extraordinary was Hoover's public announcement the next day that, yes, Coolidge *had* offered him the Secretaryship of Agriculture, but that he had declined it.[30]

Historians have generally considered Coolidge's unusual job offer as evidence of his confidence in Hoover and of their ideological compatibility on farm policy. Indeed, this was the case. But there may have been more to this denouement than met the eye. A few days earlier, Coolidge had announced that Ambassador to Great Britain Frank B. Kellogg would shortly replace Charles Evans Hughes as secretary of state—a move that completely stunned official Washington. For months, rumors had circulated that Hughes might soon retire, and many political figures had believed that Hoover would succeed him. According to the *New York Times*, there was no evidence that Hoover was disappointed at being passed over for the more elevated Cabinet position. But if a political insider at the Republican National Committee was correct, Hoover was more than disappointed; he was furious. According to this source (who was evidently very close to Coolidge), Hoover was so upset at the selection of Kellogg—who he felt had slighted him on some matter in the past—that he immediately wrote a letter resigning from the Cabinet. Hoover was persuaded not to send the letter, and an intermediary notified the White House of the crisis. To assuage Hoover's angry ego, President Coolidge promptly offered him the Secretaryship of Agriculture and permission to disclose this fact publicly.[31]

If this version of the event is correct, it revealed how highly Coolidge regarded his secretary of commerce and how much the president wished to retain him in the Cabinet. It also may be evidence for a rumor that was to recur repeatedly in Washington in the next two years: that Hoover, with his heart set ultimately on the presidency, wanted badly to be secretary of state.

The net result of the January 1925 offer was that Hoover emerged with enhanced bureaucratic prestige. In the end, Coolidge made Jardine (Hoover's candidate) secretary of agriculture. Unlike the deceased Wallace, Jardine worked well with the secretary of commerce, whose sphere of influence once again expanded.

On March 4, 1925, Calvin Coolidge took the presidential oath of office for a new term. No longer Warren Harding's legatee, the man from Vermont was now chief executive in his own right, and his priorities were not necessarily those of his secretary of commerce. Coolidge's prized goals were tax-cutting, debt reduction, and economy in government—conservative goals. The Cabinet officer on whom he most relied to implement them was Secretary of the Treasury Andrew Mellon. As the economic boom known as "Coolidge prosperity" took hold in the mid-1920s, Mellon's influence at the White House flourished.

This did not mean that Hoover's influence necessarily waned. In size, reputation, and effectiveness, the Department of Commerce continued to grow. Between 1921 and 1928, the department increased its staff by more than 50 percent and almost doubled its congressional appropriation. In 1925, in response to Hoover initiatives, President Coolidge transferred the Patent Office and Bureau of Mines from the Department of the Interior to the Department of Commerce. In aviation, radio, labor disputes, settlement of the Allies' World War I debts, and much else, Hoover was in the very thick of the federal government's policy making.[32]

By late 1925, the nation's press had begun to take notice. The Washington correspondent of the *New Republic* doubted "whether in the whole history of the American government a Cabinet officer has engaged in such wide diversity of activities or covered quite so much ground [as Hoover]. . . . There is more Hoover in the administration than anyone else. Except in the newspapers and the political field there is more Hoover in the administration than there is Coolidge." A few weeks later a lengthy profile in the *New York Times Magazine* reached the same conclusion: "No man in the administration plays so many parts" as Hoover.[33]

If Coolidge resented his secretary of commerce's ubiquity, there was as yet no sign of it. In April 1925, for instance, Coolidge invited Hoover (among others) to spend a weekend cruising down the Potomac River on the presidential yacht, the *Mayflower*. Throughout the Coolidge years, in fact, the two men conferred frequently on public affairs—often for an hour or more at a time, at the White House after dinner. To all appearances the relationship between them was businesslike and amicable.[34]

Temperamentally, of course, the gap between them persisted. While Hoover appreciated Coolidge's "high intellectual honesty," "moral courage," and other personal qualities, he surely found the Yankee president a little too conservative for his taste. Coolidge, wrote Hoover years later, was "a fundamentalist in religion, in the economic and social order, and in fishing." To the horrified disdain of Hoover (an expert fly fisherman), Coolidge, when he took up fishing as president, initially baited his hook with worms.[35]

Yet for all the evidence that the secretary of commerce was a valued member of the Coolidge administration, in late 1925 and 1926 signs multiplied that Hoover was becoming disenchanted. One source of his anxiety was growing speculation in the stock market and real estate—trends fueled, in his opinion, by the "easy money" policies of the Federal Reserve Board. Unwilling, because of his Cabinet status, to intervene directly with the Fed, he persuaded Senator Irvine Lenroot to address a set of sharp inquiries to Federal Reserve officials. (Hoover helped to draft Lenroot's questions.) Hoover himself, without mentioning the Fed by name, publicly criticized Wall Street's "fever of speculation" in his December 1925 review of economic prospects for 1926. Lenroot's letters (with their not-too-subtle hint of a possible congressional investigation) may have caused the Federal Reserve Board to tighten its monetary policy for a time. It certainly revealed Hoover in a characteristic role: the bureaucratic wirepuller, working discreetly through willing intermediaries. The developing bull market, however, drew no remonstrance from the White House.[36]

On other fronts, too, Hoover was growing restive. In mid-1926, he complained privately that Coolidge was not being a sufficiently energetic leader, particularly in the ongoing struggle over farm relief. In 1925 and early 1926, Hoover conducted a loud campaign against foreign monopolies, notably the British rubber-control policy known as the Stevenson Plan. His agitation infuriated the State Department. To at least one official in the department, Hoover's very public denunciation of the British was a blatant attempt to further his presidential ambitions.[37]

Resentment of Hoover's "self-advertising" began to build in Washington in early 1926, especially at the State and Treasury departments. To William R. Castle Jr., a senior State Department official, Hoover's "whole campaign at the present time" was "a personal publicity campaign" designed to establish him as "the great figure in American life, the one man in the administration who has completely at heart the good of the American people. He seems to be insanely ambitious for personal power." In Washington, in December

1925, a report circulated that Hoover had been promised the Secretaryship of State the following June, in return for promising not to interfere in the presidential campaign of 1928.[38]

This sensational rumor was probably false. But there is little doubt that Hoover's recent burst of newspaper publicity had rankled some Republican leaders. According to a profile of Hoover in the New York *World* some months later, the Republican Party's "delegate slatemakers" were saying that no man since Theodore Roosevelt had such a large entourage of "personal press agents" as Hoover.[39]

Did Calvin Coolidge share this developing sentiment? The record, predictably, is silent. But Coolidge was an assiduous reader of the press, and in his own papers at the Library of Congress is the very New York *World* article just cited. "HOOVER BOOSTED AGAIN AS LEADER," ran the headline. "Called Best Fitted Man for Presidency but Professional Politicians, Generally, Fight Shy of Him." Most interestingly of all, perhaps, the *World* article contained a direct quotation from Coolidge's good friend and booster, Dwight W. Morrow: "If the President is not a candidate [in 1928] the logical Republican nominee is Herbert Hoover." At the top of this clipping, deposited today in the Coolidge Papers, someone wrote: "File here under Hoover," and so it was. Someone in the White House was watching the secretary of commerce.[40]

A month later, the *New York Times* published a glowing profile of the secretary of commerce as a veritable "one man Cabinet." More than any other person in American history, it said, either inside or outside the government, Hoover was "the recognized leader of all business America." Although the *Times* quoted Hoover's closest associates as insisting that he was "utterly without political ambition" and that his aspirations were "satisfied in his present position," the *Times* reported that Hoover "probably would not grumble" if he were "kicked upstairs."[41]

For his part, despite his private reservations about his chief, Hoover continued to play the role of loyal lieutenant. When, in mid-1926, a, friend suggested that Hoover resign and escape Washington for awhile, the secretary of commerce replied that he had this in mind but that he first had much to do for the administration before the November 1926 elections. In the ensuing campaign, he spoke vigorously for Republican candidates from coast to coast and hailed President Coolidge's "great work" for "national rehabilitation." By being such a good political soldier, Hoover could, perhaps, allay conservative Republican doubts about his party regularity. He could also win points with his boss in the White House.[42]

By the end of the campaign, there were signs that he needed to do just that. In mid-October, Secretary of the Treasury Mellon somehow got the notion that Hoover was refusing to campaign in Massachusetts, where President Coolidge's closest political friend and adviser, William M. Butler, was embroiled in a desperate race for the Senate. Anxious to dispel this dangerous impression, Hoover made a written denial to the president. At the request of Coolidge's secretary, Hoover sent a letter to Massachusetts publicly endorsing Butler.[43]

A few days later, while on a campaign tour in the West, Hoover received a startling telegram from the president—the first known sign of discord between them: "Press reports indicate you are going to make addresses and hold conference on matters that come under the Interior Department. I suggest that you take no action of that kind until you have conferred with Secretary Work and me. Acknowledge." Hoover was stunned. "Not a word of truth in the report given you," he wired back; "have never heard of any such question." "Greatly mystified," he asked Secretary of Interior Hubert Work to find the source of the "pollution."[44]

What had happened? Earlier in the year, in speeches on the west coast and elsewhere, Hoover had unveiled a comprehensive scheme for the development of the nation's water resources. Years later, Hoover disclosed in his memoirs that President Coolidge was "not very enthusiastic" about certain of these proposals because of their high cost, and in fact refused to sanction some of them. Then, in the waning days of the 1926 election campaign, press reports circulated that advocates of a Columbia River–basin development project were organizing to promote their cause in Congress and that a "waterways bloc" would be active in the next congressional session. The press reports also evidently suggested that Hoover was going to confer with some of these activists. To Coolidge, already at war with a feisty "farm bloc" over McNary-Haugenism, the thought of battling yet another special interest group eager to spend taxpayers' money must have been anathema. It evidently displeased him that Hoover was apparently in league with these interests—and on an issue seemingly outside his jurisdiction.[45]

In a lengthy telegram to Work and a lengthier letter to Coolidge, Hoover insisted that he had done nothing to exceed his statutory authority, to encroach on the Interior Department's turf, or to misstate the official water policy of the administration. He pointed out that Coolidge himself, in messages to Congress, had already formally endorsed all but one of Hoover's specific water development projects. He even suggested that creation of a "bloc" to support Coolidge's water proposals would be a good thing. He also denied having any improper contacts with the Columbia River enthusiasts. Perhaps Hoover did not yet realize that Coolidge was not as enamored of expensive public works projects as his engineer at the Department of Commerce. In a terse reply, Coolidge acknowledged Hoover's letter and enclosures. The president did not say, however, that he believed Hoover's elaborate explanations.[46]

Hoover never forgot the admonitory telegram that the man in the White House dispatched to him in October 1926. It was an unmistakable lesson to the "one man Cabinet" that, if he was not careful, he could alienate his boss. In the months ahead, Hoover did not cease to be a useful servant to his president. But the trajectory of their friendship had definitely reached its zenith.[47]

Early in 1927, Hoover had an opportunity to help the president when Congress passed a new version of the McNary-Haugen farm bill. Relying in part upon ammunition supplied by the commerce secretary, Coolidge vetoed the legislation. This did not mean that Coolidge was thrilled with Hoover's alternatives (he was not). But at least in their opposition to what they perceived as a noxious panacea, the two men shared common ground.[48]

Behind the scenes, however, new evidence of friction between the president and his secretary of commerce soon appeared. Once again the issue was waterway development. In his annual message to Congress, Coolidge had pronounced himself in favor of the "necessary legislation" to expedite development of the lower Colorado River.[49] On Capitol Hill, this legislation had taken the form of the Swing-Johnson bill, which would authorize $125 million for a gigantic dam at Boulder Canyon. The Swing-Johnson bill was vehemently opposed by private power interests, who argued that it would permit the federal government to generate and sell electricity at the dam site on an unprecedented scale in direct competition with private enterprise. Partly for this reason, the bill was bottled up in the House of Representatives Rules Committee.

Enter now Richard B. Scandrett Jr.—friend of Calvin Coolidge, nephew of Dwight Morrow, vice president of the American Gas and Electric Company, and opponent of the Swing-Johnson bill. On a trip to Washington in early January, Scandrett called upon his old friend Bertrand H. Snell, chairman of the House Rules Committee. Snell had his own reasons for delaying the bill, but he told Scandrett that he was under great pressure from Hoover to release it so that the full House could take action. And Hoover, Snell presumed, was representing the White House.

The eager young Scandrett told Snell that the bill was in conflict with the 1924 Republican Party platform, which had stoutly opposed government enterprise in competition with the private sector. Hoover, who was also militantly opposed to socialism, evidently did not share the private power companies' interpretation of the bill's potential. In any event, Scandrett and Snell promptly prepared a memorandum—which Scandrett swiftly delivered to the White House—stressing the bill's socialistic character, its alleged incompatibility with past Republican pronouncements, and Hoover's *approval* of the bill in his conversations with members of Congress. According to Scandrett, when Coolidge learned what Hoover was doing, the president was "mad as the devil."[50]

Coolidge's irritation may have been matched by Hoover's own. On January 21, the secretary of commerce told a friend that big business, basking in prosperity and favored by the Coolidge administration, had become arrogant. In fact, he added, big business needed to be curbed more now than in Theodore Roosevelt's day. Among Hoover's grievances was the opposition of big business to the creation of a Boulder Dam.[51]

It was not domestic policy, however, but foreign policy—coupled with Hoover's apparent political ambition—that provided the occasion for the most public and most dangerous display of presidential displeasure in their entire relationship. Early in 1927, Secretary of State Frank B. Kellogg was seventy years old. Known as "Nervous Nellie" to his detractors, Kellogg had never been popular in official Washington, and speculation had often sprouted that he would not remain long in his post. When the tense and irritable secretary of state took a vacation in February, rumors flew that he would soon quit because of ill health. The White House denied the report.[52]

By the beginning of April, rumors of Kellogg's impending resignation were again swirling in the nation's press, along with suggestions that Herbert Hoover would succeed him. The Baltimore *Sun* reported that it was "well known" that Hoover would like to hold the preeminent Cabinet position and that it was "no secret" that his friends were ready to "exert influence" for him at the "proper time." A few days later, the *Washington Post* declared that Hoover would become secretary of state within a few weeks and that Dwight Morrow would succeed him at the Commerce Department. Meanwhile, up in Boston, the *Independent*—edited by Hoover's former secretary, Christian Herter—opined that Kellogg's days "seem numbered" and that Hoover "stands head and shoulders above all others" as the best person to inherit Kellogg's job.[53]

To at least one Washington observer, the rising flood of Kellogg-will-go rumors suggested a deliberate campaign to drive him into retirement. Indeed, there is some evidence that one of Hoover's closest associates had been endeavoring to do just that in order to create a vacancy for Hoover. For its part, the White House stoutly denied the sensational reports of a Cabinet shakeup. Coolidge himself disclaimed any knowledge that Secretary Kellogg intended to resign. Some days later, the president was reported to be "weary" and "exasperated" by the incessant suggestions that Hoover replace Kellogg in order to "redeem" the State Department's lost "prestige."[54] Hoover, of course, kept mum, at least publicly. Whatever his hopes, he told a close friend on April 3 that there was no chance that Kellogg would leave. In the next twelve days, however, something evidently happened to change Hoover's assessment. On April 15, on a trip to New York City, he confided to the same friend that he might become secretary of state.[55]

As it turned out, April 15, 1927, was to be a very eventful day in Washington. For some time, the Coolidge administration had been grappling with a dangerous crisis in China, where civil war, revolution, and anarchy had created pressures for American and European intervention. In response to the murderous Nanking Incident in March, the United States had joined other powers in dispatching an identic note to the Chinese government demanding compensation for the loss of foreign lives and property in the Nanking riots.

Then, on April 15, the *Washington Herald* carried a banner headline on page one: "CABINET IS SPLIT OVER CHINA POLICY . . . HOOVER FEARS KELLOGG ERRS BY FAILURE TO TRY LONE HAND." According to the *Herald*'s article, Hoover had spoken out in a Cabinet meeting against a policy of joint diplomatic action with Great Britain and other foreign powers against China. Nevertheless, the State Department had gone ahead and issued a diplomatic protest identical to that of the British. The *Herald* quoted Hoover as denying any "official" differences between Kellogg and himself. But it noted that the tales of a policy rift between them had revived rumors that Hoover wanted to succeed the ailing secretary of state.[56]

The *Washington Herald*'s sensational story was quickly denied on all sides. The *New York Times* found "no foundation whatever" for the claim that Hoover was the "chief objector" to Kellogg's China policy. Hoover himself soon blamed the leak on Secretary of the Navy Curtis Wilbur, who had evidently told some correspondents that *he* did not approve the identic note. Worried about his indiscretion, Wilbur (according to Hoover) then told the newsmen not to publish it. One of the journalists wrote a story about

Cabinet dissension anyway, without mentioning Wilbur by name. After that story appeared, *other* journalists, whom Wilbur had not briefed, leaped to the inference that the dissident Cabinet officer must be Hoover. The tale quickly acquired new momentum.[57]

Hoover's version of the episode may or may not have been correct.[58] But even if true, in a sense it no longer mattered. Now the president of the United States had *two* embarrassing stories on his hands—China and the Hoover/Kellogg rumors—and he did not like it one bit.

On April 15, only hours after the *Herald's* article hit the streets, Coolidge held his semiweekly news conference. He was not in an affable mood. With unusual bluntness, the president denied that his Cabinet was in any way divided over China policy. "All members of the Cabinet," he declared, had agreed with Secretary Kellogg's actions in that area. In fact, the president noted pointedly, Hoover had been "the warmest advocate in the Cabinet of identic notes." Coolidge then proceeded to scold the press about "speculation" concerning the United States government's attitude toward delicate foreign problems like the crisis in China. And then, without warning, the angry president added a stinging announcement: "While I am on that, I might state again that Mr. Kellogg isn't going to resign. If he does resign, Mr. Hoover will not he appointed Secretary of State."[59]

What had happened? The usually self-controlled Coolidge was certainly not immune to fits of temper, as members of his official family knew. But why now? According to one source, during the press conference a reporter accidentally stepped on Coolidge's dog, provoking a severe presidential tongue-lashing. From then on, it was said, the president had been in a foul mood. This happenstance may have added to the asperity of the president's remarks, but it certainly did not dictate their substance. Something more had prompted the chief executive's explosion, and not a few of the correspondents who emerged from the press conference thought they knew what it was. The president of the United States, they believed, was jealous of his secretary of commerce.[60]

Coolidge's remarkable press conference—and above all, his apparent slap at Hoover—unleashed a typhoon of controversy in the nation's press. The Baltimore *Sun* called it "the most unusual, even the most sensational, incident" in the nearly four-year-old Coolidge presidency. According to the *Washington Post*, no other political utterance of Calvin Coolidge had evoked as much curiosity as this. Politicians, pundits, editorialists, and White House spin doctors promptly endeavored to explain what he meant.

On the one side, it was claimed that Coolidge (1) had intended no rebuff at all; (2) in fact, esteemed Hoover highly; (3) considered Hoover too valuable as secretary of commerce to transfer to the Department of State; (4) wanted his secretary of state to be a lawyer; and (5) meant to rebuke press rumor mongering about Hoover, not Hoover himself. According to this thrust of interpretation, the president's choice of words was merely a case of Vermont plain-speaking, not meant to convey any reproach.[61]

Other commentators were not so convinced. It was one thing for the president of the United States to be irritated at misleading reports of disagreements in his Cabinet and at the incessant gossip that his secretary of state would soon resign. But why did Coolidge then curtly say, without a word of further explanation, that Hoover would not succeed Kellogg *even if* Kellogg resigned? To the columnist Frank R. Kent, the truth was that Coolidge *did* intend to rebuke Hoover. To Kent (who detested Coolidge), "The truth is that with Mr. Coolidge and the small group of intimates who surround Mr. Coolidge there is and has been for a long time considerable jealousy of Mr. Hoover—and that fact has been well known and widely talked of in Washington." According to Kent, the "White House" had been intensely annoyed a year or so earlier when newspaper correspondents had begun habitually to refer to Hoover as the "Economic President of the United States."[62]

Chagrined at the uproar he had instigated (or so the press now reported), President Coolidge moved quickly to quell it. On April 16, he invited Hoover (who was then in New York City) to have breakfast with him in Washington, D.C., the next morning. Thoroughly upset by the president's published remarks, Hoover returned to the capital immediately. The next morning, Easter Sunday, he joined Secretary of the Treasury Mellon, among others, for breakfast with the president. Nothing happened. Hoover sat at Coolidge's left, and Mellon at his right, but no clarification, no apology, not one word about politics emanated from the president's lips. Hoover and the other invitees left more perplexed than ever.[63]

If Coolidge thought that his little gesture would placate the secretary of commerce and satisfy the press, he miscalculated. By now Hoover's friends and political supporters were reported to be incensed at the still unexplained presidential barb. The White House breakfast, which one correspondent dubbed "one of the strangest Easter feasts on record," only strengthened the speculative fever.[64]

With Washington abuzz in gossip over the "Hoover mystery" and with the *New York Times* (among others) practically demanding a clarification,

President Coolidge held his next regularly scheduled press conference on April 19. Now, once and for all, he tried to put the incident to rest:

> I didn't speak of Mr. Hoover's abilities the other day. I had rather assumed that that would be assumed by the conference. His reputation is so well established in this country, and indeed abroad, for ability and executive achievement that I doubt very much if I should be able to shake it even if I wished to. Certainly, I have no desire to do that and shouldn't want to be thought so lacking in appreciation of a man of his abilities as to think that he wasn't well qualified for any position in the Cabinet that he would be willing to accept. Of course, the place that he is in now is one of great importance and of constantly increasing importance, not only on account of our domestic commerce, but on account of our foreign commerce, which under his direction and encouragement has very greatly increased and shows promise of further increase in the future.[65]

The next day the president's explanation was front page news across the country. Never before, apparently, had the "White House Spokesman" spoken so admiringly about anyone in his administration. Pro-Coolidge papers hailed his tribute to his secretary of commerce, and the whiff of political scandal soon subsided—although not before 221 separate newspaper editorials across the country had commented on the incident. Still, nothing Coolidge had said in explanation could quite conceal one fact: Whatever the tone of his original remark, its substance remained unmodified. He had no intention of making Hoover his secretary of state.[66]

The Hoover-Coolidge relationship now returned to outward normalcy. Only three days after the president's quasi-apology before the press, he appointed Hoover chairman of a Cabinet committee to coordinate relief efforts for victims of flooding in the lower Mississippi Valley. This was no perfunctory assignment; the Mississippi River flood of 1927 was the worst natural disaster in American history. More than three hundred thousand people were forced to flee their homes and live in tent cities. That spring and summer, Hoover threw himself with characteristic zeal into organizing the public/private response to the unprecedented emergency. His leadership won him the applause of the nation and new status as a humanitarian hero. In a letter to the engineer-turned-public servant in June, Coolidge himself praised Hoover's "great service" and told him: "I do not think of anyone else that was equipped to handle it as you have done." In this same letter, Coolidge even invited Hoover to visit him during the summer at the presidential vacation site in South Dakota, if Hoover should happen to be "going west at any time."[67]

For his part, Hoover seemed anxious to furbish his credentials as a loyal lieutenant. The secretary of commerce was undoubtedly aware of the pervasive belief in political circles that Coolidge was annoyed by the maneuverings of Hoover's friends to advance his presidential prospects, and by press reports that Hoover would be Coolidge's choice to succeed him in 1928. Hoover also undoubtedly realized that any presidential ambitions he harbored could be crushed forever if he antagonized the sometimes irascible man in the White House.[68]

In the spring and summer of 1927, then, as speculation intensified about whether Coolidge would run again, Hoover did his best to proclaim his fealty. He was *not* a candidate for the presidential nomination, he told a visitor in May (who promptly informed the *New York Times*). The secretary of commerce said he was convinced that Coolidge would run again, be renominated, and win reelection. In mid-July, in Chicago, he declared: "No, I will not be a candidate. I am for Mr. Coolidge, who, I am sure, will be our president for four more years."[69]

Under the circumstances, Hoover could not have been entirely pleased when the *Des Moines Register*, on April 27, published a cartoon by J. N. Darling. The cartoon depicted a horde of pedestrians, all in the likeness of Hoover, crossing the street and creating a traffic jam. The pedestrians were identified as Hoover the secretary of commerce, Hoover the radio commissioner, Hoover the farm economist, Hoover the labor arbitrator, and more. The stopped vehicles were labeled "Sec. Kellogg," "Sec. Mellon's car," and "Congress." Standing in the middle of the parade, and acting as a traffic cop, was Calvin Coolidge, dressed as a policeman. The title of the cartoon was "The Traffic Problem in Washington, D.C."[70]

There is no evidence that Coolidge saw or commented upon this artistic suggestion that Hoover was *the* dynamic figure in Washington. Nor, apparently, did Coolidge comment in May when Hoover publicly clashed with Kellogg over the question of whether the U.S. government should restrict private American loans to foreign countries for purposes that the U.S. government deemed nonproductive. (Hoover was in favor of such a policy). A few weeks later, however, Hoover's intimate friend Hugh Gibson (fresh from a visit to Washington) provided a hint that all was not well beneath the surface. According to Gibson, President Coolidge was thoroughly irritated by the accolades Hoover was receiving for his Mississippi flood relief work.

Certainly some in the Coolidge wing of the GOP were worried by the adulation that Hoover was gaining in the deep South, whose delegates might be a decisive factor at the next Republican national convention.[71]

On July 20, Hoover arrived at the Black Hills of South Dakota, where he briefed the vacationing president about the Mississippi Valley's flood-recovery needs. The atmosphere seems to have been anything but cordial. At first the president had planned to remain at his quarters in the State Game Lodge and let his visitor come to him. Then Coolidge changed his mind and motored to the train station at Custer. But when Hoover stepped off the train, it was a Secret Service agent who met him; the president did not get out of his car. When Hoover came over to the waiting automobile, Coolidge greeted him without a smile. Later, the two men were chauffeured to the president's office in Rapid City. On the entire drive (thirty miles), neither man spoke to the other.[72]

It is impossible to know the source of the president's displeasure—if, indeed, displeasure it was. The president may have been bothered by the possibility that his omnipresent commerce secretary would demand a special session of Congress to appropriate extra money for flood relief—a course Coolidge strongly opposed. In the president's view, sessions of Congress always produced "agitations" that disturbed business. In any case, Hoover could not have been comforted by his host's frosty reticence or by the spate of political rumor mongering that the visit generated. Questioned by the press, Hoover angrily denied a report that he was about to resign and run for president regardless of Coolidge's intentions. "I am desirous and willing to serve under and with President Coolidge," he insisted.[73]

More and more, conjecture about Hoover's and Coolidge's ambitions was coloring the news coverage about the two men. No doubt with relief, Hoover departed from the Black Hills on July 21 and headed to his beloved California. Less than two weeks later, on August 2, he was vacationing at the Bohemian Grove north of San Francisco when a telegram arrived from the Associated Press. It said: "President Coolidge issued statement as follows Quote I do not choose to run for president in 1928 Unquote Please telephone or telegraph your views of Presidents statement."[74]

Suddenly the path to the White House was open. Or was it?

In reconstructing the next phase in the Coolidge-Hoover relationship, it may help to recall that Coolidge was both a stubborn Vermont Yankee and a lover of practical jokes. Certainly this least flamboyant of presidents must have relished the perplexity that his cryptic announcement produced in the nation's political elite. What did the president mean, and how much did he mean it? Had he really forsaken another term? Would he accept a draft, if offered, at the next convention? Would he publicly endorse someone else?[75]

Coolidge's stunning thunderbolt posed immediate problems for Hoover. Already under suspicion at the White House for his pushiness, the secretary of commerce could ill afford to look overly ambitious, at least not until the president's own intentions were certain. Hoover therefore immediately instructed his supporters to lie low and informed the press of his "regret" at Coolidge's statement. "I still believe," said Hoover on August 3, that Coolidge "should be renominated and re-elected."[76]

A few weeks later, when both men were back in Washington, Hoover called at the White House and tried to obtain some clarification. The secretary of commerce explained that since August 2 he had been inundated with "urgings" that he now seek the presidency. Despite this, Hoover declared that he thought Coolidge should run again. If the president would give the signal, Hoover said, he would steer his supporters into a "Draft Coolidge" effort. Hoover further offered to "stop the movement toward myself" if there were "any possibility" that Coolidge could be persuaded to accept renomination. The president answered that Hoover "ought not to stop it." When Hoover asked whether Coolidge's Black Hills declaration was "absolutely conclusive," however, the president "made no direct reply."[77]

Denied the positive assurance that he sought, Hoover felt obliged to confine his presidential maneuverings that autumn to "unofficial" activities by his friends. But if for Hoover the future still seemed murky, for Coolidge, apparently, it was altogether clear. Sometime in the autumn of 1927, the president was out on one of his frequent strolls in downtown Washington with his Secret Service escort and friend, Edmund W. Starling. Suddenly the "little fellow" (as Starling called Coolidge) spoke:

> Well, they're going to elect that superman Hoover, and he's going to have some trouble. He's going to have to spend money. But he won't spend enough.
>
> Then the Democrats will come in and they'll spend money like water. But they don't know anything about money. Then they will want me to come back and save some money for them. But I won't do it.[78]

If this anecdote is accurate (and there is no reason to doubt its essence), it was one of the most prescient remarks Calvin Coolidge ever made.

Then, on December 6, in an address before the Republican National Committee, the president broke his public silence. Prior to this speech, Hoover had gone to him again, informing him that there was "great demand" that he continue in office and that, if Coolidge would give his assent at the RNC meeting, the party would surely "go along unanimously." Ever anxious to demonstrate his loyalty, Hoover stressed that he did not want Coolidge to feel constrained by the activities of Hoover's friends. According to Hoover, Coolidge "made no very definite statement" except to give him some campaign advice. Instead, the president reserved his next bombshell for the speech he gave to the RNC:

> This is naturally the time to be planning for the future. The party will soon place in nomination its candidate to succeed me. To give time for mature deliberation I stated to the country on Aug. 2 that I did not choose to run for president in 1928.
>
> My statement stands. No one should be led to suppose that I have modified it. My decision will be respected.
>
> After I had been eliminated the party began, and should vigorously continue, the serious task of selecting another candidate from among the numbers of distinguished men available.

Once more the inscrutable figure in the White House had delivered an oracular pronouncement. This time, for most observers, its meaning seemed plain. Still, the president did not state what he would do if, in defiance of his apparent wishes, the Republican national convention should draft him anyway. On that slim reed of uncertainty, much of the politics of the next six months would pivot.[79]

The campaign of 1928 now got underway in earnest. By early February, Hoover was ready to announce his candidacy publicly. But before he did so, he went to the White House yet again. He told the president that he (Hoover) was under pressure to enter the presidential primary in Ohio, where Senator Willis had already come out as a favorite son. Hoover then asked Coolidge directly whether he intended to place his name on the Ohio primary ballot. The president replied in one word: "No." Hoover then asked whether *his* name should go on the Ohio ballot. The president replied in two words: "Why not?"[80]

With Coolidge's acquiescence, then (though hardly his blessing), Hoover publicly affirmed his candidacy for president on February 12, 1928. Somewhat disingenuously (for a man already working at full throttle behind the scenes for his objective), Hoover asserted his "conviction" that he should not "strive for the nomination." For this reason, he said, and because of his "obligations as Secretary of Commerce," he would make no "personal campaign." Hoover thereupon pledged that if he received the nomination he would "consider it my duty to carry forward the principles of the Republican Party and the great objectives of President Coolidge's policies—all of which have brought to our country such a high degree of happiness, progress, and security." Interestingly, Hoover did not precisely promise to carry forward Coolidge's policies—only the *objectives* of those policies. It was a subtle distinction that may have been deliberate.[81]

Certainly one Coolidge policy that Hoover did *not* approve was the president's indifference toward—if not outright encouragement of—the surging stock market. By early 1928, prices on the New York Stock Exchange had advanced to record levels, abetted by a staggering growth in brokers' loans. In January, the amount of such loans held by member banks of the New York Federal Reserve system approached an unprecedented $4 billion, an increase of about a billion dollars in just twelve months. On January 6, President Coolidge was asked at a news conference whether the amount of these loans was now dangerously high. Relying upon information from his Treasury Department, the president replied that he saw no signs that the amount was "large enough to cause particularly unfavorable comment." Upon hearing this presidential benediction, the stock market soared again.[82] When Hoover heard it, he was incredulous. Turning to an aide, he asked: Did Coolidge say *that?*[83]

Actually, Coolidge himself had qualms about the enormous credit expansion that was driving the stock market upward. But for a variety of reasons, he declined to intervene. As he put it to a relative a few days later, "I regard myself as the representative of the government and not as an individual." When "technical matters" arose, he said, he turned them over to the appropriate government agency and used the resulting feedback as the basis for his official stance. That, however, "does not prevent me from thinking what I please as an individual." And as an individual, he considered any loan obtained for "gambling in stocks" to be an "excessive loan." Herbert Hoover's conception of the presidential office was to be far more interventionist.[84]

Meanwhile, Coolidge's attitude toward Hoover was becoming more critical. In the autumn of 1927, the president startled William R. Castle Jr. of the State Department by remarking that he did not consider Hoover a very good adviser on State Department affairs. It was probably during this period that someone asked Coolidge what he thought of his secretary of commerce. The president replied, "How can you like a man who's always trying to get your job?" In the wake of the Mississippi River flood disaster, Coolidge began privately to disparage Hoover as the "miracle worker" and "wonder boy."[85]

Publicly, Coolidge remained scrupulously neutral in the developing presidential campaign. He even issued further renunciatory statements. In March, he declined a request from the Republican State Central Committee of Wyoming that he run again. A month later he insisted that a write-in movement for him in the Massachusetts primary be discontinued. His letter strongly intimated his displeasure at "Draft Coolidge" drives occurring in other states. Officially, at least, Coolidge was out of the contest and doing nothing to confer advantage on any would-be successor.[86]

Privately, however, an agitated Hoover was not so sure. Hoover was fully cognizant that much of the opposition to his candidacy was coming from men who were plotting for a deadlocked convention and a last-minute draft of Coolidge. As early as December 1927, Hoover believed that agents of the Republican national chairman were constantly telling Coolidge false stories about Hoover and that Coolidge was reacting angrily. A few months later, Hoover appeared to agree with the report of a friend that Coolidge was hostile to his secretary of commerce. It is impossible to know the substantive basis for these perceptions. But Hoover believed (as he later wrote a friend) that Coolidge considered him a "somewhat dangerous 'liberal.'" Hoover also believed that Coolidge preferred Senator Charles Curtis of Kansas for the nomination, and he expected Coolidge to say so publicly. From day to day, then, Hoover was condemned to live in fear that the "little fellow" would in some way deprive him of the great prize.[87]

By early May, Hoover was far in the lead in the quest for delegates but by no means certain of a majority. For a final time, he made a plea to the president. I now have abou 400 delegates, he told Coolidge. But if you will allow your name to be placed in nomination, I will release my delegates and tell them to vote for you. Hoover was certain that Coolidge would then be nominated. According to Hoover, the president replied that this (in Hoover's words) was "a fine offer, but it should not be done." As for the claim of 400 delegates, the president remarked, "If you have 400 delegates, you better keep them." He said no more.[88]

Once again, the "Great Enigma" had given his caller little relief from nervous tension, but Hoover might have derived hope from a conversation that Coolidge had at nearly the same time with Senator James Watson, a "favorite son" candidate who had recently been conspiring to renominate the president. "You and Charles Hilles [a leading pro-Coolidge Republican in New York] are bad boys, and I want you to behave yourselves," Coolidge lectured. "I have studied it all over and have finally concluded that I do not want that nomination."

"But suppose the Convention nominates you, then what?" Watson asked. Ducking this "hypothetical" question, Coolidge explained why he did not want to be president again. "I fitted into the situation that existed right after the war, but I might not fit into the next one," he said. After the war, the American people had wanted "rest"; he had given it to them, and they had prospered. But now, new circumstances were arising. "From this time on, there must be something constructive applied to the affairs of government, and it will not be sufficient to say, 'Let business take care of itself.'" "I do not feel that I am the man" to "meet the demand" for "affirmative" action that will soon arise, said Coolidge. "Somebody can do it, but I do not want to undertake it." Watson warned Coolidge that if he did not accept the nomination, Hoover would surely be selected. "Well," Coolidge replied, "that is a matter for the Convention to decide."[89]

Meanwhile, in Washington, D.C., the McNary-Haugen monster had once again reared its head. Only weeks before the Republican convention was to assemble, the Congress enacted yet another version of this farm-relief panacea so loathed by both Coolidge and Hoover. On May 23, President Coolidge vetoed the measure. In a scathing message whose ferocity astonished the press, Coolidge excoriated the "vicious," "dangerous," "repugnant," "fantastic," "delusive," "preposterous," and "intolerable" features of the McNary-Haugen bill. His veto was promptly sustained.[90]

For Hoover, the president's rebuff of McNary-Haugenism contained both good and bad news. On the one hand, it highlighted a critical issue on which he was in accord with Coolidge and the more conservative elements in the Republican Party. It also threw a roadblock in front of Hoover's rivals for the nomination, some of whom had endorsed the controversial legislation. On the other hand, the divisive controversy now threatened to bedevil the national convention and even to ignite the defection of the farm-belt states to the Democrats. In the aftermath of the president's stinging veto, enraged McNary-Haugenites vowed to carry the fight to the convention floor in Kansas City. The governor of Nebraska called for one hundred thousand farmers to march on the convention and "demand their rights."[91]

In a bid to quell the threatened agrarian rebellion, Secretary of Agriculture Jardine asked the president in May to send a special message to Congress urging enactment of an alternative farm bill sponsored by Jardine and Hoover. In this way, the farm states could be appeased. Coolidge apparently did not care for the alternative bill. Or perhaps he did not care to confer so obvious a favor on the leading contender for the nomination just weeks in advance of the party's decision. For whatever reason, Coolidge was not to be moved. When Jardine asked him outright to send the special message in support of the farm bill as a favor to Hoover (the presumptive nominee), the president exploded: "That man has offered me unsolicited advice for six years, all of it bad!"[92]

The final weeks before the convention were a time of high but covert drama, as pro- and anti-Hoover forces attempted to smoke out the sphinx in the White House. Hoover's agony was excruciating. He was so close to success, yet possibly so far. Pacing the floor in anxiety at one point, he exclaimed to an adviser, "Everything is all right. The Kansas City situation seems to hold no element of doubt. But the thing that gets me is the man there in the White House. What is his game? What cards will he play and how?" Deeply disturbed by Coolidge's continuing silence, Hoover arranged on June 8 to debrief a certain friend after the friend had lunched with the president. The friend could only report afterward that Coolidge had given no hint of his political plans. That very same day, Andrew Mellon, chairman of the powerful Pennsylvania delegation, asked the president whether there was any possibility that he would change his mind about the nomination. According to Mellon, the chief executive "looked down his nose and almost snarled his reply." "He speaks of his position and cannot change," Mellon wrote in his diary. "Is in accord with me on Hoover." What this probably meant was that Coolidge had reached the same conclusion that Mellon had: Without a draft of the president, Hoover's nomination was inevitable.[93]

Despite tremendous pressures, then, Coolidge refused to give the signal that even then could have stopped Hoover. Nor, despite repeated pleadings, did he succumb to demands that he anoint an anti-Hoover candidate or help the anti-Hoover coalition "get together." "I refused to interfere," Coolidge told a friend two years later. "There was no way for me to do so without creating a situation that would lead to my own nomination. I was determined that that should not happen."[94]

Still, in ten long, agonizingly suspenseful months, he had never issued a "Sherman statement." He had not once said unequivocally that he would refuse to accept the nomination if it were tendered to him. Why not? Because, he asserted in his autobiography, such a statement would not have been "in accordance with my conception of the requirements of the presidential office." (Just what these were, he did not say.) "I never stated or formulated in my own mind what I should do in such circumstances," he added, "but I was determined not to have that contingency arise."[95]

In the end, Coolidge did not have to face this supreme crisis of renunciation. On the eve of the balloting in Kansas City, William Vare, the boss of Philadelphia, bolted to Hoover, splitting the hitherto uncommitted Pennsylvania delegation and making any further "Stop Hoover" movement hopeless. The anti-Hoover front quickly collapsed. Coolidge himself, through his secretary Everett Sanders, requested the pro-Coolidge leaders of several state delegations not to vote for him, and they obeyed.[96]

Yet if Coolidge did not want the nomination, he was not necessarily gratified by the convention's outcome. As it happened, the president was on his way by train to Wisconsin for a summer vacation when the Republican Party chose his successor. Coolidge was in bed when, late on the evening of June 14, Hoover swept to a first ballot victory in Kansas City. The next morning, Coolidge received the news in Wisconsin, and the Secret Service agent who was with him never forgot his reaction. His face betraying anger, the president bluntly ordered the agent to get him a bottle of whiskey.[97]

At this point, one might ask: if Coolidge was so unenthusiastic about Hoover, why did he not try in some way to thwart Hoover's pursuit of the great prize? First, Coolidge appears to have sincerely believed that a sitting president should not, in most cases, attempt to influence the selection of his successor. The candidate, he later wrote, "should be the choice of the people themselves." To all external appearances, Coolidge scrupulously adhered to these convictions. A second, less abstract reason may also have intruded: the absence of acceptable, first-class alternatives. Andrew Mellon was too old. Charles Evans Hughes was not interested. Vice President Charles Dawes openly favored McNary-Haugenism and had even helped the fight for it in the Senate; besides, Coolidge had other reasons for detesting him. Frank Lowden of Illinois—an open and formidable contender—also embraced the McNary-Haugen plan, even endorsing it just six days before Coolidge's veto. By this act, Lowden made it impossible for eastern, conservative Coolidgeites to support him. Coolidge later opined that had Lowden not made that ill-timed endorsement, he might well have wrested the nomination away from Hoover.[98]

There were other candidates, of course—favorite sons and such—but these were small fry, and Coolidge did not care for some of them, either. Hoover was not the only presidential aspirant whom the president disliked. And even if he secretly preferred Senator Curtis (as both Hoover and Curtis thought), for Coolidge there was still the hurdle of principle mentioned above.[99]

This dearth of acceptable rivals of Hoover in 1928 (acceptable, that is, to party conservatives) underscores the centrality of the McNary-Haugen controversy in Republican politics in the 1920s. On this, one of the key litmus-test issues of the day, Hoover and Coolidge stood on the same side of the ideological divide. Without this essential common ground between them, it is doubtful that Hoover could have become Coolidge's successor.

Coolidge's first official response to Hoover's convention victory was a telegram that in form, at least, was more than adequate: "You have been nominated for the most important position in the world. Your great ability and your wide experience will enable you to serve our party and our country with marked distinction. I wish you all the success that your heart could desire. May God continue to bestow upon you the power to do your duty." Only one phrase—the wish for "all the success that your heart could desire"—carried a possible hint of reproach. Was this an oblique reference to what in Coolidge's eyes was Hoover's overweening ambition? If so, no one seems to have noticed. Hoover's reply to Coolidge's wire was equally dignified: "I am greatly touched by your telegram. During the last seven years you have given me unremitting friendship and my greatest hope is that it will continue to sustain me in this new task. Your high sense of duty and your devotion to public service will always be for me an inspiration." To the Republican national convention, Hoover pledged "to uphold the traditions of the Republican Party so effectively exemplified by Calvin Coolidge." On the surface, all seemed well.[100]

In the next several months, however, the now familiar Coolidge/Hoover pattern repeatedly manifested itself: public correctness, private strain. One source of tension was uncertainty over whether Hoover would visit the president in Wisconsin on a trip west to California. Early in July, reports circulated in Washington that the secretary of commerce would do so. Coolidge, who had issued no such invitation, was displeased and let the press know it: "I have no definite engagement to meet Mr. Hoover. I have no information of any kind or description as to whether he is coming here. I should assume, though, that if he was coming he would say something to me about it." The next day Coolidge's lack of knowledge of Hoover's plans was duly reported in the press. Taking the hint, the secretary of commerce speedily asked the president for an opportunity to visit him and discuss "some matters of importance in connection with the campaign." Coolidge promptly invited Hoover and his wife to stay at the president's vacation lodge on his visit.[101]

On July 16, the Republican nominee and Mrs. Hoover arrived at the presidential retreat in the Wisconsin woods. At the outset, at least, it was an awkward encounter. When the two men met, the president was unsmiling, and his handshake "the usual matter of course greeting for which he is famous." It was left to the two wives to do the smiling. A few minutes later, Coolidge and Hoover sat solemnly for the photographers. When asked by one of them to carry on a conversation, the president turned to Hoover and made some remark. Hoover smiled but made no reply. The president spoke to him again. Once more his guest smiled but said nothing. Turning to the photographers, Coolidge said, "I am sorry. I am willing, but I cannot make Mr. Hoover keep up his end of the conversation." This was a switch: Silent Cal unable to get Hoover to speak! Mrs. Coolidge and Mrs. Hoover were greatly amused. Eventually, at the president's prodding, Hoover held an informal news conference, but he said nothing about politics.[102]

The remainder of the Hoovers' two-day sojourn went well; so, at least, Coolidge told his next news conference. Much of the time the president and his guest spent fishing, a recreational activity that required neither of them to say much to the other. "He is a more expert fisherman that I am," Coolidge afterward confided to the press. But when asked whether he could be quoted on this, the president declined.[103]

One issue that the two apparently did not resolve during Hoover's visit was the timing of his resignation as secretary of commerce. Hoover had informed Coolidge of his desire to leave in a note on June 30 and had formally tendered his resignation on July 5. But Coolidge seemed in no hurry to accept it. He informed the press twelve days later that there was some Commerce Department business that he wanted Hoover to "look into a little" before the resignation became official. Was Coolidge, in this subtle way, letting Hoover know that he was still president? One cannot be sure.[104]

Hoover now went on to California, where, on August 11, he formally accepted his party's nomination in a ceremony in the Stanford University football stadium. The event was carried on nationwide radio, but Coolidge did not listen. At the time of Hoover's address, the president was out fishing—a datum that was quickly reported in the press. In fact, Coolidge did not send Hoover a congratulatory telegram for three days—and then only after his failure to do so had been noted in the newspapers. When it came, the presidential felicitation was but two sentences long: "Your speech ranks very high in political discussion. I congratulate you upon it and upon the reception which has been given to it by the country."[105]

Seven days later, Coolidge finally accepted the resignation of his secretary of commerce. In a parting telegram of thanks, the president asserted that Hoover's service had been "of great benefit to the commercial life of the Nation" and that Hoover's knowledge of "the mechanics of business and government" was "unsurpassed." "It will always be a satisfaction to me," wrote Coolidge, "to have had the benefit of your wise counsel in meeting the problems which have arisen during my administration. My best wishes will always attend you in the broader field to which you have been called." On its face it was a decent encomium, but many Republican politicians were disappointed. To them the president's message seemed "lacking in fervor."[106]

If Hoover now hoped that Coolidge would participate actively in the fall campaign against the Democrats, he soon learned differently. On August 19, the nominee asked Coolidge by letter to deliver at least two nationally broadcast speeches for the Republicans. But when Coolidge returned to Washington from Wisconsin in September, he indicated that he had reached no decision about his campaign role. He told visitors that he did not consider it dignified for a president to deliver political speeches during a campaign. Theodore Roosevelt, he pointed out, had made no partisan speeches for Taft in 1908, nor had Woodrow Wilson for his party's standard bearer in 1920. If this was indeed Coolidge's sole reason for not hitting the hustings, it showed how exalted was his conception of the office he held.[107]

Olympian dignity, of course, was not what Republican activists were seeking in the frantic autumn of 1928. By mid-October, Coolidge's reticence about the GOP ticket had become a source of comment in the press and of considerable discomfiture among Republican leaders. Would "the White House sphinx," or would he not, deliver a speech for the party? No one seemed able to find out. To be sure, in late September the president had sent a message to a Massachusetts party leader endorsing Hoover, but the endorsement had been embarrassingly formal. As one observer noted, Coolidge's "recommendation was like that one gives an employee whose departure is welcome to the endorser." Day by day the mystery mounted. Could it be, as some Democrats were openly suggesting, that the man in the White House did not really care who succeeded him? Once again, as the *New York Times* editorialized, Coolidge was "most secretive when the politicians are almost neurotic at being kept so long on needles and pins."[108]

All this speculation probably delighted the attentive reader of newspapers who inhabited the presidential mansion. Once more Coolidge the Silent was proving himself a master of suspense.

On November 1 Hoover called upon his president one more time before heading to California to vote. As the Movietone cameras recorded the scene on the White House lawn, Coolidge said: "Good-bye, Mr. Hoover. I wish you a pleasant trip to California and a safe return. Good-bye and good luck." Replied Hoover: "Good-bye and thank you, Mr. President." Nothing more.[109] But the press did not know that Hoover and Coolidge were secretly planning one last Coolidgean surprise. Since the president was unwilling to make campaign speeches, Hoover conceived the idea of a dramatic presidential telegram to the candidate late in the campaign.[110] Coolidge agreed, and on November 2—only four days before the election—he telegraphed a message in some of the most effusive words he ever wrote:

I have just heard your St. Louis speech with great satisfaction. It is the concluding address of a series which have disclosed a breadth of information, a maturity of thought, and a soundness of conclusion on public questions never surpassed in a previous presidential campaign. You have had the knowledge and judgment which enabled you to tell the people the truth. You have been clear, candid and courteous, demonstrating your faith in the people and your consciousness that the truth has a power and conclusiveness of its own which is always supreme. All the discussion has only made more plain the wisdom of the plans you have proposed for solving our political, economic, and social problems. You have shown your fitness to be President. I wish to congratulate you on the high quality of your leadership. You are able, experienced, trustworthy, and safe. Your success in the campaign seems assured and I shall turn over the great office of President of the United States of America to your keeping, sure that it will be in competent hands in which the welfare of the people will be secure.[111]

The telegram at once evoked large headlines, as both men surely knew that it would. Hoover was grateful. Republican leaders were jubilant and relieved. Not everyone, of course, was ecstatic. The *New York Times* wondered, "If the president wanted to promote the success of his sometime subordinate, why was he so unconscionably long in bringing himself to do it?"[112] Nevertheless, no one could charge that Coolidge, a faithful party man, had failed to do his political duty. And when, on November 6, Hoover was overwhelmingly elected, Coolidge telegraphed his "cordial congratulations": "The success of our party with your election to the Presidency and the endorsement of the Administration are of great satisfaction to me. With this endorsement I can now retire from office in contentment."[113]

The president's term, however, still had four months to run, and he was known to be very touchy about his prerogatives. No doubt with these sensitivities in mind, Hoover proposed on November 1 that he take a semiofficial goodwill tour of Latin America after the election. Coolidge was willing to accommodate the president-elect, although the correspondence between them betrayed a hint of disharmony. The thrifty president evidently wanted Hoover to sail on a U.S. Navy cruiser; Hoover insisted upon and ultimately received a battleship. And so, from November 19, 1928, until early January 1929, Hoover not only stayed out of Washington; better still, he stayed out of the country.[114]

On January 9, back in Washington at last, the president-elect conferred at the White House at Hoover's request and began planning his new regime. A few days later, Hoover headed to Florida for a vacation; he returned to the capital in mid-February, a full two weeks in advance of his inauguration. Both of these visits were contrary to recent precedent; Wilson and Harding had not set foot in the capital until the eve of *their* inaugurations. If Coolidge perceived Hoover's visits as undue encroachment, he evidently did not say so. To all appearances, contacts between the chief executive and his successor-in-waiting were (in one newspaper's words) "entirely correct and friendly." Coolidge even gave Hoover some "fatherly" advice about managing the White House: "You have to stand every day three or four hours of visitors. Nine-tenths of them want something they ought not to have. If you keep dead-still they will run down in three or four minutes. If you even cough or smile they will start up all over again."[115]

Still, signs were appearing that a new political era was at hand, and Coolidge could not have been entirely happy at the prospect. Throughout his term, the frugal executive had gotten along with one White House secretary (a senior position, not a clerical one). On January 11, Hoover asked Coolidge to recommend to the Congress the appropriation of money to hire two more. Coolidge went along with this request. But if Washington scuttlebutt was correct, during these final weeks, as problems came to his desk, Coolidge began to remark, "We'll leave that to the wonder boy."[116]

One such problem—in Hoover's eyes, at least—was the continuing, dizzy advance of the stock market: that "mad orgy of speculation" (as he later called it) that had begun in 1927. Upon returning from Latin America in January 1929, Hoover had been "appalled" (as he subsequently put it) by the extent to which share prices had risen during his trip. The nervous president-elect promptly called upon Coolidge and urged him to ask the Federal Reserve Board "to put the brakes upon the misuse of credit for speculative purposes." Although Coolidge (said Hoover) "could not believe that anything was really wrong," he did authorize Hoover to raise the issue with the Federal Reserve Board. Hoover did so. According to him, the board instituted some restrictions on the speculative use of credit and "got out warnings" that briefly cooled the "market fever." But to Hoover's chagrin, at a press conference some days later President Coolidge made "a bullish statement" that set off the market stampede all over again. By the time Hoover took office, it was too late (he later claimed) to do much to curb the market's "madness."[117]

Hoover's account may have been self-serving, but it did limn the contrast between his approach to the economy and Coolidge's. According to Hoover, his predecessor as president was "a strict legalist" who held that the Federal Reserve Board "had been created by the Congress entirely independent of the Executive and that he could not interfere." Hoover had no such aversion to "jawboning" the Fed, either personally or through surrogates.[118]

On March 4, 1929, fulfilling an ambition that had touched his soul for a decade or longer, Herbert Hoover became president of the United States. For an hour and a half during the ceremonies, he and Calvin Coolidge stood, sat, and walked side by side without saying a word to each other. In his inaugural address, Hoover politely paid tribute to his predecessor: "For wise guidance in this great period of recovery the nation is deeply indebted to Calvin Coolidge." When the ceremonies at the Capitol were over, the two men said goodbye, and the new president left for the White House. The ex-president took a train home to New England, where, for the rest of his days, he lived.[119]

Coolidge's exit from Washington did not mean that he had permanently left the national stage, however much he (and Hoover) may have desired it. For the next four years, as New Era prosperity curdled into depression, the puzzling Yankee in Northampton, Massachusetts, cast a troubling shadow over his successor.

As the Great Depression set in and intensified, talk of replacing Hoover in 1932 with another candidate circulated widely among Republican leaders. Hoover could never be sure when a challenge to his renomination might erupt from his party's conservatives (or, for that matter, from Republican Progressives). Hoover knew painfully well that Coolidge could have taken the prize from him in 1928 at any time and that the Coolidge faction of the party had only grudgingly acquiesced in Hoover's selection. The man in the White House therefore kept an anxious watch on the sage of Northampton.

The new president's uneasiness about his predecessor may have been reciprocated, if Washington gossip was at all on the mark. According to one hostile source, Coolidge was decidedly unhappy when Hoover, in his very first economy move, put the presidential yacht, the *Mayflower*, in mothballs. When Hoover, in another act of symbolic frugality, removed two unused riding horses from the White House to nearby Fort Myer, Coolidge supposedly gibed, "Yes, I s'pose they'll eat less hay at the fort than they will at the White House."[120]

Publicly, of course—and by now we should not expect otherwise—Hoover and Coolidge maintained a carefully respectful relationship. If the former president had reservations about his successor's policies, he did not discuss them in public. Nor did Coolidge undercut the incumbent with plans of his own to combat the depression, despite incessant pleadings that he do so. "I won't do it," he said. "I refuse to be a Deputy President."[121]

As it happened, Hoover need not have fretted about Coolidge's plans for 1932. Ever the party loyalist, and burdened by failing health, the former president had no intention whatever to run again. In late 1931 he wrote: "A retired President ought to be an example of loyal support to his successor." "In an emergency like the present," he added, "the responsible elements of our party should offer a solid front in their support of the President. That is the course I propose to pursue." The following spring he gave no encouragement when die-hard Coolidgeites attempted to draft him for the national ticket, either as president or vice president. Hoover and his supporters easily quashed the abortive insurrection.[122]

And now, in the last election campaign he would ever see, it was Coolidge's turn to be the loyal lieutenant. There was no question at all about his sentiments. "I think it would be a great calamity if Mr. Hoover was not reelected and I cannot believe that he will be defeated," he wrote to a close friend. As a contribution to the cause, he published "The Republican Case" in the *Saturday Evening Post* in September. Hoover, he said, should be reelected "for what he has done and for what he has prevented." Hoover was "safe and sound." In a note of thanks, Hoover said he found it difficult to express his "full feeling of appreciation" for Coolidge's article.[123]

But Hoover and his increasingly desperate associates wanted more. Throughout the summer and autumn, emissaries from the White House and other quarters beseeched Coolidge to make speeches to save the party from disaster. At first he resisted; his ailing throat would not stand it, he said. But the former president relented when told that his party was going to be defeated and that he must be seen to have been one of the fighters for the losing cause. "I am always ready to share the fate of my party," he replied. A few weeks later he appealed for Hoover's reelection at a rally in Madison Square Garden. Hoover was overjoyed. With almost pathetic gratitude, he thanked Coolidge for this "warming remembrance from a true friend."[124]

Coolidge, in fact, had not been well when he spoke in New York and had been afraid that he would be unable to finish. Upon learning of the ex-president's physical difficulties, President Hoover quickly dropped plans for Coolidge to deliver a campaign address in Chicago.[125] In the end, Coolidge did manage to speak again publicly—on the night before the election, on nationwide radio from his home in Northampton. For the last time, he faithfully performed his duty according to the code by which he had lived:

> When the American people make a major decision like the election of a President they do not offer themselves to the highest bidder. . . . In all our history we have never deserted our President because we were not making money. . . . Promises and good intentions are not enough. We cannot afford rash experiments. . . . For nearly twenty years our President, Herbert Hoover, has been serving our country and the world. Measured by accomplishments he holds commanding rank. . . . All the teachings of common sense require us to reelect President Hoover. . . . From my knowledge of President Hoover, after sitting at the Cabinet Table with him for eight years, after considering the difficulties he has encountered and the policies he has proposed, I believe that he is the best man for us to entrust with the Presidency in this great emergency.[126]

It was a classically conservative case for a man he had once disparaged as a meddlesome liberal.

Two months later, Calvin Coolidge died suddenly. Herbert Hoover was shocked by the news. The president immediately issued a proclamation and attended the funeral in Northampton. "I feel I no longer fit in with these times," Coolidge had said just weeks before his death. About to be consigned to exile himself, Hoover soon felt the same way. Perhaps partly in gratitude for Coolidge's valiant contribution to the Republican campaign of 1932 when his uncertain health was failing, Hoover in the years to come tended to suppress the depth and detail of their past differences. To one correspondent in 1934, he even denied that there had ever been any "friction" between Coolidge and himself. *De mortuis nil nisi bonum?* Not quite. In Hoover's memoirs and elsewhere, explicit and implicit criticism of Coolidge can be found. But the acute, underlying sense of vexation—which Hoover and Coolidge had often felt about each other—was lacking in Hoover's later reminiscences. Long after his predecessor passed away, Hoover perpetuated the patina of diplomatic correctness that had marked their relationship in life.[127]

And what more need now be said? Leaving aside differences of personality and ideology, the Coolidge/Hoover relationship illustrated this point: Political parties are alliances of factions. Only three times in the twentieth century—1908, 1928, and 1988—has an elected candidate of one party succeeded in office an elected incumbent of the same party.[128] Such intraparty successions can be fraught with peril, for they entail the ascendancy of a new faction *within the coalition*. In a subtle sense, the recent victory at the polls becomes perceived as a factional triumph more than an all-party success. Trouble can soon result, over redistribution of patronage and much else. If Coolidge had been a younger man and less of an organization man, the Republican Party might have engaged in factional warfare in 1932 as it did in 1912 and 1992, and for some of the same reasons.

The convoluted Coolidge/Hoover story illustrates something else. The Republican Party of the 1920s was no monolith. In the nuances of these two men's relationship, we can see in microcosm some of the political fault-lines of a decade far more intriguing than is usually perceived.

27

Herbert Hoover, Supply-Side Economics, and the Tax Increase of 1932

When this article was written, supply-side economics was emerging as the dominant economic ideology among American conservatives, and President Herbert Hoover's tax policies in 1932 were being cited by ardent supply-siders as an egregious example of how not to cure a depression. As a Hoover biographer, I considered this critique to be neglectful of the context in which Hoover struggled, leading to a superficial understanding of a pivotal episode in our nation's history. Hence this rejoinder, which appeared as an op-ed piece in the Wall Street Journal *on June 12, 1980, under the title "Herbert Hoover's Balanced Budget."*

For more on this issue, see Chapter 28, "Herbert Hoover's Bad Press."

To historically minded observers of American politics it appears that a specter is haunting the 1980 presidential campaign: the specter of Herbert Hoover.

On the left, Senator Kennedy compares President Carter to President Hoover and revives the stale, stereotyped imagery of the New Deal: Hoover = Republicans = Depression and hard times.

On the right, a spirited band of Lafferites portrays Hoover as a cheerless apostle of "belt-tightening," a man whose stubborn adherence to a sterile economic policy in 1932 exacerbated the Great Depression and drove the Republican Party into a half century of political exile.

Whence arises this currently popular identification of Herbert Hoover with "austerity" and no-growth economics? It derives primarily from a single episode in Hoover's presidency. In 1931–32 Hoover proposed—and a

Democratic-controlled Congress ultimately enacted—a massive tax increase in a desperate effort to balance the federal budget. It was the largest percentage peacetime tax hike in American history. Such a policy understandably does not readily appeal to today's proponents of tax cuts as economic stimulus. But it is imperative to understand the context of Hoover's decision.

In fiscal year 1932, near the nadir of the Great Depression, the U.S. government incurred its largest peacetime deficit to date in American history. The shortfall ($2.7 billion) approached a staggering 60 percent of all federal expenditures. (A comparable percentage federal deficit today would be over $300 billion—in one year.)

FORTHRIGHT HOOVER

Faced with a peacetime fiscal drain of unprecedented proportions, what was President Hoover to do? He could try to make up the deficit by borrowing and thus increase the federal debt. But Hoover forthrightly rejected this self-defeating approach; massive federal borrowing, he contended, would simply overwhelm the money markets and soak up precious capital badly needed for private investment and recovery. Such a course, he said, would only "stifle" productivity, consumption and employment. It would choke the very flow of credit and recovery that he was striving to unleash, via the Reconstruction Finance Corporation and other instruments.

Nor could Hoover simply do nothing. For 150 years the federal government had always attempted (except in wartime) to balance its budget. This was the regnant orthodoxy in 1932—an orthodoxy so powerful that Franklin Roosevelt and the Democrats denounced Hoover in the election campaign for extravagant, unsound "radical" economics, and pledged to institute both a balanced budget and a 25 percent reduction in federal expenditures if elected. While Hoover himself had not, in the past, been an inflexible adherent of a balanced budget, he, too, in early 1932 publicly declared that a balanced budget was now, under the circumstances, an "absolute necessity."

Why? In part because Hoover—and most political and business leaders—believed exactly what Hoover argued: that a balanced budget was "the very keystone of real recovery," the bedrock of restored public confidence. Confidence (with the consequent flow of credit to businesses) was, in Hoover's judgment, the key. If the U.S. government could not control its own finances, how could economic recovery begin?

But there was a second, and probably most compelling, reason for Hoover's tax decision. On September 21, 1931, Great Britain abandoned the gold standard. The U.S., however, still struggled to maintain it. This meant that every dollar was legally convertible to gold, both at home and abroad.

At once the frightening effects of Britain's action became manifest. Gold flowed in record quantities out of the United States: $712 million in six weeks. If the pound fell, could the embattled dollar be far behind? Moreover, many nervous depositors withdrew currency from American banks—thereby helping to generate a wave of bank failures. Bank reserves plummeted by over a billion dollars (an enormous sum in those days) in just six weeks. Spasms of hoarding set in. The credit structure became more paralyzed than ever.

And now, against this disconcerting backdrop, the federal government's deficit was reaching a staggering magnitude. Confronted with what treasury secretary Andrew Mellon himself in January 1932 called a "grave emergency," Hoover opted to raise taxes (and cut federal spending) in order to balance the budget.

Hoover did so, it seems clear, not only to avoid borrowing but to prevent a run on the dollar and to save the gold standard. He must demonstrate the very financial integrity of the U.S. government. Foreign and domestic confidence in the American government's commitment to sound finance would, he believed, end the hoarding, relieve the beleaguered banks, and liquefy the frozen credit structure of the country. "The first requirement of confidence and of economic recovery," said Hoover in late 1931, "is financial stability of the United States Government." And that meant a balanced budget (via new taxes). This was the prevailing doctrine throughout the country in 1931–32. This was the standard economic thinking of the time.

Hoover's call for increased taxes, in fact, won widespread bipartisan support. Few politicians (or economists) challenged his rationale. Indeed, the only real debate in the Democratic-controlled Congress was not over whether to raise taxes, but how. On whom should the burden fall? Conservatives favored a manufactures' sales tax; liberals and radicals wanted to "soak the rich." In the end, after months of haggling, compromise legislation was approved in June 1932.

Incredible though it may now seem, nobody of influence in 1932 called for a tax cut to stimulate the economy, increase revenue, and thus balance the budget. Even Andrew Mellon, hero of today's tax-cutters, endorsed a tax increase that year. On January 13, 1932, Mellon told the House Ways and Means Committee: "It is essential to raise additional revenue, not just to cover expenditures but to maintain unimpaired the credit of the United

States Government." This "last objective," Mellon went on, was "an indispensable step in our progress to a road toward recovery."

(All of Mellon's tax cuts of the 1920s, incidentally, had occurred in an era of large federal surplus.)

It is important, too, to keep some perspective on the dimensions of federal spending and taxation at the time. The federal government's tax "wedge" in the Hoover era was small. In 1929 total federal expenditures comprised a mere 2.5 percent of the Gross National Product. (Today they approach 25 percent.) In the 1970s federal deficits alone were annually several times higher than entire annual budgets in Hoover's administration.

Moreover, from 1929 to 1932 the federal income tax structure was almost unbelievably low. Of the 36.1 million families and unattached individuals in this country in 1929, scarcely 4.1 million even filed tax returns. Of these, fewer than 2.5 million actually had taxable income. Ninety percent of families and unattached individuals earned less than $4,000. At the prevailing tax rates (after deductions and credits were allowed for), they escaped income taxation almost entirely. Throughout Hoover's presidency—and even after the tax hike of 1932—the vast majority of the American people paid no income taxes whatsoever.

Even after the substantial 1932 tax increase was enacted, the resulting tax burden rose to levels that today seem nearly idyllic. Under the new law a family with four exemptions earning $20,000 in 1932 paid a federal income tax of $1,616—an effective rate of only 8.1 percent.

A family with four exemptions earning $5,000 (a quite comfortable sum in 1932) paid all of $68 in income tax. Very few Americans incurred even that much obligation. It was not until World War II that most Americans became income tax payers.

DIRE CONSEQUENCES?

One must wonder, then, whether the tax increase of 1932 had all the dire economic and political consequences now attributed to it.

My purpose, however, is not to assert the wisdom—by today's standards—of the tax increase of 1932. Seen in retrospect (after almost fifty years of changing economic orthodoxy), Hoover's decision is now generally regarded by historians and economists as a serious mistake. Tax reductions in economic slumps are now the standard prescription of Keynesians and Lafferites alike (although the form of their remedies varies). But one must remember that Hoover and his contemporaries did not have the benefit of today's presumably superior wisdom. Hoover's "battle of the budget" in 1932 was fought four years before the publication of Keynes's revolutionary "General Theory" and forty-two years before the discovery of the Laffer Curve.

So if we ponder the context of Hoover's actions, and the constraints within which he worked, a much different understanding of him emerges. And that is the point. When interpreting the past, be wary of the pitfalls of present-minded preoccupations. With Herbert Hoover or anyone else, resist the temptation to select a sliver of the past as a basis for broad historical judgment. Above all, remember the context. If we are to learn from our history, we must first understand it.

28

Herbert Hoover's Bad Press

This is a slightly modified version of an essay written early in the election year of 2004 and printed in the Spring 2004 issue of the American Road, *the newsletter of the Hoover Presidential Library Association.*

Often it seems that Herbert Hoover is the Rodney Dangerfield of American politics: He gets no respect.

Other unpopular presidents, like Woodrow Wilson and Harry Truman, have recovered their reputations posthumously. A few, like Ronald Reagan, have lived to see their ratings rise. Some presidents whom historians deem mediocre—like Grover Cleveland and William Howard Taft—are conceded in retrospect to have possessed commendable integrity.

But not Hoover—at least not in our media and political culture of 2004.

Consider the evidence. A couple of months ago, a caravan of fifty-one unemployed Americans descended on the Herbert Hoover Presidential Library-Museum in West Branch, Iowa. They were part of a national "Show Us the Jobs" tour organized by the AFL-CIO. Upon reaching the Hoover Library grounds, the travelers disembarked from their buses, lined up near the museum entrance, unfurled a "Show Us the Jobs" banner, and had themselves photographed.

Why did they stop in West Branch? Because, explained one of the organizers, "George Bush is the first president since Herbert Hoover to have a net job loss." "We're just here," she said, "to acknowledge Herbert Hoover."

Acknowledgment, indeed. The tour group did not bother to visit his museum. Having staged their photo op, the unemployed reboarded their buses and moved on. Their stay in West Branch lasted just twelve minutes.

The "Show Us the Jobs" media event is emblematic of the use to which Hoover's name is being put in this election year. Across the land, political opponents of President Bush are reciting the mantra that he is "the first president to lose jobs since Herbert Hoover and the Great Depression." Whatever one may think about the statistical basis for this charge, the intention of Bush's critics is clear: to tie him rhetorically to a man perceived by the critics to have been a presidential failure.

Even the state of Iowa—where Hoover is something of a hero and his historic site a popular tourist attraction—has not been immune from the current wave of Hoover-bashing. Recently, the governor himself joined in the refrain that the Bush administration has "the worst job creation record since Herbert Hoover." And at the state capitol in Des Moines, a portrait of Hoover that had long hung in the governor's office has now been tucked away in a closet. The portrait is said to be "in need of repair."

What is happening here? Why is Hoover suffering once again from public disparagement? At one level the answer is obvious. Like consumer confidence data and the monthly unemployment rate, Hoover has become a leading economic indicator. Whenever the economy falters, the mention of his name shoots up. Nearly forty years after his death and more than seventy years after his presidency, he remains a historical punching bag, a symbol of hard times, ineptitude, and indifference.

The development of this symbolism was not exactly accidental. During Hoover's administration the Democratic Party's chief publicist and spinmeister, Charles Michelson, orchestrated an unremitting barrage of disparagement of Hoover's shortcomings: a foretaste of what a later generation would call "the politics of personal destruction." As the economy worsened, the nation's travails were increasingly personalized. Millions of bewildered Americans looked for scapegoats, and Hoover became the target. It was not the Great Depression; it was the "Hoover Depression." Shantytowns of the homeless were named "Hoovervilles." The insides of trouser pockets were called "Hoover handkerchiefs." Newspapers were "Hoover blankets." Armadillos were "Hoover hogs."

The temptation to interpret the Depression as a giant morality play, replete with heroes and knaves, did not abate when Hoover left office. Franklin Roosevelt—whose grasp of economics was not profound—perceived the world in such judgmental terms. In his 1933 inaugural address, he roundly denounced the nation's "money changers" as the villains in the drama and vowed to restore "the temple of our civilization" to "the ancient truths." Later on he castigated "economic royalists" and pledged to make himself their "master."

For years to come, at election time, Roosevelt and his Democratic successors "ran against Hoover." In 1948 President Harry Truman (who privately admired Hoover) nevertheless lambasted him on the hustings. If the Republicans won the election, he claimed, it would bring back the era of the "Hoover cart"—"the remains of the old tin lizzie being pulled by a mule, because you couldn't afford to buy a new car [and] you couldn't afford to buy gas for the old one." The "Hoover cart," said Truman, was "the only automobile in the world that eats oats."

And so it goes whenever the economy weakens. In 1987, when the stock market suddenly plummeted, allusions to Hoover and the Crash of 1929 filled the airwaves, and films of Depression-era breadlines appeared on television. In 1992, when President George Herbert Walker Bush ran for reelection at the end of a recession, leading Democrats ridiculed him as George Herbert Hoover Walker Bush. Old habits among politicians die hard.

Today's critics of Hoover on the Left, then, are heirs to a long, and by now reflexive, tradition of political oratory. To them he is little more than an advertising slogan, a Pavlovian stimulus meant to elicit an emotional response. Hoover/Depression, Hoover/unemployment, Hoover/Republicans: it is pro-New Deal historiography reduced to a single catchword.

But if Hoover wins little respect these days among partisan Democrats, where are his defenders among the Republicans? The answer is: almost nowhere, and therein lies another curious tale.

During Hoover's long and productive ex-presidency, he came to be revered by many in the GOP. His philippics against the New Deal inspired the party faithful. His speeches at national conventions were received with rapture. A patron of *Human Events*, *The Freeman*, and other conservative causes, he was admired as a benevolent grandfather figure on the American Right. To his liberal opponents and a considerable number of voters, his name continued to connote hard times and ineffective leadership. To his conservative supporters it conveyed an image of resilient rectitude.

When Hoover died in 1964, however, his political comeback died with him, and within a decade-and-a half his image radically changed. Acclaimed in his later years as "the greatest Republican of his generation," by the 1980s he was likened on the Right to Jimmy Carter. When Ronald Reagan became president in 1981, he soon made known his admiration for Calvin Coolidge (but not Hoover). To be sure, Reagan was not publicly critical of his hapless predecessor. But among a rising generation of conservative pundits and politicians, Hoover fell completely from favor.

What happened? In the 1970s a new conservative orthodoxy known as supply-side economics was born. Led by the free-market economist Arthur Laffer, the writer Jude Wanniski, Representative Jack Kemp, and the editorial board of the *Wall Street Journal*, the supply-siders built a powerful case for the reduction of tax rates as the answer to the oppressive stagflation of the Nixon/Ford/Carter years. Their arguments became the intellectual foundation for the Reagan Revolution and the dominant economic paradigm of the Republican Party ever since.

Searching for historical precedents to buttress their policy agenda, the supply-siders extolled the tax-cutting program of Calvin Coolidge and Secretary of the Treasury Andrew Mellon in the 1920s, as well as the tax cuts propounded by John F. Kennedy forty years later. Significantly, they did not turn in the least to Herbert Hoover. In the eyes of the evangelical supply-siders, President Hoover had committed two disastrous blunders. First, in 1930 he had signed into law the Smoot-Hawley tariff, a protectionist measure which (in their view) fractured the world economy and converted the crisis of 1929 into a catastrophe. Second, in 1931–32 Hoover had proposed—and a Democratic-controlled Congress had enacted—a massive tax increase in a desperate effort to balance the federal budget. It was the largest percentage peacetime tax hike in American history. It was a precedent which naturally did not appeal to conservative Reaganites of the 1980s and 1990s.

And that was it. Supply-side theorists and publicists showed little interest in any other part of Hoover's record: his belief in voluntarism, for example, or his social philosophy grounded in the ideal of equal opportunity. Nor did they pay much attention to the historical context in which his presidential decisions occurred. In fiscal year 1932, for instance, the federal government incurred its largest peacetime deficit to date in American history, a shortfall which approached a staggering 60 percent of all federal expenditures. Faced with a peacetime fiscal drain of unprecedented proportions, what were President Hoover and the Congress to do? The financial stability of the federal government and the viability of the gold standard appeared to hang in the balance. In 1932 no one of influence advocated tax cuts under these dire circumstances. Even after the tax hike of 1932 became law, the tax rates remained astonishingly low by modern standards. The vast majority of the American people still paid no federal income taxes whatsoever.

For present-minded activists of the 1980s and 1990s, however, Hoover's overall record of public service seemed less important than the alleged effects of his tax and tariff policies. Like the do-nothing Hoover of liberal carica-ture, the Hoover of supply-side economic orthodoxy became a cardboard figure—a rhetorical weapon to deploy against political foes. In an ironic reversal, it was now Republicans who accused protectionist, high-tax Demo-crats of repeating Hoover's errors.

To Jack Kemp and other popularizers of the new doctrine, Hoover was synonymous with dour, fetishistic, old-fashioned, balance-the-budget con-servatism: a shopworn and defensive ideology which they hoped to expel from the Republican Party. Time and again Kemp contrasted his optimistic brand of Republicanism with what he derisively called "Hooverism."

The rise of supply-side economics—and the anti-Hoover history lesson associated with it—was part of a larger intellectual trend which has gathered steam since the 1970s: the proliferation of scholarly, libertarian critiques of the liberal welfare state and its antecedents. At first one might think that Hoover, the arch-critic of New Dealism from 1933 to 1964, would be hailed in this new literature as a libertarian prophet, now that the currents of his-tory have turned his way. It has not happened. In the world of free-market economists, historians, and think tanks, it is not Hoover the ex-president who commands attention, but Hoover the president, and they do not par-ticularly like what they see. If to today's liberals Hoover in the White House was a timid man who did too little, to today's libertarians and many con-servatives he was an unwise activist who did too much. In recent books of a libertarian cast, like Jim Powell's *FDR's Folly*, Hoover emerges not so much as Franklin Roosevelt's antithesis but as his wrong-headed progenitor: a well-meaning interventionist who paved the way for the even more egre-gious statism which followed.

Thus even in what might be considered his natural constituency, Hoover has become a political outcast, whose name is rarely invoked except in criti-cism. Among libertarian thinkers and those influenced by their scholarship (a large chunk of the contemporary American Right), he tends to be per-ceived not as one of "us," but as one of "them."

There are additional reasons why Hoover continues to receive a bad press—and all too often, no press at all. We live in a media world driven by sound bites, an environment not conducive to the nuanced analysis that Hoover requires. There remains a disconnect between recent Hoover scholarship—which tends to portray him as an exceptionally able and even tragic figure—and the selective, moralistic stereotyping so ingrained in our popular culture. Moreover, the narration of our nation's political history is increasingly organized around the presidency—a narrowing of focus that, in Hoover's case, omits much of importance. He was, after all, in public life for fifty years, of which only four were in the White House. In this era of perpetual campaigning for the presidency, Hoover's enormous *non*presidential achievements—notably his humanitarian relief work and creation of the Hoover Institution—are repeatedly overlooked. In the popular imagination all that seems to matter is his presidency.

Finally, Hoover continues to receive less respect than he ought because, throughout his amazingly varied public life, he often did not fit the conventional mold. At the outset of his career in politics, he called himself an "independent progressive," alienated from Democratic radicals and Republican reactionaries alike. Toward its end, he supported Barry Goldwater for president. A self-styled Progressive Republican in the 1920s, distrusted by the party's conservative wing, he conceived his White House term as a reform presidency—until Franklin Roosevelt and others outflanked him on the Left. A trenchant opponent of New Deal "collectivism," he labeled his own creed "historic liberalism," which must, he admitted, be "conservatism in contrast." He was a friend of Woodrow Wilson—and Douglas MacArthur, of Justice Louis Brandeis—and Senator Joseph McCarthy. He hated communism but fed millions of starving Russians under the Bolshevik regime. He loathed socialism yet favored stiff inheritance taxes on large fortunes. His political philosophy combined both conservative and liberal elements.

In short, Hoover was difficult to pigeonhole—"too progressive for the conservatives," it has been said, "and too conservative for the radicals." In today's increasingly polarized political climate, he is not a convenient candidate for anyone's hall of heroes.

Must those who honor Hoover's legacy resign themselves, then, to his present status as a political pariah? Not entirely. As the economy recovers, derogatory references to him will no doubt decline in frequency—until the next downturn. In one respect, in fact, time is subtly working in Hoover's favor. A recent poll conducted by the University of Pennsylvania's National Annenberg Election Survey found that only 43 percent of the nation's adults could correctly identify him. Among respondents between the ages of eighteen and twenty-nine, the figure fell to 38 percent. Most Americans, it seems, do not know who Hoover was, and the younger they are, the less they know, good or bad. Thus the current spate of aspersions about him in the media, while irritating to Hoover's defenders, are probably relatively harmless.

But for those of us engaged in historical scholarship and the propagation of historical knowledge, the rising tide of historical ignorance and amnesia is hardly a solution. It does, however, offer an opportunity to fill in the blanks in the public consciousness of Hoover's record.

But how? One strategy—embedded in the programs of the Hoover Library-Museum—is to call attention to the extraordinary range of Hoover's achievements, both before and after his troubled presidency. It is an approach worth building upon. From time to time, I lecture about Hoover to audiences around the country. Afterward people invariably say that they *had no idea* how truly accomplished he was. They had no idea, for instance, that in his far-flung humanitarian endeavors he was responsible for saving more lives than any person who has ever lived. The nonpolitical and nonpresidential parts of the Hoover legacy remain, for most of the public, terra incognita.

A strategy of "accentuating the positive," however, will not be enough by itself. As someone once remarked, our problem is not what we don't know; it's what we do know that isn't so. Paeans to Hoover's humanitarianism ("the rest of the story") will not much impress those who insist that his actions as president exacerbated and failed to mitigate the Great Depression. If advocates of a "better press" for Hoover wish to make headway, they must reappraise the policies of his presidency.

And here fresh questions abound for serious scholars. How much of what we "know" about President Hoover isn't so? How much of it is simply unexamined mythology? What, for instance, was his role in the political battle that produced the Smoot-Hawley tariff? And was the tariff as deleterious as later alleged? (Some recent scholarship on the subject raises doubts.) Was the tax increase of 1932 as much of a mistake as its detractors contend? And how do Hoover's anti-Depression measures compare with his successor's? At a juncture when the scholarly literature on Roosevelt's economic performance is increasingly critical, the time has surely come for a reassessment of Hoover's.

And by what criteria should he then be judged? On what grounds may he properly be criticized: for intervening in the economic crisis too little, or for intervening too often and too much? It is a question with profound implications for our national self-understanding and public policy. What, in short, is the lesson of the Hoover presidency? The answer is no longer self-evident.

The time has also come for a full-length documentary film about Hoover's life. In a culture dominated more than ever by images, we need a movie that truly communicates the high achievements and ironies of his long career.

There is much, then, to be done if Hoover is to appear as more than a negative blip on our national radar screen. For starters, why not indulge in a bit of theater suitable for our times? Why not invite the busload of unemployed back to West Branch—and bring in the media to cover the story?

But let the story be this. Have the visitors spend a day *inside* the Hoover museum, instead of a mere twelve minutes on the front lawn.

Part V

Whither Conservatism?

29

How Should Conservatives
Look Back on the New Deal?

*For decades conservative attitudes toward Franklin Roosevelt have ranged
from ambivalence to hostility—feelings that the economic slump of 2008–9
brought again to the center of conservative discourse. How should conservatives assess the legacy of Roosevelt's New Deal?*

*The brief essay below offers one historian's answer. It is drawn from
remarks delivered at a panel of a conference on the New Deal, held at the
Lyndon Baines Johnson Library in Austin, Texas, in March 1983, to com-
memorate the fiftieth anniversary of Franklin Roosevelt's accession to the
presidency. My presentation was then published in* Wilbur J. Cohen, ed.,
The New Deal Fifty Years After: A Historical Assessment *(Lyndon Baines
Johnson Library/Lyndon B. Johnson School of Public Affairs, 1984).*

In 1936 my father was in his early twenties. In that year, my grandfather
died, the family business closed, and my father's family confronted the
grim plague of the thirties—unemployment. The next winter, my father
obtained a job with the WPA. He was assigned to work with a crew digging
a ditch and laying a water pipeline in his hometown. This was in Massachusetts. As it happened, it was a bitterly cold winter, and with no protective
blanket of snow on the ground, the zone of frost bit deep. To dig the ditch,
it was necessary to penetrate down through three feet of frozen earth using
wedges, sledgehammers, and pick axes. It was agonizingly slow work. To dig
a section of a ditch just five feet deep in all, one-and-a-half feet wide and
eight feet long, it took two men two entire days. It was work, of course, and
the pay, though meager, was welcome.

313

But my father and his fellow workers wondered why it was necessary to dig that ditch at the worst possible time, in the dead of winter. If the WPA had simply waited until spring, the frozen earth would have thawed and the pipeline could have been laid rapidly with far more efficiency and far less cost.

Such instances of misallocation of resources, of so-called "makework projects," evoked popular ambivalence. On the one hand, the projects gave the unemployed, including my father, something to do and precious pay besides: short-term benefits. On the other hand, the projects frequently conveyed the impression that the work at hand was hardly worth doing or worth doing well. A subtle disjunction between effort and reward developed. A certain attitude of cynicism took root: long-term lessons. It was said that the initials WPA stood for "We Putter Around."

This experience of my father's illustrates in microcosm some of the principal legacies of the New Deal. In the short term, the WPA and various other New Deal agencies provided emergency assistance to millions of Americans in real distress: food, money, mortgage relief, and more. Millions benefited. In doing so, the New Deal, as George Will wrote last year, "irrevocably altered the relationship between the government and its citizens."

"We hold this truth to be self evident," declared the Democratic Party platform of 1936, "that government in a modern civilization has certain inescapable obligations to its citizens, among which is aid to those overtaken by disaster." It is a principle that is now embedded in our national consensus. Today, few dispute that one function of government is to provide, in contemporary terms, a safety net for the truly needy.

But in providing humanitarian aid and in establishing the federal government as the prime purveyor of that aid, the New Deal had a consequence that has proved increasingly problematic. In the perspective of half a century, it seems clear that the New Deal's fundamental achievement was not the restoration of prosperity, but the founding, however embryonically, of the welfare state. And the fundamental premise of the welfare state is that the redistribution of wealth is the principal purpose of government. But where, one must ask, does the wealth come from in the first place? Will there always be wealth to divide? What, after all, is the source of our prosperity? What is the engine of job creation and productivity? In what ways can we assist people in need without creating a permanent culture of dependency? How can we establish a safety net without succumbing to the demoralizing proposition that the government owes everyone a living, not just subsistence but a living? These are troubling questions and ones which increasingly impinge on our public discourse.

I would like to give you one example, and I will not choose it from the United States, partly because I don't want to get into contemporary controversy and partly because it illustrates a point I want to make, namely that the crisis of the welfare state is one that transcends the United States and is not simply due to the programs, good or ill, of the current administration. It is a problem being faced by governments throughout the industrial world.

Not long ago I came across a remarkable article on the efforts being made now by West European governments to control the welfare state which in principle has been accepted. No one disputes the principle. But the application is now coming under some scrutiny. And I came across some interesting data about Holland, which is one of the most advanced of the modern welfare states.

The unemployed in Holland receive benefits for two-and-a-half years, much longer than in the United States. Unemployed workers receive vacation pay. Holland's social security benefit program absorbs 35 percent of all government spending. But what I find most remarkable is that, under the disability insurance program currently operating in Holland, incapacitated workers are allowed to spend the rest of their working lives receiving 80 percent of their previous pay, adjusted annually for inflation.

This is a program undoubtedly noble in conception, but what has happened? It seems that it is very difficult to lay off a worker in Holland. It requires approval of government—regional councils, involving a great deal of red tape. Companies circumvent this procedure in the following fashion: they approach the worker and suggest that he declare himself disabled. The common excuse given is low back pain. The workers don't mind going on the disability program because the benefits are very generous, so they stay at home for a year on 80 percent of their pay under the government's sick-pay program. At the end of the year, it is common for the disability plan's medical service to declare the worker permanently disabled. What has happened in practice is that 750,000 workers in Holland have now declared themselves disabled. That's 15 percent of the entire work force. What has happened, I'm afraid, is that a program noble in conception has somehow become flawed in practice, and it illustrates the point I made earlier.

I am reminded of the early twentieth-century journalist Ambrose Bierce's definition of a conservative and a liberal. "A conservative," he said, "is a statesman enamored of present evils, as opposed to the liberal, who would replace them with others."

Today, fifty years after the Great Depression, it seems to me that we confront the disturbing and ironic reality that the welfare state and the principles upon which it rests have themselves become an impediment to prosperity and social well being. Improvising boldly, responding to human misery, the New Deal gave Americans hope and it gave them immediate relief if not a permanent cure. This was its fundamental achievement. But in the long run, it bequeathed also a philosophy of government that, taken alone, cannot suffice. Self-evident truths can become half-truths unless balanced by other truths gone out of fashion.

30

The Uneasy Future of American Conservatism

This essay was presented at a Reagan Symposium held at Regent University in Virginia in February 2006. It is reprinted here in slightly modified form from Charles W. Dunn, ed., The Future of Conservatism: Conflict and Consensus in the Post-Reagan Era (*ISI Books, 2007).*

In the boisterous chatter of current political debate, it is easy to forget that American conservatism has become middle-aged. In 2005 its flagship publication, *National Review*, celebrated its fiftieth anniversary. A couple of years before that, the Intercollegiate Studies Institute, another star in the conservative firmament, celebrated its own half-century of existence, along with the golden anniversary of Russell Kirk's tour de force, *The Conservative Mind*. In Washington, D.C., the Heritage Foundation—the nerve center of the conservative public policy establishment—is now more than thirty years old.

THE ANXIETIES OF MATURITY

What happens when a political movement reaches maturity? For those within its ranks, the impulse grows to proclaim success and salute its intrepid founders in festschrifts, biographies, and other acts of commemoration. For those outside its ranks, passion yields to envious curiosity: How, the critics wonder, did such a phenomenon come into prominence and power? With the advent of middle age, present-mindedness gives way slowly to increased self-consciousness and a quest for deeper understanding of one's roots.

In 2007 American conservatives are proudly conscious of their past. But mingling with their impulse to celebrate is a discernible note of unease. In part this is a consequence of the instability of the world as we now know it. Particularly since September 11, 2001, Americans of all political persuasions have lived with a heightened sense of the unpredictability of events. Whether the source of anxiety be terrorism abroad, hurricanes at home, the prospect of nuclear weaponry in the hands of Iran, or predictions of an imminent global pandemic of bird flu, many Americans at present are convinced that things are not quite under control. All this makes it risky for anyone in politics to rest on his laurels. Relaxation is impossible. The shape of the future cannot be taken for granted.

Other unsettling perceptions are peculiar to conservatives. Among many on the right, there is a growing realization that conservatism's political success in recent decades has not been matched by commensurate changes in the way we live. For two generations the critique of the liberal welfare state has been integral to conservative discourse, yet governmental expenditures and regulations continue to grow. Conservatives passionately decry the tide of moral relativism, yet year by year they perceive a further hollowing out of the moral foundations of our civilization. There is a sense, moreover, in parts of the conservative intellectual community, that "the old gray mare, she ain't what she used to be": that the conservative movement itself has been corrupted, even transmogrified, on its road to power.

Lurking beneath these anxieties is another, seldom expressed yet not far (one suspects) from the surface of conservative consciousness: When a political or intellectual movement becomes middle-aged, does this mean that its glory days are numbered? Must noonday sunshine fade inevitably into twilight? To put it bluntly: is the sun about to set on the conservative empire?

THE EVOLUTION OF FUSION

Such questions cannot be addressed in a vacuum. Before we can profitably peer into conservatism's future, it is necessary to grasp its present configuration and understand how the present came to be. In a post–9/11 world, it would be a bold person indeed who would venture to predict the contingent factors that may affect the prospects of American conservatives. In this respect the future is unknowable. What *is* knowable is conservatism's past. By examining the recent evolution of the American Right, we can identify some of the internal factors that impinge upon its present, creating the frontier where the next chapter in the conservative saga will be written. In conservatism's own history, first as an intellectual and then as a political movement, may be found important clues to its problematic present and uncertain future.

Perhaps the most important fact to assimilate about modern American conservatism is that it is not, and has never been, univocal. It is a *coalition* with many points of origin and diverse tendencies, not always easy to reconcile: a river of thought and activism fed by many tributaries. At its best, it has been driven not by petty material interests but by ideas and by a driving urge to implement them. It is a coalition, moreover, that has evolved over two generations: a datum of increasing significance.

In 1945, at the close of World War II, no articulate, coordinated conservative intellectual force existed in the United States. There were, at most, scattered voices of protest, profoundly pessimistic about the future of their country and convinced that they were an isolated remnant, standing athwart history yelling, in the words of William F. Buckley Jr. at *National Review*, "Stop!" History, in fact, seemed to be what the Left was making. The Left—liberals, socialists, even Communists—appeared to be in complete control of the twentieth century.

In the beginning, in the aftermath of the war, there was not one right-wing renaissance but three, each reacting in diverse ways to challenge from the Left. The first of these groupings consisted of libertarians and classical liberals, resisting the threat of the ever-expanding State to individual liberty, free-market capitalism, and individual initiative in the economic realm. Convinced in the 1940s that post–New Deal America was rapidly drifting toward central planning and socialism—toward what the economist Friedrich Hayek famously called "the road to serfdom"—these intellectuals offered a powerful defense of free-market economics that achieved some prominence and influence by the mid-1950s. From men like Hayek, Ludwig von Mises, and John Chamberlain in the 1940s and 1950s, to Milton Friedman and the Chicago School economists in the 1960s, to Arthur Laffer and the supply-side economists in the 1980s, and to such recent winners of the Nobel Prize in Economics as Gary Becker, the libertarian conservatives produced a sophisticated defense of free-market capitalism and exerted an enormous influence over the American Right. They helped to make the old verities defensible again after the long nightmare of the Great Depression. The Reagan administration's policies of tax-rate cutting, deregulation, and encouragement of private-sector economic growth in the 1980s were the direct product of this intellectual legacy. More recently, the current Bush administration's agenda for tax-cutting can be traced intellectually to the supply-side orthodoxy that captured the Republican Party in the Reagan era.

Much of this perspective was enunciated in powerful books, such as Hayek's masterly polemic *The Road to Serfdom* (1944), a book now recognized as one of the most influential works published in the English language in the twentieth century. Other works of note included Ludwig von Mises' *Human Action* (1949), Milton Friedman's bestselling *Capitalism and Freedom* (1962), Thomas Sowell's *Knowledge and Decisions* (1980), and George Gilder's *Wealth and Poverty* (1981). On a more popular level, the free-market fiction of Ayn Rand shaped the minds of many, including a young man named Alan Greenspan.

Concurrently, and independently of the libertarians, a second school of nonliberal thought emerged in America in the first decade after World War II: the "new conservatism" or "traditionalism" of such men as Richard Weaver, Peter Viereck, Robert Nisbet, and Russell Kirk. Appalled by totalitarianism, total war, and the development of secular, rootless mass society during the 1930s and 1940s, the "new conservatives" (as they were then called) urged a return to traditional religious and ethical absolutes and a rejection of the moral relativism that had allegedly corroded Western values and produced an intolerable vacuum filled by demonic ideologies. More European-oriented and historically minded, on the whole, than the classical liberals, the traditionalist conservatives extolled the wisdom of such thinkers as Edmund Burke, Alexis de Tocqueville, and the Anglo-American literary giant T. S. Eliot, and called for a revival of Christian orthodoxy, classical natural law, premodern political philosophy, and mediating institutions between the citizen and the state. Why? In order, they said, to reclaim and civilize the spiritual wasteland created by secular liberalism and the false gods it had permitted to enter the gates.

In provocative books like Richard Weaver's *Ideas Have Consequences* (1948) and Robert Nisbet's *The Quest for Community* (1953), the traditionalists expounded a vision of a healthy and virtuous society antithetical to the tenets of contemporary liberalism. From towering European émigré scholars like Leo Strauss and Eric Voegelin they learned new techniques for assessing the problem of secular modernity. From Russell Kirk's monumental tome *The Conservative Mind* (1953) the fledgling traditionalists acquired something more: an intellectual genealogy and intellectual respectability. After Kirk's book appeared, no longer could conservatism be dismissed, as

John Stuart Mill had dismissed British conservatives a century before, as "the stupid party." No longer could conservatism be disparaged as the philosophy of provincials and philistines. In books like *The Conservative Mind* the highbrow conservative academics of the 1950s struck a blow against the liberals' superiority complex.

Third, there appeared in the 1940s and 1950s, at the onset of the Cold War, a militant, evangelistic anticommunism, shaped by a number of excommunists and ex-Trotskyists of the 1930s, including Whittaker Chambers, James Burnham, Frank Meyer, and many more. It was also reinforced by anti-Communist exiled scholars from eastern and central Europe, including Stefan Possony and Gerhart Niemeyer. These former men and women of the Left and their European émigré allies brought to the postwar American Right a profound conviction that America and the West were engaged in a titanic struggle with an implacable adversary—communism—which sought nothing less than the conquest of the world.

Each of these emerging components of the conservative revival shared a deep antipathy to twentieth-century liberalism. To the libertarians, modern liberalism—the liberalism of Franklin Roosevelt and his successors—was the ideology of the ever-aggrandizing, bureaucratic welfare state which would, if unchecked, become a centralized totalitarian state, destroying individual liberty and private property. To the traditionalists, modern liberalism was a disintegrative philosophy which, like an acid, was eating away not only at our liberties but also at the ethical and institutional foundations of traditional society, thereby creating a vast spiritual vacuum into which totalitarianism could enter. To the Cold War anticommunists, modern liberalism—rationalistic, relativistic, secular, antitraditional, quasisocialist—was by its very nature incapable of vigorously resisting an enemy on its Left. Liberalism to them was *part* of the Left and could not effectively repulse a foe with which it shared so many underlying assumptions. As James Burnham eventually and trenchantly put it, modern liberalism was essentially a means for reconciling the West to its own destruction. Liberalism was the ideology of Western suicide.

In the late 1950s and early 1960s the three independent wings of the conservative revolt against the Left began to coalesce. The movement found its first popular embodiment in the editor of *National Review*, William F. Buckley Jr., who, apart from his extraordinary talents, personified each impulse in the developing coalition. He was at once a traditional Roman Catholic, a defender of the free market, and a staunch anti-Communist (a source of his ecumenical appeal to conservatives).

THE EVOLUTION OF DIVISION

As this consolidation began to occur, certain intellectual problems arose for those who took the name conservative. It was not enough for them to rebel against contemporary liberalism. If they were conservatives, what did they wish to conserve? What was the conservative tradition to which they professed such fealty?

It soon transpired that the conservative intellectuals (not all of whom liked the word "conservative") gave a variety of answers. Some identified conservatism with the defense of Christian orthodoxy. Some extolled what they labeled the Great Tradition of political philosophy going back to ancient Greece and Rome. Some invoked natural law in opposition to liberalism's emphasis on natural rights. Some venerated Edmund Burke as their political patron saint. Most admired America's Founding Fathers and its tradition of limited government and constitutionalism. Some, like Hayek, repudiated the conservative label entirely and styled themselves Old Whigs or classical liberals.

Complicating this quest for philosophical order was a severe challenge to the fragile conservative identity: a growing and permanent tension between the libertarians and the traditionalists. To the libertarians, the highest good in society was individual liberty, the emancipation of the autonomous self from external (especially governmental) restraint. To the traditionalists (who tended to be more religiously oriented than most libertarians), the highest social good was not unqualified freedom but decent behavior, or, as they often put it, *ordered* freedom resting ultimately on the cultivation of virtue in the individual soul. Such cultivation, argued traditionalists, did not arise spontaneously. It needed the reinforcement and guidance of mediating institutions and even of the government itself. To put it another way, libertarians tended to believe in the beneficence of an uncoerced and spontaneous social order, both in markets and morals. The traditionalists often agreed, more or less, about the market order, but they were far less sanguine about the unregulated moral order. Spontaneity was not a term of endearment in the traditionalist lexicon.

Not surprisingly, this conflict of visions generated a tremendous polemical controversy on the American Right in the 1960s, as conservative intellectuals attempted to sort out their first principles. The argument became known as the freedom-versus-virtue debate. It fell to a former Communist and chief ideologist at *National Review*, a man named Frank Meyer, to formulate a middle way that became known as fusionism—that is, a fusing or reconciliation of the competing paradigms of the "libs" and the "trads." As a purely theoretical construct, Meyer's fusionism was rickety, but as a formula for political action and as an insight into the actual character of American conservatism, Meyer's project was a considerable success. He taught libertarian and traditionalist purists that they needed each other and that American conservatism must not become doctrinaire. To be relevant and influential, especially politically, it must stand neither for an abstract, dogmatic antistatism nor for a regimenting authoritarianism but for a society in which people are simultaneously free to choose and desirous of choosing the path of virtue.

In arriving at this modus vivendi, the architects of fusionism were aided immensely by the third element in the developing coalition: anticommunism, an ideology that everyone could share. The presence in the world of a dangerous external enemy—the Soviet Union, the Evil Empire, the mortal foe of liberty *and* virtue, of freedom *and* faith—was a crucial cement for the nascent conservative movement. The life-and-death stakes of the Cold War helped to curb the temptation of right-wing ideologues to absolutize their competing insights and thereby commit heresy.

Politically, the postwar American Right found its first national expression in the campaign of Senator Barry Goldwater for the presidency of the United States in 1964. The 1964 election had three enduring consequences for conservatives. It created the Democratic congressional majorities which permitted enactment of President Lyndon Johnson's Great Society program, the greatest lurch to the Left in domestic policy since the New Deal. It led to conservative capture of the political machinery of the Republican Party. And it created a new national political figure in Ronald Reagan, whose eloquent television speech for Goldwater on the eve of the election led directly to Reagan's successful candidacy for governor of California two years later.

It was not long after the 1964 election that a new impulse appeared on the intellectual-political scene, one destined to become the fourth component of today's conservative coalition. The phenomenon became known as neoconservatism. Irving Kristol's definition conveyed its essence. A neoconservative, he said, was "a liberal who has been mugged by reality." According to another definition, a neoconservative was someone who uttered two cheers for capitalism instead of three. In any case, one of the salient developments of the late 1960s and 1970s was the intellectual journey of various liberals and social democrats toward conservative positions.

The stresses that produced this migration were many. In part, neoconservatism may be interpreted as the recognition by disillusioned denizens of the Left that good intentions alone do not guarantee good governmental policy and that the actual consequences of liberal social activism in the sixties and seventies were often devastating. In this context, it is clear that one of the key intellectual events of the 1960s was the founding of *The Public Interest* in 1965, an act of revisionist liberalism that forced many melioristic social scientists to reexamine their premises. In considerable measure neoconservatism was also a reaction of moderate liberals to the antinomian cultural upheavals of the 1960s, particularly on the college and university campuses, and to the eruption of the so-called New Left, with its tendency to blame America first for world tensions and its neoisolationist hostility to a vigorous prosecution of the Cold War.

Many neoconservatives, in fact, were former anti-Communist liberals of the Harry Truman/Henry Jackson wing of the Democratic Party who found themselves bereft of a political home after the capture of their party by the followers of George McGovern in 1972. Such names as Irving Kristol, Norman Podhoretz (the editor of *Commentary*), and Midge Decter come quickly to mind.

To the already existing conservative community, the entry of erstwhile liberals and socialists into its precincts was to have many consequences. One of these was already discernible in the 1970s. Since the days of the New Deal, American liberals had held a near monopoly on the manufacture and distribution of prestige among the intellectual and chattering classes. From a liberal perspective, the libertarian, traditionalist, and Cold War conservatives of the fifties and sixties were eccentric figures, no threat to liberalism's cultural hegemony.

The emerging neoconservatives, however, were an "enemy within" who had made their reputations while still on the Left and could not be so easily dismissed. By publicly defecting from the Left, and by critiquing it so effectively, the neoconservatives undermined a hitherto unshakable assumption in academic circles: the belief that only liberalism is an intellectually respectable point of view. By destroying the automatic equation of liberalism with intelligence, the neoconservative intellectuals brought new respectability to the Right and greatly altered the terms of public debate in the United States.

Meanwhile another development—one destined to have enormous political consequences—began to take shape in the late 1970s: the political "great awakening" of what came to be known as the Religious Right. Initially, the Religious Right was not primarily a movement of intellectuals at all. It was, rather, a groundswell of protest at the grassroots of America by aroused citizens, many of them Protestant evangelicals, fundamentalists, and Pentecostals, but including some Roman Catholics and Orthodox Jews as well. While Religious Right leaders like Jerry Falwell, Pat Robertson, and James Dobson appeared to share the foreign policy and economic perspectives of earlier conservatives, their guiding preoccupations lay elsewhere, in what became known as the "social issues": abortion, school prayer, pornography, drug use, sexual deviancy, the vulgarization of mass entertainment, and more. Convinced that American society was in a state of vertiginous moral decline, and that what they called secular humanism—in other words, modern or postmodern liberalism—was the fundamental cause of this decay, the Religious Right exhorted its hitherto politically quiescent followers to enter the public arena in defense of their traditional moral code and way of life.

In a very real sense the Religious Right was closest in its concerns to traditionalist conservatism. The Religious Right also shared the neoconservatives' revulsion against the nihilism of the sixties. But whereas the traditionalists of the 1940s and 1950s had largely been academics in revolt *against* rootless, mass society, the Religious Right of the 1980s was a revolt *by* the "masses" against the secular virus and its carriers in the nation's elites. And whereas the traditionalist conservatives of the pre-Reagan era had been disproportionately Roman Catholic and the neoconservatives disproportionately Jewish, the religious conservatives who became prominent in the Reagan era were disproportionately drawn from the ranks of long marginalized evangelical Protestants.

And whereas conservative intellectuals had heretofore concentrated most of their energies on national issues (like economic policy and conduct of the Cold War), the Religious Right was different. It addressed the moral traumas experienced by ordinary people in their everyday lives, especially those conflicts affecting the transmission of normative values to the young. Above all, the religious conservatives derived their fervor from an unremitting struggle against what most of them considered the supreme abomination of their time: legalized abortion, a practice that from 1973 to the present has taken the lives of more than forty million unborn children.

In time the Religious Right acquired intellectually influential voices. Many other conservative writers shared its disquietude about the debasement and demoralization of culture and joined in various struggles to reverse the tide. The phenomenon gained further momentum from its organic ties to a vast and growing evangelical Protestant subculture: a "parallel universe" (as one observer has called it) of Christian universities, colleges, television and radio stations, magazines, publishing houses, philanthropies, para-church ministries, crisis pregnancy centers, and bookstores. It acquired still more influence by forging an alliance with like-minded Roman Catholics and Orthodox Jews—a conservative ecumenical movement without precedent in American history. Spearheaded at the political level by the Moral Majority and then by the Christian Coalition, the Religious Right brought to American conservatism a moral intensity and populist dimension not seen since the Goldwater campaign of 1964.

RONALD REAGAN AND THE TRIUMPH OF ECUMENICITY

By the end of President Reagan's second term in office, the American Right had grown to encompass five distinct impulses: libertarianism, traditionalism, anticommunism, neoconservatism, and the interfaith Religious Right. And just as William F. Buckley Jr. had done for conservatives a generation before, so Ronald Reagan in the 1980s did the same: he performed an ecumenical function, giving each faction a seat at the table and a sense of having arrived.

Reagan also did something more. As Michael Barone has recently observed, the Great Communicator gave American conservatism a demotic voice and a more optimistic tone, evoking hope for the future rather than nostalgia for the past. In the dark days of the 1940s and early 1950s, American conservatives had occasionally sounded like General Bullmoose in the Broadway play Li'l Abner: "Progress is the root of all evil/ Bring back the good old days!" Reagan's message more nearly resembled the motto of the General Electric Company (for which he had worked as spokesman in the 1950s): "Progress is our most important product." More than any conservative leader in memory, he reaffirmed the continuing validity and vitality of the American Dream.

With Reagan's political triumph as a clinching incentive, American conservatism completed a transition, already underway in the 1960s, from a defiant, contrarian, minority posture and rhetoric to a confident identification with Middle America. Conservatives who had once perceived themselves as history's losers now saw themselves as the vanguard of the silent majority. With Reagan's presidential candidacy providing the bridge, both the neoconservatives and the Religious Right crossed the Rubicon into the arms of the conservative coalition.

As these disparate elements merged under Reagan into a political as well as intellectual force, they experienced a stirring passage from the world of theory to the world of public policy. Perhaps the most striking feature of conservative intellectual activity in the Age of Reagan was that there was so much of it. The publication of conservative books, articles, and syndicated columns—already substantial in the 1970s—attained in the Reagan era the proportions of an avalanche. Gone were the days when *National Review* and a couple of other periodicals constituted the virtual totality of intelligent conservative journalism in the United States. Increasingly, it seemed that every strand of the conservative movement had its own publication—its own branch, as it were, on the family tree.

This cascade of literature was intimately linked to a second extraordinary trend: the proliferation of a burgeoning network of conservative media, foundations, research centers, and idea-based advocacy groups, from the shores of the Potomac to the farthest corners of the country. By the 1990s literally hundreds of them had come into being. In the legal profession, a phalanx of public-interest law firms challenged overweening government in the courts. Among law students and legal scholars, the Federalist Society (founded in 1982) articulated conservative approaches to constitutional interpretation and provided an invaluable resource for networking and information exchange. In the field of environmental policy, the Political Economy Research Center (PERC), based in Bozeman, Montana, championed a paradigm shift known as free-market environmentalism. For Religious Right activists, the Focus on the Family organization, the Family Research Council, and the American Center for Law and Justice, among other groups, provided an arsenal of intellectual and legal ammunition.

The examples are legion, but the point is clear. Within a span of less than a generation, something truly remarkable occurred in American political and intellectual life: A vibrant conservative counterculture was forged. We need not dilate upon its more recent and familiar manifestations, such as the efflorescence of talk radio, the spread of homeschooling and classical Christian schools, and the birth of the blogosphere. Suffice it to note the magnitude of the change. No longer a tiny and marginalized remnant, the conservative conglomerate as we know it today—Hillary Clinton's "vast right-wing conspiracy"—is literally at our fingertips, if we but choose to tune in or log on.

Fueling this surge in programmatic conservatism was another development which the Reagan presidency accelerated: a deepening collaboration between conservative intellectuals and politicians. Such a symbiosis had long been common on the other side of the ideological spectrum. From the

327

New Deal of Franklin Roosevelt to the New Frontier of John F. Kennedy to the Great Society of Lyndon Johnson, prominent academicians have regularly supplied "idea power" to the American Left. Since 1980 this "intellectualization" of domestic politics and public policy formulation has extended to the American Right as well.

There was no more dramatic example of this trend than the appearance in the 1970s of a body of thought called "supply-side economics," initially identified with Professor Arthur Laffer of the University of Southern California. In a remarkably short time, Laffer's work was enthusiastically publicized by several influential conservative writers until, in the form of tax-reduction legislation sponsored by Representative Jack Kemp and Senator William Roth, it became the official tax policy of the Republican Party. In 1980 Ronald Reagan heartily endorsed this proposal, and he signed a modified form of it into law early in his presidency. No more could it be charged that conservative politicians were stodgy reactionaries lacking in fresh ideas. On the contrary, many of them—like Newt Gingrich, Steve Forbes, and Reagan himself—craved ideas, thrived on ideas, and found in supply-side economics a way of taking the ideological offensive. In supply-side economics, theory and practice decisively merged. The Republican Party has not been the same since.

THE AMBIGUITIES OF SUCCESS AND THE PERILS OF PROSPERITY.

The successes of the Reagan years did not come without costs, however. During the 1980s and long afterwards, conservative intellectuals (usually of a traditionalist bent) could be heard to complain at times that the conservative cause was being "reduced to politics," drained of its ethical vision, and deflected from its larger mission of cultural renewal. As the Reagan Revolution passed into history some of its intellectual architects—especially libertarians—wondered what it had really accomplished. Reagan had tarnished the intellectual pretensions of social democracy, to be sure, and had undermined the legitimacy of the liberal status quo. But he had not overturned it; "big government" was bigger than ever.

More recently, scholars such as Steven Hayward have noted that the rise of "populist" or majoritarian conservatism in the eighties (and beyond) was accompanied by a conspicuous weakening of the antistatist ideology that had long united conservatives. Still others have suggested that conservative politics, like all politics, attracts not only those who come to do good but also those who come to do well. Conservative journalist M. Stanton Evans has famously remarked that, over the years, some conservatives have gone to Washington believing it to be a cesspool, only to decide that it is really a hot tub.

From the perspective of today it is increasingly apparent that the Reagan presidency coincided with and fostered a profound, generational shift in American conservatism. Before 1980 the American Right had been primarily a movement of dissent, spearheaded by intellectuals. Its capital city (to the extent that it had one) was New York, the home of *National Review*. After 1980 it became a political movement as well, subject to the constraints and temptations of political action. Its capital city, the focus of its dreams and energies, became Washington, D.C., itself. Perhaps not coincidentally, in practice if not quite in theory American conservatism today stands well to the left of where it stood in 1980.

Yet even as conservatives in the eighties and nineties escaped the wilderness for the promised land inside the Beltway, the world they wished to conquer was changing in ways that threatened their newfound power. Ask yourself this question: aside from conservatism, what have been the most important social movements in America in the past thirty years? To this historian the answer is plain: feminism and environmentalism. Since the 1970s, the United States has been moving right *and* left at the same time. Out in the culture—both highbrow and lowbrow—the vectors of social change have not been pointing in a uniformly conservative direction.

Next, ask yourself this: what has been the most historically consequential date for conservatives in the past generation? September 11, 2001? Perhaps. But surely the other such date was November 9, 1989, the night that the Berlin Wall came down. Since 1989 one of the hallmarks of conservative history has been the reappearance of factional strains in the grand alliance.

By far the most persistent source of discontent on the right has been the status within its ranks of the neoconservatives. To an angry group of traditionalists in the late 1980s who took the label "paleoconservatives," the "neocons" were "interlopers," "impostors," and Johnny-come-latelies who, despite their recent journey to the right, remained essentially secular, Wilsonian, and welfare-statist in their underlying philosophy. In other words, said their critics, they were not truly conservative at all. During the final phase of the Cold War, and more recently during the war against Islamist terrorism, the paleocons accused the neocons of foisting on the Right a profoundly unconservative, neo-Wilsonian ideology of "global democratic capitalism." As if, said disgusted paleocons like Patrick Buchanan, Wilsonian "global democracy" were the sum and substance of the conservative vision.

Like the neoconservatives against whom it endlessly polemicized, paleo-conservatism became a discordant element in conservative circles. Fiercely and defiantly "nationalist" (rather than "internationalist"), skeptical of "global democracy" and entanglements overseas, and fearful of the impact of Third World immigration on America's Eurocentric culture, Buchanan-ite paleoconservatism increasingly resembled much of the American Right *before* 1945: before, that is, the onset of the Cold War. When Buchanan himself campaigned for the presidency in 1992 under the pre–World War II, anti-interventionist banner of "America First," the symbolism seemed deliberate and complete.

Nor were neoconservatives the only faction to come under fire from disaffected members of the pre-Reagan Right. To certain libertarians and traditionalists, it appeared that the other latecomer to the coalition, the Religious Right, was also insufficiently antistatist—too willing to use governmental power to implement its moral vision. Congressional intervention in the Terry Schiavo case in 2005 brought some of these latent conflicts to the surface.

Aside from the built-in philosophical tensions with which the conservative coalition has been living for half a century, two fundamental facts of political life explain the recrudescence of intramural debates among conservatives since the Reagan era. The first is what we might call the perils of prosperity. In the 1950s and early 1960s the number of publicly active conservative intellectuals in the United States was minuscule: perhaps a few dozen at most. Today how can one even begin to conduct such a count? Prosperity has come to conservatism, and with it a multitude of niche markets and specialization on a thousand fronts. With prosperity and specialization have also come signs of sibling rivalry and an attenuation of "movement consciousness," as the various elements in the coalition pursue their separate agendas.

Although the Heritage Foundation and others have taken important steps to coordinate conservative activism inside the Beltway, the "vast right-wing conspiracy" is now so large and dispersed that no single institution can function as its general staff, as *National Review* was able to do in its early days. No longer does American conservatism have a commanding ecumenical figure like Buckley or Reagan.

As the conservative universe has expanded, there has arisen a tendency to categorize conservatives in ever smaller subgroups. Thus we have the neocons, the paleocons, the "theocons" (theological or religious conservatives), and the "Leocons" (disciples of Leo Strauss). Certain immigrant conservative writers like David Frum and John O'Sullivan have been dubbed "immicons." Traditionalist conservatives with "green" sensibilities and countercultural tastes are called "crunchy cons." Young conservatives have been labeled "minicons." All this is rather playful and amusing, but it does suggest the sectarian impulses at work.

The second fundamental fact of political life that explains the renewal of friction on the right is one that has been hinted at already. It did not escape notice in the early 1990s that the conservatives' uncivil strife coincided with the dismantling of the Berlin Wall, the collapse of communism in Europe, and the stunning end of the Cold War. Until then most conservatives had been governed by Benjamin Franklin's prudential advice in 1776: "We must all hang together, or assuredly we shall all hang separately." Inevitably, after 1989, the question arose: could a movement so identified with unyielding anticommunism survive the disappearance of the adversary in the Kremlin? Or would long-suppressed centrifugal tendencies prevail?

THE CHALLENGE OF WILLIAM JEFFERSON CLINTON

The conservative movement, of course, did not crumble in the 1990s. Predictions of its imminent demise proved unfounded. Conservatism since 1945, after all, had always encompassed more than geopolitical anticommunism. The downfall of the Soviet Union did not render obsolete the deeper, civilizational concerns of a Friedrich Hayek, a Richard Weaver, or a Russell Kirk. Conservatives were also helped by the appearance in 1993 of a new unifying agent in the person of William Jefferson Clinton.

Nevertheless, it is undeniable that anticommunism supplied much of the glue in the post-1945 conservative coalition and that the death of communism in Europe weakened the fusionist imperative for American conservatives. As the post–Cold War era settled in during the 1990s, many conservatives appeared to be searching for a new, post-anti-Communist synthesis of their aspirations.

Indeed, much conservative intellectual activity in the past ten years or so can be interpreted as a succession of efforts to formulate a new fusionism for a new era. In the first term of President Clinton, we saw the rise of the "Leave Us Alone" coalition, united in its detestation of intrusive government, be it in the form of higher taxes, Hillary Clinton's health-care plan, gun control, or subversion of private property rights. Its galvanizing principle was that of individual liberty—the libertarian paradigm. A little later, certain neoconservatives at the *Weekly Standard* propounded something called "national greatness" conservatism, an adumbration of the muscular foreign policy of George W. Bush. Bush himself, before he was elected president, expounded what he called "compassionate conservatism." It was among other things a deliberate rebuke of the antistatist thrust of the Leave Us Alone movement and the confrontational governing style of Speaker of the House Newt Gingrich, which Bush perceived as an electoral dead-end.

More recently, the metaphor of war—with its insistent summons to unity—has returned to conservative discourse. A new enemy has appeared in radical Islam, and with it a new raison d'être for conservatives. The reemergence of foreign threats at the center of public consciousness after 9/11, and after what Charles Krauthammer has called our decade-long "holiday from history," gave American conservatism a renewed sense of mission grounded on the bedrock principle of national security. In the global war on terrorism, most American conservative intellectuals and grassroots activists found the functional equivalent for the Cold War against communism.

On the home front, the cohesion that was once supplied by anticommunism has increasingly come from another "war," one that seems ever more integral to conservative identity. This is the so-called culture war, pitting an alliance of Roman Catholics, evangelical Protestants, and Orthodox Jewish believers against a postmodern, post-Christian, even anti-Christian secular elite whom they perceive to be aggressively hostile to their deepest convictions. Every day fresh tremors break out along this fault line—over abortion, euthanasia, gay marriage, stem-cell research, the Terry Schiavo case, "the war against Christmas," and the composition of the federal courts. It is a struggle literally over the meaning of right and wrong, a battle (for conservatives) against what Pope Benedict XVI has called "the tyranny of relativism." It is a protracted and seemingly irrepressible conflict that gives few signs of ebbing, at least among the media and political classes for whom politics seems increasingly to be a form of warfare.

THE CHALLENGE OF GEORGE W. BUSH

Whatever its outcome, for the present the conduct of the "culture war" has given most conservatives a renewed sense of purpose and embattlement. Yet all is not well on the Potomac. For a full generation now, American conservatism has thrived as a coalition of five distinct components, each reacting to a perceived external challenge from the Left. Now, for the first time in its history, conservatism confronts an *internal* challenge from an utterly unexpected source: the so-called "transformative" presidency of George W. Bush.

For the Religious Right and the neoconservatives, the Bush years have been relatively congenial ones. The president himself, a born-again Christian from Texas, has assiduously cultivated the Religious Right and has rewarded it with Supreme Court nominations and various public-policy initiatives. To this crucial constituency, he has appeared to be "one of us." Together with the Religious Right, many neoconservatives have exerted a powerful influence on the Bush administration's foreign policies, and just as importantly, on the rhetorical and theoretical garb with which they have been clothed. The editor of *First Things* has even suggested that the pro-life Religious Right and the neoconservatives have become the new center of gravity in the conservative coalition, vessels for a "new fusionism" aimed at remoralizing American life and foreign policy.

Other and older parts of the conservative coalition have been more ambivalent and at times dismayed. Although happy enough with the administration's judicial appointments and tax-cutting policies, they note that, under Bush, Medicare drug benefits have been expanded, educational policy has been increasingly nationalized, and federal spending (at least until recently) has been allowed to soar unchecked. For conservatives whose intellectual roots predate the 1980s, and for whom "limited government" has been a defining mantra, Washington, D.C., in 2007 is not a pretty sight. Although "big government" conservatism—or, as they might say, Big-Government "conservatism"—may now be on the wane (at least in theory), it is painfully clear that a substantial segment of the American electorate has a vested interest in the welfare state and that anything deemed to be a frontal assault upon it is unlikely to be very successful.

Even more than its sometimes heterodox domestic policies, the Bush administration's approach to foreign affairs—especially in Iraq—has placed new stresses on the conservative coalition. The president's audacious assertion of executive power in the war on terrorism has rattled libertarians and others for whom the restraint of executive power is a settled conservative principle. His sweeping invocation of the language of democratic universalism reminds some conservatives of Eleanor Roosevelt—the epitome (for them) of platitudinous naïveté. For those who base their foreign policy outlook on the virtues of prudence and realism, Bush's "hard Wilsonianism" seems egregiously unconservative, although it must be added that, unlike Woodrow Wilson, Bush is not a supranationalist: a fact that has helped to draw conservative patriots to his colors.

With the exception of the paleoconservatives associated with Patrick

Buchanan's *American Conservative* magazine, most conservatives, especially younger ones, continue to support Bush's conduct of the War on Terror, as the recent debate over national security wiretapping suggests. The seriousness of the terrorist threat, and the stridency and near hysteria of the anti-war Left, have done much to suppress any inclination on the right to defect from the man in the White House. But some "old school" conservative intellectuals, like George Carey and Jeffrey Hart, are now openly questioning whether the Bush administration is conservative at all. Like a pool player whose opening shot scatters the billiard balls in all directions, the president has unsettled many parts of his putative base. Whether the voices of dissent on the right grow louder will probably depend on contingent events in the Middle East.

THE FUTURE OF A FRACTIOUS COALITION

And so we come to the uneasy future of American conservatism. It will be uneasy, firstly, because the global village in which we live is a troubled place, capable of altering the trajectory of our politics in unpredictable ways. It will be uneasy, secondly, because American conservatism, as it has evolved over two generations, is fundamentally a coalition, which, like all coalitions, contains within itself the potential for its own dissolution.

There is no certainty, for example, that the Religious Right—the largest demographic bloc in the right-wing alliance—will remain mobilized at the level of intensity that has brought conservative victories at the polls in recent years. In 2004 white evangelical Protestants accounted for approximately one quarter of the voters in the presidential election, and they voted overwhelmingly for Bush. One catalyst for their high turnout was the presence on the ballots in eleven states of initiatives to prohibit homosexual marriage. The existence of these ballot referenda presumably helped the president gain votes, but this is not a tactic than can be replicated at every election.

Will the religious conservatives—"the boots on the ground" of the conservative movement, as Richard Land of the Southern Baptist Convention has called them—remain in their present state of discipline and zeal? The Religious Right's agenda of moral reformation has not been easily translatable into public policy, as the "thirty-year war" over abortion abundantly attests. If, for instance, future Supreme Court decisions should thwart the religious conservatives, or should some of their foot soldiers grow weary and discouraged, enough of them might relapse into political passivity to tip the electoral balance against the Right.

Is the long foretold "conservative crackup" just around the corner? Conceivably—but it has not happened yet in fifty years. Despite the genuine (and perennial) risks of such an implosion, despite the inherent philosophical tensions and intramural squabbles that have marked its history, the disintegration of the American Right seems unlikely any time soon. For one thing, each wing of the movement has become thoroughly institutionalized. From the Beltway to the blogosphere, the clusters of purposeful energy (and funding) that social scientists call institutions continue to multiply and flourish. These are not the manifestations of a dying political army. And thanks to such weapons as e-mail, the Internet, and Rush Limbaugh, the permanent mobilization of "the boots on the ground" seems easier than ever.

A conservative crackup is also unlikely because signs of cultural renewal—or at least of hope—continue to appear. One sees it in the growing interest in Christian-oriented movies and in the multiplicity of faith-based initiatives seeking the remoralization of our society: "compassionate conservatism" at the hardy grassroots. One sees it in the rise of what one author has called a "missionary generation" of college students coming out of evangelical Protestant, Roman Catholic, and Orthodox Jewish institutions of higher learning. If the "return to religion" that is now taking place on America's campuses (even in the Ivy League) persists, in fifteen years America may be a much different nation.

Above all, the conservative coalition seems destined to endure because most of the external stimuli that goaded it into existence have not disappeared. In some respects, they have grown stronger. The Berlin Wall may be gone, and socialist economics may be discredited, but significant sectors of American society continue to move in directions antithetical to conservative beliefs. Particularly in the area of "lifestyles"—of drug use, sexual mores, acceptance of pornography, and taste in mass entertainment—popular attitudes and behavior have veered sharply in a permissive, even neo-pagan, direction in recent decades.

More than forty years ago, the conservative theorist Frank Meyer proclaimed that "the Christian understanding of the nature and destiny of man, which is the foundation of Western civilization, is always and everywhere what conservatives strive to conserve." Not everyone will accept this formulation. But those who do must admit that large swatches of American life—such as the academy, the media, and the entertainment industry—have become increasingly indifferent, even antagonistic, to the Christian faith and worldview. For defenders of Judeo-Christian ethics—and that means most conservatives—there remains much work to do. There is still a potent enemy on the left.

This precarious state of affairs raises a question. Can a national house so deeply divided govern itself effectively? Can a regime flourish in which the Right dominates the election returns and the making of public policy while the Left dominates our underlying mores and cultural transmission belts? Whether conservatives can thrive indefinitely without victory in the *final* struggle—the contest for our culture—may be the great, unanswered question about American politics.

A number of years ago, a young member of the British Conservative Party was campaigning for a seat in Parliament. At a public rally he zestfully defended the Tory platform and concluded: "These are our principles. If you do not like them, we have others!"

American conservatism in its middle age is a diverse movement with many principles, not always easily harmonized. For this reason it may appear to be an unstable coalition. But it has also proved remarkably resilient, united in part by overlapping aspirations and by a recurrent sense of mortal challenge from enemies at home and abroad.

For conservatives the wilderness years are long over. But the conservative ascendancy is incomplete, and tomorrow belongs automatically to no one. If the conservative coalition is to continue to prosper, it must remember the ecumenism of Reagan, resist the tendency to fragment, and avoid the temptation to retreat into a fatal passivity induced by disillusionment or despair. Let not the words of an unknown poet become conservatism's epitaph:

> On the plains of hesitation
> Bleach the bones of countless millions
> Who, at the dawn of victory,
> Sat down to rest,
> And, resting, died.

31

Ronald Reagan's Legacy and American Conservatism

This essay, which originally appeared in Charles W. Dunn, ed., The Enduring Reagan *(University Press of Kentucky, 2009), was delivered during the
Third Annual Ronald Reagan Symposium at Regent University. The event
occurred in February 2008.*

I

In 2008 a specter is haunting American politics: the genial specter of Ronald Reagan. More than any of our forty-three presidents—more even than
our current incumbent—Reagan's memory is on the minds and tongues of
a nation hungering for renewal. On the Republican side, presidential candidates invoke his name daily and vie to be perceived as his political heir.
On the Democratic side, pundits speculate whether Barack Obama, with his
oratorical skills, might just be a liberal Reagan. On television, on the radio,
and in the blogosphere, conservative commentators extol his legacy and ask:
what would Reagan do if he were living today?

The phenomenal wave of current interest in Ronald Reagan is a powerful
reminder of his continuing influence on American life. Almost twenty years
after he left the presidency, and nearly fifteen years after he withdrew into
the solitude of his final illness, he continues to shape the political identity
of a large sector of the American electorate. It is not the least of his legacies
to his country.

Legacy: how often we now hear this word when we think about our
presidents.[1] No longer do our chief executives confine themselves, while in

office, to performing their constitutional duties. Instead—or so the media tell us—toward the end of their tenure they become preoccupied with seeking the plaudits of posterity. Thus in 2007, more than an entire year before President George W. Bush was to leave office, the media began to assure us that he would be devoting his remaining days in the White House to creating a "legacy."[2]

The urge to build a legacy (and thereby, presumably, impress future historians) does not diminish when a president walks out of the Oval Office for the last time. One of the interesting phenomena in American politics in the past half century has been the invention and institutionalization of the hyperactive ex-presidency, dedicated in part to enhancing a president's reputation beyond his term of office and even beyond the grave. Our first modern ex-president was the energetic Theodore Roosevelt, who was only fifty years old when he left the White House in 1909. Unlike most of his successors, TR did not focus much on long-term legacy-building, perhaps because he spent so much of his time trying to become president again. A more representative figure—and arguably the true inventor of the ex-presidency—was Herbert Hoover, who left office in 1933 and lived for another thirty-one-and-a-half years, making him the longest serving former president in our history. Hoover did many things in those years, but one theme was paramount: his unflagging desire to vindicate his record in the eyes of his contemporaries, as well as of generations to come.

Now if one were to ask a leading politician (such as a president) to ruminate about his future place in the history books, most of them would probably profess to be unconcerned (no doubt because it could appear egotistical openly to admit otherwise). George W. Bush, for instance, seems nonchalant about the subject. He has pointed out with jocularity that historians are still analyzing the presidencies of George Washington and Abraham Lincoln. He has remarked that he "will be long gone before the true history of the Bush administration is written."[3] He has even suggested that it would be an act of dishonor for him to use his power to try inflate his stock among future historians. "You betray the office," he says, "if you get caught up" in "your personal standing."[4]

If Bush seems unworried about what scholars will someday say about him, few of our nation's chief executives behave this way any more. No longer do our presidents leave their presidencies alone when they vacate the White House. Instead, they create presidential libraries, museums, and public policy centers to present their story to the public. They publish memoirs big enough to be doorstops. Their closest associates produce a barrage of memoirs of their own, sometimes even before the president leaves power. Out in the country, groups of admirers organize to preserve historically significant sites associated with the life of the great man.

Increasingly, Congress chimes in with honorific initiatives of its own. In 1975, for instance, three years after the death of former President Truman, Congress created an official "federal memorial" to him to be known as the Harry S. Truman Scholarship Foundation, which to this day awards federally funded scholarships to college students intending to pursue a career in public service. In 1978 Congress established a federal memorial for Herbert Hoover, in the form of an additional building for the Hoover Institution at Stanford University. The Woodrow Wilson International Center for Scholars in Washington, D.C. has become the federal memorial to our twenty-eighth president. And so it goes.

The impulse to memorialize our presidents has even begun to extend to presidential candidates who never got to be president at all. The Hubert H. Humphrey Fellowship Program (announced by President Carter in 1978), the Barry M. Goldwater Scholarship and Excellence in Education Program (created by Congress in 1986), and the Robert J. Dole Institute of Politics at the University of Kansas come to mind. One catalyst for these ventures has undoubtedly been the example of the most famous public policy enterprise of all: Harvard University's Institute of Politics, which the Kennedy family and its friends established in the 1960s, not long after the assassination of JFK.

Increasingly, then, the history of the American presidency is not simply what historians and other academic scribblers say it is, at least not in the short run. Instead, the interpretation of a president's legacy has become a deliberate and organized undertaking, involving the former president himself.

The career of Ronald Reagan has not been exempt from this process. Like every one of his predecessors since Herbert Hoover,[5] Reagan created a presidential library and museum for his papers after he left office. In 1990 he duly published a monumental, 746-page autobiography.[6] Since the 1980s, members of his presidential team—from Cabinet officers to speechwriters, from pollsters and personal staff to ambassadors and the First Lady herself—have generated a torrent of fascinating memoirs, probably the largest and richest such trove for any president in our history. From his boyhood home in Dixon, Illinois, to his magnificent ranch near Santa Barbara, California, important parts of Reagan's "landscape" have been preserved for the edification of future generations.

Yet in one respect Reagan was decisively different from most of his immediate predecessors and successors: Except for creating a presidential library,
and the nearly obligatory memoir to go along with it, Reagan did little to
define and refine his legacy after he left the White House. Partly this was
because of his advancing age: He was nearly seventy-eight years old (and by
far the oldest of any our presidents) when he left Washington in 1989, and he
was truly ready to retire. More sadly, the onset of Alzheimer's disease in 1994
deprived him of any further opportunity—even if he had desired one—to
remain on the public stage and try to influence the verdict of history. Most
importantly, Reagan made little further effort to furbish his legacy because,
at bottom, he felt no need to do so. He was genuinely content with most of
his record at the nation's helm.

Consider his televised farewell address to the American people in early
1989, in which he acclaimed his beloved country (as he had so often) as a
"shining city upon a hill," blessed by God and chosen by Him for a noble
purpose. "And how stands the city on this winter night?" Reagan asked.
"More prosperous, more secure, and happier than it was eight years ago"—
"still a beacon, still a magnet for all who must have freedom." "We've done
our part," he said to "the men and women of the Reagan revolution." "My
friends: we did it. We weren't just marking time. We made a difference. We
made the city stronger. We made the city freer, and we left her in good hands.
All in all, not bad, not bad at all."[7]

Unlike such presidents as Hoover, Richard Nixon, Jimmy Carter, and
William Clinton, Reagan felt no compulsion to "run for ex-president" or seek
exoneration in the eyes of history. His legacy seemed to him plain enough,
and it needed no defense.

But if Reagan himself seemed serene about his accomplishments, many
of his ardent admirers were less so—and less inclined to let the judgment of
history take its course. In 1997 the conservative activist Grover Norquist and
his Americans for Tax Reform organization launched a bold and unprecedented initiative known as the Reagan Legacy Project. Its stated objective
was to honor Reagan's legacy by naming "significant public landmarks"
after him in every state of the union as well as in more than 3,000 counties
throughout the United States. In 1998 the project's organizers succeeded in
having Washington, D.C.'s National Airport officially renamed the Ronald
Reagan Washington National Airport. It was the first of a number of such
victories in the politics of memory.[8] Nor was this all. Since the 1990s there
has been talk on the Right about adding Reagan's countenance to Mount

Rushmore (much to the annoyance and trepidation of some American liberals). More recently, the conservative Heritage Foundation—the intellectual nerve center of the Reagan revolution during the 1980s—inaugurated a year-long campaign of political education on radio and the Internet. Its arresting title: "What Would Reagan Do?"[9]

Clearly the nation's fortieth president continues to appeal to the American imagination—and not just to his own devoted partisans. Type in the words "Reagan biography" at Amazon.com; one will discover more than 850 listed items. Or conduct an Internet search on Yahoo for the exact phrase "Reagan legacy"; more than 800,000 results will appear. [10] Or consult the Ronald Reagan Presidential Foundation's latest catalogue. In its thirty-two pages, one will find available for purchase Reagan books, neckties, posters, CDs, DVDs, medallions, and much else.

To some scoffers the groundswell of "Reagan nostalgia" (as they dismissively call it) is little more than a right wing equivalent of the liberal cult of John F. Kennedy's Camelot. But what is most noteworthy about this phenomenon is not its occasionally nostalgic trimmings but its unabashedly pedagogical motivation. Each year, for example, the conservative Young America's Foundation brings thousands of college and high school students to its Reagan Ranch Center in Santa Barbara, California, and to the nearby Reagan ranch itself (which the foundation now owns). There, it holds numerous lectures and classes on Reagan's life and philosophy: events often carried on C-SPAN. The foundation proudly styles its Santa Barbara facility a "Schoolhouse for Reaganism," and includes members of his administration on its Reagan Ranch Board of Directors. Similarly, the Heritage Foundation's "What Would Reagan Do?" project, initiated in early 2008, proclaims him a "role model" for present and future political leaders. Why? In the words of the foundation's president, Edwin J. Feulner Jr., Reagan was politically successful "because he spoke powerfully to the American people about conservative principles—which he would not compromise!" [11]

What is one to make of the enduring fascination with this leader? Obviously the mood of the moment has something to do with it: In 2008, the political coalition that Reagan forged is widely perceived to be in disarray, and memories of the Gipper remind embattled conservatives of better days. But current events do not fully explain a phenomenon that has been building for nearly twenty years. We must probe more deeply. Why has the celebration of Reagan's legacy become a "project"? Why the fervent determination to preserve, protect, and defend the historical reputation of this man?

II

To answer these questions, we must understand Ronald Reagan's special relationship with modern American conservatism.

Reagan was a conservative politician, of course, but there were many others during his long career, and he was by no means the most militant among them. When he ran for president in 1980, he was not even the sole conservative in the field. (Representative Philip Crane of Illinois was also a contender.) Reagan was articulate, but so were Barry Goldwater and Robert Taft. Unlike them, he succeeded in becoming president, but so too did several other Republicans during his lifetime. Yet it was Reagan who became the most revered conservative leader since Calvin Coolidge. Why?

Obviously his personal charm, wit, optimistic temperament, transparent decency, authoritative physical appearance, and oratorical talent were tremendous assets. Someone said of him that he "could get a standing ovation in a graveyard."[12] He was, in that now hackneyed phrase, a "great communicator." His sense of humor and gifts as a raconteur were legendary; not surprisingly, entire anthologies of his witticisms and stories are now in print. Thanks in large measure to Reagan, a healthy sense of humor is an attribute we now hope to find in our chief executives. Indeed, one of his subtle legacies has been what one might call the theatrical presidency: the public expectation that our presidents will in some sense entertain us even as they govern.

But Reagan's personal qualities do not definitively explain his profound appeal to the American Right. John F. Kennedy was another witty and charismatic president, and no slouch as a speaker, but he was never a favorite of the nation's conservatives. Reagan gained their favor not so much because of his winsome personality and superlative communication skills, but because they liked and believed what he said. His message was more important than the messenger.[13]

But even this observation does not completely hit the mark. Other contemporary politicians "talked the talk" just as sincerely as Reagan did, but he—not they—won the conservatives' fealty and affection. The question persists: why was he different?

First, unlike most of the Republican politicians of his day, Reagan was something of an intellectual: a man who not only spoke the language of the Right but seriously thought about it. He was, we now know, an inveterate and voracious reader of conservative literature, including Whittaker Chambers's classic anti-Communist autobiography, *Witness*, which influenced him hugely (and parts of which he committed to memory).[14] More likely than not, he read Friedrich Hayek's *The Road to Serfdom* (1944) and Henry Hazlitt's *Economics in One Lesson* (1946), two of the foundational texts of free-market philosophy after World War II. As a spokesman for General Electric between 1954 and 1962, Reagan was exposed to the cascade of libertarian, limited government, antisocialist publications that the company relentlessly disseminated to its employees. The company's brilliant public relations strategist, Lemuel Boulware, became a lifelong friend. Reagan himself referred to his work at GE as "almost a postgraduate course in political science for me."[15] Thanks perhaps to Boulware, Reagan became an early and lifelong reader of *National Review*, which he came to regard and publicly acknowledge as his "favorite magazine."[16] He also avidly read the influential conservative weekly *Human Events*, and often clipped articles from its pages.[17]

In the 1950s, in short, Reagan became—and remained ever after—a conservative by conviction, not convenience. He consumed books and tracts of the Right with zest, and he believed.

Secondly, and again unlike most Republican presidential aspirants of his era, Reagan was what activists on the Right call a "movement conservative": one who associated himself not merely with a few conservative causes and catchwords, but with the intellectuals, journalists, and public policy entrepreneurs who were steadfastly building a movement of ideas. Richard Nixon, by contrast, seemed to regard conservatives as a prickly interest group, to be handled in a gingerly manner and appeased. Reagan did infinitely more, and conservatives noticed.

Both before and during his presidency, Reagan displayed his affinity for the conservative movement in a multitude of ways. He joined the national advisory board of the conservative youth organization Young Americans for Freedom. In 1984, he awarded the Presidential Medal of Freedom posthumously to Whittaker Chambers, one of the conservative icons of the Cold War. It was an action keenly appreciated on the Right. In 1988 he conferred the same high honor on the free-market economist Milton Friedman. Two months later he gave a President's Citizens Medal to the distinguished conservative scholar Russell Kirk. Reagan was the featured speaker at *National Review*'s thirtieth anniversary gala in 1985 and at the Heritage Foundation's anniversary banquet in 1986. More tellingly still, on eight separate occasions during his presidency he addressed in person the annual Conservative Political Action Conference in Washington, D.C.: a giant gathering of the faithful from all across the land. And he instituted the custom of annually addressing his administration's political appointees at a pep rally held each January in the nation's capital. He never forgot that he represented a political and intellectual movement, and he repeatedly let its leaders know that he considered himself to be one of their tribe. Many of his gestures were symbolic, to be sure, but in politics, as in marriage, "little things mean a lot."

And here we come to the third reason for Reagan's extraordinary bond with his fellow conservatives. Before 1980, the conservative insurgency since World War II had been largely an alliance of dissenters, on the outside of the American political mainstream looking in. When Reagan won the presidency that year, he scored more than a smashing personal victory; he brought American conservatives into the "promised land" inside the Beltway. He conferred prestige upon them and legitimized them as players in the political big leagues. He secured for them a permanent beachhead in the epicenter of national politics, and they were grateful.

In assessing Reagan's legacy for conservatives, it is important to remember that the movement which came to power with him was not a monolith. It was a coalition of five distinct parts: 1) classical liberals and libertarians, apprehensive of the threat of overweening government and the welfare state to individual liberty and free-market capitalism; 2) "traditionalist" conservatives, appalled by the weakening of the ethical norms and institutional foundations of American society at the hands of secular, relativistic liberalism; 3) anti-Communist Cold Warriors, convinced that America was increasingly imperiled by an evil empire seeking the conquest of the world; 4) neoconservatives—disillusioned men and women of the Left who had been "mugged by reality" and were gravitating toward the conservative camp; and 5) the Religious Right, traumatized by the moral wreckage unleashed upon America by the courts and by the culture wars of the 1960s and 1970s.

Reagan himself seems to have been closest in his outlook and priorities to the free-market conservatives and Cold Warriors. In his first autobiography, published in 1965, he asserted that classical liberalism was "now the conservative position."[18] On another occasion he declared: "Today's conservative is, of course, the true liberal—in the classical meaning of the word."[19] But the president was astute enough to identify himself (and sincerely so) with each component of the grand coalition. To a convention of fifteen thousand evangelical Christians in 1980, for instance, he famously remarked: "I know you can't endorse me. But I want you to know that I endorse you."[20] It could even be said that Reagan was a premature neoconservative, for he had once been a very liberal Democrat. Just after the election of 1980, he warmly endorsed a new book on foreign policy by the neoconservative writer Norman Podhoretz.[21]

Thus just as William F. Buckley Jr. had done for conservatives out of power before 1980, so Reagan as president during the eighties did the same: He performed an emblematic and ecumenical function. Much of his popularity as a conservative paladin derived from his ability to embody all these impulses simultaneously.

Yet Reagan did more than simply give his fellow conservatives access to power. He also placed his own distinctive brand upon their movement— thereby cementing even further the bond between them. At the time of his accession to the presidency, the American Right was completing a transition from a dissident, minority consciousness to a perception of itself as the authentic voice of Middle America. Once upon a time, during the 1950s, many conservatives had gloomily regarded themselves as a forlorn and defeated remnant, "standing athwart history yelling Stop!" By 1980 they had begun to speak of themselves in more populist terms, as the vanguard of America's silent, moral majority.

Reagan's electoral triumph completed this mainstreaming process. More than that, he imbued it with rhetorical staying power. As Michael Barone has observed, the Great Communicator gave American conservatism a demotic voice and a more optimistic tone, evoking hope for the future instead of nostalgia for a receding past. Unlike some of the more European-oriented conservative intellectuals, he couched his social vision in the language of American exceptionalism, the lilting religious imagery of America as a chosen nation, chosen by God "to be free" and to be "the golden hope of all mankind."[22] He believed this. He believed, too, in words of Tom Paine which he loved to quote: "We have it in our power to begin the world over again."[23]

So in his inaugural address in 1981, Reagan exhorted his fellow citizens "to believe in ourselves and to believe in our capacity to perform great deeds." His invincible optimism, his unquenchable confidence in the elixir of freedom, his conviction that history "is not predetermined," inspired not only Americans in general but a generation of his fellow conservatives.

All this is not to say that American conservatives were enraptured by Reagan's performance in the presidency. Truth to tell, they were often dismayed and disappointed, although more by his advisers than by the man himself. In our current mood of celebration of Reagan's legacy, we tend to forget what contemporary observers and the burgeoning memoir literature about him attest: that in both the domestic and foreign policy arenas, the Reagan administration was often at war with itself. It was a war, as the expression of the time had it, between "pragmatists" and "ideologues"—that is, between middle-of-the road, pre–Reaganite Republicans and principled "movement conservatives" intent upon effecting a revolution. The conflict permeated the highest levels of the White House staff, it involved the president's wife (who sided with the pragmatists), and it engendered internecine feuds and manipulative policymaking processes that aptly have been described as Byzantine. It gave rise to the great conservative battle cry of the eighties: "Let Reagan be Reagan."

Particularly during the president's second term, his increasingly intensive pursuit of arms control agreements with the Soviet Union offended and alarmed many conservatives, both inside and outside his administration. Especially perturbed was the neoconservative journal *Commentary*, edited by Norman Podhoretz, which published a number of highly critical articles on this subject during the mid- and late 1980s.[24] Reagan's zealous drive for the total abolition of nuclear weapons—culminating in the roller-coaster summit conference in Reykjavik in 1986—made even Margaret Thatcher fear that he had gone wobbly.[25] On the whole, it is safe to say that Reagan's first term was more congenial to conservatives than his second.

When Reagan left the White House in 1989, not everyone on the Right was ready to give him a grade of "A." Libertarians, especially, wondered just how much had really been accomplished during his two terms. One prominent libertarian—dismayed by the administration's perceived inability (or unwillingness) "to reverse the growth of Leviathan"—published an essay provocatively entitled "The Sad Legacy of Ronald Reagan."[26] Nevertheless, most movement conservatives credited Reagan with bequeathing them a politically precious gift—a successful, conservative presidency—and their verdict was accordingly positive.[27] So, too, was that of most other Americans: In January 1989, Reagan left office with a public approval rating of well over 60 percent—the highest for any departing president since Franklin Roosevelt.

The "shining city upon a hill," it seemed, had been well served.

The looming question for conservatives was: would historians agree?

III

According to a historian of my acquaintance, scholarly appraisals of a president's legacy go through three stages: bunk, debunk, and rebunk. At the beginning of 1989 there was reason to believe that the coming historical evaluation of Reagan's presidency would skip the first phase and permanently wallow in the second. Politicians often like to say that they will let history determine the merits of their record, as if history were a disembodied, infallible force. What more sophisticated politicians realize is that historical judgment is an artifact, the product of creatures known as historians, who are not as free from bias as they like to think.

In the case of Ronald Reagan, this posed an immediate challenge. For despite his popularity with the general electorate at the end of his second term, there was one influential corner of America where he remained anathema: academe. For all of Reagan's wit, charm, and persuasiveness, his had been a highly polarizing presidency, and few academic social scientists inhabited his side of the great divide. Reagan was an unabashed conservative. The vast majority of historians and political scientists were not.

Not surprisingly, then, the leftward-tilting American intelligentsia in the 1980s largely looked upon the president as at worst a warmonger and at best (in Clark Clifford's notorious phrase) as an "amiable dunce." The septuagenarian president was pilloried as an indolent actor "sleepwalking through history." The contempt which many academics felt for him was captured in the response by the historian Henry Steele Commager to Reagan's 1983 address labeling the Soviet Union an "evil empire"—a speech roundly applauded by conservatives. According to the very liberal Professor Commager, it was "the worst presidential speech in American history, and I've read them all."[28]

Reagan himself did not seem to mind the aspersions cast upon him by his ideological enemies. As various biographers have noted, he always cared more about the "box office" (the voters) than about the critics. He also enjoyed letting his opponents underestimate him, and seemed to play along with some of their misperceptions of his temperament. "It's true hard work never killed anybody," he once reputedly remarked, "but I figure, why take the chance."[29] On his desk in the White House he kept a plaque which said: "There's no limit to what a man can do or where he can go if he doesn't mind who gets the credit." Still, the disdain which many in the professoriate expressed for him (and, even more, for his conservative political philosophy) made it seem unlikely that he would be treated favorably in the history books anytime soon.

The first scholarly evaluations of Reagan after he left the White House seemed to confirm his conservative defenders' worst fears. In 1990, the Siena Research Institute asked more than two hundred academic historians and political scientists to rank all forty American presidents. Reagan came in at an undistinguished twenty-second, just two notches ahead of Jimmy Carter.[30] Four years later the institute conducted another survey; this time Reagan inched up to twenty—four points lower than the current incumbent, Bill Clinton.[31] In 1996 the liberal historian Arthur Schlesinger Jr. asked thirty prominent historians (and two Democratic politicians) to rank the presidents anew. Although seven accorded Reagan a "near great" ranking, nine others dismissed him as "below average," and four judged him an outright "failure." In the composite ranking, Reagan placed a mediocre twenty-fifth, just behind his successor in office, George Bush, and just barely ahead of Chester Arthur. [32]

Schlesinger's poll outraged American conservatives. Nearly every participant in his survey was a left-of-center intellectual like himself; only one of the thirty-two was a known conservative. Was this—conservatives wondered—how the "impartial" judgment of history would be rendered upon Reagan? Perhaps not coincidentally, several months later Grover Norquist initiated the Reagan Legacy Project. In the next several years, conservatively inclined presidential scholars came forth with rejoinders and correctives to Schlesinger, including *Presidential Leadership: Rating the Best and the Worst in the White House*.[33] In this volume, a more ideologically diverse set of academic experts moved Reagan into the "near great" category.

In retrospect, Schlesinger's skewed 1996 survey may be seen as the last hurrah of the anti-Reagan consensus in liberal academia. Shortly afterward, a funny thing happened on Reagan's journey into the history books: His reputation among the professors began to rise. Here and there reputable scholars—hardly any of them on the political Right—began to publish books and articles containing more than a modicum of praise.[34] One sign of this new glasnost appeared in a 1999 essay in the *Washington Post* by the liberal political scientist and biographer of Franklin Roosevelt, Professor James MacGregor Burns. "When historians tally up the [twentieth] century's 'great' or 'near-great' presidents," he declared flatly, "Roosevelt and Reagan will be among them."[35] It was a remarkable accolade, particularly considering its source.

Why this rapid shifting of the tide? Every president's place in history depends to some degree upon the record of his immediate successors, and here Reagan was singularly fortunate. After the brief economic recession of 1991–92, the economic revival that had commenced on his watch resumed: the "long prosperity" (it has been called), arguably rooted in the policies he implemented in the early 1980s. One of the principal criticisms of Reagan had been that "Reaganomics" had led to huge and dangerous federal budget deficits. When the economy nevertheless grew stronger and the deficits disappeared in the 1990s, this part of Reagan's legacy came to seem far less consequential than once feared, and his free-market, low-tax philosophy seemed vindicated. The Republican capture of Congress in 1994 (including the House of Representatives for the first time in fifty-two years) ratified the "Reagan revolution" even further. Soon Bill Clinton himself was claiming that "the era of big government is over." Like the Labour Party leader Tony Blair after the "Thatcher revolution" in Great Britain during the eighties, Clinton appeared to recognize that Reagan had pulled the political center of gravity to the Right. That is one way to measure a presidential legacy.

Reagan's genuine likeability and his courageous response to Alzheimer's disease no doubt helped to dissipate some of the lingering hostility evinced by his ideological foes. His unruffled affability and dignified demeanor as chief executive contrasted favorably with the scandals and hyperpartisanship of the Clinton years (and beyond). But most of all, Reagan's reputation—and the new respect for his legacy—profited from the amazing events that occurred shortly after he left office: the liberation of eastern Europe from Communist captivity and the collapse of the USSR just two years later.

Looking back with the advantage of hindsight, we tend to forget that it was not at all obvious on January 20, 1989—the day the Reagan administration officially ended—that the end of the Soviet empire was near. Reagan, of course, had publicly prophesied communism's early demise.[36] But even he was surprised when the Berlin Wall came down less than ten months after he left office.[37] This swift and stunning geopolitical earthquake, and the attendant end of the Cold War, confronted historians Left and Right with a monumental explanatory problem: How and why did all this happen, and so unexpectedly? Who was responsible? Who deserved credit? As the scholarly investigations proceeded, nearly every serious academic investigator came to recognize that Reagan's role in these shattering developments had been substantial.

To be sure, there were—and remain—sharp differences of emphasis among the scholars. In one corner stands the "Reagan Victory School," which argues essentially that Reagan *won* the Cold War, that he *intended* to win it, and that as president he conceived and carried out a coordinated campaign to achieve this objective.[38] In another corner are those who emphasize internal Soviet conditions and decision-making, the pivotal role of Mikhail Gorbachev, and Reagan's pursuit of nuclear disarmament (over the objection of his more conservative advisers). The debate between these two "schools" is likely to continue at least until more of the Soviet archives are opened. But even the academic disparagers of Reaganite "triumphalism" seem inclined to grant that the Gipper was at the very least the "best supporting actor" in Gorbachev's drama and that Reagan's policies helped to push the Soviet Union toward irreversible reform.[39] Some would go further. There is no better example of Reagan's change of fortune in academic scholarship than the judgment pronounced in 2004 by the dean of America's diplomatic historians, John Lewis Gaddis of Yale University. In his considered opinion, Reagan should be remembered as a highly skilled and effective geopolitician—indeed, as the most successful American strategist of the Cold War.[40]

If events after 1989 encouraged a fresh and favorable interpretation of Reagan's legacy, another development proved nearly as important. Sooner or later, historical scholarship must be grounded not on the quicksand of political or academic fashion but upon the solid bedrock of archival research. In the case of Reagan, the archival record turned out to be more effulgent than anyone dreamed.

Early in 2001 three scholars—Kiron Skinner, Martin Anderson, and Annelise Anderson—published a remarkable book of Reagan's own writings drawn from a previously unknown file in his personal papers.[41] Between 1975 and 1979, Reagan had delivered more than 1,000 daily syndicated radio broadcasts, each about 500 words long, on nearly every public policy issue and controversy imaginable. It turned out that he composed 670 of these essays by himself, in his own handwriting, and that he personally edited them as well. A large sampling from this cache of primary sources comprised the bulk of the volume *Reagan, In His Own Hand,* which Skinner and the Andersons assembled. It revealed a dimension of Reagan hitherto hidden from view. In 2003, the three scholars published an equally impressive sequel: *Reagan: A Life in Letters,* a compendium of more than 1,000 substantive letters—entirely written by Reagan himself—out of an estimated 10,000 such letters that he is believed to have composed during his long life.[42]

More than any other scholarly publications in the past twenty years, the Skinner/Anderson anthologies demolished the old, demeaning stereotypes and propelled the upward arc of Reagan's reputation. The nation's fortieth chief executive stood revealed as a prolific and capable writer, skillful editor, disciplined worker, wide-ranging reader, and intelligent, even visionary, thinker. Before his presidency he wrote nearly all of his own speeches—a notable accomplishment in itself. Even in the White House he drafted many of his major addresses himself and carefully edited his speechwriters' submissions. This was not the Reagan that his detractors (and even some admirers) thought they knew.

The surge of scholarly reappraisal was now approaching high tide. In 2004 Paul Kengor published *God and Ronald Reagan*, a "spiritual biography" which argued that in Reagan's religion lay the key to his character and much of his conduct as president. Far from being a merely nominal Christian, Reagan (in Kengor's account) was a deeply committed, if self-effacing, man of faith who was convinced that God had a plan—indeed, a mission—not only for America as a nation but for himself as its president. According to Kengor, Reagan came to believe that God's purpose for him was to confront and defeat atheistic communism. [43]

Just how Reagan fulfilled this mission Kengor explained in his next book, *The Crusader: Ronald Reagan and the Fall of Communism*.[44] Here Kengor portrayed Reagan as a man with a "sense of destiny," who sought to become president for a specific purpose: to effect the collapse of communism and the breakup of its evil empire. Once in power, Reagan (claimed Kengor) pursued this goal relentlessly to victory.

Meanwhile, in 2005, Paul Lettow published a monograph, *Ronald Reagan and His Quest to Abolish Nuclear Weapons*, which illuminated an even less familiar part of Reagan's psyche: his lifelong loathing of nuclear weapons and his growing determination as president to rid them from the earth. It seemed that Reagan was not only a Cold Warrior but also a nuclear abolitionist who "was convinced that it was his personal mission to avert nuclear war."[45]

In 2007 Reagan scholarship took another leap forward with the publication of his presidential diary, which he faithfully kept between 1981 and 1989.[46] Although this much-awaited tome yielded no spectacular revelations, it enhanced Reagan's stature as a genuinely decent person, and reinforced the growing sense among scholars that he had been an astute and competent chief executive.

By the beginning of 2008 Reagan's historical reputation had soared to heights that few conservatives had thought attainable. It was now commonplace for academics and media commentators alike to acclaim him as one of America's most successful presidents. The new consensus did not mean that scholars agreed on what it was that made him so estimable. In fact, the more his reputation rose, the more contested his legacy became. By 2004, in the wake of the war in Iraq, American neoconservatives and their "realist" critics were arguing over who was the legitimate heir of Reagan's policies.[47] On the Left, certain liberals—unable to deny Reagan's catalytic role in concluding the Cold War—began to assert that Reagan had succeeded because he had given up his hardline conservative ideology. It was Reagan's "pragmatism," they asserted, and his willingness to negotiate with the Soviets, that had led him to "end" the Cold War rather than "win" it.[48]

The most audacious of the liberal revisionists was the historian John Patrick Diggins, in *Ronald Reagan: Fate, Freedom, and the Making of History* (2007). Diggins, who detested neoconservatives like Norman Podhoretz, set out to "rescue" Reagan from the "neocon hawks" and other "so-called Reaganites" who had allegedly taken the United States down a "trail of blunders" in the Middle East. In flat contravention of the Reagan Victory School, Diggins claimed that Reagan had been a "reluctant cold warrior," whose greatness lay in turning himself from a hawk into a dove.[49]

Nor did Diggins stop there. In the sweep of modern history, he asserted, Reagan was not a conservative at all (at least by Burkean standards) but a freewheeling liberal in the tradition of Thomas Paine and Ralph Waldo Emerson. "Far from being a conservative" (wrote Diggins), "Reagan was the great liberating spirit of modern American history, a political romantic impatient with the status quo."[50]

Diggins' controversial book—colored, as it was in part, by current contentions—intrigued but failed to persuade most conservative reviewers.[51] His insistence, for instance, that Reagan was a radically "Emersonian optimist" who believed man to be innately good seemed to neglect the depth of Reagan's Christian upbringing and convictions, including his belief in prayer and his serene assurance that God had a purpose for his life.[52] But the liberal historian was correct to notice in Reagan a romantic, even utopian streak, which shocked and at times mortified his advisers. Nowhere was this trait more in evidence than in his increasingly bold pursuit of the abolition of nuclear weapons.[53]

"Dick, you know what I really want to be remembered for?" he said out of the blue to his pollster, Richard Wirthlin, one evening in 1983. "I want to be remembered as the president of the United States who brought a sense and reality of peace and security. I want to eliminate that awful fear that each of us feels sometimes when we get up in the morning knowing that the world could be destroyed through a nuclear holocaust." Astonished by this remark, Wirthlin became convinced that Reagan was "a man who was *obsessed* with peace."[54] On another occasion, during a conversation in 1986 with his hard-line arms-control adviser, General Edward Rowny, Reagan blurted out, "I have a dream. I have a dream of a world without nuclear weapons. I want our children and grandchildren particularly to be free of these weapons."[55] And what is more, he pursued this vision all the way to the fateful summit conference with Gorbachev in Reykjavik. What was the engine driving Reagan's unwavering quest? In his 1990 autobiography he gave his answer. He disclosed how he came to believe after the assassination attempt upon him in 1981 that God had spared his life for a reason. His brush with death led him to believe that he had discerned this reason. The experience made him feel that "I should do whatever I could in the years God had given me to reduce the threat of nuclear war."[56]

Thus, just when it seemed that Reagan's triumphant march into the history books was secure, and conservatives could say "mission accomplished," the spin-doctoring of his legacy took a most unusual turn. Until 2004 or so, conservatives had labored with increasing success to rescue Reagan from the sneering incomprehension of left-wing academics. Now a new battle for his legacy loomed, with liberals striving to claim at least a part of it for themselves. [57]

And so the question arose, as it had so often during Reagan's lifetime: in Peggy Noonan's words, "Who was that masked man?"[58] Had there, in fact, been two Reagans behind that good-humored façade? If so, how did the two of them fit together? And which, if either, was the dominant part of his innermost self? The "ideologue" or the "pragmatist"?[59] The crusader against communism or the crusader against the Bomb? The persistent Cold Warrior and scourge of the "evil empire" or the peace-seeker who (in his own words) "placed a lot of faith in the simple power of human contact in solving problems"?[60]

One conclusion was certain: "the riddle of Reagan" (as his close aide Michael Deaver once put it) [61] had not yet been totally solved. Historians of his life and presidency were not about to become unemployed. The argument about the man and his legacy had only just begun.

IV

So how stands the legacy of Ronald Reagan in 2008? Historical interpretation is a never-ending process, subject to ideological crossfire and the vicissitudes of bunk-and-debunk. Still, it seems likely that five achievements of

Reagan will stand out in the fullness of time. First, at a moment of dangerous drift and national malaise, he restored his country's sense of self-confidence and its will-to-greatness. Secondly, he bequeathed an ineffaceable example of optimism, grit, serenity, wit, and constructive use of the life he had been given to live. Reagan himself did not believe that his own personality was of much historical importance. He once remarked that he could understand why, two hundred years from now, people would be interested in his presidency, but not why they would be interested in him. [62] Here, perhaps, his modesty misled him. Like other notable American presidents, his personal qualities will continue to fascinate and inspire. He may not make it to Mount Rushmore, but he will long survive in the Mount Rushmore of our collective memory.

Thirdly—and for this conservatives especially will always be indebted—he transmuted American conservatism from theory to practice, gave conservatives a successful presidency to defend (and a statesman to honor), and shifted the paradigm of political discourse for at least a generation. Fourth, he mobilized the resources—rhetorical, military, diplomatic, economic, and spiritual—that in one way or another put communism and its Soviet empire on the road to extinction.

Finally, and perhaps most importantly, he gave us his words. With incandescent prose he revived America's sense of itself as a sweet land of liberty, selected by God for a great purpose. For so long as the United States of America survives as a free and independent polity, his vision of America's meaning will tug at our souls.

Of this legacy, historians will likely say: not bad, not bad at all.

32

How Firm a Foundation?
The Prospects for American Conservatism

This essay is adapted from an address on October 24, 2008, at Belmont Abbey College, where I received the Richard M. Weaver Prize for Scholarly Letters from the Ingersoll Foundation. The essay was published in the Spring 2009 issue of the Intercollegiate Review.

The occasion of this award has prompted me to reflect about the influence of Richard Weaver on my own life. The other day, while rummaging through an old desk drawer, I came upon a list of the books that I had read in high school. It was a list that I had compiled at the time, recording the date that I completed my reading of each volume. There I found that on August 14, 1963, just a month before entering college, I finished *Ideas Have Consequences* for the first time.

Weaver's book fortified me for the experience of attending a very liberal liberal-arts college in the 1960s—and particularly for my freshman-year English composition course, which was steeped in the theories of the semantics movement that Weaver abhorred. Like Russell Kirk's *The Conservative Mind*, which I read a year later, *Ideas Have Consequences* provided an intellectual foundation for dissent from the collegiate zeitgeist. *Ideas Have Consequences* was one of the first serious books that I ever read a second time. And if memory serves, it was the first book that I ever gave to someone other than a family member to read.

Looking back, I now realize that it was not just Weaver's writings that impressed me. His sense of vocation, his example of being in liberal academia but not of it, were, I believe, among the influences that encouraged me to pursue a scholarly career. So I feel especially moved to receive this high honor to which his name is attached.

We have gathered to consider the future of American conservatism. Until a few weeks ago, it did not appear to have much of a future at all. Writing in the September issue of *The American Prospect*, the liberal columnist E. J. Dionne declared flatly that "the conservative era" in American politics is "in its final days." The "conservative project," he said, is "exhausted." Meanwhile, in the September 10 issue of the *New Republic*, Sam Tanenhaus, the editor of the *New York Times Book Review*, asserted that the conservative movement "has never been in poorer shape than it is today." Indeed, he claimed, it has entered "its last and genuinely decadent phase."

Such sentiments are by no means confined to the American Left. In the past three years, an increasing number of conservative commentators have wondered aloud whether the long foretold "conservative crackup" was finally at hand. Jeffrey Hart, for example, in his 2006 history of *National Review*, perceived a movement succumbing to a tide of doctrinaire, unconservative ideology and a reckless politics of imprudence. William F. Buckley Jr. reportedly believed in his last years that the conservative movement he had so tirelessly championed was (in Hart's words) "probably finished"—a case of "intellectual suicide." A leading conservative journalist of my acquaintance remarked a couple of years ago that the movement is suffering a nervous breakdown—a consequence, he said, of the end of the Cold War. A few on the Right have even suggested that if the movement is not already dead, then it ought to be. "Is the Conservative Movement Worth Conserving?" was the title of a posting at a prominent conservative website just a couple of months ago.

Earlier this year the *New York Times'* technology columnist David Pogue listed the five stages of grieving when you lose your computer files: Denial, Anger, Bargaining, Depression, and Moving to Amish Country. It sounds like a fair description of the mood gripping many American conservatives in 2008. Certainly, evidence abounds of a political and intellectual movement in crisis. One sign of this is the growing tendency on the Right to classify conservatives into ever-smaller sectarian groupings: neoconservatives, paleoconservatives, big government conservatives, leave-us-alone conservatives, "national greatness" conservatives, compassionate conservatives, crunchy conservatives—and the list goes on. Another sign is the sharp intramural polemicizing in which some of these elements have indulged in recent years. Thus the paleoconservatives relentlessly pound the neoconservatives, Straussians exchange fire with anti-Straussians, devotees of Abraham Lincoln debate his detractors, libertarians take issue with religious conservatives, and neo-agrarians critique capitalism and free marketeers. A once relatively disciplined band of brothers (or so it used to appear in the Age of Reagan) has seemingly devolved into a rancorous jumble of factions. It calls to mind Napoleon's answer when asked against whom he preferred to fight. He replied: against his allies. They were the ones who caused him the most trouble.

Several adventitious factors have strengthened the impression among many observers that American conservatism has come to a cul de sac. The deaths of Milton Friedman in 2006, Jerry Falwell in 2007, and William F. Buckley Jr. in 2008 precipitated an outpouring of anxious retrospection and an intensified awareness that nearly all of modern conservatism's founding fathers have now gone to the grave. Coupled with this generational changing of the guard has been the phenomenal upsurge of popular interest in the life and achievements of Ronald Reagan. More than any of our forty-three presidents, Reagan has been on the minds and tongues of a nation hungering for renewal in 2008. From conservatives in particular has come the cry, "What would Reagan do?" Critics scoff at this as mere nostalgia, the right-wing equivalent of the liberal cult of John F. Kennedy. It is much more than that, but memories of the Gipper remind embattled conservatives of better days and reflect the feeling of disorientation that many on the Right now feel.

A more subtle ingredient in this mix has been the efflorescence in the past decade of historical scholarship about American conservatism since World War II—much of it written by young liberal historians. This is not necessarily a sign of declension, but it certainly testifies to the growing passage of time: The conservative movement has now been around long enough to be the object of academic inquiry. To put it another way, modern American conservatism—a marginalized orphan in academia when I began research on it a generation ago—has become middle-aged. Which, of course, raises the uncomfortable question: are old age and remarginalization just around the corner?

Clearly, many conservative thinkers and activists are determined to avoid any such outcome. One of the notable features of the conservative landscape at present is the quest by the intellectual Right to revitalize its roots and recover its philosophical moorings. Last year, for example, the conservative quarterly *Modern Age* devoted one of its fiftieth anniversary issues to

"Conservative Reflections on Neglected Questions and Ignored Problems." Next spring the Philadelphia Society, the nation's oldest society of conservative intellectuals, will focus its entire national meeting on the legacy of the luminaries of twentieth-century conservatism. Meanwhile, younger authors like Ryan Sager, Michael Gerson, and Ross Douthat have written books attempting to reformulate conservatism for a new generation. In and of themselves, these efforts might be considered a token of vitality. Taken together, however, they convey the impression that the condition of conservatism has become problematic.

Current explanations of the conservative predicament tend to fall into two distinct categories. The first stresses the movement's political failure and frustrations during the presidency of George W. Bush. With the exception of its Supreme Court nominations and tax-cutting policies, Bush's administration now seems to many conservative stalwarts to have been in large measure a liberal Republican administration—more akin to Rockefeller and Nixon than to Reagan. At home, Medicare drug entitlements have been expanded, education policy has been nationalized, and federal deficit spending has been allowed to soar unchecked. The administration's abortive immigration reform initiative in 2007 further alienated most conservatives from the man in the White House. The concurrent wave of congressional scandals and the battle over earmarks have reminded rueful conservatives of the temptations from which even Right-minded politicoes are not always immune.

Even more than its sometimes heterodox domestic policies, the Bush administration's approach to foreign policy has placed severe strains on the conservative coalition. The president's audacious assertion of executive power in the war on terrorism has rattled libertarians and others for whom the restraint of executive power is a settled conservative principle. His sweeping invocation of the language of democratic universalism has gratified neoconservatives but has struck some other conservatives as an exercise in platitudinous naiveté. For those on the Right who base their foreign policy outlook on the virtues of prudence and realism, Bush's "hard Wilsonianism" has seemed disturbingly utopian and unconservative.

There can be little doubt that the war in Iraq proved to be vexing to the American Right. It exacerbated what is now a nearly thirty-year war between the neoconservatives and the paleoconservatives. It led William F. Buckley Jr. to announce in early 2007 that if he were a member of Congress he would vote against the proposed troop surge in Iraq. Buckley did not live to see the surge's success—at least for the time being—but his pessimism about Iraq and his negative verdict on the Bush presidency exemplified a broader mood of disillusionment on the Right with the fruits of its political ascendancy.

This feeling of disenchantment was all the more agonizing because political victory had been so long in coming. The conservative movement as we know it began to coalesce more than half a century ago, but it was not until 2002—just six years ago—that the nominally conservative political party in the United States gained simultaneous control of both houses of Congress and the presidency. Not even Ronald Reagan had the influence over Congress that George W. Bush possessed between 2003 and 2006. Although we must not overlook the paralyzing tactics of liberal Democrats in the U.S. Senate during those years, this fact did not keep many conservatives from concluding that their leaders in Washington had squandered a historic opportunity for conservative reform.

The second cluster of explanations for conservatism's present malaise focuses not so much on external, political circumstances but on internal factors—that is, the structure and dynamics of the conservative movement itself. Perhaps the most important thing to understand about modern American conservatism is that it is not, and has never been, univocal. It is a *coalition,* with many points of origin and diverse tendencies that are not always easy to reconcile with one another. Historically, it has been a river of thought and activism fed by many tributaries: a wide and sometimes muddy river, but one with great power, so long as the tributaries flowed into the common stream.

So long as the Cold War continued, this coalition held together reasonably well. Anticommunism—a conviction shared by nearly everyone—supplied much of the essential unifying cement. But with the end of the Cold War in the early 1990s, and the departure from office of the ecumenical Reagan, long-suppressed centrifugal tendencies resurfaced on the American Right. What had once appeared to be creative tensions began to look to some like irreconcilable differences. Without a common foe to concentrate their minds and tongues, it became easier to succumb to the bane of all coalitions: the sectarian temptation, the tendency to go it alone and accentuate disagreements with one's former collaborators.

Cropping up in both of these sets of explanation, from time to time, has been a kind of historical determinism: the notion that political and intellectual movements, like individuals and nations, have immutable life cycles. Just as it was once believed that civilizations ineluctably pass from barbarism to Arcadian bliss to urban prosperity and eventual rot and decline, so, it sometimes seems, must the conservative movement itself pass—in Jacques Barzun's phrase—from dawn to decadence. This half-articulated theory of social entropy underlies much of the current giddiness on the Left about conservatism's prospects—and perhaps some of the angst that one finds among some commentators on the Right.

There is one other explanatory framework that has recently arisen to account for conservatism's success and, inferentially, for its supposedly imminent demise. It is the thesis—popular among some left-of-center academics—that in political terms American conservatism arose in reaction to the tumult of the 1960s and that as the traumatic sixties recede into the past, so will the voting patterns associated with it. Put more bluntly, it is the thesis—again, popular among some on the Left—that the key to the conservative ascendancy since 1968 has not been conservative ideas or the failures of liberalism but something uglier: the racial prejudice of white people.

Although most scholars, I believe, would reject this line of historical analysis as crudely simplistic, nevertheless, on both sides of the political divide one detects at times a sense—of hope on the Left and fear on the Right—that conservatism is doomed to political decrepitude as America becomes more multiracial in character. It is one more manifestation of the nervousness with which some conservatives are facing the future.

So, then, are Dionne, Tanenhaus, and other declinists correct? Is the house of conservatism in shambles and about to collapse? When addressing such questions, historians are expected to be judicious, and accordingly, I begin with the judicious words of Mark Twain. When informed in 1897 that a newspaper in New York had reported that he had died, he told a visiting journalist: "Just say the report of my death has been grossly exaggerated."

How firm are the foundations of modern American conservatism? Let us look further. Perhaps they are sturdier than many observers now think.

There are several reasons for considering this possibility. First, when examining the epiphenomena of contemporary politics—especially in our era of ever more frenzied and frothy news cycles—it is helpful to remember the adage "this, too, shall pass away." The divisive Bush presidency is nearly over and the Iraq war gives signs of winding down. Slowly, some of the "external" political circumstances that so dismayed conservatives in recent years have begun to dissipate.

As George Orwell reminded us years ago, one of the temptations to which intellectuals are susceptible is to assume that whatever is happening right now will continue to happen—that tomorrow will inevitably look just like today. In some ways it will, but in some ways it won't. Certainly the future is preconditioned by the past, but it is not *predetermined* by the past. We are creatures of our mental constructs and our life experiences, yes, but we are not robots. The longer I study history, the more impressed I am by the importance of contingency—the unforeseen and the unforeseeable—in the shaping of human events. American conservatives, I suspect, instinctively look upon our history in this way: not simply as a burden and constraint but as possibility. They should therefore take heart in 2008 from the knowledge that this, too, shall pass away.

Secondly, in their obsession with the sound and fury of the stormy present, it is easy for conservatives to overlook and undervalue one of their most impressive achievements during the past forty years: the creation of a veritable conservative counterculture, a burgeoning infrastructure of alternative media, foundations, research centers, think tanks, publishing houses, law firms, homeschooling networks, and more. From the Beltway to the blogosphere, these clusters of purposeful energy continue to multiply and flourish. From the perspective of a historian, this flowering of applied conservatism, this institutionalization of conservative ideas, is a remarkable intellectual and political development.

Think of it: when Richard Weaver was writing in the 1950s and early 1960s, the number of publicly active, professing conservative intellectuals in the United States was minuscule—perhaps a few dozen at most. Today how can we even begin to count? Since 1980 prosperity has come to conservatism, and with it, a multitude of niche markets and specialization on a thousand fronts.

Does this mean that all is well in the conservative parallel universe? Not necessarily. A few months ago the neoconservative columnist David Brooks accused the conservative think tanks of being "sclerotic." Other conservatives have quoted Eric Hoffer's pungent aphorism that every cause begins as a movement, becomes a business, and then a racket. Still, the fruit of a generation of successful conservative institution building appears to have reached a critical mass that is unlikely to crumble anytime soon. This augurs well for the continued influence of conservatism on our national conversation.

A third source of durability for conservatives is this: on the home front, the cohesion that was once supplied by Cold War anticommunism has increasingly come from another "war," one that seems integral to the identity of most Americans on the Right. This is the so-called culture war, pitting an alliance of conservative Roman Catholics, evangelical Protestants, and Orthodox Jewish believers against a post-Judeo-Christian, even anti-Christian, secular elite whom they perceive to be aggressively hostile to their deepest convictions. Every day, fresh tremors break out along this fault line—over abortion, euthanasia, stem cell research, gay marriage, and the composition of the federal courts. It is a struggle literally over the meaning of right and wrong.

During the past year it became commonplace in the media to suggest that the culture wars are over as a salient feature of American life. It was said, for example, that young evangelical Protestants are tiring of the old battles and turning to new causes like global warming and relief for AIDS victims in Africa. But oh, the unpredictable contingencies of history: In the past two months the culture wars have returned to the national arena with a vengeance. We shall see how this latest episode in the contest for our culture plays out. For now, at least for a season, the seemingly irrepressible conflict between conservative people of faith and the secular Left has resumed, especially among the media and chattering classes for whom politics seems increasingly to be a form of warfare.

Fourthly, the conservative coalition seems likely to endure for a while because most of the external stimuli that goaded it into existence have not disappeared. In some respects, they have recently grown stronger. The Berlin Wall may be gone, and unvarnished socialist economics may be discredited in theory, but the Russian bear under Vladimir Putin is growling again, while at home the drive for redistribution of wealth and a nationalized medical care system gathers force. Large swatches of American life—notably the universities, the major media, and the entertainment industry—seem more hostile than ever to the Christian faith and worldview. For defenders of Judeo-Christian ethics—and that means most conservatives—there remains much work to do. There is still a potent enemy on the Left.

This awareness of external challenge from the Left is, I believe, integral to the prospects for American conservatism in the years ahead. If anyone doubts this, the phenomenal events of the past two months should be persuasive. If the conservative movement earlier this year seemed anemic and in need of fresh energy, it received it massively on August 29, 2008, when Senator John McCain introduced Governor Sarah Palin to the nation, and a few days later, on September 3, when Palin addressed the Republican national convention. I do not think we will soon forget the emotional intensity of those six days—an intensity not felt on the American Right since the presidential campaign of Barry Goldwater. To the amazement of much of the punditocracy, the conservative grassroots turned out to be alive after all.

But Governor Palin's nomination did more than bring joy and rejuvenating vigor to most conservative hearts. The ferocious and mocking assault on her by many in the media reminded indignant conservatives of who they are and, even more vividly, of who their opponents are. It restored to conservatives a sense of their cause as a fighting faith. Moreover, at least temporarily it relieved some of the internal, structural stresses in the conservative camp and tended to pull the fractious coalition back together. From the paleoconservative Patrick Buchanan to the neoconservative William Kristol, from ardent free marketeers like Lawrence Kudlow to the crunchy conservative Rod Dreher and a legion of social conservatives, with just a few conspicuous exceptions leading spokesmen for the American Right rallied to the Palin candidacy.

Whether this turnabout will prove to be a fleeting spasm or a precursor to a conservative revival, one cannot say. As I mentioned earlier, it is always risky to presume that tomorrow's headlines will necessarily resemble today's. But it does appear significant that in the fiery furnace of political and cultural contention this autumn, an insurgent spirit has returned to American conservatism. If this persists, it will likely buttress the movement's foundations.

Nevertheless, spirit alone cannot do it all. Ideas, too, have consequences, as Richard Weaver long ago reminded us, and it is in this realm that conservatives face challenges that should curb any temptation toward triumphalism. Consider, for example, the phenomenon known as globalization. When we use this word, we tend to think first of the globalization of markets—of free trade in goods and services across national borders. But far more significant, I think, is the accelerating globalization of human migration patterns, with cultural and political consequences that we have scarcely begun to fathom. More people are now on the move in the world than at any time in the history of the human race, and more and more of them are making America their destination. The number of international students, for instance, attending American colleges and universities is now approximately 600,000 per year—a figure more than double what it was in 1980.

Meanwhile, increasing numbers of Americans are electing to live outside the United States. At least four to six million Americans are now permanent residents abroad. Among American college students, particularly those matriculating at elite institutions, it is now quite common to spend one's junior year overseas—something very few could afford to do just a generation ago.

This unprecedented intermingling of peoples and cultures—abetted by rising prosperity, expanding air travel, and the incredible velocity of mass communication—has already begun to have ideological ramifications. In the United States, it has been accompanied by the emergence of multiculturalism as the driving philosophy of our educational system. It has been accompanied by the deliberate dilution of traditional civic education and the resultant explosion of cultural illiteracy about America's heritage. It has been accompanied in the field of historiography by narratives which accentuate the failures and blemishes of the American experience. It has been accompanied by the rise of a liberal, cosmopolitan elite imbued with a post-national, even antinational sensibility and motivated by what the historian John Fonte calls "transnational progressivism"—an ideology profoundly antithetical to conservative beliefs.

What does all this portend for the party of the Right? For generations, American conservatives have been united in their defense of our nation, of our inherited constitutional order, against enemies both foreign and domestic—something relatively easy to do during the Cold War but increasingly difficult today. Traditionally, American conservatives have been Eurocentric in their political and cultural discourse, but how can conservatives convincingly articulate this perspective to non-European immigrants and to millions of superficially educated young Americans at a time when Europe itself no longer seems Eurocentric?

These are not idle questions. The political scientist James Ceaser recently observed that for thirty years the conservative movement in the United States has been defending ideas "that almost all other nations in the West are abandoning": "the concept of the nation itself," "the importance of [b]iblical religion," and "the truth of natural right" philosophy. Traditionally Americans have adhered to a form of national self-understanding that scholars term "American exceptionalism." Ronald Reagan did, and he carried the country with him. Now, increasingly, the Reaganite vision of American goodness and uniqueness that most conservatives embrace seems both more exceptional and more vulnerable than ever.

With what arguments, symbols, rituals, and vocabulary can conservatives make their case for the American way of life that they cherish to those for whom the traditional arguments, symbols, rituals, and vocabulary are either unfamiliar or seem hopelessly passé? Again, this is not a trivial concern. It lies at the very heart of our current election campaign. Behind the disputes over public policy and personal fitness for the presidency, behind the vehemence of the culture war surrounding Governor Palin, lurks the question: What kind of a polity does America desire to become? As the conservative British commentator Gerard Baker recently noted, the election of 2008 has turned into a "struggle between the followers of American exceptionalism and the supporters of global universalism." Whatever the outcome on November 4, American conservatives have not yet adequately articulated their convictions in terms that can appeal to people outside their own camp and particularly to those whom James Burnham called the "verbalizers" of our society.

This leads me to a final observation. I am a historian of American conservatism, and I can happily report that sophisticated discourse is thriving on the American Right—in journals like *Modern Age*, the *Intercollegiate Review*, the *New Criterion*, the *University Bookman*, the *Claremont Review of Books*, and *Humanitas*, to name a few. *National Review*, the *American Spectator*, and the *Weekly Standard* continue to flourish. But it also appears to me that conservatives spend much of their time (in current parlance) "cocooning" with one another and that, in this Age of the Internet, too much conservative advocacy has been reduced to sound-bite certitudes and sterile clichés. What do conservatives want? Limited government, they answer; free enterprise, strict construction of the Constitution, fiscal responsibility, traditional values and respect for the sanctity of human life. No doubt, but I wonder: How much are these traditional catchphrases and abstractions persuading people anymore? How much are they inspiring the rising generation? How much are they resonating with America's dominant professional classes, particularly those in the more secularized and urbanized regions of this country?

It is not a new problem. In fact, it is a perennial problem, the essence of which Whittaker Chambers captured long ago. "Each age," he wrote, "finds its own language for an eternal meaning."

What do conservatives want? To put it in elementary terms, we want to be free, we want to live virtuous and productive lives, and we want to be secure from threats beyond and within our borders. We want to live in a society that sustains and encourages these aspirations. Freedom, virtue, safety: goals reflected in the libertarian, traditionalist, and national security dimensions of the conservative movement. But to achieve these perennial goals, we must communicate in language that connects not only with our own coterie but with the great majority of the American people.

Can it be done? I think it can. If there is one thing that virtually all conservatives hold in common, it is the conviction that there is indeed an "eternal meaning," a fount of wisdom to be drawn upon through thick and thin. Believing this, we can smile and persevere. The immediate future may prove unsettling to American conservatives, but in the words of William F. Buckley Jr. nearly fifty years ago, "the wells of regeneration are infinitely deep."

Notes

Introduction

1. George Packer, "The Fall of Conservatism," *New Yorker* 84 (May 26, 2008): 47–53; E. J. Dionne, "The Right in the Rearview Mirror," *American Prospect* 19 (September 2008): 42–49.

2. Quoted in Packer, "Fall of Conservatism," 49.

3. Jonah Goldberg, "Conservatives, Fear Not . . . ," *USA Today*, June 3, 2008, 9A.

4. Austin Bramwell, "Is the Conservative Movement Worth Conserving?" posted at http://www.takimag.com on August 14, 2008.

5. Quoted in Parker, "Fall of Conservatism," 49.

6. Sam Tanenhaus, "The Movement's Remains," *New Republic* 239 (September 10, 2008): 16–23.

7. Sam Tanenhaus, "Conservatism Is Dead," *New Republic* 240 (February 18, 2009): 12–17.

8. Jeffrey Hart, "The GOP Must Change or Die," posted at http://www.thedailybeast.com on November 12, 2008.

9. Claes Ryn, "The Conservative Movement in Chapter 11," March 29, 2009, posted at http://phillysoc.org.

10. Rod Dreher, "Here Comes the Conservative Civil War," posted at http://www.realclearpolitics.com on November 10, 2008.

11. David Brooks, "Darkness at Dusk," *New York Times*, November 11, 2008, A29.

12. For an overview, see Tobin Harshaw, "Weekend Opinionator: The Party of Limbaugh? A Conservative Debate," posted at http://opinionator.blogs.nytimes.com on March 6, 2009.

13. John Derbyshire, "How Radio Wrecks the Right," *American Conservative* 8 (February 23, 2009): 6–7, 34.

14. David Frum, "Why Rush Is Wrong," *Newsweek* 153 (March 16, 2009): 26–32.

15. The quoted words are by Richard Lowry, editor of *National Review*, in a blog posted at http://corner.nationalreview.com on March 3, 2009.

16. Howard Kurtz, "GOP Fights Back Over Criticism of Limbaugh," *Washington Post*, March 6, 2009, A1.

17. Whittaker Chambers to William F. Buckley Jr., September 1954, quoted in William F. Buckley Jr., ed., *Odyssey of a Friend: Whittaker Chambers' Letters to William F. Buckley Jr., 1954–1961* (New York: Putnam, 1970), 83.
18. Patricia Cohen, "Conservative Thinkers Think Again," *New York Times*, July 20, 2008, "Week in Review" section, 3.
19. Ronald Brownstein and David Wasserman, "The Diploma Belt," *National Journal* 41 (February 21, 2009): 18–23.
20. Michael Barone, "Obama's 21st Century Campaign Stuck in a Mid-20th Century Program," posted at http://www.washingtonexaminer.com on March 17, 2009.

CHAPTER 8: THE PLACE OF WILLMOORE KENDALL IN AMERICAN CONSERVATISM

1. Henry Wells to Willmoore Kendall, July 15, 1946; copy in my possession.
2. See Yvona Kendall Mason, ed., *Oxford Years: The Letters of Willmoore Kendall to His Father* (Bryn Mawr, PA: Intercollegiate Studies Institute, 1993). Since the publication of this volume, its publisher has relocated to Wilmington, Delaware.
3. Mason ed., *Oxford Years,* 459, 477.
4. Kendall, July 15, 1946. In this letter, Wells referred to Kendall in these terms. In an interview with the author, Professor Wells said that Kendall did not explicitly talk about himself as an American Veblen but that this was implicit in his strong sense of mission to correct errors and get the truth to prevail.
5. Willmoore Kendall to Francis Wilson, n.d. (but Spring 1963), Francis Wilson Papers, University of Illinois-Urbana.
6. Jeffrey Hart, "Willmoore Kendall: American," in Nellie D. Kendall, ed., *Willmoore Kendall Contra Mundum* (New Rochelle, NY: Arlington House, 1971), 26.
7. George H. Nash, "Conservative Iconoclast (I)," *Modern Age* 19 (Spring 1975): 127–35; George H. Nash, "Conservative Iconoclast (II)," *Modern Age* 19 (Summer 1975): 236–48; George H. Nash, *The Conservative Intellectual Movement in America Since 1945* (New York: Basic Books, 1976), 227–48.
8. Charles S. Hyneman, "In Memoriam," *P.S.: Newsletter of the American Political Science Association* 1(Winter 1968): 56.
9. Hart, "Willmoore Kendall: American," 9.
10. Willmoore Kendall and George W. Carey, *The Basic Symbols of the American Political Tradition* (Baton Rouge: Louisiana State University Press, 1970).
11. This volume was edited by Kendall's widow.
12. Nash, "Conservative Iconoclast (I), 127–35; "Conservative Iconoclast (II)," 236–48. See also Nash, *Conservative Intellectual Movement,* 227–48.
13. John P. East, "The Political Thought of Willmoore Kendall," *Political Science Reviewer* 3 (1973): 201–39.
14. Gregory Wolfe, introduction to Willmoore Kendall, *The Conservative Affirmation in America* (Chicago: Gateway Editions, 1985), ix–xxi; Samuel Francis, "Prophet of the Heartland," *The World and I* 1 (February 1986): 662–69, reprinted in Samuel Francis, *Beautiful Losers: Essays on the Failure of American Conservatism* (Columbia, MO: University of Missouri Press, 1993), 79–87.
15. For example: Harry Jaffa, *How to Think About the American Revolution* (Durham, NC: Carolina Academic Press, 1978), 13–48; Harry Jaffa et al., *Original Intent and the Framers of the Constitution* (Washington, D.C.: Regnery Publishing, 1994), 27, 31; Garry Wills, *Lincoln at Gettysburg* (New York: Simon & Schuster, 1992), 39, 145, 146.

16. Saul Bellow, "Mosby's Memoirs" (1968), reprinted in Saul Bellow, *Mosby's Memoirs and Other Stories* (New York: Viking Press, 1968), 157–84. See also Garry Wills, *Confessions of a Conservative* (Garden City, NY: Doubleday, 1979), 17–25.

17. Two of Kendall's books are collections of essays and book reviews: *The Conservative Affirmation* (Chicago: Henry Regnery Company, 1963) (reprinted in 1985) and *Willmoore Kendall Contra Mundum.*

18. A small fraction of these letters constitutes the volume *Oxford Years,* a book more than 500 pages long.

19. Willmoore Kendall to Austin Ranney, n.d. (but probably early 1965); copy in my possession.

20. Garry Wills used the word "volatile" to describe Kendall's mind; see Wills, *Confessions,* 23.

21. Wills, *Confessions,* 17.

22. Mason, *Oxford Years,* 477.

23. Garry Wills, "Domini Canis," *Modern Age* 7 (Fall 1963): 439.

24. Hyneman, "In Memoriam," 56.

25. "In both his writings and lectures he invited dispute and never shied away from a good fight. Indeed, he seemed to thrive in debating situations." George W. Carey, "Willmoore Kendall, 1909–1967," *Western Political Quarterly* 20 (September 1967): 799.

26. Even friends used words like "difficult" and "perverse" to describe him. Nash, *Conservative Intellectual Movement,* 247.

27. [University of Dallas] *University News,* September 28, 1963, 4.

28. William F. Buckley Jr., *Cruising Speed: A Documentary* (New York: Putnam, 1971), 74.

29. Leo Paul S. de Alvarez, "Difficult, Singular and Legendary," *National Review* 23 (August 24, 1971): 935.

30. Most of Kendall's writing on this subject can be found in *The Conservative Affirmation* and *Willmoore Kendall Contra Mundum.*

31. Kendall in *American Political Science Review* 57 (June 1965): 473; Kendall, *Contra Mundum,* 393.

32. Kendall, *Contra Mundum,* 332, 333.

33. This is a categorization developed in my book *The Conservative Intellectual Movement in America Since 1945.*

34. John B. Judis, *William F. Buckley, Jr.: Patron Saint of the Conservatives* (New York: Simon and Schuster, 1988), 62.

35. Kendall, *Contra Mundum,* 601.

36. Kendall to William F. Buckley Jr. (received July 23, 1963), William F. Buckley Jr. Papers, Yale University Library; Kendall, "Quo Vadis, Barry?" *National Review* 10 (February 25, 1961): 107–8, 127.

37. Kendall, *Contra Mundum,* 393.

38. Kendall, *The Conservative Affirmation,* xi.

39. Kendall, *Contra Mundum,* 393.

40. Willmoore Kendall and George W. Carey, "Towards a Definition of 'Conservatism,'" *Journal of Politics* 26 (May 1964): 406–22.

41. Kendall, *The Conservative Affirmation,* ix.

42. Kendall, *Contra Mundum,* 396.

43. Kendall to Francis Wilson (received April 11, 1963), Wilson Papers.

44. Kendall to Francis Wilson (received April 11, 1963), Wilson Papers. The Long passage quoted above in the text (see note 41) may have been aimed at Kirk.

45. See Kendall, *Contra Mundum,* 29–57, 386–402.

46. Kendall to Francis Wilson, n.d. (but probably March 1963), Wilson Papers.

47. In an interview with the author some years ago, Professor Charles S. Hyneman recalled that Kendall advocated preventive war during the early Cold War years. In a speech in Europe in 1957, Kendall asserted that "American Europe" could "become free . . . only by liberating itself from every form of subjection to communism. And this it can do only by destroying the military power of the Soviet Union." Quoted in Rafael Calvo-Serer, "They Spoke for Christian Europe," *National Review* 4 (July 27, 1957): 109.

48. Nash, *Conservative Intellectual Movement,* 404, note 49. Kendall gave substantial help to William F. Buckley Jr. and L. Brent Bozell in the preparation of their book *McCarthy and His Enemies* (Chicago, 1954). Kendall to Austin Ranney, April 13, 1954, copy in my possession; Judis, *William F. Buckley, Jr.,* 106.

49. Kendall, *Contra Mundum,* 621. The other root of the American conservative movement, according to Kendall, was "Buckleyism." This may not have been a neutral observation; in 1963 the Buckley-Kendall friendship ruptured and never recovered. Judis, *William F. Buckley, Jr.,* 211–12.

50. Kendall to Francis Wilson, August 4, 1960, Wilson Papers.

51. See Kendall, *Contra Mundum,* 29, 40, 57; Nash, *Conservative Intellectual Movement,* 244, 245; Henry Regnery, *Memoirs of a Dissident Publisher* (New York and London: Harcourt Brace Jovanovich, 1979), 186.

52. A task that in any case has been undertaken elsewhere by this author (in *The Conservative Intellectual Movement in America Since 1945*) and by John P. East, among others. The purpose of the present chapter, of course, is not a textual analysis of Kendall's finished product as a conservative but an examination of his place within the conservative community to which (with so many misgivings) he belonged.

53. William F. Buckley Jr., "Hold on to Your Hats," *National Review* 14 (April 23, 1963): 324.

54. Kendall called himself an "Appalachians-to-the-Rockies patriot."

55. See Samuel Francis, "Prophet of the Heartland," 662–69.

CHAPTER 9: THE LIFE AND LEGACY OF RUSSELL KIRK

1. George A Panichas, ed., *The Essential Russell Kirk* (Wilmington, DE: ISI Books, 2007).

CHAPTER 13: THE INFLUENCE OF RICHARD WEAVER'S *IDEAS HAVE CONSEQUENCES* ON AMERICAN CONSERVATISM

1. For a sampling of tributes to Weaver soon after his death, see: Russell Kirk, "Richard Weaver, RIP," *National Review* 14 (April 23, 1963): 308; Kendall Beaton [Weaver's brother-in-law], "Richard M. Weaver: A Clear Voice in an Addled World" (typescript, August 5, 1963), copy enclosed with Beaton to Louis H. T. Dehmlow, August 11, 1963, Richard M. Weaver Collection, Division 1, File 4, Hilldale College, Hillsdale, Michigan; Ralph T. Eubanks, "Richard M. Weaver: In Memoriam," *Georgia Review* 17 (Winter 1963): 412–15; Wilma R. Ebbitt, "Richard Weaver, Teacher of Rhetoric," ibid., 415–18. Eubanks called Weaver "one of the ablest cultural critics of our times."

2. Nisbet's comment was printed on the front cover of the paperback edition of *Ideas Have Consequences* published by the University of Chicago Press in 1984.

3. Henry Regnery, "Richard Weaver: A Southern Agrarian at the University of Chicago," *Modern Age* 32 (Spring 1988): 111–12.

4. Eugene Genovese, "Ideas Had Consequences," *New Republic* 214 (June 17, 1996): 36.

5. Joseph Scotchie, *Barbarians in the Saddle: An Intellectual Biography of Richard M. Weaver* (New Brunswick, NJ and London: Transaction, 1997), x.

6. *New York Times,* June 2, 1983, C13.

7. The three books published by Weaver in his lifetime were: *Ideas Have Consequences* (Chicago: University of Chicago Press, 1948), *The Ethics of Rhetoric* (Chicago: Henry Regnery Company, 1953), and *Composition: A Course in Writing and Rhetoric* (New York: Henry Holt, 1957). The four that appeared between 1964–70 were: *Visions of Order: The Cultural Crisis of Our Time* (Baton Rouge: Louisiana State University Press, 1964), *Life Without Prejudice and Other Essays* (Chicago: Henry Regnery Company, 1965), *The Southern Tradition at Bay: A History of Postbellum Thought* (New Rochelle, NY: Arlington House, 1968), and *Language Is Sermonic: Richard M. Weaver on the Nature of Rhetoric* (Baton Rouge: Louisiana State University Press, 1970).

8. George M. Curtis III and James J. Thompson Jr., eds., *The Southern Essays of Richard M. Weaver* (Indianapolis: Liberty Press, 1987).

9. Richard M. Weaver, "Up from Liberalism" (1959), reprinted as a Heritage Foundation *President's Essay* (Washington, D.C., 1987), with a Foreword by Edwin J. Feulner Jr.

10. Richard M. Weaver, *Visions of Order: The Cultural Crisis of our Time* (Bryn Mawr, PA: Intercollegiate Studies Institute, 1995).

11. A recent bibliographic search yielded doctoral dissertations by Jing-Ling Jenny Lin (Ohio State University, 1991), Brenan R. Nierman (Georgetown University, 1993) and Fred Douglas Young (Georgia State University, 1994), as well as master's theses by Phillip Roy Ballard (East Texas State University, 1987), Christopher Todd Carver (Texas Tech University, 1993), Robert J. Drumm (Texas Tech University, 1995), Edward C. Reilly (University of Maine, 1990), and Lisa Jane Tyree (University of Arkansas, 1989). The two biographies of Weaver that have been published so far are Fred Douglas Young, *Richard M. Weaver, 1910–1963: A Life of the Mind* (Columbia, MO and London: University of Missouri Press, 1995), and Joseph Scotchie, *Barbarians in the Saddle* (already cited). A relevant monograph is Bernard K. Duffy and Martin J. Jacobi, *The Politics of Rhetoric: Richard M. Weaver and the Conservative Tradition* (Westport, CT: Greenwood Press, 1993). An excellent anthology of appreciative essays is Joseph Scotchie, ed., *The Vision of Richard Weaver* (New Brunswick, NJ and London: Transaction, 1995). Two articles of note are George A. Panichas, "Irving Babbitt and Richard Weaver;" *Modern Age* 38 (Summer 1996): 267–76, and R. V. Young, "Juliet and Shakespeare's Other Nominalists: Variations on a Theme by Richard Weaver," *Intercollegiate Review* 33 (Fall 1997): 18–29.

12. E. Victor Milione, "The Uniqueness of Richard M. Weaver," *Intercollegiate Review* 2 (September 1965): 67. See also Willmoore Kendall, "'How to Read Richard Weaver: Philosopher of 'We the (Virtuous) People,'" ibid., 77–86. According to Kendall, Weaver was "much eulogized but seldom if ever subjected to analysis and, what is more important, seldom if ever really listened to" (79).

13. Russell Kirk, *The Sword of Imagination* (Grand Rapids, MI: William B. Eerdmans, 1995), 173.

14. "In This Issue," *National Review* 14 (April 23, 1963): 303.

15. Eliseo Vivas, "Introduction" to *Visions of Order,* ix.

16. Clifford Amyx, "Weaver the Liberal: A Memoir," *Modern Age* 31 (Spring 1987): 106; Thomas Landess, "Is the Battle Over . . . Or Has It Just Begun?" *Southern Partisan* 3 (Spring 1983): 19; Eliseo Vivas, "The Mind of Richard Weaver," *Modern Age* 8 (Summer 1964): 307, 310; Edwin J. Feulner Jr., "Foreword" to his 1987 *President's Essay* cited above,

page 1; Eugene Davidson, "Richard Malcolm Weaver—Conservative," *Modern Age* 7 (Summer 1963): 229.

17. Eugene Davidson and Henry Regnery both spoke of Weaver in these terms. Davidson, "Richard Malcolm Weaver—Conservative," 227; Regnery, "A Southern Agrarian," 112.

18. The friend was Bernard Iddings Bell. Kirk, *Sword of Imagination,* 174.

19. Ralph T. Eubanks, "Richard M. Weaver, Friend of Traditional Rhetoric: An Appreciation," in Weaver, *Language Is Sermonic,* 4; Donald Davidson, "The Vision of Richard Weaver: A Foreword," in Weaver, *Southern Tradition at Bay,* 15.

20. Eubanks, "Richard M. Weaver, Friend of Traditional Rhetoric," 4.

21. Eugene Davidson, "Richard Malcolm Weaver—Conservative," 229–30.

22. Richard M. Weaver, "Up from Liberalism," *Modern Age* 3 (Winter 1958–59): 23.

23. Eugene Davidson remarked that "everything Weaver did evidenced his patient, stubborn battle on behalf of this core of values that he taught and by which he lived." Davidson, "Richard Malcolm Weaver–Conservative," 227.

24. Landess, "Is the Battle Over . . . ?" 19.

25. Eugene Davidson, "Richard Malcolm Weaver–Conservative," 227; Henry Regnery, *Memoirs of a Dissident Publisher* (New York and London: Harcourt Brace Jovanovich, 1979), 191–92; Fred Douglas Young, *Richard M. Weaver,* 166; Ted J. Smith III (Weaver's biographer) to the author, June 21, 1998.

26. Richard H. King, "Anti-Modernists All!" *Mississippi Review* 44 (Spring 1991): 194.

27. Walter Sullivan, *In Praise of Blood Sports and Other Essays* (Baton Rouge and London: Louisiana State University Press, 1990), 28.

28. Regnery, "A Southern Agrarian,"111; Feulner, Foreword to his 1987 *President's Essay,* 4; R. V. Young, "Juliet and Shakespeare's Other Nominalists," 18.

29. Nisbet comment on the cover of the 1984 paperback edition of *Ideas Have Consequences.*

30. Richard M. Weaver to Cleanth Brooks, January 28, 1948, Cleanth Brooks Papers, Box 15, Beinecke Rare Book and Manuscript Library, Yale University.

31. Weaver, Foreword to paperback edition of *Ideas Have Consequences* (Chicago, 1959 and 1984), v; list of reviews of *Ideas Have Consequences* provided to the author by Professor Ted J. Smith III.

32. Weaver to Donald Davidson, February 28, 1948, Donald Davidson Papers, Special Collections, Heard Library, Vanderbilt University.

33. Ibid.

34. Eliseo Vivas, "Historian and Moralist," *Kenyon Review* 10 (Spring 1948): 346.

35. Willmoore Kendall in *Journal of Politics* 11 (February 1949): 261.

36. Kirk, *Sword of Imagination,* 172; Kirk, "Ten Exemplary Conservatives" (lecture at the Heritage Foundation, Washington, D.C., December 11, 1986: Heritage Lecture 83), 8.

37. Russell Kirk, *Beyond the Dreams of Avarice* (Chicago: Henry Regnery Company, 1956), 80.

38. Ibid., 81.

39. Kirk, "Ten Exemplary Conservatives," 8.

40. Kendall in *Journal of Politics* 11 (February 1949): 260.

41. Frank S. Meyer, "Richard M. Weaver: An Appreciation," *Modern Age* 14 (Summer–Fall 1970): 243, 244.

42. Tillich's comment was printed on the jacket of the original hard-cover edition of *Ideas Have Consequences* and on the back cover of subsequent paperback editions.

43. Weaver, *Ideas Have Consequences,* 1.

44. Ibid.

45. Ibid., 2–3.
46. 1bid., 94.
47. Ibid., 98.
48. Ibid., 85, 89, 91.
49. Whittaker Chambers's essay about Toynbee was the cover story of the March 17, 1947, issue of *Time*. Chambers's piece is reprinted in Terry Teachout, ed., *Ghosts on the Roof: Selected Journalism of Whittaker Chambers, 1931–1959* (Washington, D.C.: Regnery Gateway, 1989), 141–49.
50. Arnold Toynbee, *Civilization on Trial* (New York: Oxford University Press, 1948).
51. Whittaker Chambers to William F. Buckley Jr., August 5, 1954, printed in William F. Buckley Jr., ed., *Odyssey of a Friend: Whittaker Chambers's Letters to William F. Buckley Jr., 1954–1961* (New York: Putnam, 1969), 67–68.
52. George R. Geiger, "We Note . . . The Consequences of Some Ideas," *Antioch Review* 8 (Spring 1948): 251–54; Dixon Wecter, "Can Metaphysics Save the World?" *Saturday Review* 31 (April 10, 1948): 7–8, 30–32; Herbert J. Muller; "The Revival of the Absolute," *Antioch Review* 9 (March 1949): 99–110; S. I. Hayakawa, *Symbol, Status, and Personality* (New York: Harcourt, Brace & World, 1963): 154–70. The epithet "Divine Doctors of the Great Books Movement" was Hayakawa's.
53. Hayakawa, *Symbol, Status, and Personality*, 155, 158–60.
54. Weaver's master's thesis was entitled "The Revolt against Humanism." He completed it at Vanderbilt University in 1934. See Fred Douglas Young, *Richard M. Weaver*, 56–58, for a discussion of the thesis.
55. Weaver, *Ideas Have Consequences*, 62, 130.
56. Willmoore Kendall, in his *Journal of Politics* review cited above, remarked that Weaver "on a number of counts . . . invites comparison" with Ortega y Gasset. One of Weaver's biographers has written that *Ideas Have Consequences* was "similar in both its theme and structure" to *The Revolt of the Masses*. (Scotchie, *Barbarians in the Saddle*, 44.) Weaver was undoubtedly familiar with Ortega's book. In Weaver's introduction (33) to *The Southern Tradition at Bay*, which he wrote shortly before *Ideas Have Consequences*, he discussed Ortega's concept of the "spoiled child" psychology and specifically mentioned *The Revolt of the Masses*.
57. For Weaver's conversion to Southern Agrarianism and to what he called "the poetic and ethical vision of life," see his autobiographical essay "Up from Liberalism" (cited above) and the biographies by Scotchie and Young.
58. One historian of the South has written of Weaver: "What was he saying in *Ideas Have Consequences* that Ransom, Tate, and Davidson had not said in *God Without Thunder*, *I'll Take My Stand*, *Who Owns America?* and *The Attack on Levithan?*" Fred Hobson, *Tell About the South* (Baton Rouge and London: Louisiana State University Press, 1983), 326.
59. John Crowe Ransom, for instance, directed Weaver's master's thesis.
60. Weaver, *Ideas Have Consequences*, 10.
61. Weaver to Donald Davidson, February 28, 1948.
62. The terms "'cultural pessimism'" and "declinist" come from Arthur Herman, *The Idea of Decline in Western History* (New York: Free Press, 1997). See especially pages 7–9, for his distinction between them. Herman's treatment of post-1945 "cultural pessimism" focuses on its manifestation on the Left, where, he argues, the "antimodern chorus in America today" has its "leading voices" (8). Herman does not mention Richard Weaver or (except in passing) other right-of-center declinists and cultural pessimists of the post-World War II period.

63. Weaver, *Ideas Have Consequences*, 1.

64. E. Victor Milione, "Ideas in Action: Forty Years of 'Educating for Liberty,'" *Intercollegiate Review* 29 (Fall 1993): 56.

65. Muller, "Revival of the Absolute," 106–7.

66. Weaver, *Ideas Have Consequences*, 162–63.

67. Ibid, 4.

68. Ibid, 52.

69. The text of Young Americans for Freedom's manifesto, known as the Sharon Statement, is printed in John A. Andrew III, *The Other Side of the Sixties* (New Brunswick, NJ and London: Rutgers University Press, 1997), 221–22.

70. Weaver, *Ideas Have Consequences*, 53, 21.

71. Ibid, 36.

72. Ibid, 131.

73. Ibid, 2.

74. W. E. Garrison, "Unraveling Mr. Weaver," *Christian Century* 65 (May 5, 1948): 416.

75. W. A. Orton, review in *Commonweal* 48 (May 14, 1948): 126.

76. Wecter, "Can Metaphysics Save the World?" 31; John Lewis, "Ideas and Consequences," *Science and Society* 14 (Winter 1949–50): 68–76. Weaver himself asserted in *Ideas Have Consequences*: "The way was prepared for the criteria of comfort and mediocrity when the Middle Ages abandoned the ethic of Plato for that of Aristotle. . . . In Thomism, based as it is on Aristotle, even the Catholic church turned away from the asceticism and the rigorous morality of the patristic fathers to accept a degree of pragmatic acquiescence in the world" (119). It should be noted that comfort and pragmatism were not terms of approval in Weaver's vocabulary.

77. Ted J. Smith III to the author, June 21, 1998. In his eulogy of Weaver, Russell Kirk asserted that Weaver attended Episcopal church services in Chicago just once a year (Kirk, "Richard Weaver, RIP," 308). Without a doubt, Weaver's churchgoing in Chicago was infrequent. Although raised in the Methodist/Disciples of Christ tradition, Weaver did not belong to a church in his Chicago years. According to Professor Smith, Weaver once told a University of Chicago colleague that if he joined a church it would be the Episcopal church.

78. John P. East, *The American Conservative Movement: The Philosophical Founders* (Chicago and Washington, D.C.: Regnery Books, 1986), 46–52. Of original sin, for example, Weaver wrote that "there is no concept that I regard as expressing a deeper insight into the enigma that is man" ("Up from Liberalism," 29).

79. A number of commentators have noticed this. See, for example, East, *American Conservative Movement*, 46; Jeffrey B. Gayner, "The Critique of Modernity in the Work of Richard M. Weaver," *Intercollegiate Review* 14 (Spring 1979): 99; Fred Douglas Young, *Richard M. Weaver*, 102, 167.

80. Fred Douglas Young, *Richard M. Weaver*, 20, 34, 102. Weaver once wrote: "Literalism is the materialism of religion. . . ." He claimed that his native region, the South, had "shunned" this materialism, "except in the crudest exhibitions of Fundamentalism." Weaver, *Southern Tradition at Bay*, 43.

81. Among the leading conservative intellectuals after World War II who converted to Roman Catholicism were Russell Kirk, Willmoore Kendall, and Frank S. Meyer, all of whom admired Weaver. I have found no evidence, however, that *Ideas Have Consequences* had any direct influence on their decisions to convert.

82. Weaver, *Ideas Have Consequences*, 3.

83. George H. Nash, *The Conservative Intellectual Movement in America Since 1945* (rev. ed. Wilmington, DE: Intercollegiate Studies Institute, 1996), 42–49.

84. Weaver, *Ideas Have Consequences,* 129.

85. Ibid., 1. Man is "free," said Weaver here, and "those consequences we are now expiating are the product not of biological or other necessity but of unintelligent choice."

86. Weaver, *Southern Tradition at Bay,* 394.

87. Weaver, *Ideas Have Consequences,* chapter 7. The quotations occur on pages 165 and 166.

88. Ibid., 69.

89. Ibid, 53.

90. Ibid, 62.

91. Ibid, 37–38.

92. Ibid, 107.

93. Ibid, 74–75, 110.

94. Ibid, 75.

95. Ibid, 105.

96. Ibid, 116, 105.

97. As an instructor at Texas A&M University in the late 1930s, Weaver (as he later put it) "encountered a rampant philistinism, abetted by technology, large-scale organization, and a complacent acceptance of success as the goal of life" ("Up from Liberalism," 24). It was, by all accounts, an unhappy time in his career, and it led directly to what he himself described as a conversion experience (ibid.). Already exposed to anticorporate, anti-Republican, and Socialist thinking as a college student (he became a Socialist in the year he graduated) Weaver then discovered another strand of antimodernism in the Southern Agrarians at Vanderbilt. In 1940 he left behind Texas A&M University—and all it stood for in his mind—and immersed himself in the literature of the postbellum South. This great turning in Weaver's life was, in the words of Donald Davidson, "the experience of a change of heart, of mind, of life" (Davidson, Foreword to *Southern Tradition at Bay,* 15). See also Fred Douglas Young, *Richard M. Weaver,* 61–67.

98. Weaver, *Ideas Have Consequences,* 132–33.

99. Ibid, 134. One reason Weaver opposed "finance capitalism" was that its "aggregation of vast properties under anonymous ownership" was "a constant invitation to further state direction of our lives and fortunes" (133).

100. Ibid, 134, 135.

101. Weaver to Donald Davidson, February 28, 1948.

102. Richard M Weaver, *The Ethics of Rhetoric* (Chicago: Henry Regnery Company, 1953).

103. Weaver was an enthusiastic supporter of *National Review.* Weaver to William F. Buckley Jr., June 14, 1956, William F. Buckley Jr., Papers, Box 4, Yale University Library.

104. Weaver to Cleanth Brooks, March 30, 1944, Brooks Papers, Box 15.

105. See Scotchie, *Barbarians in the Saddle,* 151–55, for a list of Weaver's contributions to *National Review* and most of his other published writings.

106. Weaver to Buckley, March 9, 1961, Buckley Papers, Box 17. See also Weaver to Buckley, September 14, 1962 and October 31, 1962, ibid., Box 23.

107. For Weaver's contributions to *Modern Age,* see Scotchie's bibliography.

108. Weaver to Donald Davidson, September 7, 1960, and October 5, 1961, Davidson Papers; Weaver to Robert Ritchie, March 30, 1963, Weaver Collection, Division 1, File 3; Regnery, "A Southern Agrarian," 112.

109. Weaver to Donald Davidson, September 7, 1960.

110. Information supplied by the Intercollegiate Studies Institute, March 10, 1998. Weaver remained on the board until his death.

111. The pamphlets were *Education and the Individual* (1959), *Relativism and the Crisis of Our Time* (1960), and *Academic Freedom: The Principle and the Problems* (1963). A fourth Weaver essay—originally a 1962 speech entitled "The Role of Education in Shaping Our Society"—was published by ISI several years after his death. For more on Weaver's work with ISI, see his correspondence with E. Victor Milione, Don Lipsett, and other ISI representatives, 1959–63, in the Weaver Collection, Division 1, File 3.

112. Weaver to Charles R. Hoeflich, April 19, 1961, Weaver Collection, Division 1, File 3. See also Weaver to Don Lipsett, January 23, 1962, in the same file.

113. Weaver to E. Victor Milione, March 14, 1963, Weaver Collection, Division 1, File 3.

114. Weaver to Robert Ritchie, March 30, 1963.

115. E. Victor Milione to Weaver, January 29, 1959, Weaver Collection, Division 1, File 3.

116. Information supplied by the Intercollegiate Studies Institute, March 10, 1998.

117. Weaver, Foreword to 1959 paperback edition of *Ideas Have Consequences,* vi. At about this time, Weaver had completed the first draft of another book of cultural criticism, the posthumously published *Visions of Order.* It had many similarities in perspective with *Ideas Have Consequences,* particularly in its view that the West had suffered an undeniable cultural decline in the past half century. (Weaver, *Visions of Order,* 3–5.)

118. Nash, *Conservative Intellectual Movement,* 383–84.

119. Weaver, *Ideas Have Consequences,* 181. Weaver wrote here: "Individualism, with its connotation of irresponsibility, is a direct invitation to selfishness, and all that this treatise has censured can be traced in some way to individualist mentality."

120. Weaver to Hoeflich, April 19, 1961.

121. Masthead of *New Individualist Review,* April 1961–Spring 1963. Weaver was much admired by the journal's young editors and contributors. See "In Memoriam: Richard M. Weaver," *New Individualist Review* 2 (Spring 1963): 2.

122. Richard M. Weaver, "How to Argue the Conservative Cause" (typescript of a speech before an ISI group in Chicago, September 22, 1962), copy in Weaver Collection, Division 3. This is an abridged and slightly variant version of a public lecture, "The Conservative Cause," which Weaver first presented at the University of Wisconsin, under the auspices of the Wisconsin Conservative Club, on April 22, 1959. Audio recordings of the 1959 speech are in the Weaver Collection at Hilldale College. Both versions (1959 and 1962) made the same points discussed in my text.

123. Richard M. Weaver, "The Southern Phoenix," *Georgia Review* 17 (Spring 1963): 6–17. In early 1963, Weaver was preparing to teach at Vanderbilt University in the academic year 1963–64 (and very possibly longer). Fred Douglas Young, *Richard M. Weaver,* 175–76; Scotchie, *Barbarians in the Saddle,* 15.

124. Kirk, "Richard Weaver, RIP," 308.

125. Scotchie's bibliography is the best introduction to this expanding literature.

126. Frank S. Meyer, ed., *What Is Conservatism?* (New York: Holt, Rinehart and Winston, 1964), dedication page.

127. Kendall, "How to Read Richard Weaver," 77–86.

128. Ibid, 80.

129. For Weaver's principal articles on Southern themes, see Curtis and Thompson, eds., *Southern Essays of Richard M. Weaver.* See also Weaver, "Integration Is Communization," in *National Review* 4 (July 13, 1957): 67–68; and Weaver, "The Regime of the South," *National Review* 6 (March 14, 1959): 587–89.

130. Lewis P. Simpson, "The Story of M. E. Bradford," *Southern Literary Journal* 26 (Spring 1994): 103.

131. M. E. Bradford, *Remembering Who We Are: Observations of a Southern Conservative* (Athens, GA: University of Georgia Press, 1985): 88. See also Bradford, "The Agrarianism of Richard Weaver: Beginnings and Completions," *Modern Age* 14 (Summer–Fall 1970): 249–56.

132. Landess, "Is the Battle Over . . . ?" 17.

133. Documentation on this effort may be found in the Weaver Collection, Division 1, File 6.

134. Scotchie, *Barbarians in the Saddle,* 155; Landess, "Is the Battle Over . . . ?"

135. For example: Hobson, *Tell About the South,* 323–35; George Core, "One View of the Castle: Richard Weaver and the Incarnate World of the South," *Spectrum* [School of Arts and Sciences, Georgia State University] 2 (June 1972): 1–9; William C. Havard, "Richard M. Weaver: The Rhetor as Philosopher," in Mark Royden Winchell, ed., *The Vanderbilt Tradition* (Baton Rouge and London: Louisiana State University Press, 1991), 163–74.

136. Chilton Williamson Jr., "Richard Weaver: Stranger in Paradise," *National Review* 37 (December 31, 1985): 96, 98, 100.

137. For a brief summary of the controversy, see Nash, *Conservative Intellectual Movement,* 337–39.

138. See Scotchie, *Barbarians in the Saddle,* particularly chapters 3 and 8, for a good expression of this point of view.

139. Eugene Genovese, *The Southern Tradition: The Achievement and Limitations of an American Conservatism* (Cambridge, MA and London: Harvard University Press, 1994), 35.

140. Weaver, *Ethics of Rhetoric,* 212, 215.

141. Ben C. Toledano, "Up from Capitalism," *National Review* 48 (January 29, 1996): 64–65.

142. Richard M. Weaver, "The Meaning of Name and Place" (address at the Weaver family reunion, August 10, 1950), printed in a pamphlet entitled *Two Unpublished Essays by the Late Richard M. Weaver* (Glendale, SC: Foundation for American Education, 1978). This essay was reprinted in the Spring–Summer 1981 issue of the *Southern Partisan.* In this address Weaver wrote: "I have been condemned for the past six years to earn my living in that most brutal of cities, a place where all the vices of urban and industrial society break forth in a kind of evil flower. I sometimes think of the University to which I am attached as a missionary outpost in darkest Chicago. There we labor as we can to convert the heathen, without much reward of success. But of course we learn many things about what is happening to this country."

143. In 1996, the neoconservative editor Richard John Neuhaus called Weaver "an intellectual saint in the conservative cult called Southern Agrarianism." Neuhaus immediately added: "We have had our problems with some who claim to profess that creed, but in Weaver's thought it is undeniably attractive, often compellingly so." Neuhaus thereupon reprinted an excerpt from Weaver's essay "Up from Liberalism" and hoped that some of its readers would be inspired to read *Ideas Have Consequences,* "a closely reasoned and elegantly argued conservative classic" (*First Things,* no. 60 [February 1996]: 87–88).

144. During his career Weaver occasionally had been criticized by fellow conservatives on a few issues, notably his interpretation of Edmund Burke and Abraham Lincoln. But he had never been subjected to a frontal assault.

145. R. Emmett Tyrrell Jr., *The Conservative Crack-Up* (New York: Simon & Schuster, 1992), 33.

146. Samuel Francis, *Beautiful Losers: Essays on the Failure of American Conservatism* (Columbia, MO: University of Missouri Press, 1993), "Ideas and No Consequences," especially 1–4.

147. Weaver, *Southern Tradition at Bay*, 391.

148. Jeffrey Hart, "Dream Weaver," *National Review* 48 (March 25, 1996): 60–61.

149. Weaver, *Ideas Have Consequences*, 187.

150. Kirk, *Beyond the Dreams of Avarice*, 81.

151. Robert Bork, *Slouching Towards Gomorrah: Modern Liberalism and American Decline* (New York: ReganBooks, 1996). Note the subtitle.

152. Weaver, *Ideas Have Consequences*, 10.

CHAPTER 15: HILLSDALE COLLEGE: A MODEL FOR CONSERVATIVES

1. *Chicago Tribune*, July 18, 1937, 15.

CHAPTER 17: GOD AND MAN AT YALE REVISITED

1. See John Judis, *William F. Buckley, Jr.: Patron Saint of the Conservatives* (New York: Simon & Schuster, 1988).

2. The text of Buckley's proposed Alumni Day address of February 22, 1950, is printed in William F. Buckley Jr., *God and Man at Yale* (Chicago: Henry Regnery Company, 1951), 222–27, as well as in subsequent editions of this book.

3. Ibid., 129–30; William F. Buckley Jr., *Miles Gone By: A Literary Autobiography* (New York: Regnery Publishing, 2000), 106; Judis, *William F. Buckley, Jr.*, 76–78.

4. Buckley, *Miles Gone By*, 106.

5. Buckley, *God and Man at Yale*, xii–xiii.

6. Buckley, *God and Man at Yale*, ix.

7. Ibid., xi–xiii, xv.

8. Ibid., 9.

9. Ibid., 25.

10. Ibid., 26–34.

11. Ibid., 46–57.

12. Ibid., 46, 113.

13. Ibid., 114.

14. Ibid., 114–15.

15. Ibid., 116, 134–35, 175, 185. According to Buckley, "every citizen of a free economy, no matter the wares that he plies, must defer to the sovereignty of the consumer" (185). Colleges and universities were no exception.

16. Ibid., 175, 194.

17. Ibid., 43.

18. Ibid., 151, 154–55, 186.

19. Ibid., 181.

20. Ibid., 197, 195–96, 195, 190.

21. Ibid., 193.

22. *New York Times*, October 30, 1951, 27.

23. Regnery to William F. Buckley Sr. (Buckley's father), April 14, 1952, Henry Regnery Papers, Box 11, Hoover Institution Archives, Stanford University; copyright page for the December 1968 paperback edition of Buckley's book (for the listing by date of the various printings between 1951 and 1968).

24. "Secular, Collectivist Yale?" *Newsweek* 38 (October 22, 1951): 70; "Rebel in Reverse," *Time* 58 (October 29, 1951): 57–58; "God, Socialism and Yale," *Life* 31 (October 29, 1951): 32.
25. "Isms and the University," *Saturday Review* 34 (December 15, 1951): 18–19, 44–45.
26. See Judis, *William F. Buckley, Jr.,* 89, and the following correspondence: Regnery to William F. Buckley Jr., September 24 and 29, 1951, and October 22, 1951; and Regnery to William F. Buckley Sr., January 8 and 28, 1952. All in Regnery Papers, Boxes 10 and 11.
27. Henry Regnery, *Memoirs of a Dissident Publisher* (New York: Harcourt Brace Jovanovich, 1979), 168; Judis, *William F. Buckley, Jr.,* 88–89.
28. "God, Secularism and Yale," 32.
29. "Rebel in Reverse," 57.
30. Buckley, *God and Man at Yale,* xii.
31. Buckley to the editor, *Yale Daily News,* November 26, 1951, William F. Buckley Jr. Papers, Yale University Library.
32. Dwight Macdonald, "God and Buckley at Yale," *Reporter* 6 (May 27, 1952): 36.
33. Buckley to the editor, *Yale Daily News,* November 26, 1951; Judis, *William F. Buckley, Jr.,* 93; Buckley, introduction to the 1977 reissue of *God and Man at Yale.* This lengthy (forty-six page) introduction can be found in his *God and Man at Yale* (South Bend, IN: Gateway Books, 1986), v–l. It is reprinted also in Buckley, *Miles Gone By,* 57–94. Page citations below will be from the 1986 printing.
34. *New York Times,* October 12, 1951, 25, and February 18, 1952, 1, 12; Buckley introduction to *God and Man at Yale,* 1977 edition, xxvii.
35. McGeorge Bundy, "The Attack on Yale," *Atlantic Monthly* 188 (November 1951): 50–52.
36. William F. Buckley Jr., "The Changes at Yale," *Atlantic Monthly* 188 (December 1951): 78–82; Bundy, "McGeorge Bundy Replies," ibid., 82–83; Judis, *William F. Buckley, Jr.,* 93.
37. Judis, *William F. Buckley, Jr.,* 93; Buckley, introduction to *God and Man at Yale,* 1977 edition, xxvii.
38. Buckley, "Changes at Yale," 78.
39. Theodore M. Greene, quoted in *Time* 58 (October 29, 1951): 58, and in Buckley, introduction to *God and Man at Yale,* 1977 edition, xxxv.
40. Quoted in Buckley's 1977 introduction to *God and Man at Yale,* xxxi.
41. Robert Hatch, "Enforcing Truth," *New Republic* 125 (December 3, 1951): 19.
42. S. Vernon McCasland in *Journal of Bible and Religion* 20 (April 1952): 135.
43. Quoted in Regnery, *Memoirs,* 169.
44. Fred Rodell, "That Book About Yale: The Attack on Free Universities," *Progressive* 16 (February 1952): 14–16.
45. Vern Countryman review in *Yale Law Journal* 61 (February 1952): 272–83.
46. Frank Ashburn review in *Saturday Review* 34 (December 15, 1951): 44–45.
47. Buckley, *Miles Gone By,* 106.
48. Henry Regnery to Buckley, September 24, 1951.
49. Buckley, *God and Man at Yale,* 194. See also 195.
50. In the fiscal year 1950–51, which ended on June 30, 1951, contributions to Yale University's Alumni Fund exceeded $1,000,000—a record for Yale and apparently "an all-time record for any university" (*New York Times,* July 9, 1951, 23; Macdonald, "God and Buckley at Yale," 37). A possible loss of $1,000,000 in donations (because of Buckley's book) would have been a humiliating blow to Yale's fundraisers.
51. *New York Times,* June 12, 1951, 1, 25.
52. Countryman review, 283.
53. Buckley, introduction to *God and Man at Yale,* 1977 edition, xxviii.
54. In a private letter that came to Buckley's attention, Yale's president claimed that Buck-

ley's forthcoming book (which he had not yet seen) was an attack on academic freedom from a "militant Catholic viewpoint" (a charge Buckley stoutly denied). Buckley, letter to the editor, *Yale Daily News,* November 26, 1951.

55. Bundy, "McGeorge Bundy Replies," 84; Bundy, "The Attack on Yale," 50.

56. Rodell, "That Book About Yale," 15.

57. Bundy, "The Attack on Yale," 50.

58. Quoted in Buckley, introduction to *God and Man at Yale,* 1977 edition, xxi, and in William F. Buckley Jr., *Nearer, My God: An Autobiography of Faith* (New York: Doubleday, 1997), 30n.

59. Buckley, letter to the editor, *Yale Daily News,* November 26, 1951; Judis, *William F. Buckley, Jr.,* 93–94.

60. Quoted in Judis, *William F. Buckley, Jr.,* 93.

61. George Marsden, *The Soul of the American University: From Protestant Establishment to Established Nonbelief* (New York: Oxford University Press, 1994), 13–14.

62. Sidney Hook, *Heresy, Yes; Conspiracy, No* (New York, 1953), 220.

63. Paul Blanshard, *American Freedom and Catholic Power* (Boston: Beacon Press, 1949).

64. Buckley, *God and Man at Yale,* 18.

65. John T. McGreevy, *Catholicism and American Freedom: A History* (New York: W. W. Norton & Company, 2003), 166–68.

66. Christopher E. Fullman, "God and Man and Mr. Buckley," *Catholic World* 175 (May 1952): 104–8; Macdonald, "God and Buckley at Yale," 36; "Yale vs. Harvard," *Commonweal* 56 (June 27, 1952): 285.

67. Such right-wing publications as the *Chicago Tribune,* the *Freeman, Barron's,* and the *American Mercury* published favorable reviews. Around the beginning of 1952, Buckley compiled a dossier of these and other positive responses to his book. A copy of this document is in the Regnery Papers, Box 11. Buckley did not lack for sympathizers in the popular press.

68. Regnery to Buckley, November 20 and 30, 1951, Regnery Papers, Box 10.

69. Russell Kirk, *Academic Freedom: An Essay in Definition* (Chicago: Henry Regnery Company, 1955), 118–26. See also Kirk's introduction to William F. Buckley Jr., *Rumbles Left and Right* (New York: Putnam, 1963), 14.

70. Macdonald, "God and Buckley at Yale," 36. Years later Buckley noted: "I think it is safe to say that no fully integrated member of the intellectual community associated himself with my position on academic freedom." Buckley, introduction to *God and Man at Yale,* 1977 edition, xxxix.

71. Buckley, "Changes at Yale," 82.

72. Buckley, introduction to *God and Man at Yale,* 1977 edition, xlv, xxxix.

73. William F. Buckley Jr., "Father Fullman's Assault," *Catholic World* 175 (August 1952): 332.

74. Buckley, "Changes at Yale," 80; Buckley, introduction to *God and Man at Yale,* 1977 edition, xxi–xxii.

75. Buckley, introduction to *God and Man at Yale,* 1977 edition, xix.

76. Ibid., xlvi and xlvii.

77. Interview of Buckley in *Civil Liberties Review* 4 (March–April 1978): 48–49; interview of Buckley in *Prospect* (March 1984): 12.

78. Macdonald, "God and Buckley at Yale," 37; Buckley, introduction to *God and Man at Yale,* xxviii.

79. M. Stanton Evans, *Revolt on the Campus* (Chicago: Henry Regnery Company, 1961), 2.

80. *New York Times,* July 5, 1952, 23; Regnery, *Memoirs,* 170.

81. Buckley, introduction to *God and Man at Yale,* 1977 edition, xxviii.

82. Buckley, *God and Man at Yale,* 114; Buckley, "Changes at Yale," 80.

83. Buckley, Foreword to *God and Man at Yale,* 1951 edition, xiv.

84. *New York Times,* October 21, 1967, 1, 35; ibid., October 29, 1967, E9; ibid., March 9, 1968, 31; ibid., June 17, 1968, 1, 26. See also Buckley, "What Makes Bill Buckley Run," *Atlantic Monthly* 221 (April 1968): 65–69. Buckley lost to Cyrus R. Vance, who later became President Jimmy Carter's secretary of state.

85. John Chamberlain, *A Life with the Printed Word* (Chicago: Regnery Gateway, 1982), 147.

86. William F. Buckley Jr., *Let Us Talk of Many Things* (New York: Forum, 2000), 249–50. Professor Fred Rodell, who called himself an "old friend" of Chamberlain, nevertheless publicly charged that it had been "irresponsible" of Chamberlain to write an introduction to Buckley's book. Rodell alleged that it was "tragic" that "men like John Chamberlain . . . should lend their influence to what is essentially a know-nothing campaign" against the "spirit of free inquiry." Rodell, "That Book about Yale," 16. The passions surrounding the Buckley book ran deep.

87. Buckley, *Let Us Talk of Many Things,* 249.

88. Regnery to Buckley, December 5, 1951, Regnery Papers, Box 10; Regnery, *Memoirs,* 170–73; *New York Times,* June 23, 1996, 33; Buckley, *Let Us Talk of Many Things,* 192.

89. George H. Nash, *The Conservative Intellectual Movement in America Since 1945,* rev. ed. (Wilmington, DE: ISI Books, 2006), 69–70.

90. Ibid., 213.

91. Benjamin Hart, *Poisoned Ivy* (New York: Stein and Day, 1984), with a Foreword by Buckley; Roger Kimball, *Tenured Radicals: How Politics Has Corrupted Our Higher Education* (New York: Harper & Row, 1990); Dinesh D'Souza, *Illiberal Education: The Politics of Race and Sex on Campus* (New York: Free Press, 1991).

92. Buckley, "Changes at Yale," 82.

93. Buckley, *Rumbles Left and Right,* 134.

94. Buckley gave a commencement address at Grove City College on May 18, 1991 and received an honorary degree.

95. Cited in note 61.

96. Buckley, interview in *Civil Liberties Review* 4 (March–April 1978): 49.

CHAPTER 22: JEWS FOR JOE MCCARTHY

A Note on Sources

The location, if any, of the records of the American Jewish League Against Communism is unknown. But its remarkable story can be traced through a rich array of published and unpublished sources, cited below. I wish to acknowledge and thank the following institutions for facilitating my research: the Jacob Rader Marcus Center of the American Jewish Archives, the Klau Library of Hebrew Union College, the Hoover Institution Archives, Library of Congress, Mount Holyoke College Library, Yale University Library, and YIVO Institute for Jewish Research.

1. For biographical information on Benjamin Schultz (1906–78), see: *New York Times,* April 25, 1978, 40, and "The Strange Career of Rabbi Schultz," *New York Post,* December 6–10, 1954 (a critical but informative five-part series).

2. Benjamin Schultz, letter to the editor, *New York Times,* June 13, 1946, 26; Schultz,

"American Jews Show CP the Door," *New Leader* 30 (July 19, 1947): 4, 15; *New York Post,* December 8, 1954.

3. *New York Post,* December 8, 1954; *New York Times,* March 6, 1970, 39.

4. S. Andhil Fineberg memorandum to Louis Bennett, October 23, 1947, American Jewish Committee (hereinafter AJC) Records, GEN-12 series, Box 13, "American Jewish League Against Communism 47–49" folder, YIVO Institute of Jewish Research, New York City.

5. *National Jewish Post,* October 24, 1947, 5. The *World-Telegram* promised "a startling revelation of the foothold which Communists have gained in our churches."

6. *New York World-Telegram,* October 14, 15, 16, 1947 (a three-part series).

7. Ibid., October 14, 1947.

8. Ibid., October 15, 1947.

9. Ibid., November 7, 1947.

10. Ibid.

11. See, for example, *New York Times,* April 3, 1948, 7.

12. Quoted in Melvin I. Urofsky, *A Voice that Spoke for Justice: The Life and Times of Stephen S. Wise* (Albany: State University of New York Press, 1982), 358.

13. According to Wise's biographer: "Perhaps indiscriminately Wise allowed his name to be used by a number of 'peace committees' later charged with being Communist front groups." Ibid., 359.

14. Schultz, "American Jews Show CP the Door," 15.

15. *New York World-Telegram,* October 15, 1947.

16. *New York Post,* December 8, 1954. See also Schultz's column, "A Weekly Digest of the Yiddish Press," in *National Jewish Post,* April 5, 1946, 15, and May 24, 1946, 14.

17. In April 1947 Wise told Schultz of his "disgust" for Schultz's column in the *National Jewish Post* and informed him that Wise was "thoroughly ashamed of your performances and to have to admit that you are an alumnus of the Jewish Institute of Religion." Undeterred, Schultz replied that he would "continue my discussion of attempted Communist domination of the American Jewish Congress, an organization which I have praised on occasion; and of which you are unhappily the president at the moment." Quoted in *New York Post,* December 8, 1954.

Schultz's "Uptown and Downtown" column on April 11, 1947, contained a passage captioned "The A. J. Congress and Communists." It quoted a source alleging that Communists and fellow travelers continued to belong to (and feel "at home" in) the American Jewish Congress (which Wise, of course, headed). *National Jewish Post,* April 11, 1947, 4.

18. *National Jewish Post,* October 24, 1947, 5. Wise added that Schultz "knows that his articles contain a minimum of truth and a maximum of untruthful propaganda in behalf of his Red-baiting employers."

19. S. Andhil Fineberg to Eugene Lyons, September 5, 1951, in AJC Records, GEN-12 series, Box 13, "American Jewish League Against Communism 51" folder. In 1947, Fineberg—a rabbi and a member of the staff of the American Jewish Committee—was a friend of Schultz and a resident of a neighboring city. Schultz consulted him during the controversy touched off by the *World-Telegram* articles. See ibid. and Fineberg's memorandum of November 30, 1972, entitled "Solomon Andhil Fineberg Archives: Communism–American Jewish League Against," in S. Andhil Fineberg Papers, Box 4–7, Jacob Rader Marcus Center of the American Jewish Archives (hereinafter AJA), Hebrew Union College-Jewish Institute of Religion, Cincinnati, Ohio.

20. *National Jewish Post,* October 24, 1947, 5; Civil Rights Division of the Anti-Defamation League of B'nai B'rith, memorandum on American Jewish League Against Com-

munism, Inc., enclosed with J. Harold Saks to ADL Regional Offices, April 15, 1948, copy in AJC Records, GEN-12 series, Box 13, "American Jewish League Against Communism 47–49" folder.

21. Fineberg memorandum to Bennett, October 23, 1947; Fineberg to Lyons, September 5, 1951; Fineberg to Lyons, September 24, 1951, Fineberg Papers, Box 4–7.

22. *National Jewish Post,* October 31, 1947, 3.

23. Fineberg memorandum, November 30, 1972. The rabbi who pointed out the necessity for a public hearing—and thereby saved Schultz from immediate expulsion—was Fineberg himself. In his 1972 memorandum Fineberg also recorded that he succeeded in discouraging a similar effort to expel Schultz from the Central Conference of American Rabbis.

24. *New York Times,* October 23, 1947, 25; *National Jewish Post,* October 31, 1947, 3, 14; *New York Post,* December 8, 1954.

25. *New York Times,* October 23, 1947, 25; *National Jewish Post,* October 31, 1947, 3.

26. So claimed both Schultz and the newspaper which printed his series. *New York World-Telegram,* November 7, 1947; *National Jewish Post,* November 14, 1947, 3. According to the *World-Telegram:* "Since their publication, not a single statement" in Schultz's articles had been "challenged from a factual standpoint." Schultz contended that his articles were "based on facts." *National Jewish Post,* October 31, 1947, 3.

27. Fineberg to Lyons, September 24, 1951.

28. American Jewish Committee memorandum on Rabbi Benjamin Schultz, September 22, 1952, AJC Records, GEN-12 series, Box 12, "American Jewish League Against Communism 52–53" folder; *New York Post,* December 8, 1954.

29. *National Jewish Post,* October 31, 1947, 3; [S. Andhil Fineberg], "The American Jewish League Against Communism" (typescript, January 9, 1950), in AJC Records, GEN-12 series, Box 13, "American Jewish League Against Communism 50" folder; *New York Post,* December 8, 1954.

30. *New York Times,* October 22, 1947, 31; *New York Herald-Tribune,* October 22, 1947.

31. Ibid. Two days later the board's chairman admitted that the board's decision to move against the rabbi at this particular juncture had been "bad timing," creating an erroneous impression that "we were defending Communists or might be Communists ourselves. Nothing could be more wrong." He insisted that Schultz's newspaper series "had nothing to do with the trustees' decision to ask him to resign. We feel that for years he has neglected his duties and that feeling just boiled over" (*National Jewish Post,* October 31, 1947, 3).

32. *New York World-Telegram,* October 22, 1947.

33. Ibid., November 7, 1947.

34. *National Jewish Post,* October 31, 1947, 3.

35. *New York Post,* December 8, 1954.

36. Fineberg memorandum, November 30, 1972.

37. *National Jewish Post,* October 31, 1947, 3; *New York Times,* November 8, 1947, 18; *New York Post,* December 8, 1954.

38. *New York World-Telegram,* November 7, 1947; *New York Times,* November 8, 1947, 18; *National Jewish Post,* November 14, 1947, 3.

39. Fineberg to Lyons, September 5, 1951.

40. Benjamin Schultz testimony, July 13, 1949, in U.S. Congress, House of Representatives, Committee on Un-American Activities, 81st Congress, 1st Session, *Hearings Regarding Communist Infiltration of Minority Groups–Part I* (Washington, D.C., 1949), 435. At the

time of his resignation from his position in Yonkers in 1947, Schultz announced that he would "continue to fight communism as strongly as before through my writing and lecturing." He added that he was completing a book "on the truth about Jews in Russia" (*National Jewish Post*, November 14, 1947, 3).

41. Joseph Keeley, *The China Lobby Man: The Story of Alfred Kohlberg* (New Rochelle, NY: Arlington House, 1969), 196–99; Isaac Don Levine, ed., *Plain Talk: An Anthology from the Leading Anti-Communist Magazine of the 40s* (New Rochelle, NY: Arlington House, 1976), xii.

42. Nathan Glazer, *The Social Basis of American Communism* (New York: Harcourt, Brace & World, 1961), 130–31; Arthur Liebman, "The Ties That Bind: The Jewish Support for the Left in the United States," *American Jewish Historical Quarterly* 66 (December 1976): 306–7. For extended discussion of American Jews and the Communist Party, see: Glazer, *Social Basis*, 130–68; Harvey Klehr, *Communist Cadre: the Social Background of the American Communist Party Elite* (Stanford, CA: Hoover Institution Press, 1978), 37–52; and Arthur Liebman, *Jews and the Left* (New York: Wiley, 1979), 57–66.

43. Liebman, "The Ties That Bind," 296, 307.

44. Ibid., 306.

45. *New York Post*, December 9, 1954; Keeley, *China Lobby Man*, 248; *Jews Against Communism* 6 (Autumn 1953): 3. The latter source—the official newsletter of the American Jewish League Against Communism—stated flatly that the league was founded at a meeting in Eugene Lyons's home in November 1947. However, it was not formally incorporated until February 1948.

46. *New York Post*, December 9, 1954.

47. The league's platform of March 1948, printed in *Jews Against Communism* 8 (Summer 1955): 4, 6.

48. *New York Post*, December 9, 1954.

49. Ibid.; masthead of form letter ("Dear friend") by Rabbi Benjamin Schultz (executive director of the nascent league), April 21, 1948, in AJC Records, GEN-12 series, Box 13, "American Jewish League Against Communism 47–49" folder.

50. American Jewish Committee memorandum, "Rabbi Benjamin Schultz," July 27, 1950, in AJC Records, GEN-12 series, Box 13, "American Jewish League Against Communism 50" folder; Max J. Merritt to George Sokolsky, January 25, 1962, Marvin Liebman Papers, Box 8, Hoover Institution Archives, Stanford University. According to the former source, David Dubinsky (the head of the union) was among the league's three principal contributors. According to the latter source, Dubinsky's union gave the league $5,000 on one occasion.

51. Keeley, *China Lobby Man*, 248–49.

52. Kohlberg, quoted in *New York Post*, December 9, 1954.

53. *New York Times*, March 15, 1948, 7.

54. *New York Post*, December 9, 1954; Keeley, *China Lobby Man*, 248–49.

55. *New York Times*, March 15, 1948, 7; copies of press clippings enclosed with Rabbi Benjamin Schultz's form letter of April 21, 1948.

56. *New York Times*, December 6, 1954.

57. *Jews Against Communism* 1 (July–August 1948): 1; ibid., 1 (High Holy Days, 1948): 6; [S. Andhil Fineberg], "The American Jewish League Against Communism." As mentioned above, *Jews Against Communism* was the league's newsletter.

58. *New York Times*, April 26, 1948, 4.

59. *Jews Against Communism* 1 (July–August 1948): 2.

60. *New York Times,* May 16, 1948, Section I, 17.

61. Ibid.; *Jews Against Communism* 1 (July–August 1948): 1; ibid., 1 (High Holy Days, 1948): 2.

62. *New York Times,* July 26, 1948, 6; *Jews Against Communism* 1 (High Holy Days, 1948): 1, 4; Benjamin Schultz testimony, July 13, 1949, 433–44 (cited in note 40); *New York Times,* July 14, 1949, 1, 16.

63. Benjamin Schultz testimony, May 18, 1949, in U.S. Congress, Senate, Subcommittee of the Committee of the Judiciary, 81st Congress, 1st Session, *Control of Subversive Activities* (Washington, D.C., 1949), 124.

64. American Jewish League Against Communism, *Jews Against Communism* (pamphlet, n.d., but probably early 1949), copy in AJC Records, GEN-12 series, Box 12, "American Jewish League Against Communism 52–53" folder; *Jews Against Communism* 1 (July–August 1948): 3; *New York Times,* September 20, 1948, 12. See also *New York Times,* July 25, 1949, 7, and September 15, 1949, 30.

65. Gregor Aronson, *Soviet Russia and the Jews* (New York: American Jewish League Against Communism, 1949); *Jews Against Communism* 6 (Autumn 1953): 3 (referring to Aronson's study as "the pioneer pamphlet in the field"); Benjamin Schultz testimony, September 25, 1954, in U.S. Congress, House of Representatives, Select Committee on Communist Aggression, 83d Congress, 2d Session, *Treatment of Jews by the Soviet* (Washington, D.C., 1954), 94.

66. American Jewish League Against Communism, Foreword to Aronson, *Soviet Russia and the Jews.*

67. *Jews Against Communism* (pamphlet, n.d.), cited above.

68. Benjamin Schultz testimony, May 13, 1948, in U.S. Congress, Senate, Committee on the Judiciary, 80th Congress, 2d Session, *Control of Subversive Activities* (Washington, D.C., 1948), 361–62.

69. Benjamin Schultz testimony, May 18, 1949, in U.S. Congress, Senate, Subcommittee of the Committee on the Judiciary, 81st Congress, 1st Session, *Control of Subversive Activities* (Washington, D.C., 1949), 120–21.

70. *Jews Against Communism* (pamphlet, n.d.).

71. American Jewish League Against Communism letter to New York City Board of Education, January 13, 1949, copy in AJC Records, GEN-12 series, Box 13, "American Jewish League Against Communism 47–49" folder; *New York Times,* January 14, 1949, 25, and January 21, 1949, 23.

72. Ibid.; Liebman, "The Ties That Bind," 297.

73. League letter to Board of Education, January 13, 1949; *New York Times,* January 14, 1949, 25.

74. *New York Times,* January 21, 1949, 23.

75. [Fineberg], "The American Jewish League Against Communism."

76. Ibid.; *New York Times,* September 21, 1949, 20.

77. Schultz testimony, July 13, 1949, 444.

78. [Fineberg], "The American Jewish League Against Communism."

79. *Congressional Record* 95 (May 11, 1949): A2862–63.

80. American Jewish Committee memorandum on Schultz, July 27, 1950; *New York Times,* February 20, 1952, 31.

81. American Jewish Committee memorandum on Schultz, July 27, 1950.

82. *New York Times,* April 12, 1948, 19.

83. See, for example, *New York Times,* July 6, 1949, 23.

84. Ibid., January 27, 1950, 14, and January 30, 1950, 5.

85. Ibid., August 15, 1948, Section I, 4; Schultz testimony, May 18, 1949, 124. Even before the league was founded, Schultz urged the National Conference of Christians and Jews to create a "committee of national religious leaders . . . to investigate communism in the churches." *New York Times,* November 15, 1947, 19.

86. *New York Times,* January 13, 1949, 14.

87. Washington, D.C. *Times-Herald,* March 20, 1949; *New York Post,* March 22, 1949; [Fineberg], "The American Jewish League Against Communism."

88. Anti-Defamation League, Civil Rights Division, memorandum on American Jewish League Against Communism, ca. April 15, 1948 (cited in note 20).

89. Joseph Woolfson memorandum to David Danzig, December 15, 1949, AJC Records, GEN-12 series, Box 13, "American Jewish League Against Communism 47–49" folder; [Fineberg], "The American Jewish League Against Communism"; Fineberg memorandum to David Danzig, January 10, 1950, AJC Records, GEN-12 series, Box 13, "American Jewish League Against Communism 50" folder. See also the critical editorial in *National Jewish Post* June 11, 1948, 8. The *Post* asserted that the league's press releases "lead the unwary non-Jewish reader to believe that communism is so important among U.S. Jewry that an organization had to be founded to carry on a full-fledged struggle against it." The *Post* also declared that Jewish Communists were an "infinitesimally small minority."

90. *Jews Against Communism* (pamphlet, n.d.).

91. *Jews Against Communism* 1 (July–August 1948): 2.

92. Ibid.; [Fineberg], "The American Jewish League Against Communism"; Benjamin R. Epstein (national director of Anti-Defamation League of B'nai B'rith) to Leon Lowenstein, March 26, 1951, copy enclosed with Alfred Kohlberg to Meier Steinbrink, April 20, 1951, in George E. Sokolsky Papers, Box 74, Hoover Institution Archives; S. Andhil Fineberg memorandum to John Slawson, April 17, 1953, in AJC Records, GEN-12 series, Box 12, "American Jewish League Against Communism 52–53" folder.

93. Stuart Svonkin, *Jews Against Prejudice: American Jews and the Fight for Civil Liberties* (New York: Columbia University Press, 1997), 126–27, 131.

94. [Fineberg], "The American Jewish League Against Communism"; unsigned American Jewish Committee memorandum, September 1, 1950, in AJC Records, GEN-12 series, Box 13, "American Jewish League Against Communism 50" folder.

95. Fineberg memorandum to Danzig, January 10, 1950.

96. Merle Miller, *The Judges and the Judged* (Garden City, NY: Doubleday, 1952), 154–55; *Jews Against Communism* 5 (Passover 1952–5712): 3; ibid., 6 (Autumn 1953): 4.

97. American Jewish Committee memorandum, "Rabbi Benjamin Schultz," September 22, 1952, in AJC Records, GEN-12 series, Box 12, "American Jewish League Against Communism 52–53" folder. This memorandum was evidently written by, or at the suggestion of, the director of the Civil Rights Department of the American Jewish Committee, Edwin J. Lukas. See notation by S. Andhil Fineberg on his copy of an expanded version of this memorandum prepared in October 1954, in Fineberg Papers, Box 4–7. Another copy of the October 1954 version is in AJC Records, GEN-12 series, Box 144, "Schultz, Rabbi Benjamin 47–61" folder.

98. *Jews Against Communism* 1 (July–August 1948): 2.

99. For example: *Congressional Record* 95 (May 11, 1949): A2863; Schultz testimony, July 13, 1949, 434.

100. Eugene Lyons to Edwin J. Lukas, February 4 and 9, 1951, in AJC Records, GEN-12 series, Box 13, "American Jewish League Against Communism 51" folder. Alfred Kohl-

berg noted that Earl Browder (head of the Communist Party of the United States from 1930 to 1945) had often claimed: "Anticommunism and anti-Semitism are two different names for the same thing." Keeley, *China Lobby Man,* 247.

101. Fineberg memorandum to Danzig, January 10, 1950.

102. Svonkin, *Jews Against Prejudice,* 152–53, 163.

103. Fineberg memorandum, November 30, 1972; Fineberg memorandum to John Slawson, April 17, 1953, in AJC Records, GEN-12 series, Box 12, "American Jewish League Against Communism 52–53" folder.

104. Fineberg memorandum to Danzig, January 10, 1950. As of March 1950 the AJC had not yet taken any final action. See Selma Hirsh memorandum to Alfred Bernheim, March 13, 1950, attached to Fineberg's memorandum.

105. Minutes of the AJC's Staff Policy Committee, January 11, 1950, in AJC Records, GEN-12 series, Box 13, "American Jewish League Against Communism 50" folder.

106. American Jewish Committee memorandum on Schultz, July 27, 1950; George Kellman memorandum to George Hexter, August 21, 1950, in AJC Records, GEN-12 series, Box 13, "American Jewish League Against Communism 50" folder.

107. For example, see: Alfred Kohlberg to Jacob Blaustein, July 12, 1950; Kohlberg to Irving M. Engel, August 14, 1950; Kellman memorandum to Hexter, August 21, 1950; George J. Hexter to Kohlberg, August 31, 1950. All in AJC Records, GEN-12 series, Box 13, "American Jewish League Against Communism 50" folder.

108. Unsigned American Jewish Committee memorandum, September 1, 1950; Edwin J. Lukas to Walter White, September 8, 1950, AJC Records, GEN-12 series, Box 13, "American Jewish League Against Communism 50" folder.

109. *New York Times,* August 28, 1950, 1.

110. Ibid., 34.

111. Ibid., August 29, 1950, 1, 50.

112. Eugene Lyons, "Our New Privileged Class," *American Legion Magazine,* September 1951, 37. See also Lyons to Jacob Blaustein, November 25, 1950, in AJC Records, GEN-12 series, Box 13, "American Jewish League Against Communism 50" folder.

113. *New York Times,* September 7, 1950, 1, 34; Jacob Blaustein to members of the American Jewish Committee, November 9, 1950, copy enclosed with Edwin J. Lukas to Irving M. Engel, June 12, 1953, in AJC Records, GEN-12 series, Box 12, "American Jewish League Against Communism 52–53" folder; Lyons to Blaustein, November 25, 1950; Alfred Kohlberg to the members of the American Jewish League Against Communism (printed letter), February 1951, Sokolsky Papers, Box 74. Copies of the latter document are in the Klau Library at Hebrew Union College and in AJC Records, GEN-12 series, Box 13, "American Jewish League Against Communism 51" folder.

114. *Newsweek* 36 (September 11, 1950): 51–52; Miller, *Judges and the Judged,* 155–56.

115. Miller, *Judges and the Judged,* 153–57; Merlyn S. Pitzele, "Is There a Blacklist?" *New Leader* 35 (May 12, 1952): 21–23; Merle Miller, "'I Accept Responsibility . . . ,'" *New Leader* 35 (June 16, 1952): 12–15; Merlyn S. Pitzele, "'This Book Is a Bad Mistake,'" *New Leader* 35 (June 16, 1952): 15–18.

116. Joint Statement of the American Jewish Committee, American Jewish Congress, and Anti-Defamation League of B'nai B'rith re Communism and Civil Liberties, December 26, 1950, enclosed with Jules Cohen memorandum to the NCRAC membership, December 26, 1950, in AJC Records, GEN-12 series, Box 13, "American Jewish League Against Communism 50" folder.

117. Cohen memorandum to the NCRAC membership, December 26, 1950.

118. *New York Times,* November 20, 1950, 9; Svonkin, *Jews Against Prejudice,* 176–77, 298.

119. This controversy may be traced in the following documents in the AJC Records, GEN-12 series, Box 13, American Jewish League Against Communism folders for 1950 and 1951: Benjamin Schultz to Edwin J. Lukas, December 21, 1950; Lukas to John Slawson, December 26, 1950; Lukas to Schultz, January 3, 1951; George Kellman memorandum to John Slawson et al., January 5, 1951; Schultz to Lukas, January 11, 1951; Alfred Kohlberg to Lukas, February 7, 1951; Lukas to Kohlberg, February 8, 1951; Kohlberg to Lukas, February 9, 1951; Eugene Lyons to Lukas, May 4, 1951; Lukas to Lyons, May 10, 1951; Lyons to Lukas, May 11, 1951. See also Lyons to S. Andhil Fineberg, April 10, 1953, in AJC Records, GEN-12 series, Box 12, "American Jewish League Against Communism 52–53" folder. In addition, see Kohlberg to the members of the American Jewish League Against Communism (printed letter), February 1951, and Benjamin R. Epstein to Leon Lowenstein, March 26, 1951, cited above.

120. Svonkin, *Jews Against Prejudice,* 127.

121. *New York Times,* January 24, 1951, 1, 12.

122. Ibid., October 28, 1951, 1, 38; ibid., October 29, 1951, 22.

123. American Jewish League Against Communism press release, January 27, 1951, in AJC Records, GEN-12 series, Box 13, "American Jewish League Against Communism 51" folder; *Cincinnati Enquirer,* January 28, 1951, clipping in Cincinnati, Ohio—Jewish Community Relations Council Records, Box 48–21, AJA; Kohlberg to the members of the American Jewish League Against Communism, February 1951. The latter source contains a transcript of the portions of Rabbi Schultz's speech referring to Marshall and Nimitz. Schultz's remarks were briefly reported in the *Washington Post,* January 28, 1951, M11, and the *Los Angeles Times,* January 28, 1951, 27.

124. NCRAC statement, January 30, 1951, enclosed with Jules Cohen memorandum to NCRAC membership and CJFWF Member Communities, January 30, 1951, in AJC Records, GEN-12 series, Box 13, "American Jewish League Against Communism 51" folder; Washington, D.C., *Sunday Star,* February 11, 1952, A6. Copies of the NCRAC statement and the *Sunday Star* article are in SC-11055, AJA.

125. New York Board of Rabbis resolution, January 31, 1951, quoted in a memorandum enclosed with Edwin J. Lukas to Walter Rothschild, February 9, 1953, in AJC Records, GEN-12 series, Box 12, "American Jewish League Against Communism 52–53" folder.

126. See, for example, editorial in *Cincinnati Enquirer,* February 4, 1951, copy in Cincinnati, Ohio—Jewish Community Relations Council Records, Box 48–21.

127. George Kellman memorandum to John Slawson, Edwin J. Lukas, and David Danzig, February 6, 1951, and to Slawson, February 7, 1951, both in AJC Records, GEN-12 series, Box 13, "American Jewish League Against Communism 51" folder; Kohlberg to the members of the American Jewish League Against Communism, February 1951.

128. See particularly Kohlberg to Steinbrink, April 20, 1951 (plus enclosure); Lukas to Lyons, May 10, 1951; Kohlberg to George E. Sokolsky, February 1, 1952 (plus enclosures), Sokolsky Papers, Box 74. See in general AJC Records, GEN-12 series, Box 12, "American Jewish League Against Communism 52–53" folder, and Box 144, "Schultz, Rabbi Benjamin" folder.

129. Kohlberg to the members of the American Jewish League Against Communism, February 1951; Kohlberg to the members of the league, February 26, 1953, copies in Sokolsky Papers, Box 74, and in AJC Records, GEN-12 series, Box 12, "American Jewish League Against Communism 52–53" folder.

130. George E. Sokolsky telegram to Alfred Kohlberg, February 18, 1952; Kohlberg to

Sokolsky, February 21, 1952; handwritten notes by Sokolsky and his secretary, February 26 and 28, 1952; Meier Steinbrink to Kohlberg, November 7, 1952; Kohlberg to Steinbrink, November 14, 1952; all in Sokolsky Papers, Box 74. Also: Benjamin R. Epstein memorandum to all ADL regional directors, November 10, 1952, in Sokolsky Papers, Box 47, and in AJC Records, GEN-12 series, Box 13, "American Jewish League Against Communism 52–53" folder.

131. Victor Lasky to John Slawson, April 9, 1953; Eugene Lyons to S. Andhil Fineberg, April 10, 1953; Fineberg memorandum to Slawson, April 17, 1953; Edwin J. Lukas to Irving M. Engel, June 12, 1953 (plus enclosures); Lukas to Engel, June 25, 1953; all in AJC Records, GEN-12 series, Box 12, "American Jewish League Against Communism 52–53" folder.

132. Lukas to Engel, June 25, 1953.

133. Engel to Lukas, July 17, 1953; Engel to John Slawson, September 3, 1953; both in AJC Records, GEN-12 series, Box 12, "American Jewish League Against Communism 52–53" folder.

134. *New York Times,* September 12, 1950, 15. Levine later said that he "got out when I felt that the committee [the league] had gotten off the track by neglecting the education of many Jewish people in the facts about Communism." Levine, quoted in Keeley, *China Lobby Man,* 249.

135. Jewish War Veterans press release, February 1, 1951; Kohlberg to Julius Klein, February 20, 1951; copies of both in AJC Records, GEN-12 series, Box 13, "American Jewish League Against Communism 51" folder.

136. *New York Post,* December 9, 1954.

137. Ibid.

138. *National Jewish Post,* May 25, 1951, 3. For Schultz's rejoinder, see ibid., June 1, 1951, 9, 10. Schultz asserted that the league was "going strong," that its membership was increasing, and that history was "on our side." He applauded other Jewish organizations' adoption of what Fineberg called "intelligent anti-Communist programs" but insisted that this "aping" of the league had not gone "far enough." Schultz attributed Jewish defense agencies' professional staffs' "resentment" of the league to "a damaged ego plus a feeling of guilt."

139. *New York Times,* November 16, 1951, 52, and January 15, 1952, 19.

140. Ibid., February 7, 1952, 29, and April 12, 1952, 8; unsigned memorandum, September 18, 1952, in AJC Records, GEN-12 series, Box 12, "American Jewish League Against Communism 52–53" folder.

141. *New York Times,* November 8, 1951, 32.

142. Ibid., December 5, 1951, 34.

143. Ibid., November 16, 1951, 52; Eugene Lyons to S. Andhil Fineberg, September 26, 1951, in AJC Records, GEN-12 series, Box 13, "American Jewish League Against Communism 51" folder.

144. Lyons to Fineberg, September 26, 1951.

145. Ibid.; Lyons, "Our New Privileged Class," 37.

146. *New York Times,* February 20, 1952, 31.

147. Keeley, *China Lobby Man,* 1–9, 98–112.

148. *New York Times,* April 8, 1960, 31.

149. Ibid., December 11, 1952, 27.

150. *Jews Against Communism* 5 (Autumn 1952): 1. The award to Cohn was for "outstanding Americanism and Judaism."

151. *New York Times,* September 15, 1953, 14.

152. Ibid., May 8, 1953, 12; *Jews Against Communism* 6 (Autumn 1953): 1, 4.

153. *Jews Against Communism* 6 (Autumn 1953): 5.

154. *New York Times,* July 29, 1954, 9; *Time* 64 (August 9, 1954): 15; Frank Gibney, "After the Ball," *Commonweal* 60 (September 3, 1954): 531–35. Technically, the Cohn dinner was given by the Joint Committee Against Communism in New York, not the AJLAC. But the league identified itself with the event; Kohlberg, the league's chairman, spoke at the banquet.

155. Quoted in Thomas C. Reeves, *The Life and Times of Joe McCarthy* (New York: Stein and Day, 1982), 642. Rabbi Schultz introduced Senator McCarthy as "my hero" (*Time* 64 [August 9, 1954]: 15).

156. *New York Times,* October 7, 1954, 24. Also: Leon M. Birkhead to Rabbi Louis Newman, October 21 and 24, 1954; Newman to Birkhead, October 24, 1954; Newman to Rabbi Morris Kertzer, October 26, 1954; all in AJC Records, GEN-12 series, Box 144, "Schultz, Rabbi Benjamin 47–61" folder.

157. *New York Times,* October 7, 1954, 24, October 8, 1954, 10, and November 12, 1954, 11.

158. Ibid., November 12, 1954, 11; Walter Goodman, "'Nobody Loves Joe . . . (But the Peepul),'" *New Republic* 131 (November 29, 1954): 12–14.

159. *New York Times,* November 13, 1954, 9.

160. Isaiah M. Minkoff to NCRAC membership and CJFWF agencies, December 22, 1954 (plus enclosures), in AJC Records, GEN-12 series, Box 144, "Schultz, Rabbi Benjamin 47–61" folder.

161. *New York Post,* December 6–10, 1954; Rabbi Morris N. Kertzer to Rabbi Gershon B. Chertoff, December 9, 1954, in AJC Records, GEN-12 series, Box 144, "Schultz, Rabbi Benjamin 47–61" folder.

162. Sokolsky to Victor Emanuel, August 13, 1954, Sokolsky Papers, Box 46.

163. Kohlberg to Morrie Ryskind, July 14, 1954, Alfred Kohlberg Papers, Box 151, Hoover Institution Archives.

164. *Jews Against Communism* 8 (Summer 1955): 4.

165. *Cincinnati Enquirer,* January 28, 1951. The author has found no corroborative evidence for his claim. Schultz's figure was nearly 100 times the figure (300–400 members) that the American Jewish Committee's investigation of the league had yielded in 1950.

166. *New York Post,* December 9, 1954.

167. *New York Times,* February 14, 1955, 6.

168. Ibid., April 21, 1955, 16; *Congressional Record* 101 (April 25, 1955): 5060–61.

169. *New York Times,* May 2, 1955, 12.

170. *Jews Against Communism* 8 (Summer 1955): 1; Victor Lasky, "Benjamin Schultz: The Rabbi the Reds Hate Most," *American Mercury* 81 (November 1955): 85.

171. Victor Emanuel to Sokolsky, December 22, 1955; Sokolsky to Emanuel, January 4, 1956; both in Sokolsky Papers, Box 46.

172. Emanuel was listed as a director on the league's masthead in *Jews Against Communism* 8 (Summer 1955): 2. See also ibid., 10 (Winter 1957–58): 3.

173. Sokolsky to Emanuel, January 4, 1956. According to Sokolsky, Baruch contributed $1,000 to the league every year.

174. Victor Emanuel to Schultz, December 7, 1956; Bennett Cerf to Emanuel, December 12, 1956; Emanuel to Sokolsky, December 18, 1956; all in Sokolsky Papers, Box 46. Also: *Jews Against Communism* 10 (Spring 1957): 6, and 10 (Winter 1957–58): 2, 5.

175. *Jews Against Communism* 9 (Spring 1956): 3, 4, and 10 (Spring 1957): 1.

176. Sokolsky to Kohlberg, August 2, 1956, Kohlberg Papers, Box 160.

177. Ibid.

178. *New York Times,* April 17, 1956, 13; March 11, 1957, 17; May 6, 1957, 18; May 6, 1958, 4; and October 31, 1958, 3.

179. Kohlberg to Sokolsky, January 13, 1958, Kohlberg Papers, Box 160.

180. Ibid.; Keeley, *China Lobby Man,* 251. In his letter of resignation Kohlberg did not specify the reasons for his decision.

181. W. H. Smyth to Kohlberg, May 5, 1958, enclosed with Kohlberg to Sokolsky, May 9, 1958, Sokolsky Papers, Box 74. See also Sokolsky to William F. Buckley Jr., June 22, 1961, William F. Buckley Jr. Papers, Box 13, Yale University Library.

182. Sokolsky form letter, May 3, 1961 (plus attached memorandum), Liebman Papers, Box 8; draft memorandum from John Slawson to Irving M. Engel, February 5, 1962, in AJC Records, GEN-12 series, Box 12, "American Jewish League Against Communism 54–62" folder.

183. *New York Times,* April 8, 1960, 31.

184. See Sokolsky to Schultz, December 23, 1959, copy in Kohlberg Papers, Box 160. Sokolsky was upset when Schultz took a trip to Europe without notifying him and without leaving the office keys behind. Sokolsky was so disturbed that he began to review his own involvement in the league as well as the question of the organization's future. Shortly thereafter Sokolsky suspended the league's operations.

185. Sokolsky to Buckley, August 24, 1960, Buckley Papers, Box 12; Sokolsky to Buckley, June 22, 1961.

186. Fineberg to Lukas, May 18, 1961, in AJC Records, GEN-12 series, Box 12, "American Jewish League Against Communism 54–62" folder.

187. Ibid.

188. Max J. Merritt to members of the Los Angeles chapter of the American Jewish League Against Communism, August 8, 1961, enclosed with Merritt to Sokolsky, August 10, 1961, Sokolsky Papers, Box 88; draft memorandum from Slawson to Engel, February 5, 1962. The former source says that Schultz resigned; the latter source says he was dropped because of lack of money to pay him.

189. Schultz to Sokolsky, May 26, 1960, Sokolsky Papers, Box 103; Fineberg to Lukas, May 18, 1961; Fineberg to Schultz, November 20, 1962, Fineberg Papers, Box 4–7; Marvin Liebman to Robert D. Bring, January 30, 1963, Liebman Papers, Box 8. Rabbi Schultz evidently threatened to file a lawsuit against the league for his back salary (Liebman to Bring, January 30, 1963). Schultz's friend Fineberg felt that Schultz's right-wing allies had idolized him, only to let him down later (Fineberg to Schultz, November 20, 1962).

190. George Sokolsky said that he had Rabbi Joshua L. Goldberg (a prominent Jewish naval chaplain) locate a job for Schultz in the rabbinate (Sokolsky to Buckley, August 24, 1960). But S. Andhil Fineberg said that *he* facilitated Schultz's return to a rabbinical career (Fineberg to Lukas, May 18, 1961). Probably both rabbis assisted Schultz's transition. Schultz served in Brunswick, Georgia, from 1960 to 1962.

191. Schultz to Fineberg, June 28, 1962, Fineberg Papers, Box 4–7.

192. Memphis, Tennessee, *Commercial Appeal,* October 25, 1962, 37, copy in Fineberg Papers, Box 4–7; *The Citizen,* October 1962, 7, copy in SC-11055, AJA.

193. (Jackson, Mississippi) *Clarion Ledger,* February 1, 1963, clipping enclosed with Rabbi Perry E. Nussbaum to Schultz, February 1, 1963, copy in Fineberg Papers, Box 4–7.

194. Nussbaum to Fineberg, November 23, 1962, Fineberg Papers, Box 4–7; Rabbi Robert Blinder memorandum to SoFTy advisors et al., May 14, 1963, SC-11055, AJA. See also

numerous letters to/from Fineberg, 1962–63, concerning Schultz, in Fineberg Papers, Box 4–7, and numerous letters to/from Nussbaum, 1963, regarding Schultz, in SC-11055, AJA.

195. See Fineberg to Schultz, November 20, 1962; Nussbaum to Schultz, February 1, 1963; and the correspondence files cited in the preceding footnote.

196. *The Citizen,* October 1962, 7; Nussbaum to Fineberg, November 23, 1962; Nussbaum to Schultz, February 1, 1963.

197. Schultz to Fineberg, November 27, 1962, Fineberg Papers, Box 4–7; Schultz to Jacob R. Marcus, March 25, 1971, SC-11056, AJA.

198. Schultz to Marcus, March 25, 1971 (plus enclosed clipping from [Clarksdale, Mississippi] *Press-Register,* April 8, 1968).

199. The 1962–63 correspondence in the Fineberg Papers, Box 4–7, and SC-11055, AJA, presents the story in detail.

200. *Jewish Post and Opinion* clippings, February 12, 1971; Morrie Ryskind column in Memphis, Tennessee, *Commercial Appeal,* February 28, 1971; Fineberg memorandum on American Jewish League Against Communism, November 30, 1972; all in Fineberg Papers, Box 4–7. Also: *New York Times,* April 25, 1978, 40.

201. Liebman to Sokolsky, August 12, 1960, Sokolsky Papers, Box 239; Sokolsky to Buckley, August 24, 1960.

202. Sokolsky form letter, May 3, 1961 (plus attached memorandum).

203. Isaiah Terman memorandum to AJC area directors and executive assistants concerning the American Jewish League Against Communism, May 22, 1961, in AJC Records, GEN-12 series, Box 12, "American Jewish League Against Communism 54–62" folder.

204. *Information from the Jewish Community Council* [of Metropolitan Boston], May 15, 1961, copy in AJC Records, GEN-12 series, Box 12, "American Jewish League Against Communism 54–62" folder.

205. Masthead of Liebman memorandum to the league's officers and directors, January 5, 1962, Sokolsky Papers, Box 8; Sokolsky to Bernard Baruch, April 6, 1962, Sokolsky Papers, Box 22.

206. Liebman memorandum to the league's officers and directors, January 5, 1962; American Jewish League Against Communism press release, January 11, 1962, Liebman Papers, Box 8; *New York Times,* February 14, 1962, 20; Sokolsky to Baruch, April 6, 1962,

207. American Jewish League Against Communism press release, February 28, 1962; Liebman memorandum to members and friends of the AJLAC, February 28, 1962 (plus enclosure); both in Liebman Papers, Box 8.

208. *B'nai B'rith Messenger* [Los Angeles], March 16, 1962, 25.

209. For the Schwarz controversy see: Marvin Liebman to Sokolsky, May 2, 1962, Liebman Papers, Box 8; Fred Schwarz to Arnold Forster, June 6, 1962, and to Label Katz, June 6, 1962, copies enclosed with Arnold Forster to Sokolsky, June 7, 1962, Sokolsky Papers, Box 266; *National Review* 12 (June 5, 1962): 398–99, and 12 (June 19, 1962): 433–34; *New York Times,* June 29, 1962, 5; Marvin Liebman, *Coming Out Conservative* (San Francisco: Chronicle Books, 1992), 158; Frederick Schwarz, *Beating the Unbeatable Odds* (Washington, D.C.: Regnery Publishing, 1996), 323–31, 335–52.

210. William F. Buckley Jr. to Sokolsky, May 10, 1962; Sokolsky to Buckley, May 29, 1962; both in Sokolsky Papers, Box 31. Also: Sokolsky syndicated column, June 30, 1962, copy in Sokolsky Papers, Box 266. Publicly, Sokolsky wondered why Schwarz, an Australian, did not become an American citizen. Said Sokolsky: "I believe that an alien should mind his own business about the United States." Privately, Sokolsky considered Schwarz's anti-Communist gospel to be infantile and ineffective. But Sokolsky's hostility to Schwarz

seemed to go beyond these stated objections. Both Liebman and *National Review* stated that Sokolsky "loathed" Schwarz, for whom (Liebman claimed) Sokolsky had a deep "hatred." Liebman, *Coming Out Conservative*, 158; *National Review* 12 (June 5, 1962): 399. The magazine added that Sokolsky was "apparently obsessed" about Schwarz.

211. Merritt to Sokolsky, January 25, 1962; Liebman to Buckley, May 9, 1962, Buckley Papers, Box 21 (copy in Liebman Papers, Box 8).

212. Morrie Ryskind to Buckley, July 27, 1962, Buckley Papers, Box 22.

213. Liebman to Buckley, May 9, 1962.

214. Ryskind to Buckley, July 27, 1962; bulletin of the Jewish Council Against Communism (based in Los Angeles), May 1963, copy in Liebman Papers, Box 93. According to Ryskind, the Los Angeles chapter had been dropped from the league because of Sokolsky's disagreements with Merritt.

215. Liebman to Sokolsky, May 2, 1962; Liebman to Buckley, May 9, 1962.

216. Ibid.

217. Liebman to Sokolsky, May 2, 1962.

218. Sokolsky to Liebman, May 4, 1962, Liebman Papers, Box 8. For Liebman's published account of this episode see his *Coming Out Conservative*, 158.

219. *New York Times*, June 29, 1962, 1, 5.

220. Ibid., December 14, 1962, 16.

221. Ibid., May 6, 1963, 29, and May 13, 1963, 22; *New York Post*, May 27, 1963.

222. *New York Post*, May 27, 1963. The columnist was James A. Wechsler.

223. On April 26, 1978, the day after the *New York Times* reported the death of Rabbi Schultz, it printed the following correction: "An obituary of Rabbi Benjamin Schultz reported yesterday that the American Jewish League Against Communism had ceased operations in 1960. The organization is still active, and Roy M. Cohn has been its president since 1962" (*New York Times*, April 26, 1978, B1). Despite this statement (presumably made at the request of Cohn), I have found no evidence of any activity by the league after 1966, when it gave an award to William F. Buckley Jr. See William F. Buckley Jr., *Let Us Talk of Many Things* (Roseville, CA: Forum, 2000), 108.

224. *New York Times*, August 3, 1986, Section I, 1, 33 (obituary of Roy M. Cohn). The obituary did not mention the American Jewish League Against Communism.

225. *Jews Against Communism* 10 (Spring 1957): 3.

226. Ibid.

227. Svonkin, *Jews Against Prejudice*, 114.

228. American Jewish Committee memorandum on Rabbi Schultz, July 27, 1950.

229. American Jewish Committee memoranda on Schultz, September 22, 1952, and October 1954.

230. See, for instance, Fineberg memorandum to Danzig, January 10, 1950.

231. Svonkin, *Jews Against Prejudice*, 165–67.

232. A recent account of the struggle to expel the JPFO from the Jewish community council in Los Angeles in 1948–51 contains no reference to the league. Deborah Dash Moore, *To the Golden Cities: Pursuing the American Jewish Dream in Miami and L.A.* (New York: Free Press, 1994), 202–5.

233. *New York Post*, December 6, 1954. According to the *Post*, Isaac Don Levine thought Schultz "had been designated to propagate anticommunism among the Jews; instead, he appointed himself a Jewish spokesman to the world" (Ibid., December 9, 1954). This development was probably attributable in part to Schultz's rejection by his fellow rabbis and the Jewish defense agencies.

234. Sokolsky to Buckley, August 24, 1960. In 1954 Kohlberg admitted that at the time of the league's founding in 1948 his "relationships in the Jewish field were limited to the United Jewish Appeal and the Federation of Jewish Philanthropies" (*New York Post,* December 9, 1954).
235. Unsigned American Jewish Committee memorandum, September 1, 1950; Lukas to Walter White, September 8, 1950; George J. Hexter to Sydney M. Kaye, September 1, 1950, in AJC Records, GEN-12 series, Box 13, "American Jewish League Against Communism 50" folder.
236. Fineberg to Lyons, September 24, 1951.
237. Ibid.; joint statement by the American Jewish Committee, American Jewish Congress, and Anti-Defamation League of B'nai B'rith on communism and civil liberties, December 26, 1950.

CHAPTER 23: FORGOTTEN GODFATHERS

1. See for example, John Judis, *William F. Buckley, Jr.: Patron Saint of the Conservatives* (New York: Simon & Schuster, 1988), and George H. Nash, *The Conservative Intellectual Movement in America Since 1945,* rev. ed. (Wilmington, DE: ISI Books, 1996).
2. *National Review* 1 (November 19, 1955): 3. The names were Frank Chodorov, Eugene Lyons, Frank S. Meyer, Morrie Ryskind, and William S. Schlamm.
3. James T. Patterson, *Mr. Republican: A Biography of Robert A. Taft* (Boston: Houghton Mifflin, 1972), 326–28.
4. Recorded oral history interview of William F. Buckley Jr., September 27, 1996, by Timothy S. Goeglein; copy in the Motion Picture, Broadcasting, and Recorded Sound Division, Library of Congress, Washington., D.C.
5. *National Review* 2 (December 8, 1956): 7; ibid., 12 (June 5, 1962): 398–99; ibid., 12 (June 19, 1962): 433–34: ibid., 12 (July 3, 1962): 469; ibid. 16 (October 6, 1964): 855–56, 858; ibid., 18 (April 19, 1966): 352; William F. Buckley Jr., to Fred C. Schwarz, March 6, 1963, William F. Buckley Jr. Papers, Box 27, Yale University Library. See also Arnold Forster and Benjamin R. Epstein, *Danger on the Right* (New York: Random House, 1964), 47–67, and Frederick Schwarz, *Beating the Unbeatable Foe* (Washington. D.C.: Regnery Publishing, 1996), 315–31.
6. Forster and Epstein, *Danger on the Right,* 241.
7. Buckley to Morrie Ryskind, September 6, 1960, Buckley Papers, Box 11.
8. Nash, *Conservative Intellectual Movement,* 133; William F. Buckley Jr., "Willi Schlamm, RIP," *National Review* 30 (September 29, 1978): 1196; Buckley, "Willi Schlamm," *National Review* 32 (December 31, 1980): 1636–37; John Chamberlain, A *Life with the Printed Word* (Chicago: Regnery Gateway, 1982), 145.
9. Chamberlain, A *Life,* 145; Judis, *William F. Buckley, Jr.,* 117.
10. William F. Buckley Jr., "Morrie Ryskind, RIP," *National Review* 37 (September 20, 1985): 19–20; Buckley oral history interview (1996); Morrie Ryskind (with John H. M. Roberts), *I Shot an Elephant in My Pajamas* (Lafayette, LA: Huntington House Publishers, 1994), 183. Wrote Buckley in his 1985 obituary notice for Ryskind: "'Without him it is doubtful that this journal [*National Review*] would ever have been launched."
11. Buckley oral history interview (1996). Buckley's father was the greatest single contributor ($100,000 of the $290,000 Buckley raised). Judis, *William F. Buckley, Jr.,* 118, 121. In his 1996 interview Buckley stated that the principal place where he succeeded in his fundraising was Morrie Ryskind's home.

12. Buckley, "Morrie Ryskind, RIP," 20. Buckley's sister Priscilla, who was *National Review's* managing editor for many years, has stated that Morrie Ryskind was a "very important" figure for *National Review* and a "very good and faithful friend." Telephone interview by the author of Priscilla L. Buckley, January 13, 1999. Ryskind remained on *National Review's* board of directors for the rest of his life.

13. Eugene Lyons, *Assignment in Utopia* (New York: Harcourt, Brace and Company, 1937).

14. Frank Chodorov, "A Fifty-Year Project," *analysis* 6 (October 1950); Chodorov, *A Fifty-Year Project to Combat Socialism on the Campus* (Intercollegiate Studies Institute pamphlet, ca. 1952, copy in the author's possession); *Human Events* 9 (May 14, 1952): 7.

15. But not for long. Chodorov soon deposed him (and made himself president) because, he wrote humorously to Buckley, "Easier to raise money if a Jew is president. You can be V-P." William F. Buckley Jr., *The Jeweler's Eye* (New York: Putnam, 1968), 347–48.

16. Ralph de Toledano, ed., *Notes from the Underground; The Whittaker Chambers–Ralph de Toledano Letters: 1949–1960* (Washington, D.C.: Regnery Publishing, 1997), 198. Toledano had a wife and two sons to support and did not feel he could take such a risk. Nor was he certain that he, Buckley, and Schlamm could "work together." (Note: Toledano was living when this article originally appeared. I have inserted his year of death in the text for this reprinting.)

17. Toledano's first signed contribution to *National Review* appeared in its April 18, 1956 issue. His name went on the magazine's masthead in its June 18, 1960 issue, where he was listed as a contributor. Nearly forty years later he remains on the masthead as a contributing editor.

18. Marvin Liebman, letter to the editor, *National Review* 1 (December 7, 1955): 30.

19. Marvin Liebman, *Coming Out Conservative* (San Francisco: Chronicle Books, 1992), 144. The phrase "agitation-propaganda" was used by Buckley in reference to Liebman.

20. Interview of Priscilla L. Buckley by the author, January 13, 1999.

21. Buckley to Morrie Ryskind, March 24, 1959, Buckley Papers, Box 9. As early as January 1958 Buckley had thought of publicly attacking the *American Mercury* in the pages of *National Review* (Ryskind to Buckley, March 6, 1959, Buckley Papers, Box 9). Years later Buckley recalled that he "was tracking the scene" at the *American Mercury* "pretty carefully" in the 1950s (Buckley to the author, March 3, 1999). See also Buckley to Ryskind, March 31, 1959, Buckley Papers, Box 9.

22. William F. Buckley Jr., confidential memorandum to writers for *National Review,* April 1, 1959, Buckley Papers, Box 8. Buckley also disclosed that each of *National Review's* editors had agreed not to contribute to the *Mercury* until it acquired new management. See also Buckley to Ryskind, May 27, 1959, Buckley Papers, Box 9, and Nash, *Conservative Intellectual Movement,* 378.

23. Buckley to Alice F. Peppard, March 9, 1960, Buckley Papers, Box 10. For more on the *American Mercury* controversy, see "The American Mercury and Russell Maguire," *Facts* 13 (October–November, 1959): 143–46; *New York World Telegram and Sun,* March 1, 1960, 6; *Newsweek* 55 (March 14, 1960): 92.

24. Even Buckley's friend the conservative Jewish columnist George Sokolsky seemed to have this impression. Buckley to George Sokolsky, August 12, 1959, Buckley Papers, Box 9.

25. Interview of Priscilla L. Buckley, January 13, 1999. Miss Buckley recalled that her brother was seeking a prestigious and non-Catholic religion editor since so many Catholics were "on board" *National Review* already.

26. Ibid.

27. Marvin Liebman later declared, "I firmly believe that Bill [Buckley] opposed any of the open or hidden anti-Semitism, anti-intellectualism, and bigotry that seemed to dog the American Right" (Liebman, *Coming Out Conservative,* 144).

28. Buckley to Dore Schary, June 27, 1967, Buckley Papers, Box 45. His letter was in response to Schary to him, June 22, 1967, in the same file. Buckley had a similar exchange with the editor of the *Jewish Forum* in 1962. On this occasion Buckley remarked, "Nothing is more tiresome than the charge that every member of the American Right is ex-officio anti-Semitic." See Charles Ruddock to Buckley, January 4, 1962, and Buckley to Ruddock, January 16, 1982, copies in George E. Sokolsky Papers, Box 31, Hoover Institution Archives, Stanford University,

29. Toledano was born of American parents in the International Zone of Tangier and came to the United States at the age of five. Lyons was born in Russia and emigrated to the United States with his parents at the age of nine.

30. Years later Ryskind recalled that his life "began in a two-room apartment on the top floor of a five-story walkup tenement"—a building with no heat, no gas, no electricity, no telephone, and no indoor bathroom. "It was," he remarked, "the Jewish equivalent of a log cabin on the frontier" (Ryskind, *I Shot an Elephant,* 5).

31. Chodorov, Ryskind, Lyons, and Toledano attended Columbia University. Liebman briefly attended New York University. Meyer (whose background was the most affluent) attended Princeton and ultimately graduated from Oxford. Schlamm, meanwhile, attended the University of Vienna.

32. The autobiographies are Frank Chodorov, *Out of Step: The Autobiography of an Individualist* (New York: Devin-Adair Company, 1962); Liebman, *Coming Out Conservative;* Lyons, *Assignment in Utopia;* Ryskind, *I Shot an Elephant;* and Ralph de Toledano, *Lament for a Generation* (New York: Farrar, Strauss and Cudahy, 1960). Toledano's *Notes from the Underground,* cited earlier, is also a valuable source.

The biographical details in the text and in the preceding note have been gleaned from these autobiographies and a variety of other sources, including *New York Times* obituaries and *Who's Who* entries. In addition see, for Chodorov, Charles H. Hamilton, ed., *Fugitive Essays: Selected Writings of Frank Chodorov* (Indianapolis: Liberty Press, 1980), 11–30.

For Liebman: his "Professional Notes" (May 1974), Marvin Liebman Papers, Box 139, Hoover Institution Archives; Liebman memorandum to "all concerned" (plus attachments), November 24, 1980, William A. Rusher Papers, Box 52, Library of Congress.

For Lyons: entry in *Current Biography: Who's News and Why* (New York: H. W. Wilson Company, 1944), 426–30; "Biographical Notes on Eugene Lyons (for H. R.)," Eugene Lyons Papers, Box 1, Hoover Institution Archives; *Contemporary Authors,* vols. 9–12, first revision (Detroit: Gale Research Company, 1974), 547–48.

For Meyer: his congressional testimony, February 26, 1957, printed in U.S. Congress, Senate, Committee on the Judiciary, *Hearings before the Subcommittee to Investigate the Internal Security Act and Other Security Laws,* 85th Congress, 1st Session, 1957, 3577–3609.

For Ryskind: Joseph Adamson III, "Morrie Rykind," *Dictionary of Literary Biography,* vol 26: *American Screenwriters* (Detroit: Gale Research Company, 1984), 269–75.

For Schlamm: *Contemporary Authors,* vols. 93–96 (Detroit: Gale Research Company, 1980), 472–73; *Deutsches Literatur-Lexikon,* vol. 15 (Bern, Switzerland: K. G. Saur Verlag, 1993), 76–77.

For Toledano: *Current Biography Yearbook* 1962 (New York: H. W. Wilson Company, 1962), 424–26; *Contemporary Authors,* New Revision Series, vol 31 (Detroit: Gale Research, Inc., 1990), 431–32.

33. Chodorov entitled one of his books *One Is a Crowd: Reflections of an Individualist* (New York: Devin-Adair Company, 1952).

34. Chodorov, *Out of Step,* 83, 87–88.

35. Chodorov, *One Is a Crowd,* 28.

36. Chodorov, *Out of Step,* 104.

37. Chodorov, *One Is a Crowd,* 20–21.

38. Ibid., 20–22.

39. Ryskind, *I Shot an Elephant,* 21–36.

40. For a glimpse of Ryskind's political views in the 1920s and early 1930s, see ibid., 164. According to one authority, Ryskind's "zealous antiwar tirades convinced George S. Kaufman that they should collaborate on a pacifist musical." The result was *Strike Up the Band* (1930) (Adamson, "Morrie Ryskind," 271).

41. Morrie Ryskind, "Move Over, Mr. Frankenstein," *The Nation* 147 (September 10, 1938): 245.

42. Morrie Ryskind, "The Hollywood Tea Party," *The Nation* 142 (May 6, 1936): 581.

43. *Der Spiegel* 14 (May 11, 1960): 30; ibid., 32 (September 11, 1978): 252 (obituary for Schlamm).

44. Lyons, *Assignment in Utopia,* 6.

45. Ibid., 8.

46. Ibid., 8–9.

47. Ibid., 37.

48. Ibid., 48.

49. Meyer's congressional testimony, February 16, 1957, 3578–79; telephone interview by author of John C. Meyer (Frank Meyer's son), January 14, 1998.

50. Liebman, *Coming Out Conservative,* 27–30.

51. Toledano, *Lament for a Generation,* 14.

52. Ibid., 12–17; Ralph de Toledano, "The Road to Anti-Communism," *American Mercury* 78 (April 1954): 31.

53. Toledano, *Lament for a Generation,* 40; Toledano, "Road," 30.

54. Chodorov, *One Is a Crowd,* 22; Chodorov, *Out of Step,* 50.

55. Frank Chodorov, "Educating for a Free Society," *Scribner's Commentator* 9 (February 1941): 36–37. Chodorov extolled George as "the apostle of individualism," exponent of private property, opponent of socialism, and philosopher of "free enterprise, free trade, free men."

56. Ibid., 37–42; Chodorov, *Out of Step,* 78–79; *Time* 32 (August 22, 1938): 32.

57. Nash, *Conservative Intellectual Movement,* 13; Frank Chodorov, *The Income Tax: Root of All Evil* (New York: Devin-Adair Company, 1954).

In 1936 Chodorov met Albert Jay Nock, founder of the legendary *Freeman* magazine in the 1920s and author of *Our Enemy, the State.* To Chodorov, the elderly libertarian was "the most civilized man I ever knew," an "intellectual warehouse" and fount of libertarian wisdom. The two became close friends. See Frank Chodorov, "My Friend's Education," *The Freeman* 5 (August 1954): 63; Frank Chodorov, "Gentle Nock at Our Door, *Fragments* 4 (April–June 1966): 2.

58. Nash, *Conservative Intellectual Movement,* 14, 347–48.

59. Ibid., 133; Chamberlain, *A Life with the Printed Word,* 90–91.

60. *New York Times,* April 14, 1949, 19: Frank S. Meyer's congressional testimony, February 26, 1957, 3578–87, 3600; Frank S. Meyer, "Champion of Freedom," *National Review* 8 (May 7, 1960): 305; interview of John C. Meyer by the author January 14, 1998. According to Meyer, *The Road to Serfdom* "played a "decisive part in helping me free myself from Marxist ideology."

61. Morrie Ryskind, "Report for Ike," *The Freeman* 3 (December 29, 1952): 247; Ryskind, "Move Over, Mr. Frankenstein," 244–45.

62. Louis Waldman, letter to the editor, *The Nation* 142 (April 1, 1936): 431; Ryskind, "Hollywood Tea Party," 581. In the latter article Ryskind applauded Waldman's letter as "a magnificent declaration of principles." Waldman's letter objected to a Socialist united front with the Communists and attacked the Communists for their opposition "by philosophy and practice" to civil liberties.

63. Mary H. Ryskind (Morrie Ryskind's wife) to Eugene Lyons, January 6, 1938, Lyons Papers, Box 6; Ryskind, "Move Over, Mr. Frankenstein," 245.

64. Ibid.; Morrie Ryskind, "The Fallen Idol," *National Review* 1 (April 11, 1956): 26.

65. Toledano, *Lament for a Generation,* 16, 21–29; Ralph de Toledano, "Epitome of the Thirties," *National Review* 23 (April 20, 1971): 435. Toledano recalled in 1971 that Lyons's *Assignment in Utopia* had "shaken me to the core in my college days for its scrupulous exposure of the Soviet myth." Thus did one premature Jewish conservative help to beget another.

66. Toledano, *Lament for a Generation,* 37.

67. Toledano, "Epitome of the Thirties," 435.

68. Toledano, *Lament for a Generation,* 37.

69. Ibid., 41–42; *Current Biography Yearbook 1962,* s.v. "Tolodano, Ralph de."

70. Toledano, *Lament for a Generation,* 61–64.

71. Chamberlain, *A Life with* the *Printed Word,* 67–68, 91; Judis, *William F. Buckley, Jr.,* 115.

72. "Biographical Notes on Eugene Lyons (for H. R.)."

73. Lyons became a contributing editor of *Plain Talk* with its March 1947 issue. The magazine's first issue appeared in October 1946.

74. *Plain Talk* 1 (October 1946): inside front cover; Toledano, *Lament for a Generation,* 91.

75. Ralph de Toledano and Victor Lasky, *Seeds of Treason* (New York: Funk & Wagnalls Company, 1950); Frank S. Meyer, *The Moulding of Communists* (New York: Harcourt, Brace & World, 1961). Somehow Lyons found the time to ghostwrite another anti-Communist classic, *I Chose Freedom* (1946), by the Soviet defector Victor Kvavchenko. Eugene Lyons oral history interview (1968), 5, Hoover Institution Archives; Lyons to Robert Conquest, May 7, 1969, and Joan Colebrook to Lyons, March 26, 1974, both in Lyons Papers, Box 1.

76. Ryskind, *I Shot an Elephant,* 163–66; Ryskind, "Heraclitus and Hollywood," *Human Events* 10 (August 26, 1953).

77. Morrie Ryskind testimony, October 22, 1947, printed in U.S. Congress, House of Representatives, Committee on Un-American Activities, *Hearings Regarding the Communist Infiltration of the Motion Picture Industry,* 80th Congress, 1st Session, 1947, 181–88.

78. Ryskind, *I Shot an Elephant,* 166, 171; Ryskind to Henry Regnery, December 28, 1953, Henry Regnery Papers, Box 66, Hoover Institution Archives; Ryskind, "Dolph Menjou," *National Review* 15 (November 19, 1963): 440; Toledano, *Lament for a Generation,* 147. In his autobiography Ryskind wrote, "After I testified against the Hollywood Ten, I was never again to receive one single offer from any studio, and the same fate befell [three other cooperative witnesses]" (166). Ryskind told Regnery that in all about a dozen Hol-

lywood anti-Communists were blacklisted by the industry for their congressional testimony.

Ryskind was not the only premature Jewish conservative to suffer reprisals for his strenuous anticommunism. In 1947, Ralph de Toledano was fired as editor of the Ethical Culture Society's monthly magazine in part because of his association with the anti-Communist periodical *Plain Talk* (Toledano, *Lament for a Generation*, 91).

79. Liebman, *Coming Out Conservative*, 52.

80. Ibid, 70–71, 76, 80, 86–87.

81. Ibid, 81–112.

82. Ryskind, *I Shot an Elephant*, 170–71; Ryskind, "Reflections from Bedlam," *National Review* 4 (November 2, 1957): 402; Mary Ryskind to William F. Buckley Jr., July 15, 1967, Buckley Papers, Box 45.

83. Ryskind, *I Shot an Elephant*, 174–79.

84. Ibid., 177–78.

85. Eugene Lyons, *The Red Decade: The Stalinist Penetration of America* (Indianapolis: Bobbs-Merrill Company, 1941); Nash, *Conservative Intellectual Movement*, 76–77.

86. *Current Biography* (1944), s.v. "Lyons, Eugene."

87. Eugene Lyons, "In Defense of Red-Baiting," *New Leader* 29 (December 7, 1946): 8.

88. Eugene Lyons, letter to the editor, *New York Times,* June 26, 1949, section 4, 8; Lyons, "Who's Hysterical?" *American Legion Magazine* (March 1950), 20, 56–59; Lyons, "Is Freedom of Expression Really Threatened?" *American Mercury* 76 (January 1953): 22–33.

89. Lyons, "Is Freedom of Expression Really Threatened?" 33.

90. Toledano, "Road to Anti-Communism," 34; Toledano, *Lament for a Generation*, 146.

91. Ralph de Toledano, "The Liberal Disintegration—A Conservative View," *The Freeman* 1 (November 13, 1950): 109–10.

92. Toledano, *Lament for a Generation*, 126–27.

93. Ibid., 132, 149.

94. Many pages in *Lament for a Generation* expound upon these themes. See also Toledano, ed., *Notes from the Underground* (especially his foreword); Toledano, "Let Only a Few Speak for Him," *National Review* 11 (July 29, 1961): 49–51; Toledano, "Ten Years Dead," ibid., 22 (July 27, 1971): 793.

95. Eugene Lyons, *Our Unknown Ex-President: A Portrait of Herbert Hoover* (Garden City, NY: Doubleday, 1948). See also his *Herbert Hoover: A Biography* (Garden City, NY: Doubleday, 1964).

96. Lyons oral history interview (1968), 9; Lyons to William F. Buckley Jr., September 1 and 14, 1964, Buckley Papers, Box 31; Lyons, letter to the editor, *New York Times,* August 15, 1974, 32.

97. Toledano, *Lament for a Generation*, 189–90, 196–97; Toledano, *Notes from the Underground*, 181; Toledano, "Herbert Hoover at 90—A Small Tribute," printed in Toledano, *America, I Love You* (Washington, D.C.: National Press, 1968), 52–54.

Although Frank Meyer apparently never met ex-President Hoover, he adopted a thoroughly Hooverian perspective on recent American history. A "quiet and undramatic revolution" had commenced in America in the early 1930s, Meyer asserted in the 1950s. Since that time the United States had undergone a "collectivist transformation" of tremendous magnitude. Frank S. Meyer, "The Meaning of McCarthyism," *National Review* 5 (June 14, 1958): 565; Frank S. Meyer, "Call for a Third Party," *The Freeman* 4 (April 5, 1954): 494.

98. William S. Schlamm to William F. Buckley Jr., January 11 and 30, 1962, Buckley

Papers, Box 65; "Eugene Lyons, RIP," *National Review* 37 (February 8, 1985): 21. Toledano, in particular, came to feel painfully ambivalent about McCarthy and ultimately unable to defend him. Toledano, *Lament for a Generation*, 205–12.

99. See Morrie Ryskind, "For Joe McCarthy," *The Freeman* 2 (September 8, 1952): 832; *New York Times*, April 6, 1953, 7; ibid, November 16, 1954, 28; William S. Schlamm, prologue to William F. Buckley Jr. and L. Brent Bozell, *McCarthy and His Enemies* (Chicago: Henry Regnery Company, 1954), vii–xv; Frank S. Meyer to Henry Regnery, March 10, 1954, Regnery Papers, Box 51; William S. Schlamm, "Across McCarthy's Grave," *National Review* 3 (May 18, 1957): 469–70; Frank Chodorov, "McCarthy's Mistake," *Human Events* 9 (November 12, 1952).

Schlamm long regretted not having gone to work for McCarthy in 1952, when given the chance (Schlamm to Buckley, January 11, 1962). Meyer did work with the Wisconsin senator on some matters. Interview of John C. Meyer by the author, January 14, 1998.

100. In 1959 or thereabouts, Ryskind joined a new "conservative organization to fight collectivism" called the John Birch Society despite concerns about some of the private views of its founder, Robert Welch. For a time Ryskind was content with the low-key, anti-Communist educational work of the new organization. But then Welch's bizarre conspiracy theories (for example, that President Eisenhower was a Communist agent) became public knowledge. An embarrassed Ryskind eventually (and quietly) resigned. A year or two later, when Welch himself *publicly* asserted that Eisenhower was a Communist, Ryskind publicly rebuked him in a newspaper column for his "foul blow" to the conservative cause. See Ryskind, *I Shot an Elephant*, 198–200; Ryskind newspaper column (an open letter to Robert Welch), October 30, 1963, copy in Buckley Papers, Box 26.

Schlamm, a self-described McCarthyite, was more flamboyant. When Welch initiated his monthly magazine, *American Opinion,* in February 1958 the lead article was written by none other than Schlamm himself. For nearly five more years Schlamm served as one of the journal's associate editors, and his "European Survey" column appeared regularly in its pages. Even after Buckley informed him in 1962 that Welch was now "greatly damaging the anti-Communist cause," Schlamm (now living in Europe) counseled against public criticism of him. When Buckley proceeded to do so anyway, Schlamm replied that Buckley had made a fatal mistake. The right thing to do, the ex-Communist argued, was to collaborate with Welch and steer him away from his errors. Buckley thought this hopeless; perhaps Schlamm came to think so, too. At the end of 1962, his name disappeared from *American Opinion's* masthead. See *American Opinion* 1 (February 1958); 1–6; Buckley to Schlamm, January 2, 24, 1962; February 1, 19, 1962, Buckley Papers, Box 65; Schlamm to Buckley, January 11, 30, February 9, 1962, Buckley Papers, Box 65. Schlamm's name appeared on *American Opinion's* masthead (as one of the journal's associate editors) from February 1958 through November 1962. No explanation was offered for the disappearance of his name after that. It is not known who or what precipitated the break.

101. Buckley, "Willi Schlamm," 1636.

102. Toledano's encomium (and two others) are contained on an undated typed sheet in the George E. Sokolsky Papers, Box 31. The author does not know whether the blurb appeared on the dust jacket of the Buckley/Bozell book.

103. Meyer to Regnery, March 10, 1954; Morrie Ryskind to Henry Regnery, January 17 and 30, 1954, Regnery Papers, Box 66. Meyer considered Schlamm's prologue to the book to be one of the greatest essays of his time.

104. Toledano, *Lament for a Generation*, 99.

105. Toledano, "Road to Anti-Communism," 35.

106. Toledano, *Lament for a Generation,* 177.

107. Toledano, "Road to Anti-Communism," 35.

108. Frank S. Meyer, *In Defense of Freedom* (Chicago: Henry Regnery Company, 1962), 106.

109. Frank S. Meyer, "The Rotten Apple in Our Schools," *The Freeman* 5 (September 1954): 101.

110. Frank S. Meyer, "What Time Is It?" *National Review* 6 (September 13, 1958): 180.

111. Toledano, *Lament for a Generation,* 99, 222, 230, 241, 261.

112. See, for example, ibid., 172, and Ryskind, *I Shot an Elephant,* 169. Wrote Toledano: "In the context of morals, politics, and economics, liberalism was corrupt. And its corruption stemmed from one corrupting influence: the doctrine that all absolutes are evil with the exception of the absolute State." Wrote Ryskind: "Liberalism was the banner that I marched under so proudly all those years ago . . . while the labels have indeed changed my principles haven't. In my day, a liberal was one who stood for the rights of the individual against the encroachments of the state." See also Liebman, *Coming Out Conservative,* 143: "From the time I quit the Communist party, I have been a firm believer in the importance of the individual over any state, political party, or religious hierarchy. To me the individual is all, subservient only to God." Liebman added: "Bill's [Buckley's] style of conservatism won me over. His orbit of friends . . . all embraced a conservatism that defended the primacy of the individual over the state" (144).

113. Meyer, *In Defense of Freedom,* 1.

114. Ibid., 27. Meyer warned a strictly limited state, a *desanctified* state, confined to providing for the common defense, the administration of justice, and the protection of citizens against assault and violence. Otherwise the government should leave people alone.

115. *Out of Step,* of course, was the title of Chodorov's autobiography.

116. Priscilla L. Buckley, in her interview of January 13, 1999, with the author, recalled that the Jewish conservatives around *National Review* did not "make a big thing" about the fact that they were unrepresentative of the political sentiments of their fellow Jews. William F. Buckley Jr. has recalled that Frank Meyer "discussed everything including his despondency that the overwhelming number of American Jews backed the Democratic Party and [that] like himself, many had backed the Communists." But this "demographic datum," said Buckley, "was simply accepted as a challenge in life." William F. Buckley Jr. to the author, March 3, 1999.

117. For a recent and sensitive memoir on this subject by one of them, see Toledano, "Among the Ashkenazim," *Commentary* 101 (June 1996): 48–51.

118. Ryskind, *I Shot an Elephant,* 51.

119. Liebman, *Coming Out Conservative,* 41–47.

120. Toledano, *Notes from the Underground,* 101.

121. Interview of John C. Meyer, January 14, 1998.

122. Toledano (in 1955), quoted in "The American Mercury and Russell Maguire," 145. Toledano also said on the same occasion: "Anti-Semitism is vicious and stupid. Anybody who drags it into the anti-Communist fight not only confuses the issue but destroys other anti-Communists. It gives the Communists the chance to use the old line that the only people who oppose them are anti-Semites."

123. Ryskind to Buckley, March 26, 1959; Ryskind to Alfred Kohlberg, February 5, 1959, Alfred Kohlberg Papers, Box 151, Hoover Institution Archives.

124. Liebman, *Coming Out Conservative,* 135–36, 154–56.

125. Eugene Lyons, "The Myth of Jewish Communism," *Pageant* (April 1947): 20–25;

Lyons, "American Jews and the Kremlin Purges," *New Leader* 36 (March 2, 1953): 14–15; Lyons, "'Jewish Ordeal in Russia," *Catholic Digest* 17 (May 1953): 107–11.

126. Victor Lasky, "Benjamin Schultz—The Rabbi the Reds Hate Most," *American Mercury* 81 (November 1955): 85. According to Lasky, the league was founded in Lyons's apartment.

127. Ibid., 83.

128. Liebman, *Coming Out Conservative*, 157.

129. Toledano, *Lament for a Generation*, 272.

130. Garry Wills, *Confessions of a Conservative* (Garden City, NY: Doubleday, 1979), 42.

131. Frank Chodorov, "How a Jew Came to God: An Intellectual Experience," *analysis* 4 (March 1948): 1. (Reprinted in *One Is a Crowd*, 8–33.)

132. Chodorov, *Out of Step*, 79. He was also a friend of Albert Jay Nock, who in 1941 published a highly controversial article in the *Atlantic Monthly* entitled "The Jewish Problem in America." If Chodorov was aware of the ensuing uproar and of suspicion that Nock was anti-Semitic, he apparently never let it upset his friendship with a man he considered a mentor. In 1945, when Nock died, Chodorov became administrator of Nock's estate. See Albert Jay Nock, "The Jewish Problem in America," *Atlantic Monthly* 167 (June 1941): 699–706, and 168 (July 1941): 68–76; James Marshall, "The Anti-Semitic Problem in America," *Atlantic Monthly* 168 (August 1941): 144–49; Chodorov, *Out of Step*, 144.

133. Ryskind, *I Shot an Elephant*, 175. Ryskind later met Taft and was convinced both that Taft was sincerely anti-Nazi and that Taft had acted out of conscience on defensible constitutional grounds.

134. Articles by Lyons appeared in the March 1951 and February, April, and May 1953 issues of the *Catholic Digest*. See also Eugene Lyons, book review of Arnold Beichman, *Nine Lies about America*, in *Twin Circle*, July 14, 1972, copy in Lyons Papers, Box 4. A Catholic publishing house, Twin Circle brought out a paperback edition of *Assignment in Utopia* in 1967.

135. Toledano, *Lament for a Generation*, 91–92.

136. Eugene Lyons, "Our New Privileged Class," *American Legion Magazine* (September 1951): 37.

Both Lyons and Ryskind continued to support the American Jewish League Against Communism long after it had become a virtual pariah among Jewish organizations. In 1962 they were listed as vice presidents of the League. Marvin Liebman at that point was its executive secretary. American Jewish League Against Communism press release, February 28, 1962, Marvin Liebman Papers, Box 8, Hoover Institution Archives.

137. Eugene Lyons to Arnold Forster, June 7, 1962, Lyons Papers, Box 1, printed in *National Review* 12 (July 3, 1962): 469; Lyons to Forster, June 13, 1962, copy in George E. Sokolsky Papers, Box 266; *New York Times*, June 29, 1962, 1, 5.

138. William S. Schlamm, *Wer ist Jude?* (Stuttgart, Germany: Seewald, 1964), 60. The quotations are translated from the German.

139. Toledano, "Negro 'Hate Groups' Turn Openly on the Jews," ca. February 27–28, 1965, typescript copy enclosed with Toledano to Buckley, March 2, 1965, Buckley Papers, Box 34. Toledano's syndicate decided not to distribute this column.

140. Chodorov, *One Is a Crowd*, 12.

141. Chodorov, review of Elmer Berger, *A Partisan History of Judaism*, in *Human Events* 8 (December 19, 1951): no pagination; Chodorov, "Some Blunt Truths about Israel," *American Mercury* 83 (July 1956): 55–59. Chodorov also applauded Alfred Lilienthal's anti-Zionist polemic *What Price Israel?* in *Human Events* 10 (November 11, 1953).

142. Chodorov in *Human Events* 10 (November 11, 1953): no pagination. In 1956, a few months before the Suez war, Chodorov urged Americans to "keep out of" the Arab-Israeli imbroglio (Chodorov, "Some Blunt Truths about Israel," 59).

143. Ryskind to Buckley, March 26, 1959.

144. Buckley to the author, March 3, 1999. Schlamm may have helped to edit Alfred Lilienthal's book *What Price Israel?* in 1953. See Henry Regnery to Schlamm, February 9, 1953, and Schlamm to Regnery, April 9, 1953, both in Regnery Papers, Box 67. After reading Lilienthal's manuscript, Schlamm was quite willing to edit it and expressed sympathy with Lilienthal's intent.

145. Interview of John C. Meyer by the author, January 14, 1998.

146. Ibid.; interview of Priscilla L. Buckley, January 13, 1999. According to Buckley, Meyer was pro-Israel partly because he was Jewish and partly because of anti-Communist (Cold War) considerations. Meyer's son mentioned his father's support of Israel because it was an outpost of Western civilization.

147. Among our group of seven, Eugene Lyons seems to have been publicly silent about Israel—at least in those of his writings with which the author is familiar. As a prolific writer for magazines, Lyons specialized in the Communist issue and conditions in the Soviet Union.

148. Liebman, "Professional Notes"; Liebman, *Coming Out Conservative,* 55–79.

149. In 1967, just after the Six Day War, Liebman organized an ad hoc Council on Communist Anti-Semitic Policy and Practice to educate American Jews about Communist China's "venomous campaign of denunciation against Israel and against Jews in general." See Marvin Liebman to Benjamin Mandel, June 21, 1967; Liebman to Maxwell Steinhart (plus enclosure), August 10, 1967; Liebman to Donald A. Feder, September 1, 1967; all in Liebman Papers, Box 27. Among those who joined the council were Will Herberg and Eugene Lyons.

150. Toledano, *America, I Love You,* 307–11.

151. Toledano to Dr. and Mrs. David de Sola Pool, October 25, 1969, Ralph de Toledano Papers, Box 1, Hoover Institution Archives. Toledano wrote several syndicated columns while visiting Israel in March 1969; copies are in his papers, Box 3.

152. Toledano to Walter Minton, January 28, 1970, Toledano Papers, Box 1.

153. Ryskind received religious instruction prior to his bar mitzvah as a boy. Ryskind, *I Shot an Elephant,* 12–13. Many years later he remarked in a letter that he was about to commence his Yom Kippur fast. Ryskind to Buckley, September 27, 1963, Buckley Papers, Box 27. Evidently he remained observant.

154. Chodorov, *One Is a Crowd,* 15.

155. Interview of John C. Meyer by the author, January 14, 1998.

156. Toledano, "Among the Ashkenazim," 48; Toledano, *Notes from the Underground,* 72.

157. Toledano, *Lament for a Generation,* 8–9, 218, 247–48, 252–53; Toledano, "These Things I Believe," *The Standard* 33 (November 1946), 1.

158. Eugene Lyons to T. P. Curry, February 19, 1938; Lyons to Walter Hogan, June 6, 1938; both in Lyons Papers, Box 6. The author has found no evidence that Lyons ever altered his views.

159. Lyons, *Assignment in Utopia,* 7.

160. Liebman, *Coming Out Conservative,* 220.

161. Chodorov, *One Is a Crowd,* 22–29.

162. After suffering a massive stroke in 1961, Chodorov was eventually placed in a Roman

Catholic nursing home. (His close friend William F. Buckley Jr. arranged this, at the request of Chodorov's daughter.) There he lived out his last days and even attended church on Sunday. But though he had come to believe in the doctrine of natural law, he never joined a religious group, and he stipulated that his burial service not be religious in character. Fittingly, though, there was a eulogy offered by William F. Buckley Jr. Had it not been for the encouragement and editorial help that Chodorov had given him with his first book *(God and Man at Yale)*, it is "quite unlikely," Buckley later wrote, that he would ever have "pursued a career as a writer," See Grace Klein to Buckley, July 30 and October 31, 1965; Buckley to Grace Klein, August 3, 1965 (all in Buckley Papers, Box 35); Buckley, *Jeweler's Eye*, 343–49; Buckley to E. Victor Millone, June 6, 1960, Buckley Papers, Box 10. The transfer of Chodorov from another nursing home (where he was unhappy) to the Catholic one did not appear to have any religious significance.

163. Toledano, *Lament for a Generation*, 243–59.

164. Toledano to Whittaker Chambers, December 14, 1951, printed in Toledano, *Notes from the Underground*, 71–72. See also 304.

165. See, for example, Toledano, "The Masses of Victoria," *National Review* 9 (October 8, 1960): 216–17. In this essay he remarks, "The Mass is a door to God." One of Toledano's favorite poets was the Spanish mystic St. John of the Cross. In 1966, Toledano published a religious poem of his own in an ultraconservative Catholic magazine edited by William F. Buckley Jr.'s brother-in-law. See Toledano, *Lament for a Generation*, 127, 250; Toledano, *Notes from the Underground*, xxii, 60; Toledano, "The Small Gospel of Peter," *Triumph* 1 (November 1966): 33.

166. Toledano, *Lament for a Generation*, 252.

167. Toledano, "Among the Ashkenazim," 50–51.

168. Toledano, *Notes from the Underground*, 242.

169. Ibid., 304. In this passage Toledano writes of Whittaker Chambers's "failure to come to terms with the Roman church—a failure shared by me for I could never forget what the church and state had done to my ancestor Daniel de Toledo—the particle of nobility having been granted by Ferdinand and Isabella—and to his family." See also "Among the Ashkenazim," 48.

On a more mundane level, Toledano was also annoyed by the negative reaction of some Catholics to a passage they deemed offensive in his 1955 novel *Day of Reckoning*. "The brethren have dropped me cold," he reported to Whittaker Chambers in 1956. "No more invitations to speak at Communion Breakfasts, no more friendly hints about conversion, no more conspiratorial chattiness." *Notes from the Underground*, 223; see also 192, 242.

170. Toledano, *Notes from the Underground*, 50, 164–5.

171. William F. Buckley Jr., to the author, March 3, 1999. The quoted words are Buckley's but may have been Schlamm's actual self-description also.

172. Schlamm, quoted in *Der Spiegel* 14 (May 11, 1960): 31.

173. Buckley oral history interview (1996).

174. Cited in note 138.

175. Carlo Schmid, " . . . Wer Jude Sein Will," *Der Spiegel* 19 (June 2, 1965): 117–18, 120.

176. Erik von Kuehnelt-Leddihn, "William S. Schlamm, RIP," *National Review* 30 (October 13, 1978): 1284.

177. Ibid.

178. Liebman, *Coming Out Conservative*, 219–23; William F. Buckley Jr., "Marvin Liebman, RIP," *National Review* 49 (April 21, 1997): 18; interview of Priscilla L. Buckley by

the author, January 13, 1999. There is a sequel to this story. In 1990, Liebman publicly declared himself a homosexual in a letter to William F. Buckley Jr. which was published in *National Review* 42 (July 9, 1990): 16–18. For the rest of his life, Liebman was a gay rights activist as well as a conservative. In protest at the Roman Catholic Church's position on homosexuality, Liebman stopped attending mass. But both Buckley (in his obituary notice in *National Review)* and his sister (in her interview with the author) have indicated that Liebman did not renounce his Catholic faith.

179. Interview of John C. Meyer by the author, January 14, 1998.

180. "Frank S. Meyer," *National Review* 24 (April 28, 1972): 467, 473 (reminiscences by Peter P. Witonski and L. Brent Bozell).

181. Interview of John C. Meyer, January 14, 1998.

182. Ibid.

183. Wills, *Confessions of a Conservative,* 42. According to Wills, the "problem he [Meyer] had with Judaism" was "its feel for supporting *community.*"

184. Ibid.

185. Interview of John C. Meyer, January 14, 1998; Frank S. Meyer to Rose Wilder Lane, December 11, 1953, "Meyer, Frank. S., 1953–55," Correspondence and Subject File, Rose Wilder Lane Papers, Herbert Hoover Presidential Library, West Branch, Iowa. In 1962, in his aptly titled *In Defense of Freedom*, Meyer declared himself "certain" that "Christianity, which informs Western civilization, is the highest and deepest relationship to the Divine that men can attain . . . but I am not able to say that any single institutional church is the bearer of God's spirit on earth" (165). In a column in *National Review* in 1962 (later reprinted) Meyer asserted that "the Christian understanding of the nature and destiny of man, which is the foundation of Western civilization, is always and everywhere what conservatives strive to conserve" (Frank S. Meyer, *The Conservative Mainstream* [New Rochelle: Arlington House, 1969], 54). It seems revealing that he did not say "the Judeo-Christian understanding," a formulation that became common among conservatives in the generation after him.

186. "Frank S. Meyer," 466 (reminiscence by William F. Buckley Jr.).

187. Ibid.; Wills, *Confessions of a Conservative,* 42.

188. Interview of Priscilla L. Buckley, January 13, 1999. Buckley recalled that Meyer was quite libertarian about abortion. He believed that the government should not tell people whether or not they could have abortions.

189. Meyer to Rose Wilder Lane, December 11, 1953; Wills, *Confessions of a Conservative,* 42.

190. He did not find the Church's position on suicide convincing, he told a priest two days before his death. *One* day before his death he informed William F. Buckley Jr. that he did not like the collectivist sound of the Christian doctrine of "the communion of the saints." "Frank S. Meyer," 466 (Buckley reminiscence); Buckley to the author, March 3, 1999; Buckley, "Frank S. Meyer," *National Review* 32 (December 31, 1980): 1639.

191. "Frank S. Meyer," 467 (Buckley reminiscence).

192. Schlamm, *Wer Ist Jude?*, 56. The quoted words are translated from the German. It is interesting that Frank Chodorov, who did not convert to Christianity, maintained that being Jewish was compatible with a philosophy of individualism; Chodorov contended that it was "the tendency toward self-expression which we call individualism" which "has got the Jew into difficulties" over the years. He asserted that "the Jewish child has drilled into him almost from birth the importance of self-improvement through self-help." He insisted that "Jewish culture is definitely not socialistic, even though tribal adherence has always been emphasized as a matter of self-preservation" (Chodorov, *One Is a Crowd,* 32).

Similarly, Eugene Lyons (who also did not convert) wrote in 1947, "Totalitarianism in any form, in the final analysis, is alien to the spirit of the Jewish people, who are anything but collectivist" (Lyons, "Myth of Jewish Communism," 23).

193. Liebman did visit some Protestant churches in his search for a spiritual home, but his interest in them seems to have been brief and casual. Liebman, *Coming Out Conservative,* 219.

194. Buckley did discuss these matters with Frank Meyer shortly before be died, but Meyer had already spoken with a priest and, of course, had been attracted to Catholicism for years, even before he knew Buckley. Liebman had been a virtual member of the Buckley family for years, but he seems to have reached his decision before discussing it with Buckley. In neither case (Meyer and Liebman) can one say that Buckley was a decisive figure in their religious conversion.

195. Nash, *Conservative Intellectual Movement,* 70–71, 114, 136.

196. Murray Friedman, "Right of Passage," *Moment* (October 1997): 51–52.

197. Kuehnelt-Leddihn, "William S. Schlamm, RIP," 1284; Kuehnelt-Leddihn, "The Phenomenon of Willi Schlamm," *National Review* 9 (September 24, 1960): 177–79; *Der Spiegel* 14 (May 11, 1960): 14, 28–34, 36–42; *American Opinion* 3 (June 1960): 27–28; *New York Times,* February 12, 1960, 10; *Der Spiegel* 32 (September 11, 1978): 252. Schlamm was often the subject of critical coverage in *Der Spiegel,* which featured a full-page photograph of "Demagoge Schlamm" on the cover of its May 11, 1960 issue.

198. "Frank S. Meyer," 471 (reminiscence by M. Stanton Evans).

199. Buckley, "Marvin Liebman, RIP," 18; Buckley column on Liebman in *National Review* 44 (October 5, 1992): 71.

200. Liebman, *Coming Out Conservative,* 90.

201. Among them were Milton Friedman, David Lawrence, and George Sokolsky.

CHAPTER 24: JOINING THE RANKS

1. Book-length treatments of neoconservatism include (in order of appearance) Peter Steinfels, *The Neoconservatives* (New York: Simon and Schuster, 1979); Gary Dorrien, *The Neoconservative Mind: Culture and the War of Ideology* (Philadelphia: Temple University Press, 1993); John Ehrman, *The Rise of Neoconservatism: Intellectuals and Foreign Affairs, 1945–1994* (New Haven, CT: Yale University Press, 1995); and Mark Gerson, *The Neoconservative Vision: From the Cold War to the Culture Wars* (Lanham, MD: Madison Books, 1996). Neoconservatives are a major subject of David Hoeveler, *Watch on the Right: Conservative Intellectuals in the Reagan Era* (Madison, WI: University of Wisconsin Press, 1991). A lively compendium is Christopher De Muth and William Kristol, eds., *The Neoconservative Imagination: Essays in Honor of Irving Kristol* (Washington, D.C.: AEI Press, 1995). Several neoconservatives have written highly illuminating memoirs. These include Irving Kristol, *Neoconservatism: The Autobiography of an Idea* (New York: Free Press, 1995) and Midge Decter, *An Old Wife's Tale: My Seven Decades in Love and War* (New York: ReganBooks, 2001). Of crucial importance for the history of *Commentary* are four volumes by Norman Podhoretz: *Making It* (New York: Random House, 1967), *Breaking Ranks: A Political Memoir* (New York: Harper & Row, 1979), *Ex-Friends* (San Francisco: Encounter Books, 2000), and *My Love Affair with America: The Cautionary Tale of a Cheerful Conservative* (New York: Free Press, 2000). For accounts of the "New York intellectuals" that contain significant discussion of *Commentary*'s history, see Alexander Bloom, *Prodigal Sons: The New York Intellectuals and Their World* (New York: Oxford

University Press, 1986); Alan M. Wald, *The New York Intellectuals: The Rise and Decline of the Anti-Stalinist Left from the 1930s to the 1980s* (Chapel Hill, NC: University of North Carolina Press, 1987); and Neil Jumonville, *Critical Crossings: The New York Intellectuals in Postwar America* (Berkeley, CA: University of California Press, 1991).

2. Podhoretz's *Breaking Ranks, Ex-Friends,* and *My Love Affair with America* treat his disillusionment with, and revolt from, the Left at length. See also Norman Podhoretz, "The 'Commentary' Case," *Quadrant* 31 (August 1987): 29–32, and his essay "Neoconservatism: A Eulogy," *Commentary* 101 (March 1996): 19–27. For Podhoretz's use of the phrase "the cultural revolution of the 60's" quoted in the text, see his article "What the Voters Sensed," *Commentary* 55 (January 1973): 6.

3. Norman Podhoretz, "A Certain Anxiety," *Commentary* 52 (August 1971): 4, 6, 8, 10.

4. As a further sign of the magazine's new direction, Podhoretz introduced into the June 1970 issue an editorial column of his own, entitled "Issues." *Commentary* 49 (June 1970): 26, 28. He continued the column through December 1972.

5. Podhoretz, *My Love Affair with America,* 180.

6. See, for example, Louis Harap, " 'Commentary' Moves to the Right," *Jewish Currents* 25 (December 1971): 4–9, 27–30; Merle Miller, "Why Norman and Jason Aren't Talking," *New York Times Magazine,* March 26, 1972, 34–35, 104–111.

7. "Come On In, the Water's Fine," *National Review* 23 (March 9, 1971): 249–50.

8. James Burnham, "Selective, Yes. Humanism, Maybe," *National Review* 24 (May 23, 1972): 516.

9. Podhoretz's correspondence with Buckley may be found in the William F. Buckley Jr. Papers, Manuscripts and Archives, Yale University Library. The earliest item in the Podhoretz file is a letter from him to Buckley dated March 2, 1972.

10. Buckley to Podhoretz, March 28, 1972, Buckley Papers.

11. Podhoretz to Buckley, February 1, 1973, and Buckley to Podhoretz, April 26, 1973, Buckley Papers. Because of illness Buckley was unable to contribute to the symposium.

12. Dwight Macdonald, "Scrambled Eggheads on the Right," *Commentary* 21 (April 1956): 367–73; recorded oral history interview of William F. Buckley Jr., September 27, 1996, by Timothy S. Goeglein, copy in the Motion Picture, Broadcasting, and Recorded Sound Division, Library of Congress, Washington, D.C.

13. Richard H. Rovere, "The Conservative Mindlessness," *Commentary* 39 (March 1965): 38–42.

14. Podhoretz, *Ex-Friends,* 167–68.

15. Podhoretz, "A Certain Anxiety," 6, 10.

16. This is a phrase that I used in 1976 to describe the new political orientation then arising at *Commentary* and at the publication *The Public Interest.* George H. Nash, *The Conservative Intellectual Movement in America Since 1945* (New York: Basic Books, 1976), 324–27.

17. Podhoretz, "The 'Commentary' Case," 31.

18. Lewis A. Coser and Irving Howe, eds., *The New Conservatives: A Critique from the Left* (New York: Quadrangle, 1974).

19. Podhoretz, "Neoconservatism: A Eulogy," 20. Michael Harrington was not the first person to use the word "neoconservatism" (which can be traced back to the 1950s), but he and some of his colleagues on the Left were evidently the first, or among the first, to apply it specifically to the phenomenon represented by *Commentary.*

20. Podhoretz, *Breaking Ranks,* 354–56; Midge Decter, contribution to "What Is a Liberal—Who Is a Conservative?" *Commentary* 62 (September 1976): 50–51.

21. *New York Times*, December 7, 1972, 14; Podhoretz, *Breaking Ranks*, 339, 344; Ehrman, *Rise of Neoconservatism*, 60–61.

22. Podhoretz, *My Love Affair with America*, 180–81; *Ex-Friends*, 224–25; Elliott Abrams, contribution to "Liberalism and the Jews," *Commentary* 69 (January 1980): 17.

23. Daniel Patrick Moynihan, "The United States in Opposition," *Commentary* 59 (March 1975): 31–44.

24. Podhoretz, *Breaking Ranks*, 351–54.

25. Ibid., 16, 356–57; Ehrman, *Rise of Neoconservatism*, 90–92.

26. Ehrman, *Rise of Neoconservatism*, 92–96, 131–35.

27. Established in 1965 by Irving Kristol and Daniel Bell, *The Public Interest* put forth a steady stream of critical analysis of Great Society liberalism, both in theory and practice. *The Public Interest*'s focus, however, was on public policy, not on the wider political and cultural turbulence associated with the sixties Left. *Commentary*—although receptive to *The Public Interest*'s outlook—was not a policy journal aimed at social scientists. Its paramount concerns included foreign policy and what later became known as the "culture wars."

28. Podhoretz, "Neoconservatism: A Eulogy," 21. It was precisely because Senator James Buckley of New York appeared to Podhoretz to be an enemy of the New Deal and the "liberal welfare state" that Podhoretz deemed Buckley "a radical of the Right." Podhoretz, *Breaking Ranks*, 356, 358.

29. Podhoretz, "Neoconservatism: A Eulogy," 21.

30. Ibid. It is noteworthy that when Podhoretz "broke ranks" with the Democratic Party of the McGovernites, he allied himself for a time with the Social Democrats, a small Socialist group linked to the anti-Communist leadership of the AFL-CIO. Podhoretz, *My Love Affair with America*, 180. Podhoretz's wife also briefly became affiliated with the Social Democrats; see Midge Decter, "Socialism's Nine Lives," *Commentary* 113 (June 2002): 30.

31. Podhoretz, *Breaking Ranks*, 27.

32. In 2002 Midge Decter asserted that in the 1970s American "ideological conservatives, who by decade's end would be preparing to take power, were with only a few exceptions still sulking in their cultural tents" (Decter, "Socialism's Nine Lives," 30). One suspects that many other "neoconservatives" at that time shared Decter's view of the "ideological conservatives."

33. Lionel Trilling, *The Liberal Imagination: Essays on Literature and Society* (New York: Viking Press, 1950), ix.

34. Podhoretz, *My Love Affair with America*, 189–90.

35. Jeffrey Hart, "New Directions: Catholics and Jews," *National Review* 30 (April 28, 1978): 517–20.

36. Podhoretz, *Breaking Ranks*, 307; "Neoconservatism: A Eulogy," 22.

37. As late as 1979, Podhoretz was using the words "centrist" and "centrist liberal" to describe his political position; Podhoretz, *Breaking Ranks*, 16.

38. Ehrman, *Rise of Neoconservatism*, chapter 4: "Searching for Truman: 1976–1980," 97–136.

39. Ibid., 131–35.

40. Norman Podhoretz, "The Riddle of Reagan," *Weekly Standard* 4 (November 9, 1998): 22–24.

41. Podhoretz, *Ex-Friends*, 100.

42. Ibid.; Norman Podhoretz, *The Present Danger* (New York: Simon and Schuster, 1980);

Michael Kramer, "The Book Reagan Wants You to Read," *New York* 13 (December 1, 1980): 23–24, 26.

43. Norman Podhoretz, "The New American Majority," *Commentary* 71 (January 1981): 19–28.

44. Among the *Commentary* contributors and other supporters who took important positions in the Reagan administration were Elliott Abrams (Podhoretz's son-in-law), William Bennett, Linda Chavez, William Kristol, Richard Perle, and Richard Pipes.

45. Jeane Kirkpatrick, "Dictatorships and Double Standards," *Commentary* 68 (November 1979): 34–45; Podhoretz, "The 'Commentary' Case," 30.

46. Podhoretz, *Ex-Friends*, 98; Norman Podhoretz, "The Neo-Conservative Anguish Over Reagan's Foreign Policy," *New York Times Magazine,* May 2, 1982, 30.

47. It was in the early 1980s that neoconservatives lost what Irving Kristol called their "social democratic wing." Although most of the original "neoconservatives" moved to the right on economic issues, a few remained on the left-of-center. Senator Daniel Patrick Moynihan also left the *Commentary* orbit. Years later Norman Podhoretz observed that in making an intellectual case for capitalism the neoconservatives had been positively "heretical" toward the socialist tradition of the "New York intellectuals" out of whose milieu so many neoconservatives had come. Podhoretz, *Ex-Friends,* 229.

48. Irving Kristol, "Ideology and Supply-Side Economics," *Commentary* 71 (April 1981): 48–54.

49. As Podhoretz later put it, "It was the neoconservatives who decided that the time had come to drag capitalism out of the closet." Podhoretz, "Neoconservatism: A Eulogy," 23. See also Podhoretz, *Ex-Friends,* 229, and "The New Defenders of Capitalism," *Harvard Business Review* 59 (March-April 1981): 96–106.

50. George Gilder, *Wealth and Poverty* (New York: Basic Books, 1981).

51. Michael Novak, *The Spirit of Democratic Capitalism* (New York: Simon and Schuster, 1982). *Commentary's* reviewer hailed Novak's book as a "stunning achievement." Samuel McCracken, "A Theology of Capitalism," *Commentary* 74 (July 1982): 74, 76–77.

52. See, for example, Podhoretz, "Neo-Conservative Anguish," 30–33, 88–89, 92, 96, 97; "Appeasement By Any Other Name," *Commentary* 76 (July 1983): 25–38; "The Reagan Road to Detente," *Foreign Affairs* 63, no. 3 (1985): 447–64.

53. Podhoretz, "Riddle of Reagan," 25.

54. The words "impostor" and "interlopers" were used by the paleoconservative professors Clyde Wilson and M. E. Bradford, respectively, in *Intercollegiate Review* 21 (Spring 1986): 7, 15.

55. On the Bradford-Bennett controversy, see: George F. Will, "A Shrill Assault on Mr. Lincoln," *Washington Post,* November 29, 1981, C7; John B. Judis, "The Conservative Wars," *New Republic* 195 (August 11 and 18, 1986): 15–16; Paul Gottfried, *The Conservative Movement,* revised edition (New York: Twayne Publishers, 1993), 74–75; Gerson, *Neoconservative Vision,* 312–13. Among paleoconservatives Bradford's defeat produced great bitterness that persists to this day. See, for example, Samuel Francis, "Inhospitable Neos," *National Review* 41 (April 7, 1989): 43; Joseph Scotchie, *Revolt from the Heartland: The Struggle for an Authentic Conservatism* (New Brunswick, NJ: Transaction, 2002), 56–58; and Samuel Francis, "The Paleo Persuasion," December 16, 2002, posted at *The American Conservative's* website (available at <http://www.amconmag.com>).

56. "The State of Conservatism: A Symposium," *Intercollegiate Review* 21 (Spring 1986): 3–28; Jeffrey Hart, "Gang Warfare in Chicago," *National Review* 38 (June 6, 1986): 32–33; Judis, "Conservative Wars," 16.

57. See, for example, Hart, "Gang Warfare in Chicago," 32–33; Judis, "Conservative Wars," 15–18; Paul Gottfried, "Notes on Neoconservatism," *The World and I* 1 (September 1986): 573–82; Edward Shapiro, "Conservatism and Its Discontents," ibid., 565–72; Brigitte Berger and Peter L. Berger, "Our Conservatism and Theirs," *Commentary* 82 (October 1986): 62–67; Ernest van den Haag, "The War between Paleos and Neos," *National Review* 41 (February 24, 1989): 21–23; "Paleolithics," ibid., April 7, 1989, 43–44, 46; David Frum, "Cultural Clash on the Right," *Wall Street Journal*, June 2, 1989, A16; Robert Moynihan, "Thunder on the Right," *30 Days* (September 1989): 66–72; John B. Judis, "The War at Home," *In These Times* 14 (March 14–20, 1990): 12–13, 22; Llewellyn H. Rockwell, Jr., "A New Right," *Rothbard-Rockwell Report* 1 (April 1990): 8–12; John P. Judis, "The Conservative Crackup," *American Prospect* 1 (Fall 1990): 30–42; Jacob Weisberg, "Hunter Gatherers," *New Republic* 205 (September 2, 1991): 14–16. The neo-paleo feud is also discussed in detail in the books by Dorrien and Gerson (cited earlier) and in Gottfried, *Conservative Movement,* 142–66. See also Sara Diamond, *Roads to Dominion: Right-Wing Movements and Political Power in the United States* (New York: Guilford Press, 1995), 279–89. For an excellent analysis of the intellectual tensions between neoconservatives and paleoconservatives, see Edward S. Shapiro, "Jews and the Conservative Rift," *American Jewish History* 87 (June and September 1999): 195–215. An astute account of paleoconservatism is Edward Ashbee, "Politics of Paleoconservatism," *Society* 37 (March-April 2000): 75–84.

58. Paul Gottfried, "Scrambling for Funds," *Rothbard-Rockwell Report* 2 (March 1991): 9–15; Gottfried, *Conservative Movement,* 118–41.

59. Russell Kirk, *The Politics of Prudence* (Bryn Mawr, PA: Intercollegiate Studies Institute, 1993), 187. Kirk's charge is contained in a chapter entitled "The Neoconservatives: An Endangered Species" (172–90). This essay was originally a lecture delivered at the Heritage Foundation in Washington, D.C., in 1988.

60. Stephen J. Tonsor, "Why I Too Am Not a Neoconservative," *National Review* 38 (June 20, 1986): 55.

61. Van den Haag, "War between Paleos and Neos," 21.

62. Shapiro, "Conservatism and Its Discontents," 569; Shapiro, "Jews and the Conservative Rift," 204.

63. Kirk, *Politics of Prudence,* 187.

64. Kirk accused many of the neoconservatives of being "cultural and economic imperialists"; ibid.

65. Tonsor, "Why I Too Am Not a Neoconservative," 54–56. Said Tonsor: "Unbelief is incompatible with Conservatism" (ibid., 55).

66. Dan Himmelfarb, "Conservative Splits," *Commentary* 85 (May 1988): 54–58.

67. Norman Podhoretz, "The Hate That Dares Not Speak Its Name," *Commentary* 82 (November 1986): 21–32; Norman Podhoretz, "What Is Anti-Semitism? An Open Letter to William F. Buckley Jr.," *Commentary* 93 (February 1992): 15–20; Norman Podhoretz, "Buchanan and the Conservative Crackup," *Commentary* 93 (May 1992): 30–34. See also Podhoretz, *My Love Affair with America,* 202–4. Additional details about these controversies may be found in most of the sources cited in note 57.

68. Podhoretz, "What Is Anti-Semitism?" 16–17; "Buchanan and the Conservative Crackup," 30–4. See also Joshua Muravchik, "Patrick J. Buchanan and the Jews," *Commentary* 91 (January 1991): 29–37.

69. Patrick J. Buchanan, "Conservatives heading for a crack-up," *Boston Herald,* May 1, 1991, 31.

70. Podhoretz, "Buchanan and the Conservative Crackup," 30–34; letters to the editor in *Commentary* 94 (September 1992): 2, 4–6, 8–10, 12; Norman Podhoretz, "Buchanan and Anti-Semitism," *Wall Street Journal,* October 25, 1999, A52; Patrick J. Buchanan, letter to the editor, *Wall Street Journal,* November 5, 1999, A19; Norman Podhoretz, letter to the editor, *Wall Street Journal,* November 8, 1999, A51.

71. Podhoretz, "Buchanan and the Conservative Crackup," 32; John O'Sullivan letter to the editor, *Commentary* 94 (September 1992): 2, 4; Podhoretz rejoinder to O'Sullivan, ibid., 10.

72. William F. Buckley Jr., *In Search of Anti-Semitism* (New York: Continuum, 1992).

73. Podhoretz, "What Is Anti-Semitism?" 15–20.

74. Ibid., 15, 20.

75. It is called *The American Conservative.*

76. Podhoretz, "The Hate That Dares Not Speak Its Name," 32; Moynihan, "Thunder on the Right," 71; Gottfried, "Scrambling for Funds," 9–15; Gottfried, *Conservative Movement,* 118–41; Gottfried, "Conservative Crack-up Continued," *Society* 31 (January–February 1994): 23–9.

77. Burnham, "Selective, Yes. Humanism, Maybe," 516.

78. In mid-1979, Irving Kristol remarked that "the gap is closing" between Reaganite conservatives and the neoconservatives. In his judgment, conservatives were "gradually becoming, I would say, somewhat neoconservative." In his opinion, Reagan and "the Republican Party as a whole" were moving toward an acceptance of "the welfare state principle" coupled with criticism of the welfare state's "size and shape"; in other words, the neoconservative position. Irving Kristol, remarks at National Public Radio's "National Town Meeting: 'The Neoconservatives," Washington, D.C., July 19, 1979 (transcript in the author's possession). Kristol's comments proved prophetic of the practice (if not, perhaps, the theory) of applied Reaganite conservatism in the 1980s.

79. In 1996 Norman Podhoretz suggested that many traditional conservatives moved toward acceptance of the principles of the (early) civil rights movement "under the tutelage of the neoconservatives." Podhoretz, "Neoconservatism: A Eulogy," 24.

80. Ibid., 23–24.

81. Thus, Podhoretz's book *My Love Affair with America* contains considerable discussion of the "culture wars" of the 1990s. It also seems emblematic of his evolving interests that his latest book focuses on religion. See Podhoretz, *The Prophets: Who They Were, What They Are* (New York: Free Press, 2002). It is also noteworthy that during the 1990s, Podhoretz's wife, Midge Decter, was affiliated for five years with the Institute on Religion and Public Life, publisher of the religiously oriented journal *First Things.* Decter, *An Old Wife's Tale,* 176–81.

82. David Cantor, *The Religious Right: The Assault on Tolerance and Pluralism in America* (New York: Anti-Defamation League, 1994); *New York Times,* July 23, 1994, 26.

83. *New York Times,* July 23, 1994, 26.

84. See, for example, Arnold Forster and Benjamin R. Epstein, *Danger on the Right* (New York: Random House, 1964).

85. *New York Times,* July 23, 1994, 26; ibid., August 2, 1994, A21 (for the advertisement). See also Midge Decter, "The ADL vs. the 'Religious Right,'" *Commentary* 98 (September 1994): 45–47, and letters to the editor, *Commentary* 99 (January 1995): 10–14.

86. Norman Podhoretz, "In the Matter of Pat Robertson," *Commentary* 100 (August 1995): 27–32. Podhoretz remarked here that "in my view Robertson's support for Israel trumps the anti-Semitic pedigree of his ideas about the secret history of the dream of a new world order," (32).

87. Norman Podhoretz, "The Christian Right and Its Demonizers," *National Review* 52 (April 3, 2000): 30–32.

88. Midge Decter, "A Jew in Anti-Christian America," *First Things*, no. 56 (October 1995): 25–31. See also Irving Kristol, "The Future of American Jewry," *Commentary* 92 (August 1991): 21–26. According to Kristol, "The real danger is not from a revived Christianity, which American Jews (if they are sensible) can cope with, but from an upsurge of anti-biblical barbarism that will challenge Christianity, Judaism, and Western civilization altogether" (26).

89. Richard John Neuhaus, "Introduction" to "The End of Democracy? The Judicial Usurpation of Politics," *First Things*, no. 67 (November 1996): 18–20. The ensuing symposium contained essays by five contributors. Although the "Introduction" was signed by "The Editors," Neuhaus himself (the editor in chief) evidently wrote it. Podhoretz, *My Love Affair with America*, 204.

90. Podhoretz, *My Love Affair with America*, 204–5, 208–9; contribution to "On the Future of Conservatism," *Commentary* 103 (February 1997): 35–37.

91. Ibid.; Gertrude Himmelfarb, letter to the editor, *First Things*, no. 69 (January 1997): 2.

92. The two were Gertrude Himmelfarb and Peter Berger. A third contributor, Walter Berns, also resigned. *First Things*, no. 69 (January 1997): 2, 3; and Jacob Heilbrunn, "Neocon v. Theocon," *New Republic* 215 (December 30, 1996): 22.

93. The *First Things* symposium generated a huge outpouring of commentary, much of which has been collected in two volumes: Mitchell S. Muncy, ed., *The End of Democracy?* (Dallas: Spence, 1997); Mitchell S. Muncy, ed., *The End of Democracy? II: A Crisis of Legitimacy* (Dallas: Spence, 1999).

94. Heilbrunn, "Neocon v. Theocon," 20–24; David Glenn, "The Schism," *Lingua Franca* 7 (February 1997): 24–26; Michael Rust and David Wagner, "GOP Philosopher-Kings Battle for Soul of the Party," *Insight* (February 3, 1997): 12–15; *Chronicle of Higher Education*, February 7, 1997, A14–15.

95. Rabbi Mayer Schiller, quoted in *Insight* (February 3, 1997): 15.

96. Podhoretz, *My Love Affair with America*, 215–20.

97. Ibid., 220.

98. Ibid., 232–35.

99. Podhoretz, contribution to "On the Future of Conservatism," 36.

100. Podhoretz, *My Love Affair with America*, 209.

101. Ibid.

102. Podhoretz, "Neoconservatism: A Eulogy," 19, 25.

103. Ibid., 26, 25, 23.

104. Arthur Hertzberg, *A Jew in America: My Life and a People's Struggle for Identity* (San Francisco: HarperSanFrancisco, 2002), 284–85.

105. Murray Friedman, "Rights of Passage," *Moment* (October 1997): 51–52.

CHAPTER 26: THE "GREAT ENIGMA" AND THE "GREAT ENGINEER"

1. *New York Times*, April 4, 1923, 1; [Ray Thomas Tucker], *The Mirrors of 1932* (New York: Brewer, Warren & Putnam, 1931), 65; James E. Watson, *As I Knew Them* (Indianapolis and New York: Bobbs-Merrill Company, 1936), 233.

2. *New York Times*, August 5, 1923, 5; Robert K. Murray, *The Harding Era: Warren G. Harding and His Administration* (Minneapolis: University of Minnesota Press, 1969), and

Robert K. Murray, "Herbert Hoover and the Harding Cabinet," in Ellis W. Hawley, ed., *Herbert Hoover as Secretary of Commerce: Studies in New Era Thought and Practice* (Iowa City, IA: University of Iowa Press, 1981), 19–40.

3. For Coolidge's background, see Claude M. Fuess, *Calvin Coolidge: The Man from Vermont* (Boston: Little, Brown and Company, 1940); Donald R. McCoy, *Calvin Coolidge: The Quiet President* (Lawrence, KS: University Press of Kansas, 1988); Donald R. McCoy, unpublished paper, "Herbert Hoover's Relations with Warren G. Harding and Calvin Coolidge," delivered at George Fox College, October 1993 (copy in possession of the author).

4. R. V. Oulahan, "Hoover, the Handy, Plays Many Parts," *New York Times Magazine*, November 22, 1925, 3; Hendrik Booraem V, *The Provincial: Calvin Coolidge and His World, 1885–1895* (Lewisburg, PA: Bucknell University Press, 1994), 36–37.

5. John Hiram McKee, *Coolidge Wit and Wisdom* (New York: Frederick A. Stokes Company, 1933), 121.

6. "Memoirs of Robert G. Simmons" (typescript, n.d.), 15, in Robert G. Simmons Papers, Herbert Hoover Library, West Branch, Iowa; H. L. Mencken, *A Carnival of Buncombe* (Baltimore: Johns Hopkins Press, 1956), 124.

7. James H. MacLafferty, "A Visit to Calvin and Grace Coolidge at 'the Beeches,' Northampton, Massachusetts, September 24, 1930" (typescript, n.d.), 7, in James H. MacLafferty Papers, Herbert Hoover Library.

8. Russell Lord, *The Wallaces of Iowa* (Boston: Houghton Mifflin Company, 1947), 253.

9. McCoy, *Calvin Coolidge,* 290.

10. George H. Nash, *The Life of Herbert Hoover: The Humanitarian, 1914–1917* (New York: W. W. Norton & Company, 1988), 370.

11. Dwight Morrow to J. P. Morgan Jr., ca. August 19, 1927, quoted in Harold Nicolson, *Dwight Morrow* (New York: Harcourt, Brace and Company, 1935), 291.

12. Howard H. Quint and Robert H. Ferrell, eds., *The Talkative President: The Off-the-Record Press Conferences of Calvin Coolidge* (Amherst, MA: University of Massachusetts Press, 1964), 9.

13. A. H. Ulm, "Hoover Emerges as a Cabinet," *New York Times,* September 19, 1926, sec. 4, 1.

14. Herbert Hoover, *The Memoirs of Herbert Hoover,* vol. 2: *The Cabinet and the Presidency* (New York: Macmillan Company, 1952), 56.

15. Ibid., 55–56.

16. Brand Whitlock diary, February 26, 1921, in Allan Nevins, ed., *The Journal of Brand Whitlock* (New York: D. Appleton-Century Company, 1936), 652; Murray, "Herbert Hoover and the Harding Cabinet," 30–33; Edward L. Schapsmeier and Frederick H. Schapsmeier, "Disharmony in the Harding Cabinet: Hoover-Wallace Conflict," *Ohio History* 75 (Spring–Summer 1966): 126–36, 188–90.

17. Oswald Garrison Villard, "Presidential Possibilities: IV. Herbert C. Hoover," *The Nation* 126 (February 29, 1928): 235.

18. The use of the epithets "Great Enigma" for Coolidge and "Great Engineer" for Hoover may be seen in *Mirrors of 1932,* 56.

19. C. Bascom Slemp to Herbert Hoover, October 19, 1923, "President Coolidge: 1923, October," Commerce Papers, Herbert Hoover Papers, Herbert Hoover Library; McCoy, *Calvin Coolidge,* 200–2.

20. Hoover, *Memoirs,* 2: 115–16, 122; Calvin Coolidge to Hoover, March 14, 1924, "President Coolidge," Commerce Papers, Hoover Papers.

21. Hoover's remarks before Business Men's Commission on Agriculture, National Industrial Conference Board, April 15, 1927, Public Statements File, Hoover Papers.

22. McCoy, *Calvin Coolidge*, 234–35; Edgar Rickard diary, January 23, 1925, Hoover Library.

23. *New York Times*, November 20, 1923, 21; Hoover, *Memoirs*, 2: 56; Ralph Arnold, "Laying Foundation Stones: Part II," *Historical Society of Southern California Quarterly* 37 (September 1955): 243–60; Richard Dale Batman, "The Road to the Presidency: Hoover, Johnson, and the California Republican Party, 1920–1924" (Ph.D. dissertation, University of Southern California, 1965), 239–305; Hoover telegram to *California Republican*, April 26, 1924, "President Coolidge," Commerce Papers, Hoover Papers.

24. Mark Sullivan diary, March 25, 1924, Mark Sullivan Papers, Hoover Institution Archives, Stanford University; *New York Times*, May 29, 1924, 1; June 8, 1924, sec. I, 3; June 10, 1924, 1–2; June 11, 1924, 1.

25. Coverage of the Republican national convention can be found in the *New York Times* and other newspapers for June 10–13, 1924. See also "The Old Guard Plunges Through," *Independent* 112 (June 21, 1924): 329–30, for an account probably written by Hoover's friend and former secretary, Christian Herter, as well as McCoy, *Calvin Coolidge*, 245–47.

26. *New York Times*, June 13, 1924, 1; Hoover to Grosvenor Clarkson, June 21, 1924, "Clarkson, Grosvenor," Commerce Papers, Hoover Papers.

27. Hoover to C. Bascom Slemp, October 7, 1924; Slemp to Hoover, October 8, 1924. Both in Calvin Coolidge Papers, case file 482, Library of Congress, and in "President Coolidge," Commerce Papers, Hoover Papers.

28. Hoover to Coolidge, November 5, 1924, and Coolidge to Hoover, November 5, 1924, "President Coolidge," Commerce Papers, Hoover Papers; Mark Sullivan diary, November 18, 1924, Sullivan Papers; *New York Times*, November 21, 1924, 3.

29. Hoover to C. Bascom Slemp, November 3, 1924, "President Coolidge," Commerce Papers, Hoover Papers.

30. *New York Times*, January 16, 1925, 1; January 17, 1925, 1, 2. Privately Hoover worried that if he became secretary of agriculture he would be unable to win the loyalty of that department's bureau chiefs for at least two years. Edgar Rickard diary, January 23, 1925, Hoover Library. Some of the late Secretary Wallace's associates had been bitter opponents of Hoover—and vice versa.

31. *New York Times*, January 17, 1925, 1; William R. Castle Jr. diary, April 15, 1925, microfilm copy at the Hoover Library.

32. Ellis W. Hawley, "Herbert Hoover, the Commerce Secretariat, and the Vision of an 'Associative State,' 1921–1928," *Journal of American History* 61 (June 1974): 116–40; Coolidge, executive order 4239, June 4, 1925, "President Coolidge," Commerce Papers, Hoover Papers. See also Joseph Brandes, *Herbert Hoover and Economic Diplomacy: Department of Commerce Policy, 1921–1928* (Pittsburgh: University of Pittsburgh Press, 1962); Hawley, *Herbert Hoover as Secretary of Commerce*; Carl E. Krog and William R. Tanner, eds., *Herbert Hoover and the Republican Era: A Reconsideration* (Lanham, MD: University Press of America, 1984); R.V. Oulahan, "Hoover, the Handy, Plays Many Parts"; Philip T. Rosen, *The Modern Stentors: Radio Broadcasters and the Federal Government, 1920–1934* (Westport, CT: Greenwood Press, 1980); Robert Zieger, *Republicans and Labor, 1919–1929* (Lexington, KY: University Press of Kentucky, 1969); and Benjamin D. Rhodes, "Herbert Hoover and the War Debts, 1919–33," *Prologue* 6 (Summer 1974): 130–44.

33. "Washington Notes," *New Republic* 44 (September 2, 1925): 43; Oulahan, "Hoover, the Handy, Plays Many Parts," 3.

34. *New York Times,* April 26, 1925, sec. I, 25; Hoover, *Memoirs,* 2: 55; Richard Scandrett, "Remembering Calvin Coolidge: An Oral History Memoir," *Vermont History* 40 (Summer 1972): 209.

35. Hoover to Arthur McKeogh, January 23, 1935, Herbert Hoover Collection, Box 314, Calvin Coolidge folder, Hoover Institution Archives; Hoover to William Allen White, January 25, 1938, Post-Presidential Individual File, Hoover Papers; Hoover, *Memoirs,* 2: 55–56.

36. Hoover, *The Memoirs of Herbert Hoover,* vol. 3: *The Great Depression* (New York: Macmillan Company, 1952), 7–10; Herbert F. Margulies, "The Collaboration of Herbert Hoover and Irvine Lenroot, 1921–1928," *North Dakota History* 45 (Summer 1977): 40–41; Herbert F. Margulies, *Senator Lenroot of Wisconsin: A Political Biography, 1920–1929* (Columbia, MO and London: University of Missouri Press, 1977), 391; *New York Times,* December 31, 1925, 4.

37. Rickard diary, June 29–30, 1926, September 25–26, 1926; Brandes, *Herbert Hoover and Economic Diplomacy,* 84–128; Brandes, "Product Diplomacy: Herbert Hoover's Anti-Monopoly Campaign at Home and Abroad," in Hawley, ed., *Herbert Hoover as Secretary of Commerce,* 186–214; William R Castle Jr. to Alanson B. Houghton, January 7, 1926, "England: January–March 1926," William R. Castle Jr. Papers, Hoover Library; Castle diary, January 21, 1926.

38. Castle to Houghton, January 7, 1926; Castle diary, December 4, 1925, January 7 and 11, 1926.

39. Castle diary, December 4 and 5, 1925; New York *Evening World* article by Robert Barry, August 18, 1926, Coolidge Papers, case file 3.

40. Robert Barry article.

41. Ulm, "Hoover Emerges as a Cabinet."

42. Rickard diary, June 29–30, 1926; *New York Times,* October 17, 1926, 1, 3, and October 3, 1926, 9.

43. Hoover to Coolidge, October 19, 1926, "President Coolidge," Commerce Papers, Hoover Papers; *New York Times,* October 23, 1926, 9.

44. Coolidge to Hoover, October 25, 1926, and Hoover to Coolidge, October 25, 1926, Coolidge Papers, case file 3; [?] Burlew, telegrams (in behalf of Hoover) to Hubert Work, October 26 and 28, 1926, Coolidge Papers, case file 3.

45. Hoover, *Memoirs,* 2: 56, 112–16; Work to Hoover, October 28, 1926, "President Coolidge," Commerce Papers, Hoover Papers; Hoover to Work, October 29, 1926, Coolidge Papers, case file 3.

46. Hoover to Work, October 29, 1926; Hoover to Coolidge, November 2, 1926, Coolidge Papers, case file 3; Coolidge to Hoover, November 9, 1926, Coolidge Papers, case file 3.

47. In his *Memoirs,* Hoover stated that it was after a speech of his in Seattle on August 21, 1926, on "water conservation" that President Coolidge sent him a "sharp telegram . . . objecting on the ground that my proposals would improperly increase expenditures" (*Memoirs,* 2: 56). I have found no Coolidge-to-Hoover telegram fitting this description. Hoover's recollection here was probably inaccurate. In all likelihood, he was referring to the presidential telegram (quoted in my text) that he received in Tulsa, Oklahoma, on October 25, 1926.

48. A draft presidential veto message, heavily edited by—and apparently written by—Hoover, is in "President Coolidge," Commerce Papers, Hoover Papers. It is dated February 14, 1927. At the top of the page, in Hoover's handwriting, are the words: "Next to Final Draft Sent President Feb. 16_1927." A comparison of this draft with Coolidge's final

veto message (February 25, 1927) shows that Coolidge used some of Hoover's sentences and paragraphs. Coolidge thus incorporated parts of Hoover's draft verbatim. See also McCoy, *Calvin Coolidge,* 308–10, 324.

49. Coolidge message to Congress, December 7, 1926, printed in *New York Times,* December 8, 1926, 14–15.

50. Richard B. Scandrett Jr. to Dwight W. Morrow, February 26, 1927 (plus enclosures), Dwight W. Morrow Papers, Series I, Box 41, folder 25, Amherst College Archives; Scandrett, "Remembering Calvin Coolidge," 209; Richard B. Scandrett Jr. oral history (typescript, ca. 1966), 205–7 and supplemental memorandum, 11–12 (regarding Hoover and the Boulder Dam), Cornell University Libraries.

51. Rickard diary, January 21, 1927.

52. *New York Times,* March 5, 1927, 2.

53. Baltimore *Sun* clipping, March 31, 1927, copy in Clippings File, Hoover Papers; press summary for March 1927, Clippings File, Hoover Papers; *Washington Post,* April 3, 1927, sec. I, 1, 4; *Independent* 118 (March 26, 1927): 325–26.

54. Daily Press Summary, April 6, 1927, 6, Clippings File, Hoover Papers; [Charles W. Hilles], memorandum regarding George Barr Baker, May 14, 1927, in Dwight W. Morrow Papers, Series I, Box 26, folder 14; *New York Herald Tribune,* April 4, 1927, 5; transcript of President Coolidge's news conference, April 5, 1927, in Press Conferences of Calvin Coolidge, the Forbes Library, Northampton, MA; Baltimore *Sun* clipping, April 17, 1927, Clippings File, Hoover Papers.

55. Rickard diary, April 3 and 15, 1927.

56. *Washington Herald,* April 15, 1927, 1, clipping attached to Daily Press Summary for April 15, 1927, Clippings File, Hoover Papers.

57. Ibid.; *New York Times,* April 15, 1927, 4, April 16, 1927, 6; Castle diary, April 21, 1927.

58. For a report that it was Wilbur (not Hoover) who initially objected to Kellogg's China policy, see *New York Herald Tribune,* April 20, 1927, 1.

59. Transcript of President Coolidge's news conference, April 15, 1927, Press Conferences of Calvin Coolidge, Forbes Library.

60. Rickard diary, April 16, 1927. According to "T. R. B." in the *New Republic,* the word "jealousy" was "on the lips of every correspondent who came out of the White House conference" on April 15. *New Republic* 50 (May 4, 1927): 300. The possibility that Coolidge was jealous of Hoover also appeared in articles in the Baltimore *Sun* (including Frank R. Kent's column "The Great Game of Politics") on April 17, 1927. Copies in Clippings File, Hoover Papers. On May 6, 1927, Clinton W. Gilbert published an article headlined "Why People Are Jealous of the Secretary of Commerce" in the *New York Post.* A copy of this item is in "President Coolidge—Statement to the Press . . . ," Commerce Papers, Hoover Papers.

61. Baltimore *Sun* clipping, April 17, 1927, in Clippings File, Hoover Papers; press summary entitled "President Coolidge's Statement on the Secretaryship of State" (April 18, 1927), Clippings File, Hoover Papers. For other examples of this cluster of interpretations, see *New York Times,* April 16, 1927, 1, 6; *New York Herald Tribune,* April 17, 1927, sec. I, 1, 3; *Boston Post* clipping, April 17, 1927, in "President Coolidge—Statement to the Press . . . ," Commerce Papers, Hoover Papers; *New York Times,* April 19, 1927, 8; press summary entitled "The President's Statement on the Secretaryship of State" (April 20, 1927), Clippings File, Hoover Papers; "Back Stage in Washington," *Independent* 118 (May 21, 1927): 541.

62. Frank R. Kent, "The Great Game of Politics," Baltimore *Sun,* April 17, 1927, copy in Clippings File, Hoover Papers.

63. *Boston Post* clipping, April 17, 1927; press summary for April 18, 1927, Clippings File, Hoover Papers; *New York Times,* April 17, 1927, sec. I, 4, and April 18, 1927, 21; Rickard diary, April 16, 1927; New York *World,* April 18, 1927, 1, 2.

64. *New York Times,* April 19, 1927, 8; Baltimore *Sun* clipping, April 19, 1927, in "President Coolidge–Statement to the Press . . . ," Commerce Papers, Hoover Papers; press summary entitled "The President's Statement on the Secretaryship of State" (April 20, 1927), 1, in "President Coolidge–Statement to the Press . . . ," Commerce Papers.

65. New York *World,* April 18, 1927, 1, 2; *New York Times,* April 19, 1927, 8; Mark Sullivan's column in Portland *Morning Oregonian,* April 19, 1927, copy in "President Coolidge–Statement to the Press . . . ," Commerce Papers, Hoover Papers; transcript of President Coolidge's news conference, April 19, 1927, in Press Conferences of Calvin Coolidge, Forbes Library.

66. Press summary entitled "The President's Statement on the Secretaryship of State" (April 20, 1927); Hoover's staff's press summary and tabulation for the month of April 1927 (especially 13–15), in Clippings File, Hoover Papers. According to "T. R. B." in the *New Republic,* Coolidge neither retracted the "slur" nor removed "the ban on Hoover for promotion." *New Republic* 50 (May 4, 1927): 300. For a similar observation, see New York *World,* April 20, 1927, 2.

67. *Washington Post* clipping, April 23, 1927 (with annotations), in "Mississippi Valley Flood–Relief Work–Miscellaneous–1927–April," Commerce Papers, Hoover Papers; Bruce A. Lohof, "Herbert Hoover, Spokesman of Humane Efficiency: The Mississippi Flood of 1927," *American Quarterly* 22 (Fall 1970): 690–700; Coolidge to Hoover, June 20, 1927, "President Coolidge," Commerce Papers, Hoover Papers.

68. Press summary entitled "The President's Statement on the Secretaryship of State" (April 20, 1927), 2; *New York Herald Tribune,* April 17, 1927, sec. I, 1, 3; *New York Times,* May 9, 1927, 23.

69. *New York Times,* May 8, 1927, sec. I, 9, May 9, 1927, 23, and July 21, 1927, 13.

70. *Des Moines Register,* April 27, 1927, 1.

71. (Charleston, South Carolina) *Post* editorial, May 5, 1927, copy in "President Coolidge–Statement to the Press . . . ," Commerce Papers, Hoover Papers; New York *Sun* editorial, May 5, 1927, copy in Morrow Papers, Series I, Box 34, folder 18; Hoover, *Memoirs,* 2: 89–90; Rickard diary, June 3, 1927; New York *World,* July 21, 1927, 5.

72. New York *World,* July 21, 1927, 5; George C. Drescher oral history (1967), 6, Hoover Library. Drescher was a Secret Service agent who accompanied the president and Hoover on the drive to Rapid City.

73. *New York Times,* July 22, 1927, 3; also see July 21, 1927, 13.

74. Associated Press telegram to Hoover, August 2, 1927, "President Coolidge," Commerce Papers, Hoover Papers.

75. For Coolidge's love of practical jokes (and its significance for understanding him), see Booraem, *The Provincial,* 44, 162–63, 204–5, and McCoy, *Calvin Coolidge,* 157–58. Hoover, in his *Memoirs,* 2: 190, recalled that Coolidge "certainly enjoyed the amazing volume of curiosity and the discussion that his statement had evoked and apparently did not want to end it. Nor did he ever do so."

76. Rickard diary, August 3, 1927; *New York Times,* August 4, 1927, 1.

77. Hoover to William Allen White, January 25, 1938; Hoover, *Memoirs,* 2: 190.

78. Edmund W. Starling, *Starling of the White House* (New York: Simon & Schuster, 1946), 263.

79. Hoover to William Allen White, January 25, 1938; *New York Times,* December 7, 1927, 1.

80. Donald R. McCoy, "To the White House: Herbert Hoover, August 1927-March 1929," in Martin L. Fausold and George T. Mazuzan, eds., *The Hoover Presidency: A Reappraisal* (Albany, NY: State University of New York Press, 1974), 29–49, 197–99; Rickard diary, February 11, 1928; Hoover, *Memoirs*, 2: 191.

81. Rickard diary, February 11, 1928; *New York Times*, February 13, 1928, 1, 2.

82. Coolidge statement to the press, January 6, 1928, in Quint and Ferrell, eds., *The Talkative President*, 137–38; *New York Times*, January 7, 1928, 2, January 8, 1928, sec. I, 1.

83. Bradley Nash oral history (1968), 79–80, Hoover Library. Nash dated this incident as probably occurring in the autumn of 1927, but the episode seems to have occurred on January 6, 1928. See also Hoover, *Memoirs*, 3: 13, note 8.

84. McCoy, *Calvin Coolidge*, 319–20; William Allen White, *A Puritan in Babylon: The Story of Calvin Coolidge* (New York: Macmillan Company, 1938), 390–91. According to Hoover, Coolidge was a "strict legalist" who "insisted that the [Federal] Reserve Board had been created by Congress entirely independent of the Executive and that he could not interfere." Hoover disagreed. Hoover, *Memoirs*, 3: 11.

85. Castle diary, October 4, 1927; George Creel, *Rebel at Large* (New York: G. P. Putnam's Sons, 1947), 265–66; White, *A Puritan in Babylon*, 353.

86. *New York Times*, March 11, 1928, 1, 8, and April 11, 1928, 1, 5. Coolidge later wrote: "In the primary campaign I was careful to make it known that I was not presenting any candidate." Coolidge, *The Autobiography of Calvin Coolidge* (New York: Cosmopolitan Book Corporation, 1929), 245.

87. Rickard diary, December 31, 1927, May 6, 1928; Hoover, draft letter to William Allen White, January 25, 1938, Post-Presidential Individual File, Hoover Papers; Henry L. Stoddard, *It Costs to Be President* (New York and London: Harper & Brothers, 1938), 89.

88. Hoover to William Allen White, January 25, 1938; Hoover, *Memoirs*, 2: 193.

89. Watson, *As I Knew Them*, 255–56.

90. *New York Times*, May 24, 1928, 1, 10, 11, and May 26, 1928, 1; McCoy, *Calvin Coolidge*, 327.

91. *New York Times*, May 24, 1928, 1.

92. White, *A Puritan in Babylon*, 400.

93. Ibid., 401; Rickard diary, June 8, 1928; Robert J. Rusnak, "Andrew W. Mellon: Reluctant Kingmaker," *Presidential Studies Quarterly* 13 (Spring 1983): 275.

94. Stoddard, *It Costs to Be President*, 91.

95. Coolidge, *Autobiography*, 243–44.

96. Ibid., 244, 246; *New York Times*, June 15, 1928, 1, and April 10, 1929, 60; New York *Evening Post* article, April 9, 1929, copy in Clippings File, Hoover Papers; Charles D. Hilles to Cyril Clemens, August 23, 1944, Calvin Coolidge Papers, Miscellaneous Collection, Box 2, folder 10, Forbes Library.

97. Drescher oral history, 4–5; *New York Times*, June 16, 1928, 2.

98. Coolidge, *Autobiography*, 245; Stoddard, *It Costs to Be President*, 91–93; *New York Herald Tribune*, May 18, 1928, 7.

99. "If Coolidge disliked Herbert Hoover, it must be remembered that he disliked many men." McCoy, *Calvin Coolidge*, 391; Hoover, draft letter to William Allen White, January 25, 1938; Hoover, *Memoirs*, 2: 194.

100. Coolidge to Hoover, June 15, 1928, Calvin Coolidge Personal Files, PPF 1360, Forbes Library; Hoover to Coolidge, June 15, 1928, "Coolidge, Calvin," General Correspondence, Campaign and Transition Papers, Hoover Papers; Hoover, *Memoirs*, 2: 196.

101. *New York Times*, July 4, 1928, 2; Coolidge statement to the press, July 3, 1928, Press

Conferences of Calvin Coolidge, Forbes Library; Hoover to Coolidge, July 5, 1928, Everett Sanders to Hoover, July 7, 1928, Hoover to Sanders, July 7, 1928, Calvin Coolidge Personal Files, PPF 1360; Sanders to Hoover, July 9, 1928, Coolidge Papers, case file 3.

102. *New York Times,* July 17, 1928, 1, 2; New York *World,* July 17, 1928, 1, 2.

103. Transcript of Coolidge press conference, July 17, 1928, in Press Conferences of Calvin Coolidge, Forbes Library.

104. Hoover to Coolidge, June 30 and July 5, 1928, "Coolidge, Calvin," General Correspondence, Campaign and Transition Papers, Hoover Papers; transcript of Coolidge press conference, July 17, 1928.

105. *New York Times,* August 14, 1928, 24; Coolidge to Hoover, August 14, 1928, "Coolidge, Calvin," General Correspondence, Campaign and Transition Papers, Hoover Papers.

106. Coolidge to Hoover, August 21, 1928, "Coolidge, Calvin," General Correspondence, Campaign and Transition Papers, Hoover Papers; *New York Times,* August 22, 1928, 1, 2.

107. Hoover to Coolidge, August 29, 1928, Calvin Coolidge Personal Files, PPF 1360; *New York Times,* September 14, 1928, 6, September 15, 1928, 4, and November 4, 1928, sec. I, 1.

108. *New York Times,* September 30, 1928, sec. I, 1, October 5, 1928, 3, October 6, 1928, 18, October 7, 1928, sec. 3, 1, 2, October 20, 1928, 16, and October 26, 1918, 24.

109. Ibid., November 2, 1928, 2.

110. E. D. Adams, "Notes on Hoover" (November 6 and 7, 1928), E. D. Adams Papers, Box 8, Stanford University Archives.

111. Coolidge to Hoover, November 2, 1928, "Coolidge, Calvin," General Correspondence, Campaign and Transition Papers, Hoover Papers. Printed in *New York Times,* November 3, 1928, 1.

112. Hoover to Coolidge, November 3, 1928, Coolidge Papers, case file 4450; *New York Times,* November 4, 1928, sec. I, 1, and November 5, 1928, 22.

113. Coolidge to Hoover, November 7, 1928, "Coolidge, Calvin," General Correspondence, Campaign and Transition Papers, Hoover Papers.

114. Castle diary, July 6, 1928; transcript of Coolidge press conference, November 9, 1928, Press Conferences of Calvin Coolidge, Forbes Library; *New York Times,* November 10, 1928, 2; Coolidge to Hoover, November 8 and 9, 1928; Hoover to Coolidge, November 8 and 9, 1928. The Coolidge-Hoover exchanges are in Coolidge Papers, case file 4450. See also Hoover, *Memoirs,* 2: 211.

115. *New York Times,* January 10, 1929, 1, January 22, 1929, 28, February 17, 1929, sec. 3, 1, 2; Everett Sanders memorandum for Mrs. Coolidge, January 15, 1929, Coolidge Papers, case file 4450; Hoover, *Memoirs,* 2: 55.

116. Hoover to Coolidge, January 21, 1929 (plus enclosure), Everett Sanders to Hoover, January 21, 1929, Sanders memorandum, January 21, 1929, Coolidge Papers, case file 4450; *Mirrors of 1932,* 61.

117. Hoover, *Memoirs,* 2: 56; Hoover to William Allen White, January 25, 1938. See also Hoover, *Memoirs,* 3: 16–17.

118. Hoover, *Memoirs,* 3: 11.

119. *New York Times,* March 5, 1929, 5, 6.

120. *Mirrors of 1932,* 59; *New York Times,* March 23, 1929, 1.

121. Richard Norton Smith, "Calvin Coolidge: The Twilight Years," in *The Real Calvin Coolidge,* 4 (Plymouth, VT: Calvin Coolidge Memorial Foundation, 1986), 26.

122. Calvin Coolidge, "Party Loyalty and the Presidency," *Saturday Evening Post* 204 (October 3, 1931): 3–5, 102. For anti-Hoover maneuverings of certain Coolidge supporters in 1932, see James H. MacLafferty diary, June 9, 1932, MacLafferty Papers, and

Edward T. Clark to Coolidge, June 11, 1932, in John L. Blair, ed., "The Clark-Coolidge Correspondence and the Election of 1932," *Vermont History* 34 (April 1966): 86–88.

123. Coolidge to Edward T. Clark, September 11, 1932, in "Clark-Coolidge Correspondence," 99; Calvin Coolidge, "The Republican Case," *Saturday Evening Post* 205 (September 10, 1932): 3–5, 68–70, 72; Hoover to Coolidge, September 7, 1932, "Coolidge, Calvin," President's Personal File, Hoover Papers.

124. Stoddard, *It Costs to Be President,* 136–39; *New York Times,* October 12, 1932, 1, 16; Hoover to Coolidge, October 12, 1932, "Coolidge, Calvin," President's Personal File, Hoover Papers; Edward T. Clark to Coolidge, October 13, 1932, in "Clark-Coolidge Correspondence," 104. For Coolidge's concern about his inability to make speeches because of his throat, see "Clark-Coolidge Correspondence," 99, 105, 106.

125. Coolidge to Clark, October 16, 1932, in "Clark-Coolidge Correspondence," 106; Fuess, *Calvin Coolidge,* 460; Hoover to Fuess, August 22, 1938, in Fuess, *Calvin Coolidge,* 460–61.

126. Coolidge's speech to the nation on November 7, 1932, in *Campaign Speeches of 1932 by President Hoover [and] Ex-President Coolidge* (Garden City, NY: Doubleday, Doran & Company, 1933), 262–68.

127. Theodore G. Joslin diary, January 5 and 7, 1933, Hoover Library; Hoover to Mrs. Calvin Coolidge, January 5, 1933, "Coolidge, Calvin," President's Personal File, Hoover Papers; Coolidge interview, December 14, 1932, in Stoddard, *It Costs to Be President,* 145; Hoover to William Allen White, January 25, 1938; Hoover to Arthur McKeogh, November 7, 1934, Herbert Hoover Collection, Box 314, Coolidge folder, Hoover Institution Archives.

128. I am not referring to presidential succession following the death or resignation of the incumbent but to succession by election. In the case of succession as a result of a presidential death, of course, factional troubles can also become acute. The woes of Harry Truman and Lyndon Johnson are notable examples.

CHAPTER 31: RONALD REAGAN'S LEGACY AND AMERICAN CONSERVATISM

1. In January 2008, when this essay was written, a Google search of the Internet for "presidential legacy" yielded 17,700 results.

2. In January 2008, an Internet search for "Bush legacy" produced 136,000 results.

3. George W. Bush interview with Nadia Bilbassy-Charters, January 4, 2008, excerpt provided by the White House Office of Public Liaison.

4. George W. Bush interview with Nahum Barnes and Shimon Shiffer, January 2, 2008, excerpt provided by the White House Office of Public Liaison.

5. Franklin Roosevelt established the first presidential library in 1941, and every succeeding president has done the same. In 1962 Roosevelt's immediate predecessor in office, Herbert Hoover, dedicated his own presidential library, which then became part of the system of presidential libraries administered by the National Archives.

6. Ronald Reagan, *An American Life* (New York: Simon & Schuster, 1990).

7. Ronald Reagan's farewell address, January 11, 1989, available online at http://www.reaganlibrary.com.

8. The project maintains a weblog, *Reagan's Legacy,* at http://reaganlegacy.blogspot.com.

9. For more on this, log on to the Internet at http://www.heritage.org.

10. As of mid-January 2008.

11. Quoted in Rebecca Hagelin, "What Would Reagan Do?" (a column dated January 9, 2008, and posted online at http://www.townhall.com).

12. Thomas W. Evans, *The Education of Ronald Reagan* (New York: Columbia University Press, 2006), 195.

13. See Jeffrey Bell, "The Candidate and the Briefing Book," *Weekly Standard* 6 (February 5, 2001): 21–26, especially 26.

This point deserves emphasis. Long ago, John Henry Cardinal Newman asserted that Toryism is "loyalty to persons." In the case of modern American conservatives, one must respond: not necessarily so. For them conservatism is loyalty to principle. Where putatively conservative politicians appear to deviate too far or too often from these beliefs, the politicians lose their following on the Right. When, for example, Senator Barry Goldwater—a conservative hero in the 1960s—appeared to move toward the left (on social issues) in the 1970s and 1980s, his popularity among conservatives declined. As mentioned in the text below, the same thing happened (to a lesser extent) to President Reagan during his second term.

14. Paul Kengor, *God and Ronald Reagan: A Spiritual Life* (New York: ReganBooks, 2004), 76–88.

15. See Evans, *Education of Ronald Reagan,* especially 74–80; Lee Edwards, *The Essential Ronald Reagan* (Lanham, MD: Rowman & Littlefield Publishers, 2005), 54; Reagan, *An American Life,* 129.

16. Reagan remarks at a reception honoring *National Review,* February 21, 1983, in the Public Papers of President Ronald W. Reagan, available online at http://www.reagan.utexas.edu/archives/speeches/publicpapers.html.

17. Lou Cannon, *President Reagan: The Role of a Lifetime* (New York: Simon & Schuster, 1991), 180.

18. Ronald Reagan, *Where's the Rest of Me?* (New York: Dell, 1965), 297.

19. Kiron K. Skinner, Annelise Anderson, and Martin Anderson, eds., *Reagan: A Life in Letters* (New York: Free Press, 2003), 272.

20. Stephen F. Hayward, *The Age of Reagan: The Fall of the Old Liberal Order, 1964–1980* (Roseville, CA: Forum, 2001), 680.

21. Michael Kramer, "The Book Reagan Wants You to Read," *New York* 13 (December 1, 1980): 23–24, 26.

22. Skinner et al., eds., *Reagan: A Life in Letters,* 256, 257, 259.

23. Ibid., 259. The quotation is from Paine's pamphlet *Common Sense* (1976).

24. See, for example, Norman Podhoretz, "The Neo-Conservative Anguish Over Reagan's Foreign Policy," *New York Times Magazine* (May 2, 1982), 30–33, 88–89, 92, 96–97; Podhoretz, "Appeasement By Any Other Name," *Commentary* 76 (July 1983): 25–31; Patrick Glynn, "Reagan's Rush to Disarm," *Commentary* 85 (March 1988): 19–28; Walter Laqueur, "Glasnost and Its Limits," *Commentary* 86 (July 1988): 13–24; John Ehrman, *The Rise of Neoconservatism* (New Haven and London: Yale University Press, 1995), 146–49, 174–76.

25. Margaret Thatcher, *The Downing Street Years* (New York: HarperCollins, 1993), 470–73. The British prime minister was greatly alarmed by how far Reagan and his colleagues "had been prepared to go." It seemed to her "as if there had been an earthquake beneath my feet." She soon flew to Washington, D.C., and persuaded Reagan to issue a joint statement of clarification with which she was "well pleased."

26. Sheldon L. Richman, "The Sad Legacy of Ronald Reagan," *Free Market* 6 (October 1988).

27. For example, see "A Fond Farewell to the 'Gipper,'" *Human Events* 49 (January 21, 1989): 1, 17.

28. Quoted in Charles Krauthammer, "Reluctant Cold Warriors," *Washington Post,* November 12, 1999, A35.

29. Slight variations of this aphorism are in circulation, all attributed to Reagan. The historian John Lewis Gaddis has shrewdly noted "Reagan's artful artlessness: his habit of appearing to know less than his critics did, of seeming to be adrift even as he proceeded quietly toward destinations he himself had chosen." John Lewis Gaddis, "Strategies of Containment: Post–Cold War Reconsiderations" (address at the Elliott School of International Affairs, the George Washington University, April 15, 2004). Transcript available online at http://www.gwu.edu.

30. Siena Research Institute press release, August 19, 2002, accessible online at http://www.siena.edu.

31. Ibid.

32. Arthur Schlesinger Jr., "The Ultimate Approval Rating," *New York Times Magazine* (December 15, 1996), 46–51; Arthur Schlesinger Jr., "Rating the Presidents: Washington to Clinton," *Political Science Quarterly* 112 (Summer 1997): 179–90.

33. Alvin S. Felsenberg et al., "'There You Go Again,'" *Policy Review*, no. 82 (March–April 1997): 51–53; James Taranto and Leonard Leo, eds., *Presidential Leadership: Rating the Best and the Worst in the White House* (New York: Free Press, 2004). According to the scholars polled by Taranto and Leo, Reagan placed eighth among all the presidents, just behind Harry S. Truman and just ahead of Dwight D. Eisenhower.

34. Paul Kengor, "Reagan Among the Professors," *Policy Review*, no. 98 (December 1999–January 2000): 15–27.

35. James MacGregor Burns, "Risks of the Middle," *Washington Post*, October 24, 1999, B7.

36. Notably in his commencement address at the University of Notre Dame (May 17, 1981) and his address to the National Association of Evangelicals (March 8, 1983).

37. See Marc Fisher, "The Old Warrior at the Wall," *Washington Post*, September 13, 1990, D1–D2, and Fred Barnes, "Covering the Gipper," *Weekly Standard* 6 (February 5, 2001): 29.

38. See especially Peter Schweitzer, *Reagan's War* (New York: Doubleday, 2002) and Paul Kengor, *The Crusader: Ronald Reagan and the Fall of Communism* (New York: Regan, 2006).

39. Edmund Levin, "Reagan's Victory?" *Weekly Standard* 10 (November 15, 2004): 31–34.

40. Gaddis, "Strategies of Containment."

41. Kiron Skinner, Annelise Anderson, and Martin Anderson, eds., *Reagan, In His Own Hand* (New York: Free Press, 2001).

42. Cited in note 19.

43. Kengor, *God and Ronald Reagan: A Spiritual Life* (cited in note 14).

44. Cited in note 38.

45. Paul Lettow, *Ronald Reagan and His Quest to Abolish Nuclear Weapons* (New York: Random House, 2005), 243.

46. Douglas Brinkley, ed., *The Reagan Diaries* (New York: HarperCollins, 2007).

47. See, for example: Stefan Halper and Jonathan Clarke, "Would Ronald Reagan Have Attacked Iraq?" (June 15, 2004) and Peter J. Wallison, "Reagan, Iraq, and Neoconservatism" (June 16, 2004), both posted at http://www.spectator.org. See also Halper and Clarke's article, "Neoconservatism Is Not Reaganism," *American Spectator* 37 (April 2004): 20–24, and Jacob Heilbrunn, "A Uniter, Not a Decider," *National Interest*, no. 90 (July–August 2007): 79–87.

48. John Patrick Diggins, "How Reagan Beat the Neocons," *New York Times*, June 11, 2004, A27.

49. John Patrick Diggins, *Ronald Reagan: Fate, Freedom, and the Making of History* (New York: W. W. Norton & Company, 2007), xxi, xxii, 34; interview of Diggins in *Washington Times*, February 7, 2007, A2.

50. Diggins, *Ronald Reagan*, xvii.

51. For respectful but critical assessments of Diggins' book by conservative scholars and journalists, see: Rich Lowry, "The Liberal Reagan," *New York Times Book Review,* February 18, 2007, 21; Katherine Ernst, "Was Reagan a Liberal?" (March 2, 2007), posted online at http://www.city-journal.org; Dan Seligman, "Warriors," *Commentary* 125 (April 2007): 71–74; Peter J. Wallison, "Reagan Co-Opted," *American Spectator* 40 (July–August 2007): 68–75; Steven F. Hayward, "Reagan and the Historians," *Claremont Review of Books* 7 (Fall 2007): 14–18. For Diggins's subsequent argument with Wallison, see "Whose Reagan? An Exchange," *American Spectator* 40 (October 2007): 8–11.

52. Interestingly, the most systematic study of Reagan's religious faith—Paul Kengor's *God and Ronald Reagan*—contains not a single reference to Ralph Waldo Emerson.

53. On this point, see Lettow, *Ronald Reagan and His Quest to Abolish Nuclear Weapons,* 132–34, 234–35; Edward Rowny interview, May 17, 2006, 14–16, Ronald Reagan Oral History Project, Miller Center of Public Affairs, Presidential Oral History Program, University of Virginia, transcript online at http://www.millercenter.virginia.edu/scripps/digitalarchive/oralhistories/reagan; Kenneth Adelman, *The Great Universal Embrace: Arms Summitry—A Skeptic's Account* (New York: Simon & Schuster, 1989), 20, 67–70. Adelman, who served (by Reagan's appointment) as director of the U.S. Arms Control and Disarmament Agency from 1983 to 1987, described Reagan as an antinuclear "mystic" with a "visionary streak."

54. Richard Wirthlin, *The Greatest Communicator* (Hoboken, NJ: John Wiley & Sons, 2004), 113–15. According to Wirthlin, this conversation occurred "just as his [Reagan's] economic policies were beginning to kick in and produce what would later become unprecedented economic growth." This would have been at the end of 1982 or (more likely) 1983.

55. Lettow, *Ronald Reagan and His Quest to Abolish Nuclear Weapons,* 196; Rowny oral history (2006), 14.

56. Reagan, *An American Life,* 269.

57. In his review (cited above) of John Patrick Diggins's book, Rich Lowry remarked that "across the political spectrum we are beginning to agree that Ronald Reagan was an important, even admirable, figure. What liberals and conservatives will probably never agree on is why."

58. This was the title of chapter 8 in Peggy Noonan's memoir, *What I Saw at the Revolution: A Political Life in the Reagan Era* (New York: Random House, 1990).

59. One of Reagan's most thorough biographers to date, Lou Cannon, has written that "on nearly all issues" Reagan "was simultaneously an ideologue and a pragmatist" (Cannon, *President Reagan,* 185).

60. Reagan, *An American Life,* 567.

61. Michael K. Deaver, *A Different Drummer: My Thirty Years with Ronald Reagan* (New York, HarperCollins, 2001), 2.

62. He so expressed himself at a dinner of presidential biographers (at which I was present) in Washington, D.C., on February 14, 1983.

Acknowledgments

As every author knows, writing a book can be an intensely solitary endeavor. But *publishing* one's writing is a more communal task. It is a pleasure to acknowledge here those people who have assisted me in bringing this volume to fruition.

My acknowledgments begin with Jeffrey O. Nelson, who, as editor in chief of ISI Books in 2005, invited me to assemble a collection of my historical writings for publication. I felt honored indeed by his suggestion. Although I did not see my way to act upon it immediately, the idea intrigued me, and from time to time I let him know of my interest in following through in due course. From time to time also, our mutual friend John J. Miller of *National Review* added his words of encouragement, which helped to persuade me that there might be an audience for these writings beyond academic circles. To Jeff Nelson, then, I offer my warm thanks for being the catalyst of this volume, and to John Miller I say thank you as well, for enthusiastically seconding the motion.

Meanwhile ISI Books, under Jeff's successor as editor, Jeremy Beer, brought out in 2006 a handsome, updated, thirtieth-anniversary edition of my first book, *The Conservative Intellectual Movement in America Since 1945*. The response to its republication further convinced me of the wisdom of compiling the principal essays that I have written on this subject since that volume first appeared—pieces tucked away in all sorts of scholarly journals and opinion magazines. (And in several instances, not yet published.) By early 2009, after writing and delivering still more such reappraisals of conservatism's past and possible future at various forums, I concluded that the moment had come to transmute these scattered writings into a single, accessible, and increasingly timely volume.

ISI Books' new editor in chief, Jed C. Donahue, readily agreed and has expertly paved the path toward publication. It has been a pleasure to work with him, Jennifer Connolly, Chris Michalski, and their colleagues in this undertaking.

Most of the chapters in this book originated as conference papers and lectures in academic settings. I am grateful to those who, over a number of years, have provided me these opportunities and am pleased to acknowledge, with thanks, the individuals and institutions—listed formally on a separate page—who have kindly given permission to print or reprint the items found in this book.

For skillfully scanning the thirty-two chapters into a format required for submission to the publisher, I thank Dawn Larder. Before the book took shape, the ever efficient Emma Kuipers had typed many of its eventual components and provided disks for future use. After Emma moved away to distant places, I was blessed to find a competent successor in Jennifer Hale, who assisted me with a multitude of computer-related tasks. When Jen left for a semester of study at the University of St. Andrews, Sandra Hull-Hale ably helped me put the remainder of the manuscript into final form. Hearty and appreciative thanks to you all!

For expert proofreading and copy editing assistance, I thank Kara Beer and Erica Ford. To Erica my thanks also for meticulous preparation of the index. At the Mount Holyoke College Library in South Hadley, Massachusetts (my home town), where I wrote and edited many of the essays in this volume, a team of conscientious librarians created a congenial environment for which I am grateful. And always, through the long and sometimes laborious publishing process, my sister Nancy, a writer herself, has been there with her unflagging support.

Finally, for many years Annette Y. Kirk has tirelessly promoted the study of reflective conservatism through her programs at the Russell Kirk Center for Cultural Renewal, named after her late husband (a figure a who appears frequently in the preceding pages). More recently, Professor Charles W. Dunn, the author and editor of several valuable books on American conservatism, has established at Regent University an annual Reagan Symposium, where the assessment of conservative thought (and related subjects) has proceeded with distinction. One of my great pleasures as an independent scholar has been the opportunity to participate in these two projects. To their impresarios, who are also my friends, *Reappraising the Right* is dedicated.

Permissions

The author would like to acknowledge the following publications, sources, and individuals for granting permission to reprint his work in this volume.

Chapter 1: "Pilgrim's Progress: America's Tradition of Conservative Reform" originally appeared in *Policy Review* (Fall 1991). Reprinted by permission of *Policy Review*.

Chapter 2: "Engines of 'Idea Power': The Rise of Conservative Think Tanks" was originally delivered as a speech at an Indiana Policy Review Foundation dinner in 1991. Reprinted by permission of the Indiana Policy Review Foundation.

Chapter 3: "Modern Tomes: Conservative Writings that Changed Our Minds Between the 1970s and 1990s" originally appeared in *Policy Review* (July–August 1997). Reprinted by permission of *Policy Review*.

Chapter 4: "The Quiet, Libertarian Odyssey of John Chamberlain" originally appeared in *The American Spectator* (March 1983) and is reprinted by permission of *The American Spectator*.

Chapter 5: "Whittaker Chambers: The Ambivalent Icon" originally appeared in *The American Spectator* (May 1997) and is reprinted by permission of *The American Spectator*.

Chapter 6: "Searching for Conservatism's Essence: The Investigations of John P. East" originally appeared as an introduction to John P. East, *The American Conservative Movement: The Philosophical Founders* (Regnery Books, 1986). Reprinted by permission of Regnery Publishing, Inc.

Chapter 7: "Friedrich Hayek and the American Conservative Movement" is printed by permission of the author, George H. Nash.

Chapter 8: "The Place of Willmoore Kendall in American Conservatism" originally appeared in *Willmoore Kendall: Maverick of American Conservatives,* John A. Murley and John E. Alvis, editors (Lexington Books, 2002), 3–15. Reprinted by permission of Rowman & Littlefield Publishing Group.

Chapter 9: "The Life and Legacy of Russell Kirk" was originally delivered as a lecture at the Heritage Foundation on June 22, 2007. Reprinted by permission of The Heritage Foundation.

Chapter 10: "The Memoirs of Forrest McDonald, Conservative Historian" originally appeared as a review of Forrest McDonald's memoir *Recovering the Past* in *Modern Age* (Spring 2005). Reprinted by permission of *Modern Age.*

Chapter 11: "E. Victor Milione (1924–2008)" is printed by permission of the author, George H. Nash.

Chapter 12: "Ernest van den Haag (1914–2002)" originally appeared in the *University Bookman* (Spring 2003). Reprinted by permission of the *University Bookman.*

Chapter 13: "The Influence of Richard Weaver's *Ideas Have Consequences* on American Conservatism" originally appeared in *Steps Toward Restoration,* Ted J. Smith III, editor (ISI Books, 1998), 81–124, and is reprinted by permission of ISI Books.

Chapter 14: "Francis Graham Wilson: A Conservative Scholar's Wisdom" originally appeared as a review of Francis Wilson's book *The Case for Conservatism* in the *University Bookman* (1991). Reprinted by permission of the *University Bookman.*

Chapter 15: "Hillsdale College: A Model for Conservatives" originally appeared as a Foreword to *The Permanent Things: Hillsdale College 1900-1994* by Arlan K. Gilbert (Hillsdale College Press, 1998). Reprinted by permission of Hillsdale College Press.

Chapter 16: "The New Counterculture: Rod Dreher and the Crunchy Cons" originally appeared as a review of Rod Dreher's book *Crunchy Cons* in the *Wall Street Journal,* February 21, 2006. Reprinted by permission of the author, George H. Nash, and the *Wall Street Journal.*

Chapter 17: "*God and Man at Yale* Revisited" was presented as a paper at a conference at Grove City College in April 2009. This previously unpublished essay is printed by permission of the author, George H. Nash, and Paul Kengor.

Chapter 18: "William F. Buckley Jr. the Writer" originally appeared as the Introduction to *William F. Buckley Jr.: A Bibliography,* edited by William F.

Chapter 27: "Herbert Hoover, Supply-Side Economics, and the Tax Increase of 1932" originally appeared as the op-ed piece "Herbert Hoover's Balanced Budget" in the *Wall Street Journal* (June 12, 1980). Reprinted by permission of the author, George H. Nash, and the *Wall Street Journal*.

Chapter 28: "Herbert Hoover's Bad Press" originally appeared in *The American Road* (Spring 2004), the newsletter of the Hoover Presidential Library Association. This essay is reprinted by permission of the Hoover Presidential Library Association.

Chapter 29: "How Should Conservatives Look Back on the New Deal?" was originally a speech at a New Deal conference held at the Lyndon Baines Johnson Library in 1983 and published in *The New Deal Fifty Years After: A Historical Assessment*, edited by Wilbur J. Cohen (Lyndon Baines Johnson Library and Lyndon B. Johnson School of Public Affairs, 1984). Reprinted by permission of the Lyndon Baines Johnson Library and Lyndon B. Johnson School of Public Affairs.

Chapter 30: "The Uneasy Future of American Conservatism" originally appeared in *The Future of Conservatism*, edited by Charles W. Dunn (ISI Books, 2007). Reprinted by permission of ISI Books.

Chapter 31: "Ronald Reagan's Legacy and American Conservatism" originally appeared in *The Enduring Reagan*, edited by Charles W. Dunn (University Press of Kentucky, 2009), and is reprinted by permission of the University Press of Kentucky and Charles W. Dunn.

Chapter 32: "How Firm a Foundation? The Prospects for American Conservatism" originally appeared in the *Intercollegiate Review* (Spring 2009). Reprinted by permission of the *Intercollegiate Review*.

Index

About the Author

George H. Nash is a historian, lecturer, and the author of six other books, including *The Conservative Intellectual Movement in America Since 1945* and a three-volume biography of Herbert Hoover. He is a senior fellow at the Russell Kirk Center for Cultural Renewal and an associate of the Hauenstein Center for Presidential Studies. He has also been a visiting fellow at the Hoover Institution on War, Revolution and Peace. The 2008 recipient of the Richard M. Weaver Prize for Scholarly Letters, Nash graduated summa cum laude from Amherst College and received his Ph.D. in history from Harvard University. He lives in South Hadley, Massachusetts.